EDMUND CAMPION

For all my dearest friends

Edmund Campion
A Scholarly Life

GERARD KILROY
University College London, UK

ASHGATE

Published by
Ashgate Publishing Limited
Wey Court East
Union Road
Farnham
Surrey, GU9 7PT
England

Ashgate Publishing Company
110 Cherry Street
Suite 3-1
Burlington, VT 05401-3818
USA

www.ashgate.com

British Library Cataloguing in Publication Data
A catalogue record for this book is available from the British Library

The Library of Congress has cataloged the printed edition as follows:
Kilroy, Gerard, 1945–
    Edmund Campion: a scholarly life / by Gerard Kilroy.
        pages cm
    Includes bibliographical references.
Summary: "Edmund Campion has always been the leading Elizabethan martyr, an accolade that overshadowed his early life. This biography assesses the power of Campion's spoken word, in Prague and in England, the disastrous impact of the invasion of Ireland on the Jesuit mission, and the drama of his capture, 'conferences' in the Tower and trial. The warm affection he everywhere inspired, was almost submerged in the controversy that surrounded his execution" – Provided by publisher.
    ISBN 978-1-4094-0151-3 (hardcover: alk. paper) 1. Campion, Edmund, Saint, 1540–1581. 2. Campion, Edmund, Saint, 1540–1581 – Influence. 3. Christian martyrs – Great Britain – Biography. 4. Jesuits – Great Britain – Biography – 16th century. 5. England – Intellectual life – 16th century. 6. England--Church history – 16th century. I. Title.

BX4705.C27K55 2015
272'.7092 – dc23
[B]
                                                                    2015002221
ISBN 9781409401513 (hbk)

MIX
Paper from
responsible sources
FSC
www.fsc.org   FSC® C013985

Printed in the United Kingdom by Henry Ling Limited, at the Dorset Press, Dorchester, DT1 1HD

Contents

List of Illustrations

Colour Plates

Black and White Figures

List of Abbreviations

ABSI	Archivum Britannicum Societatis Iesu (Farm Street, London)
APMC	Archive of Prague Castle, Metropolitan Chapter Library
ARSI	Archivum Romanum Societatis Iesu (Rome)
ARCR	A.F. Allison and D.M. Rogers, *The Contemporary Printed Literature of the English Counter-Reformation between 1558 and 1640*, vol. 1: *Works in Languages Other than English*; vol. 2: *Works in English* (Aldershot, UK and Burlington, VT, 1989–94)
BL	British Library
Bodl.	Bodleian Library, Oxford
CCC	Corpus Christi College, Oxford
CRS	Catholic Record Society (with number of volume)
CSP	*Calendar of State Papers*
CWE	*Collected Works of Erasmus*, University of Toronto
Dillingen	Studienbibliothek Dillingen
Folger	Folger Shakespeare Library
Holleran	James V. Holleran, *A Jesuit Challenge: Edmund Campion's Debates at the Tower of London in 1581* (New York: Fordham University Press)
HUO	*The History of the University of Oxford*, 8 vols (Oxford: Clarendon Press, 1584–2000), vol. 2, *Late Medieval Oxford*, ed. J.I. Catto and Ralph Evans (1992); vol. 3, *The Collegiate University*, ed. James McConica (1986).
LMA	London Metropolitan Archives
NLI	National Library of Ireland
ODNB	*Oxford Dictionary of National Biography*
OHS	Oxford Historical Society
Opuscula	Edmund Campion, *Decem Rationes Propositae in Causa Fidei et Opuscula Eius Selecta* (Antwerp: Plantin Moretus, 1631), ARCR 1. 170
PRO	Public Record Office, the National Archives
SZ	Książnica Cieszyńska, Biblioteka Leopolda Jana Szersznika
Simpson	Richard Simpson, *Edmund Campion: A Biography*, 2nd ed. (London: John Hodges, 1896)
Strahov	Strahov Monastery Library, Prague
STC	W.A. Jackson, F.S. Ferguson and Katharine F. Panzer, *A Short-Title Catalogue of Books Printed in England, Scotland and Ireland and of English Books Printed Abroad, 1475–1640*, 2nd ed., 3 vols (London: Bibliographic Society, 1976–91)
TCD	Trinity College Dublin

Preface

When Edmund Campion sent his manuscript of *Rationes Decem* to Stonor Park, Robert Persons was surprised and moved by the number of scholarly references in the margins. Campion spent a year in Prague trying to recover the manuscript of his *Histories of Ireland*, whose marginal glosses specified even the provenance of the various sources he had used. When, on the run, Campion agreed to go to Norfolk for his own safety, he said he could not live without his books, which he had left in Lancashire. In the opening minutes of the first disputation in the Tower, Campion offered to send to two of the best libraries in Europe, those of the Emperor and Wilhelm, Duke of Bavaria, for an early edition of Luther. Even among men of learning, Campion was outstanding in the precision of his scholarship.

Others were more aware of the sound of his voice. Eighty years after his mission, the memory in the north was still preserved, of men camping out in neighbouring barns to hear Campion preaching at dawn. We have accounts of only a few of his sermons, but on the best-documented occasions at Lyford, everyone, including the man about to betray him, was weeping. Campion was still a London schoolboy when he addressed Queen Mary; he addressed Queen Elizabeth in Oxford, and became the favourite preacher at the court of the Emperor, Rudolf II, in Prague. Even when he faced large popular audiences, primed to be hostile, in the Tower, in Westminster Hall and at Tyburn, Campion was able to win them over. On several recorded occasions, Campion received the ultimate, and rare, accolade of an Elizabethan audience: stunned silence. The readers of Campion's most famous work, the *Rationes Decem*, felt they were *hearing* Campion. Hard as it is to recover the sounds of an earlier culture, this book attempts to convey the way Campion's preaching won the hearts, as well as the minds, of 'emperor and clown alike'.

Affection is the most consistent element in Campion's life. Fatherless by the age of 12, Campion was virtually adopted by elders of the city of London; he continued to attract patrons, from London Mayors to the Earl of Leicester, the Queen, the Emperor and the Duke of Bavaria; significantly, he turned down an offer of preferment in Rome from Cardinal Alfonso Gesualdi. The devotion he inspired among his fellow students at St John's College, Oxford, lasted till his death, and well beyond; letters from them always begin with endearments in the superlative form; Dr Allen writes that he cannot find a term adequate to express his affection. The servants of Mrs Yate followed Campion's closely guarded procession to the Tower, weeping. Even Anthony Munday, one of his hostile witnesses, acknowledged how much affection Campion inspired among 'the learned'; his betrayer, George Elyot, came to the Tower to beg his forgiveness. Thirty years after his death, princes, papal nuncios and English nobles went on their knees when they entered his former cell in Prague.

Like many a medieval scholar, Campion travelled across Europe. At Oxford he wrote a long poem on the Rome of the apostles and early martyrs: he enacted this intellectual journey when he left Douai to walk a thousand miles as a pilgrim to Rome, where he visited the shrines of those apostles and martyrs, and joined a new missionary order. This decisive rejection of the political ambitions of his Oxford contemporaries, Dr Nicholas Sander and Dr William Allen, secured for him the most productive period of his life, in the court of Rudolf II, and the city of Prague. Many of his works have survived in the provinces of Bohemia, Germania and Polonia, where his teaching was so revered that, a hundred years later, Boluslav Balbin, S.J., records that he was not alone in tracing a 'genealogy' that stretched back to Campion through five generations of teachers.

At the moment when he was most happily engaged as priest and scholar in Prague, he was recalled to lead the first Jesuit mission to England. With a hearty aversion to political 'meddling', he lingered on his way to Rome, notably in the library of Duke Wilhelm in Munich. In Rome, he again visited the shrines, turned down the leadership of the mission, dressed as a pilgrim, and walked without flinching another thousand miles to Calais, knowing he was 'going to be hanged'. Only when Campion reached Rheims, did Dr Allen tell him that Dr Sander had led a military expedition to Ireland. There was no turning back, so Campion landed in a country that was preparing to withstand the combined threat of invasion by foreign forces and rebellion by its Catholic subjects.

Unable to follow the original plan, Campion and Persons spent a year in disguise, trying to maintain a programme of preaching in the face of constant spying and harassment. The personal style of *Rationes Decem* shows that it was a continuation in print of Campion's commitment to preaching. The book is a chivalric address to the 'most powerful queen', not a challenge to the authority of the regime. Nevertheless, the materiality of print – the procurement of paper, the noise of the press, the transport of books – raised the level of danger. *Rationes Decem* remains a unique phenomenon in the history of the book: printed on a secret press, it is a book about which we know almost everything, from the time and place where it was suggested, to the way in which it was first received and read. The recent reappearance of the only copy still in its original binding helps us understand the physical conditions under which it was read, as it passed from hand to hand. It secured for Campion the unique distinction of four public disputations in the Tower. Over the next 100 years, it was published in some 90 editions across Europe.

Campion has his name on more warrants for torture than any other person in English legal history, and his treatment attracted criticism from lawyers at home and courts abroad, forcing the Queen herself to issue a proclamation declaring the trial and execution just, and the Lord Treasurer to defend his torture in several European languages. The dust of the *melée* that followed his death obscured Campion's scholarly and priestly integrity. If his life sometimes seems to follow the pattern of Jonah (forced to return to an unwilling people), Campion is, in other ways, the opposite. Every cause has wanted Campion to be on their boat; even his opponents called him the 'champion', and chose him to represent the opposition.

The earliest sources for Campion's life are far from simple. Campion's fellow missionary, Robert Persons, S.J., one of the greatest Catholic writers of the period, was commissioned to write a life by the Jesuit General, Claudio Acquaviva. He began writing in 1593, but gave up within a year of starting. He also wrote about these events in several other scattered 'memoirs', and a host of letters, but his memory of dates is not good. For all his skill as a writer, he was a biased participant, knew little of Campion's London background, suppressed the full horror of Sander's invasion of Ireland and abandoned his story of Campion as the Uxbridge conference ended in November 1580, the very moment when Sander's Spanish reinforcements were being massacred. There is no evidence that Persons was involved in political conspiracy before August 1581, but it seems unlikely he knew nothing of Sander's plans before he reached Rheims.

Persons passed his incomplete 'Of the life and martirdome', and his 'Notae breves' (Brief notes) for the unfinished chapters, to Paolo Bombino, S.J. and was personally at his elbow in Rome for at least some of the time Bombino was writing. Bombino published his *Vita et Martyrium* in Antwerp in 1618, and then in an elegant edition in Mantua, in 1620. Bombino drew on several sources other than Persons, and used at least one manuscript still extant in the English College in Rome. Richard Simpson, the outstanding modern biographer, made full use of Bombino (as his notebooks show), but denigrated him for his 'bombast', a negative verdict echoed by the Propositor in the *Cause of Canonization*, who based his own criticisms of Bombino's style on the poor 1618 edition, disowned by the author. Persons was not Bombino's only source: he also had access to other information, especially of the capture at Lyford Grange, the first disputation, the secret meeting with the Queen, and the trial. Many priests who were eyewitnesses survived long after the death of Persons: Richard Stanihurst till 1618, Henry Holland till 1625, John Colleton till 1635 and Thomas Fitzherbert, S.J., till 1640. A contemporary translation of Bombino into English, extant in a sadly incomplete Bodleian manuscript, adds details that only a participant, like Colleton, can have known, so I have treated this, Bodl. MS Tanner 329, as a primary source. Three historians of the Society of Jesus, Daniel Bartoli (1608–85), Boluslav Balbin (1621–88) and Joannes Schmidl (1693–1762), provide important evidence of the growing esteem in which Campion was held in Europe, especially in Bohemia.

Richard Simpson consulted many original sources for the first edition of his *Edmund Campion* in 1867, but several manuscripts unknown to him, and recently discovered in London, Dublin, Oxford, Rome, Prague, Dillingen and Cieszyn, modify parts of his account, and give material form to the European dimension of Campion's life. Evelyn Waugh's gripping *Edmund Campion*, first published in 1935, and written with style in five months, elegantly captures the courage and glamour of Campion, even if his assessment of the political context now seems historically, and personally, conditioned. All references to Waugh are to the first English edition of 1935; all those to Simpson are to the posthumous, second edition of 1896, which was based on Simpson's own revisions.

This book has taken care to describe the scholarly life of Campion, before he was summoned to England, so the historical context of London, Oxford, Ireland and Prague, occupies more space than in Waugh, Simpson, Bombino or Persons. Nevertheless, the drama of his last year in disguise, his capture, torture, disputations, trial and execution, still occupies half the book, and the last chapter offers a glimpse of the complex legacy of these events. There seems no reason to dispute Simpson's final judgement that the failure of the English mission of 1580 had its roots in Dr Allen's divided intentions. Campion himself did all he could to fulfil the instructions of his Jesuit superiors, which were innocent of political ambition. In recent scholarship, however, there has been a shift towards a political reading of Campion's own part in the mission. The evidence presented here suggests that Campion was reluctant to be drawn into the English muddle of politics and religion, that he was aware of the broad strategic aims of Dr Allen and Dr Sander, and did all he could to avoid being caught in their schemes. If, as contemporary chronicles implied, the English mission of 1580 was entangled in the marriage negotiations with the Duke of Anjou, it was even more fatally undermined by the Irish invasion of Dr Sander. By 1580, when he received the summons to the English mission, Campion had surrendered himself, through his Ignatian vow of obedience, to the service of God and of others. There was clearly a painful struggle between his intellectual perception of the political realities and the religious commitment he had made, which is why he stressed, again and again, that he had been 'sent' (*missus*).

This book is intended to reach the many admirers of Campion who are outside the academic community. In order not to interrupt the flow of the narrative for the general reader, I have tried to confine to the footnotes responses to important recent studies of Campion, the English mission and martyrdom, but some have crept into the text. Dr Sander's presence at the Council of Trent reminds us that the policy of refusing to attend Protestant services was adopted long before the Jesuits arrived. While not directly confronting the debate on the continuity of English Catholicism, I note that many Marian priests weave in and out of the Campion story. My principal concern has been to reimagine Campion's life as a scholar and priest, to provide documentary evidence for every assertion, and to show Campion as a human being. Many of the critical decisions in his missionary year he made at the point of departure, or sometimes, just afterwards.

Campion remained committed to a vision of the catholic, apostolic and missionary church until his last words on the scaffold. While he consistently voiced his opposition to the papal bull and fully accepted the Queen's civil authority, he was interrogated, on the rack, not on his own *Rationes Decem*, but on Sander's monumental book, *De Visibili Monarchia*, and the subversive views it expressed. The contemporary historian William Camden concluded that the Queen herself did not blame 'these wretched little priests' (*misellis his sacerdotibus*), bound by their vow of obedience, but their superiors: the first name on Campion's indictment was that of Dr Allen.

I have tried to preserve the sound of his original words, to enable the reader to hear his voice; for this reason, in quotations, I have preserved the original spelling and punctuation, only modernizing (in English) the *i/j* and *u/v* graph and silently expanding abbreviations. I have quoted Fr Christopher Grene's manuscript copy of Persons's *Life of Campion*, the earliest surviving text, which also contains his notes for the unfinished chapters, rather than the printed version, in *Letters and Notices*, by the great scholar, John Hungerford Pollen. This is scarcely more accessible, does not include the 'Notae breves', and frequently modifies the meaning by modernizing the spelling and punctuation. For Campion's letters, I have used a combination of the rough drafts in manuscript and the beautiful octavo edition of the *Opuscula*, published in Antwerp by Balthasar Moretus (1574–1641) on the Plantin press, in 1631. I have tried to preserve a sense of the bilingual culture so central to Campion's international life: he had to defend his use of Latin on the scaffold, but his English rhetoric was an unostentatious mixture of the formal and the idiomatic. His last words at Tyburn were in Latin, the language in which he spoke, wrote and prayed.

William Byrd wrote several pieces of music that reflected grief at the execution of Campion; Philippe de Monte, *Kapellmeister* in Prague, sympathetically sent Byrd a setting of *Super flumina Babylonis*, to which Byrd responded in kind, with a promise never to forget: *si non meminero tui*. Much of Byrd's music was sung behind the closed doors of English country houses, but these notes soared to the roof in the cathedral of St Vitus in Prague. It is a good image of Campion's own life: his memory, concealed in the attics of remote English houses, was placed on altars in Prague, Lyons and Rome, and treasured in libraries and colleges across Europe, transcending the insularity that was gradually separating England from its continental cultural heritage.

Gerard Kilroy

Acknowledgements

This book was written with the help, support, patience and hospitality of more people than I can name. I wish first to thank the Grocers' Company, who have enabled me, over 12 years, to follow Campion's trail, the Catholic Record Society which enabled me to travel to Rome and Valladolid, and the Folger Shakespeare Library, whose four fellowships have enabled me to enjoy its wonderful collections. Gail Kern Paster, Michael Witmore, Daniel De Monte, Richard Kuhta, Georgianna Ziegler, Goran Proot, Steve Galbraith, Erin Blake, Ron Bogdan, Deborah Leslie, Heather Wolfe, Betsie Walsh and Laetitia Yendle have all educated me by their kindness and warmth. A Fellowship at Marsh's Library, and the help of Jason McElligott, Hiram Morgan, Maria O'Shea and Nirvana Flanagan, enabled me to explore all the libraries of Dublin, including Farmleigh House, Trinity College, the National Library of Ireland and the Chester Beatty Library, to visit Smerwick on the Dingle Peninsula, and the University of Cork. A term's Fellowship in the welcoming SCR at St Catherine's College, Oxford, enabled me to explore fully the Oxford of Campion's day. I wish particularly to thank Charlie Dingwall for so generously welcoming me to Lyford Grange, Georgina Stonor for sharing her knowledge of Stonor Park, Lord Petre for showing me round Ingatestone Hall, Brendan Callaghan, S.J. and Joseph Munitiz, S.J., for making me so welcome at Campion Hall, Sir Bernard de Hoghton at Hoghton Tower, Abbot Aidan Bellenger and Simon Johnson for making me so welcome at Downside, Anna Edwards and Rebecca Volk for allowing me to rifle through the Archives of the British Province of the Society of Jesus at Farm Street, Jan Graffius for sharing the rich treasures at Stonyhurst College, especially Campion's autograph dramatic fragments, Peter Harris for introducing me to the English College at Valladolid, Colin Harris and the patient staff of Bodley's Duke Humfrey Special Collections, now in the Weston Library, the staff of the British Library Manuscript Room, Giles Mandelbrote, in Lambeth Palace Library, the staff of the Jesuit Archives in Rome, Julia Chadwick, formerly in Exeter College Library, Christine Ferdinand in Magdalen College Library, Catherine Hilliard, Ruth Ogden and Stewart Tiley in St John's College Library, Marek Suchý and Tomas Zubéč in the Prague Castle Archive of the Metropolitan Chapter Library, and Małgosia Habuda in the Dominican Library, Krakow.

In Poland it has been a privilege, over 25 years, to visit Krakow, where the kindness and hospitality of Bishop Gzegorz Ryś has been so welcoming, and to be part of a research project working alongside Teresa Bela, Jolanta Rzegocka, Katarzyna Gara and Clarinda Calma, who invited me to share the excitement of finding the Campion *Concionale* in Książnica Cieszyńska, Biblioteka Szersznika, to teach in the Jagiellonian and Tischner Universities and the Ignatianum, to explore the Jagiellonian, Czartoryski and Czapski Libraries, the Warsaw

University Library and the Studienbibliotek Dillingen in Bavaria. I also wish to thank František and Dagmar Halas, Petr and Klara Osolsobě and Radek and Iva Vasinova, whose hospitality over more than ten years enabled me to teach Shakespeare to delightful students at Masaryk University while tracing Campion's life in Brno and Prague, and to Václav Dlapka, S.J., who enabled me to visit the Strahov Monastery Library and the Clementinum.

I wish to thank particularly those who have led me to newly located manuscripts: Peter Beal, who led me to Exeter College MS 166, Hilton Kelliher, who located two copies of Campion's poem, in Bodleian Rawl. poet. D. 289, and in Holkham Hall MS 437, Daniel Andersson who located the two manuscripts in the Prague Castle Archive, and shared with me his extensive knowledge, Peter Blayney, who introduced me to the manuscripts linked to Edmund Campion senior, Andrew Hegarty, who introduced me to the Berington papers and shared with me his knowledge of St John's College before his *Biographical Register* was published, Thomas McCoog, S.J., who alerted me to many archives, Jan Pařez, who introduced me to new material in the Strahov Monastery Library, Paul Townsend and Stephen Morgan, who allowed me free access to the Winchester copy of the *Rationes Decem*, and Martin Wiggins, who generously sent me a copy of the manuscript of *Ambrosiana* in Rome, Wilfred and Anne Hammond whose guidance and hospitality provided many happy days tramping the hills and woods of Lancashire in search of recusant houses, Frances Scarr and Richard Wilson, whose enthusiasm first prompted me to begin this project so many years ago.

This book has involved much 'travail', in every sense, and I am conscious of huge debts to many people. I wish particularly to thank my colleagues, past and present, in the Department of English at University College London, especially Helen Hackett, Chris Laoutaris, John Mullan, Alison Shell, John Sutherland, René Weis and Henry Woudhuysen. There are many others whose companionship, kindness and guidance has been essential: Timothy Billings, Nancy Pollard Brown, Michael Caines, Vincent Carey, James Carley, Bernard and Armelle Chevignard, Alex and Elizabeth Chisholm, Anne Coldiron, Peter Davidson, Anne Dillon, Eamon Duffy, Sonja Fielitz, Thomas S. Freeman, Danny Friedman, Ian Gadd, Anna Gialdini, Andrew Gordon, Jan Graffius, Stephen Greenblatt, Christina Hardiment, Earle Havens, Thomas Herron, Victor Houliston, Arnold Hunt, Ann Hutchison, Hannibal Hamblin, Phebe Jensen, James E. Kelly, Michael Kiernan, Dosia Kurtyanek, Colm Lennon, Carole Levin, Arthur Marotti, Agnes Matuska, Steven May, Jean-Christophe Mayer, Richard McCoy, Hiram Morgan, Raz Chen Morris, Mary Morrissey, Alan H. Nelson, John and Julia O'Connor, John O'Malley, S.J., Evangelia Papoulia, David Pearson, Nicholas Pickwoad, Aysha Pollnitz, Goran Proot, Michael Questier, Mark Rankin, Tom Rist, Donald Russell, Alec Ryrie, Mark Sawicki, Lois Schwoerer, Tim Sheehy, Clothilde Thouret, David Trim and Chris and Ding Xiang Warner. I am indebted to each of them in profound and incalculable ways.

An earlier form of parts of Chapter 1 appeared in 'Edmund Campion in the Shadow of Paul's Cross: The Culture of Disputation', in *Paul's Cross and the*

Culture of Persuasion in England, 1520–1640, ed. Torrance Kirby and P.G. Stanwood (Leiden and Boston: Brill, 2014), 263–87. I thank Torrance Kirby for his kind permission to publish parts of this. A greatly extended form of parts of Chapter 2 appeared in 'The Queen's Visit to Oxford in 1566', *Recusant History* 31.1 (2013), 331–73; I thank Anne Dillon and the Council of the Catholic Record Society for their permission. An extended form of parts of Chapters 4, 5 and 6, appeared as '"Paths Coincident": The Parallel Lives of Dr Nicholas Sander and Edmund Campion, SJ', in the *Journal of Jesuit Studies* 1 (2014), 520–41. I thank James E. Kelly and Brill for their kind permission to publish. An earlier form of parts of Chapter 12 appeared in 'A Tangled Chronicle: The Struggle over the Memory of Edmund Campion', in *The Arts of Remembrance in Early Modern England*, ed. Andrew Gordon and Thomas Rist (Burlington and Farnham: Ashgate, 2013), 141–59. I wish to thank Erika Gaffney, Alyssa Berthiaume and Kathy Bond Borie for all their dedicated work in steering this biography so expertly from proposal to publication. Finally, I wish to thank those who read various chapters and over several years helped solve many problems, Thomas McCoog, S.J., and Nigel Ramsay, and finally, Clare Asquith, who patiently read through the whole book and wisely saved me from many deviations, errors, repetitions and a thousand excesses of various sorts.

Chapter 1
A Spectacle to all the Realme

Edmund Campion was born on 25 January 1540, in the north-east end of Paul's Churchyard, next to Paul's Cross, the open-air pulpit that was the ancient focal point for the City of London.[1] Edmund Campion was, therefore, like 'the most famous martyrs of England, Thomas à Becket and Thomas More', a Londoner.[2] When John Foxe, the martyrologist, who was later to plead for Campion's life to be spared, was invited to speak from Paul's Cross, he referred to it as 'that renowned theatre' (*tam celebre videlicet theatrum*).[3] From the age of thirteen Campion was chosen to address queens and emperors in London, Oxford and Prague.[4] Although Campion consistently chose the simple life (walking to Rome as a pilgrim, for example), he was constantly thrust forward to take the lead, as at his trial. Campion's last words on the scaffold (in the passive voice) show that he felt he had been forced to play his part in the tragedy of English religious politics:

> *Spectaculum facti sumus Deo, Angeli[s], & hominibus* saying, These are the wordes of S. Paule, Englished thus: We are made a spectacle, or a sight unto God, unto his Angels, and unto men: verified this day in me who am here a spectacle unto my lorde god, a spectacle unto his angels and unto you men.[5]

---

[1]   Paolo Bombino, *Vita et Martyrium Edmundi Campiani* (Mantua: Osanna Brothers, 1620), 1, gives this date; the translation, Bodl. MS Tanner 329, fol. 1r, mentions only the year. Robert Persons, 'Of the life and martyrdom of Father Edmond Campion', ABSI Collectanea P. I, fol. 76b; printed by J.H. Pollen, in *Letters and Notices*, 11 (1876), 219–42; (1877), 308–39; 12 (1878), 1–68 (219), merely says 'in about the yeare of God 1540'. Daniel Bartoli, S.J., *Europeae Historiae Societatis Iesu Pars Prior Anglia,* trans. Ludovicus Janinus, S.J. (Lyons: Adam Demen, 1671), p. 75, specifies the day and month, and is followed by Joannes Schmidl, S.J., *Historiae Societatis Jesu Provinciae Bohemiae Pars Prima Ab Anno Christi MDLV Ad Annum MDXCII*, 2 vols (Prague: Charles University Press, 1747), I, 336. No records of births, marriages or deaths have survived from St Faith's parish.

[2]   ABSI Collectanea, P. I, fol. 76b; Bombino, *Vita et Martyrium*, 2; Bodl. MS Tanner 329, fol. 1r.

[3]   BL MS Harley 417 (John Foxe's Papers, vol. 2), fol. 129r (my translation).

[4]   ABSI Collectanea P. I, fol. 77b; Persons confirms that Campion was 13 when he addressed the new Queen, Mary Tudor.

[5]   [Thomas Alfield], *A true reporte of the death and martyrdome of M. Campion Jesuite and preiste, & M. Sherwin, & M. Bryan preistes, at Tiborne the first of December 1581 Observid and written by a Catholike preist, which was present therat Whereunto is annexid certayne verses made by sundry persons* ([London: Verstegan, 1582]), STC 4537, ARCR II. 4, sigs B8v–C1r.

The very time and place of Campion's birth propelled him towards his role as a leading orator and preacher. At Paul's Cross, the religious divisions were publicly debated on a stone pulpit before an audience that included all the livery companies and, sometimes, so many volatile and unstable apprentices that armed guards were required.[6] Both the date and place of his birth determined that Campion's early years should be spent at the epicentre of the violently moving plates of religious and political conflict. The son of a radical stationer, he was surrounded by printers, publishers and booksellers; from beginning to end, he spent his life in the world of the book.

By the time he was twenty, London, where 'the experience of Reformation had been most intense and most immediate', had borne the brunt of four alterations of religion; parishes were instructed to smash statues and tear down altars, only to be forced, later, to restore and demolish them again in a bewildering whirligig.[7] The Aldermen helped the young King Edward to avoid armed conflict at the end of his reign, while a calm Lord Mayor, Sir Thomas White, who became Campion's surrogate father, enabled a city of divided loyalties to survive an armed rebellion that brought cannon fire to Charing Cross, and threatened Southwark with destruction in the first year of Mary's reign, 1554.[8] Campion's other patron, Sir William Chester, is recorded in Foxe's *Acts and Monuments* as the Sheriff who 'sheede tearese at the death of Christes people'.[9]

Persons and Bombino both relate the year of Campion's birth to the suppression of the monasteries.[10] Campion was to receive most of his education in the restored ruins of two religious houses. The dissolution of the monasteries, administered by Thomas Cromwell and completed in 1540, destroyed the entire educational, medical and social structure of England, and affected London badly. 'The streates & lanes in London began to swarme with beggers & roges'.[11] The city's Aldermen and rich merchants, with the help of Bishop Ridley, were able to persuade King Edward VI, in February 1552, to allow them to set up Christ's Hospital for

---

[6]   Charles Wriothesley, *A Chronicle of England*, ed. W.D. Hamilton, 2 vols (London: Camden Society, 1875), II. 97–8.

[7]   Susan Brigden, *London and the Reformation* (Oxford: Clarendon Press, 1989), p. 637.

[8]   John Stow, *The Chronicles of England, from Brute vnto this present yeare of Christ, 1580* (London: Henry Bynneman, 1580), STC 23333, pp. 1078–90, for a vivid account of Wyatt's rebellion.

[9]   Foxe, John, *The first (second) volume of ecclesiasticall history contaynyng the Actes and monuments*, 2 vols (London: J. Daye, 1570) STC 11223, p. 1804. All references will be to this edition.

[10]   Bombino, *Vita et Martyrium*, p. 1; Bodl. MS Tanner 329, fol. 1r, talks of 'a year famous for two revolutions which chaunced to religious orders, the ancient being put downe, in one place, & other new rising up elsewhere'.

[11]   William Lemprière, ed., *John Howes' MS., 1582, "A brief note of the order and manner of the proceedings in the first erection of" The Three Royal Hospitals of Christ, Bridewell and St. Thomas the Apostle* (London: Septimus Vaughan Morgan, 1904), p. 6.

fatherless children.[12] The 12-year-old Campion, who had recently lost his father, appears to have been presented to the 'hospital', when it opened on 23 November 1552, and spent nearly five years in the restored ruins of Greyfriars, until he joined Sir Thomas White's new foundation of St John's in June 1557, founded in the restored ruins of St Bernard's College, the Cistercian house of studies in Oxford. It is significant that Campion's first sermon in English (in May 1580) focused on 'how many goodly churches, monasteries & other monuments of piety' the fire that had swept England 'had devoured in an instant'.[13]

London's distinguished merchants and Lord Mayors played a central role in Campion's life. For the first 30 years of his life *Edmundus Campianus Anglus Londinensis*, as he later styled himself, benefited from their determined action.[14] His entire education at St Paul's School, founded by John Colet, and at the two new foundations of Christ's Hospital and St John's College, Oxford, was funded by the Aldermen and livery companies whose civic responsibility and private benevolence lay behind the foundation of three hospitals and the incorporation of a fourth (St Bartholomew's) between 1552 and 1557. This was a network of Hospitals: St Thomas's Hospital for 'Sore and sicke persons', Bridewell for 'ydell vagabondes' and Christ's Hospital for 'ffatherless children'.[15] The Mercers' Company funded and governed St Paul's, while Sir William Chester, Lord Mayor and Draper, Anthony Hussey, Governor of the Merchant Adventurers and of the Russia Company, and Sir Thomas White, Lord Mayor and Merchant Taylor, all helped personally to fund Campion's education; the Grocers' Company, at the request of Sir William Chester, gave Campion a scholarship in 1566, which he kept for two years.[16] The city and livery companies were justly proud of their schools: the 'men-chyleryn of the hospetall, and after the chylderne of sant Antonys and then all the chltheryn of Powlles and all ther masters and husshers', attended in their colourful uniforms the series of Easter sermons at St Mary's Spital, and took part in processions, coronations and all major civic occasions.[17]

---

[12] Lemprière, ed., p. 6.

[13] ABSI Collectanea P. I, fol. 115a.

[14] ARSI Anglia 38/1, fol. 31r. Campion also styles himself in this way on the title page of the book he acquired at Douai, the *Summa* of Thomas Aquinas, now at Heythrop College (see Chapter 3).

[15] J.A. Kingdon, *Richard Grafton: Citizen and Grocer of London* (London: privately printed, 1901), p. 8.

[16] The records of the Court of Assistants of the Grocers' Company are now in Guildhall MS 11.588, fols 156r–189r (fol. 156 for Chester's request). W.H. Stevenson and H.E. Salter, *The Early History of St John's College, Oxford* (Oxford: Clarendon Press for the Oxford Historical Society, 1939), 181–4, were the first to make full use of one of the best documented episodes in Campion's life.

[17] *The Diary of Henry Machyn*, ed. by John Gough Nichols (London: Camden Society, 1848), 87. This is just one of many public events featuring the three schools.

Campion was, in this sense, a child of the City of London, supported by its funding, paraded in its ceremonies and rewarded in its competitions. In a city that was at the heart of the Reformation struggle, the most continuous and stable element in Campion's life was his love of learning. Supported by the leading merchants and livery companies, Campion rapidly emerged as the leading schoolboy orator in London, winning at least two public competitions, and he was chosen to address the new Queen in 1553.[18] Campion's aesthetic and intellectual appreciation of classical authors must have been sharpened by their comparative stability in a world of volatile political and religious change.

The turbulence of this period is epitomized by a sequence of events that occurred in the year Campion was born. In February 1540, the conservative Bishop of Winchester, Stephen Gardiner, launched an attack on three radical reformers, Dr Robert Barnes, William Jerome and Thomas Garrett.[19] This began what Barnes himself called the 'Cockfight'.[20] When Barnes replied, Gardiner went to the King to complain how 'he being a bishop and a Prelate of the realme, was handled and reviled at Paules crosse'.[21] From the same pulpit, William Jerome also replied with a seditious sermon on 7 March. By April, all three preachers were in the Tower. On 28 July 1540, the day the King married his fifth wife, he also executed Thomas Cromwell, the man whom he had recently made Earl of Essex as a reward for overseeing the dissolution of all religious houses and the transfer of their wealth to the Crown. Two days later, on 30 July 1540, the King had Dr Robert Barnes, Thomas Garret and William Jerome burned, ostensibly for their views on transubstantiation; their radical political demands may have been more offensive, since Dr Barnes asked that

> where hys grace hath received into his hands all the goods and substance of the Abbeys … Would it to God that it might please his grace to bestow the sayd goods to the comforte of hys poore subjects who surely have great need of them.[22]

On the same day, in an ostentatious display of what Susan Brigden calls 'scrupulous equity', the King had three Catholic priests hanged, drawn and quartered for their denial of the Royal supremacy.[23] Stow glosses the event in the margin: *Sixe Priestes, three brent, three hanged.*[24] The death of Dr Barnes was immortalized

---

18   Bombino, *Vita et Martyrium*, p. 3; Bodl. MS Tanner 329, fol. 1v.

19   Foxe, *Actes and Monuments*, p. 1370.

20   Foxe, *Actes and Monuments*, p. 1371. Barnes used the term 'in a pleasant allegory'.

21   Foxe, *Actes and Monuments*, p. 1371.

22   Foxe, *Actes and Monuments*, p. 1373. Susan Brigden, *London and the Reformation* (Oxford: Clarendon Press, 1989), highlights this event as a significant moment, pp. 316–24, describing the ballad controversy that broke out, p. 322, and Grafton's part in printing some of them, p. 323.

23   Foxe, *Actes and Monuments*, p. 1374; Brigden, *London and the Reformation*, p. 315.

24   John Stow, *The Chronicles of England, from Brute vnto this present yeare of Christ, 1580* (London: Henry Bynneman, 1580), STC 23333, p. 1019.

by Foxe.[25] It became a landmark long remembered by contemporaries, which unleashed a frenzy of printed ballads.[26] Forty-one years later, a similar ballad war was to break out after Campion's death, but it was to develop into a war in print that raged in several languages across Europe, since a scholar of European renown had been executed on a manifestly false indictment.[27]

> 1° Vocor Edmundus Campianus, Anglus Londinensis, Annos natus 34 / 2° Ex legitimo Matrimonio, & Parentibus ab antiquo Christianis, & in Catholica fide, ut speratur, defunctis. Pater vocabatur Edmundus, Mater N. conditione cives & bibliopolae, mediocri fortuna.

> [1st: My name is Edmund Campion. I am English and a Londoner, now in my thirty-fourth year / 2nd: I was born from parents who were legitimately married, had long been Christian, and who have now died (it is to be hoped) in the Catholic faith. My father was called Edmond, my mother N., and they were free citizens and stationers of modest means.][28]

Edmund Campion's written answers to the 'Examen' on 26 August 1573, when he entered the Society of Jesus in Prague, confirm the importance of his London background, the date of his birth and suggest that his mother, Alice, took over the business when his father died, sometime before November 1552.[29] His guarded statement that his parents 'had long been Christian', but had died, he hoped, in the Catholic faith, tells us a great deal that can now be corroborated from other sources. He was clearly not present when they died, but the statement conceals the pain of a son divided by religion from both his *patria* (London) and his parents, able only to hope (and not to know) that his parents had died in the Catholic faith. Robert Persons, apparently unaware of Campion's reservation, later asserted that his parents were 'very honest & catholick'.[30]

The father who 'was called Edmond Campion' and whose house seems to have been only feet from Paul's Cross, was a stationer (*bibliopola*) the profession involved in publishing, printing and selling books, which was undergoing a radical transformation during Campion's lifetime. We now know exactly where in London his parents lived. Edmund Campion senior is registered in the Subsidy Roll of 1541 as living in St Faith's parish, and his wealth is assessed at £40: 'of modest wealth',

---

25 John Foxe, *Actes and Monuments*, pp. 1363–74 (p. 1374, with woodcuts).

26 Brigden, *London and the Reformation*, pp. 322–4.

27 See Chapter 12.

28 ARSI Anglia 38/1, fol. 31r, a copy of a lost original, with significant differences from the continuous statement in Schmidl, *Historiae*, I. 338–9. We know his mother's name from the nuncupative will discussed below.

29 Paolo Bombino, *Vita et Martyrium*, p. 3; Bodl. MS Tanner 329, fol. 1v, must be mistaken when he states that Campion was still 12 at Mary's accession: 'no sooner was he twelve yeares old'.

30 ABSI Collectanea P. I, fol. 77a (Fr Christopher Grene, S.J., has numbered the openings, not the leaves, so I have used *a* for the verso, and *b* for the recto).

mediocri fortuna, as his son later said.[31] It was even more modest in 1544, when his wealth was assessed at only £10; his fortunes continued to decline.[32] On 30 June 1545, 'Edmundus Campyon Stacyoner' was brought before the Court of Aldermen, and bound on a recognizance of £40, on condition that he appear in person at the next Court of Aldermen, and then at each subsequent meeting until further notice.[33] His offence is not recorded, but his attendance was reported at every meeting until 3 November, when he was discharged of his obligation, and Robert Toy, James Holyland and Thomas Petyt each had to offer sureties of £20 for him.[34] Twenty-four years later, Humphrey Toy and William Norton stood surety for the young Edmund Campion when he compounded for the first fruits of a benefice.[35] Of the two parishes attached to the colossal cathedral, 'Seynt Faythes-under-Paules' was the one with a 'cluster of recognizable stationers', and they seemed to have formed a tight-knit, fiercely loyal, if frequently irascible, family.[36]

The cathedral, with its bustling, noisy churchyard, where gossip, booksellers, printers and publishers competed with the episcopal and civic authorities, must have dominated the first 17 years of Campion's life, providing a rich visual and auditory backcloth to Campion's childhood. Stow says that the spire rose to 520 feet, until it was struck by lightning in 1561, while the cathedral towered over the tightly packed city, as it still does over contemporary maps of the city (Plate 1).[37] Paul's Churchyard, a busy and crowded precinct measuring 900 by 600 feet, was almost filled by the massive cathedral, so large that most people cut through the path from the north to the south door, sometimes bringing their animals with them. Throughout this period, 'Paules' was the central space for Londoners, where you could catch the latest news or gossip; at his trial with Campion, Thomas Cottam protested that the fact that he 'walked daylye in Paules' was a sign of his 'innocency'.[38] The church of St Faith's was located in the crypt (sometimes called the Crowds or Shrouds) along with the confraternity of the Brotherhood of Jesus.

---

[31] R.G. Lang, ed., *Two Tudor Subsidy Assessment Rolls for the City of London: 1541 and 1582* (London: London Record Society, 1993), p. 72. 'The Parte of Seynt Faythes Parishe' in the 1541 Subsidy Roll is number 107. I thank David Trim for alerting me to this valuable document.

[32] Peter W.M. Blayney, *The Stationers' Company and the Printers of London, 1501–1557*, 2 vols (Cambridge: University Press, 2013), p. 530. Blayney introduced me to this episode in personal communication, led me to the documents and then set them all out in his monumental study.

[33] Blayney, *Stationers' Company*, 534 and 598 n. 109.

[34] LMA, COL/CA/01/01/011, fols 205v, 218v, 219v, 221v and 241v.

[35] See Chapter 2.

[36] Blayney, *Stationers' Company*, p. 534.

[37] Wilberforce Jenkinson, *London Churches before the Great Fire* (London: SPCK, 1917), p. 5, cites Dugdale's *History of St. Paul's*.

[38] BL MS Harley 6265, fol. 20v.

It was here that the Stationers met for worship, and the only counter-Reformation sodality founded in England, the Brotherhood of Jesus, held its grand funerals.[39]

The parish of St Faith's consisted mainly of the houses in Paternoster Row, the northern boundary of Paul's Churchyard, and the centre of the printing industry, inhabited by many of the best known stationers, the term that had come to embrace the entire company of printers, publishers and booksellers, even before they were incorporated as a livery company in 1557. Some parishioners had houses and shops in the Cross Yard, where John Colet had founded his school between 1509 and 1512, close to Paul's Cross. The evidence suggests that Edmond and Alice Campion lived in the north-east end of the churchyard.[40] This is supported by a remarkable will of 1549 that was made 'in the Mansion house of the scholemaster of Paules' by Richard Jones when he was 'suffering from a peculiar quartan fever running in his blood'.[41] Richard Jones was the third Master of St Paul's, who had been at the school since 1522, when William Lyly died, and he succeeded Lyly's son-in-law, John Ritwise, as Master. Since the will was nuncupative (oral), there was clearly a crisis in his fever, which had necessitated the summoning of eight witnesses, who were all close neighbours, and included the Surmaster (usher) James Jacob.[42] The late Henry Jacob, presumably his father, had owned the shop next to the school; the musician called John Jacob, who was arrested with Campion at Lyford Grange in 1581, may have been the son of James.[43] There were four women present, which was most unusual: Denys, the wife of James Jacob; Anne, wife of Thomas Dockwray, notary and Proctor of the Court of Arches, and, in 1557, first Master of the Stationers' Company; Elizabeth (born Scampion), wife of Robert Toy; and Alice, wife of Edmond Campion.[44] Actually, Richard Jones

---

[39]   Brigden, *London and the Reformation*, p. 582.

[40]   The basis for nearly all this detailed knowledge is Peter W.M. Blayney, *The Bookshops in Paul's Cross Churchyard* (London: Bibliographic Society, 1990), 35, 45, 50–51. His study mapped the exact location of most of the printers and publishers in the Churchyard. In a personal letter of 7 July 2009, Blayney supplemented this by a list of those in St Faith's parish who owned houses in Paternoster Row. Since Edmund and Alice Campion were not there, they must have been in the north-east end of the Churchyard, the only other habitation in the parish. Peter Blayney writes that 'Most of the last dozen natives listed for St Faith's [in the Subsidy Roll of 1541] can be located in the houses lining the north side of the Cross Yard, so it's quite likely that Campion was somewhere in that range – but there's not enough evidence to pinpoint him'.

[41]   Michael McDonnell, 'Edmund Campion, S.J. and St Paul's School', *Notes and Queries* 194 (1949), 46–9, 67–70, 90–92 (91); Blayney, *Stationers' Company*, pp. 693–4.

[42]   Blayney, *Stationers' Company*, p. 693.

[43]   Blayney, *Stationers' Company*, p. 693.

[44]   Blayney, *Stationers' Company*, p. 693 (where Campion's mother is named Alice) and p. 898 n. B (where he suggests that Elizabeth Scampion may have considered herself a relative of the Campion family). There are no women named in the 40 examples of wills given in Henry R. Plomer, *Abstracts from the Wills of English Printers and Stationers from 1492 to 1630* (London: Bibliographic Society, 1903).

survived a few months more, but his will confirms what we know from other sources: that Campion's family lived on the eastern side of the Churchyard, were close to St Paul's School (and its schoolmasters), and to Robert Toy and Thomas Dockwray.

Campion grew up, surrounded by printers, just as English printing, still lagging behind the big continental centres like Venice, Paris and Basel, and still heavily dependent on foreign craftsmen, began to make an independent mark.[45] The majority of stationers, like Campion's father, were of a 'godly' persuasion, as suggested by the fact that so many disappear from view or go into exile under Mary Tudor (no light decision for a printer).[46] Thomas Dockwray, first master of the newly incorporated Stationers' Company in 1557, stands out as a committed Catholic and member of the revived Brotherhood of Jesus, but he was a notary; William Rastell, John Cawood and Robert Caly are exceptions in a largely reformist profession.

Edmond Campion senior published, around 1548, an octavo volume of four virulently anti-papist tracts, under the title, *Newes from Rome concerning the blasphemous sacrifice of the papisticall Masse with dyvers other treatises very Godlye & profitable.*[47] The book, written by Randall Hurlestone, was 'Prynted at Cantorbury by J. Mychell. for E. Campion'; John Mychell was one of Archbishop Cranmer's printers, who had also worked for Edward Whitchurch, the partner of Richard Grafton in the enterprise of the 'Great Bible' of 1539.[48] The book that Campion senior published, which contains fierce attacks on the Mass, on vestments and ceremonies, on saints and, crucially, on transubstantiation, perhaps the most controversial issue of the period between 1540 and 1547 when Henry VIII was trying to maintain an orthodox view on all Catholic doctrine, 'leaves no doubt about where his religious sympathies lay'.[49] It was ostensibly for his views on the sacrament of the Eucharist that Cromwell was executed in 1540.[50]

We do not know what his mother or the young Campion believed during these early years, but his father's publication and the dominant reformist atmosphere among printers, publishers and their apprentices, suggest that he grew up in an atmosphere that was predominantly godly, and may have been conflicted.

---

[45]   Andrew Pettegree, 'Printing and the Reformation: The English Exception', in *The Beginnings of English Protestantism*, ed. Peter Marshall and Alec Ryrie (Cambridge: University Press, 2002), pp. 157–79 (p. 162), stresses the dominance of Latin in books published in Europe.

[46]   Pettegree, 'Printing and the Reformation', pp. 176–7.

[47]   See note 62, and Blayney, *Stationers' Company*, p. 32. Both the STC and Blayney think 1548 the most likely date. Blayney, *Stationers' Company*, p. 32, thinks it was issued 'early in the reign of Edward VI'.

[48]   Blayney, *Stationers' Company*, p. 655, puts Campion among publishers who had others print for them.

[49]   Blayney, *Stationers' Company*, p. 655 n. B.

[50]   Brigden, *London and the Reformation*, p. 314.

The freedom enjoyed by printers and the heady excitement experienced by young readers of the English Bible during the reign of Edward, when Campion was at grammar school, must have been infectious. William Maldon of Essex was a young apprentice when the Scriptures were set forth 'to be rede in all churches in ingelonde', and recounts that he joined readers of the New Testament at the back of the church in Chelmsford, and was so gripped by it that he and his father's apprentice 'layed our money to gether' and bought a copy themselves and 'and hydde it in our bedstrawe & so exercysed it at convenyent tymes'.[51] When his irate father discovered the bedstraw Bible, he thrashed William and threatened him with an impromptu hanging, accusing him, as he recalls, of speaking against 'the kynges injunctiones'.[52] Although the date is not precise, the time must have been shortly after the year of Campion's birth, 1540, and before the death of Henry VIII in 1547.

The lethal programme of repression under Mary was not calculated to win the hearts and minds of the young. Several edicts suggest the authorities were particularly worried about unrest among apprentices in London.[53] It is possible that Campion went up to Oxford more godly than Catholic, and that his gradual and rather uncertain embrace of Catholicism may not have been just a dangerous and costly 'coming out', as it has been portrayed ever since Persons and Bombino, but a real intellectual conversion that occurred gradually between 1557, when he began to grow close to the remarkable Sir Thomas White, and 1571, when he finally left for Douai. Campion spent the first 30 years of his life in the midst of passionate religious conflict, in institutions which had endured 'fower chaunges in religion, all fower capitall, all 4 within litle more then 14 yeare'.[54] The public allegiances of men in these institutions may have differed from their private beliefs.

Edmond Campion, stationer, lived opposite Thomas Berthelet, Thomas Dockwray, Reyner Wolfe and Richard Jugge, and was a neighbour to Toy, Petyt and John Cawood. Toy and Petyt are registered in St Faith's parish in the Subsidy Roll of 1541; Toy is valued at £20, and Petyt at £100.[55] We know they were close neighbours of Campion's on the east side of Paul's Churchyard from descriptions of their premises in wills.[56] Robert Toy, Thomas Petyt and Thomas Berthelet were

---

[51] Charles C. Butterworth, *The English Primers (1529–1545): Their Publication and Connection with the English Bible and the Reformation in England* (Philadelphia: University of Pennsylvania Press, 1953), p. 202.

[52] Butterworth, *English Primers*, p. 202, quoting BL MS Harley 590.

[53] Brigden, *London and the Reformation*, pp. 599–600.

[54] The quotation comes from Sir John Harington, whose father had a house in the west end of Paul's Churchyard, in the treatise he sent Tobie Matthew, then Bishop of Durham, in 1602, York MS XVI.L.6, 239; printed in *A Tract on the Succession to the Crown (1602 A.D.)*, ed. Clements R. Markham (London: Roxburghe Club, 1880), p. 106.

[55] R.G. Lang, ed., *Two Tudor Subsidy Assessment Rolls for the City of London: 1541 and 1582* (London: London Record Society, 1993), p. 107.

[56] Plomer, *Wills of English Printers*, pp. 12–13, 15 (for the wills of Robert Toy and his widow, Elizabeth).

all involved, along with Richard Grafton and Edward Whitchurch, in the publishing of English and Latin primers. The repressed book trade experienced a period of liberation for the reformist writers from 1547, so that *Newes from Rome* would fit very well into the efflorescence of print in the year 1548. This was the year the Reformation in England went into full swing. The high altar in St Paul's was dismantled, statues smashed, the rood-screen destroyed, pictures whitewashed and a thousand years of piety swept away in one of the most iconoclastic episodes in history. The Injunctions of 31 July 1547 affected every parish in London, including the two schools that Campion attended:

> At St Paul's school the picture of Jesus was removed, along with the tablet over the tomb of Colet, its founder … At the dissolved Grey Friars all the altars were pulled down, the tombs of the nobility in alabaster and marble carried away, the walls and stalls of the choir demolished. One by one, the churches were transformed, reformed from idolatry: the brightly painted walls now whitelimed, pulpits replaced tabernacles, Scriptural messages replaced wall paintings, plain glass stood in the windows.[57]

On 27 November 1547, the preacher at Paul's Cross, displaying in front of the pulpit a statue of Our Lady hidden by the parishioners and found by the visitors, attacked 'the great abhomination of idolatrie in images', and then invited the boys of St Paul's to smash the statue.[58] Campion may have been too young to be selected for the team of iconoclasts, but he must have watched. The Marian reimposition of statues and rood-screens aroused equal resistance. On 15 October 1555, the Governors of Christ's Hospital, including Sir Thomas White, complained about being asked to pay for 'the reedifienge of a Rode lofte'.[59] For the largely Protestant publishing profession Edward's reign was a brief golden era, brought to a dramatic end with the arrival of a Catholic queen in 1553. The new queen, after allying herself with the Spanish throne, attempted to reverse the changes of the previous 20 years.

For Campion, the smell of ink and damp paper, as the sheets were hung up to dry, and the noise of the presses must have been as much a part of his life as the sound of preachers at Paul's Cross. When he went to Christ's Hospital (the restored Greyfriars) in 1552, his journey was no more than 300 yards: out of Paul's Gate, along Paternoster Row, up Ivy Lane and across Newgate Market. All the way were printers and booksellers. The situation in the old Greyfriars itself must have been bizarre. The type and presses of Richard Grafton, which he had rescued from Paris, were confiscated and given to the Catholic printer Robert Caly, usually known as 'Papist Robin the promoter [informer]'. Yet Grafton who, like Campion's father, had worked with John Mychell, stayed on as a governor of Christ's Hospital.[60]

---

[57]   Brigden, *London and the Reformation*, pp. 428–9.
[58]   Wriothesley, *Chronicle*, II. 1.
[59]   Kingdon, *Richard Grafton*, p. 74.
[60]   Brigden, *London and the Reformation*, p. 623.

It was Campion who, according to Persons, first suggested that the Jesuit missionaries acquire a press, came down to supervise the printing, and first printed a book on the Greenstreet House press in Roman type.[61] Campion's last public act before his capture, in 1581, was to instruct William Hartley to place 400 copies of *Rationes Decem* on the seats of academics gathered for the annual Commencement ceremony in the university church of St Mary the Virgin, Oxford. It is a fitting climax to the life of the son of a publisher of controversial literature. It is hardly surprising that the most consistent element in the life of a London boy who early won competitions in Latin oratory was his love of disputation, nor that the son of a man who had published *Newes from Rome*, a radical reformist book, should challenge the two universities to public debate with a book printed in an attic on a secret printing press.[62] This is a perfect illustration of the tempest of religious change that divided cities, universities, schools and families.[63]

London was at this time an independent and burgeoning mercantile centre, opening up new trade routes to Russia, Persia and Africa. To understand Campion it is important to imagine just how enclosed the city was, and how international the Thames made it feel. Londoners combined a hostile attitude to foreigners (especially Spaniards) with a restless zeal for trade and travel.[64] The bishops who went into exile under Mary spent their time in Geneva or Frankfurt and brought back with them the books of Calvin, Luther and Zwingli. The Venetian Ambassador, Giovanni Michiel, in the fourth year of Mary's reign, 1557, when Edmund Campion was 17, describes London as a vibrant city of 185,000 inhabitants. He picks out one political and two striking, architectural features:

> It has handsome streets and buildings, especially the bridge, which has nineteen arches, all of solid stone, over the river, and the cathedral church of St Paul. And yet most beautiful is the site of the City placed, as it is, advantageously on the banks of the Thames, from which, besides beauty, it derives great wealth (*gran commodita*) from the vast concourse of ships, of three and four hundred Venetian tons burthen, which enter the river from every quarter, being aided by the strong ebb and flow of the sea, although more than sixty miles from the city. Above all, London is most opulent, not only from her trade and great commerce with other countries, but by the many privileges enjoyed by all the inhabitants themselves, without exception, that is to say, by the commonalty, merchants,

---

[61] ABSI Collectanea, P. I, fol. 152b.

[62] Randall Hurlestone, *Newes from Rome concerning the blasphemous sacrifice of the papisticall Masse with dyuers other treatises very Godlye and profitable* (Prynted at Cantorbury for E. Campion [n.d., 1548?]), STC 14006; Edmund Campion, *Rationes Decem* ([Stonor Park: S. Brinkley, 1581]), STC 4536.5, ARCR I. 135.1.

[63] For the difficulty of determining allegiance in this period, see Alec Ryrie, 'Counting Sheep, Counting Shepherds: The Problem of Allegiance in the English Reformation', in *The Beginnings of English Protestantism*, ed. Peter Marshall and Alec Ryrie (Cambridge: University Press, 2002), pp. 84–110.

[64] As instructions from the livery companies make clear; Brigden, *London and the Reformation*, p. 556.

and artificers, from amongst whom some twenty-five persons, called Aldermen (elected from amongst the wealthiest and most monied amongst them) rule the city with supreme power, almost like a Republic, neither the King nor his ministers interfering in any way. I have used the term commonalty (*huomeni populari*), because the nobility, according to the custom of France and Germany, all live in the country remote from the city.[65]

When Cardinal Pole landed at Whitehall in the royal barge in 1554, it was with all the pomp of a man who had spent years among Italian humanists in Padua, and only narrowly missed being elected Pope in 1549. Yet, the London that prepared for the arrival of Philip in 1554, had very nearly joined the rebellion led by Sir Thomas Wyatt. While they wished to be part of the learning and reforms of continental Europe, Londoners had no wish to be ruled by the future King of Spain.

If the Thames was the source of London's trading wealth, Paul's Churchyard was its hub. Monarchs came there before going to Westminster to be crowned; the Lord Mayor and Aldermen processed there on Sundays or sat in hierarchical ranks for the sermons, and the Bishop of London, *ex cathedra Sancti Pauli*, attempted to control the religious views of the capital and, therefore, of the country. The Cross Yard was dominated by Paul's Cross, which was both the focal point of the City of London and the site of large civic sermons, attended by the Lord Mayor, Aldermen, livery companies and all the crafts and trades in their distinctive costumes, together with the 'boys of Paules'. Several sources suggest the audience (which was by no means passive) could number six or seven thousand.[66] Campion was the child of a city where the culture of the spoken word, whether in sermons at St Mary's Spital, Paul's Cross, or any of the 123 parish churches, or in public disputations and schoolboy competitions, dominated the landscape. It was here that some of the biggest dramas of the reformation were to be played out during Campion's childhood and schooldays. As religious opinions went through their most complex and conflicted time in history, Paul's Cross became the public barometer of the nation's views. As Arnold Hunt has argued:

> By the end of the sixteenth century, Paul's Cross sermons had become distinctively 'London' occasions, in which preachers addressed their exhortations to the mayor and aldermen in particular, offering them moral guidance on the government of the City and drawing their attention to sins and divisions within the civic community.[67]

---

[65]   *CSP Venetian, 1556–1557*, VI. 1045, no. 884.

[66]   Mary Morrissey, *Politics and the Paul's Cross Sermons, 1558–1642* (Oxford: University Press, 2011), p. 102.

[67]   Arnold Hunt, *The Art of Hearing: English Preachers and Their Audiences, 1590–1640* (Cambridge: University Press, 2010), pp. 320–42 (p. 323). The whole section is a superb analysis of the role and continuing importance of Paul's Cross.

During Edward's brief reign, the reformers enjoyed something like religious freedom. Trouble lay ahead when, on Monday, 15 January 1554, Mary announced to the Mayor and Aldermen her decision to marry a foreigner, and coupled it with a demand that they ensure that God's religion 'which they had yett verie slacklye sett forth' be better kept 'within the cittie that they might be a spectacle to all the realme'.[68] London was to be the stage on which a pattern of the revived religion would be played, in processions, sermons and large competitions in public disputation.

Some of the most dramatic scenes occurred at the beginning of Mary's reign. Edmund Bonner, Bishop of London, and Stephen Gardiner, Bishop of Winchester, whose diocese stretched to Southwark, attempted to reimpose orthodoxy, with 'a concerted campaign of preaching' the focus of which 'was London's major preaching venue Paul's Cross'.[69] Bishop Bonner made sure that there was 'the highest possible attendance, the Lord Mayor and aldermen in their robes leading the way', and even attempted to silence London streets by telling churchwardens that 'during the Paul's Cross sermons there should be no "ryngynge of belles, playinge of Children, cryenge or making lowd noyse, rydynge of horses, or otherwyse, so that the Preacher there or his audience was troubled thereby"'.[70] On Sunday, 13 August 1553, only 10 days after Mary's entry into London, an incident described in several contemporary chronicles, shows how major currents crystallized round this stone pulpit, especially during the hot days of August. Dr Gilbert Bourne, Bonner's chaplain, mounted the pulpit to denounce the long imprisonment of his bishop during Edward's reign. Bourne managed to rouse the indignation of his audience in such a way that they were 'showtyng at hys sermon, as yt [were] lyke madpepull'.[71] The crowd tried to drag him from the pulpit and someone threw a dagger at him; it struck the wooden post of the pulpit and 'rebounded back a great waye'.[72] When the Lord Mayor, Sir George Barnes and Aldermen failed to restore order, two evangelical preachers, later to be among the first martyrs of Mary's burning, John Rogers and John Bradford, found themselves trying to restrain the crowd of young men and women.[73] After the dagger was thrown, Bradford gave up trying to calm the crowd and, with the help of Rogers, managed to get Bourne inside the safety of Paul's School.

---

[68] Wriothesley, *Chronicle*, II. 106.

[69] Eamon Duffy, *Fires of Faith: Catholic England under Mary Tudor* (New Haven and London: Yale University Press, 2009), p. 19.

[70] Duffy, *Fires of Faith*, p. 19, quoting Edmund Bonner, *Interrogatories upon which ... Churchwardens shall be Charged* (London, 1558), STC 10117, no. 47.

[71] Morrissey, *Paul's Cross*, p. 7, citing *Diary of Henry Machyn* (1848), p. 41; *Chronicle of the Grey Friars of London*, ed. John Gough Nichols (London: Camden Society, 1852), p. 83.

[72] Stow, *Chronicles*, p. 1068.

[73] Wriothesley, *Chronicle*, II. 98.

This busines was so heynously declared to the Quene and her Counsell, that my Lord Mayor and Aldermen were sent for to the Quenes Counsell to the Tower the 14 and 15 of August, and yt was sore layd to theyr charge, that the liberties of the city had lyke to [haue] bene taken away from them, and to depose the Lord Mayor, straightly charginge the Mayor and Aldermen to make a direct ansere to them on Wednesday the 16 of August whether they would rule the city in peace and good order, or ells they would sett other rulers ouer them.[74]

The Mayor, Sir George Barnes, summoned 'the Commons of the liverye' to pass on the warning, and the Common Council pledged loyalty and a tough line on offenders. The edicts that followed make clear that the authorities associated the trouble with young apprentices (like William Maldon), set free from authority by reading the Bible in English. On 16 August, apprentices and servants were ordered to attend their parish churches and on no account to 'wear dagger nor other weapon'. On the following Sunday, 20 August, when Dr Watson, soon to be Bishop of Lincoln preached, no chances were taken. 'A troop of two hundred men accompanied the preacher to the pulpit and stood around it all through the sermon', and many of the Privy Council were present, while the Mayor, Sheriffs, Aldermen and all the Livery Companies and Crafts, sat in separate ordered rows.[75] The Cross, which had acted as a flashpoint of riot and disorder, was now made to represent civic hierarchy. All this happened outside Campion's front door.

In 1554, the Lord Mayor, Sir Thomas White, successfully saw off Wyatt's rebellion, which brought cannon to Charing Cross.[76] The heads of the traitors were taken down only when the city prepared for the marriage of Philip and Mary, an event that brought many Spaniards to London, and a great deal of tension. Campion was 14 when, outside his door, on Sunday, 10 June 1554, just over a month before the royal marriage:

> there was a gonne shotte nere Powlles cherch-yerd that the pellyt came nere the prechers face that preched at Powlles crosse.[77]

The pellet narrowly missed Sir Thomas White who was attending the sermon, sitting in his accustomed place below the pulpit, 'the pellet hittinge the churche wall next where the Lord Mayre satt'.[78] The intended target was Dr Pendleton, a man who had been 'an itinerant protestant preacher' in Edward's reign, who had conformed under the new Queen to become a notable Catholic persuader, preacher and disputant'.[79] Perhaps the pistol-shot expressed a sense of betrayal at the 'conversion' of this famous preacher.

---

[74]   Wriothesley, *Chronicle*, II. 98.

[75]   Morrissey, *Paul's Cross*, p. 7.

[76]   See below for full discussion of the rebellion.

[77]   *Chronicle of the Grey Friars*, p. 90.

[78]   Wriothesley, *Chronicle*, II. 117.

[79]   Duffy, *Fires of Faith*, pp. 12–13.

> The x. of June, Doctoure Pendleton preached at Paules Crosse, at whome a
> Gunne was shotte, the pellet whereof went very neare him, and lighte on the
> Churche wall. But the shooter coulde not be founde.[80]

It was a violent indication of the strength of the reform movement in London.
Stow records that on 22 June 'was Proclamation made forbidding the shooting
of handgunnes, and bearing of weapons'.[81] This event, disrupting the order of the
City and the tradition of preaching, must have lingered long in the memory.

Campion, who had spent his formative years in Paul's Churchyard, developed
a lifelong devotion to disputation, and a belief that intellectual argument was the
only solution to the theological differences of the period. If he was unlucky in
being born into the epicentre of religious conflict, where printing and preaching
alike battled with changes of royal policy, he was extremely fortunate to benefit
from an education at London schools that enabled him to become the leading
schoolboy orator.

Campion would have joined St Paul's School around 1547, when Richard
Jones, described by Polydore Virgil as 'a learned and discreet man' (*homo doctus
atque modestus*) was still Master.[82] After the nuncupative will discussed above,
he seems to have lingered on till he was replaced on 8 October by Thomas
Freeman, who had been the first Master of the Mercers' other London school,
in the old Hospital of St Thomas Acon. Freeman was dismissed by the Mercers
on 27 May 1559, on the grounds that he 'was not seen or learned in the Greek
tongue as was well known at his first entrance'.[83] The real reason appears to have
been that he was not sympathetic to the reformed religion.[84] Although the school
had to follow all the regulations that accompanied each change of regime and
religion, we cannot know what was the dominant religious belief in St Paul's
School while Campion was there under Richard Jones and Thomas Freeman.
One account of a Bodmin school at the same time, shortly before the so-called
Prayer Book rebellion of 1549, gives us a glimpse of how the religious divisions
permeated school life. The boys divided themselves into 'two factions, the one
whereof they called the old religion, the other the new' until real harm was
caused and the fighting suppressed.[85] As Alec Ryrie argues, 'by 1553 the English
had come, like the schoolboys of Bodmin, to see themselves as a nation divided
by religion'.[86]

---

[80]   Stow, *Chronicles*, p. 1091.

[81]   Stow, *Chronicles*, p. 1091.

[82]   Michael McDonnell, *The Registers of St Paul's School 1509–1748* (London:
privately printed, 1977). p. 27.

[83]   McDonnell, *Registers of St Paul's*, p. 32.

[84]   McDonnell, *Registers of St Paul's*, p. 32.

[85]   Ryrie, 'Counting Sheep', p. 109.

[86]   Ryrie, 'Counting Sheep', p. 110.

In 1509, St Paul's school was founded for 153 boys (the number of fish in St Peter's catch) by one of the greatest deans of St Paul's, John Colet. Colet asked the help of his friend Erasmus in drawing up a plan of study, and the books Erasmus supplied, quickly became standard textbooks. The *De ratione studii* was written specially for Colet in 1511, and Erasmus gave two other works to Colet, the *De copia*, dedicated to Colet in 1512, and the book of John Lyly's that he heavily revised at Colet's request; first published in 1513, it was always known as 'Lyly's Grammar'.[87] By the 1540s when Campion joined the school, St Paul's and its curriculum had become the model for all the other major schools in the country. A decade later, the new grammar schools set up under Edward VI in towns like Stratford, Southampton, Birmingham and Bath, all followed this pattern. The emphasis on learning to speak well in Latin was to play a central role in Campion's life. By 1540, Colet's school was at the height of its influence. Eton, Winchester, Westminster and Canterbury were all following the same curriculum, using 'Lyly's Grammar' and Erasmus's *De Copia* as their textbooks.

Central was the study of the great classics of Greek and Latin literature. Since these works formed the basis of the last four years of school, under the heading of rhetoric, the first four years were spent mastering the grammar that would enable the pupil to read, to write and, above all, to speak the languages fluently. The sixteenth-century school was dominated by speaking aloud: debating, argument, composition, verse recitation and variation. What made Erasmus's method particularly successful was his emphasis on learning as a game: 'I'm not sure anything is learned better than what is learned as a game'.[88] He goes on to recommend competitions as an incentive, 'a mock contest', though he deplores the use of chess or dice, as these games are too complicated.[89] He cites Quintilian to associate his theory of play with the importance of the early learning of languages:

> After the first elements have been imparted I should personally prefer a boy to be encouraged to practise speaking right from the start. For since young children can pronounce any language, however barbarous, within months, is there any reason why the same thing should not occur in Greek or Latin?[90]

---

[87]   Erasmus, *De ratione studii, ac legendi, interpretandique auctores libellus aureus, Officium discipulorum ex Quintiliano. Qui primo legendi, ex eodem*, 2nd ed. (Strasbourg: Schurer, 1513); *Collected Works of Erasmus*, 24, *De Copia*, trans. Betty I. Knott; *De Ratione Studii*, trans. and annot. Brian McGregor (Toronto: University of Toronto Press, 1978). 'Lyly's Grammar' was first published in 1513 by Richard Pynson, King's Printer, and later by Thomas Berthelet, who had succeeded him, in 1540.

[88]   *CWE*, vol. 40, *Colloquies*, trans. and annot. Craig R. Thompson (Toronto: University of Toronto Press, 1997), p. 1098.

[89]   *CWE*, vol. 26, *De pueris Statim ac liberaliter instituendis declamatio*, trans. and annot. Beert C. Verstraete (Toronto: University of Toronto Press, 1985), p. 339.

[90]   *CWE*, vol. 24, *De ratione studii*, p. 675.

Erasmus points out that children are naturally imitative and can learn languages more easily than adults, 'especially when the subject is taught in the guise of play by a wise and sympathetic instructor'.[91]

The canon of writers established by Erasmus formed the basis both of the curriculum in schools, and of the two universities. When, in 1517, Bishop Fox founded Corpus Christi College, Oxford, when Sir Thomas Pope wrote the statutes for Trinity College, Oxford, in 1555, and when Sir Thomas White founded St John's College, Oxford, in 1557, they laid down a syllabus that followed the recommendations of Erasmus. Campion's London schooling and his university education, in that sense, were remarkably continuous. Not only was the syllabus in both cases devised by the most influential educational theorist of all time, but the personnel were also the same. Sir Thomas White, even as he was founding St John's, was still working as an active Governor of Christ's Hospital, where he is listed as a Governor in the earliest extant Court minute from 25 November 1556. Campion's schooling, even before he arrived at St John's, enabled him to speak fluently in Latin, whether in formal orations or in rhetorical disputation. The groundwork for a brilliant career as an orator was firmly and carefully laid before Campion reached Oxford.

All the school registers, like the records of St Faith's parish, perished in the Great Fire of 1666. John Evelyn's diary of account of 7 September 1666, describes how 'that goodly Church of St Paul' has now become 'a sad ruin':

> The ruines of the vaulted roof, falling, broke into St Faith's, which being filled with the Magazines of bookes belonging to the Stationers, and carried thither for safety, they were consumed, burning for a week following. Thus lay in ashes that most venerable church, one of the most antient pieces of early piety in the Christian World.[92]

Campion seems to have been at Colet's school until he was 12, before moving to Christ's Hospital. Robert Persons's statement that Campion was in 'the grammar schooles of London' is, therefore, correct.[93]

Campion's life as a schoolboy was anything but dull. He won more than one school competition, probably in 1552, while at St Paul's, and in 1555, while at Christ's Hospital.[94] The first evidence comes from Persons's recollections:

---

[91]   *CWE*, vol. 26, *De pueris instituendis*, p. 346.

[92]   Quoted by Wilberforce Jenkinson, *London Churches Before the Great Fire* (London: SPCK, 1917), p. 37.

[93]   ABSI Collectanea P. I, fol. 77a.

[94]   Michael McDonnell, 'Edmund Campion, S.J. and St Paul's School', *Notes and Queries* 194 (1949), 46–9, 67–70, 90–92, particularly in the second section (67–70) makes a convincing case. Since there is no evidence of any competition in 1553 or 1554, I suggest the above dates.

The tokens of his future good talents and excellency of witt & ability in learning were diverse wayes discovered in the tender yeares of his first studies in London, for that being eminent above the rest he bare away ever commonly the game in all contention of learning proposed by the schooles of London to their schollers, whereof himself somtimes afterwards would merrily make mention & name the rewards that there were given to him, though ever with great modesty, for that they touched his own praise and commendation.[95]

John Stow tells us that these competitions were originally held in the churchyard of St Bartholomew's Priory, 'where vpon a banke boorded about vnder a Tree, some one Scholler hath stepped vp, and there hath apposed and answered, till he were by some better Scholler ouercome and put downe', but that, after the property had been surrendered to Henry VIII, the disputations had ceased until they were:

> in the raigne of *Edward* the 6. revived in the Cloystre of *Christes Hospitall*, where the best Schollers, then stil of S. *Anthonies* schoole, howsoever the same be now fallen, both in number and estimation, were rewarded with bowes and arrowes of silver, given to them by *Sir Martin Bowes, Goldsmith*. Nevertheless, howsoever the encouragement fayled, the [schollers of Paules, meeting with them of S. Antonies, would call them Anthonie pigs, and they againe would call the other pigeons of Paules, because manie pieigons were bred in Paules Church, and Saint Anthonie was alwayes figured with a pigge following him: and] children mindfull of the former usage, did for a long season disorderly in the open streete provoke one another with *Salue tu quoque, placet tibi mecum disputare, placet?* and so proceeding from this to questions in Grammar, they usually fel from that to blowes [with their Satchels full of bookes], many times in so great heapes that they troubled the streets, and passengers: so that finally they were restrained [with the decay of Saint Antonies schoole].[96]

The first record of a competition in Mary's reign, is on Bartholomew Eve, 23 August 1555, by which time Campion was certainly at Christ's Hospital, the new location, and the prizes have been changed: three silver pens for three games.[97] Behind this change may have been the Sheriff for that year, William Chester, who was Campion's patron. Both as an individual, and as part of these schools, Campion became used to being on the stage that public events in London then required.

It was presumably because of his success in competitions that Campion was chosen to address the new Queen, Mary Tudor, as she first entered London, on 3 August 1553:

---

[95]   ABSI Collectanea P. I, fol. 77a.

[96]   *A Survay of London* (London: John Wolfe, 1598) STC 23341, pp. 55–6, with additions [in square brackets] from *A Survay of London* (London: John Windet, 1603) STC 23343, pp. 74–5.

[97]   Stow, *Chronicles*, pp. 1097–8.

And when her highnes came against St Buttolphes church there was a great stage covered with canvas where all the children of Christes Hospitall sat, with all the governours and officers belonging to the same: one of the children saluting her highnes kneelinge on his knees made an oration to her highnes in Latin.[98]

Persons, presumably remembering conversations with Campion, tells us that the Queen:

coming to the citty of London, she was to be receaved in triumphant manner with a publick oration att the grammer school of St Paul in the yeare of grace 1553 Edmund Campion being then but 13 yeares of age was chosen among all the youths of London to make that oration, though att that time he were no scholler of the schoole, which is a publick testimony of his towardlynesse at that age.[99]

The event is recorded by the Imperial Ambassadors, writing back to the Emperor, who describe the initial joy at the arrival of Mary:

We will add that a scaffolding was erected at the town gate, where about one hundred poor little children were placed, all dressed in blue, with red caps upon their heads. They were given to the Queen to nourish and care for them, the eldest being not being over twelve or fourteen. One of them addressed a prayer to her Majesty that she might take them under her care, such, they say, being the custom in England at the royal entries.[100]

Since Campion was (as Persons states) no longer at St Paul's on 3 August 1553, it seems likely that he had been presented by one of the 30 governors at the foundation of Christ's Hospital in November 1552. The school, established in the old Greyfriars and designed for 'poor fatherless' children, had been set up by the Aldermen of the City of London, and narrowly escaped being closed down within its first year by the arrival of a Queen who wished to restore the Franciscan friars to their old house.[101] From the time he was presented to Christ's Hospital, Campion seems to have been virtually adopted by a succession of mayors and aldermen – Sir William Chester, Sir Thomas White, Anthony Hussey and the

---

[98] Wriothesley, *Chronicle*, II. 93–5; McDonnell, 'Campion and St Paul's School', p. 47.

[99] ABSI Collectanea P. I, fol. 77a; Bombino, *Vita et Martyrium*, 2; Bodl. MS Tanner 329, fol. 1v. Persons's comment that the welcoming speech was 'at the grammar school of St Paul' seems mistaken. It is just possible that Campion could have greeted the new Queen on 30 September, the day before her coronation, but this seems unlikely, since Stow's account of that day specifically names 'one Maister Heywod' as the orator on that occasion.

[100] *CSP Spanish, 1553*, XI. 151, 6 August. The official historian of Christ's Hospital records the same incident, but with the unique (and scarcely credible) detail that when 'a childe of the free schoole' made 'an oraction to hir', 'shee cast hir eie another waie', Lemprière, ed., p. 64.

[101] Lemprière, ed., pp. 63–74.

Company of Grocers are among his official patrons – and that sense of being part of the establishment never left him. Even in exile, Campion, unlike many of his Catholic contemporaries, never deviated from a benign acceptance of civic order and civil authority.

Equally, Campion's presentation to the Hospital as it opened in the ruins of the old Greyfriars, established a pattern. Within a year of his arrival, Christ's Hospital had to adapt to a complete change of religion, and within a year of his arrival in Oxford, St John's College (the restored St Bernard's) had to adapt to the new regime of Elizabeth I. Sir Thomas White pursued outward conformity in response to this reversal. White's last instructions to the College, given in tears to Campion, began with the encouragement that 'we should nourish mutual charity among ourselves' (*mutuam inter nos charitatem aleremus*).[102] Anthony Munday, trying to denigrate Campion, only confirms his fame and popularity:

> Edmund Campion, as it is by men of sufficient credit reported, at what tyme he spent his studie heere in Englande, both in the Hospital, and also at the university of Oxenford: was alwaies addicted to a mervailous suppose in himselfe, of ripe judgement, prompt audacitie, & cunning conveyaunce in his Schoole pointes, wherethrough, he fell into a prowde and vaineglorious judgement, practising to be eloquent in phrase, and so fine in his quirkes and fantasticall conjectures; that the ignorant he wun by his smoothe deuises, some other affecting his pleasaunt imaginations, he charmed with subtiltie, and choaked with Sophistrie.[103]

Christ's Hospital was a remarkable triumph of civic responsibility, and a tribute to the men who formed the backbone of the City of London, like Sir Thomas White and Sir William Chester. It contained an unusual mixture of street children and orphans alongside children from families of 'modest wealth' presented, like Campion, by Aldermen and city merchants.

The foundation of Christ's Hospital by the Lord Mayor and Aldermen of the City of London undoubtedly helped form Campion's character and attitudes to authority. The men involved in setting up and running the new school were all merchant pioneers: Sir William Chester, who was to sponsor the entire course of Campion's Oxford education, was a leading Merchant Adventurer. Richard Grafton, a Grocer and the first Treasurer of Christ's Hospital, had pioneered the printing of the Great Bible in England in 1539, in the cloisters of the old Greyfriars and, as the appointed printer of Prince Edward, of the first authorized primer in 1545. Grafton continued to live in the cloisters from 1539 till he died, old, infirm and poor, in May 1573. During this period the old Greyfriars was transformed

---

[102]   Stevenson and Salter, *Early History of St John's*, p. 409.

[103]   A[nthony]. M[unday]., *A Discouerie of Edmund Campion, and his Confederates, their most horrible and traiterous practises, against her Maiesties most royall person, and the Realme* (London: J. Charlewood for Edwarde White, 29 January 1582), STC 18270, sig. G1v–G2r.

into a school for the poor children of the city, and Grafton was deeply involved as Treasurer in the establishment and running of this institution for the 'fatherlesse or poore mans childe'.

The suppression of the monasteries, completed in 1540 by Thomas Cromwell, had left a massive gap in the social and educational provision of the country. The city of London became vividly aware of this, because of the steady rise in the number of poor on the streets of a rapidly expanding London:

> The number of the poore did so encrease of all sorts, that the churches, streates and lanes were fylled daylye with a number of loathsome Lazars botches and sores so that St Bartholomews hospital was not able to receyve the tenthe part of those that then were to be provided for. Whereuppon the preachers in theire pulpitts moved the people to provide and gyve liberally to the relefe of those poore people.[104]

Nicholas Ridley, Bishop of London, stirred the young King, Edward VI, with a Sunday sermon in February 1552. With the king's support, the bishop immediately engaged the Mayor, Sir Richard Dobbes, who formed a committee of 30, which by July had raised sufficient funds for the poor of London, whom they divided into three main categories. The Committee determined to make St Thomas's and Christ's Hospital 'swete and redye to receyve the poore', '300 persons' at St Thomas's, '500 persons' at Christ's Hospital. Repairs began, Stow tells us in the *Chronicles*, on 26 July.[105] For Christ's Hospital, they ordered '500 ffeatherbeds & 500 padds of strawe' as many blankets and 1,000 sheets. On 23 November, the Hospital took in 380 children, Campion presumably among them. Some died from the shock of the change:

> A number of the children being taken from the dunghill when they came to swete and cleane keping & to a pure dyett dyed downe righte and so lykewyse the poore aged & other in the hospitalles dyed.[106]

By the standards of any age, this colossal achievement, within nine months, of fund-raising, planning and restoration, reveals the strength of the structure of the City of London. Of the five former Lord Mayors now involved in the administration of the London Hospitals, two, Sir Thomas White and Sir William Chester, became personal patrons of Campion, and Sir Martin Bowes must have known him through the competitions.

The children of 'the Hospital' quickly became a central part of civic life, and Campion would have been part of their public appearances. The first was on Christmas Day 1552. Stow describes the moment:

---

[104] Lemprière, ed., p. 6.
[105] Stow, *Chronicles*, p. 1053.
[106] Lemprière, ed., p. 39.

On Christmasse daye in the afternoone, when the Lorde Maior and Aldermen rode to *Paules*, al the children of *Christes Hospitall*, stoode in array from *Saint Laurence* Lane in Cheape toward Paules, al in on Lyverie of Russet Cotten, the men children with red Caps, the women children kerchiefs on their heades, all the Maisters of the Hospitall formeost: nexte them the Phisitions and four Surgeons, and between every twentie children one woman keeper, whych children were in number 340.[107]

The central event of the London liturgical and social calendar was the annual series of five sermons around Easter, which Stow describes:

time out of minde, it hath bin a laudable custome that on good friday in the after noone some especial learned man by appoyntment of the prelate doth preache a sermon at *Paules crosse*, treating of *Christs Passion*. And upon the three next Easter holidayes, Monday, Tuesday, and Wednesday, the like learned men by the like appointment doe use to preach on the forenoon at the said Spittle, to perswad the articles of *Christs* resurrection, and then on low Sunday before noon one other learned man at Paules crosse is to make rehersall of those fowre sermons, either commending or reproving them, as to him by judgment of the lerned divines is thought convenient. And that done he is to make a sermon of himselfe, which in all were five Sermons in one.[108]

The Greyfriars children were soon part of the 'shewe', and by Easter 1553, wearing their trademark 'plonket Coates', the blue woollen coats that gave them their name:

The thirde of Aprill, being Monday after Easter daye, the children of Christs Hospitall in *London*, came from thence thorough the Citie to the Sermon kepte at *Saint Marie Spittle*, all clothed in plonket Coates, and red Cappes, and the maiden children in the same Lyverie, with kerchefs on their heades, all whiche with their matron and other governors were there placed on a Scaffolde of eight Stages, and there sate the same time, whiche was a goodly shewe.[109]

In St Mary's Spital, there was a special two-storey house, built on the south side in 1488, in whose loft 'the Ladies and Aldermens wives doe stand at a large window or sit at their pleasure', and the crowds were even greater than at the Cross.[110] So important was the presence of Christ's Hospital that, when a new pulpit was built in 1594, a 'large house on the east side of the said pulpit was

---

[107] Stow, *Chronicles*, p. 1055. This may be their only recorded public appearance in red.

[108] Stow, *Survay of London* (1598), pp. 129–30; *Survay of London* (1603), p. 169; see Morrissey, *Paul's Cross*, p. 21.

[109] Stow, *Chronicles*, pp. 1056–7.

[110] Stow, *Survay of London* (1598), p. 129; *Survay of London* (1603), p. 169 (which adds that, in times past, 'the Bishop of *London* and other Prelates' used to sit in the loft).

then builded for the governors and children of *Christes* Hospital to sit in'.[111] In 1557, Dr Henry Pendleton, undaunted by the earlier attempt on his life, and Dr John Young, were the star preachers, with the Lord Mayor, Aldermen, 'alle the masters of the hospetall with grenstayffes in ther handes, and all the chylderyn of the hospetall in bluw garmenttes', and more than '20,000 people' on Easter Monday, and the 'whole city' (we are told) on Easter Tuesday.[112] Campion, in blue coat, and in his last year of school (and perhaps already selected by Sir Thomas White for St John's) would surely have enjoyed this competition between two famous preachers. He might have stayed afterwards for the game of barley break, when 'ever was master parsun in the fyre', but probably not for drinking in the Swan, or the dinner in Westminster with the Duke of Muscovy, which followed.[113]

A dark cloud overshadowed that Easter's festivity. On Monday of Holy Week, 12 April 1557, three men and two women had been burned at Smithfield: Thomas Loseby, Henry Ramsey, Thomas Thirtell, Margaret Hide and Agnes Stanley.[114] Smithfield is not more than 200 yards from Christ's Hospital: close enough to hear the cries and the noise of the crowd, as well as smell the smoke and, certainly in the case of the burning of five people, the charred flesh. One has to ask what impact the burning had on the consciousness of Campion. In a campaign masterminded by Cardinal Pole, 284 men and women were burned at the stake in a way that still causes revulsion. Some of these were certainly known to Campion. The first man to be burnt at Smithfield, on 4 February 1555, was John Rogers, one of the two men who, outside Campion's home, had saved Dr Bourne from certain death on 13 August 1553; the other saviour of Dr Bourne, John Bradford, was burnt at Smithfield on 1 July 1555.[115] The burnings normally took place in the morning, by which time the school day would have started. London was one of the strongholds of Protestant resistance, and Smithfield one of the main stages for these gruesome dramas. The protests of young apprentices, many of whom Campion must have known, worried the authorities, so that the Privy Council ordered the Mayor and aldermen to 'see to it that "no housholdeer suffer any of his apprentices or other servants to be abrode" at the time of any burning'.[116] The horror of these barbaric acts done in the name of religion would have left its mark on young boys trying to learn their grammar or imitate Cicero.

Although we cannot know what these 300 boys thought or felt, or what their masters and ushers said, Campion is unusual among Catholics in twice using the word *persecution* of Mary's campaign to extirpate heresy. In the second disputation he said:

---

[111]   Stow, *Survay of London* (1598), p. 130; *Survay of London* (1603), p. 170.

[112]   Machyn, *The Diary*, pp. 131–2; cited in Duffy, *Fires of Faith*, 19.

[113]   Machyn, *The Diary*, p. 132.

[114]   Foxe, *Actes and Monuments*, p. 2161.

[115]   Duffy, *Fires of Faith*, pp. 159–60, points out that the 'rescue' was interpreted in a hostile way, as part of the incitement to rebellion.

[116]   Duffy, *Fires of Faith*, pp. 159–60.

For although persecution be in one place, yet this complaint may be done in divers other places. As for example, the Protestants in Queen Mary's time being persecuted in England, yet might they have this remedy in Germany where their relligion was used.[117]

Since the masters of Christ's Hospital had all been appointed by godly Aldermen, it seems likely that their reactions would have been similar to that of Julius Palmer, who was, according to Foxe, so shocked by the burning of Latimer and Ridley in Oxford that he resigned his fellowship at Magdalen, and was himself burned for heresy.[118] When the noise of the burning reached them, would the masters and pupils have paused to pray for the martyrs? The Queen's sudden death, in November 1558, brought another complete reversal. The printer, John Day, published, in four colossal editions, the book that permanently etched these burnings on the English consciousness. Foxe's *Actes and Monuments*, 'the Book of Martyrs', full of compelling and unforgettable details, successfully portrayed Catholicism as foreign, subversive and cruel.[119] One woodcut in Foxe showed Dr John Story, attempt to stop the singing of M. John Denley, martyred on 8 August 1555, with a burning fagot.[120] 'The notoriety that Foxe's narrative and the woodcut of 1570, had given to Story's treatment of Denley and others almost certainly contributed to the excruciating savagery used in Story's own execution' in June 1571.[121] Campion, who would have known Story as a neighbour in St Faith's, encountered him again in the Hospital, since Story used Greyfriars for interrogating suspects.[122] He brought Thomas Greene, a young apprentice of John Wayland, to Christ's Hospital for distributing a pamphlet, *Antichrist*.[123] Story knew that his punishment, whipping, would be anathema to Grafton, the Bible's printer, so he tried to see that 'the matter should not be lightly handled'.[124] Wayland, a Catholic printer, had reported his own apprentice, to whom Elizabeth Young gave

---

[117] BL MS Harley 422, fol. 152v; Holleran, p. 104.

[118] Foxe, *Actes and Monuments*, p. 2118.

[119] The 1570 edition is a colossal work, which runs to 2,300 pages in two folio volumes. The woodcuts were to provide a visual record of the brutal scenes that has etched them on the English imagination.

[120] Foxe, *Acts and Monuments*, p. 1867.

[121] Duffy, *Fires of Faith*, p. 123 (see plate 23). Persons says that Campion was present at Story's trial on 26 May and his execution on 1 June 1571, which cannot be correct, since it conflicts with the dates given in the dedications at the start of Campion's *Two Bokes of the Histories of Ireland* (see below, Chapter 3).

[122] Brigden, *London and the Reformation*, p. 623.

[123] Brigden, *London and the Reformation*, p. 623, quoting CLRO, Repertory 13, fol. 135r; Guildhall MS 12819/1, fol. 123r.

[124] Brigden, *London and the Reformation*, pp. 623–4. The full account of this episode of imprisonment, interrogation and scourging is in Foxe, *Actes and Monuments*, pp. 2262–3.

the book imported from Emden.[125] Foxe lets Greene recount how he was brought into Christ's Hospital, and then kept in a 'stinking dungeon' for a month, until Story commanded him

> to be stripped, he standing by me, and called for two of the Beadels, and the whippes to whip me; and the two Beadels came with a corde, and bound my handes together, and the one end of the cord to a stone piller. Then one of my frendes, called Nicholas Priestman, hearyng them call for whips, hurled in a bundell of rods, which semed something to pacifie the mind of his cruelty: and so they scourged me with rods.[126]

All the other Hospital boys must have heard the scourging of Greene. Greene refused to incriminate Elizabeth Young, but admitted finally to giving one copy to John Beane, an apprentice of Richard Tottell. In the small world of stationers, Campion may even have known Greene and his friend John Beane. Foxe makes it clear that Story's cruelty is moderated by two Stationers, who were apparently there to protect the apprentice.[127] The proximity of the Hospital to Smithfield and to Paul's Cross, the presence of Story and Grafton, meant that the Hospital boys were inextricably entangled in these barbaric events.

We have no idea what Campion thought of his former neighbour, this 'bloody Nimrod', but he could not have enjoyed hearing that, when he was being butchered, Story, in his late sixties in 1571, 'did not only roare and cry like a helhound, but also strake the executioner doing his office, and resisted as long as strength did serve him, beinge kept downe by three or foure men, until he was deade'.[128] He must have been horrified at the cruel and barbarous reciprocity of 'an ideological struggle inscribed in the quivering flesh of suffering human beings'.[129]

For the Governors or masters of the Hospital, there was justifiably, great pride in their achievement. Londoners felt a great affinity for the Hospital, since it figured frequently in their wills.[130] This was particularly true of stationers: in 1593, William Norton, who stood surety for Campion when he compounded for the first fruits of Sherborne in 1568, left to all scholars of Christ's Hospital that had gone

---

[125]   Foxe, *Actes and Monuments*, p. 2262. The book was *Antichrist, that is to saye: a true reporte, that Antichriste is come*, tr. out of Latin by J. Olde (Sothwarke: Christopher Trutheall [Emden: E. van der Erve], 1556) STC 25009. For Elizabeth Young, see Foxe, *Acts and Monuments*, p. 2268.

[126]   Foxe, *Actes and Monuments*, p. 2263.

[127]   I am grateful to Thomas S. Freeman for this suggestion.

[128]   Wiiliam Fulke, *A Retentive, to Stay good Christians, Against the Motives of R. Bristowe*, (London: T. Vautrollier for George Bishop, Entered in Stationers' Register, 9 February 1580), STC 11449, p. 59.

[129]   Duffy, *Fires of Faith*, p. 123.

[130]   Ian W. Archer, *The Pursuit of Stability: Social Relations in Elizabethan London* (Cambridge: University Press, 1991), table 5.6, p. 176. Bequests to the Hospital totalled over 600 pounds in 1570–73, and £2,600 in 1594–97.

on to either Oxford or Cambridge their choice of his books to the value of 20s.[131] He also left lands to the Governors of Christ's Hospital to pay for an interest-free loan for a young Stationer for three years.[132] If Campion lost a father, he gained several devoted patrons and the patronage of the city of London. As John Bossy argues, 'Campion was a product of the Christian humanism taught in the London schools'.[133]

Sir William Chester was still funding Campion, when he went up to Oxford, as revealed in a codicil added to the will of Anthony Hussey, who was not only a wealthy Draper in St Faith's parish, but also Principal Registrar of the Archbishop of Canterbury and, as such, the principal executor for the will of Gabriel Dunne, last Abbot of Buckfast, a former student of 'the late Barnard college'.[134] Campion was suitable for the terms of the abbot's will, which was specially directed to those 'disposed to be preestes and ministers of Christes Churche'.[135] By a codicil of this will, dated 27 May 1560, Hussey gave 'to Campion, Sir William Chester's scholar, forty shillings a year so long as he is a student in Oxford'.[136] Campion's education was, thereby, partly funded by a pre-reformation abbot who died when the Marian restoration was at its height (on 5 February 1558).[137] Chester was elected Master of the Drapers' Company five times between 1553 and 1569.[138] Alderman of several London wards, knighted by Queen Mary in 1557, and elected Lord Mayor in 1560,

---

[131]   Plomer, *Wills*, pp. 11, 24 and 31.

[132]   Plomer, *Wills*, p. 32.

[133]   John Bossy, *The English Catholic Community, 1570–1850* (London: Darton, Longman & Todd, 1975), p. 15.

[134]   Katherine M. Longley notes this in a letter in the Propositor's file for Campion's canonization.

[135]   Dunne had left a clause in his will that his executors should 'bestow the residee of his goods and chattels "at the discrecion to the advancemente of poore maidens marriages Releef of Scolleres And Students, specially to soche as my Executors shall thinke metest as shalbe towarde lerninge disposed to be preestes and ministers of Christes Churche"' (16 Welles & 59 Mellershe – P.C.C.). See also Leslie Campion, *The Family of Edmund Campion* (London: The Research Publishing Co., 1975), p. 39. Gabriel Dunne left 38 of his books to 'the late Barnard College', where he had been a student; Stevenson and Salter, *Early History of St John's*, 44. See McDonnell, *Notes and Queries*, p. 90.

[136]   *Index of Wills Proved in the Prerogative Court of Canterbury. 1558–1583, vol. III, and now preserved in the Principal Probate Registry, Somerset House London*, Compiled by S.A. Smith, M.D., and edited by L.L. Duncan, F.S.A. (London, 1898), P.C.C., 52 Mellershe, p. 168.

[137]   *Oxford Dictionary of National Biography* (hereafter *ODNB*), 'Gabriel Dunne' (c.1490–1558), by Nicholas Orme.

[138]   A.H. Johnson, *The History of the Worshipful Company of the Drapers of London*, 2 vols (Oxford: Clarendon Press, 1915), pp. 470–71. There is a gap in the list of Masters for the year 1561, when it is most likely that it was Chester, since he alternated with Richard Champion for 10 years.

Chester took trade to Russia, Persia and west Africa.[139] He was a founding member of the Russia Company, and was granted concessions by the Tsar in 1567, and was one of the Merchant Adventurers 'riding in velvet coates and chaines of golde', who welcomed the Duke of Muscovy in 1557.[140]

He was also very compassionate. As Governor of St Thomas's, Bridewell and Bethlem hospitals, he personally ensured that a young starving girl was admitted.[141] Foxe records Chester releasing his godly apprentice, Laurence Saunders, who was 'ravished with the love of learning, and especially wyth the reading of Gods word' and 'geving him his Indenture', so that he could pursue his studies of Latin and Greek.[142] As Sheriff of London in February 1555, Chester famously gave permission for Dr Rowland Taylour, on his way to martyrdom, to 'speake with hys wyfe', and 'wept apace' as Dr Taylour, his wife and his daughters knelt together in prayer.[143]

Sir Thomas White was a Governor of Christ's Hospital from 25 November 1556, and like Chester, rescued individual children from the streets: he presented 'Brigide Barton bourne in Southwerke' to Christ's Hospital on 8 November 1557.[144] Campion became closer than anyone else to the founder of St John's, received his dying wishes and delivered White's funeral oration in 1567.[145] White began his year as Lord Mayor on 28 October 1553. He was knighted on 10 December 1553, but was buying in reserves of cheap coal and wood for the poor, to combat excessive prices at Christmas.[146] The coronation had taken place on 1 September 1553 and passed off splendidly, so the mayoral year must have looked set for the restoration of many abandoned Catholic ceremonies and rituals, but the Queen, as we have seen, told the Lord Mayor and Aldermen on 15 January of her marriage intentions 'for the great preferment of this realme'.[147]

On 1 February, the proposed marriage caused a formidable rebellion by Sir Thomas Wyatt. The Mayor and Aldermen were in charge of mustering men, so White took his dinner 'in harnis'.[148] The next day, Candlemas, 'most of the householders of London' were in arms, accoutred in homespun white coats emblazoned with the red cross of the City of London. When Wyatt crossed the Thames at Kingston, 12 carts, full of powder and shot, were stored in Paul's Churchyard.[149] Campion,

---

[139] Johnson, *Company of Drapers*, II. 189.

[140] Stow, *Chronicles*, 1103; *ODNB*, 'Sir William Chester' (*c*.1509–1595?), by J.D. Alsop.

[141] Kingdon, *Richard Grafton*, Minutes, pp. 1–10.

[142] Foxe, *Actes and Monuments*, p. 1664.

[143] Foxe, *Actes and Monuments*, p. 1700.

[144] Kingdon, *Richard Grafton*, transcripts, p. 11.

[145] See Chapter 2.

[146] Wriothesley, *Chronicle*, II. 105. Both events are recorded here.

[147] Wriothesley, *Chronicle*, II. 106.

[148] Wriothesley, *Chronicle*, II. 109.

[149] Stow, *Chronicles*, p. 1083.

just 14, must have been vividly aware of the crisis, even before it erupted into cannon fire at Charing Cross.[150] Fighting took place on 7 February at Hyde Park Corner, and Wyatt's men advanced, swords drawn, down Fleet Street, when 'divers of his men took the Queen's men by the hand as they went toward Ludgate'.[151] By five o'clock, Wyatt had surrendered, and Sir Thomas Pope took the leading turncoat, Alexander Brett, 'by the bosome saying: oh Traitoure, howe couldest thou finde in thy hearte to worke such a villany'.[152] The handshakes of rebels and defenders of the city, the closeness of Pope and Brett, and the interiority of the language of treason could be an emblem for this whole period. The apprentices had remained loyal, perhaps more because they trusted their Mayor than because they approved of the Spanish marriage.

The Queen responded savagely to disloyal Londoners. Some 60 rebels were hanged (and many quartered) all round London, despite the efforts of one of White's sheriffs, Sir Thomas Offley, who became a Governor of Bridewell, who 'saved many who should have died'.[153] The bodies were removed only for the royal wedding in September. In March 1554, a month after taking Brett captive, Sir Thomas Pope founded Trinity College, Oxford; in July of the same year, Sir Thomas White began buying rectories around Oxford.[154] On 11 December 1554, White drew up 'an article of agreement' with Christ Church for a lease of the lands and grove of the late Bernard College, a suppressed Cistercian house. If Campion benefited from a vibrant school culture and some remarkable aldermen, his early life was defined by conflicted loyalties and violent religious change. He was educated in a city, which the Queen made a 'spectacle to all the realme' and tainted with the barbaric theatre of public executions. Early thrust onto the stage of public speaking, he was to return to London in disguise, to become one of the most famous preachers in the country and, on the scaffold at Tyburn, 'a spectacle unto his angels and unto you men'.[155]

---

[150]   Stow, *Chronicles*, pp. 1078–88.

[151]   Machyn, *The Diary*, p. 54; quoted in Brigden, *London and the Reformation*, pp. 544–5.

[152]   Stow, *Chronicles*, p. 1087.

[153]   Brigden, *London and the Reformation*, p. 552, quoting Thomas Fuller, *The Worthies of England* (1662).

[154]   Stevenson and Salter, *Early History of St John's*, p. 1.

[155]   Alfield, *A true reporte*, sigs B4v–C1r.

Chapter 2
Among the Ruins

Edmund Campion was among the first group of scholars at the restored college in Oxford, which Sir Thomas White dedicated to St John the Baptist on 24 June 1557.[1] Oxford must have presented an extraordinary landscape to the 17-year-old student. The colleges and halls of the medieval university were almost entirely contained by the city walls, and surrounded by tributaries of the Thames and the Cherwell, beyond which, on the meadows to the south and west of the city, were now the ruins of what had been the largest collection of religious houses anywhere in England.[2]

From the south-west to the north-east, a swathe of halls, libraries and churches inhabited by Dominicans, Franciscans, Cistercians, Benedictines, Carmelites and Austin Friars, had defined the city.[3] On a large island to the west of the city, had been Oseney Abbey, home of the Augustinian canons and the most powerful house in Oxford.[4] Its church had been 'not only the envy of other religious houses in England but also beyond the seas'.[5] With its own mill, fishponds, dove-houses and 'orchards and arbours ... divided with cunning meanders', this must have been, even in Campion's time, an idyllic spot.[6]

When he arrived, Oxford was busy restoring a city damaged by the depredations of Thomas Cromwell. The Abbot of Rewley had appealed to Cromwell in September 1536 'that our house may be saved, although it be converted into a college, to have both learning and learned men go forward therein'.[7] Cromwell did not heed his appeal, but others, 20 years later, did what they could. John Feckenham, a former monk of Gloucester College, and now Abbot of the restored Westminster Abbey, whom Sir Thomas White called 'my deare frende', was a pivotal figure both for White and for Sir Thomas Pope, who was busy drawing

---

[1]   Stevenson and Salter, *Early History of St. John's*, p. 118. Andrew Hegarty, *A Biographical Register of St John's College, Oxford, 1555–1660* (Woodbridge: Boydell Press, 2011), OHS, NS 43, p. 5.

[2]   R.B. Dobson, 'The Religious Orders 1370–1540', in *The History of the University of Oxford*, vol. 2, *Late Medieval Oxford*, ed. J.I. Catto and T.A.R. Evans (Oxford: Clarendon Press, 1992), pp. 539–79 (p. 541).

[3]   Dobson, 'Religious Orders', *HUO*, II. 541.

[4]   Dobson, 'Religious Orders', *HUO*, II. 542.

[5]   Bodl. MS Wood F. 29a, fol. 218v; Anthony Wood, *City of Oxford*, 3 vols (Oxford: Oxford Historical Society, 1890), vol. 2, *Churches and Religious Houses*, p. 218.

[6]   Bodl. MS Wood F. 29a, fols 214r and 215v; Wood, *City of Oxford*, II. 195, 209.

[7]   Dobson, 'Religious Orders', *HUO*, II. 545, citing *Reg. canc.* 1434–69, ii.81.

up the foundation documents for Trinity College in March 1555, the very month when Feckenham was petitioning the Queen to allow him and 15 other monks to return to the religious life in Westminster.[8] Two months later, on 1 May 1555, Sir Thomas White was given the royal Letters Patent to found a college 'in the house commonly called Bernerd Colledge' for a President and 30 members.[9]

Dr George Owen, M.D., physician to Henry VIII, Edward VI and Mary, and mentor of George Etheridge, acquired, as gifts or purchases, a large number of monastic properties, which he then proceeded to donate to colleges.[10] The most notable was Durham College, which he held for only a year before passing it to Sir Thomas Pope.[11] Owen worked with both White and Pope to help Dr William Tresham in 'the saving of St Marie Colledge', the former house of study of the Augustinian canons, from 'spoile'.[12] Campion himself benefited from this coherent policy of purchasing land and restoring the buildings for 'learned men'.[13] On 2 February 1560 (the year that Campion graduated as Bachelor of Arts), Sir Thomas White bought the entire nine acres of White Friars (opposite St John's), where only the great hall was still standing.[14] On 13 June 1560, he also acquired the remains of Feckenham's old house of studies, Gloucester College.[15] As late as 1573, George Owen's son, Richard, sold to St John's College, the manors of Wolvercote and Walton, many farms and some 500 acres that had belonged to Godstow Priory, Oseney Abbey and Rewley Abbey, as well as houses belonging to the chantry of St Mary Magdalen in the parish of St Giles.[16] Richard Owen's two sons, Walter and John, were later among the party of 10 fellows to leave Oxford, in 1583, for Dr Allen's college in Rheims; they were led by Edward Stransham, a fellow of St John's, who was born in the parish of St Mary Magdalen.

---

[8]   David Knowles, *The Religious Orders*, 3 vols (Cambridge: University Press, 1948–61) vol. 3, p. 427, sees Feckenham as the inspiration; Hegarty, *Register*, pp. 15–16, is sceptical, but evidence supports Knowles; see White's letter to Bramston, 'Mr Fecknam ys my deare frende whose request I may not denye hym, Stevenson and Salter, *Early History of St John's*, pp. 420–21.

[9]   Stevenson and Salter, *Early History of St John's*, p. 114.

[10]   These included Godstow, Rewley, Durham, the chantry of St Mary Magdalen, New Hall and Alban Hall, *ODNB* 'George Owen', by Sidney Lee, rev. Patrick Wallis.

[11]   Bodl. MS Wood F. 29a, fol. 270v; Wood, *City of Oxford*, II. 274, and note 2.

[12]   Bodl. MS Wood F. 29a, fols 251r–252v; Wood, *City of Oxford*, II. 240–44.

[13]   White's letter of 1565 to the President, Stevenson and Salter, *Early History of St John's*, p. 417.

[14]   Bodl. MS Wood F. 29a, fols 190v–191; Wood, *City of Oxford*, II. 444–5. Edmund and Isabell Powell of Sandford, had bought the estate in 1542, clearly intending to rescue it. The hall was pulled down only in 1596, when the stone was used to build the new library at St John's; Stevenson and Salter, *Early History of St John's*, pp. 430–32.

[15]   Stevenson and Salter, *Early History of St John's*, pp 432–9; Dobson, 'Religious Orders', *HUO*, II. 579 n. 134.

[16]   Stevenson and Salter, *Early History of St John's*, pp. 527–9.

Campion's own view of the Henrician destruction emerges (with uncharacteristic vehemence) in his *Narrative of the Divorce of Henry VIII*, where he describes an inscription in the original lodge of Christ Church, addressed to Elizabeth during her visit of 1566, which called the college 'the unfinished monument of your father':

> I have never seen anything more wretched than the memory of an outstanding patron being obliterated and conferred on a man who has destroyed all honesty, completely confused the human and divine, and destroyed, root and branch, both religion and the monarchical republic of Britain.

> (Quo nihil vidi miserius; obliterari memoriam praestantissimi partroni; conferri in eum, quo omnem honestatem profuderit, divina & humana omnia miscuerit, religionem & rem BRITANNIAE publicam exciderit).[17]

Numbers in the university had fallen to just over 1,000 in 1552, but they steadily rose over the next 15 years. The departure of monks and friars who came from France, Spain, Portugal, Italy and Ireland, had heralded 'an increasing academic insularity which was soon to be harnessed to the creation of a highly insular post-reformation English church'.[18] The Marian foundations of Trinity and St John's were meant to help restore theology, and they certainly helped to restore numbers in the university to a total of 1,764 students by 1568, when Campion became proctor.[19] Campion was one of 47 graduating Bachelor of Arts on 20 November 1560.

The importance Queen Mary attached to Oxford is shown by her appointment of Cardinal Pole as Chancellor. Under his guidance, she gave new endowments to the university, and restored the 10 *scholae publicae* established by Abbot Hooknorton of Oseney in 1440, and the Divinity Schools; both were ready in the same year as Campion came up to Oxford, 1557. The university responded with a fervent acknowledgment of its gratitude to the queen.[20] The restoration was overshadowed by Pole's campaign to extirpate heresy. A visitation, in 1556, of Magdalen, New College and Corpus, which included confiscation of books and many expulsions by Stephen Gardiner, Bishop of Winchester, and the papal nuncio, Nicholas Ormanetto, set a bad precedent for the next decade. Worse still, between 14 and 18 April 1554, a series of disputations had taken place in St Mary

---

[17] *Narratio de Divortio Henrici VIII. Regis ab Uxore Catharina et Ab Ecclesia Catholica Romana Discessione*, Scripta ab EDMUNDO CAMPIANO, added by Richard Gibbons, S.J., to Nicholas Harpsfield, *Historia Anglicana Ecclesiastica* (Douai: M. Wyon, 1623), ARCR I. 639, p. 737.

[18] Dobson, 'Religious Orders', *HUO*, II. 559.

[19] Folger MS V.a.176, fols 173r–174r.

[20] Claire Cross, 'Oxford and the Tudor State from the Accession of Henry VIII to the Death of Mary', in *The History of the University of Oxford*, vol. 3, *The Collegiate University*, ed. James McConica (Oxford: Clarendon Press, 1986), pp. 117–49 (p. 142).

the Virgin, with Hugh Latimer, Nicholas Ridley and Thomas Cranmer. Although the doctors of divinity from the two universities attended in their elaborate gowns, the academic splendour ended in tragedy, and bathos: Bishops Latimer and Ridley were burned in a ditch outside Balliol on 16 October 1555 and, on 21 March 1556, on 'a foul and rainy day', Archbishop Cranmer retracted his recantation but was nonetheless burned 'in the Towndditch at Oxford'.[21] These events, the year before Campion arrived, were to exact a 'tribal, intimate revenge' on all who had participated.[22]

Campion is named in the earliest extant Foundation Deed of 5 March 1558 (the year of Mary's death), when St John's was a very small college.[23] Only in 1612 did the college attain to something like a full complement of '1 President, 50 Fellows (including probationer scholars), 43 Commoners, 20 poor scholars and 14 other servants'; in the first few years, there may well have been only half that number.[24] Campion was to spend 13 years in Oxford, graduating Master of Arts and *Junior in Comitiis* (with a special role in disputations) on 3 July 1564.[25] He was Reader in Rhetoric at St John's from 1564 to 1570, a post that exempted him from taking orders, he served as Dean of Arts, and was elected Proctor in 1568.[26] A student was required to spend seven years before the MA, and then he could go on to study Theology for a further seven years.[27] This is the process Campion describes in his 'Examen' (fifth section) in Prague:

> I first studied Christian morals in my home country (*patria*); then, at Oxford, I spent seven years studying Philosophy, and devoted about six years to Theology: to Aristotle, positive Theology and the Fathers.[28]

It was in theology that the most serious effect of the departure of the monks and friars was felt. In the period between 1500 and 1535, there had been some 750 monks and friars living and studying in Oxford, and it was 'to the advanced study of theology or canon law that all but a minute proportion of the regulars of late

---

[21]   John Foxe, *The first (second) volume of ecclesiasticall history contaynyng the Actes and monuments*, 2 vols (London: J. Daye, 1570) STC 11223, pp. 2063–4, and 2067 (woodcut); Cross, 'Oxford and Tudor State', *HUO*, III. 142–4.

[22]   Seamus Heaney, 'Punishment', in *New Selected Poems 1966–1987* (London: Faber and Faber, 1990), p. 72.

[23]   Stevenson and Salter, *Early History of St John's*, p. 119.

[24]   Hegarty, *Register*, p. xlii, citing Bodl. MS Tanner 338, fol. 28r–v.

[25]   Hegarty, *Register*, p. 28.

[26]   Hegarty, *Register*, pp. 28–31.

[27]   Bartoli, *Europeae Historiae*, p. 75, explains the seven-year period as 'the custom at Oxford' (*Oxonii mos*).

[28]   ARSI Anglia 38/1, fol. 31v; see Schmidl, *Historiae*, I. 339. It is striking that Campion includes Aristotle in Theology. See Chapter 12 for details of the composite book, now in Campion Hall, which he owned in Oxford, of two commentaries on Aristotle by Johannes de Janduno and Frater Dei Gratia Esculanus, O.P.

medieval Oxford devoted most of their academic energies'.[29] The consequences of losing all this theological expertise, and so many excellent libraries, were lamented throughout Campion's time in Oxford.[30] On 1 June 1560, Bishop Jewel complained in a letter to Peter Martyr that 'every thing [in Oxford] is falling into ruin and decay; for the colleges are now filled with mere boys and empty of learning'.[31] Queen Elizabeth herself 'wrote to the Lord Keeper, Nicholas Bacon', to say how concerned she was that 'the study of divinity was much decayed through lack of maintenance, and because of 'the alterance of the times'.[32] As Anthony Wood wrote of the Lady Margaret Chair of Divinity in 1562, 'There were few or none capable of that lecture at this time, occasion'd by the fewness of theologists, and emptiness of houses of learning in the university'.[33] In 1586, in an ironic twist, Sir Francis Walsingham established a theological lecture to be preached by John Rainolds so that 'the common places of the Scripture, the Principles of Religion, and matters of controversye might be handled and expounded, like as at Rhemes and other places beyond the seas'.[34]

In 1554, Sir Thomas White was led 'by divine inspiration in a dream to restore this building'.[35] White's dream placed him in the tradition of the foundress of Godstow Priory, who had a dream, and also dedicated her foundation to St John the Baptist.[36] It was only, as Campion said, when the founder 'recognized the ancient structure, recognized the remains of the two walls, and recognized an orderly row of trees' that White settled on St John's.[37] Sir Thomas White's purpose in founding the College was 'the increase of the orthodox faith and of the Christian profession in so far as it is weakened by the damage of time and the malice of men'.[38] This purpose was restated in 1562 when the statutes were transcribed afresh by John Bereblock. Sir Thomas still included the clause in 1566, seven years after the Act of Supremacy.[39] Although Sir Thomas aimed to establish a college that was to train scholars in biblical and scholastic theology, he was an irenic man, close to

---

[29]   Dobson, 'Religious Orders', *HUO*, II. 571; Cross, 'Oxford and the Tudor State', *HUO*, III. 130.

[30]   Dobson, 'Religious Orders', *HUO*, II. 562–6, specifies the outstanding libraries of Greyfriars, Durham and Canterbury Colleges.

[31]   C.M. Dent, *Protestant Reformers in Elizabethan Oxford* (Oxford: University Press, 1983), p. 20.

[32]   Dent, *Protestant Reformers*, p. 21.

[33]   Anthony Wood, *Fasti Oxonienses*, 2 vols, ed. P. Bliss (London: Rivington, 1815), I. 160.

[34]   S.L. Greenslade, 'The Faculty of Theology', in *HUO*, III. 295–334 (p. 312).

[35]   Folger MS J.a.1, fol. 44v; Stevenson and Salter, *Early History of St John's*, p. 408.

[36]   Bodl. MS Wood E. I, fol. 72r–v.

[37]   Folger MS J.a.1, fol. 44v; Stevenson and Salter, *Early History of St John's*, p. 408.

[38]   Statute 16, quoted by Stevenson and Salter, *Early History of St John's*, p. 146.

[39]   Stevenson and Salter, *Early History of St John's*, p. 394.

Sir William Chester.[40] We learn from Campion's funeral oration that, on his deathbed, Sir Thomas White embraced Campion and, in tears, begged him 'that we should nurture charity among ourselves', and make sure that the college suffered no harm, he asked them to pray, not for his recovery, but for a strong faith in Christ.[41]

The accession of Elizabeth in 1558 affected Oxford profoundly. The Queen followed the Act of Supremacy of 1559 with an attempt to purge a largely Catholic university where there were 'few gospellers ... and many papists'; two heads of houses resigned immediately, three more were deprived in 1559, and three more in 1561.[42] Within two years of the Act, only one head elected under Mary remained in office, and all the Regius Professors had been replaced. Robert Horne, the Calvinist bishop of Winchester, became the official visitor of New College, Magdalen, Trinity and Corpus. The return of Marian Calvinist exiles, like John Jewel, a pupil of Peter Martyr, Thomas Sampson and Laurence Humphrey, Professor of Divinity and President of Magdalen, was to shape the university. Religious differences between the colleges became marked; Magdalen was as Calvinist under Humphrey, as St John's remained Catholic under its first three Presidents.

Sir Thomas White secured his restored college with a network of former monks, Marian priests and leading Catholics, which ensured that his original aims continued well after the Act of Supremacy. At least eight of those connected with the early years of the college had links with Abbot Feckenham: William Ely, Alexander Belsyre, Richard Eden, Thomas Bramston, Thomas Paynell, Gabriel Dunne, Henry Cole and Henry Holland. Alexander Belsyre, the first President of St John's, had been a canon of Christ Church at Oseney; the second President, William Ely, had been chaplain to Bishop Bonner, while William Stocke, a Marian priest, was the first principal of Gloucester Hall, and he retained the lease granted on 13 June 1560 until it was transferred to Henry Russell on 12 April 1576.[43] Russell was arrested with Campion and accused of harbouring him, and the returns of 1577 make clear he was thought to harbour many recusants at Gloucester Hall; he recorded none, even though 'Sir William Catesbie lyeth there'.[44] By then, Francis Willis, a close friend of Henry Russell and Sir William Cordell, was the sixth President of the

---

[40]   Foxe, *Actes and Monuments*, p. 1804.

[41]   Bodl. MS Rawl. D. 272, fol. 7r; Stevenson and Salter, *Early History of St John's*, p. 409.

[42]   Penry Williams, 'Elizabethan Oxford: State, Church and University', in *HUO*, III. 397–440 (p. 406).

[43]   Andrew Hegarty, *A Biographical Register of St John's College, Oxford* (Oxford: Boydell Press, 2011), *OHS*, n.s. vol. XLIII. pp. 15–16, 51, 126–7, 143; Stevenson and Salter, *Early History of St John's*, p. 124. Stocke was vicar of Sherborne, Gloucestershire (where Campion accepted a benefice) in 1554.

[44]   Stevenson and Salter, *Early History of St John's*, p. 437.

College.[45] By the time Campion returned to Lyford Grange in 1581, Willis had also become vicar of nearby Cumnor, and rector of Kingston Bagpuize.[46]

Two of the largest donors to St John's library, Gabriel Dunne and Richard Eden, had been monks.[47] Gabriel Dunne, a Cistercian, had been the last Abbot of Buckfast, and left to 'the late Bernard Colledge such nombre of my bookis as myne executor shall thinke good'.[48] Thomas Paynell, who gave the library 152 volumes, was an Augustinian canon, formerly at St Mary's College.[49] White appointed Richard Eden, a former monk of Hailes Abbey and St Bernard's, to be Principal of Gloucester Hall in 1563. Eden gave the library a ten-volume *Opera* of Saint Augustine, which is still there.[50] Dr Henry Cole, another donor, helped to launch a major controversy (which ran to 64 books) with his reply to Bishop Jewel in 1560.[51]

Henry Holland, Feckenham's nephew, became a Fellow in 1570 and left for Douai in 1573, at about which time Thomas Bramston, (who had been a novice at Feckenham's restored Westminster, and was allowed to attend Feckenham in the Tower) also left the College to become a priest *'in ultramarinis partibus'* (overseas).[52] Holland went on to help Gregory Martin with his translation of the New Testament, wrote a Latin elegy for Campion, in which he praised Campion for 'carrying away the prize as the adornment of his age' (*Qui decus et palmam temporis huius habes*), and is mentioned affectionately as 'our Holland' (*Hollandus noster*) in several of Martin's letters to Campion.[53] Sir Thomas sidestepped the savage visitations that Bishop Horne gave to New College and Corpus, by

---

[45]   Hegarty, *Register*, p. 168.

[46]   Stevenson and Salter, *Early History of St John's*, pp. 326–40; Hegarty, *Register*, p. 168.

[47]   J.F. Fuggles, 'A History of the Library of S. John's College, Oxford from the Foundation of the College to 1660' (Dissertation for Oxford University, 1975), pp. 20–22; Stevenson and Salter, *Early History of St John's*, pp. 135–6; *Edmund Campion: Memory and Transcription* (Aldershot, UK and Burlington, VT: Ashgate, 2005), pp. 42–3.

[48]   Gabriel Dunne, the son of a grocer, studied at St Bernard's College, supplicated for the BTh, having studied logic, philosophy, and theology for 12 years. He died on 5 December 1558, and bequeathed 45 volumes to St John's, including works of classical literature and theology, Stevenson and Salter, *Early History of St John's*, p. 122; *ODNB*, 'Gabriel Dunne', by Nicholas Orme.

[49]   Stevenson and Salter, *Early History of St John's*, pp. 133–6.

[50]   Benefactors' Register, col. XXI. The *Opera*, printed in 1532 in Paris, has an entire volume devoted to a superb index. See N.R. Ker, 'Oxford College Libraries in the Sixteenth Century', *Bodleian Library Record* 6 (January 1959), 459–515 (p. 511).

[51]   A.C. Southern, *Elizabethan Recusant Prose, 1559–1582* (London: Sands, 1950), pp. 60–64.

[52]   Stevenson and Salter, *Early History of St John's*, pp. 332–3.

[53]   BL MS Harley 3258, fol. 78r–v: I thank Hilton Kelliher for alerting me to this elegy. For letters, see *First and Second Diaries of the English College, Douay*, ed. T.F. Knox (London: Nutt, 1878), pp. 308–20.

entrusting the college, in 1566, to two visitors for life.[54] One was William Roper, the son-in-law of Sir Thomas More, with whom Sir Thomas Pope, the founder of Trinity, had wept on the day of his death, 5 July 1535.[55] The other was Sir William Cordell, a Marian Privy Councillor, to whom, as Campion's oration confirms, Sir Thomas particularly entrusted the care of the College. He was made an executor with Sir Thomas's widow, Dame Joan White, and received £100 in White's will.[56] Cordell amply repaid this trust, taking care over the College till his death in 1581.[57]

Despite the change of monarch and the Act of Supremacy of 1559, the College, throughout Campion's time, continued to promote the 'old religion'. Campion himself describes White as 'not only an unlearned man, but one of a simple and open intelligence'.[58] White shared Feckenham's concern for social justice, his desire to restore the religious houses and his respect for civil authority. Feckenham had played a key part in the coronation of Elizabeth; White seems to have done all he could to sustain the old religion without confrontation with the civil power.[59] Campion's own schooling, and his success in rhetorical eloquence (*ars bene loquendi*), seems now to have evolved into a commitment to intellectual freedom and theological debate. Campion returned to England in 1580 asking for debate in his 'Letter to the Council'; his last act before arrest was to print secretly a book that demanded a disputation.[60]

The whole university had been wondering if the Calvinists, led by Laurence Humphrey at Magdalen, and Thomas Sampson and James Calfhill at Christ Church, and locked in a bitter conflict over vestments with the Queen and her archbishop, would gain control.[61] Campion's was not a simple solitary choice between Catholic and Protestant (as it has always been presented since Bombino), but part of a larger struggle between the conflicting groups competing for ascendancy in a divided university.[62] Archbishop Parker, under pressure from the Queen, had summoned Humphrey, Sampson and Calfhill to Lambeth on 3 March 1565; when they refused to back down on 29 April, Sampson was ejected from Christ Church.[63] Humphrey, supported by his fellows, survived at Magdalen, even though a letter to Leicester makes it clear that he believed, 'as late as 2 June 1566, that he might be deprived'.[64]

---

[54]   Stevenson and Salter, *Early History of St John's*, pp. 129 and 206.

[55]   *ODNB*, 'Sir Thomas Pope', by Clare Hopkins.

[56]   Stevenson and Salter, *Early History of St John's*, p. 405.

[57]   Stevenson and Salter, *Early History of St John's*, p. 206.

[58]   Stevenson and Salter, *Early History of St John's*, p. 409.

[59]   *ODNB*, 'John Feckenham', by C.S. Knighton.

[60]   See Chapter 7.

[61]   Williams, 'State, Church and University', *HUO*, III. 409–10; Jennifer Loach, 'Reformation Controversies', *HUO*, III. 363–96 (p. 384).

[62]   As suggested by Bombino, *Vita et Martyrium*, p. 5.

[63]   Williams, 'State, Church and University', *HUO*, III. 416.

[64]   Dent, *Protestant Reformers*, p. 38.

As the Queen, an active participant in the controversy, arrived on 31 August 1566, she made a witty but barbed comment to Dr Humphrey:

> Master doctoure umphrey me thinckethe this gowne becummeth yu verye well & I marvell that you are so straighte laced in thes poyntes but I cam not nowe to chide.[65]

Sir Thomas White, Sir William Chester and Anthony Hussey remained Campion's patrons in Oxford. Campion was summoned to attend to the dying founder and receive his dying wishes.[66] In his funeral oration for White in 1567, the dominant note of the speech is affection, but Campion confirms Wood's gloomy verdict on Oxford, saying 'the arts are despised, made captive, unkempt and almost drowned in sorrow'.[67] They have been deprived, Campion says, of a father, whose childlessness has enabled him to treat them all as his children; others are sorrowing, but they are grieving; the word 'love' is inadequate to describe his attitude to them, which is more than *amor, caritas, pietas* or *amicitia*.[68] Everything suggests White had become almost a father to Campion. Many copies of this attractive eulogy have survived; with a variety of rhetorical figures, the warmth of its natural language embraces the audience.[69] Campion says that Sir Thomas's death has been felt across the land: by his widow, of course, by the whole of the order of knights, and by the world of letters. The generosity of the tribute is matched by the depth of feeling, expressed in emotive *iteratio* (repetition) – *illum illum (inquam)* (he, he, I say) – and *exclamatio* – *dii boni* (good God!) – and in the constant reminders that they, the hearers, and he, the speaker, having shared the same benevolence, now share the same grief.[70] Campion emphasizes the achievement of the man who, during Wyatt's rebellion, 'won universal acclaim for the way he carried out the duties of the Mayor of London during the greatest crisis of the state'.[71] His benefactions to Bristol and 30 other cities, his generosity to the Merchant Taylors, his restoration of Gloucester Hall, are all singled out.[72] But the climax of the speech is praise for White as a man. Campion asserts that

---

[65]   CCC MS 257, fol. 117r; Bodl. MS Twyne 17, p. 158. Twyne's copy has minor variants: 'Mr Dr Umfrey, me thinkes this gowne & habit becometh you very well, & I mervayle that you are so straight laced in this poynt; but I come not now to chyde, & then gave him her hande to kisse'.

[66]   Stevenson and Salter, *Early History of St John's*, p. 138.

[67]   Bodl. MS Rawl. D. 272, fol. 7v.

[68]   Folger MS J.a.1, fol. 44r; Stevenson and Salter, *Early History of St John's*, pp. 407–8.

[69]   Folger MS J.a.1, fols 44r–45v; Folger MS V.a.173, fols 35r–37r; Bodl. MS Rawl. D. 272, Auct. F. 5. 13, Arch. IV. Westmon. II. See Stevenson and Salter, *Early History of St John's*, pp. 407–11.

[70]   Stevenson and Salter, *Early History of St John's*, p. 407.

[71]   Stevenson and Salter, *Early History of St John's*, p. 409.

[72]   Stevenson and Salter, *Early History of St John's*, p. 409.

they all, wearing the badges of learning as masters of art or doctors, have been outclassed by this simple man; that they who have combed the poets, orators and philosophers, have been outdone by a man who had none of those advantages.[73] Among other patrons of the arts, he, who only competed in humility and modesty, carried off the prize; while most other founders of colleges were nobles or bishops, he (like Sir Thomas Pope) was a private man, a merchant.[74] Campion ends by saying that, while he was expected to say these things,

> that particular judgement of his about me and the perpetual zeal with which he embraced me, demanded in their own right that I say these things.[75]

Campion's funeral speech for Sir Thomas White is evidence both of Campion's rhetorical genius and of his remarkable gift for friendship. Campion attracted the patronage of monarchs, nobles, churchmen and merchants, and repaid it with warmth and affection.

In the early 1560s, Sir Thomas White seems to have been hoping that the latest alteration in religion would be as impermanent as the previous three.[76] The appointment of the Earl of Leicester as Chancellor, his *nova statuta* of 1565, and a whole series of episcopal visitations by the Calvinist Bishop Horne and his commissary, George Ackworth, gradually extinguished such hope.[77] By the time White died in 1567, the balance of power was tilting towards the small band of Calvinists, like Laurence Humphrey, Robert Horne and James Calfhill, who were supported by Leicester, and away from the large number of 'papists'. The steady stream of Catholic scholars leaving for Louvain in the early years of the reign, especially from New College, developed into a flood after 1565.[78]

Between the Act of Supremacy in 1559 and the visit of the Queen in 1566, Oxford was an ideological battleground. During Campion's time in Oxford, Leicester was 'the most influential single figure in Elizabethan Oxford', and uncertainty over whether the Queen would marry him was a factor in determining which way the religious issue would go.[79] From 19 June 1559, the Spanish Ambassador was reporting to Philip II that the Queen was pretending to be interested in a match with Archduke Charles in order to 'reassure somewhat the Catholics', and told the King that 'if it were not for your Majesty, the Pope would proceed against the Queen'.[80] By 31 January 1562, Lord Robert Dudley was asking the Spanish

---

[73] Stevenson and Salter, *Early History of St John's*, p. 410.

[74] Stevenson and Salter, *Early History of St John's*, p. 410.

[75] Stevenson and Salter, *Early History of St John's*, p. 409.

[76] Stevenson and Salter, *Early History of St John's*, p. 394.

[77] Dent, *Protestant Reformers*, 40–41.

[78] James McConica, 'The Catholic Experience in Tudor Oxford', in *The Reckoned Expense*, 2nd ed., ed. Thomas McCoog, S.J. (Rome: IHSI, 2007), pp. 58–9.

[79] Williams, 'State, Church and University', *HUO*, III. 423.

[80] *CSP Spanish, 1558–1567*, I. 77.

ambassador, Bishop de Quadra, to persuade the king to 'write to the Queen in his favour'.[81] Three years later, on 20 October 1565, while negotiations on 'the free exercise of their religion' were still going on with the Emperor Maximilian, the King was instructing the new Spanish ambassador, Bishop Guzman de Silva, that all marriage negotiations with the Queen were futile because she 'will either not marry or else marry Robert, to whom she has always been so much attached'.[82] Philip II instructed his ambassadors to make support for marriage to Dudley dependent on his promising to 'reduce the kingdom to our true ancient Catholic religion'.[83] In a letter of 28 January 1566, de Silva wrote that the Queen openly discussed 'the Earl's suit', and 'said laughingly, two neighbouring Queens would be married in the same way'.[84] Right up to her visit to Oxford from 31 August to 6 September 1566, the Queen was keeping both the Archduke and the Earl of Leicester in doubt as to her intentions. Guzman de Silva reported, immediately after the visit, that the Queen was negotiating with the Archduke's ambassador on the question of religious toleration.[85] Once it became clear that 'toleration of a Mass in the royal household was a prerequisite of a Catholic marriage', there was no future for a scheme by which the Queen hoped (in de Silva's eyes) to acquire 'both the king of Spain and emperor as her protectors': religion was to be the stumbling block in subsequent negotiations.[86]

This complex diplomacy explains Catholic attempts to win the Queen's favour during her visit.[87] Courtship was in the air, even if it may, in part, have been put on to impress (or confuse) the Spanish ambassador. On 4 February 1566, de Silva records being brought into an intimate garden conversation, in which the Queen 'very affectionately' told Leicester that 'if he were a King's son she would marry him to-morrow'.[88] Stow records the Queen's public display of affection when Leicester returned to London on 2 April 1566: 'She cam owt of hir coche in the highe way, and she imbrased the earle and kyssed hym thrise, and they rode togythar to Grenewytche'.[89] Oxford Catholics, like John Bereblock, Thomas

---

[81]   *CSP Spanish, 1558–1567*, I. 224–5.

[82]   *CSP Spanish, 1558–1567*, p. 492. See Susan Doran, *Monarchy and Matrimony: The Courtships of Elizabeth I* (London and New York: Routledge, 1996), pp. 78–95 (p. 81), for a full account of the endless tergiversations of this fruitless marriage negotiation, which lasted from 1565 till the end of 1567.

[83]   *CSP Spanish, 1558–1567*, I. 371.

[84]   *CSP Spanish, 1558–1567*, I. 514.

[85]   *CSP Spanish, 1558–1567*, I. 579 (14 Sept 1566).

[86]   Doran, *Monarchy and Matrimony*, p. 96.

[87]   For detailed account of this visit see Gerard Kilroy, 'The Queen's Visit to Oxford in 1566: A Fresh Look at Neglected Manuscript Sources', *Recusant History* 31.3 (2013), 331–73.

[88]   *CSP Spanish, 1558–1567*, I. 523.

[89]   John Stow, 'Historical Memoranda', in *Three Fifteenth-Century Chronicles*, ed. James Gairdner (London: Camden Society, 1880), p. 137.

Neale and George Etheridge tried to court the Queen with gifts, which supports Christopher Haigh's argument that 'Catholics came to think that the Queen might be won over, and in 1564–65 a spate of Catholic books dedicated to Elizabeth was published by exiles at Antwerp'.[90] Added urgency had been given to the issue by the birth of a son to Mary Stuart in June 1566.[91] Leicester was seen as a possible candidate 'until the mid-1560s, and beyond', and 'figures in Spain and the Roman Curia' saw him as a supporter of Catholicism until at least 1565.[92]

Campion (now 26) was chosen to open three days of disputations, beginning on Tuesday 3 September 1566, all of which the Queen attended.[93] Campion by common consent was acknowledged to be the best orator in the university, and 'so excelled in a style of eloquence that was both polished and vigorous that those who excelled in either virtue were called Campionists'.[94] The disputations were *spectacula* on a grand wooden stage inside the university church of St Mary the Virgin. John Bereblock, Campion's contemporary, who has a good sense of audience, has left the best eyewitness account of the drama and excitement of these disputations, and of Campion's performance.[95] Bereblock conveys the drama of the occasion, describing the extra wooden tier put into the church, so that the Queen, her nobles and the ladies of the court, having processed through the church, could ascend to an elevated tier. On the ground floor the seating was hierarchical: masters of art on stools, proctors on a raised platform, doctors on both sides of the amphitheatre on larger and higher benches, and 'bachelors of art, and the younger scholars besieging this wooden structure'.[96] The exotic costumes of both courtiers and academics were elaborately theatrical. The proctors, who stage-managed these debates, clearly chose their best Master of Arts to open them:

---

[90]   Christopher Haigh, *Elizabeth I*, 2nd ed. (London: Pearson Education, 1998), p. 37.

[91]   Doran, *Monarchy and Matrimony*, p. 85.

[92]   Doran, *Monarchy and Matrimony*, p. 212; see also pp. 66–7 for Leicester's shifting religious loyalties.

[93]   For Cecil, Leicester and the Spanish Ambassador, there must have been something like 17 hours of disputations: ABSI Collectanea P. I, fol. 149[*bis*]; CCC MS 257, fol. 109v.

[94]   Daniel Bartoli, S.J., *Europeae Historiae Societatis Iesu Pars Prior Anglia*, trans. Ludovicus Janinus, S.J. (Lyons: Adam Demen, 1671), p. 75. Simpson, p. 6, elaborates on Bartoli, whom he does not name as his source, to include imitation of 'speech, gait and diet'; in Waugh, *Edmund Campion*, p. 10, this is further developed to include 'his habits of speech, his mannerisms and his clothes'.

[95]   Three manuscripts survive: Folger MS V.a.109, fols 1r–21r (autograph); Bodl. MS Rawl. D. 1071, pp. 1–49 (paginated); Bodl. MS Add. A. 63, fols 1r–20r (autograph). The text is printed in Charles Plummer, *Elizabethan Oxford: Reprints of Rare Tracts* (Oxford: Clarendon Press, 1887), pp. 115–50, and in John Nichols, *The Progresses and Public Processions of Queen Elizabeth I: A New Edition of the Early Modern Sources*, 3 vols, ed. Elizabeth Goldring and others (Oxford: University Press, 2014), vol. 1, pp. 611–65, translated by Sarah Knight.

[96]   Bodl. MS Add. A. 63, fol. 9r; Plummer, *Elizabethan Oxford*, p. 130.

But when the Queen came into view from her higher position, a shout went up from the whole theatre, growing louder and louder as it was repeated and went down through the heads of houses and the distinguished professors of the arts. While the eyes of everyone were locked with intense concentration on the appearance of the doctors, suddenly Campion, with a remarkably serene countenance and composed demeanour, processed up to the decorated podium of the Respondent. He was wearing a very elaborate costume: a long dalmatic with wide flowing and unfastened sleeves. On top of this was a gown that was entirely enclosed except for one opening for his right arm. On top of this, his shoulders were completely covered with white fur, gleaming bright. All the Masters of Art were similarly dressed.[97]

Bereblock provides a unique glimpse of Campion's remarkable presence, a natural authority that made him the obvious choice for the first respondent; he was already *primus* (first), the *princeps gregis* (leader of the flock) as a contemporary poem has it.[98]

Bereblock describes what follows in the Natural Philosophy disputation as a gripping gladiatorial contest in words. As soon as the proctors signalled the start of the contest, the first opponent, John Day of Magdalen, stepped forward and proposed two topics, whether lower bodies are controlled by higher, and 'whether the moon is the cause of the ebb and flow of the sea'.[99] As Campion was opening the event, he started by greeting the Queen and subtly pleading for funds and support.[100] He addressed the Queen and the Earl of Leicester as equals, linked by a series of parallel clauses, for which he must have had Leicester's permission.[101]

O Jupiter, preserve, I beseech you, these advantages for us: your majesty, your honour; you as a parent and you as our patron; you who thus advise us, you who carry out policy; you who have responsibility for these things and you who adorn our university; you, [Chancellor] who make us secure, and you [Your Majesty] who make us blessed.

---

[97]   Bodl. MS Add. A. 63, fol. 9r; Plummer, *Elizabethan Oxford*, p. 131 (my translation).

[98]   [John Gibbons and John Fen], eds, *Concertatio Ecclesiae Catholicae in Anglia Adversus Calvinopapistas et Puritanos* (Trier: Bock, 1588), fol. 66v; Edmund Campion, *Decem Rationes Propositae in Causa Fidei et Opuscula Eius Selecta* (Antwerp: Plantin Moretus Press, 1631), ARCR I. 170, p. 205.

[99]   Folger MS V.a.176, fol. 168v. The text of the speech is in Folger MS V.a.173, fols 29v–30v, which also contains Campion's speech on Sir Thomas White, fols 35r–37r, and Tobie Matthew's welcome to Robert Dudley as Chancellor, fols 37r–39v, and in Bodl. MS Rawl. D. 272, fols 11r–12r.

[100]   Bodl. MS Rawl. D. 272, fol. 11r; Folger MS V.a.173, fol. 29v.

[101]   The Bishops' Bible given to William Cecil by Archbishop Parker two years later has a hand-painted engraving of the Earl added to the beginning of the second part; the Queen's engraving remains unadorned, *The. holie. bible. conteynyng the olde testament and the newe* (London: R. Jugge, [1568]), STC 2099, Folger copy 3. This beautiful book is described by Peter W. M. Blayney in *Elizabeth I: Then and Now*, ed. Georgianna Ziegler (Washington, DC: Folger Shakespeare Library, 2003), p. 43.

[O Jupiter serva (obsecro) haec nobis bona: maiestatem tuam; honorem tuum: te parentem, et te patronum; te qui sic mones, te quae sic facis; te qui haec curas, te quae nos ornas; te qui nos securos, te quae nos beatos facis.][102]

The Queen was amused, and 'smylinge sayde unto my Lord of Leycester, you my Lord must still be one'.[103] Campion then widened the focus to make a powerful case for philosophy (both for the arts, and for Elizabeth as the '*literata princeps*'), encouraged her to emulate both her grandfather Henry VII, and father (although we know what Campion really thought of this 'founder'). He exhorted the Queen to tend, nourish and adorn both philosophy and 'the rest of the disciplines of the most prosperous arts': the adjective *florentissimarum* here seems optative rather than indicative.[104] The Elizabethan bishops were too busy marrying, acquiring livings and leaving wealth for their children, to endow any colleges, and had not matched their Henrician predecessors (of whom 'twelve had founded twenty-two schools or colleges') in donations to learning.[105]

Campion's speech is a masterpiece of diplomacy, especially against the background of an interventionist Leicester. While it starts with fulsome flattery of both Queen and Chancellor, it uses the moon and the earth as an instructive analogy of the ideal relationship of the monarch to the university: a subtle plea to support without interfering.

> From all these things we can draw this conclusion. When the moon draws closer, the sea, just like water in oil put on a fire, begins to boil and seethe, with all the gasses of which it is composed and mixed turned to liquid, in such a way as the sea at fixed times, with the water made thinner miraculously displays an increase, and then little by little, as the rays of the moon decrease, gathers itself together and goes back into its own basin. This is what our scholars call the ebb and recession of the sea. I have come to the end of the first part of my talk.[106]

Campion then confronts the second question, the hierarchical nature of the universe and moves from a play on *coelum* (heaven) and *celsitudo* (loftiness) to praising the ruling dignitaries while gently reminding them that everything other than God decays and dies. The extant manuscripts record one long speech, whereas Bereblock indicates a fierce contest that flows back and forth, in which first Day, then John Meyrick, Richard Bristow and Adam Squire, 'drove hard at, struck, and closed upon his opponent like an assailant' (*premit, impellit, urget*), and Campion like 'an armed and well-prepared man' shook off his attackers

---

[102]   Bodl. MS Rawl. D. 272, fol. 11r (where the scribe has had problems with the complex structure of the sentence); Folger MS V.a.173, fol. 29v.

[103]   CCC MS 257, fol. 109r; Bodl. MS Twyne 17, p. 162.

[104]   Bodl. MS Rawl. D. 272, fol. 11r; Folger MS V.a.173, fol. 29v.

[105]   Felicity Heal, *Of Prelates and Princes: A Study of the Economic and Social Position of the Tudor Episcopate* (Cambridge: University Press, 1980), p. 96.

[106]   Bodl. MS Rawl. D. 272, fol. 11v (my translation).

effortlessly.[107] After John Belly was unexpectedly called to arbitrate (*repentinus iudex*), Campion descended from the podium and everyone prepared to leave. But the Queen had enjoyed it so much that she asked for the debate to continue, and John Wolley (a rising palace servant), was called on to propose a topic, while James Leech launched the attack. Although the topic proposed was more daring (whether a prince is to be declared by succession or by election) Bereblock gives the impression that Campion's contest was much more exciting.[108] At six o'clock, it was decided to postpone the evening's drama, to spare the Queen's health, 'because she had been detained by the long debate'.[109]

Campion, it seems, had completely captivated the Queen, since Leicester was deputed to offer him preferment and patronage on an unlimited scale:

> Robert Dudley, Earle of Leister, a man much favoured, as then by Queene Elizabeth, some say for other gifts, but most for his flourishing youth & comely personaage, calling Campian unto him, after many exquisitie prayses. Verily (Ingenious young man) sayd hee, you are much beholding to the Queens Majesty. No one would beleeve what a care shee hath to pleasure & preferre you. In so much that I am commanded to aske what you would have her doe for you, or any of your friendes, *Make use of her royal generosity, knowing that you have been safely taken under her protection, and may expect, day be day, more and more benefits.* Be not now childishly bashfull to doe your selfe good in any thing shee may bestead you. In very deed I myselfe am so much taken with your deserts that not only by the Queenes command, but of my owne free will, I shall be ready evermore to promote you. Thus much for the present. Henceforth leave us to care & provide for you.[110]

The following morning Campion was chosen to dispute again in Merton College in front of Leicester, Cecil, Guzman de Silva, when the Spanish Ambassador, who had asked for an impromptu debate, declared, 'It is no wonder that they are getting heated: they are disputing about fire' (*non mirum si incalescant, disputant enim de igne*).[111] Four more hours of public disputations followed on Wednesday afternoon and five on Thursday, including a final discussion, in Divinity, on whether 'it is not permissible for a private man to take up arms against a prince, even an unjust one'. The Queen, not surprisingly, 'taried til the ful end', especially as the Respondent was the anti-vestiarian Dr Humphrey (perhaps hoping to regain her favour by

---

[107]   Bodl. MS Add. A 63, fol. 10r; Nichols, *Early Modern Sources*, I. 479 and 651, where Sarah Knight's translation brings out the combative nature of the disputation superbly. I thank her for this and many helpful suggestions.

[108]   Bodl. MS Add. A 63, fol. 10r–v; see Folger MS V.a.176, fol. 168v.

[109]   Bodl. MS Add. A 63, fol. 11v; Nichols, *Early Modern Sources*, I. 625 and 653.

[110]   Bombino, *Vita et Martyrium*, p. 7; Bodl. MS Tanner 329, fol. 3r–v. I have translated (in italics) a sentence omitted by the translator.

[111]   ABSI Collectanea, P.I, fol. 149b; see also Miles Windsor in CCC MS 257, fol. 110r.

arguing against assassination).[112] Finally, at the request of the Spanish Ambassador, the Earl of Leicester, the Earl of Ormond and the Secretary, William Cecil, the Queen herself made a speech in Latin.[113] These disputations are not just fascinating glimpses of early modern pedagogy, but indicators of a vigorous oral culture that was central to every stage of the public life of the rhetorical 'champion', from his childhood in Paul's churchyard to the disputations in the Tower and the trial in Westminster Hall.

In the end, Leicester's choice of Laurence Humphrey as his representative in Oxford ensured that by 1571, 'the only Marian exile of significance', would become the most powerful man in the university: President of Magdalen, Regius Professor of Divinity *and* Vice-Chancellor.[114] Anthony Wood is careful to emphasize that Humphrey was not elected, but appointed 'by virtue of letters from the chancellor' in 1571, and he continued as commissary (or vice-chancellor), 'without any nomination or designation', until he finally resigned in 1576.[115]

Leicester's patronage had a darker side. The records of Convocation and Congregation show that Leicester intervened continuously, from the moment of his appointment, in the affairs of the university.[116] In September 1566, while the Queen left Oxford to stay with the staunchly Catholic family of Lord Windsor, George Ackworth began a new series of visitations for the Bishop of Winchester, of the four colleges under his aegis.[117] By 1567, the Earl of Leicester had begun turning the elected office of commissary (vice-chancellor) into his own appointment.[118] The university archives reveal Leicester intervening in the elections, first of the commissary, and then of the proctors.[119]

'All – if at least sixteen years of age – were to take the oath to observe the university's statutes', but it was not till 14 November 1581, that all matriculands were required to take the oath of supremacy and sign up to the articles of religion, which 'finally brought into being a Protestant, undergraduate, collegiate university'.[120] St John's was living a double life: outwardly obeying the statutes, inwardly carrying on with the mission it kept restating in its own statutes.[121] The *nova statuta* of 1565 combined with no less than six visits by Leicester – three while Campion was there – on 6 January 1565, with the Queen in August 1566,

---

[112]   Folger MS V.a.176, fol. 169r–v.

[113]   CCC MS Twyne 17, pp. 166–7.

[114]   Dent, *Protestant Reformers*, p. 23.

[115]   Wood, *Fasti Oxonienses*, I. 187–95.

[116]   Oxford University Archives, *Calendar of the Register of Congregation and Convocation* (1564–82), housed in the Tower of the Bodleian Library (hereafter Reg. Cong.).

[117]   Dent, *Protestant Reformers*, pp. 40–43.

[118]   Williams, 'State, Church and University', *HUO*, III. 423.

[119]   Reg. Cong. 1564–82, fols 39v–69v.

[120]   McConica, 'Catholic Experience in Tudor Oxford', p. 58.

[121]   Stevenson and Salter, *Early History of St John's*, p. 394.

and again in 1569, when Campion was proctor.[122] The year in which the Queen paid her visit to Oxford could be seen as a watershed, and coincided with the period when Leicester ceased to be seen as a protector of Catholicism. After 1566, the situation became increasingly difficult for all colleges, as episcopal visitations imposed conformity.[123] Leicester's selection of Calvinists to rid Oxford of papistry gave them disproportionate power. If the voices of puritan protest were easy to suppress, it proved much harder to eradicate papistry, and Oxford remained resolutely papist till the end of Leicester's life. In 1580, he wrote to his newly appointed vice-chancellor and 'the rest of the convocation':

> So for that it is a thinge wheare with the universitie hathe bin and is yet more then I wolde wishe specially touched, I ernestlie praye you all that all advise and authoritye maye be used to remove all pupilles from any tutors suspected of popery, as allso that no suspected papestes be shrowded ether in the universite or towne, as I heare with greefe they are of late more then heare to fore, and especially in the haules.[124]

Leicester did his best to turn the university into a private fiefdom, as portrayed in *Leicester's Commonwealth*: 'no man daring to contrary or interrupt the least word or signification of his will but with his extreme danger.[125] Campion's description of the arts 'unkempt and almost drowned in sorrow' agrees with the picture painted in *Leicester's Commonwealth*, which accused him of destroying all academic order: 'the public lectures abandoned (I mean of the more part) the taverns and ordinary tables frequented, apparel of students grown monstrous'.[126] Leicester found the university flourishing, Wood pithily comments, and left it in disorder.[127]

The pressure from Leicester, Bishop Horne and Dr Ackworth, drove Catholics abroad and underground. A letter of the Privy Council on 14 August 1581 'to the Vicechauncelour and Doctors of the Universitie of Oxforde' complained that most

---

[122] The first date is from Reg. Cong. 1564–82, fol. 6v; the others from Williams, 'State, Church and University', *HUO*, III. 424.

[123] For the slow eradication of papists, see Williams, 'State, Church and University', *HUO*, III. 407–15.

[124] Reg. Cong. 1564–82, fol. 311v.

[125] *Leicester's Commonwealth: The Copy of a Letter Written by a Master of Art of Cambridge (1584)*, ed. D.C. Peck (Ohio: University Press, 1985) p. 117. Peter Beal has found 90 manuscripts of this book, and alerted me to one copied by Sir John Harington, his brother Francis and his 'servant', Thomas Combe, now in Exeter College, Oxford, MS 166. See my 'Advertising the Reader: Sir John Harington's "Directions in the Margent"', *English Literary Renaissance* 41.1 (2011), 64–110 (pp. 87–95).

[126] Bodl. MS Rawl. D. 272, fol. 7v (Campion); Peck, ed., *Leicester's Commonwealth*, p. 116.

[127] Williams, 'State, Church and University', *HUO*, III. 424, citing Wood, *Annals*, II. 231ff.

of the seminary priests have been 'heretofore schollers of that Universitie'.[128] Of course, many left for the Continent. 'All told, something over a hundred fellows and other senior members left Oxford during the first decade of the reign of Elizabeth, a great percentage of them into the priesthood and the work of the English mission'.[129] By 1585 the number must have been close to 170, nearly one tenth of the university. Of the 116 priests executed under Elizabeth, 51 were Oxford graduates. Between 1565 and 1580 some 54 fellows from only four colleges, New College, the newly founded Colleges of St John's and Trinity, and Exeter College (virtually refounded by Sir William Petre in 1567), left Oxford for Douai or Rheims.[130] Of those who crossed the Channel on the Jesuit mission in 1580, nine were Oxford men.[131] Campion's two fellow martyrs were both Oxford men, but when Alexander Briant talked of 'his being in *Oxford*', the crowd shouted back, 'What have we to do with *Oxford?*'[132]

The situation at St John's itself was even more striking, especially for such a small college. Even when Campion returned to Oxford in 1581, many members of St John's were still adhering to the old religion. Over 30 members of the college and two chaplains left Oxford to become Catholic priests at Rheims or Douai.[133] These include six who were among the original 20 members of the College: Alexander Belsyre, William Ely, John Bavand (Campion's tutor), Campion himself, Gregory Martin, Leonard Stopes and Ralph Wyndham.[134] At least nine members of the college, including Campion, were put to death for their religious beliefs, and others appear to have died in prison.[135] To these must be added a wider group of men who had close contact with Campion, who left the college '*alterata religione*' (with religion altered): John Bereblock, who taught law in the English College in Rome, Thomas Bramston (who first went to work with Sir Thomas Tresham as a tutor), Robert Charnock, Humphrey Ely (brother of the President), Henry Holland, Jonas Meredith, Henry Russell (probably the 'Russell M.A.' at Campion's Mass at Lyford Grange), Henry Shaw, Edward Stransham and William Wigges.[136] Two of the chaplains of the college were martyred: in 1577, Cuthbert

---

[128]   *APC, 1581–82*, xxiii, p. 170. See Chapter 8 for full text.

[129]   McConica, 'Catholic Experience in Tudor Oxford', pp. 51–2.

[130]   These figures have been obtained by analysing the lists of John S. Wainwright, 'Elizabethan Recusant Fellows of Oxford Colleges', *Downside Review* 94 (1913), 41–68.

[131]   Edmund Campion (St John's), Robert Persons (Balliol), Edward Rishton and Thomas Cottam (Brasenose), Ralph Sherwin and John Paschal (Exeter), Dr Humphrey Ely (St John's), Thomas Briscow (Oxford college not known), John Hart (Oxfordshire man, said to be Oxford graduate, but college not known).

[132]   Alfield, *A true reporte*, sig. D3r; for full exchange, see Chapter 11.

[133]   Hegarty, *Register*, p. xliv.

[134]   Stevenson and Salter, *Early History of St John's*, p. 394, focusing on 1567–74.

[135]   Hegarty, *Register*, p. xliv.

[136]   See Henry Holland's, *In Chronologiam Edmundi Campiani Jesuitae viri eloquentissimi*, in BL Harley MS 3258, fol. 78r.

Mayne (a *contubernalis*, or room-mate, of Campion), was the first priest to be martyred in Elizabethan England.[137] William Hartley, the other chaplain, took 400 copies of *Rationes Decem* to Oxford, distributed them in St Mary's on 27 June 1581, and returned triumphant to Stonor Park, where he was arrested with Stephen Brinkley and John Stonor on 6 August 1581.[138] After being sentenced to death, reprieved and finally banished on 21 January 1585, he returned, within a few months, to distribute books, was tried and condemned at the Middlesex Sessions at Newgate on 18 September 1588, and executed in the frenzy of anti-Catholic feeling that followed the Armada on 5 October 1588.[139] It is a remarkable story of persistent and determined courage. William Wigges (*Wigsaeus noster*), suspected of helping Mayne had to flee abroad in 1577, left behind his family, and (after his wife's death) was ordained a priest in 1582.[140] The entry against Henry Shaw in the College *Catalogus Sociorum* is typical. It reads, 'religion having been changed, he departed, became a priest and was imprisoned in the prison at Wisbech.'[141] The neat ambiguity of the phrase *alterata religione* (is it the college or the fellow who has altered?) captures the anomalous position of these early fellows: having joined a college founded to promote the Catholic faith, they are swearing, within two years, to do exactly the opposite. In view of the small size of the college, the number who left to go abroad to become priests is all the more remarkable.[142] Adversity bound these men, scattered across Europe, closely together: Campion and Martin address each other as *dulcissime* or *suavissime*, and attach the affectionate possessive *noster* (our) to other fellows: 'our Wiggsy', 'our Holland', 'our Bramston': a society as closely bound together, over 20 years, as the Society of Jesus, which has always used the term 'our men' (*nostri*).

Less well known than the story of these Catholic exiles, is that of other fellows in the university, who resigned, but continued teaching within the city, or just outside, in a network of what amounted to safe houses. Edmund Rainolds, one of five remarkable brothers, incepted Master of Arts alongside Campion and Martin in 1564.[143] He resigned from Corpus in 1568, 'because he was popishly affected, retired to Glocester hall, where being a noted Tutor for 60 years or thereabouts, grew very rich', accumulating property at Wolvercote, Eynsham and Cassington.[144]

---

[137]   Anstruther, *Seminary Priests*, I. 155–6.

[138]   *APC*, XIII, 151. *Diarium Rerum Gestarum in Turri Londinensi* in *De Origine Schismatis Anglicanae De Origine ac Progressu Schismatis Anglicani, aucti per Edouardum Rishtonum* (Ingolstadt: Ederus, 1587), ARCR I. 974, sig. 2l7v, suggests they were brought to the Tower on 13 August.

[139]   Hegarty, *Register*, p. 304.

[140]   Hegarty, *Register*, p. 165.

[141]   Stevenson and Salter, *Early History of St John's*, p. 335.

[142]   Hegarty, *Register*, p. xliv.

[143]   Wood, *Fasti*, I. 165. For the five brothers, see Kilroy, 'Queen's Visit to Oxford', pp. 336–7.

[144]   Bodl. MS Wood, E. 1, fol. 160r–v.

He bought the freehold of Moat Farm, Cassington in 1610.[145] Under two miles across the meadows from Godstow, the moated manor house and church were outside the university boundaries.

With him at Cassington was Thomas Neale, a Marian priest. Neale 'did quietly enjoy' an exhibition of £40 per annum from St John's.[146] Neale remained rector of Hanborough, where he had been ordained a Catholic priest under Mary, until 1567, but let his uncle, Alexander Belsyre, the first President of St John's College, a 'stubborn recusant', live in the rectory from 1562 to 1567.[147] In 1566, Neale and Bereblock had presented the Queen with two book gifts.[148]

> The Queen and the Court set out again to the disputations. And while she was on her way, Thomas Neale, the Reader of Hebrew met her in the gardens of the college, and gave her a gift of the Rabbinical commentaries on the twelve prophets, translated from Hebrew into Latin. He was ready with a Hebrew gratulatory speech which he had written for her arrival, and he added to that a Dialogue in verse, and a topography of the whole university, with genuine pictures of each of the individual schools and colleges, indicating their natural site and form. Bereblock of Exeter College made these with his own pen, and everyone admired the work. But the Queen was greatly moved by the kindness of Neale, and by such a gift as his, and she seemed never to have received a better or more generous gift, and she gave him very fulsome and personal thanks.[149]

Although Neale was appointed Regius Professor of Hebrew in 1559, Christ Church paid him only under pressure from the Privy Council, so he became a commoner of Hart Hall and built himself lodgings next to New College, where he did his teaching.[150] In 1569, Neale finally resigned the chair of Hebrew, and moved to Cassington, and appears to have taught there for the next 20 years. Before Neale died, sometime after 1590, he placed in the church at Cassington some remarkable memorial verses for himself around a shroud brass (Figure 2.1). The position of the brass, above a side-altar, suggests that Neale may have said Mass there. At a

---

[145]   *VCH, Oxford*, vol. 12, *Wootton Hundred (South) Including Woodstock*, ed. Alan Crossley (Oxford: University Press, 1990): 'Cassington', Janet Cooper (pp. 36–54), pp. 41 and 46.

[146]   Stevenson and Salter, *Early History of St John's*, p. 422: letter of Sir Thomas White, 12 December 1566.

[147]   Hegarty, *Register*, pp. 528–9.

[148]   BL MS Royal 2 D. XXI: *Rabbi Davidis Kimhi commentarii super Hoseam, Joelem, Amos, Abdiam, Jonam, Micheam, Nahum, Habacuc & Sophonian; Latine redditi per Thomas Nelum, Hebraicae Linguae Professorem Oxonii; et R. Elizabethae inscripti.* This is a beautiful book, with text in Neale's own hand, in black ink, with biblical quotations in red.

[149]   Folger MS V.a.109, fol. 15r (my translation); Plummer, *Elizabethan Oxford*, pp. 139–40.

[150]   Hegarty, *Register*, p. 529. See Wood, *Athenae Oxonienses*, I. 576–7 n. 9.

Figure 2.1   Thomas Neale, Professor of Hebrew: his shroud brass at St Peter's Church, Cassington, Oxfordshire, 1590. Photograph by the author.

time when prayers for the dead had been forbidden, Neale openly asks those he has 'succoured', to pray for him now that he is 'tongueless' in the grave:

Hic iacet elinguis qui linguis pluribus olim
Usus, Hebraismi publica lingua fuit.
Graeca quid hic? quid Hebraea iuvat? quid lingua Latina?
Si qua alios iuvit, nunc ea sola iuvat.
Vos ergo Thomae Neli quos lingua iuvabat,
Elinguem lingua (quaeso) iuvate pia.
Subscriptio ipsi authoris
Hos egomet versus posuit mihi sanus, ut esset
Hinc praevisa mihi mortis imago meae.
Etiam si occiderit me
In ipsum tamen sperabo. Job, ca. 13.
Anno. Domini. 1590. aetatis vero meae. 71.

[Here lies tongueless a man who used many languages, and was the official reader of Hebrew. But what help is there in Greek, what in Hebrew, what in the Latin language? If his skill in languages ever gave succour to others, that alone gives him protection now. You, therefore, whom the tongue of Thomas Neale used to help, help him, voiceless as he now is, with your holy tongue. *Subscription of the author himself*: While still healthy, I placed these verses here for myself, so that an image of my death might thereby be seen by me in advance. *Even if he kills me, I shall still put my hope in him.* Job. c. 13. A.D. 1590, my 71st year.][151]

In the heart of the university, opposite St Mary's, another leading scholar, whom Campion must also have known, was teaching. George Etheridge, appointed Regius Professor of Greek in 1547, was a protégé of George Owen, and himself an eminent physician, who published a key medical textbook.[152] In April 1559, he was deprived for his part in the trial of Latimer and Ridley and, on the accession of Elizabeth, he refused the oath of supremacy.[153] Thenceforward

He mostly lived and kept a family in an ancient decay'd place of literature called George-hall, opposite almost to the south end of Catstreet in St Mary's parish in Oxon ... He constantly adhered to the R. Catholic religion, wherein he has been zealously educated, for which he suffered at the Reformation ... An eminent musician, an eminent Hebritian, Grecian and poet.[154]

---

[151]   This text is taken from the plaque itself, and the translation is mine. Juvenal uses *iuvo* with 'nudum hospitio tectoque', *Saturae*, 3.211, and Ovid with 'aliquem portuque locoque', *Heroides*, 2.55.

[152]   *In libros aliquot pauli Aeginetae, hypomneta quaedam, seu observationes medicamentorum* (London: T. East, 1588) STC 7498; see G.D. Duncan, 'Public Lectures and Professorial Chairs', in *HUO*, III. 335–61 (p. 355).

[153]   Wood, *Athenae Oxonienses*, I. 546–7.

[154]   Wood, *Athenae Oxonienses*, I. 546.

The recusant returns of 1577 confirm that 'he receiveth preystes in serving mens apparel disguysed, besides a great number of the towne and contrey that suspitiously resort to his house, to heare a masse'.[155] For over 25 years from 1559, Etheridge taught 'the sons of diverse Catholic gentlemen' in what was in effect an unregistered hall, numbering William Gifford and Thomas Belson among his pupils.[156] Etheridge was imprisoned and interrogated frequently.

The leading Aristotle scholar, Dr John Case, a contemporary of Campion's, resigned his fellowship at St John's in 1574, and began teaching in two adjoining houses, numbers 2 and 4, in Magdalen Street:

> In 1564 he was elected scholar of St. John's coll. and was afterwards fellow, master of arts, and the most noted disputant and philosopher that ever before set foot in that college. But so it was, that being Popishly affected, he left his fellowship and married, and with leave from the chancellor and scholars of the university, he read logic and philosophy to young men (mostly of the R.C. religion) in a private house in St. Mary Magdalen parish, particularly in his latter days in that large tenement on the north-side of the inn called the George; wherein, having had disputations, declamations, and other exercises, as in colleges and halls, many eminent men issued thence.[157]

Like Etheridge, Case was running a papist hall, notable for its disputations.[158] Two letters of Sir Henry Cobham, ambassador in Paris, confirm that John Case provided a safe house to men departing for the priesthood and priests arriving from abroad.[159] William Byrd dedicated a book of music to him, with verses by Thomas Watson.[160] Case dedicated the first book officially printed in Oxford by Joseph Barnes, *Speculum moralium quaestionum*, to the Earl of Leicester, who was obviously unaware what Case was doing.[161] Three leading scholars, in Hebrew, Greek and Aristotle, were teaching in Oxford, outside the official structure.

Other safe houses in the city itself were inns and taverns: the Mitre, the Catherine Wheel (where later four martyrs were arrested), the George and the Star. In the large tenement at the back of the George, Marian priests frequented the

---

[155]   CRS 22, *Early Recusants*, ed. Patrick Ryan (London: Catholic Record Society, 1921), p. 97.

[156]   Wood, *Athenae Oxonienses*, I. 547. For Belson, see Christine Kelly, *Blessed Thomas Belson: His Life and Times 1563–1589* (Gerrards Cross: Colin Smythe, 1987), p. 54.

[157]   Wood, *Athenae Oxonienses*, I. 685–8.

[158]   Wood's assertion is far from being 'an unlucky guess', as asserted by Stevenson and Salter, *Early History of St John's*, p. 202. See Hegarty, *Register*, p. xxxiv.

[159]   *CSP Foreign, January 1581–April 1582*, ed. A.J. Butler (London: HMSO, 1907), no. 541 (p. 486) and no. 550 (p. 492).

[160]   William Byrd, *A gratification unto master John Case, for his learned booke, lately made in the praise of musicke* (London: T. East, 1589), STC 4246.

[161]   Williams, 'State, Church and University', *HUO*, III. 430; *Speculum moralium quaestionum in universam ethicen Aristotelis* (Oxford: Jos. Barnes, 1585), STC 4759. Barnes printed nine other books by Case.

Star (now the Randolph Hotel), and here Mass was said, attended by the leading Catholic families of Oxfordshire:

> Mrs Williams, at the signe of the starre commeth not to the churche at all, as some saie. Others saie once in the yere, and that on tuesdaie before Easter and secretely receiveth communion. Her husband is an alderman and a Justice of peace, and thoughe he come him selfe to the churche, yet he is a common receiver of professed enemies, as of Marshall a priest, of Chamberleine aforenamed, Powel of Sandford, Owen of Godstoe, Palmer, Cletherowe and a number more.[162]

Marshall was a Marian priest, mingling at the Star with the gentry and aldermen of Oxford. The parish of St Mary Magdalen, which formed part of the property sold to St John's by Richard Owen of Godstow, was the nursery of several 'plebeian' priests. Fr John Filby, son of a 'curryer' of St Mary Magdalen, used as a base a house at Stanton St John, which Etheridge had leased to 'Mr Ambrose ... a Lawyer'. John Filby's brother, William, was the priest arrested when he came to see Campion as he passed in captive bonds through Henley.[163] In the same parish was Stransham who 'receiveth Lovanistes' and had two sons who became priests, one of whom, Edward, matriculated at St John's in 1575, and arrived at Douai two years later, having been born 'of good, honest Catholic parents', in the parish of St Mary Magdalen, and had been working in Oxfordshire.[164] Ordained at Rheims in 1580, Edward left for England at almost the same time as Campion, in June 1581, but escaped capture.[165] On 15 June 1583, Stransham, leading a large party of 'certaine students of Trinitye Colledge and certaine of other Colledges', departed for Rheims.[166] He returned again to England, accompanied by Walsingham's leading spy, Nicholas Berden, in July 1585, and was captured soon after arrival, without suspecting the treachery of his companion.[167] He was held in the Clink, tried on 19 January 1586, and executed at Tyburn two days later.[168] Two simple families of St Mary Magdalen's parish produced between them four priests and two martyrs.

---

[162]   CRS 22, p. 98.

[163]   See Chapter 7.

[164]   Alan Davidson, 'Roman Catholicism in Oxfordshire from the Late Elizabethan Period to the Civil War (c. 1580–c. 1640)', Ph.D. thesis presented to the University of Bristol in 1970, p. 654, citing PRO 12/118, no. 37; see CRS 22, p. 99.

[165]   Davidson, 'Catholicism in Oxfordshire', p. 412.

[166]   Davidson, 'Catholicism in Oxfordshire', pp. 653–4, full list, citing PRO 12/161, no. 13.

[167]   For Berden, see CRS 5, *English Martyrs*, ed. John Hungerford Pollen (London: Catholic Record Society, 1908), pp. 122–5; and CRS 21, *Ven. Philip Howard, Earl of Arundel, English Martyrs*, vol. 2, ed. John Hungerford Pollen, S.J. and William MacMahon, S.J. (London: Catholic Record Society, 1919), p. 69.

[168]   Anstruther, *Seminary Priests*, I. 337, citing BL MS Harley 360, fol. 35.

In Oxford, gentry like the Napiers of Holliwell Manor, and the Owens of Godstow, plebeian families like the Stranshams and Filbys, old Marian priests like Marshall, Jesuits, seminary priests, deprived Regius Professors and leading Aristotelians, were woven together in a tight fabric of manors, inns, farms and private halls that was unique.[169] An anonymous complaint, to the Bishop of Winchester and the Earl of Bedford, confirms this:

> For amongst us an huge garrisoon, & mighty multitude dothe remaine, which coovertlye dothe encline unto papistrie, whoo in their obscure dens, dimme caves, secret closets, merck clowdie taverns, darck mistie victuallinge howses bothe loorckinge hydinge & absenting them selves, arr even on their ale benches in the midst of their tipplinge jugges. & quaffing pottes, great reasoners and talkers (a gods name) of devine matters & of thinges appending unto the same.[170]

When Campion returned in 1581, it was to this underground network. Thomas Ford caught up with him at a 'publike Inne' near Oxford, surrounded by 'a notable troope of principall Catholikes', 'many university men' and a 'knotte of speciall friendes'.[171] In Oxford, Catholicism was embedded in the masonry of the city and closely tied with the surrounding county, which had suffered at the hands of William, Lord Grey for its part in the Prayer Book rebellion of 1549.[172] The fact that some of the best scholars in Oxford had resigned their chairs to teach unofficially, and many of the rest were in Louvain, Rheims or Rome, steadily transformed Oxford during the years between Campion's speech to the Queen in 1566 and his return to Oxford in 1581.

On 28 September 1566, immediately after Leicester's offer of royal patronage, Sir John White, Sir William Chester, Laurence Humphrey and Dr Godwin, Dean of Christ Church proposed that the exhibition of the Company of Grocers, 'be granted unto one Edmond Campion'; he would receive 'X marks' (£6, 13s, 4d) under the usual conditions that 'he shal ones in the yere preche at paulls crosse'.[173]

Campion was elected proctor on 18 April 1568, and almost immediately came under pressure from the Grocers' Company. By July, Campion had not 'to the Companies knowledge made one sermon anywhere', and was 'suspected to be of no sound judgement in religion'; the Company held five separate meetings to try

---

[169] Dom Bede Camm, *Forgotten Shrines* (London: Macdonald & Evans, 1910), pp. 149–82, describes movingly the arrest and execution of George Napier in 1610, and the importance of Holywell Manor.

[170] Bodl. MS Ashmole 1537, fols 38r–39r (English); Loach, 'Reformation Controversies', *HUO*, III. 395.

[171] Bombino, *Vita et Martyrium*, p. 154–6; Bodl. MS Tanner 329, fols 58r–59v.

[172] *ODNB*, 'Grey, William, Thirteenth Baron Grey of Wilton (1508/9–1562)', by Julian Lock, confirms the order to hang four priests from Bloxham and Chipping Norton steeples.

[173] *Orders of the Court of Assistants*: 19 June 1556–18 June 1591, Grocers' Company Records, Guildhall Library MS 11.588, fol. 156r.

to insist that Campion should preach.[174] Circumstantial evidence suggests that the source of the complaint was Humphrey. So the Grocers challenged Campion to preach at Paul's Cross, 'that he may utter his mind in favouring the religion now authorized'.[175] On 2 August 1568, Campion appeared in person before the Court of Assistants where the Court 'well lyking that he did not utterly refuse to preche did farther consider of him and of his answer that he wold be loth to preche to so notable a place at the first', decided to grant him an extension till 17 October and an easier pulpit in 'the pithy church of St Stephen's Walbrook'.[176] Before this date arrived, Campion wrote a letter to the Company:

> wherein he thanked the Company for the benefit he had receyved at their handes and frankly yielded up the same unto them, aledging that he dare not, he cannot, neither was it expedyent he shuld preche as yet declaring in his letter dyvers reasons for the same.[177]

What 'dyvers reasons' Campion gave, remain unknown, but the apparent quotation from Campion's own words of his reluctance give us a glimpse of the emotional intensity surrounding London pulpits. The next meeting of the Court of Assistants lists a Mr Dorset as one of the two new candidates for the scholarship, with Humphrey as his first backer.

Preachers from the two universities were reluctant to incur the expense of travelling and lodging for what must have been at least four days' travel. Between June 1565 and November 1566 (when Campion accepted the Grocers' scholarship), most of the preachers at Paul's Cross were 'London ministers and senior clerics'; only 8 out of 70 preachers are described as from Oxford and Cambridge.[178] But Campion's anxiety about mounting the pulpit in Paul's Cross undoubtedly owed less to the cost, and more to two current controversies, both at their height between 1566 and 1568.

The anti-vestarian controversy may have led in Oxford to resignations, but in London it caused serious disorder. Congregations reacted angrily to Archbishop Parker's edicts that surplices and hats must be worn by ministers. On Sunday 7 April, there were such violent arguments between ministers and parishioners that the doors of many churches were closed.[179] On Whit Monday, 3 June, a preacher at St Margaret's Pattens was attacked: 'a certayne nombar of wyves threw stons at hym and pullyd hym forthe of the pulpyt, rentyng his syrplice and scrattyng his

---

[174] Guildhall MS 11.588, fols 184r–89r.

[175] Guildhall MS 11.588, fol. 184r.

[176] Guildhall MS 11.588, fol. 185v.

[177] Guildhall MS 11.588, fol. 188r, quoted by Stevenson and Salter, *Early History of St John's*, 182–4.

[178] Morrissey, *Paul's Cross*, 30, citing Bodl. MS Tanner 50.

[179] Stow, *Memoranda*, p. 138.

face, &c'.[180] On 26 January 1567, when Bishop Grindal himself came to preach at St Margaret's, Old Fish Street, 'the people (especially the wymen) that ware in the sayde churche unreverently howtyd at hym with many oprobrious words shouting, "Ware horns", in reference to his cornered hat'.[181] It is no wonder that, when Grindal invited John Foxe to preach at Paul's Cross, Foxe wrote to him to voice his fear that he would be 'howled off by the hisses of the mob'.[182]

Paul's Cross had come to be associated with a particularly populist style of preaching. It was also the site of another controversy reaching its height at exactly the same time. In 1559, Bishop Jewel had launched his 'Challenge' sermon at Paul's Cross, in which he argued that the Mass, the Pope and Transubstantiation were not part of the primitive church, sparking off one of the biggest controversies of the age; Dr Henry Cole, closely involved with Sir Thomas White, had written three replies before he was imprisoned in May 1560.[183] Throughout the 1560s, preachers at Paul's Cross attacked the printed works of Jewel's opponents, all New College contemporaries of Campion's who were now in Louvain. The doyen of Paul's Cross was Alexander Nowell, Dean of St Paul's, who was simultaneously attacking Thomas Harding from the pulpit, and Thomas Dorman and Nicholas Sander in print.[184]

At the Cross, Nowell had to apologize for an earlier, inadequate, sermon against Harding's latest book: he explained that, although he had had the book only for two days, he had answered it because the book 'was come in all mens hands almost'.[185] From Louvain, Dorman and Harding accused their opponents of preaching at Paul's Cross, 'among the unlearned and simple people', because they did not dare to engage in serious academic debate.[186] For here, 'a peculiarly aggressive and populist style of preaching predominated' that was despised and derided by the Louvain theologians.[187] John Martial argued that, at Paul's Cross, 'the precher talking against the papistes, saieth, the Lord confounde them', to which

---

[180]   Stow, *Memoranda*, p. 139; quoted by Arnold Hunt, 'Preaching the Elizabethan Settlement', in *Oxford Handbook of the Early Modern Sermon*, ed. Peter McCullough, Hugh Adlington and Emma Rhatigan (Oxford: University Press, 2011), pp. 366–86 (p. 373).

[181]   Stow, *Memoranda*, p. 140; Hunt, 'Preaching the Elizabethan Settlement', p. 373.

[182]   Foxe's Papers, BL MS Harley 417, fol. 129r (my translation).

[183]   A.C. Southern, *Elizabethan Recusant Prose, 1559–1582* (London: Sands & Co., [1950]), pp. 60–67 gives one some sense of the magnitude of the controversy, and lists the 64 books.

[184]   Alexander Nowell, *A Confutation, as wel of M. Dormans last Boke entituled A Disproufe. &c as also of D. Sander his causes of Transubstantiation* (London: Henrie Bynneman, 1567), STC 18739.

[185]   Bodl. MS Tanner 50, fol. 38v, cited by Hunt, 'Preaching the Elizabethan Settlement', p. 375.

[186]   Thomas Dorman, *A Proufe of Certyne Articles in Religion, Denied by M. Juell, Sett furth in Defence of the Catholyke Beleef therein* (Antwerp: J. Latius, 1564), STC 7062, p. 127; cited by Hunt, 'Preaching the Elizabethan Settlement', p. 372.

[187]   Hunt, 'Preaching the Elizabethan Settlement', p. 382.

'the prentises and dentye dames ... answer Amen'.[188] The 'great controversy' initiated by Bishop Jewel's 'Challenge' sermon was, therefore, a triangular debate between the populist preachers at Paul's Cross, the Louvain theologians and an academic audience in Oxford, where their books circulated as soon as they were printed.[189] The controversy ran to a total of 64 books, but Jewel's annotated copy of *A Defence of the Apologie of the Churche of Englande*, published on 27 October 1567, shows how visceral this debate was.[190] His marginal apostrophes to Harding (Figure 2.2) reveal the passionate quality of this debate over the papacy, as if handwritten words in the marginal space mimic the words echoing in the air around Paul's Cross.[191] Campion may have been reluctant to preach from a pulpit associated with anti-Catholic ranting, with violence, and with attacks on his Oxford contemporaries.[192]

While Campion was proctor, he tried to enable Robert Persons, then a fellow of Balliol, to take his BA on 31 May 1568, without swearing to the oath of Supremacy.

> Campion promised to do his best to that effect. However, as he had a companion in office [James Charnock of Brasenose], who watched all his proceedings, and the affair had to come off in a public assembly, the thing could not be managed.[193]

This might explain why Leicester complained to Convocation about the election of proctors on 2 November 1568.[194] This was two weeks after Campion resigned his Grocers' scholarship. Leicester's attempts to control the election of proctors was, after proper discussion by a committee, rejected: John Bereblock, who had moved to Exeter College, and was soon to leave for Rome, was one of those elected proctor for the following year.[195]

---

[188]   John Martial, *A Replie to M. Calfhills Blasphemous Answer Made Against the Treatise of the Crosse* (Louvain: Fowler, 1566) STC 17497, p. 60, cited by Hunt, 'Preaching the Elizabethan Settlement', p. 376.

[189]   Loach, 'Reformation Controversies', *HUO*, III. 386; Hunt, 'Preaching the Elizabethan Settlement', p. 372.

[190]   Southern, *Elizabethan Recusant Prose*, pp. 62–6, lists the controversy in print. See Hunt, 'Preaching the Elizabethan Settlement', pp. 374–6, for the pulpit aspects.

[191]   John Jewel, *A Defence of the Apologie of the Churche of Englande, Conteininge an Answeare to a certaine Booke lately set foorthe by M. Hardinge, and Entituled, A Confutation of & c* (London: Wykes, 1567), STC 14600, Magdalen College Library, shelf-mark 0.17.8, and was presumably inherited by Dr Humphrey. This book has 742 folio pages, but from 126 to 132, where the subject is papal supremacy, Jewel has filled virtually every marginal space with apostrophes to M. Hardinge.

[192]   See Chapter 1.

[193]   CRS 2, *Miscellanea II*, 'The Memoirs of Father Robert Persons', ed. J.H. Pollen, S.J. (London: Catholic Record Society, 1906), p. 19.

[194]   Reg. Cong. 1564–82, fol. 63r.

[195]   Reg. Cong. 1564–82, fol. 63r.

Figure 2.2　Bishop Jewel's annotated *A Defence of the Apologie*, 1567, STC 14600, Magd. O.17.8. By permission of the President and Fellows of Magdalen College, Oxford.

Campion's religious beliefs may have been shifting but in March 1569, he did three things that suggest he was still trying to pursue a career within 'the religion now established'. On 3 March 1569, he compounded for the first fruits of the idyllic parish of Sherborne, in the Windrush valley, worth £15, 6s, 8d, which (being in the diocese of Bristol) fell within the jurisdiction of the Bishop of Gloucester, Richard Cheyney.[196] On 19 March 1569, Campion supplicated for his degree in bachelor of theology. In a letter he wrote to Cheyney from Douai, dated 1 November 1571, there are references to regular visits, three years earlier (*ante triennium*), to Cheyney's library and study, 'So often was I with you at Gloster, so often in your secret chamber, so many houres in your places of retirement, your private librarie', and to dining together in the manor house of Thomas Dutton:

> You remember the serious and solemn answer you gave to me myselfe some 3 yeares since (*ante triennium*), when wee were about to dine togeather at Sherborne (*pransuri*) in the house of Thomas Dutton, a worthy gentleman, when falling by chance upon St Cyprian, I, to try what your opinion was of Councells, objected that of Carthage, which erred about the baptisme of heretikes; when you answered according to the truth, that it was not to one only province that the holy Ghost was promised, but to the universall Church, represented fully in a general Councell, and that it could not ever be shewd that any such councell erred in any poynt of doctrine.[197]

If the dating of the letter is correct, Campion was dining at Thomas Dutton's house before March 1569. Campion's sureties for the first fruits were two stationers from Paul's Cross Yard: Humphrey Toy (whose father, Robert, had stood surety for Campion's father) and William Norton, a wealthy publisher, and therefore a good surety.[198] Campion was still 'part of the family' of stationers.

There is no record of when Campion was ordained deacon.[199] Bombino tells us that Campion frequently related that he later suffered agonies of conscience over this decision.

> Campion narrated several times to friends that he had scarcely taken on such a sinful office than he began to experience a completely unaccustomed agony of a disturbed mind, as if he appeared not so much to have entered on a sacred order as drunk all the disturbing furies of that order.[200]

---

[196]   Clerical Database, E. 334/8, fol. 69.

[197]   *Opuscula*, pp. 370–71; Bodl. MS Tanner 329, fols 10v–11r.

[198]   In 1582, *Tudor Subsidy Rolls*, no. 307, William Norton was listed first in St Faith's parish, and assessed at £70. Humfrey Toy published Grafton's *Chronicle*, 'Anno. 1569. The last of March', according to the colophon. Campion's successor, Alexander Read, was non-resident and refused to pay for the first fruits, but we do not know when Campion ceased officially to be the incumbent. Presumably, Cheyney sought a replacement when Campion fled to Douai.

[199]   It may even have been before accepting the Grocers' scholarship, as Stevenson and Salter suggest, *Early History of St John's*, pp. 181–2.

[200]   Bombino, *Vita et Martyrium*, p. 17 (my translation).

The ceremony is likely to have been before he received the benefice.[201] Campion's choice of bishop is significant. Cheyney believed in the Real Presence and the councils of the church, and compared the reformers unfavourably with the fathers of the church. Bishop Jewel, in a letter of 24 February 1567 to the Calvinist reformer, Henry Bullinger, singled Cheyney out for his divergent views on the Eucharist: 'one alone of our number, the bishop of Gloucester'.[202] Campion was moving further from his father's anti-Catholic stance, but he seems, in March 1569, to have found the last refuge within the recently established church. Cheyney's conservative views were anathema (as Campion reminds him in a letter he wrote from Douai) to Laurence Humphrey, Thomas Sampson and Thomas Cooper.

> You will not achieve anything except to be mashed by eternal tortures perhaps a little less horribly than Judas, or Luther or Zvingli or those very adversaries of yours, Cooper, Humphrey and Sampson.[203]

The zealous Calvinism of Cheyney's 'adversaries' (*antagonistae*) must have made Campion, now clearly a protégé of Cheyney, a marked man in Oxford. In 1568, Humphrey sharply criticized a sermon by Cheyney on free will, and wrote to his old patron, the Earl of Bedford, urging him to bring the matter before the Privy Council; on 13 March 1571, Humphrey was installed as dean of Gloucester, apparently in an effort to surround Cheyney with 'reliable' churchmen.[204]

Campion ended his year as proctor, on 20 April 1569. Despite this, he did not come forward to complete his theology degree at the university Act on 11 July, when he would have had to dispute publicly two questions of theology (as the *nova statuta* required) before Cooper and Humphrey, having affixed the questions to the door of St Mary's 14 days earlier.[205] Instead, on 6 October 1569, he was given leave by St John's to travel abroad for five years, starting on 1 May 1570, while retaining his fellowship.[206] Campion had clearly found himself in an impasse of indecision. He did not make use of this permission, and it had to be renewed on 7 August 1570, with the fellowship to take effect from 30 September. The signatories include at least six fellows with known Catholic sympathies. Two later joined the seminary at Douai (William Wigges and Henry Shaw), two were later implicated later in harbouring priests (Henry Russell and Francis Willis) and two later taught recusants (Thomas Jenkins and John Case). The fellowship was designed to help Campion avoid taking orders in the newly established church:

---

[201]   No record survives of the ceremony, but Sherborne was in the Bristol diocese (then under the care of the Bishop of Gloucester) which 'has pretty poor records', according to Alec Ryrie; I thank him for all his help. 'Cheyney had generally poor administrative skills', *ODNB*, 'Richard Cheyney', by Jane Reedy Ladley.

[202]   *ODNB*, 'Richard Cheyney', by Jane Reedy Ladley.

[203]   *Opuscula*, pp. 366–7.

[204]   *ODNB*, 'Laurence Humphrey', by Thomas S. Freeman.

[205]   Stevenson and Salter, *Early History of St John's*, p. 184.

[206]   Stevenson and Salter, *Early History of St John's*, p. 185.

And forsomuche as we the saide Presidente and fellowes by the wordes of our Statutes do verily perswade and assure our selves that the sayed Edmonde Campione during all the terme of his abydynge beyonde the seas is not bownde to enter into holy orders but may undoubtedly continew fellowe of the colledge and receave all such commodityes as appertayne therto from tyme to tyme, althoughe he enter not into holye orders att all, we do therfore with one assente and consente assure and confirme unto him his fellowshippe with the fruicts and commodityes thereof, yearely to be paid unto him, or his assigne, durynge the forsayed terme of five yeares, without any maner limitation or exception.[207]

Campion left the college, still a deacon and still a fellow, sometime between 7 August and 30 September 1570.[208] This supports Bombino's assertion of a *'fluctuantis animi'*: a mind twisting and turning. From 1567, when he spoke at the funeral of Sir Thomas White till 1570, when he left for Ireland, we know little more than the external facts.[209] 'Nothing has been handed down for certain about his interior life' (*nihil privatim pro certo traditur*), as Bombino, succinctly says:

> Whatever the case, this much is certain: that Campion did not wholly adhere to the side of the heretics (even though they thought he did). Rather he was hesitating between the two, inclining this way and that, and suffered torment from having his opinions in this divided state. As for a long time he was oppressed by the waves of a fluctuating mind, it would be a bonus to know by what means he finally broke out.[210]

His letter to Gregory Martin from Prague makes clear that Martin had written to him in his last year at St John's:

> I remember too how earnestly you called me from Ireland to Douai, how you admonished me, and how effective were your words. Before that, I remember how from the Duke of Norfolk's house you dealt with me to keep me from the ecclesiastical dignity, which, as a friend, you feared might betray me into serving these wretched times.[211]

Bombino even quotes Martin as inviting him to Douai with characteristic emphasis on the frugality of the new seminary: 'Come, come; we can live on very little'.[212] Campion's night battle was a complex one, since it is clear that both church and

---

[207]   *St John's College*, Reg. Col. i. 92; see Stevenson and Salter, *Early History of St John's*, p. 187.

[208]   Bombino, *Vita et Martyrium*, p. 18, gives no dates. See Chapter 3.

[209]   *M. Campiani oratio coram regina*: Bodl. MS Rawl. D. 272, fols 11r–12r; Folger MS V.a.173, fols 29v–30v.

[210]   Bombino, *Vita et Martyrium*, pp. 4–5 (my translation).

[211]   Gregory Martin had been writing from the Duke of Norfolk's house begging him not to yield to the blandishments of worldly success, ABSI Anglia, A. I, fols 20v–21r; printed in Simpson, p. 126.

[212]   Bombino, *Vita et Martyrium*, p. 18.

university were in a state of uncertainty and tension. Campion's decision to take a licence to travel for five years allowed him to gain time. It is not surprising that Campion found it hard to cut adrift from an establishment that had sustained him since he was 12. Campion, a child of the city of London, and fellow of St John's, was still supported financially by Sir William Chester and Anthony Hussey.

The Jewel 'Challenge' debate, especially as it developed between Jewel and Harding, focused on the primacy of Peter in the early church, the issue most heavily annotated (as we have seen) by Jewel in his own 1567 edition of his *A Defence of the Apologie*.[213] While this controversy was at its height, Campion wrote a long poem in Latin hexameters on the first 70 years of the church's life, *Sancta salutiferi nascentia semina verbi*, showing that Peter's primacy as bishop of Rome existed from the beginning. The dedication of the poem to Anthony Browne, Viscount Montague, is headed *Edmundus Campianus Oxoniensis*, which suggests he wrote it before he arrived at Douai in June 1571, when he began to sign himself *Edmundus Campianus Anglus Londinensis*.[214] More than 130 marginal glosses locate the first 70 years of the church in biblical and historical texts, as Campion emphasizes the historical reality of these events, the transience of the *imperium Romanum*, and the everlasting glory of the *ecclesia Romana*.[215] Campion uses Virgilian echoes to contrast the historical apostles with the mythical heroes of the *Aeneid*.

Campion's interest in the early church became a consistent feature of his life, revealed in his pilgrimage to Rome in 1573, and his brief time there in 1580; in both cases he visited only the shrines of the apostles and martyrs. Campion's journey of assent, like John Henry Newman's, was an intellectual one, informing a calm certainty in all his controversial writings. The early church was for him an historical truth, held down by a network of references to contemporary historians; his last words on the scaffold confirmed that he was dying for his belief in the 'Catholic and Apostolic church', as he invited the crowd to say with him the *Symbolum Apostolorum* (Apostles' Creed).[216]

Campion's use of the word *salutifer* in the first line of the poem proclaims, from the start, Campion's preference for an Ovidian vision of salvation, which acts as a counterpoint to the Virgilian references. The word is used by Ovid exclusively of Aesculapius, who is addressed at the beginning of the *Metamorphoses* as *salutifer orbi* (bringing salvation to the world) and arrives disguised as a snake to be *salutifer*

---

[213] See above, note 180, and Figure 2.2.

[214] BL Add. MS 36529, fol. 70r.

[215] For text, translation, analysis and discussion, see Kilroy, *Edmund Campion: Memory and Transcription* (Aldershot, UK and Burlington, VT: Ashgate, 2005), pp. 47–58, 149–93. I thank Hilton Kelliher, who located two presentation copies, Holkham MS 437, and Bodl. MS Rawl. D. 289. Holkham MS 437 had been 'anonymous' only because the names of Campion and Viscount Montague had been deleted, fol. 2r.

[216] *L'Histoire de la Mort que le R.P. Edmond Campion* (Paris: G. Chaudiere, 1582), ARCR I. 197, pp. 26–7. See Chapter 12.

urbi (bringing salvation to the city) at the end.[217] Campion seems fascinated by the analogy of Aesculapius with Christ, and keen to show that salvation is to come to the world through the spiritual transformation of the Eucharist, not through political power or military force. The placing of this Ovidian word in the first line of a Virgilian epic becomes much more important when one sees Campion reverting to it, like Ovid, twice at the end of the poem:

> ille opifex rerum nostroque salutifer aevo ...
> [This creator of the world, this bringer of salvation to our age].

> nate dei patris nostroque salutifer aevo ...
> [Son of God the Father, and bringer of salvation to our time].[218]

Everything suggests that Campion's struggle in Oxford was a painful and hesitant journey of theological assent, in which the apostles, gospels, fathers of the church and councils, became – and remained – his guiding lights. For Campion the church was always that of the missionary apostles and martyrs, and not the church of a political papacy. The vision of the church in the poem is a decisive reversal of worldly power: the emperors are portrayed as both transient and cruel, while St Thomas spreads the gospel to India 'rich in gently soothing breezes', and James dies joyfully proclaiming Christ as 'bringer of salvation to our epoque' (*nostroque salutifer aevo*).[219] Later, Campion joined the missionary Society of Jesus, and clearly thought, as he said at his trial, that he might be 'sent to the Indians'.[220]

In August 1570 Campion took up his travelling fellowship and an invitation to go to Dublin. His 13 years in Oxford had begun in the full fervour of restoration, continued as Calvinists and papists struggled for the soul of the university, and ended as Catholics were being driven underground or abroad. During this time, Campion had progressed from being a prize-winning London schoolboy to becoming the most admired orator in Oxford, and an accurate historian whose insistence on detailed marginal glosses would become a constant feature of his works. If his scholarly verse exploration of the early church and his theological discussions with Bishop Cheyney led him to what seemed an inescapable conclusion, his own background as a protégé of mayors and aldermen seems to have made him unwilling to break with the established religion, or to abandon a career fostered both by the Queen and the Earl of Leicester.

---

[217] P. Ovidi Nasonis, *Metamorphoses*, ed. R.J. Tarrant (Oxford: Clarendon Press, 2004), II. 642–8, and XV. 742–4. See Chapter 4 for further discussion of these passages, and their influence on Campion.

[218] Kilroy, *Memory and Transcription*, lines 618 and 719, pp. 170, 172 and (trans.) 190, 192.

[219] *Memory and Transcription*, pp. 169 (Latin) and (trans.) 189.

[220] BL MS Harley 6265, fol. 17v. John O'Malley, S.J., *Saints or Devils Incarnate? Studies in Jesuit History* (Leiden and Boston: Brill, 2013), pp. 217–24, explains the importance of *mission* for the first Jesuits.

Chapter 3
Pilgrim to Rome

The invitation to Dublin came through Richard Stanihurst.[1] He was a young fellow of University College, Oxford, whom Campion had encouraged to complete, and publish with Reyner Wolfe in June 1570, a study of Porphyry, called *Harmonia seu Catena Dialectica, in Porphyrianas Institutiones*, so he had good reason to be grateful.[2] Stanihurst had been presented to Sir Henry Sidney when he visited University College in 1565, as the opening sentence of his dedication to Sir Henry reveals. The *Harmonia*, 'probably the first original work by an Irish writer to appear in print', is prefaced with 12 dedications, starting with Laurence Humphrey, and ending with Thomas Twyne, William Rainolds and Edmund Campion.[3] Campion's own dedication, with a valediction from St John's College, dated 1 December, ends the preliminary matter and, with its decorated capital, is given pride of place. Campion may have effected the introduction to Reyner Wolfe, whose shop, the Brazen Serpent, was on the north side of the Cross Yard.[4]

Campion, still a fellow of St John's College, Oxford, a deacon in the established church, and the official incumbent of Sherborne in the new diocese of Bristol, left the college sometime 'between 7 August and 30 September'.[5] With a licence to spend five years abroad, he could have expected a period where he could quietly resolve his religious dilemma. Persons later wrote that 'his devotion in Ireland was very singular though yet he was not in the church'.[6] It seems as if it was only just before he left Ireland the following June that Campion altered his religion, and

---

[1]   ABSI Collectanea, P. I, fol. 83b; *ODNB*, 'Richard Stanihurst' (1547–1618), by Colm Lennon.

[2]   Richard Stanihurst, *Harmonia seu Catena Dialectica, in Porphyrianas Institutiones* (London: Reyner Wolfe, June 1570), STC 23229. The colophon gives the date as 'viij. nonas. Iun'.

[3]   Reyner Wolfe, when editing Holinshed's *Chronicles*, went to Stanihurst for Campion's Irish history; he must have dealt with both men over the edition of Porphyry: Campion as sponsor, Stanihurst as author.

[4]   Blayney, *Bookshops in Paul's Cross Churchyard*, 19.

[5]   ABSI Collectanea, P. I, fol. 83b. Persons, unusually precise about the day and the month, says he arrived in Dublin on 25 August 1569; Bombino, Simpson and others followed. The decisive evidence is that Campion signed documents in college on 5 and 27 June 1570, as argued by Stevenson and Salter, *Early History of St John's*, 185, who fix the departure between the two dates in the licence to travel, Reg. Col. i. 73.

[6]   ABSI Collectanea P. I, fol. 150a.

finally adopted the faith of Saint Patrick (to whom he had a special devotion) and of the early church fathers.[7]

Campion probably sailed from Bristol, in which case he may have passed Painswick, where Bishop Cheyney had his residence.[8] The ride from Oxford to Bristol could have taken only three or four days, so Campion would have taken the opportunity to discuss his position (and their shared *antagonistae*) with his bishop and mentor. One certain fact is that John Felton was executed on 8 August, and news of his death must have reached Campion. By posting the papal bull of excommunication, *Regnans in excelsis*, on the gates of the Bishop of London, at the west end of St Paul's, Felton brought a policy that turned all Catholics into potential traitors, into the heart of London.[9] Campion's rural ride would be his last journey as a free man in England: the papal challenge to the Queen's authority, now given 'canonical effect' by its publication in England ensured that all subsequent journeys would be in disguise.[10]

Ireland was 'within one daies sailing', according to Richard Stanihurst.[11] In August, the crossing should have been calm, and the ship would have taken him up the Liffey and into the ancient port of Dublin, then the heartland of the English administration of Ireland. For the first time in his life, Campion was 'beyond the seas', with time to resolve his conflict. Persons portrays this as a simple battle between 'preferments' in the university and 'conscience', between 'good fellowship and conversation with protestants' and 'the reading of the books of certain auncient fathers of the primitive church'.[12] Campion consistently returns to the fathers – the ancient doctors of the church – as a deciding factor in his decision-making, but he reveals in his letter to Cheyney from Douai in 1571, that Cheyney had, in their many conversations, recommended him to 'follow the royal highway confidently and in full view, in the footsteps of the church, the councils and the fathers'.[13] Cheyney's advice complicated the decision, Campion argues, because

---

[7]   Bombino, *Vita et Martyrium,* p. 19, assumes that Campion was now practising as a Catholic 'freely and openly'. Simpson, p. 41, correctly repeats Persons's assertion that he 'was not then received into the church'. Vossen, in his introduction to *Histories of Ireland*, pp. 8–11, dissents.

[8]   *ODNB*, 'Richard Cheyney' (d. 1579), by Jane Reedy Ladley.

[9]   J.H. Pollen, *Act of English Martyrs Hitherto Unpublished* (London: Burns and Oates, 1891), 'Blessed John Felton', pp. 209–12, describes his courageous martyrdom; Pollen is one of the few Catholic historians to include him; see also, Patrick McGrath, *Papists and Puritans Under Elizabeth I* (London: Blandford Press, 1967), p. 101. He was beatified in 1886.

[10]   *ODNB*, 'John Felton' (d. 1570), by Julian Lock.

[11]   Richard Stanihurst, 'A Treatise Conteining a plaine and perfect description of Ireland', in Raphael Holinshed, *The First and Second Volume of Chronicle*s (London: J. Harrison, G. Bishop et al., 1587), STC 13569, II. 9.a.49.

[12]   ABSI Collectanea, P. I, fols 80b–81a.

[13]   Edmund Campion, *Decem Rationes Praepositae in Causa Fidei et Opuscula Eius Selecta* (Antwerp: Plantin Moretus, 1631), p. 363.

it allowed him to put a 'shaded consideration' (*umbratilem existimationem*) of his 'honour' before his 'eternal good'.[14] 'Shaded' would certainly have fitted the idyllic benefice of Sherborne, sleeping gently beside the river Windrush, but Campion was under pressure in Oxford as a known disciple of Cheyney.

Although Campion spent only nine months there, Ireland was to shape his life, and to determine his death. Campion was under the protection of two key figures in the English administration in the Pale, both engaged in a programme of reform, at the centre of which was education. Sir Henry Sidney, appointed Lord Deputy in 1565, wielded considerable power, both in Ireland and in England, partly as brother-in-law to the Earl of Leicester: Hooker records the Queen seeing Sir Henry Sidney arriving at Hampton Court with 'two hundred men attending upon him'.[15] James Stanihurst, 'speaker of the Irish House of Commons and recorder of Dublin', had impressive literary and historical interests that were to help Campion, and came from one of the oldest families in the Pale.[16] Both men saw education as the key to promoting civility in Ireland, and at the centre of this was a scheme for a university in Dublin.

Campion would have been the ideal person to help launch a university in Dublin: he had already attracted a great following at Oxford, and his appointment as proctor and lecturer in rhetoric gave him enough necessary status. As Colm Lennon argues, 'Campion's new interest in the history of Ireland may have been a response to the need for him to be sensitive to local traditions and cultural aspirations in the event of his being appointed'.[17] When the university scheme collapsed, Campion began writing the first history of Ireland in English.[18] Campion's *Two Bokes of the Histories of Ireland* end with his account of the parliament, dominated by the speeches of the Speaker and the Deputy: his history and the idea of a university in Dublin were, from the start, intricately connected.[19]

---

[14] *Opuscula*, p. 363.

[15] Holinshed, *Chronicles* (1587), II. 118.a.10–15 [For ease of reference, I have treated the *Chronicles* (1587) as if they were bound in three separate volumes, so that the second volume contains the 'Historie of Ireland' augmented by Hooker, while the third volume contains the 'Continuation']; *ODNB*, 'Sir Henry Sidney' (1529–86), by Wallace T. MacCaffrey.

[16] *ODNB*, 'Richard Stanihurst', including James Stanihurst (1521/2–73), by Colm Lennon.

[17] Colm Lennon, *Richard Stanihurst The Dubliner 1547–1618* (Blackrock, Dublin: Irish Academic Press, 1981), p. 31.

[18] A.F. Vossen, *Two Bokes of the Histories of Ireland* (Assen: Van Gorcum, 1963), pp. 16–20, argues against the idea of a university, and presents it as a recent idea of Richard Simpson. See below for contrary evidence.

[19] The best manuscript of Campion's *Two Bokes of the Histories of Ireland* is Bodl. MS Jones 6, which Vossen used as his copy text; all references refer to the foliation in this, which Vossen has preserved. Farmleigh MS IV.E.6 is a recent bequest to Marsh's Library, Dublin, from the Benjamin Iveagh Library and is kept in Farmleigh House, the official residence of the Irish President. This appears to be copied from the same sources as

Campion later thanked James Stanihurst for giving him, a virtual fugitive, a peaceful haven and academic space in his library, and asserts in the address 'To the Loving Reader' at the beginning of *Two Bokes of the Histories of Ireland*, that the library enabled him to write his carefully documented history:

> My speciall meanyng was to gather so mutch as I thought the cyvill subjectes could be content to reade, and withall to gyve a light to the learned antiquaries of this contrye birthe, who maye hereafter at good leysure supply the want of this fowndacion and polishe the stone rowgh hewed to their handes.[20]

Richard Stanihurst 'never stopped informing' Bombino that Campion behaved 'as if he were leading his life in a religious cloister', and was known 'among Dubliners' as 'the angel' (*Angeli nomen*) because of his unblemished life and reputation for purity.[21] This academic calm was not to last, because news of Campion's dissident religious position in Oxford had, it seems, reached Dublin, and soon the Chancellor and his commissioners 'resolved to apprehend him'.[22] The searchers were restrained only by the fact that Campion was Stanihurst's guest, and by 'his great credit' with

> Sir Henry Sydny, the Lord Deputy & Governor of that Iland, whome they also knew to be a very honourable, calme and civil gentleman, and nothing hott in their new religion, and rather a great friend to Catholicks, who had tould also Mr Stanihurst in secret that while he was Governor, *no busy knave of them all* (for those were his words) should trouble him for so worthy a guest as Mr Campian was.[23]

Sidney's phrase, 'busy knave', would certainly fit the zealous lawyer, who had taken up his appointment as Chancellor in 1567, an appointment funded by transferring the endowments of St Patrick's Cathedral to him.[24] Campion's nemesis was Dr Robert Weston, who was both Chancellor of Ireland and Speaker of the

---

Bodl. MS Jones 6, contains the *Topographia* of Giraldus Cambrensis, and so deserves to be ranked alongside Bodl. MS Jones 6.

[20]   *Histories of Ireland*, fol. 6v; see Campion's letter to James Stanihurst, *Opuscula*, p. 353.

[21]   Bombino, *Vita et Martyrium*, p. 20. Schmidl, *Historiae*, I. 338.

[22]   ABSI Collectanea, P. I, fol. 84a.

[23]   ABSI Collectanea P. I, fol. 84a. Bombino, *Vita et Martyrium*, 22, talks of waves of searchers being sent into every part of the kingdom, including Ireland, in the wake of the rebellion of the Northern Earls and the papal bull, *Regnans in Excelsis*, published on 25 February 1570.

[24]   *Calendar of State Papers Irish of the Reign of Elizabeth, 1574–1585*, ed. Hans Claude Hamilton (London: HMSO, 1867). 10 June 1567, p. 335; *ODNB*, 'Robert Weston', by Andrew Lyall.

upper house.[25] Hooker describes Weston as 'a man so bent to the execution of justice, and so severe therein'.[26] Stanihurst later 'wrote to f. Campian to Doway after his departure of the great sorrow the chancellor D. Weston etc. shewed of his escape & c'.[27] In January 1568, Weston had been appointed commissioner to enquire into irregularities in the oaths taken by all clerics, swearing to the Acts of Supremacy and Uniformity.[28] Campion's record as proctor may have made him suspect. The penurious Weston complained that he received 'spiritual livings for temporal service' and vigorously opposed surrendering the lands of St Patrick's for the university scheme. In Dublin, where the winters are rarely bitter, but often damp, Stanihurst's library was a scholarly hearth for Campion, protecting him from more than the weather.

Campion's dedication shows that he sees his history as promoting Leicester's interest in Ireland, and that he wrote it 'that my travaile into Ireland might seeme neyther cawseless nor frutelesse'.[29] Campion was already in hiding by the time he wrote the dedication, after the university scheme had been rejected, but he offered 'a humanist's vision of a unified English approach to the pacification and civilising of the island's communities'.[30] Campion, by then, was endorsing the need for a programme of civility. From start to finish, Campion was supported, housed and protected by men involved in promoting reform in Ireland. It is even possible that either Leicester or Mabel Browne, Countess of Kildare, had suggested Campion stay in Dublin so that if the education reforms went ahead, he could take a leading role. Campion's dedication enabled him both to thank Leicester for his 'severall curtesies' at Oxford, at Court, at Rycote and at Windsor, and to persuade him to 'become a patrone to this noble realme', and 'to undertake the tuition of lerning and lerned men'.[31] The speeches of Henry Sidney and James Stanihurst that end Campion's *Histories of Irelande* both focus on the scheme for a university and reform. Stanihurst begins his speech by referring to 'the zeale which I have to the reformacion of this realme', and Sidney ends by advising the parliament of the Pale to consulte 'of such good and substantiall reformacion'.[32] Reform and education frame the debate, and inform the entire book.[33]

---

[25] Holinshed, *Chronicles* (1587), II. 119.a.30.

[26] Holinshed, *Chronicles* (1587), II. 116.b.36–41. Vossen, *Histories of Ireland*, p. 20, writes that 'it is doubtful if Weston was a real opponent even for pecuniary reasons'.

[27] ABSI Collectanea P. I, fol. 150a.

[28] *ODNB*, 'Robert Weston', by Andrew Lyall.

[29] *Histories of Ireland*, fol. 4r. All references to Campion's text will be to the foliation in Bodl. MS Jones 6, which has been faithfully preserved by Vossen.

[30] Colm Lennon, 'Campion and Reform in Tudor Ireland', in *The Reckoned Expense*, 2nd ed, ed. Thomas M. McCoog, S.J. (Rome: IHSI, 2007), pp. 75–95 (p. 95).

[31] *Histories of Ireland*, fol. 4r–v.

[32] *Histories of Ireland*, fol. 96r and fol. 102r.

[33] Lennon, 'Campion and Reform', p. 81; *Histories of Ireland*, fol. 4v.

In the Chancery Rolls for Ireland, the charter for restitution of property to St Patrick's Cathedral, made in the first year of Philip and Mary, has been filed under '11 Elizabeth', as if its stated intention, 'that the youth of the kingdom should be instructed in civility of manners and the rules of moral virtue', was being revived in 1570.[34] We know from Persons that Campion wrote while there, *De homine academico*, a treatise that has now disappeared, but which indicates that the idea of a university was very much on his mind.[35]

> While there is no conclusive evidence of Campion's active involvement it is clear that he would have been attracted to a post in a university where his religious leanings might have been accommodated. Sir Henry Sidney would undoubtedly have been aware of the value of such an outstanding scholar in the new institution.[36]

The schemes of reform were blocked in the parliament, where the opposition of 'the knights and burgesses of the English Pale' was to the presence in the parliament of the so-called 'new English', of whom John Hooker was the spokesman.[37] In his 'Supplie of the Irish Chronicles', Hooker claimed that the behaviour of the Palesmen was 'altogether disordered, being more like to a bearebaiting of loose persons than an assembly of wise and grave men in parlement'.[38] The scheme for an Irish university fell, like all the other horses running in this race for reform, because the Anglo-Irish challenged the legality of a parliament full of non-resident 'Englishmen'. The scheme also ran into the very practical problem that the use of St Patrick's lands, would have cut into Dr Weston's already fragile income, and makes plausible the idea of Weston's 'underhand opposition'.[39] Campion specifies the major problem as land:

---

[34]   *Calendar of the Patent and Close Rolls of Chancery in Ireland of the Reigns of Henry VIII, Edward VI, Mary and Elizabeth* (Dublin: HMSO, 1861), I. 524–5. The original is date 15 June, 1st and 2nd Philip and Mary (1553–54), but glossed as 11 Elizabeth (1569–70).

[35]   ABSI Collectanea P. I. fol. 84a. We have his *De Iuvene Academico Oratio R. P. Edmundi in promotione seu renovatione studiorum habita*, preserved in the Cieszyn manuscript, SZ MS DD.V.8, fols 400r–405r, and in all printed editions of Campion's works from 1602 onwards (see Chapter 4 for details). Although Simpson, pp. 41–2, was the first directly to suggest that Campion's presence in Ireland was part of this scheme for a university, Vossen's arguments against it are inconclusive. Neither Persons nor Bombino knew Campion at this time, nor was either interested in circles of patronage at the English court. It is impossible to understand what happened to Campion in Ireland without a sense of the immense influence of the Earl of Leicester, and his ambition to extend this sphere of influence in both Ireland and Wales.

[36]   Lennon, *Stanihurst the Dubliner*, p. 31.

[37]   Holinshed, *Chronicles* (1587), II. 120.a.14–19.

[38]   Holinshed, *Chronicles* (1587), II. 121.a.54–71.

[39]   Simpson, p. 41.

A motyon was made in this laste parliament to erect it againe, contribucions layde together. Sir Henry Sydney, then Lorde Deputye, proffered twentie pounde landes and one hundred poundes in mony, other followed after their abilityes and devocions; the name devised Mr. Acworthe Plantolinum of Plantagenett and Bullyne. But while they disputed *of a convenient place for it* and other circumstances, they lett fall the principall.[40]

In the final speeches of the Parliament of 1571, which Campion dates as proclaimed on 28 January, both the Speaker and the Lord Deputy single out the collapse of the university scheme for regret, but Sidney portrays it as a temporary setback, and suggests that location was the problem: 'though the place be not al so commodious'.[41] Campion, who wrote up the 'notes' he took on 'comming home to my lodginge', gives us two good speeches, and all the details.[42] Hooker provides no date, fails to mention education and is carried away by castigating his opponents, Barnewall and the Palesmen, for their unsuitable behaviour. Campion left Ireland after nine months, a firm friend of the Stanihursts, the Barnewalls, and in the Earl of Kildare's livery. 'Before he completed his *Histories*, Campion's official protector while in Dublin, Sir Henry Sidney, had returned to England'.[43]

'The only 'fixed objective' in the English policy of 'successive governments', as Canny argues, was 'that of maintaining a secure foothold in Ireland without any cost to the crown'.[44] While control of the Pale was reasonably secure, the English control over the rest of Ireland was fitful and fragile. This resulted in what Ciaran Brady describes as 'highly erratic' intervention in areas outside the Pale.[45] Campion's *Histories of Ireland*, a work of enlightened history, records the last appearance of a policy of reform (soon to be replaced by savage repression), and makes no mention of the first Desmond rebellion in Munster, which was ruthlessly crushed by Sir Humfrey Gilbert, appointed Colonel of Munster by Sidney in 1569. Gilbert, educated at Eton, Oxford and the royal court, where 'hir Majestie had a special good liking of him', was 'as valiant and couragious as no man more'.[46] In 1579, Thomas Churchyard recommends Gilbert as a model of how to deal with the rebellious Irish, since the 'stiff necked must be made to stoupe, with extremitie of Justice':

---

[40]   *Histories of Ireland*, fol. 60v (my emphasis).

[41]   *Histories of Ireland*, fol. 98r.

[42]   *Histories of Ireland*, fol. 95r.

[43]   Lennon, 'Campion and Reform', p. 82.

[44]   Nicholas Canny, *The Elizabethan Conquest of Ireland: A Pattern Established 1565–76* (London: Harvester, 1976), p. 31.

[45]   Ciaran Brady, 'Court, Castle and Country: the Framework of Government in Tudor Ireland', in *Natives and Newcomers: Essays on the Making of Irish Colonial Society 1534–1641*, ed. Ciaran Brady and Raymond Gillespie (Dublin: Irish Academic Press, 1986), pp. 22–49 (pp. 38–9).

[46]   Holinshed, *Chronicles* (1587), II. 132.b.22–45.

> His maner was that the heddes of all those (of what sort soever thei were) whiche were killed in the daie, should bee cutte of from their bodies and brought to the place where he incamped at night, and should there bee laied on the ground by eche side of the waie leadyng into his owne Tente: so that none could come into his tente for any cause but commonly he muste passe through a lane of heddes which he used *ad terrorem*, the dedde feelyng nothyng the more paines thereby: and yet did it bryng greate terrour to the people, when thei saw the heddes of their dedde fathers, brothers, children, kinsfolke, and freendes, lye on the grounde before their faces, as they came to speake with the saied Colonell.[47]

Campion, who must have heard of these barbarities during the first Desmond rebellion, from the 'daily table talk' in Stanihurst's house, chose instead to give a sympathetic account of the 'mere [native] Irish', and to emphasize reform through education, laws and the Dublin parliament.[48]

If Campion spent the wintry months of February and early March in the warmth of James Stanihurst's library and the scholarly companionship of Richard, exploring records and rolls, and writing up his account of the parliament that ended on 28 January, his claustral calm was rudely interrupted on the night of 17 March 1571.

> The Commissioners then of Ireland having determined to apprehend Mr. Campian the next day in Divelin, Sir Henry Sidny the Lord Deputy having notice therof, sent a servant of his at midnight to warne Mr James Stanihurst of the danger, wherupon Mr. Campian was forced to depart presently with all hast.[49]

Stanihurst reacted immediately. His two sons, Richard and his married brother, Walter, conducted Campion on horseback, probably by the more secluded coastal route, to Turvey, 11 miles north of Dublin.[50] Campion, in his letter thanking Richard for 'staying up' (*noctu vigilas*) all night, jokes that his brother, Walter, has been 'torn from his wife's arms' (*avulsus ab uxore*).[51] As they would have had to ride slowly in the dark, they could not have arrived much before three o'clock in the morning at the house of 'a Catholick knight', Sir Christopher Barnewall of Grace Dieu.[52]

---

[47] Thomas Churchyard, *A generall rehearsall of warres* (London: J. Kingston f. [1579]), STC 5235, sig. Q3v; Nicholas Canny, *The Elizabethan Conquest of Ireland: A Pattern Established 1565–76* (London: Harvester, 1976), p. 122, drew my attention to this shocking passage.

[48] Christopher Highley, *Catholics Writing the Nation in Early Modern England and Ireland* (Oxford: University Press, 2008), pp. 123–31. Unimpressed by Campion's sympathy with the Irish and plans for reform, Highley sees the book as supporting a 'British imperial' view, redeemed only by Campion's admiration for St Patrick.

[49] ABSI Collectanea, P. I, fol. 85b.

[50] *Opuscula*, pp. 358–9.

[51] *Opuscula*, pp. 358–9.

[52] ABSI Collectanea P. I, fol. 85b.

Patrick Barnewall, his father, had been a protector of the Augustinian convent of Grace Dieu, and had led the opposition to the dissolution of the monasteries in 1537. The Anglo-Norman families feared that Cromwell would give the monastic property to the new English settlers. In the event, Barnewall himself took charge of Grace Dieu, and continued to protect the nuns by rehousing them at Portrane, on his estate, but a mile nearer the coast, where they remained till 1577. He and his son secured the monastic lands of Turvey by exchanging them for a Tipperary monastery with the Earl of Ormond.[53] Sir Christopher continued to protect the nuns at Portrane, and built a new manor-house for himself at Turvey in 1565 'on an isthmus between the inlets of Malahide and Donabate'.[54]

The Barnewall household itself was vigorously Catholic. Campion describes Sir Christopher as 'a most distinguished man', and his wife, Marion Sherle, as 'a most devout and humble woman'; they had 5 sons and 15 daughters, whom they married successfully to other members of the Catholic nobility and gentry, including Richard Stanihurst, Patrick, Baron Dunsany and Nicholas, Lord Howth. In the 10 weeks from 18 March to 27 May, Campion lived in what he describes (in his letter to Richard) as 'an inner room' (*interiori cubiculo*), where he wrote during the day, dining at night with the family.[55]

> I find it very hard that I cannot show the gratitude I feel to you. But I know that it is not your character nor your fortune to seek repayment; so I only give you my wishes for the present; the rest when I have come back to life. Meanwhile if any of these buried relics have any flavour of the old Campion, their flavour is for you; they are at your service. I truly love you and your brother Walter for the trouble you recently took for me. You were kept up all night and he was, in addition, torn from his wife's arms! In all seriousness, I owe you an enormous debt. I have nothing to write about, unless you have time and inclination to laugh. Tell me – you say nothing. Listen, then. The day after I came here, I sat down to read. Suddenly there broke into my chamber a poor old woman who wanted to tidy up the room. She saw me on her left, and knowing nothing about me, she thought I was a ghost. Her hair stood on end, her colour fled, her jaw

---

53   NLI MSS D 2329, Ormond Papers Deeds IV, No. 247, 1 May 1540; D 2568–9, 12 February 1555 (with Sir Christopher), Ormond Deeds V, No. 47; D 2569, Indenture dated 20 March; D 2612: Deeds V, 5 September 1555; Deeds V, No. 65, 12 June 1556. The whole process shows the Barnewalls, father and son, as determined and skilful negotiators, as stewards of these estates for the Earl of Ormond, protecting the convents, in return for rent and the provision of post-horses for the Earl when he visits Dublin.

54   Vossen, *Histories of Ireland*, p. 47. The house, one of the oldest manor houses in Ireland, survived until 1987, when, with the approval of Dublin's planning office, it was demolished to make way for a golf clubhouse; time has brought in its revenges for this destruction, since the pastiche pillars of the mauve *hacienda* now stand derelict. I thank Colm Lennon for guiding me round this sad relic, recorded now only in a box of plans, photographs and protest letters in the Irish Architectural Archive, Merrion Square, Dublin.

55   *Opuscula*, 351–60. 'XIII Kal. April M.D.LXXI'. Simpson, p. 55, dates this as 19 March 1571.

fell, she was struck dumb. What is the matter? I asked. Frightened to death, she almost fainted; she could not speak a word; all she could do was to throw herself out of the room; she could not rest till she had told her mistress that there was some hideous thing, she thought a ghost, writing in the garret. The story was told over supper; the old woman was sent for, and made to tell her fright; everybody died laughing, and I proved to be among the living.[56]

Vivid evidence of Campion's humour, and his image of himself as half-dead, and beyond the grave, gives one an insight into Campion's state of mind as he exchanged a life in the limelight of Leicester's favour and his position at Oxford for a life in hiding. Campion's room seems to have been an attic garret (*cellula*, or servant's room) with enough room for a table, books and bed, and still cleaned by the servants.[57]

At Turvey, he was reunited with his books. Campion's life, both in Dublin and at Turvey, was an agreeable mixture of scholarship and dialogue, solitude and the company of two of the oldest Anglo-Norman families of the Pale. At Turvey, safe on an isthmus from the pursuivants of the Chancellor, he was surrounded by a large, intelligent and pious family, supported by a community of nuns, and perhaps a number of 'the womankind of the whole Englishry of this land', who were still being educated by the nuns. On the same day as he wrote to Richard, Campion wrote to his father. The letter gives one an insight into Campion's state of mind at this time, as he thanks James Stanihurst for all his kindness:

when I was pretty well turned out of house and home, you considered me worthy not only of your hospitality, but of your embrace ... It was your generosity and goodness to receive an unknown stranger; to look after me sumptuously; to take as much care of my health as your son Richard's, who deserves all your love; to make available for me every convenience of place, time, and company as the occasion arose; to supplement my library from your own; to create such space and time for my study, that away from my rooms at Oxford I never retreated into the Muses more pleasantly. After such great generosity, one would think there was nothing more that could be added; but there was more. As soon as I knew you sensed the first gust of the storm, which would become more threatening the longer I stayed under the gaze of the heretics at Dublin, you tucked me away in this hideaway among your closest friends in a remote country estate. Up till then, I had merely to thank you for conveniences; now I have to thank you for my safety and the breath of my body – I use the word breath deliberately. For those who struggle with the persecutors are commonly thrust into horrible chambers, where they take in filthy vapours, and are not allowed to breathe wholesome air.

---

[56]   *Opuscula*, pp. 359–60.

[57]   It cannot have been the priest's hiding-hole, described by Vossen and photographed by the local historian, Peadar Bates, before the demolition, where there would have been no space for a desk and books, nor could the servant have broken in unawares on Campion. See Vossen, *Histories*, p. 47, and Peadar Bates, *Donabate and Portrane: A History* (Dublin: Bates, 2001), p. 31.

But now through you, and your children's kindness I shall live, please God, completely free from this peril, and my mind tells me, most happily. First of all, your friend Barnewall has guaranteed me every kind of support. When he had read your letter, he was sorry for the dreadful times we live in, but made me feel as if I were doing him a favour by coming to stay. As he had to go into Dublin, he commended me to his wife, who treated me most kindly. She is surely a very devout and modest woman. I was shut up in a convenient place within an inner chamber, where I made friends again with my books. With these companions I lie concealed in my little garret. XIII Kal. April. MDLXXI [19 March 1571].[58]

This letter shows that the families of James Stanihurst and Christopher Barnewall were close; the Stanihurst country house was at nearby Corduff, so the Stanihurst brothers would have known the route from Dublin well.[59] Campion stayed with the Barnewalls 10 weeks, from 18 March to 27 May. It seems likely that Richard Stanihurst stayed there during this time, if only to act as a messenger to his father; he was soon to marry Janet, the third Barnewall daughter.[60]

Since Campion tells us that he 'had not in all the space of tenne weekes' for the writing of his *Histories of Ireland*, it is tempting to think that he wrote the entire history there.[61] Yet Campion mentions in the preface the benefits he had from the archival library sources of James Stanihurst:

> Notwithstanding as naked and simple as it is, it could never have growen to any proportion in such post hast except I had lighted into familiar societie and daly table talke with the worshupfull esquyer James Stanyhurst, Recorder of Dyvelyn, who beside all courtesies of hospitalytie, and thowsand loving turnes not heere to be recited, both by word and written monumentes and by the benefyte of his owne librarie, norished most effectually myne endevour.[62]

Among his sources, Campion mentions 'rols and recordes', which turn out to include exchequer rolls.[63] If Campion had written rough drafts in Dublin, one can imagine him using his enforced captivity in the inner room at Turvey to turn this into a continuous narrative. In the dedication to the Earl of Leicester, Campion says: 'For wheras it is well knowen to the learned in this land how late it was or I could meete with Gerald of Wales'.[64] One possibility is that he wrote the second book first, in February, which ended with the speeches while they were fresh in the memory, and where the early history is based on the *Expugnatio* of

---

[58]   *Opuscula*, pp. 351–6. These three letters to the Stanihursts were passed to Robert Turner, S.J., by Richard Stanihurst before 1591, and first printed in 1602; see Chapter 12 for details.

[59]   Lennon, *Stanihurst the Dubliner*, p. 32.

[60]   Lennon, *Stanihurst the Dubliner*, p. 32.

[61]   *Histories of Ireland*, fol. 4r.

[62]   *Histories of Ireland*, fol. 6v.

[63]   *Histories of Ireland*, fols 63v and 64.

[64]   *Histories of Ireland*, fol. 4r.

Giraldus Cambrensis, and much of the later on an anonymous author (whom Campion calls 'Phil. Flatsbury') given him in 'three much different copies sent me the one by my Lord of Trimleston, another from Mr Agard, the third from Mr. Stanihurst'.[65] Then, when he had been given a copy of the Giraldus's *Topographia*, which was 'delivered me by James Stanihurst', he wrote the first book.[66] Certainly, Campion's rich choice of copies of Flatsbury suggests the Stanihurst household, not an attic room, and 'delivered' fits Turvey better than the library in Dublin, but the chronology of composition is likely to remain obscure.

Campion is remarkable as an historian for the scholarly precision with which he specifies even the provenance of his sources: even his Oxford poem on the early church, *Sancta salutiferi nascentia semina verbi*, had been unusual in the number and variety of sources listed in over one hundred marginal glosses: scriptures, doctors of the church, Greek and Roman historians. Stanihurst obviously put at Campion's disposal a fine library, which included records and rolls. Nevertheless, Campion is at his best where he is basing his recent history on accounts given him by those who knew the participants: 'From henceforward I have followed relacion of the wysest and most indifferent persons that I could aquaint myselff withall in Ireland'.[67] This is likely to have included Sidney, since the Stanihurst family had held public office in Ireland since 1399. Persons says that 'their exercise was every friday to dispute of controversies', a practice Campion may have introduced.[68] The Stanihurst household clearly provided a great deal of 'daily table talk'.[69]

His method, both of reconstructing speeches and of using independent witnesses, seems very close to that of the great Greek historian, Thucydides.[70] In the encounter between the Earl of Kildare and Cardinal Wolsey, Campion introduces a picture as detailed and complex as Tacitus into the middle of a dramatic exchange, where even the audience is brought to life:

> At theis gyrdes the Counsell would have smyled and they durste, but eche man byt his lippe and helde his countenaunce, for howsoever some of them enclined to Butler, they hated all the Cardinall, a man undoubtedly borne to honor: I thinke some Princes basturde, no butchers sonne, exceding wise, fayre spoken, highe mynded, full of revenge, vicious of his bodye, loftye to his enimyes, were they never so bigge, to those that accepted and sought his frindeshippe wonderfull curteous, a ripe scholeman, thrall to affeccions, brought abedde with flatterie, insatiable to gette, and more princelike in bestowing, as appeareth by his two Colledges at Ipswich and Oxenforde, the one suppressed with his fall, the other unfinished and yet as it lyeth for an house of Studentes, considering all

---

65 *Histories of Ireland*, fol. 54r–v.

66 *Histories of Ireland*, fol. 7r.

67 *Histories of Ireland*, fol. 72v.

68 ABSI Collectanea P. I, fol. 150a.

69 *Histories of Ireland*, fol. 6v; Lennon, *Stanihurst the Dubliner*, p. 28.

70 Thucydides, *History of the Peloponnesian War*, 4 vols (London: Heinemann, 1919), Loeb classical series, I. 38–41.

appurtenances incomporable through Christendome, wherof Henry the eight is nowe called Founder, because he let it stande. He helde and enjoyed at once the bisshoprickes of York, Duresme, and Winchester, the dignities of Lord Cardinal, Legate, and Chancellor, the Abbey of Saint Albans, divers Priorye, sondrye fat benefyces in commendam, a greate preferrer of his servauntes, advancer of learning, stoute in every quarrell, never happy till hys overthrowe. Therein he shewed such moderation and ended so perfectly, that the hower of his death did him more honour, than all the pompe of his life passed.[71]

While it uses the tropes of classical rhetoric (the parallelism of the last sentence hammering home the moral irony), it conceals its art beneath juxtapositions that are allowed to build up a portrait that convinces by contradiction, where each paradox takes the reader by surprise.[72] The message that power is transitory and brings no security is encapsulated in Campion's phrase that 'he was never happy till hys overthrowe'. When we turn to the encounter itself, Campion holds the reader gripped by the drama of the enforced listener:

Whilest the Cardinall was speaking the Earle chafed and chaunged colour and sondrye profers made to answere every sentence as yt came. At last he brake oute and interrupted him thus.[73]

The attempted interruption, preserved by Stanihurst in 1577, was lost in the 1587 Holinshed.[74] Nothing can diminish the savage force with which Campion conjures up an Irish warlord, who knows no other rule but that of the sword:

As touching my Kingdome (my Lord) I would you and I had exchanged Kingdomes but for one moneth, I would trust to gather up more crummes in that space, then twice the revenues of my poore Earledome; but you are well and warme, and so hold you, and upbraide not me with such an odious storme. I sleape on a cabbin, when you lye soft in your bed of downe; I serve under the top of heaven, when you are served under a Canapye; I drinke water out of a skull, when you drinke wine out of golden Cuppes; my courser is trained to the filde, when your genet is taught to amble; when you are begraced and be Lorded, and crowched and kneeled unto, then finde I small grace with our Irish borderers, except I cut them off by the knees.[75]

---

[71]   *Histories of Ireland*, fols 79v–80v; Raphael Holinshed, *The Chronicles of England, Scotlande, and Irelande*, 2 vols (London: George Bishop, 1577), STC 13568a, I. 1556.a.1–28.

[72]   Compare the description of Agricola, in *Tacitus in Five Volumes* (London: Heinemann, 1970), Loeb Series, vol. 1, *Agricola*, c. 23, pp. 68–9; for Tacitus at this time, see Blair Worden, *The Sound of Virtue: Philip Sidney's* Arcadia *and Elizabethan Politics* (New Haven and London: Yale, 1996), pp. 256–61.

[73]   *Histories of Ireland*, fol. 77r.

[74]   Holinshed, *Historie of Irelande* (1577), II. 82.a.48–52; Holinshed, *Chronicles* (1587), II. 85.b.43–6.

[75]   *Histories of Ireland*, fols 79v–80r.

No wonder 'the Counsell would have smyled'. But Campion allows no time for the reader to join in the pleasure of seeing the mighty mocked, because the wheel of fortune spins suddenly, and 'the next yeare Wulsie was cast owte of favour'.[76]

Matthew Parker thought much could be made of him when he read the confiscated manuscript: here was a man who was writing history as well as Hall, Holinshed, Stow, Grafton and Camden, but doing so with an imaginative and dramatic eye. Campion's fame as a writer of English could be justified from this piece alone, which contains as much drama as the *Ambrosiana*. The portrait of Wolsey is great writing, and passes, robbed of its dramatic context, through the 1577 Holinshed into the 1587 *Chronicles of England*, where Fleming even indexed it separately under 'Campians description of cardinall Wolseie'.[77] The survival of this passage, given Campion's status as traitor in the 1587 *Chronicles*, is a tribute to its power, but Campion's humane history, completed on 9 June 1571, was harnessed first to Stanihurst's Pale perspective in 1577, then interleaved with Hooker's savage history of retribution in 1587, and finally yoked incongruously with Edmund Spenser's brutal *A View of the State of Ireland* in 1633. Richard Stanihurst used Campion's admission that the work was 'rowgh hewed' to justify, in his dedication to Sidney in the 1587 edition, the fact that it then 'in mitching wise wandred through sundrie hands'.[78] What happened to Campion's texts reflects the brutal colonization of Ireland between 1571 and 1633. Campion's text emerged from the culture of reform that characterized Sidney's first term of office in Ireland, and reflected his own more compassionate approach to the Irish people; the texts of Hooker and Spenser emerge during a brutal colonial resettlement. Whereas Campion began his 1571 chapter on the 'meere Irish' by asking the reader not to impute to the Irish of today the 'faultes of their ancestours', John Hooker's 'Supplie' ends with famine: 'a heavie, but a just judgement of God upon such a Pharoicall and stifnecked people'.[79]

Campion's conception of history is clear, since he ends with a *parliament*, and with the two speeches of the Lord Deputy and the Speaker advocating reform. Campion's faith in disputation is not shaken by the fact that the aims were not achieved, as the Deputy argued, 'at the first daie'.[80] Where Campion has omitted a catalogue of massacres, Hooker's 'lamentable ... historie of Ireland, and especially this tragedie of Mounster', ends in a land where only wolves survive, with the judgement of God on the practices of 'the two doctors, Allen and Sanders' and that 'sonne of Sathan' (the pope).[81]

---

[76]   *Histories of Ireland*, fol. 81v.

[77]   Holinshed, *Chronicles* (1587), III. 917.b.20–45.

[78]   Holinshed, *Chronicles* (1587), II. 7.

[79]   Campion, *Histories of Ireland*, fol. 18r; Holinshed, *Chronicles* (1587), II. 183.a.24–5.

[80]   Campion, *Histories of Ireland*, fol. 98r.

[81]   Holinshed, *Chronicles* (1587), II. 182.b.33–183.b.22.

Although Stanihurst saw it more as 'a woorke roughlie hewed, than smoothlie planed', he considered it good enough to include in Holinshed's *Chronicles*.[82] Whereas Campion takes his history right up to the beginning of 1571, the first edition of Holinshed (1577) finishes with the end of the reign of Henry VIII (1547). The whole of Campion's final section, with its agenda of reform in the two defining speeches of Sidney and Stanihurst, was lost. The exclusion of all of the sixteenth century after the death of the Earl of Ormond in 1546 robbed Campion's text of 'the optimistic and unitive coda of Campion's *Histories*, which adumbrates a Christian humanist programme of reform through education'.[83] In 1587, Hooker's 'Supplie', which takes the *Chronicles* from 1546 to 1586, transformed the history into a moral story of papal interference and rebellion punished by 'horrible massacres and bloodie persecutions' in Munster.[84] Campion has been relegated from first to last on the list of authorities, just before 'Records and rolles divers', Cambrensis has been brought back to replace Campion's belief in the education and reform of the 'meere Irish', and Campion's 'Christian humanist thought and Stanihurst's pro-Geraldine civic patriotism', now has a 'coda that espouses English Protestant imperialism in Ireland'.[85]

Campion's *Histories of Ireland* were severely cut for the 1587 edition of Holinshed's *Chronicles*, and replaced with a narrative that justifies the colonial savagery of Sir Walter Raleigh and Lord Grey of Wilton by portraying the Irish as a barbarous nation of cannibals. The account of Campion's own trial, by contrast, *begins* with Sander's invasion, which now taints the chronicle of his trial.[86] The account of Lord Grey's massacre is ruthlessly unemotional, and gives no indication that this event was morally indefensible.[87] The whole 'Irish Historie' is now dedicated to Sir Walter Raleigh, who, as one of the two captains in charge of the massacre at Smerwick, had a great deal of blood on his hands. Sander's invasion, the very event that more than any other undermined the mission of Campion and Persons was, by a peculiar irony of historiography, now bound together, in Holinshed's *Chronicles*, with Campion's sympathetic account of the Irish people, their history and their land.

---

[82]   Holinshed, *Chronicles* (1587), dedication to Sir Henry Sidney, II. 7.

[83]   Colm Lennon, 'Ireland', in *The Oxford Handbook of Holinshed's Chronicles*, ed. Paulina Kewes, Ian W. Archer and Felicity Heal (Oxford: University Press, 2013), pp. 663–78 (p. 668).

[84]   Holinshed, *Chronicles* (1587), II. 183.a.44–5.

[85]   Richard A. McCabe, 'Making History: Holinshed's Irish Chronicles, 1577 and 1587' in *British Identities and English Renaissance Literature*, ed. David J. Baker and Willy Maley (Cambridge: University Press, 2002), p. 65.

[86]   Holinshed, *Chronicles* (1587), III. 1322.b.40–49; see Chapter 6 for the quotation in full.

[87]   For more on how Hooker and Spenser represented the massacre, see Chapter 6, pp. 181–4.

Holinshed, Hooker and Spenser, show how different was the optimistic nature of Campion's history from anything that came before or after. Campion's work was first printed in full in 1633, when Sir James Ware bound Campion's work in Dublin between the same covers as Edmund Spenser's work of 1596, *A View of the State of Ireland*.[88] While Campion's enquiries into the early history of Ireland display the same generous curiosity as Herodotus, Spenser's dialogue is a counsel of despairing brutality. No plan of 'reformation' for 'that salvage nation' can 'prosper'.[89] Ware, as editor, has even had to exercise the 'moderation' that he wishes Spenser had shown, and omits the word 'salvage'. It makes no difference. Where Campion's portrait of the 'meere Irish', by contrast, shows them with their own system of law and learning, Spenser portrays them as 'destitute of learning'; in the original manuscript, Spenser describes them as 'havinge bene allwaies without Lettres' (making much of the legendary Scythian background).[90] Campion, by contrast, portrays a long period of schooling:

> Witheowt either preceptes or observation of congruitie they speake Latten like a vulgar language, learned in their common scholes of leachcraft and lawe, whereat they begynn children, and hold on sixtene or twentie yeares, connyng by roate the aphorismes of Hipocrates and the civill institutes ... .[91]

When it comes to poetry, 'they esteeme their poetes, who wright Irish learnedly, and penne therein sonettes heroicall, for the which they are bountefully rewarded'.[92] Spenser claims that these 'Irish Bardes' use their writings to praise 'the most dangerous and desperate', and so corrupt the young.[93] Campion's portrait of the people balances vices with virtues:

> The people are thus enclyned: religious, francke, amorous, irefull, sufferable of paynes infinite, veary glorious, many sorseres, excellent horsemen, delighted with warres, great almesgivers, passing in hospitalitie.[94]

Spenser's grim determinism is monochrome black – 'it is vaine to speake of planting lawes, and plotting policie, till they be altogether subdued' – and leads

---

[88]   *The Historie of Ireland, Collected by Three Learned Authors Viz. Meredith Hanmer, Edmund Campion and Edmund Spenser* (Dublin: Societie of Stationers, 1633), STC 25067a. This appears to be a revised edition of STC 25067, but the textual variants of this edition are many. All four editions of the work in the National Library of Ireland place the texts in a different order, and have different title pages.

[89]   Edmund Spenser, *A View of the State of Ireland*, ed. Andrew Hadfield and Willy Maley (Oxford: Blackwell, 1997), p. 143. The table at the end shows Ware's attempts to soften Spenser's text.

[90]   Spenser, *A View of the State of Ireland*, p. 47 (MS p. 171).

[91]   *Histories of Ireland*, fol. 20r.

[92]   *Histories of Ireland*, fol. 16v.

[93]   Spenser, *A View of the State of Ireland*, p. 76.

[94]   *Histories of Ireland*, fol. 16v.

to the conclusion that 'there is no hope of their amendment or recovery'.[95] Linked to this bleak prediction, Spenser provides the one twisted hope that the warres will soon be over, because, from a famine caused not by their conquerors but by their own 'spoyle of others', they will quickly 'consume themselves and devour one another'.[96] This racial denigration of the Irish as cannibals (a view shared by Hooker) is what enables Spenser to justify the massacre at Smerwick, where he was present as Lord Grey's secretary.[97]

When Campion prepared to depart from Turvey in disguise, he left his manuscript with Richard Stanihurst, who was 'fully resolved to enriche M. Campion his Chronicle with further additions'.[98] Stanihurst had Campion's manuscript copied, and by 1572 there were (at least) two or three copies. Archbishop Parker had obtained a manuscript of the *Histories of Ireland* by 8 November 1572, when he wrote to Lord Burghley to tell him of an 'intercepted' package of letters 'being directed to Papists here, in order to carry on some Papistical Designs'.[99] Parker wrote:

> We have examined dyverse partyes and find no grete matter. The boke of Irelands history we opteyned, which here I send to your Lordship which your honour maye direct to my Lord of Leycestre, for it is dedicated to him, and if this Campion cowd be reclaymed or recoverd, I see bi this wyt that he were worthi to be made up.[100]

Richard Stanihurst, it seems, was working on the manuscript Campion had left with him when Raphael Holinshed asked him to join the Holinshed project. Holinshed's dedication to 'sir Henry Sydney, Knight', suggests that Wolfe also had his own copy:

> At length yet as Maister Woulfes yse was to imparte to me all such helpes as he might at any hande procure for my furtherance, in the collections of the other Histories, wherewith I specially dealte, his happe was to light also upon a copie of two Bookes of the Irish Histories, compiled by one Edmond Campion, fellow somtime of S. John Baptists Colledge in Oxforde, very well penned certenly, but so briefe, as it were to be wished that occasion had served him to have used more leysure, and thereby to have delivered to us a larger discourse of the same Histories: for as he himselfe confesseth, hee had not paste tenne weekes space to gather his mater: a very shorte time doubtlesse for such a peece of worke.[101]

---

[95]   Spenser, *A View of the State of Ireland*, pp. 21 and 101.

[96]   Spenser, *A View of the State of Ireland*, p. 101.

[97]   Spenser, *A View of the State of Ireland*, p. 105.

[98]   Holinshed, *Chronicles* (1587), II. 7.

[99]   John Strype, *The Life and Acts of Matthew Parker* (London: John Wyat, 1711), p. 375.

[100]   BL MS Lansdowne 15/46 (my transcription). Campion's 'boke' may not have been confiscated at Drogheda, as assumed by Simpson, p. 59. Vossen, *Histories of Ireland*, p. 22, summarizes the problem.

[101]   Holinshed, *Chronicles* (1587), II. sig. A2r.

The secluded life at Turvey came to an end. When Campion realized that the searchers had 'laid wait over all the realm of Ireland for him', and that the pursuit might now engulf the Barnewall family, he resolved 'to disguise himself in apparel and to returne againe into England'.[102] He added a dedication to Leicester as he was leaving Turvey and, keeping his location secret, signed it: 'from Dyvelin 27. Maij 1571'.[103] There was grief at Campion's departure, but the tears and embracing, the corollary of the affection he felt and inspired, must have been kept out of sight:

> whose hart in like manner could not be but much afflicted to depart from such dear frends, which ever after he loved most intirely and they him. And now it was no lesse grievous to leave Ireland than it had been before to leave England.[104]

It was a pattern to be repeated many times: travelling in disguise, writing in remote country houses and tearful departures. The time in Ireland had been for Campion a series of contrasts. Never before had he been threatened with arrest, or so embedded in a family hearth. Here, in the large Barnewall household, Campion must finally have accepted the authority of the Catholic church. Persons's statement about Campion's time in Ireland that 'he was not in the church', cannot be true of his departure: his choice of St Patrick as a patron and his final decision to leave England for Douai indicate that Grace Dieu lived up to its name. Campion was still a deacon in the established church and a fellow of St John's when he arrived in Ireland; by the time he left in June 1571, he appears to have become both a Catholic and a profound devotee of St Patrick, 'a fellow exile in Ireland', who 'provided a road-map for Campion's own aspirations as a missionary priest'.[105]

Up till now, Campion had been trying to remain within the established church; he had certainly resisted appeals to join the growing crowd of Oxford men gathering at Douai, in Flanders. Bombino reflects on the way Campion's word and example influenced the people with whom he stayed, but these two remarkable families had a powerful impact on Campion.[106] While the ruins of Grace Dieu may have been a familiar experience after Greyfriars and St Bernard's College, his stay with the Barnewalls is the first time Campion was part of a large Catholic family, and in the presence of a religious community of educated women. Until now, Campion had spent 18 years in completely male environments. Turvey was no *hortus conclusus*, but it must have been a 'heaven-haven', giving Campion time to give emotional assent to what his reason had already accepted.

---

[102] ABSI Collectanea P. I, fols 85r–v [Grene's foliation here is, uniquely, conventional].

[103] Farmleigh MS. IV.E.6 [p. 440], fol. 43v.

[104] ABSI Collectanea, P. I, fol. 86b.

[105] Highley, *Catholics Writing the Nation*, pp. 125–6, in a fine passage, movingly describes the way St Patrick, the archetypal *peregrinus Christianus*, may have inspired Campion, who walked as a pilgrim to Rome.

[106] Bombino, *Vita et Martyrium*, p. 20.

He crossed from Drogheda with Melchior Hussey, steward to the Earl of Kildare, 'apparelled in a Lackyes weade'.[107] Campion 'put on a livery sute of the Earl of Kildare's foot-men, for he at that time, both for riches & honour, was in Ireland much remarkable'.[108] The Countess of Kildare, Mabel Browne, was a sister of Viscount Montague, dedicatee of Campion's poem, *Sancta salutiferi nascentia semina verbi*.[109] She and Jane Dormer, the Duchess of Feria (niece of Sir Henry Sidney) had been 'companions in court in Queen Mary's time'; in her Catholic household she maintained a refuge and library for three priests.[110] Kildare's own sister, Lady Elizabeth (dubbed the 'Fair Geraldine' by Henry Howard, Earl of Surrey), had married Sir Anthony Browne, Mabel's father, in 1542, so the Kildares were doubly tied to the Montague family.[111]

Melchior Hussey had made a major contribution to the recovery under Philip and Mary of the Kildare property, confiscated after the rebellion of 'Silken Thomas' in 1534; he had been richly rewarded with extensive lands in co. Meath, so he may have been taking rolls and deeds to England to establish the Kildare claims.[112] James Stanihurst travelled to England in August 1571, only two months later, with eight bundles of statutes, containing 170 acts of the Irish parliament, to be printed there.[113] The Stanihursts, Barnewalls, Kildares, Hussey and the Lord Deputy all helped Campion to escape; never can a fugitive have had so many powerful protectors. Campion went up the coast to the port of Drogheda, where he wrote the address, 'To the Loving Reader', which is faithfully copied in two of the best manuscripts of *The Two Bokes of the Histories of Ireland*: 'Ffare well ffrom Droghdagh the .9. of June. 1571'.[114]

Someone had obviously tipped off the authorities:

> Scarcely was Campion on board, but he sees the hereticall searchers, speeding thitherwards, & allmost on his backe: you would even have deemed them houndes, following their prey in hotte chase. In so much that the swiftnesse of the pursuers, strooke a terrour into the pursued & prevented all endeavours of escape. No sooner were they come abroad the shippe, but they viewed all about,

---

[107]   ABSI Collectanea P. I, fol. 86a.

[108]   Bombino, *Vita et Martyrium*, p. 23; Bodl. MS Tanner 329, fol. 6r.

[109]   Kilroy, *Memory and Transcription*, p. 155.

[110]   Vincent P. Carey, *Surviving the Tudors: The 'Wizard' Earl of Kildare and English Rule in Ireland, 1537–1586* (Dublin: Four Courts Press, 2002), pp. 76 and 193–4. For names and details of the priests, see Chapter 6.

[111]   *ODNB*, 'Sir Anthony Browne (c. 1500–1548)', by William B. Robinson.

[112]   Carey, *Surviving the Tudors*, pp. 71–2.

[113]   Lennon, *Stanihurst the Dubliner*, p. 34.

[114]   Farmleigh MS IV.E.6 [p. 442], fol. 44v; Bodl. MS Jones 6, fol. 6v. The confirmation of the dates in *both* manuscripts leaves no room for the doubt expressed by Vossen, that the date is wrongly copied. Both of these manuscripts appear to be using an autograph original, since the same pagination is preserved throughout the text of Bodl. MS Jones 6 and (most of) Farmleigh MS IV.E.6.

peeped in every corner, gazd upon the shipmen, turned all things upside down & ever & anon threatned Campian, not only with their words, but with bended browes, rowling eyes, & ghastly lookes.[115]

Stanihurst must have given Bombino this eyewitness account. Campion, despairing of all human help, and realizing his false name and apparel were in danger, prayed fervently to St. Patrick, a fellow exile, and his chosen alias.[116] Miraculously, as he felt, the searchers did not see through his disguise, and Campion set sail: the passage 'was indifferent prosperous though full of sorrow for being forced to abandon so good Catholics & harty friends'.[117]

Bristol was again the most likely port in England. If Melchior Hussey was registering claims at the Exchequer, Campion would probably have travelled with him to London. They could have accomplished the journey in three days, but they could not have risked staying in London long. Persons cannot be correct in saying he was present at Dr John Story's brutal execution on 1 June.[118] He may well have witnessed the aftermath, Dr Story's freshly butchered head and quarters, and we know 'he found nothing but fears, suspitions, arrestings, condemnations, tortures, executions & the like'.[119] The northern rebellion, Felton's posting of the papal bull on the Bishop of London's gate, and the Ridolfi plot

> made the Queen & Councel so troubled as they could not tell whome to trust, and soe fell to rigorous proceeding against all, but especially against Catholics whome they most feared, soe as Mr Campian could not tell where to rest in England, all men being in feare & jealousy the one of the other; for which cause he resolved to fly again and to retire himself for good and all into foreign countries seing that in his own there was no secure living now any longer for a Catholick man.[120]

Campion 'was everywhere sought for' and, 'driven therefore to his last refuge', resolved to go to Flanders.[121] At Douai were 'divers learned and grave men of our English nation'.[122]

Campion set sail from Dover, only to run into more danger. As he crossed the Channel, his ship was intercepted by the *Hare*, an ageing 10-gun ship, one of two ships of the Queen appointed to sail up and down the Channel on patrol against invasion and to detect those leaving the country without licence; the warship fired

---

[115]   Bombino, *Vita et Martyrium*, p. 24; Bodl. MS Tanner 329, fol. 6r.

[116]   Bombino, *Vita et Martyrium*, p. 24; Bodl. MS Tanner 329, fol. 6v.

[117]   ABSI Collectanea P. I, fol. 86b.

[118]   Vossen, *Histories of Ireland*, p. 24, concludes that 'Persons may err in this date as he did in others'.

[119]   ABSI Collectanea P. I, fol. 87a.

[120]   ABSI Collectanea P. I, fol. 87a.

[121]   Bombino, *Vita et Martyrium*, p. 25; Bodl. MS Tanner 329, fol. 6v.

[122]   ABSI Collectanea P. I, fol. 88a.

a warning shot, and ordered Campion's ship to strike sail.[123] For the second time in a month, searchers leapt aboard the ship carrying Campion. Because Campion had no 'publike licence', the Queen's searchers took him back to England 'with great jolity and triumph', where the captain delivered Campion to the magistrates who, in turn, committed him to a 'keeper' to take him to London.[124] Luckily, the 'keeper' was corrupt. After robbing Campion of all the money intended for his journey, he 'so negligently guards his prisoner, affords so many wayes, through his feyned sleepinesse & sluggishnesse, for him to escape' that Campion could see 'his keeper more feard his staying in durance, then his flight'.[125] Campion took advantage of this 'crafty negligence' to escape, borrowed more money from his friends (some of whom must have stayed with him throughout), and set sail a second time for France.[126] This time, the voyage was untroubled, and Campion reached Calais, from where he had a further 75 miles to travel to Douai, then in Flanders. Campion could hardly have guessed that over the next 10 years, like a medieval scholar, he would travel some 5,000 miles, at least half of that distance on foot, and return to his own country only in disguise.

He arrived at Douai in June 1571, just as Dr Nicholas Sander (in nearby Louvain) was finishing his *De Visibili Monarchia* with two dedications: one dated 29 June, to Pope Pius V, and another dated 30 June, to three Cardinals: Giovanni Morone, Stanislaus Hosius and Giovanni Commendone, in which he asked the *illustrissimi cardinales* to help free their brethren from the "dreadful tyranny in England".[127] Sander ended his long defence of the right of the pope's *Civitas Dei* to depose monarchs in Book VII, with the most recent transgression of the *Civitas Diaboli*: the state-sponsored kidnapping in Antwerp on 25 May 1571, and the execution in London on 1 June 1571, of Dr Story.[128] This monumental work (844 folio pages), published a year after the papal bull, *Regnans in Excelsis*, shaped the theology and politics of English Catholic exiles over the next decade, and 122 copies of this first edition, published in Louvain by John Fowler, another New College exile, still survive.[129]

---

[123] Bombino, *Vita et Martyrium*, p. 26; Bodl. MS Tanner 329, fols 6v–7r.

[124] Bombino, *Vita et Martyrium*, p. 26; Bodl. MS Tanner 329, fol. 7r. Cf. ABSI Collectanea P. I, fol. 88a. Bombino's more complex version of this is obviously correct. Persons reduces the captain, magistrate and keeper to one person: the captain. The Tanner translator sounds as if he has an eyewitness source, as the phrase 'with great jolity & triumph' is not in the original Latin.

[125] Bombino, *Vita et Martyrium*, p. 26; Bodl. MS Tanner 329, fol. 7r.

[126] Bombino, *Vita et Martyrium*, pp. 26–7; Bodl. MS Tanner 329, fols 7r–v.

[127] *De Visibili Monarchia Ecclesiae, Libri Octo* (John Fowler: Louvain, 1571), ARCR I. 1013, sig. 2r–4v.

[128] Sander, *De Visibili Monarchia*, pp. 737–8.

[129] There is an urgent need for a new study of Sander; the best work is by Thomas McNevin Veech, *Dr Nicholas Sanders and the English Reformation 1530–1584* (Louvain: University Library, 1935). See also T.F. Mayer's *ODNB* article, 'Nicholas Sander', and Freddy Cristobal Dominguez, '"We must fight with paper and pens": Spanish Elizabethan

Sander had resigned from New College in 1560, and was ordained in Rome by Bishop Thomas Goldwell.[130] There he drafted a key report on the state of Catholics in England, for Giovanni Morone, the Cardinal Protector of England, which was to form the basis for papal estimates of the strength of Catholicism in England, and made Sander well known in Rome. Cardinal Hosius, the leading authority on the Eucharist, took Sander as his secretary to the last session of the Council of Trent, which began in 1562, where he and Goldwell represented English Catholics.[131] They pressed for excommunication of the Queen and for a rigid position to be taken on attendance of Protestant services by Catholics.[132] Pope Pius IV made two attempts to invite Elizabeth to send a legate to the Council; when neither succeeded, he recommended excommunication, which the legates considered during June 1563.[133] Sander was almost certainly the author of a secret document advocating a bull of excommunication; the Emperor Ferdinand, who would have to execute the bull, was sent a copy, and angrily instructed his ambassadors to oppose any such plan.[134] He was supported by Philip II, who (as we have seen) was still hoping to use diplomacy to try to persuade Elizabeth to grant toleration.[135]

When Cardinal Michele Ghislieri was elected Pope Pius V on 7 January 1566, he appointed Thomas Harding and Nicholas Sander as Apostolic Delegates to promulgate the decision that Catholics should not attend Protestant services, and gave them faculties to absolve Catholics who had attended Protesant services, so-called 'schismatics'; they in turn deputed the task to Laurence Vaux.[136] These decisions determined the shape of English Catholicism long before the Jesuit mission arrived in England in 1580.[137] As Dr Humphrey Ely was accurately to write: 'The true opinion of not going to heretical services came not from the Jesuits as they boast. It came from beyond the seas I confess, but yet out of a secular priest's shop'.[138]

Polemics, 1585–1598' (Princeton: Ph.D. Dissertation, 2011). I am deeply indebted to long discussions with Dr Mark Rankin, whose work on the different editions and extant copies of *De Visibili Monarchia* (1571 and 1578) and *De Origine Schismatis* (1585 and 1586), is helping to elucidate the influence of Sander on both the politics and the historiography of Catholic exiles.

[130]   Veech, *Sanders*, p. 23. For this important figure, see *ODNB*, 'Thomas Goldwell' (d. 1585), by T.F. Mayer, and Chapter 5.

[131]   Veech, *Sanders*, p. 31.

[132]   Veech, *Sanders*, p. 42.

[133]   Veech, *Sanders*, pp. 42–6.

[134]   Veech, *Sanders*, p. 44.

[135]   See the King's instructions to Bishop de Quadra, *CSP Spanish, 1558–1567*, pp. 371–2.

[136]   Veech, *Sanders*, pp. 38–9.

[137]   Peter Holmes, *Resistance & Compromise: The Political Thought of the Elizabethan Catholics* (Cambridge: University Press, p. 84, also traces the beginnings of recusancy to Trent in 1562, and the active campaign to Laurence Vaux in 1566.

[138]   Wood, *Athenae Oxonienses*, I. 470 n. 2.

After the Council, Cardinal Commendone invited Sander to come with him to Poland, to help Hosius promote the implementation of the Tridentine decrees and, on a ride through the woods in Ermland, suggested to Sander, that he write the book that became *De Visibili Monarchia*.[139] Sander returned from Poland and, in 1564, joined the other New College exiles in Louvain, in the great controversies with Bishop Jewel and Bishop Horne.[140] The Spanish ambassador, Guzman de Silva talked of 'the books which are constantly coming from Louvain'.[141]

So, while Campion had been lecturing in rhetoric, and acting as proctor in Oxford, Sander had been campaigning for a tough policy on Elizabeth. The anonymous *A particular declaration*, published by the Privy Council in 1582 to denigrate Campion, and the first attempt to justify the torture of Campion, contains all the texts that formed the basis of the interrogations; four are extracts from Book VII of Sander's *De Visibili Monarchia*.[142] The most subversive of these is the quotation from *Regnans in Excelsis*, which absolves subjects from allegiance to the Queen.[143] Campion, during his first interrogation on the rack on 1 August 1581, was asked to repudiate Sander's views.[144] Campion was also asked to repudiate Richard Bristow's 'Motives': consisting of 48 articles, Bristow too, in Motives 6 and 40, endorsed the power of the Pope to excommunicate and depose monarchs.[145] Although this was published just after Campion left Douai, it was circulating in manuscript long before Bristow, at Allen's request, put together the book for publication. The attack on the authority of the sovereign contained in these two books endorsed both the rebellion of the northern earls and the papal bull.[146] Sander remained in Louvain until he was summoned to Rome at the beginning of 1572. When Sander, accompanied by five or six companions, rode out of the gates of Louvain for Rome at the end of January 1572, everyone expected him to be given a cardinal's hat, but Pius V died on 1 May.[147]

---

[139]   Veech, *Sanders*, pp. 47–8.

[140]   For these controversies see Southern, *Elizabethan Recusant Prose*, pp. 59–140; Hunt, 'Preaching the Elizabethan Settlement', pp. 366–86, and Chapter 2.

[141]   To King Philip II from London, 14 April 1565: *CSP Spanish, 1558–1567*, p. 418.

[142]   *A particular declaration or testimony, of the undutifull and traiterous affection borne against her Majestie by Edmond Campion Jesuite, and other condemned Priestes, witnessed by their own confessions: in reproof of those slanderous bookes & libels delivered out to the contrary by such as are malitiously affected towards her Majestie and the state* (London: C. Barker, 1582), STC 4536.

[143]   Sander, *De Visibili Monarchia*, p. 734.

[144]   *A particular declaration*, p. 7.

[145]   Richard Bristow, *A Briefe Treatise of Diverse plaine and sure wayes to finde out the truthe in this doubtful and dangerous time of Heresie: conteyning sundry worthy Motives unto the Catholike faith* (Antwerp: John Fowler, 1574), STC 3799, ARCR II. 67.

[146]   *De Visibili Monarchia*, p. 730.

[147]   Veech, *Sanders*, p. 110. Veech gives the date as 25 January, but Tom Birrell (in a marginal gloss in the London Library copy) suggests that it was a week earlier.

Campion must have arrived at Douai just as copies of Sander's book reached the college, founded in Michaelmas 1568 by Dr William Allen to train priests for the English mission. At the beginning of the college's life, 'five or six Englishmen of great ability and promise', in a modest house near the theology schools of the university of Douai, were living together in a 'regular and frugal fashion'.[148] Frugality was the order of the day, and the early diaries are full of references to the loaves and fishes.[149] Oxford men predominated. When Campion arrived, he found, among these exiled scholars, Dr Richard Bristow of Exeter and Edward Rishton of Brasenose, John White, Thomas Stapleton and Thomas Dorman, Fellows of New College, the last three also veterans of Louvain. Gregory Martin had arrived in 1570, and had been sending letters to Campion begging him to come, and there were several old Oxford friends and contemporaries, who arrived about the same time: Thomas Ford of Trinity, John Hart and William Rainolds, the brother of Edmund, of New College.[150] The camaraderie among this small group of exiles (about 15 in number at this stage) was intense, as Bombino indicates:

> They livd no lesse mutually united in mindes, then in house. Their life lead in learning, their mindes in heaven. Nothing each man tooke more to heart, then obedience to the president, & yet more manifest was his authority in the will of the obeyers, then in any right of government. Joyned together they were in one table, under one roofe, in one & the selfe same forme of life.[151]

Under the terms of his licence to travel, Campion continued to receive his St John's stipend, until Michaelmas 1572.[152] 'At Douai I spent nearly two years studying Scholastic Theology', Campion wrote in his Prague 'Examen' in 1573.[153] His friends persuaded him to take the degree of Bachelor of Theology: 'hee, sweet and facill as he was of disposition, obeyd them'.[154] The Douai Diaries show that Campion took the three stages of the degree, roughly every six months, and alongside Gregory Martin: on 21 March 1572, 27 November 1572 and 21 January 1573.[155] Campion had begun his study of St Thomas Aquinas by 13 August 1571, since that is the date he inscribed a copy of the fine edition of the *Summa Totius Theologiae* of St Thomas Aquinas, which had just emerged from Christopher

---

[148]   T.F. Knox, ed., *The First and Second Diaries of the English College* (London: Nutt, 1878), xxix.

[149]   *Douay Diaries*, pp. 4–5.

[150]   ABSI Collectanea P. I, fol. 90a.

[151]   Bombino, *Vita et Martyrium*, p. 28; Bodl. MS Tanner 329, fol. 7v.

[152]   Stevenson and Salter, *Early History of St John's*, pp. 189–90. Stevenson says that 'there is no reason why he should not have received his stipend until 25 March 1573', although he notes the reduction.

[153]   ARSI Anglia 38/I, fol. 31v.

[154]   Bombino, *Vita et Martyrium*, pp. 28–9; Bodl. MS Tanner 329, fol. 8r.

[155]   *Douay Diaries*, p. 273; Stevenson and Salter, *Early History of St John's*, p. 189.

Plantin's press in Antwerp in 1569.[156] Campion annotated this copy, and added his name on the title page, styling himself, *Edm. Campianus Anglus Londinensis*.[157] The three volumes are extensively annotated, though the second volume is annotated only as far as *De peccato blasphemiae*.[158] Campion has ignored the other sins, and gone straight to the third volume, where he omits the Christological sections, on the birth, death, resurrection and ascension of Christ, and begins QUAESTIO LX. *De Sacramentis*.[159] Campion must have been doing this reading during 1571 and 1572. Both the purchase and the survival are significant: Campion was as devoted to dogmatic theology as Sander was to controversy.

Campion, encouraged by Dr Allen, wrote to Bishop Cheyney, urging him to join the Catholic church.[160] As we have seen, the letter shows that Campion had already spent a great deal of time with Bishop Cheyney, dining at Thomas Dutton's house, even before he compounded for the first fruits of the benefice of Sherborne on 3 March 1569. Alongside the zeal of the letter, is a characteristically affectionate tone:

> I love you entirely, as a man of an excellent nature, learned, noble, courteous, one to whom I am for your many favours, & good offices, infinitely endeared.[161]

Campion arrived at Douai at the end of June 1571, and left 18 months later, soon after taking the third part of his Bachelor of Theology in early 1573. It was enough time to sense the apostolic fervour for the reclamation of England present in Dr Allen's college. Allen, Stapleton and Bristow set the tone for the small group at Douai, but Sander's radical view on the monarchical papacy was the dominant voice among all the English exiles in Flanders. Campion was always sceptical about papal deposition and never showed any support for military intervention; his departure from Douai after such a short time must reflect the discomfort he felt at the mingling of religious and political aims. There is no indication that he ever

---

[156]   The inscription is: '*a. d. 1571. Idib. Augusti*'. The cost of three copies sold directly by Plantin at this time was 4½ florins (unbound) and 5½ florins (bound): my thanks to Julianne Simpson, Special Collections, John Rylands Library, for this information.

[157]   Now in Heythrop College, where the library still belongs to the British province of the Society of Jesus. There is no record in Plantin's detailed ledgers of the purchase. The quarto book is in four volumes bound as three, still in their contemporary binding.

[158]   This is on p. 43, *Quaestio Decimatertia*.

[159]   *Summa*, p. 220; for analysis of the annotations, see Canon Didiot, 'La "Somme" d'un Martyr', in *Revue des Sciences Ecclesiastiques* (1887), 193–212; and John Morris, S.J., 'Blessed Edmund Campion at Douay', *The Month* (1887), 1–17.

[160]   For Martin's letter to Dr White of New College, see Gregory Martin (Licentiate and late reader of Divinitie in the English Coleadge at Remes), *A Treatise of Christian Peregrination. Wherunto is adjoined certen epistles* (Paris: R. Verstegan, 1583), STC 17507, ARCR II. 523.

[161]   Bombino, *Vita et Martyrium*, pp. 37–8; Bodl. MS Tanner 329, fol. 12v; *Opuscula*, p. 379.

went back on what Persons describes as his decision to leave England 'for good and all'.[162] Campion's views on papal supremacy, excommunication and the authority of the Queen were completely at odds, as Simpson argued, with the views of Dr Allen at Douai and Dr Sander at Louvain.[163] It may be true, as Allen often asserted, that political talk was not encouraged in the seminary at Douai, but the books of Sander and Bristow, published at this time, put forward subversive views of the English crown and of papal power to depose monarchs. Allen later argued that Sander and Bristow were exceptions to the rule of moderation, 'Which moderation was kept in al places and persons of our Nation; (two onelie learned men of great zeale & excellencie indeed, D. Saunders and D. Bristowe, excepted)'.[164] Yet Allen himself had petitioned the Pope to implement the bull of excommunication as early as 1572; by 1576, Allen was involved in full-scale plans for an invasion of England.[165]

In early February 1573, Campion left Douai and walked a thousand miles to reach the seven great basilicas of *Roma Sancta* as it prepared for the Jubilee of 1575.[166] It was a significant gesture: Campion decided to go alone and 'dressed as a beggar' (*mendici peregrinatoris habitu*) so as 'to make himselfe more like to Christ in extreme poverty', but he 'never made knowen any thing that hapned' on this profound spiritual journey.[167] Campion left the city, accompanied for a short distance by a crowd of friends before emotional farewells. This solitary pilgrimage, very much in the pattern of St Patrick, was a deliberate and conscious surrender of himself:

> Thus it was: It fortund at that time, that a countryman of Campians, an heretike, one of his old friendes, & familiar acquayntance at Oxford, came out of curiosity to see Rome; and in his return homeward mette Campian, cladde as he was in a poore pilgrims weede. Campians face so well knowen, in so unknowen a habit put him first in doubt (posting by him on horsebacke) whether it were hee or no. Whereupon he stopd, turning his eyes upon him, & first stole a looke, afterward eyd the pilgrim more freely, & not only knew him absolutely, but leapd downe from his horse & in friendly sort saluted him. After some solemne complements at their first meeting, this man, seeming by his countenance, & outward semblance, much troubled & astonisht, askes Campian, what was the cause of that his so unwonted poverty, perhaps imputing this which had indeed

---

[162]   ABSI Collectanea P. I, fol. 87a. Persons tells us a few pages later that Campion (in letters now lost) expressed the desire to help in the conversion of England, 'though in the meane space he were well contented where he was', ABSI Collectanea P. I, fol. 98b.

[163]   Simpson, p. 71, talks of the 'divergence between his views and those of Dr. Allen'.

[164]   Allen, *A True, Sincere and Modest Defence*, p. 64.

[165]   *ODNB*, 'William Allen', by Eamon Duffy.

[166]   Etienne du Pérac produced his engraving, 'Roma Sancta', in 1575, which shows a picture-map of pilgrims visiting the 'Seven Churches' of Rome. I am grateful to Evangelia Papoulia for sharing this, and her research into Gregory XIII, with me.

[167]   Bombino, *Vita et Martyrium*, pp. 38–9; Bodl. MS Tanner 329, fol. 13r–v.

proceeded from his pious resolution, to the iniury of some highway robbers. But when he understood from himselfe, that hee had of his owne accord, undertaken so austere a life, & so sharpe a pilgrimage, he seemed (as a man wise only according to flesh and blood) to hold it an indignity, & even allmost a madnesse, for Campian, one that he had knowen at home to live in good fashion, & to have a body of constitution, none of the strongest, voluntarily to abandon himselfe to so great misery; & withall tooke to his purse & was about to relieve him till Campian, laying his hand upon him, sayd; Nay sir, there is no need of that.[168]

Campion explained he was following Christ's example, who had made himself poor for our sake; his contemporary was in tears by the time he left, and regaled all his Oxford friends with this story. The encounter tells us a great deal both about Campion's state of mind, his intentions in this 'pilgrimage', and of his reputation among other Oxford men.

When Dante addresses the pilgrims in Rome in chapter XL of *La Vita Nuova*, he distinguishes three kinds of pilgrims: *peregrini* (pilgrims, in the strict sense) are those who go 'to the house of St James', in Galicia; pilgrims who return from Palestine are *palmieri* (palmers), while pilgrims to Rome are called *romei* (romeos).[169] Campion decision to become a *romeo* was a momentous turning point in his life. Why did Campion leave the English mission at Douai after only 18 months, and go on foot and in poverty to Rome? Bombino follows Persons in explaining Campion's pilgrimage as an attempt to expiate the guilt that Campion had from receiving the diaconate at Cheyney's hands, which he now saw as 'the character of the beast'.[170] Their interpretation has to be conjectural because Campion 'never made known anything that hapned' on this long walk; and Persons is the last person to whom Campion could have expressed his concern about the involvement of Allen and Sander in political activity. Campion's solitary pilgrimage suggests a need to find a path other than Catholic political 'meddling'.

Sander had ridden from Louvain to Rome exactly one year earlier, expecting a cardinal's hat, and after the death of Pius V died, stayed in Rome to work in the office of the Secretary of State, Tolomeo Galli, Cardinal of Como, who 'did all in matters of state'.[171] So Sander was with the Cardinal of Como, planning political and military responses to the English tyrant, while Campion spent two months there 'in visiting those holy churches & memories of the blessed Apostles and

---

[168] Bombino, *Vita et Martyrium*, pp. 40–41; Bodl. MS Tanner 329, fols 13v–14r.

[169] Dante Alighieri, *La Vita Nuova* (Turin and Rome: Roux and Viarengo, 1902), pp. 158–60; *Tutte le opere* (Rome: Newton Compton, 1997), pp. 712–13; I thank Prof. Petr Osolsobě for alerting me to this passage.

[170] ABSI Collectanea P. I, fol. 94a; Bombino, *Vita et Martyrium*, p. 38; Bodl. MS Tanner 329, fol. 12v–13r.

[171] CRS 2, *Miscellanea II*, ed. J.H. Pollen, S.J. (London: Catholic Record Society, 1906), Persons, 'Domesticall Difficulties', p. 64; Veech, *Sanders*, p. 217.

infinit other martyrs & saints'.[172] Their actions reflect two radically different views of Rome, and of the church.

The Jubilee of 1575 was close at hand and pilgrimage was in the air, certainly in the consciousness of three former members of St John's College, who were all at Douai in early 1573. The papal bull 'which denounced to the Christian world the last Jubilie' was found on Campion's *contubernalis*, Cuthbert Mayne, in 1577; because it was a bull (though not the hated *Regnans in excelsis*) he was condemned for high treason.[173] It was probably in year of the Jubilee when his closest friend, Gregory Martin, wrote *A Treatise of Christian Peregrination*.[174] Martin follows Dante in focusing on Jerusalem, Rome and Compostella, and defends the practice of pilgrimage to Rome 'to visit the bodies of the Apostles lying there'.[175]

There was a recognized pilgrimage route to Rome, the *Via Francigena*.[176] At a steady 20 to 25 miles a day, with extra days for stopping longer at holy shrines, this would have taken about 40 days; Campion reached Rome by Easter Sunday, 22 March 1573.[177] A pilgrim to Rome traditionally visited the seven Constantinian basilicas. Campion treated this first month as a time for serious pilgrimage and prayer 'to begge of God that answer which he well remembers he was promisd'.[178]

Campion declared at his trial that, 'at my fyrst arryvall into Rome (which is now about tenne yeares paste) it was my happe to have accesse' to Alfonso Gesualdi, Cardinal of St Cecilia, 'who having some lyking of me, would have beene the meanes to preferre me to anie place of service, wherunto I should have

---

[172]   ABSI Collectanea, P. I, fol. 95a.

[173]   William Allen, *A true, sincere and modest Defence of English Catholiques* (Rouen: George Flinton, 1584), STC 373, ARCR II. 14, p. 2. See Richard Challoner, *Memoirs of Missionary Priests*, ed. J.H. Pollen, S.J. (London: Burns Oates and Washbourne, 1924), pp. 1–6 (p. 3), and Sacred Congregation of Rites, *Cause of the Canonization of Blessed Martyrs John Houghton, Robert Lawrence, Augustine Webster, Richard Reynolds, John Stone, Cuthbert Mayne, John Paine, Edmund Campion, Alexander Briant, Ralph Sherwin and Luke Kirby* (Rome: Vatican Polyglot Press, 1968), p. 146: the indictment for 'bringinge of the Bull'.

[174]   Gregory Martin, *A Treatise of Christian Peregrination. Wherunto is adjoined certen epistles* (Paris: R. Verstegan, 1583), STC 17507. The treatise was published posthumously in 1583, but the colophon of one of the letters bears the date 1575, and it seems likely that Martin wrote the treatise for the Holy Year.

[175]   Martin, *Christian Peregrination*, sig. A6r.

[176]   Babette Gallard, *Via Francigena: Canterbury to Rome* (France: EURL Pilgrimage Productions, 2013). This walker's guide is based on the 79 *submansiones* where Archbishop Sigeric the Serious stayed on his way from Rome to Canterbury in 990, still extant in BL Cotton MS Tiberius B.V., fols 23v–24r.

[177]   Simpson is unusually wide of the mark here; he says that Campion arrived 'in the autumn of 1572' (p. 73). Bombino, it is true, says he arrived in Rome in 1572 (o.s.), but 22 March would be 1573 (n.s.).

[178]   Bombino, *Vita et Martyrium*, p. 42; Bodl. MS Tanner 329, fol. 14v.

most fanncye'.[179] As he declared at his trial, Campion politely declined the offer, telling Gesualdi he had decided 'to vow and to be professed' in the Society of Jesus:

> being demanded further what opinion I had conceyved of the Bull, I sayd it procured much severytye in England and the heavye hand of her majestie agaynste the Catholikes, wherunto the Cardinall replied, that he doubted not but it should bee mittigated in such sorte as the catholykes should acknowledge her highness and their Queene without daunger of excommunicatione.[180]

As he insisted, his 'pryvitye enforceth not my consenting, nay rather it proved my disagreement' with the bull.[181] Campion consistently maintained this position till the end of his life. The ambiguous 'mitigation' did not come till 14 April 1580, when Sander was still fighting under a papal banner; amidst the dust and noise of war, Campion's clear-sighted precision was inaudible and invisible.[182]

In Rome, Campion taking full advantage of the 'sacraments of penance and Eucharist, dayly prayer and chiefely the visiting of most holy churches', received the answer he had been promised: he applied to join the Society of Jesus, which already had missions in Bavaria, Austria, Italy, Spain, India, Japan and Brazil, but none in England.[183] Campion's Roman Easter coincided with a Jesuit general congregation, which was taking place to elect a new general, because St Francis Borgia had died on 1 October 1572.[184] The choice of the provincials fell on Everard Mercurian, on 23 April 1573. A few days later Campion became the first postulant for the new General. There was some competition for the eminent scholar among the 47 provincials present at this meeting.[185] The congregation ended in the middle of June 1573, and Campion 'was by divine providence designed to the province of Austria', of which Bohemia then formed a part, and left with the provincial, Lorenzo Maggio, for Vienna.[186]

During the month or so that followed this momentous step, Campion received help from his old tutor, John Bavand, who was in Rome. In his letter to Bavand (in late 1577), Campion refers eight times to the spiritual death he now embraced, and to England as Egypt, a place of exile:

---

[179] BL MS Harley 6265, fol. 16v. Reading 'my fyrst arryvall' to mean 'as soon as I arrived', Simpson, p. 74, dismisses the accounts of Campion's soul-searching in Rome as 'great exaggerations, if not pure fancies'.

[180] BL MS Harley 6265, fol. 16v.

[181] BL MS Harley 6265, fol. 17r.

[182] See Chapter 5.

[183] Bombino, *Vita et Martyrium*, p. 42; Bodl. MS Tanner 329, fol. 14v. By 1580, there were already 21 Jesuit provinces, 144 colleges and 5,000 Jesuits, John O'Malley, S.J., *Saints or Devils Incarnate? Studies in Jesuit History* (Leiden: Brill, 2013), p. 68.

[184] ABSI Collectanea P. I, fol. 95a.

[185] Schmidl, *Historiae*, I. 335.

[186] Bombino, *Vita et Martyrium*, p. 43; Bodl. MS Tanner 329, fols 14v–15r.

When I was in Rome, did you not altogether spend yourself on me? Did you not give me introductions, help and money? And that to one who, as you knew, not only would never repay you, but who was on the point of leaving the world, and so to speak, of death. One of the greatest works of mercy is to bury the dead, for they help those towards whom neither flesh, blood, nor goods, nor hope, nor favour, nor any thought of earthly convenience attracts them. You were magnificent to me when I was going to enter the sepulchral rest of religion. Add one further kindness, my dear father; pray for me, that in this seclusion, far from the noise of all vanity, I may be buried really and meritoriously. For it was the Apostle's declaration, 'You are dead, and your life is hidden with Christ in God'. I remember how, on the eve of your leaving England, you bade me farewell with the words, 'I go to die'. For you had determined to let death overtake you anywhere rather than in Egypt. We must seek to die once for all, and happily, but we must seek it also daily and faithfully. But whither have I wandered?[187]

Campion had been in Rome for only three months, but this pilgrimage had transformed his life. He had given himself in obedience to his superiors, and was 'comforted to think that now he was no more his own man, nor to dispose of himself or of his own affaires, but in the hands of others who by Gods holy assistance & blessed providence would dispose of him far better every way to Gods glory & his own salvation than he could of himself'.[188] His talents were to flourish in Prague as never before, and he can hardly have imagined that 'the hands of others' would send him not to India but, like Jonah, back to the country he had so decisively left, in Persons's words, 'for good and all'.[189]

[187]   ABSI Anglia I/6, fols 18r–19r; Simpson, pp. 121–3.
[188]   ABSI Collectanea, P. I, fol. 95b.
[189]   ABSI Collectanea, P. I, fol. 87a.

Chapter 4
Et in Arcadia Ego

'Colleges', Ignatius had replied when Peter Canisius, appointed to the new province of Upper Germany, Bohemia and Austria, had asked how the society might best help Germany.[1] It was a shrewd perception of the way to win back an area where Jan Hus and Martin Luther had made such headway.[2] The letters of Peter Canisius reveal a man of enormous energy and determination; at the Emperor's request, he founded a college in Vienna in 1552, and colleges in both Prague and Ingolstadt in 1556.[3] By 1580, there were 26 Jesuit colleges from Munich to Innsbruck and Olomouc with over 1,000 Jesuits in the three provinces. In 1573, Campion, aged 33, joined one of the most dynamic educational missions in history.

When he arrived in Vienna, Campion was sent to Prague with a Spanish Jesuit, Fr James Avellianedo, who had been appointed confessor to the devout Empress, Maria Augusta.[4] Campion entered the Society in Prague, the capital of Bohemia, on 26 August 1573.[5] In the fifth section of the 'Examen' on his education, (after dealing with his time in Oxford) he replied :

> Then I spent nearly two years at Douai studying Scholastic Theology. At Oxford I was promoted to Master of Arts, and at Douai to the Baccalaureate in Theology. I have a memory that is, in every way, extremely good, an intellect that is also sufficiently perceptive, and a mind that is naturally inclined to study. I have the necessary strength required for these and all the other duties of the Society.[6]

After only two months, on 10 October 1573, Campion left Prague with the Master of Novices, Giovanni Paolo Campani, and his Socius, John Vivarius,

---

[1]   John W. O'Malley, S.J., *The First Jesuits* (Cambridge, MA: Harvard University Press, 1993), p. 207, and O'Malley, *Saints or Devils Incarnate? Studies in Jesuit History* (Leiden: Brill, 2013), pp. 58–68, 199–215.

[2]   J. Brodrick, S.J., *Saint Peter Canisius, S.J., 1521–1597* (Baltimore, MD: Carroll, 1950), pp. 254–5, gives a good summary of the way Bohemia yielded to the influence of Wycliffe and Hus.

[3]   Staatsbibliothek Munchen, MS. Cod. Lat 2202, contains copies of many of these letters. For the foundation of Ingolstadt, see Brodrick, *Canisius*, pp. 262–72.

[4]   Howard Louthan, *The Quest for Compromise: Peacemakers in Counter-Reformation Vienna* (Cambridge: University Press, 1997), p. 131.

[5]   Joannes Schmidl, *Historiae Societatis Iesu Provinciae Bohemiae*, 2 vols (Prague: Charles University Press, 1747), I. 336.

[6]   ARSI Anglia 38/1, fol. 31v, a copy of the original 'Examen', now lost, which differs from Schmidl, *Historiae*, I. 339, the customary source.

to establish a new novitiate in Brno. They were given a house on the Petrov, a high promontory that looks over the plains towards Hungary on one side, and Austria on the other, at the south-west corner of the city, by Jan Grodesky, the Bishop of Olomouc, then the capital of Moravia.[7] The previous bishop, Vilém Prusinovsky, had invited the Jesuits to Olomouc in 1566, and established a college and seminary.[8] The 17 novices were settled in the Bishop's House, slightly below the top of the hill. Just below that is the site of an ancient vegetable market. The Petrov is a beautiful breezy spot, now occupied by the diocesan buildings of the Bishop of Brno.

The reasons for this move were financial, but this *felix culpa* (fortunate fault) provided Campion began with one of the happiest years in his life. We know this from the first letter he wrote from Prague to his fellow-novices still at Brno, on 26 February 1575: it is one of the most exuberant letters he ever wrote.[9] One of the sources of vitality at Brno was the ethnic diversity of the 17 novices. There was John, from Castum, Charles Benedict Tinensis, the Bohemian, Stephen Drnoczky, the Slav, Stephen Nagius, the Hungarian, Sallitius, Finnit and George Rous from Spiro, Tobias, the Bohemian and Caspar from Puschmann.[10] The nostalgia exhibited in this letter is an indication of how much this untroubled time in the novitiate meant to Campion, to whom affectionate friendship and camaraderie came easily. He was at home in a collegiate setting, and the mundane tasks here must have been a welcome contrast to the embattled religious situation in Oxford:

> How much I love you in the heart of Jesus Christ, my dearest brothers, you may gather from the fact that in the middle of my daily duties, which hardly leave me time to draw breath, I decided I must steal some time for myself so that I could write to you. What else was I to do as soon when I heard that a reliable courrier was going to Brno? How could I not be inspired by the memory of that house in which so many souls have been set on fire, where there is fire in the spirit, fire in the body, fire in words, the fire which God came to send to the earth so that it should always burn. I remember its precious walls, which once embraced both you and me, its calefactory where we had so many blessed conversations, its beautiful kitchen where the dearest John and Charles, the two Stephens, Sallitius and Finnit and George, Tobias, and Caspar compete in unfeigned charity and humility over the pots and pans. How often do I see in my mind's eye one of you coming laden from the farm, another coming from the vegetable market with the left-overs, another one bravely and enthusiastically sweating under some other

---

[7]   Schmidl, *Historiae*, I. 347.

[8]   R.J.W. Evans, *Rudolf II and His World: A Study in Intellectual History 1576–1612* (Oxford: Clarendon Press, 1973), p. 112.

[9]   Boluslav Balbin, S.J., *Miscellanea Historica Regni Bohemiae Decadisi Liber IV Hagiographicus* (Prague: G. Czernoch, 1682), is the first to print these two letters, pp. 190–94, the second from 20 February 1577, later copied, annotated with helpful notes on the nationalities of the novices by Schmidl, *Historiae*, I. pp. 369–74, and translated by Simpson, pp. 97–101.

[10]   Schmidl, *Historiae*, I. 370.

task. Believe me, my dearest brothers, the angels rejoice to see your labours, brooms, spades and burdens and, because of them, ask more from God for you than if you carried instead sceptres, gems and gold in your bundles ... I have been about one year in religion and thirty five in the world; I wish it were the other way round, and that I had had one year in the world and thirty five in religion, that I had never known any father except the Fathers of the Society; no brothers except you and my other brethren; no work except the sweet task of obedience, no knowledge except that of Jesus crucified ...

I have been allowed this time to write to you: I have just heard the first bell for classes. I am called away and tomorrow is the feast [of St Matthew] when I shall be even busier and will have no time to write any more ... Please thank my dearest brother Cantensis, whose letter gave me the greatest possible pleasure, and I thank God for giving him such a good a mind at his age. I received from him the pictures, the Agnus Dei tablets, and the relics of our holy father Ignatius: a great treasure for which I return great thanks. I greet you all fondly in Christ Jesus from my soul ... Prague, 26 February 1575.[11]

The area immediately beneath Petrov then consisted of fields and orchards, and many shops built into the side of the hill. Just below the cobbled streets, which now surround the cathedral of St Peter and Paul, is a medieval vaulted cellar, belonging to the canons. Outside is an enclosed garden with fruit trees and spectacular blossoms in the spring. It was in the garden of the bishop's house that Campion is reputed to have had a vision of Our Lady, prophesying his death and martyrdom. He is said to have seen the Blessed Virgin in the form portrayed in a painting in Rome, copies of which had been commissioned by St Francis Borgia, who had given one to Campani.[12]

Campion performed the Spiritual Exercises under the direction of Campani, and formed a profound bond with his confessor broken only by death. He devoted one month to service of the sick, another to begging alms, another to menial tasks about the house, and the last to catechesis. The six 'experiments' must all have been something of a relief; for the first time in his life, he was in a place free of violent religious strife, and not trying to decide between fraught alternatives. One would not know from Campion's letters to Brno that after Bishop Grodesky's death, early in 1574, a lawsuit developed between the Canons of the Petrov and the Bishop of Olomouc over the land and property given to the Jesuits.[13] On his solitary pilgrimage to Rome, it seems, Campion had gradually emancipated himself from all politics; freedom of spirit was his pilgrim's badge.

---

[11]   Balbin, *Miscellanea*, pp. 190–92; Schmidl, *Historiae*, I. 369–70 (my translation); Simpson, pp. 97–9.

[12]   Schmidl, *Historiae*, I. 361–2. Neither Persons nor Bombino mentions this hagiographic incident; Schmidl insists on the authenticity of a tradition still honoured, in his time, in Brno.

[13]   Schmidl, *Historiae*, I. 353–7.

On 7 September 1574, his novice-master was appointed Rector of the house at Prague.[14] So, although Campion had completed only the first year of his novitiate (*altero Tyrocinii anno nondum completo*) at the beginning of October, Campani took Campion with him to teach rhetoric in the Clementinum, and travelled to Prague, with two other novices, in the carriage of the Chancellor, Vratislav Pernštein.[15] Pernštein had stepped in to help the Jesuits after the sudden death of their patron, Bishop Grodesky, and he acted as their protector both in Brno and in Prague.[16] The journey to Prague would have taken about eight days; if they had travelled by the road that winds peacefully along the river Sladka, they may have taken in the great castle at Pernštein on a beautiful autumnal journey.

Campion now began the most demanding, and the most glamorous, phase of his life: he arrived in Prague with the head of one of the largest noble families of Bohemia, frequently preached to the Emperor and court, and left in the carriage of Prince Ferdinand of Bavaria. At the same time, he was teaching, writing plays, giving a weekly sermon in Latin, running a sodality and speaking on numerous festive or funereal occasions, as well as being occupied in a hundred mundane tasks such as waking the house. As he himself was to say, with *sprezzatura*, to Dr Allen, 'I was not idle nor unemployed'.[17] The letter already quoted reveals how quickly tasks were loaded on him, a fact mentioned by both Persons and Bombino, and confirmed by three recently discovered manuscripts of his students' lecture notes and nearly eighty of his sermons.[18] Studies in Prague solemnly commenced on 18 October 1574. Campion was made professor of Rhetoric and opened the school with 'a glorious panegyric' (*oratione panegyrica illustri*), which was still extant when Schmidl was writing, but has now vanished.[19]

When the Archduke, Ferdinand II, of the Tyrol (as he is usually styled), was appointed regent of the Bohemian lands in 1547, he had made his seat at Prague Castle, refounded the archbishopric of Prague in 1561, selected the moderate Antonio Brus of Mohelnice for the seat, which had been vacant for 150 years, and

---

[14]   Schmidl, *Historiae*, I. 361.

[15]   Schmidl, *Historiae*, I. 361.

[16]   Simpson, p. 104.

[17]   ABSI, Collectanea, P. I, fol. 114b.

[18]   Dr Daniel Andersson located the two manuscripts in the Prague Castle Archive of the Metropolitan Chapter Library (APMC): M42, *Logic*, and M65, *Physics*, and described them in 'How to Teach Philosophy', *TLS* (8 March 2013), 14–15. I thank him for many long conversations, and Marek Suchý and Tomas Zubéč of APMC for allowing me to spend several days studying them. Dr Clarinda Calma located the *Concionale* in Książnica Cieszyńska, Biblioteka Leopolda Jana Szersznika, SZ MS DD.V.8, and generously invited me to examine the 439 leaves of this beautifully restored volume. It is clearly the manuscript seen by Schmidl, *Historiae*, I. 436: '*M.T. Ciceronis Partitiones annotata, cum aliis operibus, Pragense Archivum in thesauris habet*' (the title on the original spine). Schmidl follows this note with a reference to Campion teaching Aristotle's *Logic* and *Physics*.

[19]   Schmidl, *Historiae*, I. 362.

invited Peter Canisius to found a Jesuit academy in Prague in 1556.[20] Archbishop Brus, who became Campion's confessor and close friend, outlined his plan for the re-conversion of the country in a memorandum of 1563, aimed at reconciliation with Old-Utraquist priests.[21] The Archduke, the Archbishop and the Jesuits put their faith in the noble families: Rožmberk, Pernštein, Hradec, Dietrichstein, Lobkovic. As Campion wrote to John Bavand, his old tutor:

> Do you want to know about Bohemia? συμμιξις και κοινωνια αιρησιων, a hotch-potch and fellowship of heresies. While all the nobles are Catholics, the lower orders are a mixture, so it is a pleasant and varied harvest. For my part, I labour in it with more pleasure, since an Englishman, Wycliffe, infected the people.[22]

Rudolf II had spent eight years at the Spanish court of his uncle Philip II, from 1563 to 1571, and 'maintained his Spanish manners and fashion to the end of his days'.[23] He placed great trust in advisers with close Spanish connections; the most important was Adam Dietrichstein, who as Maximilian's ambassador in Madrid, had looked after the young Rudolf.[24] He was married to Marguerite, daughter of the Maria de Cardona, at whose funeral Campion spoke in 1577; their daughter, Polyxena, married Vilém Rožmberk in 1587.

Pernštein, who died in 1582, was Chancellor throughout Campion's time in Prague, had known the Emperor Maximilian II as early as 1545, and had also been in Spain in 1547–50, where he married Maria Henriquez de Lara.[25] These noble families were all convinced Catholics and supporters of the Jesuits, and this *facción española* was a 'potent political force'.[26] Nevertheless, Rožmberk, who had carried the crown at Rudolf's coronation as King of Bohemia in 1575, was a moderate, who left others to exercise their religion in freedom.[27] As well as the strong influence of the Spanish court, there were powerful Italian influences. When the 21-year-old Vratislav Pernštein and Vilém Rožmberk returned from Italy (where they had gone to meet Maximilian II and Maria Augusta), they rebuilt their chateaux in the Italian style.

When Maximilian II suddenly died at Regensburg on 12 October 1576, Rudolf succeeded to an Empire that stretched 600 miles from the city of Trent in the south,

---

[20]   Evans, *Rudolf II*, p. 34, citing Archivum Prazkeho Hradu (APH) UK MS I A I ('Historia Collegii S.J. Pragensis ad S. Clementinum ann. 1555–1610'); Brodrick, *Canisius*, pp. 254–62.

[21]   Evans, *Rudolf II*, p. 35.

[22]   ABSI Anglia I/6, fol. 18r–v; trans. Simpson, pp. 121–3.

[23]   Eliška Fučikova, 'Prague Castle under Rudolf II, His Predecessors and Successors, 1530–1648', in *Rudolf II and Prague*, ed. Eliška Fučikova et al. (Prague, London, Milan: Thames and Hudson, 1997), pp. 2–71 (pp. 13–14).

[24]   Evans, *Rudolf II*, p. 66.

[25]   Evans, *Rudolf II*, p. 66.

[26]   Louthan, *Quest for Compromise*, p. 157.

[27]   Evans, *Rudolf II*, p. 66.

to the university town of Breslau in the north. The Emperor had seniority over all the other monarchs of the Continent, and his lands were 'linked by a nexus of contacts at many social and political levels with all the significant countries of the day'.[28] Maria Augusta, the Dowager Empress, was still a powerful figure during Campion's time in Prague, and the Clementinum diaries record that it was she who requested a second performance of his play *Ambrosiana*.[29]

The decision of the new Emperor, Rudolf II, to make Prague the capital of the Empire meant that from 1577, he was bringing artists, architects, designers and craftsmen to Prague. The unusual religious freedom promoted by his father ensured that the city was a perfect place for the Jesuits to promote their educational and missionary agenda. When Campion came to Prague, both the court and the city had reached a level of religious toleration that was very different from the murderous conflicts in France and England. The Emperor Ferdinand, who died in 1564, had begun the search for an irenic solution to religious difference, but it was his son, Maximilian, who organized 'one of the first ecumenical confessions'.[30] Maximilian II came to Prague to attend discussions of Lutherans and Czech brethren to see if a united position could be agreed by the Evangelical church; the discussions in Prague Castle lasted from March to May 1575, and culminated in the *Confessio Bohemica*, presented to Maximilian on 18 May 1575 and signed the following day.[31] Designed to bring peace between the Utraquists (who made up three-quarters of the population) and the Bohemian Brethren *(Unitas Fratrum)*, the *Confessio* effectively promoted an equilibrium between all the various groups, including Lutherans, Calvinists, Utraquists, neo-Utraquists and Catholics.[32]

Soon after the *Confessio* was signed, the 24-year-old Rudolf II was crowned King of Bohemia on 22 September 1575, a dazzling spectacle that Campion must have witnessed.[33] Next to the Emperor was the Burgrave, Vilém Rožmberk, supported by Chancellor Pernštein. Rudolf inherited his father's irenic attitude, as his father's physician, Johannes Crato, argued in his funeral oration.[34] Born in 1519, Crato became personal physician to Ferdinand I in 1556, and close counsellor and religious adviser to Maximilian. For 12 years Maximilian kept Crato by his side,

---

[28]   Evans, *Rudolf II*, p. 1.

[29]   Strahov MS DC.III.16, fol. 99r. The diaries also note that, shortly afterwards, the Bishop of Ross dined in the refectory; there is no indication that Campion had any 'conference' with him. See Chapter 10.

[30]   Louthan, *Quest for Compromise*, p. 101.

[31]   Ivana Čornejova, 'The Religious Situation in Rudolfine Prague', in *Rudolf II and Prague: The Imperial Court and Residential City as the Cultural and Spiritual Heart of Central Europe*, ed. Eliška Fučikova, et al. (Prague, London, Milan: Thames and Hudson, 1997), pp. 310–22 (p. 315).

[32]   Louthan, *Quest for Compromise*, p. 101.

[33]   Evans, *Rudolf II*, pp. 79–80.

[34]   Louthan, *Quest for Compromise*, p. 136, citing Johannes Crato, *Oratio Funebris de Divo Maximiliano Imperatore Caesare Augusto II* (Frankfurt: A. Wechel, 1577), sig. B2v.

and appointed him to the Privy Council. Crato retired to his home in Breslau on the death of Maximilian, but, within a year, he was summoned back to deal with a crisis in Rudolf's health, which lasted from 1578 to 1580, Campion's most productive period in Prague.[35] Crato was the major healing influence, and he composed a funeral address for Maximilian (which was published but not delivered) where he related that Maximilian had said to the Bishop of Olomouc, 'No sin is more serious than the desire to tyrannize in matters of conscience'.[36] Another key figure in this circle of moderates was Andreas Dudith; born in Hungary in 1533, he had studied in Breslau, and worked with Antonio Brus at the Council of Trent; both were conciliatory spokesmen for Ferdinand.[37] He too retired to Breslau, 'lived there quietly, a close friend of Crato and member of his circle', and died there in 1589.[38] He had contacts with Hubert Languet, Sir Philip Sidney and the astronomer, Tadeáš Hájek, and wrote on the comet of 1577 in a treatise published in 1579.[39]

Rudolf's first public act was the magnificent funeral of his father, which began in Vienna in November 1576, and continued to January 1577, when the bier was carried by ship along the Danube to Linz and then taken overland to St Vitus Cathedral in Prague, where there were elaborate theatrical events.[40] In Prague, the fact that 'religious conflicts remained restricted to verbal and written polemics' meant that Campion's skills as orator, preacher, poet and playwright found their perfect milieu.[41] It is no wonder that he laboured at this harvest with such pleasure, or that most of his extant works were, as Boluslav Balbin, the historian of the Bohemian province, says, 'conceived and written beneath a Prague sky' (*sub Coelo Pragensi concepta primum, & scripta fuisse*).[42] If Rudolf's court had absorbed artistic and literary influences from Spain and Italy, the city itself was unusually bookish; in the Old Town, 'ten per cent of the libraries had more than a hundred volumes'.[43] Since books were usually transported in sheets and bound locally, binding gives one a better guide to the scale of reading: the number of bookbinders in Prague rose from 11 in 1550, to over 100 in 1620.[44] Demand was clearly stimulated by religious debate; Luther, Erasmus and Melanchthon were all popular, and print included broadsheets that could be posted on the doors of

---

[35] Louthan, *Quest for Compromise*, pp. 92–3; Evans, *Rudolf II*, p. 99.

[36] Louthan, *Quest for Compromise*, p. 134.

[37] Evans, *Rudolf II*, p. 110.

[38] Evans, *Rudolf II*, p. 106.

[39] Evans, *Rudolf II*, p. 107.

[40] Louthan, *Quest for Compromise*, p. 141; Evans, *Rudolf II*, pp. 60–61.

[41] Jiri Pešek, 'Prague between 1550 and 1650' in *Rudolf II and Prague*, pp. 252–69 (p. 258).

[42] Balbin, *Miscellanea*, p. 195.

[43] Vaclav Ledvinka and Jiri Pešek, 'The Public and Private Lives of Prague's Burghers', in *Rudolf II and Prague*, pp. 287–301 (p. 297).

[44] Radim Vondraček, 'Bookbinding: Style and Ornament', in *Rudolf II and Prague*, pp. 340–44 (p. 340).

an inn, or leaflets to be distributed.[45] This is the sort of print world reflected in the publication, by popular demand, of Campion's sermon on Maria Cardona in 1577:

> Howbeit two monuments of his witte were above the rest most highly commended, the one a tragedie, under the title of Ambrosiana: the other a funeral oration, whereby in Latine, before a most honourable assembly, he commended Mary Requesene, a principall woman, governesse of the chamber to Mary the Emperesse. The first being beheld with mighty applause of the whole theater, & this later heard with great approbation, that long the coppy thereof could not be withheld from coming abroad, so earnest was it sued for by people of all sorts. And when it was printed (a thing rarely seene) it pleased no lesse the eyes of the Readers, then it had before the eares of the hearers.[46]

Persons mentions this as the only speech of Campion's he has seen in print, but all complete copies had disappeared by the time Robert Turner's *Posthuma* were published in 1602, and the earliest surviving printed copy of the whole text is in the Plantin Moretus edition of 1631; the text appears to be based on the manuscript of Campion's sermons, the *Concionale* that was still in the Rector's library at Prague in 1747, and is now in Cieszyn.[47]

Campion's funeral oration for Maria Cardona, provides a glimpse of his life at court, and shows his ability to speak personally to his audience. Maria Cardona's husband, Antonio, was Viceroy of Sardinia, but she herself, as Campion argues, had an even grander lineage, since her father, Don Luis de Requesens, was the conciliatory governor of the Spanish Netherlands from 1573 to 1576.[48]

> She herself was the scion of a most noble father, grandparents, ancestors, a family which had always been highly renowned in the kingdom of Catalonia, and had built and endowed a monastery from its beginnings. She admired and imitated the simplicity of virgins and the humility of the poor.[49]

Later, Campion highlights how she had looked after Rudolf II '*a teneris*' (from his youth), and he, as an '*alumnus*' (pupil), had drunk the rain-drops of her goodness and piety. He praises both her father, Requesens, and Adam Dietrichstein:

---

[45] Mirjam Bohatcova, 'Book-Printing and Other Forms of Publishing in Prague', in *Rudolf II and Prague*, pp. 332–9 (p. 333).

[46] Bombino, *Vita et Martyrium*, pp. 59–60; Bodl. MS Tanner 329, fol. 16r.

[47] SZ MS DD.V.8, fols 405v–407v; the text appears to be identical to that in Plantin. Compare the fragment in the first printed edition, Edmund Campion, [bd. w. Robert Turner, *Posthuma*] *Orationes, Epistolae Tractatus de imitatione Rhetorica a Roberto Turnero Campiani discipulo collecta* (Ingolstadt: A. Angermarius, 1602), ARCR I. 1263, p. 45: '*Solum hoc fragmentum extabat*'. In this edition the title page, signatures and pagination are separate.

[48] Louthan, *Quest for Compromise*, p. 143.

[49] Campion, *Opuscula*, p. 301.

Worthy of the noble governor of Belgium, on whose counsel and bravery the wellbeing of many peoples depended; worthy of Adam Dietrichstein, her son-in-law, in whose authority, loyalty, wisdom, once two Emperors, and today the Emperor Rudolf, wished to invest so much of their power, as everyone knows.[50]

A court dominated by intelligent, cultivated and bookish nobles, with strong Spanish and Italian cultural influences, in a city where religious controversy was conducted through debate and processional display, must have been Arcadia to Campion, coming from a country violently riven by bitterly contested religious positions.

When Campion arrived in Prague in 1574, the Jesuit college had become part of the life of the court and the city, contributing to public processions, displays of learning and dramatic interludes. As Rudolf started to move his court to Prague Castle in 1577, Campion found himself in one of the most artistic and ecumenically religious cities in Europe. The Jesuit college, the Clementinum, had been opened in 6 July 1556 with a public declamation in Hebrew, and rapidly attracted the notice of all the noble families of Prague. The Jesuits were allocated a place in the dilapidated Dominican monastery of St Clement in the Old Town near the Moldava river.[51] There they found themselves in a strong position to compete with the ancient Charles University, which was in a period of decline after the departure of large numbers of Germans had led to a near-collapse in the faculty of theology.[52] By 1559, Henrik Blyssem, an outstanding theologian from Cologne, was teaching theology and Hebrew, the Bishop of Olomouc had offered a sum of money to set up a school of music so that they could sing in the Cathedral of S. Vitus, and 'the youth, both in numbers and nobility, exceeded all previous years'.[53]

On 15 March 1562, Ferdinand granted the college a charter for a lower school (grammar school) and an upper school (a university with faculties of philosophy, theology and the arts or *facultas linguarum*); Maximilian II conferred more privileges upon them in 1567, and Rudolf II on 1 April 1581.[54] Canisius had four new classrooms built to take the first intake of 200 pupils in 1562.[55] By 1573, the college was attracting an annual intake of about 50, including non-Catholics.[56] The Jesuits, supported by leading Catholic noble families, certainly used every sort of public event to advertise their learning and religious devotion.[57] The importance of

---

[50]   Campion, *Opuscula*, pp. 308–9.

[51]   Brodrick, *Canisius*, pp. 258–62.

[52]   Ivana Čornejova, 'Education in Rudolfine Prague', in *Rudolf II and Prague*, pp. 323–31 (p. 324); see Brodrick, *Canisius*, p. 254, who explains the rise of nationalism in Charles University.

[53]   Schmidl, *Historiae*, I. 134.

[54]   Čornejova, 'Education in Rudolfine Prague', p. 324.

[55]   Brodrick, *Canisius*, p. 262.

[56]   Čornejova, 'Education in Rudolfine Prague', p. 325, bases this on the fact that the overall number between 1573 and 1617 was 1,836; see Brodrick, *Canisius*, p. 828, for Canisius's policy: 'They should be led gently and gradually'.

[57]   Čornejova, 'Education in Rudolfine Prague', p. 326.

the Jesuit college to the Emperor, the Catholic nobility and the burghers of Prague, meant that, from the start, its academic life was involved in the life of the city, and the competition had the effect of giving new life to the Utraquist Charles Academy.[58] While Campion was in Prague, a unique combination of circumstances created an atmosphere of religious tolerance and academic competition that contributed to a literary, artistic and theatrical flowering.

At the Clementinum, Campion began to combine the scholarly interests familiar to him from his life in Oxford with a pastoral impulse that seems to have given full expression to his natural affections. Being a priest and a scholar seems, for him, to have been the perfect combination:

> Well known it is that Campian, from the very cradle (as I may say) of his Religious life, was evermore by the authority of his superiours imployd in matters of learning, appertayning to the good of soules.[59]

As well as waking 'in the morning the rest of the house', he was 'withall injoyned to teach Rhetoricke and to preach in Latin to the people'.[60] He was also made *Praefectus morum*, and put in charge of 'the Sodality of the Salutation of the most Blessed Virgin', which included members from the court and the city.[61] His discourse to this sodality, *De tutela B.V. Mariae* (On the protection of the Blessed Virgin Maria) is the first discourse in the Cieszyn manuscript, immediately following his 12 lines of *Litaniae B. Virginis* (Litanies of the Blessed Virgin), as it is in the *Orationes* collected by Robert Turner.[62] It is clear from these that his devotion to the Blessed Virgin was an important part of his spiritual life, and he recommends the 'most distinguished hearers' (*praestantissimi auditores*) of the Sodality, which obviously included outsiders, to 'run to her' in every sort of difficulty.[63]

Bombino makes it clear that Campion's willingness 'to performe all' meant that quickly he was stretched to the limit.[64]

> His usuall saying to his superiours was (when, overburdened before, they heaped upon him more & more businesse & even almost overwhelmed him) no other then this. Father, doe you, even out of your owne opinion, thinke me any way able to performe all this. And if he sayd he did, without any more dispute, he accepted it.[65]

---

[58]   Čornejova, 'Education in Rudolfine Prague', p. 325.

[59]   Bombino, *Vita et Martyrium*, p. 44; Bodl. MS Tanner 329, fol. 15r.

[60]   Bombino, *Vita et Martyrium*, p. 45; Bodl. MS Tanner 329, fol. 15v.

[61]   Bombino, *Vita et Martyrium*, p. 45; Bodl. MS Tanner 329, fol. 15v.

[62]   *Litaniae*, SZ MS DD.V.8, fol. 392r–v; *De tutela B.V. Mariae*, fols 392v–396r; Campion, *Orationes* (1602), *De Tutela et Defensione B.V. Mariae*, pp. 1–11.

[63]   SZ MS DD.V.8, fol. 394v, and Campion, *Orationes* (1602), p. 7. See also 'fflower of roses, Angells joy', in Arundel Harington MS, fol. 31v, which immediately precedes, 'Why doe I use my paper, ynke and pen' (see Chapter 12).

[64]   Bombino, *Vita et Martyrium*, p. 45; Bodl. MS Tanner 329, fol. 15v.

[65]   Bombino, *Vita et Martyrium*, p. 45; Bodl. MS Tanner 329, fol. 15v.

Recently discovered manuscripts in Prague and Cieszyn, containing his weekly sermons in Latin, and student notes on his lectures on Aristotle's *Logic* and *Physics*, all from late 1578 to early 1580, have provided documentary evidence of what this account suggests.[66] For the first four years, Campion was the professor of rhetoric.[67] His main task was to teach the young scholars how to write and speak in Latin, so Cicero was the model.[68] The pattern of teaching was still based on the principles laid down by Erasmus. In the lower school they were using the *De Copia Verborum* of Erasmus, but in 1559 the book was proscribed, all the copies taken in, and the money restored to the parents, because it seemed wrong that 'a man who had opened such a great window to heresy, should be so honoured in his book'.[69]

School always began in October (as it did when Campion started teaching Rhetoric in 1574), with very public, even civic ceremonies, so the school was from the start a significant part of the life in Prague. Campion delivered the speech for the start of the year, as he did in 1576, when he made the oration, a panegyric of St Wenceslas, the patron of Bohemia, whose feast it was (Figure 4.1).[70] The headings of two other speeches, *De Iuvene Academico Oratio R. P. Edmundi in promotione seu renovatione studiorum habita* (Speech of Reverend Father Edmund on the Young Scholar given at the start or renewal of the academic year) and *De foedere Virtutis et Scientiae Oratio P. Edmundi* (Speech of Father Edmund on the bond between Virtue and Knowledge) and the constant address to 'iuvenes' (the young) suggest these are contemporary copies, made while Campion was still alive, of speeches for the start of the academic year.[71] All sat on benches according to rank (*Nobilissimi in sublimi sedentes*), but the names of the most learned in each class were read out, saluted in verses and ordered to rise. Every Saturday there were public competitions between the classes,

---

[66] SZ MS DD.V.8, fols 3r–174v, contains records of nearly 80 sermons delivered from the First Sunday of Advent, 30 November 1578, to Quinquagesima, 14 February 1580; APMC M42 contains notes on Aristotle's *Logic*, from 15 December 1578 to 14 July 1579; APMC M65 contains notes on Aristotle's *Physics*, from 11 August 1579 to 9 February 1580; Fr Paul Neukirch took over the teaching the *Physics* on Tuesday, 23 February 1580. All three manuscripts confirm that Campion had left Prague after Monday 15 February, and before Monday, 22 February, 1580.

[67] Bombino, *Vita et Martyrium*, p. 44; Bodl. MS Tanner 329, fol. 15r.

[68] SZ MS DD.V.8 contains a long section entitled, *In M.T. Ciceronis Partitiones Annotata*, fols 342r–388v.

[69] Schmidl, *Historiae*, I. 135.

[70] SZ MS DD.V.8, fols 408r–414v.

[71] SS MS DD.V.8, fols 400r–405r and 417r–421r; the title would have included the surname and *Beati Martyris* if they had been later. Only the first was printed in Campion, *Orationes* (1602), pp. 29–44.

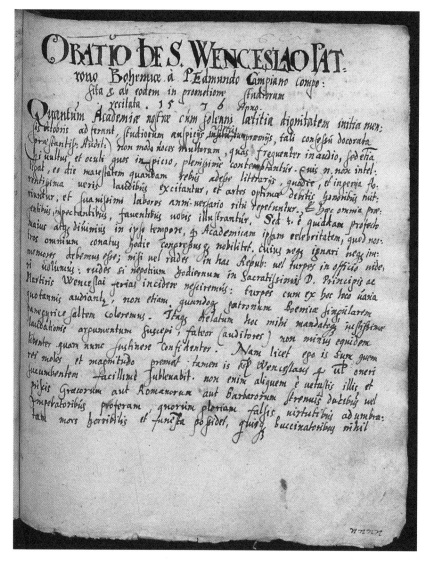

Figure 4.1   *Oratio De S. Wenceslao Patrono Bohemiae a P. Edmundo Campiano Composito et ab eodem ... recitata 1576*: SZ MS DD.V.8, fol. 408r. © Książnica Cieszyńska, Biblioteka Szersznika.

and these were popular public events.[72] In rhetoric, theses were put up each week, and there were debates on every kind of literature. All this 'ardour for learning' quickly spread and attracted other pupils.[73]

Prague was a multi-lingual city, so sermons every week were in German, Spanish, Italian, Bohemian and Latin; Campion was entrusted with the Latin sermon on Sundays and feast days. These sermons were obviously remarkable; Balbin relates that the nobility, the Archbishop, Papal Nuncio, Dowager Empress and the Emperor himself, were among his devoted audience, as confirmed by Sir Philip Sidney in 1577.[74] Language learning was central, and the catechism (*Summa doctrinæ Christianæ*) of Peter Canisius, the first book brought out by the Prague press, was published in Latin, Bohemian and German.[75] Daily 'variation' (*variatio*), the exercise that Erasmus helped to promulgate, was the means by which the art of rhetoric was learnt. The lecturer in rhetoric would expound a passage, perhaps from one of Cicero's speeches, elucidate his art and tricks of composition, and provide parallels from other authors. Then the boys would set about their own versions. There were two hours in the morning, and two hours in the afternoon, the second of which was devoted to Greek.

If one reads Campion's drafts for dramatic performances, or his eulogy of Maria Cardona, or the effect of his sermons on all who heard him, he was clearly busy. The situation in Bohemia was one where the Catholic minority had to win over the Protestant majority, but Campion's known associates all saw moderation as a way of winning over their opponents. His charm was a pleasure to them: 'he was always the same, whether speaking, teaching or writing'.[76] Persons adds to the preaching, funeral orations and lecturing the fact that Campion 'heard confessions, visited prisons & hospitals of sick men'.[77]

The Jesuits in Prague tapped into an existing tradition of dramatic performance. Archduke Ferdinand II, Governor of Bohemia between 1547 and 1567, enjoyed allegorical theatre performances in the Castle, in one of which the Archduke 'presented himself as Jupiter' and defeated huge paper giants, which went up in flames.[78] From the beginning the Jesuits had staged theatrical spectacles where

---

[72]   Staatsbibliothek Munchen, MS Cod. Lat. 1554, *Declamationes in Ducali Gymnasio Societatis Iesu Habitae, Monachii*, 1582, shows the range of speeches, *carmina* and *dialogi* given before princes and emperors, and gives one an idea of how the Jesuits won such public support.

[73]   '*Ardor discentium*', Schmidl, *Historiae*, I. 136.

[74]   Balbin, *Miscellanea*, p. 195; for Sidney, see below in this chapter.

[75]   Brodrick, *Canisius*, pp. 234–40, describes the 193 poorly printed octavo leaves of the first edition of the *Summa doctrino Christiann. Per Qu Qutiann tradita, & in vsum Christiann pueritii nunc primum edita* (Vienna: M. Zimmerman, 1554 [*vere* 1555]), which was published in 15 different languages before 1597.

[76]   Bartoli, *Europeae Historiae*, p. 81.

[77]   ABSI Collectanea P. I, fol. 99b.

[78]   Madeline Simons, 'Archduke Ferdinand II of Austria, Governor in Bohemia, and the Theatre of Representation', in *Rudolf II, Prague and the World: Papers from*

sacramental worship merged with public theatre. On the arrival of Ferdinand in 1558, they staged an allegory in which 'peace and justice overpowered the bound figure of Mars'; in 1562, they greeted Emperor Maximilian II by erecting a triumphal arch 'bearing an image of the Blessed Virgin', and adorning it with boys dressed as angels; in 1567, for Corpus Christi, over 40 boys were dressed as angels (including the archangels Michael and Gabriel) and stood completely still so that 'many doubted whether they were statues or men' until with one movement they all bowed their heads and adored the Real Presence in verses learnt by heart.[79] Mimesis crossed from representation to the real, straddling the boundary between theatre and ritual. The nobility and wealthier burghers supplied painted banners, and bought their sons white robes decorated with gold and precious stones for the occasion, while the verse was often accompanied by string orchestras and sung by choirs.[80] For the funeral reception of the body of Maximilian II in Prague in early 1577, they staged an allegory that showed Maximilian being 'led heavenward by the goddess Astraea' and bestowing 'his imperial blessing' on the new emperor.[81] Bishop Lambert Gruter, invited to give the funeral oration at Regensburg for the Emperor Maximilian II, compared him to Theodosius and himself to Ambrose, 'who had composed funeral addresses for the Emperors Valentinian II and Theodosius the Great'.[82]

Rudolf II returned to Vienna for the Corpus Christi procession in May 1578.[83] Because the Eucharist was the most contested area between the Utraquists and Calvinists, and Utraquists and Lutherans at least believed in the Real Presence, Corpus Christi processions were a particularly important part of the Jesuit mission. Some of these productions were very elaborate and spectacular. As part of the Corpus Christi celebrations of 1575, the Apostolic Nuncio and the Spanish ambassador, and other nobles of the Court carried the canopy over the monstrance 'in the Italian manner', country people came in from miles away, while the walls and pavements were strewn with tapestries and flowers; the Blessed Sacrament was carried to the sick beneath an umbrella, with torches and a bell, accompanied by a large number of the Court and the nobles, and a sizeable procession of members of either sex: the 'heretics' went on their knees as the procession passed, and donated money to cover the needs of the sick and the poor.[84]

the International Conference Prague, 2–4 September, 1997, ed. Lubomir Konečny et al. (Prague: Artefactum, 1998), pp. 270–77 (p. 272). See also Simons, 'King Ferdinand I of Bohemia, Archduke Ferdinand II and the Prague Court, 1527–1567', in *Rudolf II and Prague*, pp. 80–89 (pp. 84–5).

[79]   Michal Šroněk, 'Sculpture and Painting in Prague, 1550–1650', in *Rudolf II and Prague*, pp. 353–75 (p. 355); for the living statues, see Schmidl, *Historiae*, I. 135.

[80]   Čornejova, 'Education', p. 326.

[81]   Louthan, *Quest for Compromise*, p. 141. Campion's dramatic poem 'Anima' could have been part of these ceremonies, but the manuscript says nothing to indicate that.

[82]   Louthan, *Quest for Compromise*, pp. 138–9, citing Gruter, *Oratio Funebris*, 2r and 3r.

[83]   Louthan, *Quest for Compromise*, p. 155.

[84]   Čornejova, 'Education', p. 326; Schmidl, *Historiae*, I. 359.

Some dramatic fragments reveal Campion the schoolmaster; this is most obvious in two short pieces *Doctor Ironicus* and *Dialogus Mutus*.[85] *Doctor Ironicus* was transcribed rather unwillingly by Fr Grene, who says he has had to correct much of the text, and it may not be by Campion.[86] The *Dialogus Mutus* has much better authority.[87] It is 'a series of tableaux which, if performed, would have lent themselves to dumb show, commentary and chorus'.[88] These ambulant emblems belong to the same tradition as the silent adoring angels mentioned above.[89]

By the time Campion came to Prague, Jesuit plays were already big public spectacles intended to win back souls to the faith, not just college dramas. Three of Campion's autograph drafts preserved at Stonyhurst show him attempting something loftier than the *Dialogi*.[90] One is an autograph fair copy of *Anima*, a verse monologue written for the feast of All Souls, with 43 lines written in his neatest hand, with only three deletions (Figure 4.2).[91] The soul is led out of Purgatory by his guardian angel, and pleads with the audience to pray for the souls of the faithful departed. It is just possible that this was performed before an emperor who had recently lost his father. The audience is invited both to feel compassion for, and to identify with, the soul (*anima*). Campion shows an unusual ability to write from within the mind of the audience; he is completely in control of his didactic and theatrical aims as he imagines the soul pleading with the audience to pray more for the faithful departed:

> O you who live above, renew your prayers and release a captive. O priestly fathers redouble your masses for the dead and take pity on us; O brothers hear me and lighten my heavy load. If Phoebus would ever allow me to return to the breezes above, knowing what I have now learnt, I would spend more than six hundred years, if life were given to me, commemorating the dead and offering pious prayers for them.[92]

---

[85]   ABSI Collectanea P. II; Grene's edited *Doctor Ironicus* appears on fols 590a–591b. The *Dialogus mutus* is on fols 591b–592b.

[86]   Fr Grene complains (in a gloss) that he has had to correct many poorly transcribed lines: '*quae quia mendose erant transcripta necesse fuit aliqua pauca corrigere meliori quo fieri potuit modo*'.

[87]   This is confirmed by SZ MS DD.V.8, where the 62 lines of *Dialogus Mutus* are copied in a beautiful hand on fols 390r–391v, and confidently headed: a *R.P. Edmundo Campiano Compositus*.

[88]   Alison Shell, 'We are Made a Spectacle: Campion's Dramas', in *The Reckoned Expense: Edmund Campion and the Early English Jesuits*, 2nd ed., ed. Thomas M. McCoog, S.J. (Rome: IHSI, 2007), pp. 119–37 (p. 120). See Martin Wiggins, with Catherine Richardson, *British Drama, 1533–1642: A Catalogue*, 3 vols (Oxford: University Press, 2012), II. 614 and 635.

[89]   I am grateful to Alison Shell for her helpful advice on these dialogues, especially on ambulant emblems.

[90]   Stonyhurst MS A.V.3, fols 1r–3v.

[91]   Stonyhurst MS A.V.3, fols 4r–5r. This may be the only extant autograph fair copy.

[92]   Stonyhurst MS A.V.3, fol. 4v.

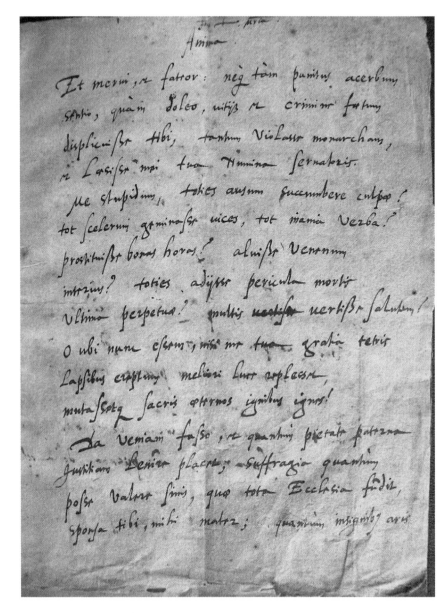

Figure 4.2 Campion's *Anima* (autograph), ABSI Stonyhurst MS A.V.3, fol. 4r.
By permission of the Trustees of the British Province of the
Society of Jesus.

The fragment ends with the soul addressing the guardian angel, and implying the presence of many other angels on the stage.[93] Two more dramatic fragments for the feast of Corpus Christi focus on another controversial theological doctrine: the Real Presence.

The first is a very brief fragment, an opening scene with seraphim, cherubim and every kind of angel, but in the second, longer draft, Campion is at his most sacerdotal, a priest wooing his audience with analogies from Ovid. He writes, deletes and then restores the phrase, *salutifer orbi*: the body of Christ is to bring salvation:

> Salve animata caro, salve cruor Inclyte Christi
> ~~Hospes, musa, cibus, Conjunx, salutifer orbi~~
> ~~Salve mihi linguam Dulcius Ambrosiae nectarisque cibo~~
> Salve dulce decus, nostroque salutifer ~~orbi~~ opus.

> [Hail, flesh filled with spirit, hail, glorious blood of Christ:
> ~~Guest, muse, food, husband, bringing salvation to the world,~~
> ~~Hail, sweeter to the tongue than the food of Ambrosia and nectar,~~
> Hail sweet ornament, the work that brings salvation ~~to our world.~~][94]

The cancels and cancellands show Campion remembering three linked passages from the *Metamorphoses*, and focusing (as we have seen) on a word that Ovid uses exclusively for Aesculapius. Ocyroe prophesies at the beginning of the *Metamorphoses*:

> aspicit infantem 'toto' que 'salutifer orbi
> cresce, puer …
> eque deo corpus fies exsangue deusque
> qui modo corpus eras, et bis tua fata novabis'.

> [She sees the infant and says: 'Grow to bring salvation to the whole world …
> From being a god, you will be made a lifeless body, and you who were just a
> body, will become a god again, and so twice renew your destiny].[95]

The god-child will become a mortal body and then a god again, and bring salvation for the whole world: Campion is clearly fascinated by the analogy of this Ovidian vision with Christ, and compares the body of Christ, *corpus Christi*, with *ambrosia* and *nectar*. Ovid himself links the idea of transformation from human to divine with *ambrosia* and *nectar* when Venus purifies the body of Aeneas of mortal elements:

---

93   Stonyhurst MS A.V.3, fol. 5r.

94   Stonyhurst MS A.V.3, fol. 6r. These deletions first aroused my interest in Campion's use of the word.

95   P. Ovidi Nasonis, *Metamorphoses*, ed. R.J. Tarrant (Oxford: Clarendon Press, 2004), II. 642–8.

unxit et ambrosia cum dulci nectare mixta
contigit os fecitque deum.

[She anointed him with ambrosia mixed with sweet nectar,
touched his mouth and made him divine.][96]

At the end of the *Metamorphoses*, Aesculapius lands quietly, in the guise of a serpent, on Tiber island to bring salvation to the city of Rome, *venitque salutifer urbi*.[97] Ovid skilfully rewrites the story of Rome, so it is Aesculapius, not Aeneas, who comes, in disguise, as *salutifer* to the *urbi* and therefore for the *orbi*.[98]

Campion, as we have seen, had used the word *salutifer* three times in his epic on the early history of the church, *Sancta salutiferi nascentia semina verbi*, written about 10 years earlier.[99] The word also occurs in the first line of the mural at Rushton Hall, followed by a bronze serpent that seems to pun on the name of Aeneas:

ECCE SALUTIFERUM SIGNUM THAU NOBILE LIGNUM
VITAE SERPENS HIC AENEUS ALTER ERAT

[Behold the salvation-giving sign of the letter Thau, noble wood,
This was the other bronze serpent of life.][100]

Here the word is in the same position in the first line as in Campion's poem, and the serpent seems to hint at its Ovidian source, suggesting the mural poem could have been written by Campion during the mission of 1580–81, and dated 1577 as a commentary on the execution of Cuthbert Mayne. These echoes of the *Metamorphoses* suggest that Campion is putting his faith in a sacramental vision of inner transformation, a salvation brought *urbi et orbi* (to Rome and the world) by the apostles and martyrs, rather than the *imperium Romanum* whose victory Virgil (with subtle qualifications) was describing.[101]

---

[96]   Ovid, *Metamorphoses*, XIV. 606–7.

[97]   Ovid, *Metamorphoses*, XV. 744; A.M. Keith, *Play of Fictions: Studies in Ovid's Metamorphoses, Book 2* (Michigan: University of Michigan Press, 1992), pp. 71–2, asserts that the word *salutifer* is an Ovidian coinage, and that the play on *orbi/urbi* goes back to Cicero.

[98]   John F. Miller *Apollo, Augustus and the Poets* (Cambridge: University Press, 2009), p. 363, discusses both *salutifer* and the *orbi/urbi* pun.

[99]   For full text of this poem and commentary, see Kilroy, *Memory and Transcription*, (pp. 121–93).

[100]   For a picture of the reredos and the context of Tresham's memorials to Campion, see plate 11 in Kilroy, *Memory and Transcription*, as well as pp. 121–4.

[101]   Kilroy, *Memory and Transcription*, pp. 49–54, discusses the poem as Virgilian epic, but does not include, I now think, sufficient consideration of Ovid.

When Campion spoke at Maria de Cardona's funeral in 1577, he described her as having followed 'the path of virtue that brings salvation' (*salutiferam virtutis viam*).[102] That Campion should bring together images from Ovid's reworking of the myth of Aeneas's founding of Rome shows how actively he was engaged with Ovid. This certainly reflects the moderate views of those around Rudolf II in the late 1570s, especially in the two years when Rudolf, in the grip of a crisis, was in the healing hands of his spiritual adviser, Crato. It seems significant that on 1 January 1581, Bartholomaeus Spranger (1546–1611) was named court painter in Prague, and began work on a series of murals of Ovid's *Metamorphoses* commissioned by Rudolf II.[103] It also reflects Campion's consistent policy; a priest and scholar, he showed no interest in the use of political power, still less of force, to restore the sacramental church in England.

In the Jubilee year of 1575, Campion was delighted to hear that Persons and a number of Oxford men had arrived in Rome and 'entred into the same religion' (the Society of Jesus): John Lane, of Corpus, William Weston, of All Souls, Giles Gallop and Henry Garnet of New College, and Thomas Stephens 'of the same university'.[104] They went on to live the life Campion seems to have expected to follow. Stephens laboured in the East Indies, Gallop in Rome, Lane in Alcala in Spain; only Weston and Garnet came to England.[105] Campion apparently corresponded with them, but none of these letters has survived, so Persons (our only, rather biased, source of information here) adds that Campion told him that he had

> still a certaine particular inward motion & inclination to be imployed towards the help of his own country then any where els, if God would move his superiors so to dispose of him, and this desire of his he imparted unto me by letters being in Rome and entred into the same Society … in the meane space he were well contented where he was; and not altogether unprofitable for England, for that now & then there passed that way, by reason of the Emperor's Court, certain English gentlemen, who, finding him there, were content to deale with him in matters of religion, & departed commonly far better instructed & persuaded than when they came thither.[106]

The most distinguished of these visitors was Philip Sidney, who came as the Queen's ambassador to the newly crowned Emperor in April 1577, and called

---

[102]   *Opuscula*, p. 297.

[103]   Eliška Fučikova, 'Prague Castle under Rudolf II, His Predecessors and Successors', in *Rudolf II and Prague*, pp. 2–71 (p. 16).

[104]   ABSI Collectanea P. I, fol. 98a.

[105]   William Weston, *Autobiography of an Elizabethan*, trans. Philip Caraman (London: Longmans, Green, 1955), left us a superb account of his mission. Philip Caraman, *Henry Garnet 1555–1606 and the Gunpowder Plot* (London: Longmans, 1964), offers a gripping account of Garnet.

[106]   ABSI Collectanea P. I, fol. 98a–b.

on Campion several times. Sidney (not yet knighted) was heir to the Earls of
Leicester and Warwick, and had once been suggested to the Queen as a possible
heir to the throne.[107]

> He came to Prague with very great state and pompe, as he was in truth a very
> goodly & noble gentleman of singular good nature, witt, curtesy, and well
> qualifyed every way: he was also of greatest expectation for greatnesse of
> fortune of any one subject of England, being heir apparent not only to his father
> Sir Henry Sidney, President of Wales & one of the Privy-Councell, but also in
> all mens sight & opinion to the two Earls of Leicester and Warwick, that were
> brothers to his mother and had no children; which two Earls, especially that of
> Leicester, were taken to be the greatest both for autority, riches and possession
> of any noble men of England.[108]

Thomas Fitzherbert records in a letter of 1 February 1628, and in another note,
that Sidney

> relating at his return of certain things remarkable and worthy of memory which
> he had noted in the time of his embassage, recounted for one an eloquent sermon
> which Father Campion had made before the Emperor in Prague while he himself
> was there, and present at the sermon.[109]

Campion's own letter to John Bavand (apparently in Rome), outlining the impact
of this meeting, survives:

> Now listen to my news. The Emperor Rudolf, a prudent, brave and good youth,
> and a sincere son of the Church, has fixed upon himself the eyes and the hearts
> of the Germans and Bohemians. If he lives, great things are expected of him.
> The Dowager Empress, Maximilian's widow, and sister of Philip of Spain, is
> living in Prague. A few months ago Philip Sidney came from England to Prague
> as ambassador, in royal style. He had a long conversation with me, I hope not
> in vain, for he seemed very enthusiastic. I commend him to your prayers at
> Mass, for he asked the prayers of all good men, and at the same time put into
> my hands some alms to be distributed to the poor for him, which I have done.
> Tell Dr Nicholas Sanders, because if any one of the labourers sent into the
> vineyard from the Douai seminary has an opportunity of watering this plant, he
> may find an occasion for helping a poor wavering soul. If this young man, so
> wonderfully beloved and admired by his countrymen, chances to be converted,

---

[107]   Michael G. Brennan, 'The Sidneys of Penshurst, the Earldom of Leicester, and the
Monarchies of England, Spain and France', in the *Sidney Journal* 22, 1–2 (2004), 25–45
(p. 43).

[108]   ABSI Collectanea P. I, fols 98b–99a.

[109]   John Hungerford Pollen, ed., *Acts of English Martyrs* (London: Burns and Oates,
1891), p. 36. This certainly implies that Campion was chosen to preach before he was
ordained.

he will astonish his noble father, the Deputy of Ireland, his uncles the Dudleys, and all the young courtiers, and Cecil himself. Keep this secret.[110]

Persons says that Sidney professed himself convinced by Campion 'that the only truth was with the Catholicks', but said that 'it was necessary for him to hold on the course which he had hitherto followed; yet he promised never to hurt or injure any Catholick, which for the most part he performed'.[111] Persons distinguishes this promise from his personal assurance to Campion that he would find him a 'trusty frend', and takes a harsh view of Sidney's later failure to intercede on Campion's behalf.[112]

When Sidney came to see him in Prague in 1577, Campion may have been affected by the news that Sidney's younger sister, Ambrosia, had died at the age of nine, two years earlier.[113] He must certainly have asked after Sir Henry, who had saved his life in Ireland, and Sidney would have told him of the fierce opposition, among Palesmen and Irish alike, evoked by his father, before he was finally recalled, his schemes for reform rejected. The bitterness over Ireland led to a dispute at court in 1578 when Philip Sidney refused to answer the Earl of Ormond, then the Queen's favourite, 'but was in dead silence on purpose', and prompted him to write 'a defence of his father's conduct' in Ireland, which appears to have convinced the Queen to accept 'his imposition of the cess' within the Pale.[114] The plight of his former protector may be what prompted Campion to consider revising his *Histories of Ireland*, so that he could defend even more vigorously Sir Henry's reform programme.[115]

During the following year, Campion made strenuous efforts to recover the manuscript of his *Histories of Ireland*. Gregory Martin first wrote to him on 22 August 1578, indicating that he has 'your Irish history from our Wiggsy, now living in Paris', but that it 'is larger ... than can easily be sent'.[116] Six months passed before Martin's next extant letter, on 13 February 1579, which he sent via Persons in Rome because so many letters had not arrived: he still cannot find a way of safely sending the manuscript, but Allen is having another copy of the *Histories* made, and 'our Holland' has carried out Campion's wish to have his heretical books burned.[117] Campion, having heard nothing, had sent his letter of January

---

[110] Simpson, *Campion*, p. 123. The draft original, much revised, is at Farm Street, ABSI Anglia, I/4, fols 18r–19r. I have adapted Simpson's translation, and tried to reflect some of the draft's deletions.

[111] ABSI Collectanea P. I, fol. 99a.

[112] ABSI Collectanea P. I, fol. 99a. See Chapter 12 for a full discussion of this issue.

[113] Campion may, in part, have chosen the title, *Ambrosiana*, to avoid touching so sensitive a nerve.

[114] *ODNB*, 'Sir Philip Sidney' (1554–1586), by Henry Woudhuysen. The 'cess' (assess) was a system of taxation.

[115] *ODNB*, 'Sir Henry Sidney' (1529–1586), by Wallace MacCaffrey.

[116] *Douay Diaries*, pp. 317–18.

[117] *Douay Diaries*, pp. 318–19.

1579 to Martin by Francis Coster, S.J., whose help he now enlisted in obtaining the bulky manuscript. Only one reply of Campion's to Martin has survived, dated '16 Kal August 1579':

> I am answering your letters, in reverse order ... I had written to Fr. Francis Coster, who is the Provincial of the Rhine Province of our Society, to ask him that, if you have my scribblings (*scriptiunculas*) on Irish affairs, to pass them to him, so that he can find a way to have them conveyed safely to me in Prague ... You ask what I am doing: I have finished the Logic of Aristotle; now I am dealing with the Physics. Soon I will be wrangling with the Bachelors, then the Master of Arts: six days of disputation followed by one of concord, because I am regarded (quite wrongly) to be 'a fluent sophist' (*sophista disertus*): what on earth does it mean (*quid refert*)?[118]

The two extant letters to Coster reveal the depth of Campion's anxiety about the manuscript of his Irish history. The first, of January 1579, begins 'I was worried about a parcel of manuscripts which I am expecting from France', and ends:

> If Martin manages to get the book to you, please could you, father, make sure it is sent to me at Prague, by the safest rather than the swiftest route. I am already saying more than I need, for I know that you will do all that is reasonably possible. I confess that I am hugely indebted to you. That book is a work still unfinished, because it was prematurely born; and if I were to lose it, I would rather it were completely destroyed than fall into the wrong hands. So I am working hard to enable it to reach you, and then it can crawl to me as slowly as you like. Farewell, from Prague.[119]

A second letter, of August 1579, to Coster indicates more lost letters:

> I enclose a letter for Martin; if you can send it on to him in France I hope that he will do his bit. I beg of you also, as Martin tells me he has no means of sending the papers to me, that if you know of any trusty person to employ, you will take the whole business upon your shoulders, and manage to have them sent from Rheims to Cologne, and from Cologne to Prague. If this cannot be done, let me know, and I will try some other plan.
>   17 Cal. Septembris ~~1569~~ 1579.[120]

These six letters of Campion and Martin reveal both the immense difficulties of correspondence in this period, and the primacy of Campion's scholarly interests.

---

[118]   *Opuscula*, pp. 397–8; ABSI Anglia I/6, fols 25v–26r; Simpson, pp. 131–2. Campion finished Aristotle's *Logic* on 14 July 1579, and began teaching the *Physics* on 11 August 1579; see below.

[119]   ABSI Anglia I, fol. 24v; trans. Simpson, pp. 117–18, who mistakenly dates this to January 1577.

[120]   ABSI Anglia I, fol. 27r; trans. Simpson, pp. 118–19, who mistakenly dates this to July 1577.

There is no request extant from him for his manuscript before 1578, so Campion's interest may have been reawakened by the visit of Philip Sidney to Prague in 1577, or by the publication of his 'Irish history' in truncated form in the 1577 Holinshed. His first letter to Coster suggests that his intention was to revise the text so that it would not forever be known by an unfinished fragment. Not till 16 October 1579, one year after his first letter, does Martin write triumphantly to 'his dearest' (*conjunctissimo suo*) Campion, to tell him that a courier has arrived from Coster to collect the manuscript:

> All of your letter fills me with delight, dear Campion, and brings you before my mind as if you were here. I seized the last one even more eagerly, because you have found a way of having your Irish history sent to you. Not only that, but the most reverend provincial, Francis Coster, has instructed me to send it to Cologne to the person you refer to as my namesake, Fr Martin. This I have done immediately, because on the next day there came a very convenient courrier, girded for the journey to Liege, so that by the fathers of your society who are there or nearby, it could be easily forwarded to Cologne. This is why I write briefly.

> The President, Dr Allen is away in Rome, having left in the month of August, and Dr Bristow is doing a profession at Douai on his behalf. Holland is glad that you are pleased with what he has done, and thinks Erasmus was not among those he spared.[121]

Martin could not have known that Dr Allen was about to ask Campion to lead the English mission, so Campion would never have a chance of revising his history. Nothing could better illustrate the gap between Campion's aims and those of Dr Allen, nor the irony that Sander's expedition, whose dreadful consequences in Munster were to close Hooker's vindictive 'Supplie' in Holinshed's *Chronicles* (1587), should be unfolding while Campion was trying to recover the text of his sympathetic history of Ireland. These letters show that Campion's circle of intimate friends still included many St John's men, now scattered across Europe: Willliam Wigges, William Stocke, Henry Holland and Gregory Martin are all honoured by the possessive pronoun: 'our' (*noster*). The most constant topic of these letters of this family of scholars is the preservation of books and the transmission of manuscripts, a world away from the encrypted political messages in the letters of Sander and Allen.

Campion said his first Mass in the college on 8 September 1578, as the Clementinum diaries record.[122] He was so troubled by scruples, Bombino tells us,

---

[121] ARSI Fondo Gesuitico 651, no. 636 contains seven letters of Martin, all printed in *Douay Diaries*, pp. 308–20. This one is the seventh, p. 320. Campion has expressed the hope that his Erasmus had been included among the books burned, p. 317. Simpson, pp. 117–19, is mistaken in his dating of Campion's letters to Coster, which has made it even harder to sort out the sequence of this interrupted correspondence.

[122] Strahov MS DC.III.16, fol. 98v; '*P. Edmundus Anglus rhetorici professor primitias in die Nat. Beatissimae Virginis cecinit*'. Schmidl, *Historiae*, I. 419, confirms the date and adds the location.

about being worthy of the priesthood, and went for confession so often to Antonio Brus, the Archbishop of Prague, that finally he had to be sent away without absolution, as there was nothing to absolve.[123] His ordination, which might have taken place 10 years earlier if there had been no 'alteration of religion' in England, seems to have released all Campion's creative energies in an *annus mirabilis* of preaching, teaching and writing. No sooner was he ordained than he presented a play for the opening of the academic year before the entire court.

The play was called *Ambrosiana*.[124] The play, under this title, is also recorded in the Clementinum diaries, by Bombino in his biography, and by Fr Alegambe, who also calls it *Nectar & Ambrosia*.[125] In the *Elogium Historicum* in the Strahov Monastery Library, the authors say that 'the tragedy Ambrosiana' received 'applause in the theatre' and 'great murmuring approval among the people' and 'without startling anyone too sharply' nevertheless managed to 'strike everyone very forcefully'.[126] It is the only play of Campion's mentioned in the *Historia Missionis Anglicanae Societatis Jesu* (1660) of Henry More, S.J., where he says that '[John] Pits, a reliable author, mentions it by the title *Nectar & Ambrosia*'.[127] Anthony Wood, apparently following Pits, twice calls it *Nectar & Ambrosia*.[128] Perhaps Pits and Wood understood the Ovidian references. There is no mention in any of Campion's surviving letters, or the letters of his contemporaries, or in the biographical works of Persons, Bombino, Ribadeneira, Alegambe, Balbin, Pits, More or Wood, of any other play by Campion.

The first mention of a play by Campion other than *Ambrosiana* occurs in Schmidl, in 1747, who confidently says that 'Campion ingeniously portrayed the

---

[123] Bombino, *Vita et Martyrium*, p. 48; Bodl. MS Tanner 329, fols 16v–17r. Bombino says Archbishop Brus 'frequently testified' (*non semel testatus*) to this; Schmidl makes no mention.

[124] *Opuscula*, p. 401; one complete copy survives in the Studienbibliothek Dillingen, MS 221, fols 135r 169v, where it is called *Ambrosia*; another, lacking title, beginning and end, is in the English College, Rome, MS C.17–v. I thank Martin Wiggins for sending me a copy of this. The long entry (three pages for the cast) in Wiggins, *Catalogue*, I. 650, makes clear the scale of Campion's play.

[125] Strahov MS DC.III.16, fol. 99r; Bombino, *Vita et Martyrium*, pp. 59–60; Philip Alegambe, S.J., ed., *Bibliotheca Scriptorum Societatis Iesu post excusum Anno M. DC.VIII Catalogum R.P. Petri Ribadaneira, S.J.* (Antwerp: Meursius, 1643), pp. 97–8, where Alegambe uses both titles: *Nectar & Ambrosia*, but notes that Bombino calls it *Ambrosiana* (p. 98). Pedro de Ribadeneira, S.J., in his influential *Illustrium Scriptorum Religionis Societatis Iesu Catalogus* (Lyons: J. Pillehotte, 1609), does not mention the play in his account of Campion, pp. 47–9.

[126] *Elogium Historicum*, Strahov MS A.J.VIII. 80, sig. B3r. See Chapter 12 for more copies.

[127] Francis Edwards, ed. and trans., *The Elizabethan Jesuits: Historia Missionis Anglicanae Societatis Jesu (1660)* of Henry More (London: Phillimore, 1981), p. 50; John Pits, *Relationum Historicarum de Rebus Anglicis* (Paris: Thierry & Cramoisy, 1619), p. 777.

[128] Wood, *Athenae Oxonienses*, I. 474–5.

conflict of Abraham with himself' in the sacrifice of *Abraham* of his son Isaac', and asserts that, 'he would hardly dare to doubt' that Campion was the author of *Saul*, performed in 1577.[129] Schmidl seems not to have known the collection of plays preserved in three linked manuscripts at Dillingen. *Isaac immolatus*, in the same manuscript as Campion's play, is elsewhere attributed to Jacob Pontanus, S.J. (1542–1626), an early *discipulus* of Campion, while *Tragoedia cui nomen inditum Saul Galboaeus* is in another Dillingen collection, and is written, in a very different style, by someone trying to imitate Aeschylus.[130]

In a letter to Campani, written from Bologna in April 1580, Campion answers his superior's request to send him a manuscript of the play, which he thinks is still in Prague where he last saw it, in the Rector's room:

> As for your query about the *Ambrosiana*, you should know, my good father, that it was not returned to me after you returned from Vienna, and I last saw it in your room. I have no doubt it is still mouldering quietly in some corner of your room, or certainly in the hands of someone who borrowed it while you were busy, so you do not remember. My only request, if the play is to be performed again, is that the production be more elaborate (*luculenta*).[131]

---

[129]   Schmidl, *Historiae*, I. 369 (Abraham); of 'Saul' he writes, I. 396: *Campianum Authorem fuisse vix ausim dubitare.* Carlos Sommervogel, *Bibliothèque de la Compagnie de Jésus* (Paris: Picard, 1891), II. 587, adds to the confusion by wrongly attributing Schimdl's statement on 'Saul' to Balbin. Schmidl's attribution of these two plays has been accepted by all the best writers on Campion, including Simpson, pp. 117 and 503; Jos. Simons, *Ambrosia: A Neo-Latin Drama by Edmund Campion*, S.J. (Assen: Van Gorcum, 1970), p. ix; and Alison Shell, '"We Are Made A Spectacle": Campion's Dramas', in *The Reckoned Expense* (2007), pp. 119–37 (p. 122); Wiggins, *Catalogue*, II. 584 and 617, accepts the attribution, with reservations.

[130]   Balbin, *Miscellanea*, pp. 195–6, makes no mention of this. Dillingen MS 221, fols 209r–231r, contains *Isaac Immolatus*, which is elsewhere found in the works of Jacob Pontanus, S.J., 'Tyrocinium Poeticum' (1594 and 1600). The play was performed on 14 December 1576, and a second time on 6 January 1577 (Fidel Radle, *Lateinische Ordensdramen des XVI* Jahrhundert, Berlin und New York, 1979). *Tragoedia cui nomen inditum Saul Galboaeus* is in an 1176-page collection of 21 Jesuit plays in Dillingen MS 219, pp. 103–86, and one can see why it took six hours. Dillingen MS 223 is a collection put together by Jacob Gretscher, S.J. of several plays by Pontanus, and miscellaneous poems and dialogues. A. Dürrwaechter, 'Aus der Fruhzeit des Jesuitendrama. Nach Dillingen Manuskripten', in *Jahrbkuch des Historischen Vereins Dillingen, IX Jahrgang* (Dillingen: J. Keller, 1897), examined the three Dillingen manuscripts. Johannes Müller, S.J., *Das Jesuitendrama in den Landern Deutscher Zunger vom Anfang (1555) bis zum Hochbarock (1665)* (Augsburge: Benno Filser Verlag, 1950), p. 51, lists both *Stratocles* and *Immolatio Isaaci* as by Pontanus. Wiggins, *Catalogue*, II. 584, posits another Campion play on the same theme, but in the German provinces of the Society of Jesus, where plays were passed from one college to another, there seems to have been a tacit convention not to repeat a theme.

[131]   *Opuscula*, pp. 401–2 (my translation). Simpson translated '*luculenta*' as 'comprehensible', whereas the sense is closer to 'spendid' or 'elaborate'.

The Dillingen manuscript heads the play:

> AMBROSIA by the Most Holy Martyr Edmund Campion Performed at Prague,
> in the presence of the Emperor, in October 1578.[132]

Campion and his Jesuit contemporaries clearly saw the play as a grand public production. The Clementinum diaries of October 1578 reveal that the play was performed twice:

> Comoediam ut Theodosianam aut Ambrosianam bis exhibuimus, in Coll. semel,
> in arce coram Imperatrice, Regina Galliaeque (eique filia) viduis, arriserunt
> caelum et spectatores.

> [We put on the comoedia *Theodosiana* or *Ambrosiana* twice: once in the College
> and once in the Castle in front of the Empress and the Queen of France, her
> daughter, both widows, and the spectators praised the play to the skies.][133]

'*S. Ambrosius Theodosium Imp. adducens ad poenitentiam Drama* (A play of St. Ambrose bringing the Emperor Theodosius to penitence)' is the way the play was recorded in Krakow.[134] Schmidl tells us that it was performed '*plausu maximo*'.[135] At another 'public performance' (*Actionem publicam*) in Kalisz, Poland, in 1592, the play was put on for the start of the academic year, and 'drew all eyes to it', and was given added weight by the fact that it was written by '*Edmundus Campianus Martyr Angliae*'.[136] Records of two other performances of the play have survived. One was in Munich in 1591, presumably before Duke Wilhelm.[137] There was another performance in the Jesuit college at Cologne in 1621, where the diary notes that 'there was staged St Ambrose excluding the Arian Valentinian and the Catholic Emperor Theodosius from entry to the church'.[138]

The play, a large civic pageant performed before the imperial Court and several members of the imperial family, with links with France and Spain, at the

---

[132]   Dillingen MS 221, fol. 135r; Jos. Simons, *Ambrosia*, p. 2. All references will be to this edition.

[133]   Strahov MS DC.III.16, fol. 99r.

[134]   Fr Jan Poplatek, S.J., 'Encyklopedia Jezuitow w XVI wieku' (a manuscript in the Ignatianum, Krakow), p. 9.

[135]   Schmidl, *Historiae*, I. 100; Simons, *Ambrosia*, p. xi.

[136]   *Annuae Litterae prov. Poloniae, 1592. Collegium Calissiense A.S.J. Pol. 50*, fol. 98v. I thank Dr Jolanta Rzegocka for this information. A Jesuit college was founded in Kalisz, near Posnan, in 1584.

[137]   Müller, *Das Jesuitendrama*, p. 51.

[138]   Jan Poplatek, S.J., located another manuscript of the play in Cologne, which he recorded as Staatsarchiv Univ. IX. 659, fols 304–340. Although the manuscript cannot now be found, the 'Liber Consuetudinum Scholae Coloniensis soc. Iesu', Historisches Archiv der Stadt Köln, Best. 150 (Universität), A 981, p. 71, records a performance, on 3 November 1621.

traditional start of the college year in October, just after Campion's ordination as a priest, presents a model of relations between the church and state, and shows the church giving good counsel to the monarch, an idea widely accepted beyond the Catholic community. As Alison Shell argues, 'Campion's exploration of the relationship between Ambrose and Theodosius reveals a conception of politics as moral persuasion', a view supported by the way the play has been recorded.[139] The cast could easily have numbered 200, since in addition to the 50 named characters, there are innumerable groups: *populus, populus Thessalonicus, Daemones, Populus innocens, chorus Angelorum, Idolotrae.* This pageant must have involved more than half the college, and some parts were clearly written for the younger boys. The rest would have been involved in the choir, the orchestra, the production of props and scenery.[140] The provision of military, ecclesiastical and imperial costumes could have involved many members of the Court and the church.

The courtyard, where the second performance took place, with the cathedral of St Vitus on one side and the royal castle on the other, provided the perfect iconography for this conflict between church and monarch. Campion's only surviving full-scale play, about the emperor Theodosius, the empress Justina and the bishop-saint Ambrose, was performed in front of another emperor, an empress and the Archbishop of Prague. Indeed, the first line of the play seems deliberately to flatter the Empress Maria Augusta, as 'Wife, parent of emperors, and ruler of a kingdom that includes Hesperia and the western region'.[141] While the three Dillingen manuscripts show that a vital and varied tradition of drama existed throughout the three linked Jesuit provinces, *Ambrosiana* is unique, among the Jesuit plays preserved there, in dealing with an historical (rather than a biblical or allegorical) topic.[142]

The struggle between church and state is resolved when the Emperor Theodosius accepts the advice of the bishop, Saint Ambrose.[143] There are other significant themes: conversion, healing and baptism, which are bound into the central theme by the drama of choice. Throughout the play, human beings, from emperors to simple soldiers, are shown as free to choose good, and reject evil.

---

[139] Shell, 'We Are Made A Spectacle', pp. 126–8, contains a superb discussion of the political thought in the play, and its relationship to the ideas of Persons. See above for the diary entries.

[140] Dillingen MS 223 contains scores for four parts, orchestras, elaborate metres and some Greek.

[141] *Ambrosia*, p. 6.

[142] The three Dillingen MSS, 219, 221 and 223, contain nearly 50 plays. Most are recorded without attribution; Campion, Pontanus and Gretscher are exceptions. Dillingen MS 223 has *sum Jakobi Gretscheri* written inside the front board and attributes several plays to *Jacob Pontanus*. For earlier Jesuit plays, see Jean-Marie Valentin, *Le théâtre des Jésuites dans le pays de langue allemande, répertoire chronologique des pièces représentées et des documents conservés (1555–1773)*, 2 vols (Stuttgart: Hiersemann, 1983–84).

[143] Alison Shell, 'We Are Made A Spectacle', p. 127.

The massacre of 7,000 innocent citizens of Thessalonica, which is at the centre of the play, is portrayed as a major crime against humanity, and Theodosius is not admitted to the church until he has repented. Music and a variety of complex poetic metres provide a counterpoint to the brutish exercise of power; the musical beauty of the church's ritual is seen as a sign of the grace rescuing mankind from the barbarism of revenge. The play consistently alternates didactic or violent scenes with light and humorous ones, and large set pieces with very personal dramas. Within the central plot of Theodosius and Ambrose, the play delights its audience with variety, humour, aesthetic beauty and a profound understanding of the importance of individual choice: free will.

The self-deprecating nature of the humour of the first scene must have won over the audience immediately, as Justina says that she would rather tolerate anyone than her enemies the 'Catholics', whom Auletes describes as 'sluggish souls' (*animas inertes*).[144] While the first two acts revolve around the conflict between church and state, they might be considered rather as rhetorical and musical pageants illustrating various aspects of the church. From the start of the play to the end, the unjustified use of force is seen as a danger for the state, whether it is the Empress Justina letting slip the dogs of war with '*nesciat modum furor*' (let fury know no measure), or the climactic horror of the massacre of 7,000 civilians at the end of Act IV. This intemperate violence is contrasted with the measured chant of Ambrose and his clerics, who sing of the bodies of the martyrs, or the calm sermon of Ambrose who preaches on the fearlessness of unarmed clerics. Ambrose's two miracles make great drama – he banishes a devil from a possessed man, and heals a blind man – but they also transform the mind of the Empress, who countermands her violent orders.

Act II introduces Saint Augustine in its first scene, which allows Campion to include the most bookish conversion in Christian literature, a scholarly reference to the *Confessions*, and to the theologian admired by Protestants and Catholics alike. The second scene reveals Augustine hearing the voice of an angel telling him to take up and read: '*Tolle, lege, tolle, lege*'.[145] Augustine is the most illustrious character in a pageant of Christian life; casting out devils, miracles of healing and of conversion displayed as the efficacious signs of the Christian church to an imperial audience. Just as they converted the Empress Justina, so they may convert the sceptical Utraquist, Lutheran and Hussite population of Prague. As a balance to the power-hungry Justina, the Empress Flaccilla is shown performing Christian works of mercy: looking after the poor and leprous Lazarus, and encouraging freedom of linguistic practice. She is the Maria Cardona figure in the play. Finally, there is a didactic scene as Augustine, together with his friend Alipius and his illegitimate son Adeodatus, all come for baptism. Ambrose catechises them on

---

[144]   *Ambrosia*, p. 6.

[145]   Campion has glossed this at the end of Act II. 2, '*Lege caput 11. et 12. lib. 8 Confessionum D. Augustini, imo totum 8. et. 9. lib., quibus D. Augustinus cuncta et conversionem suam explicat*'.

the main items of Christian belief: God as the sole creator of all, free will, grace and the importance of the Nicene Creed. This scene is immediately followed by a brief comedy of two young boys wasting time with dice, wrestling and dancing. The act ends with a stylized duet by Augustine and Ambrose, reminiscent of Greek tragedy. The message for the Utraquists, Lutherans and Calvinists of Prague is clear: two of the greatest doctors of the church are on the side of Rome.[146]

Act III, the centre of the play, proclaims its theme from the start: the struggle between power and heavenly laws, between mercy and justice. In the first scene, the young Arcadius, son of Theodosius and Flaccilla, is being instructed by his teacher Arsenius how to become worthy of his parents. In a scene clearly meant to parallel this, Theodosius has to decide what to do with the rebel Maximus. Both scenes are a prelude to the dreadful sequence of the mob of Thessalonica killing three officials in order to obtain the release of their favourite charioteer. As Ambrose advises mercy, rather than retribution, and warns Theodosius of the danger of bloodshed, an unpleasant crew of devils, close to Julian the Apostate, conspire to release *furor* (madness) in both the mob and the emperor. Demons seem to have been as popular as angels in Prague, but Campion's demons, led by Julian the Apostate, stir up human violence. The act ends, as it began, with mercy and justice: while the mob assassinates the three officials, others lament their terrible end. Act IV begins intensely as Ambrose warns Theodosius not to take vengeance on innocent people, but evil advisers win the day, and persuade Theodosius that 7,000 citizens must die for 3 murdered officials.

The role of the church in this play is to protect the innocent from the extremes of power. While violence is associated with apostasy, mercy, music and metrical order are linked with the church. Campion did not believe that the pope had *potestas ordinata* to depose a monarch, but he certainly believed that the church played an important role in reminding monarchs of a higher law, and in protecting human life. What is good for people, is necessary for monarchs: 'princes, to rule wisely, must be accountable to the Church'.[147]

Two Persian ambassadors immediately lighten the mood by speaking gobbledygook and being translated by an interpreter:

> Abrosiax Aba suattico, grundel phonu
> Off dig, um hamga persiax oister eogar.[148]

Campion's ability to alternate large set pieces with small personal dramas is shown when Arsenius, praying to be released from the 'prison' of his palace role, is approached by a swordsman sent by Arcadius. The swordsman relents and an angel advises Arsenius to escape. Mercy can operate in the individual heart. These two scenes build up the tension before the climactic massacre of Thessalonica.

---

[146] *Rationes Decem*, 'Quinta Ratio, PATRES'.

[147] Shell, 'We Are Made A Spectacle', p. 125.

[148] *Ambrosia*, p. 55.

Whether in the open space of the Castle courtyard or the Clementinum, this must have been a shocking scene. Afterwards, Ambrose prevents Theodosius, whom he calls 'a bloody prince', from entering the basilica. In the scenes that follow, Ambrose takes Theodosius through repentance and penance before he can be readmitted, but God's forgiveness is contrasted with the revenge that the Emperor has practised. Ambrose insists that Theodosius can be released only after 30 days of penance, and Theodosius submits to his command. The final forgiveness of Theodosius is accompanied by a chorus of angels, who rejoice at the return of Caesar to the heavens. All these scenes were performed in front of a modern Caesar, so one wonders whether there would have been cheers when the chorus, in Act V. 7, chant, 'The presence of Caesar makes this country blessed'. Theodosius immediately has to deal with another foreign threat in the next scene, and with the fact that all the temples of idols are still standing. Men are instructed to demolish them, but to harm no one. There must have been a lot of scope for easily destructible models of idols. The play, classified like most of the plays in these three Dillingen manuscripts, 'as a *comoedia*', ends with the Emperor and Ambrose embracing.[149] This is certainly better than the conflict between church and state that existed in England. Everything in the final scene reinforces the sense that submission to God brings happiness and order. The play ends with clerics chanting in elegiac couplets: a metrical and civic harmony. The final lines show the unity of church and state as Ambrose and Theodosius enter the church together, singing 'Glory and praise to God'. 'The play's ending is, in worldly terms, brilliantly optimistic'.[150]

This is a magnificent pageant that speaks very personally to its imperial and popular audience. The play held up a mirror to magistrates, a glass wherein Emperor and Archbishop could see the perfect balance of state and church enacted before them. It also showed the role of individual free will; each man has the ability to resist the demons of communal revenge or violence. This is an ambitious and confident *comoedia*, unique among the surviving Jesuit dramas of the period in addressing the Emperor and his family so personally through its historical theme.

Campion was much involved in the life of the court and, for the first time in his life, able to combine his scholarly interests with his priestly instincts, and so to let flower all his skills and talents. His position was also a glamorous one. He was clearly popular with the court as it settled in Prague, which became the nodal point of European monarchies, and it was from here that Campion's fame spread across Europe. This last period of 16 months is by far the best-documented period of Campion's life, since we have several of his letters, the text of his play, several dramatic fragments and many sermons and lectures. As professor of philosophy, he began lecturing first on Aristotle's *Logic*, and then on the *Physics*, and these lectures, the Clementinum diaries tell us, were attended by 'external auditors',

---

[149]   *Ambrosia*, pp. 84–5. Only three are described as *tragoediae*, like *Saul Gelboaeus*, in Dillingen MS 219, although there are many *dialogi*.

[150]   Shell, 'We Are Made A Spectacle', p. 130.

both from the court and the city.[151] We now have a record of these lectures, material evidence both of the depth of his scholarship, and of the devotion his lectures inspired in his students: we have their dictated notes from his lectures on Aristotle.[152]

The notes on Aristotle's *Logic* began simply as contemporaneous notes by Caspar Brzysky.[153] These are in a slightly untidy hand, but the same hand has returned to put in headings and dates. At a later date, another more elegant hand has added verses to the end of each section. This appears to be the hand of Adam à Winorzie, who has produced the much more decorative and decorated notes on Campion's lectures on the *Physics*, from August 1579 to the moment in February 1580 when he told his students that he was leaving for Rome.[154] The note at the beginning of the commentaries on *Logic* (Figure 4.3) reveals that:

> Edmund Campion, when leaving Prague, asked his students if he could have a copy of what they had written (and he had dictated) on Aristotle's Logic, as a memorial of his work (*in sui laboris memoriam*). Adam à Winorzie offered him his own, and when Caspar Brzysky, a scholar of the Holy Father, died a little time later, these also came to him.[155]

Campion's request for this 'memorial of his work' confirms what we know from his later letter from Bologna, that he and his students were strongly bound together, and that he found leaving Prague an emotional wrench. It appears that Campion had taught the same group of students for nearly six years, from the beginning of rhetoric into the year of philosophy. In his letter to Campani from Bologna, he wishes he had been able 'to write to them individually' (*sigillatim*), but 'overwhelmed by the number and various anxieties, I have ended up satisfying no one'.[156]

In the notes on the *Physics*, the students dramatized, in just over a hundred lines of Latin hexameters, the dialogue they had with their professor, when he told them of his imminent departure: the verse describes not just conventional sadness, but real distress at this sudden rupture.[157] The Prague fellowship was even richer now that Campion was a priest, and his teaching was incorporated into

---

[151]   Strahov MS DC.III.16, fol. 99v: '*Inchoatus Philosophiae cursus a R.P. Edmundo Campiano Anglo cum auditoribus externis*' (The philosophy course was begun by the Englishman, Reverend Father Edmund Campion, with external auditors).

[152]   APMC M42, *Logic*, and APMC M65, *Physics*. See above, n. 18.

[153]   APMC M42: the earliest date entered, 15 December 1578, is on the verso of the first front paper. The earliest date attached to the lectures is 16 January 1579, is to the end of the 'Prolegomena' and 'Commentaria ad Porphyriam', fol. 43r, so they must have begun several weeks before that.

[154]   For Adam à Winorzie, see Schmidl, *Historiae*, I. 431.

[155]   APMC M42, on verso facing title page.

[156]   *Opuscula*, 406.

[157]   APMC M65, fols 260v–263r, see Chapter 5 for date, quotation and illustration.

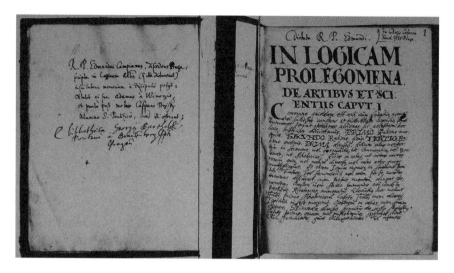

Figure 4.3   Campion's dictated notes on Aristotle's *Logic*: APMC M42, fol. 1r.
© The Prague Castle Archive, Metropolitan Chapter Library.

his devotion to the Eucharist. Evidence of the centrality of the Eucharist in his thinking can be found in the fragments he wrote for the feast of Corpus Christi, in his sermons, and in the replies he gave at his trial. He had come not as 'a Traitor to conspire the subversione of my countye' but

> as a Preyst to Mynister the Sacraments and to heare confessions the which embassaye I protest before God I would as gladye have executed and was as ready & willing to discharge, had I been sent to the Indians or uttermost region of the world, as I was beinge sent into my native countrye.[158]

The request for souvenirs of the lectures they had shared is more than a *laboris sui memoriam*; it is a record of an affectionate fellowship of learning.

A third manuscript from the Rector's library in Prague is now in the library bearing the name of Fr Leopold Szersznik (1747–1814), who rescued the work in 1773 when the Jesuits were suppressed, and took it to Cieszyn.[159] This *Concionale* (sermon book) started life as a record of nearly eighty sermons of Campion, for Sundays and feast days from the beginning of Advent 1578, till the start of 1580, made by Fr. John Aquensis, S.J., Campion's close friend who took over as lecturer in rhetoric and as Latin preacher.[160] It is a complex text in at least four different

---

[158]   BL Add. MS 6265, fols 17r–v.

[159]   This is Książnica Cieszyńska, Biblioteka Leopolda Jana Szersznika (SZ), the Szersznik Library.

[160]   SZ MS DD.V.8, fols 3r–389v (including the *In M. T. Ciceronis Particiones Annotata*). The later sermons are by Aquensis.

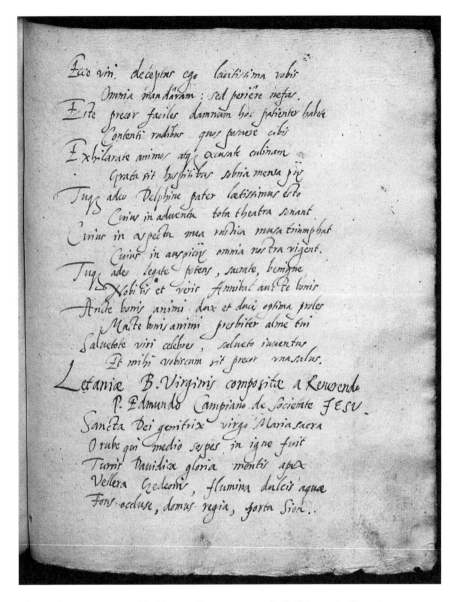

Figure 4.4   *Litaniae B. Mariae Compositae a R.P. Edmundo Campiano*,
SZ MS DD.V.8, fol. 392r. © Książnica Cieszyńska,
Biblioteka Szersznika.

hands, which has been compiled over a period of time that stretches from what appears to be contemporary transcription of the sermons, to transcriptions on much better paper and in a fair hand of nine earlier texts by Campion: the *Dialogus Mutus, Carmen ad convivas sanctae memoriae P. Edmundi, Litaniae B.M.V. Mariae* (Figure 4.4), *De tutela B.V. Mariae, De Iuvene Academico, Oratio in funere Mariae Cardonae, Oratio De S. Wenceslao, De foedere virtutis et scientiae*, and an untitled Campion sermon on the Eucharist.[161] Aquensis is the scribe of the sermons, and of the long '*In M.T. Ciceronis Partitiones Annotata*', but the scribes of the later works are unknown.[162] In the case of the sermons and Cicero, Aquensis's motives may have been purely practical, but the other transcriptions on better paper (some made during Campion's life) appear to have been gathered after Campion's death and given continuous signatures.[163]

On various kinds of paper, these different pens record both the words of Campion and their transmission; it appears that many attended his lectures and sodality, and that everyone wanted to hear him preach. His books were apparently sacred memorials even before he left Prague:

> After this he asked leave of his Rector to bestow & distribute among certain of his own schollers and fellows of his that remained in Prague some dictats & writings that he had gathered there, & some few others he carryed with him to Italy & there gave them also away; and with these and with his breviary only he took his journy on foot to Rome, being not much less distant, than his other journy afterward from Rome to England.[164]

What Campion later calls 'all this travail' was about to begin. It was certainly to be a painful departure.

While Campion was finding fulfilment as a priest and scholar, his New College contemporary, Dr Sander, was planning military intervention. Ever since Sander had been sent to Madrid in the late summer of 1573, he had been trying to persuade Philip II to use Ireland as a stepping-stone to England.[165] He was aided by the papal nuncio, Nicholas Ormanetto, and (after his death in 1577) his successor, Filippo Sega (1537–96), Bishop of Piacenza. Sander wrote from Madrid to Dr Allen on 6 November 1577 an encrypted letter that was intercepted and deciphered by the Privy Council:

---

[161]   SZ MS DD.V.8, fols 390r–428v.

[162]   Schmidl, *Historiae*, I. 436, notes in the Clementinum: '*M. T. Ciceronis Partitiones annotata, cum aliis operibus, Pragense Archivum in thesauris habet*'.

[163]   Comments on SZ MS DD.V.8 have to be tentative until it can be properly edited and published.

[164]   ABSI Collectanea P. I, fol. 105a.

[165]   Thomas M. McCoog, S.J., *The Society of Jesus in Ireland, Scotland and England 1541–1588: "Our Way of Proceeding"* (Leiden, New York, Köln: Brill, 1996), p. 92.

Therefore I beseeche you to take hould of the pope: for the king of Spaine is as fearefull of warre as a child of fyer, and all his endevor is to avoide such occasions. The pope will geve two thousand, when you there shalbe content with them. Yf they doe not serve to goe into England, at the least, they will serve to goe into Ireland. The state of Christendome dependethe upon the stowte assaillinge of Englande.[166]

By March 1578, Sander was in Lisbon trying to gain help from the King of Portugal for an expedition led by the adventurer, Sir Thomas Stuckley, but the King diverted Stuckley to Morocco for a campaign that ended in the death of both men, on 4 August 1578.[167] Persons passed this news to Campion in a letter of 28 November 1578, in the same letter that announced 'that we ar heer at Rome now 24 Inglishemen of the Societie', two of Campion's 'countrymen borne in Pater noster row' among them.[168] The news of Stuckley's disaster seems to have made Sander determined to go to Ireland himself, and he drew up a new plan around James Fitzmaurice Fitzgerald, veteran of the first Desmond rebellion in 1569. Sander intended that the *bellum sacrum* (holy war) would be fronted by an Apostolic Nuncio and English, Irish and Scottish priests, on the assumption that war would spread from one island to 'the other'.[169] By June 1579, Sander and Fitzmaurice, with the support of the papal Secretary of State, Tolomeo Galli (Cardinal of Como) and Bishop Sega, had put together a flotilla of the *San Francisco*, 3 other hired vessels and 40 soldiers under Captain Alessandro Bertone.[170] From the start it was an expedition that was richer in papal banners and friars (two Spanish and two Irish), than instruments of war.

In the Clementinum, Campion finished teaching Book I of the 'Topica' in Aristotle's *Logic* on 23 June 1579, three days after this motley collection of ships sailed north from Ferrol, in Galicia.[171] On 14 July 1579, his students recorded reaching 'the end of the entire book of Logic'.[172] Three days later, on 17 July 1579, Sander's flotilla laid anchor in the serene bay of Dingle, on the south-west corner of Ireland. James Fitzmaurice's report to the Cardinal of Como mixes colourful description with an urgent appeal:

---

[166]   CRS 26, *Miscellanea XIII* (London: Catholic Record Society, 1926), 'Some Letters and Papers of Nicholas Sander, 1560–1580', ed. John B. Wainwright, pp. 13–14 (coded words in italics), copied from BL MS 48029, fol. 50r; see also Allen, *Letters and Memorials*, p. 38, from another copy in PRO 12/118/13. The letter was used as evidence in Campion's trial, as if Allen were the author: see Chapter 10.

[167]   CRS 2, Persons, 'Domesticall Difficulties', p. 64.

[168]   ABSI Anglia I/5; CRS 39, *Letters and Memorials of Father Robert Persons, S.J.*, ed. Leo Hicks, S.J. (London: 1942), pp. 1–2.

[169]   CRS 26, p. 17.

[170]   CRS 26, pp. 19–20.

[171]   CRS 26, p. 19.

[172]   APMC M42, fol. 406v.

When we landed, which we did a little before mid-day, out of six ships (whereof we captured two on the way, hired three and had bought one) we at once uplifted the standard of the cross, and sang litanies, and in the sight of the populous town of Dingle, betook ourselves to a certain fort, with nearly forty armed men, beside four piests and the same number of monks [friars] and with the help of God ocuupied it forthwith ... Let no ship sail for Ireland from Biscaya or Galicia without bringing us something helpful, whether it be powder or lead or larger cannon or harquebuses or fresh arms or money or soldiers.[173]

'Flanked by Sander, a bishop and several friars, and in the shadow of a papal banner, James Fitzmaurice proclaimed the holy war sanctioned in letters from Pope Gregory'.[174] When Sander landed, he was enacting the resistance theory he had adumbrated in *The Rocke of the Church* (1567) and fully developed in *De Visibili Monarchia* (1571). For the Elizabethan government, it was the manifestation of its worst fears: a rebellion giving earthly reality to the papal bull, *Regnans in excelsis*. Although a small force of 40 soldiers occupied the fort, Dún an Óir, in Smerwick, Sander's ambition was to raise a large army to invade England.

On 1 August 1579, in his own house, Sir John of Desmond, brother of the Earl of Desmond, murdered Arthur Carter and Captain Henry Davell, two highly respected English officials. As Sander chillingly reported: 'This murder enabled us to go forward openly'.[175] The shocking event stirred the whole of Munster into a revolt that alarmed the Privy Council in London, which, on 10 August, established a network of extraordinary posts to carry letters between Dublin and London, via Holyhead, Tavistock and Bristol.[176] The Spanish ambassador reported on 15 August that 5,000 men had been mustered, a fleet equipped, the fortification of Dover ordered, a curfew enforced in London and the carrying of pistols forbidden.[177] The Privy Council was terrified that English Catholics would rise in sympathy, and that the loss of Ireland would lead to the loss of England.

In Prague on 11 August 1579, after a month's break, Campion began teaching Aristotle's *Physics*.[178] In Rheims, Dr Allen, leaving Dr Richard Bristow in charge, set out for Rome to ask the Jesuit General, Everard Mercurian, to lend Campion and Robert Persons to a new, entirely spiritual mission to England.[179] James Fitzmaurice Fitzgerald was killed on 18 August. We know that news of Sander's landing in Ireland had reached Rome by 27 August 1579, and Dr Allen himself was there on Monday 28 September 1579 to make a formal presentation to the Pope.[180]

---

[173]   CRS 26, pp. 24–5.

[174]   Colm Lennon, *Sixteenth-Century Ireland: The Incomplete Conquest* (New York: St Martin's Press, 1995), p. 223.

[175]   CRS 26, pp. 29–30.

[176]   *CSP Ireland, 1574–1585*, 68/27, p. 180.

[177]   *CSP Spanish, 1568–1579*, pp. 685–6.

[178]   APMC M65, fol. 1r.

[179]   *Douai Diaries*, p. 320.

[180]   CRS 53, *Miscellanea: Recusant Records*, ed. Clare Talbot (London: Catholic Record Society, 1961), pp. 222–3.

On 8 October 1579, Sander was writing to Mgr Alessandro Frumento, the papal nuncio in Portugal, giving an account of the numbers slain in the 'sacred project', and begging the Portuguese to make up the losses in ships, arms and men incurred by the Moroccan foray. From Rheims, Gregory Martin wrote to Campion, on 16 October 1579, that the manuscript of his 'Irish history' was finally being carried by special messenger to Prague, where Campion knew neither of Sander's expedition nor Allen's purpose in Rome.[181]

For the situation in Ireland had worsened. Sir John of Desmond took over the leadership of the rebellion, but his forces were badly mauled on 3 October, at Monasteranagh. On 13 November, the Earl of Desmond himself entered the fray, after he was declared a traitor, for refusing to hand over Dr Sander: he responded by sacking the coastal town of Youghal, thereby unleashing a savage series of reprisals by the Earl of Ormond and Lord Justice Pelham. On 19 November 1579, Campion began teaching Book IV of Aristotle's *Physics*, on 'Place and Time'.[182] In Ireland, over the next two months, Sander was writing desperate appeals for help.[183] When two Spanish ships put in at Dingle, with wholly inadequate supplies of money, powder, arms and wine, on 28 January 1580, Sander 'railed and reviled them for not accomplishing their former promise'.[184] The second ship was sent back within six hours to Spain, carrying Captain Bertone and letters from Sander to Bishop Sega and the Cardinal of Como, asking for help, and saying that 'all the captains regard themselves as in the pay of his Holiness'.[185]

Meanwhile, in London, opposition to the proposed marriage to François, Duke of Alençon and Anjou, always known in England as 'Monsieur', reached its peak. October was the critical month when 'queen and council engaged in an exercise at once of brinkmanship and of buck-passing'.[186] Sidney wrote his *A Letter to Queen Elizabeth Touching her Marriage with Monsieur*, perhaps before John Stubbe had his right hand cut off on 3 November 1579.[187] On 20 November 1579, the Queen commissioned four peers to 'negotiate a matrimonial treaty', despite the fact that the issue of religion was unresolved.[188] The Anjou match had created a crisis for the Queen's most faithful advisers: who would dare to give the Queen good counsel, and risk her 'extreme' rages?[189] Both 'forward Protestants' and Catholic advocates of the marriage believed that it would determine the future

---

[181] CRS 26, pp. 28–31; Gregory Martin's letter to Campion, *Douai Diaries*, p. 320.

[182] APMC 65, fol. 135r.

[183] CRS 26, pp. 35–45, letters on 26 and 27 December and 23 January.

[184] CRS 53, pp. 45–6.

[185] CRS 53, p. 43.

[186] Blair Worden, *The Sound of Virtue: Philip Sidney's* Arcadia *and Elizabethan Politics* (New Haven and London: Yale University Press, 1996), p. 149.

[187] Worden, *Sound of Virtue*, p. 111.

[188] Doran, *Monarchy and Matrimony*, pp. 174–5.

[189] Worden, *Sound of Virtue*, pp. 146–50, shows how desperate Burghley and Walsingham were.

of religion in this country.[190] Perhaps encouraged by this brief glimmer of hope, Dr Allen began negotiating with the Jesuit General, Everard Mercurian, for the participation of Campion and Robert Persons in the mission.[191]

In Prague, on 14 December 1579, Campion finished Book IV of the *Physics* by asking whether all things were in Time.[192] Time was already spinning its web in London, Smerwick and Rome, where the delayed arrival of news was central to the concatenation of events that would chain Campion to his fate.[193] Dr Allen had already pulled the thread that would tug Campion back from his scholarly explorations of Aristotle into the murderous whirlpool of English politics. As Campion returned to England, disguised, not as a serpent like Aesculapius, but as a jewel-merchant, Dr Sander was waiting impatiently for arms and men: not in Latium, but in a desolate iron-age fort:

> No mortal eye could see
> The intimate welding of their later history,
>> Or sign that they were bent
>> By paths coincident
> On being anon twin halves of one august event.[194]

---

[190]   Worden, *Sound of Virtue*, pp. 93–111 (p. 93).

[191]   Thomas M. McCoog, S.J., *"And touching our society": Fashioning Jesuit Identity in Elizabethan England* (Toronto: PIMS, 2013), pp. 66–9, argues that the French match could have been the 'framework within which the mission was discussed'.

[192]   APMC M65, fol. 168r.

[193]   McCoog, *Fashioning Jesuit Identity*, p. 68, argues that news of the collapse of marriage negotiations arrived in Rome too late 'to cancel the mission'.

[194]   'The Convergence of the Twain', in Thomas Hardy, *The Collected Poems*, ed. James Gibson (London: Macmillan, 1976), pp. 306–7 (p. 307).

Chapter 5
All this Travail

'I am summoned', his pupils record Campion as saying when, after racing through Book IV of Aristotle's *De Coelo* in one morning, he told them, at 1 p.m. on 9 February 1580, that he had been called to Rome (Figure 5.1).[1] We do not know exactly when he had first heard of the command of his General, but it seems likely that Campion knew soon after the middle of January. Adam à Winorzie has written a record of the dialogue the students had with their professor when they expressed their dismay at being abandoned in mid-course. Winorzie makes their professor defend himself against the disappointment of his students:

Inde vocor, vocor inde, via transcendere cautes
Alpeas, latiaque simul tellure potiri:
Quo me cumque dei manus inde remiserit, alta
Stat menti positum celeres inflectere cursus.

[I am summoned from there, from there I am summoned to cross the harsh Alps and at the same time occupy the land of Latium: wherever the hand of God shall send me from there, I am firmly resolved to bend my swift course.][2]

There are deliberate echoes here of Aeneas being summoned by the gods to return to his task of founding Rome. If the English mission corresponds to the solemn duty of founding Rome, then Bohemia becomes Carthage, and the wrench from his joyful and fulfilling duties, as painful as the separation of Aeneas from Dido.[3]

On 23 February, Winorzie noted that the next lecture was delivered by Fr Paul Neukirch, Campion having departed for Rome.[4] From this we know that Campion had left by Monday 22 February. All the evidence – a flurry of letters from Rector and Provincial, elaborate efforts made by his immediate superiors and princely friends to protect Campion, Campion's requests for copies of his dictated notes, the distribution of his 'dictates and writings' and, above all, the long

---

[1]   APMC M65, fol. 261r. This manuscript is a record made by his students of Campion's lectures on Aristotle's *Physics*. Adam à Winorzie seems to be the author of these hundred and one hexameter lines.

[2]   APMC M65, fol. 261r.

[3]   P. Vergili Maronis, *Aeneidos*, IV. 265–76.

[4]   APMC M65, fol. 272v. After Campion's execution, Winorzie added a prayer to Campion, to pray for his former pupil. Campion's copy letter, ABSI Anglia I/6, fol. 25r, is addressed to Fr Melchior Neuchyrch (though Campion has revised the spelling of his name); it is not clear whether they are related.

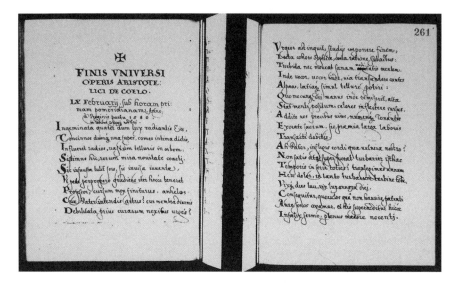

Figure 5.1   *Inde vocor*: verse dialogue of students with Campion about
              departure for Rome, from notes on lectures on Aristotle's *Physics*,
              APMC M65, fols 260v–261r. © The Prague Castle Archive,
              Metropolitan Chapter Library.

delay – suggests that Campion's departure from Prague was a moment of profound
emotional intensity.[5] At every stage of his life, from Dublin to Lyford Grange,
departure was painful for Campion. The six years in Prague, and especially the
last two after he had been ordained, had been the most richly productive in his life.
From the moment he received the summons and particularly when he received
Dr Allen's letter, Campion knew that he would be would be plunging into a
whirlpool of politics and religion, where his own belief in patient sacramental
transformation would be lost in the excited clamour of militant exiles, and he
would have to cling, in a tempestuous sea, to his vow of obedience.

The Jesuit General, Everard Mercurian, had previously turned down requests
for help with the English mission in the winter of 1575, and in January 1579.[6]
This time, when William Allen came to Rome, Pope Gregory XIII agreed to
the English mission, on 28 September 1579, and instructed Allen to approach
Mercurian, who organized a major consultation with his Assistants.[7] Persons, keen
to counter a later charge by the Privy Council 'of the lightnesse of the journy

---

[5]   APMC M42, Adam à Winorzie's note on fly paper facing title page.

[6]   McCoog, *Fashioning Jesuit Identity*, p. 55. Everard Mercurian (1514–80) was the
fourth Superior General.

[7]   McCoog, *Fashioning Jesuit Identity*, p. 66.

of F. Campion to England', devotes a whole chapter to the discussion.[8] Those taking part were Oliver Mannaerts, who was the Assistant responsible for France, Germany, Poland, Flanders and England; Benedict Palmius, Assistant for Italy and Sicily; Gonzales de Avila, Assistant for Spain and the West Indies; and Pedro de Fonseca, Assistant for Portugal, East Indies and Japan. In addition to these regional superiors, Mercurian called in Claudio Acquaviva, the provincial for Rome, who was soon to succeed Mercurian, and Persons himself.[9] The Assistants were under no illusions:

> First the very importance of the enterprise did make them doubtfull, for they did see how great & hard an affaire they were to take in hand in sending their men into to evident perils & dangers as they were to expect in England.[10]

After Allen had put forward the arguments for the mission, the case against it was presented by Persons. The first objection, surprisingly, was that the prospect of martyrdom might encourage young men to come forward.[11] The second difficulty was the central one: that 'the enimy in England according to his lying and fraudulent manner' would argue that the mission was 'not made for matter of religion but for some practise of state'.[12] Although Persons describes as 'more weighty than all the rest' the third difficulty, that it would be difficult to lead a religious life under such political repression, the consultation ended with the superiors reverting to the second objection, and offering a solution:

> It was determined for better answering of the 2nd difficulty or obloquy of the enimy about matters of State that certaine particular instructions should be delivered to them that should be sent to England, signed with the General's own hand for their religious manner of living & proceeding in England, whereby it should appeer that their coming thither was only for matter of religion & not of state wherin they were expressly willed not to meddle.[13]

With Allen, Persons, Mannaerts and Acquaviva declaring themselves in favour of the mission, Mercurian was persuaded, but he gave specific instruction that the priests were solely to minister the sacraments to Catholics and to reconcile those who had fallen away.[14] Allen's choice of a brilliant orator and someone who would become one of the best writers of the Elizabethan period suggests that he may have had a more ambitious plan.

---

[8]   ABSI Collectanea P. I, fols 102a–104b.

[9]   ABSI Collectanea P. I, fol. 102b.

[10]   ABSI Collectanea P. I, fol. 103a–b.

[11]   ABSI Collectanea P. I, fol. 103b.

[12]   ABSI Collectanea P. I, fol. 103b.

[13]   ABSI Collectanea P. I, fol. 104b.

[14]   CRS 39, pp. 316–21; McCoog, *Fashioning Jesuit Identity*, p. 66.

The spy Charles Sledd, whose reports were later edited by Thomas Norton, relates that Allen had just announced in Rome Sander's invasion of Ireland.[15] He records Persons as present at a dinner on 8 October 1579, when Allen 'thundred out in speech the arivall of D. Saunders in Irland'.[16] Sledd reports that, 'the 24 November 1579 Tuesdaye a solem diner was made' at the house of Dr Nicholas Morton, at which Allen (apparently unaware that Munster was now being put to the fire and the sword) 'declared that the spanyardes were peaseablye possesed of all Irland', and announced a mission in the spring of six more priests, saying 'how beneficial yt wold be to the Popes estate in the sendinge of their prestes, in causinge & warninge the people to be redye to receave suche as he would send here after'.[17] The simultaneous announcement of the invasion and the mission might be Sledd's invention, but there is little doubt that, when Allen was negotiating with Mercurian, the view from Rome was that Sander's expedition was on the way to success, and that the negotiations with the Duke of Anjou were likely to produce some amelioration for Catholics.[18] 'In the late spring and summer of 1579, it looked as if those in favour of the marriage had gained the upper hand', and by 24 November, Burghley, who had tried to calm opposition to the marriage by 'Penalties increased upon Recusants', had succeeded in having a marriage treaty drawn up with Simier.[19] Two days later, on 26 November, Henry Orton and Robert Johnson arrived in Rome with a copy of the royal proclamation against John Stubbe (27 September 1579): news was taking about two months to come from Ireland or England.[20] On 13 December 1579, Sledd describes a treasonable conversation between Bishop Thomas Goldwell, Dr Morton and Dr Allen, as they walk in the cloister of St Sylvester's, and talk of 'the good successe of the Spaniardes in Ireland and of the strength and multitude of there frendes in England', their

---

[15]   Sledd's report, revised probably by Thomas Norton, perhaps by Robert Beale, exists in two manuscripts. The complete text of his '2 severall Bookes' is in BL Add. MS 48029, fols 121r–142v. BL Add. MS 48023, fols 94r–109v has only the second 'book', with interesting variations, but is in a more professional hand and has a dedication to Walsingham. Although the interpretation of events may be untrustworthy, the dates and events seem plausible. The complete text has been printed (though with minor errors) in CRS 53, *Miscellanea XII, Recusant Records*, ed. Clare Talbot (London: Catholic Record Society, 1961), pp. 193–245.

[16]   BL Add. MS 48029, fol. 135r; CRS 53, p. 223. 'Persons must have heard something about Sander's arrival', McCoog, *Fashioning Jesuit Identity*, pp. 71–2.

[17]   BL Add. MS 48029, fol. 135v; CRS 53, p. 224.

[18]   McCoog, *Fashioning Jesuit Identity*, p. 61, analyzes the Council's changes in attitude to Anjou and, n. 30, examines Sledd's credibility. For the shifting sands of late 1579, see Worden, *Sound of Virtue*, pp. 99–114.

[19]   Doran, *Monarchy and Matrimony*, pp. 161–74 (p. 161), provides a detailed account of this period, of the *Gaping Gulf* and of the Queen's reactions to John Stubbe's book. See Chapter 12 for more detail on Stubbe and the proclamation.

[20]   CRS 53, p. 226. For text see Paul L. Hughes and James F. Larkin, C.S.V., eds, *Tudor Royal Proclamations*, 3 vols (London and New Haven: Yale University Press, 1969), II. 445–9.

allies the Queen Mother (Catherine de Medici), Monsieur and 'our dear friend and protector', the Duke of Guise.[21] By February 1580, when Campion was leaving Prague, the marriage negotiations had collapsed. A final round recommenced in February the following year, reaching a promising climax when Anjou came to London again on 1 November 1581, the day before Campion was racked for the last time.[22] Two days after Campion was sentenced to death, the Queen celebrated her Accession Day with what looked so like a betrothal that bonfires were lit in Antwerp.[23] But fierce religious opposition forced her to beat a retreat the next day, so that by the time Monsieur finally set sail, still a *celibataire*, for Antwerp, on 1 February 1582, Campion had become the most celebrated casualty of this protracted, fruitless and very expensive wooing.[24]

It seems likely, therefore, that the English mission of 1580 was conceived by English Catholic exiles in the brief window of optimism at the end of 1579.[25] Yet neither Dr Allen nor the Papal Secretary of State, the Cardinal of Como, can have told Mercurian of Sander's expedition. In fact, Allen had successfully overcome the reservations of the Jesuit General that it would be safe for two of his most talented priests to be sent to England only on the strict understanding that they would not 'meddle': be involved in politics. From the moment, in early December 1579, that Mercurian and Allen sent their letters to Prague, Campion (who knew of the Stuckley fiasco from Persons) showed himself detached from the political and strategic aims of the mission.[26] While Campion had grown up in a fiercely divided London, where the central religious battles of the century were fought with ferocity, Allen was from Lancashire, which the Privy Council described in 1574 as 'the very sincke of Poperie', and Persons came from a part of Somerset that was (and is still) remote from London.[27] Allen, surrounded by intellectually able and spiritually ardent men, clearly felt that the flimsily built walls of the heretical Jericho were ready to fall. Despite the experience of Cuthbert Mayne, neither Persons nor Allen seemed to have adequately imagined the horrors that awaited Campion and his fellow martyrs in 'this Tower of London ... wherein the sound of all speche and mourninge of the afflicted is shutt upp frome the eares of them that are abroade'.[28]

---

[21]   BL Add. MS 48023, fols 114r–115r. This report appears to be unique to this manuscript, which is not just a fair copy. Stephen Alford, *The Watchers: A Secret History of the Reign of Elizabeth I* (London: Allen Lane, 2012), p. 336, analyzes both manuscripts, where truth seems elusive.

[22]   Doran, *Monarchy and Matrimony*, pp. 179–89; McCoog, *Fashioning Jesuit Identity*, p. 80.

[23]   Doran, *Monarchy and Matrimony*, p. 187.

[24]   Doran, *Monarchy and Matrimony*, p. 189; McCoog, *Fashioning Jesuit Identity*, p. 81.

[25]   McCoog, *Fashioning Jesuit Identity*, p. 87, puts forward this hypothesis.

[26]   For the letter of Persons to Campion on Stuckley, see Chapter 4.

[27]   Patrick McGrath, *Papists and Puritans under Elizabeth I* (London: Blandford Press, 1967), pp. 108–9, citing *APC, 1571–73*, 27 July 1574, p. 276.

[28]   [Robert Persons], *An Epistle of the Persecution of Catholikes in Englande* (Douay: [n.p., 1582]), STC 19406, ARCR II. 627, p. 87.

On 4 December 1579, Mercurian wrote to Campion telling him to go to Padua where he would learn about his mission.[29] Mercurian did not mention England, and may have been 'silent about Campion's destination because he feared his reaction', or because he feared interception of the letter; a remarkable number of letters at this time were intercepted.[30] On 5 December, Allen himself wrote with breathless urgency and excited affection to Edmund Campion in Prague.

> My father, brother, son, Edmund Campion (I gladly take over all the terms of the highest love towards you) since the supreme Father and prefect of your Order, that is as I understand it, Christ, will summon you from Prague to Rome and furthermore into our England ... Make all haste and come, my dearest, as quickly as you can so that you may reach me in the city [of Rome] at least by the end of February, even though I should prefer you to come before the middle of the month, and that would certainly be best.[31]

It seems likely that these two letters were sent in the same bundle; news of the summons had certainly reached Vienna by mid-January, since Henrik Blyssem, the Austrian provincial, wrote to Mercurian on 18 January, to assure him that he would write to Campion's rector, Campani, but that he was worried about losing Campion when he was half-way through his course on Aristotle's *Physics*, and wondered whether he should wait till Mercurian sent a replacement; he added (in a postscript) that he had now found someone to take over the course temporarily, and had therefore written to Campani, to instruct Campion to depart as soon as possible for Padua.[32] Yet, as we have seen, Campion did not tell his students till 9 February 1580.[33]

Perhaps Campion had been hoping for a reprieve, and he and Campani were searching for a way out. On 6 February 1580, Mercurian wrote to Campion again, anxious that his first letter had not arrived, and telling Campion to proceed directly to Rome, without stopping in Padua.[34] Uncertain as to where Campion was, Mercurian may have sent a second copy of this letter to Padua, as he did for one written on 18 March 1580, when he told Campion to go straight to Milan where the party would meet him.[35] In none of these letters did Mercurian mention England.[36] On 12 February, his Provincial, Henrik Blyssem, wrote again to Mercurian to say

---

[29]   ARSI Austr. 1/1a, pp. 240–41, cited by McCoog, *Fashioning Jesuit Identity*, pp. 93–4.

[30]   McCoog, *Fashioning Jesuit Identity*, p. 96. In the letters, McCoog has unearthed evidence of significant delay. I am profoundly indebted to his research, and to many discussions with him on this issue.

[31]   ABSI Anglia A.I/7, fol. 28r; Allen, *Letters and Memorials*, p. 84.

[32]   ARSI Germ. 158, fols 31v–32r; McCoog, *Fashioning Jesuit Identity*, p. 94.

[33]   See Chapter 4.

[34]   ARSI Austr. 1/1a, p. 244.

[35]   ARSI Austr. 1/1a, pp. 255–6.

[36]   McCoog, *Fashioning Jesuit Identity*, p. 94. The three letters are in ARSI, Austr. 1/1a, pp. 244, 255–6.

how much the college would miss Campion.[37] Finally on 8 March, two weeks after Campion had left, the Rector wrote to say that Campion had departed 'a few days earlier'; and expressed the grief all felt at his departure:

> All who know his virtue, his powerful eloquence, and his other talents are affected by his loss, but obedience is as strong as death so we submit with equanimity, considering that God wills it so.[38]

Campani, who had taken Campion through the Spiritual Exercises, knew when Campion had left, and knew he intended to stay in Munich long enough for him to direct two letters there: perhaps he was trying, in some way, to paper over the slow progress of Campion. Campion received one of these letters as he was leaving Munich; the second letter he received once he had arrived in Rome.[39] Campion left Prague in the carriage of Prince Ferdinand, brother of Wilhelm, Duke of Bavaria.[40] Wilhelm had just inherited the Dukedom on the death of his father, Albert, who had erected a fine residence for the Jesuits, opened with great panache in 1561.[41] In 1581, Wilhelm himself began work on the massive St Michael's Church for the Jesuits in Munich. The Prince and his brother, the Duke, may have seen that their beloved Campion needed support at this crisis. We know that Campion gave a sermon there on the feast of St Thomas Aquinas (then, on 7 March).[42] The Duke's library contained early editions of Luther, and Campion 'copied those words very faithfully', as we know from the first disputation in the Tower.[43] Campion may have spent as long as two weeks in the Duke's library, one of the best in Europe.[44] If he left Prague by 22 February 1580, with a carriage journey from Prague of 200 miles, he could have reached Munich no later than I March. Campion told Campani in his Bologna letter, dated 30 April, that from Munich he 'was carried in the carriage of Prince Ferdinand to Innsbruck', a distance of only 90 miles.[45] From Innsbruck, Campion tells us that he went 'on foot' (*meis pedibus*) the 200 miles to Padua, which would have taken about 8 days.[46] This certainly ignores all

---

[37]   ARSI Germ. 158. fol. 47v.

[38]   ARSI Germ. 158, fol. 84v, quoted by McCoog, *Fashioning Jesuit Identity*, p. 94.

[39]   *Opuscula*, p. 400.

[40]   McCoog, *Fashioning Jesuit Identity*, p. 96.

[41]   Brodrick, *Canisius*, p. 450. Prince Wilhelm sent a stag for the occasion.

[42]   Schmidl, *Historiae*, I. 437.

[43]   Bombino, *Vita et Martyrium*, p. 228; Bodl. MS Tanner 329, fol. 96r. See Chapter 9.

[44]   Dirk Imhof, *A Never Realized Edition: Balthasar Moretus's Project of a Polyglot Bible* (Antwerp: Kockelbergh, 2014), p. 25, shows that Petrus Lansselius, S.J., found some of his best manuscripts for the projected bible in the library of the Duke of Bavaria, which in part derived from the Fugger collection.

[45]   '*Oenipontum curru Principis Ferdinandi vectus sum*', *Opuscula*, p. 404. Everything in this letter, including money given by the addressee, suggests that '*Uni ex patribus*' (p. 400) is his rector, Giovanni Campani.

[46]   *Opuscula*, p. 405.

the encouragement to speed in Allen's December letter, and suggests Campion is falling back on pilgrimage as a way of working out his crisis. Not surprisingly, in Padua, Campion received the command: 'hasten to Rome' (*Romam propera*).[47] Campion, who had now been joined by a nameless father of the society (who may have been sent from Rome to bring Campion quickly), took post-horses to Rome. The journey from Padua to Rome was about 300 miles, so Campion cannot have received Mercurian's letter of 18 March (telling him to go straight to Milan). Campion later told Campani in his Bologna letter that he had been about to give away all his money, before he received this command, but as soon as he and his fellow Jesuit began using post-horses, all his money evaporated, and he was saved only by his companion, who had plenty.[48] This part of the journey, post-haste, would have taken about seven days, especially as Campion emphasizes that he 'had scarcely time to draw breath' in the inns.[49]

Altogether, there seem to have been 9 or 10 letters about (or to) Campion at this time; none *from* him survive. The whole journey (of 800 miles), with all its different modes of travel, would have taken, at most, 32 days, but Campion did not arrive in Rome till 10 April 1580, 47 days after he left Prague, and 4 months after the summons had been sent.[50] The inescapable fact is that, whether by ducal carriage or on foot, and despite several indications of urgency, Campion had *lingered* on his journey from Prague to Padua. The word itself is used by Schmidl:

> he lingered for a little while (*aliquantisper haerebat*), whether from anxiety about the sheer immensity of the thing, or because his soul could not yet absorb the immense joy.[51]

The period from the summons to the day when Campion left Rome by the Ponte Molle for England, is swirling with unexplained delays, confused dates and missing letters. The absence of any letter from Campion himself (except to his former rector) is significant. The tradition within the Bohemian province registered what Allen, in Rheims, and Persons, in Rome, suppressed: that Campion delayed as he struggled to cope with the enormity of the task. His rector, Campani, Duke Wilhelm and Prince Ferdinand of Bavaria, seem to have steered him through the crisis, since the carriage journeys and the time in the library suggest protective care rather than ducal favouritism. The disturbance was ironed out by those who invested their lives in the English mission. It is clear that leaving the idyll of Bohemia, where every priestly and scholarly instinct was fulfilled, was a painful, emotional wrench; everything suggests that Campion was aware of Allen's political plans, and that he submitted only after a struggle, which makes him a more credible model of human sanctity.

---

[47]   *Opuscula*, p. 405.

[48]   *Opuscula*, p. 405.

[49]   *Opuscula*, p. 406.

[50]   McCoog, *Fashioning Jesuit Identity*, pp. 93–6.

[51]   Schmidl, *Historiae*, I. 437.

Henry Holland, in a letter dated 14 February 1579, suggests that Campion had ignored pleas to go to England, and that he was forgetting his friends.[52] Allen's own letter of 5 December 1579, supports this idea:

> your brothers according to the flesh also urge you [to come to England]. Even if you cannot hear their voices, God himself has heard their prayers'.[53]

Persons indicates that, although the General's first letter did not mention the reason why he was being summoned to Rome, Campion deduced the purpose from 'Dr Allen's being in Rome and of some words which both he [Persons] and Dr Allen had written unto him before he suspected the cause why he was called'.[54] Later Persons wrote that the summons 'was both suddain and strange news to him', and that Campion

> went to his chamber and there upon his knees to god satisfyed his appetit of weeping and thanksgiving & and offred himself wholy to his divine disposition without any exception or restraint, whither it were to rack, crosse, quartering or any other torment or death whatsoever.[55]

This flagrantly hagiographical account may reflect a profound psychological truth. Persons says that the night Campion received the letter, a young Silesian Jesuit rose early and

> went to F. Campians chamber dore and wrott ouer it *Campianus Martyr* whereof all men there did wounder and made great reflection therof and as I remember the sayd father tould me that his superiors had given him a pennance for doing it.[56]

Balbin names the man as Jacob Gallus, identifies the night more convincingly as the one before he left Prague, and gives the inscription as *P. Edmundus Campianus Martyr*.[57] Gallus's epigraph only highlights the dreadful reality that Campion confronted as he rode to Munich with Prince Ferdinand. Persons turns Campion's journey into that of a future martyr, and tells how 'with his breviary only he took his journey on foot to Rome ... after soe venerable a manner to Rome as he might move devotion for he came in grave priest's [garb] with long [beard and] haire

---

[52] ARSI Fondo Gesuitico 651/628, quoted by Thomas M. McCoog, S.J., '"Playing the Champion": The Role of Disputation', in *The Reckoned Expense*, ed. Thomas M. McCoog, S.J., 2nd ed. (Rome: IHSI, 2007), pp. 139–63 (p. 146).

[53] ARSI Fondo Gesuitico 651/594, published in Allen, *Letters and Memorials*, pp. 84–5, and translated in More, *Historia Missionis*, pp. 72–3.

[54] ABSI Collectanea P. I, fol. 105a.

[55] ABSI Collectanea P. I, fol. 105a.

[56] ABSI Collectanea P. I, fol. 8b.

[57] Balbin, *Miscellanea*, p. 195.

after the fashion of Germany'.[58] Priestly fashion, German or otherwise, must have been the last thing on Campion's mind.

Easter Sunday fell on 3 April 1580. Persons says that Campion reached Rome in 'Passion week' and spent 15 or 20 days there; Bombino that he arrived 'on 2nd April, that is Holy Saturday'.[59] Yet Mercurian complained to the Austrian Provincial, Henrik Blyssem, in a letter of 9 April 1580, that Campion had not yet arrived.[60] Everyone agrees that Campion left Rome on 18 April 1580.[61] The date is confirmed by a spy's note: 'Ther departed from Rome the xviiith daye of Aprell 1579 [1580] and came together into England – Father Edmond Campion, Jesuit, priste'.[62] Campion wrote to Campani: 'When I was staying in Rome about eight days, I was working hard, through lack of time, more than during the whole journey' (*denique Romae cum haererem ad circiter octo dies, plus quam toto itinere laborabam temporis peniuria*).[63] The only reasonable conclusion is that Campion arrived in Rome on 10 April 1580, and left about a week after Low Sunday.[64]

When Campion reached Rome, he went first to see Mercurian,

> & after he had bin with his General and understood his mind about the journey to England & that it should be immediately after the octaves of Easter, he made instant sute that seeing the time was so short he might be distracted with no other thing or cogitation but only to commend himself to God and visit the holy places of the citty and prepare himself for the viage. In which viage & mission he desired most earnestly & humbly that he might be charged with no temporal care or solicitude in the world, either to be superior to other or to provide for meat and drinke or the like, but that he might be left alone to his praiers and to preach & teach when occasion should be offered. And this point he urged so far forth and showed so hearty an aversion from medling with the same as it was

---

[58]   ABSI Collectanea P. I, fol. 105a. Campion, belonging to the Province that included Germany at that stage, presumably adopted the dress of his province. The Weld portrait on the cover of this book confirms the beard, but not the long hair.

[59]   ABSI Collectanea P. I, fol. 105b: '*Post Dominicam in albis egressi sumus Roma*'. Campion's Bologna letter is cross-referenced by Fr Grene to fol. 159b, highlighting the discrepancy of the date. Persons seems mistaken in the date of arrival, the liturgical calendar and the duration, of Campion's stay; see Bombino, *Vita et Martyrium*, p. 60; Bodl. MS Tanner 329, fol. 22r.

[60]   ARSI Austr. 1/1a, pp. 257–9.

[61]   *Opuscula*, p. 406.

[62]   *Douai Diaries*, p. 360. This is not Sledd, who had already reached Rheims, CRS 53, p. 242; Stephen Alford, *The Watchers: A Secret History of the Reign of Elizabeth I* (London: Allen Lane, 2012), p. 79.

[63]   Letter from Bologna, dated the last day of April, 1580, *Opuscula*, p. 406. The letter is reprinted in Simpson, pp. 155–6, who says: 'Campion left Prague on March 25', and reached Rome on 'Holy Saturday, April 5, 1580', p. 135: this would require something faster than post-horses.

[64]   As suggested by McCoog, *Reckoned Expense*, p. 146, and *Fashioning Jesuit Identity*, p. 97.

the cause that the charge of the mission was layd upon his fellow though of lesse age, standing in religion, and ability than himself.[65]

Campion was completely at one with Mercurian in his 'aversion from medling', and all the time in Rome 'he went every day to pray and say masse in different churches where Apostles or Saints bodies lay'.[66] On this second visit to Rome he could say Mass in the shrines and churches of the early Christian martyrs, and ask their prayers as he set out for his own certain martyrdom in England, where he saw himself, as we know from the letter from Bologna, as a soldier in the first rank going into battle: 'Even if we fall in the first rank, the army is full of recent recruits'.[67]

Campion's single-minded devotion to the apostolic church differed from that of Persons, who, in his first visit to Rome, was present 'at the opening of the Holy Gate by Pope Gregory the 13 in the beginning of the holy yeare 1575', but 'carried little devotion out of Rome', because he 'had attended more to see profane monuments of Cesar, Cicero and other such like then to places of devotion'.[68] We know that when Campion visited Rome in 1573, two years before the Jubilee, he had behaved very differently:

> After some daies that he had bin in Rome & satisfyed some part of his devotion in visiting those holy churches and memories of the blessed Apostles & infinit other martyrs & saints he felt his desire increased howerly to enter into the Society & order of the Jesuits.[69]

Campion visited the Rome he described in his poem, *Sancta salutiferi nascentia semina verbi*: the apostolic church of the martyrs Peter and Paul, not the Rome of Gregory XIII, where the Secretary of State, the Cardinal of Como, was managing a network of papal nuncios in Spain and Portugal, and consulting with Sander about military expeditions.[70] Campion's devotion to the church of the early martyrs was a conscious and consistent choice, expressed in his desire to avoid 'temporal care' or 'medling' (political activity). The path chosen by Nicholas Sander, with papal approval, was a dangerous meddling with the weapons of the world: money, power and the sword. It led to the deaths of 50,000 men, women and children, and the

---

[65]   ABSI Collectanea P. I, fol. 105b.

[66]   ABSI Collectanea P. I, fol. 105b.

[67]   *Opuscula*, p. 404.

[68]   CRS 2, p. 24.

[69]   ABSI Collectanea P. I, fol. 95a.

[70]   There are three extant manuscripts known of this long poem: BL Add. MS 36529, fols 69v–78r; Holkham Hall MS 437; and Bodl. MS Rawl. D 289; see Kilroy, *Memory and Transcription*, pp. 149–93, for descriptions of the first two manuscripts, text and translation. For significance of the recently discovered Bodl. MS Rawl. D. 289 in Harington's manuscript output, see Kilroy, 'Advertising the Reader: Sir John Harington's "Directions in the Margent"', in *English Literary Renaissance* 41.1 (2011), 64–110.

destruction of towns and famine throughout Munster. Campion was an incidental casualty in that 'general drama of pain'.[71]

In the 800 lines of Campion's poem on the beginnings of the church, *Sancta salutiferi nascentia semina verbi*, Campion focuses solely on the church of the apostles and martyrs, and especially St Peter:

> Hunc tibi (fabor enim quando est effabile verum)
> principe sub Christo, cui summa capescere fas est,
> nacta es christicolae primum caput urbis et orbis.
> Tu tibi nec metas rerum nec tempora ponas;
> imperium sine fine tenes sedemque perennem,
> et pia iura dabis sacrati pastor ovilis.

> [I shall speak the truth since it can be spoken: you have gained [Peter] him as the first head of the city of Christ and the world of Christ. It is he who, under Christ your prince, rightly undertakes the highest charge. Set no limits of time or space to your rule: the empire you hold is without end, your see everlasting. As shepherd of the sacred flock, you will make laws that are holy.][72]

The rule of Peter is an eternal empire, far beyond the limits of earthly power of the 'sons of Aeneas'. This is not a vision of a papacy with temporal power to depose monarchs. Like Ambrose in his play, *Ambrosiana*, the pope may advise emperors, even keep them from communion until they repent, but nowhere does Campion show interest in the power of the papacy to *depose* monarchs. This is a long way from the church, and papacy, described in the 844 pages of Sander's *De Visibili Monarchia* (1571). Sander counters the attempt by the king to take control of the church by asserting the stronger power of the pope. These two Oxford scholars would enact in their lives their contrasting visions of the church.

Campion's Roman pilgrimage is more than evidence of the piety of a future martyr: Campion insists that what is offered by the church is *spiritual* salvation through the sacraments: he had few illusions about the *political* situation into which this mission was plunging itself, and what the outcome was likely to be. Campion knew what had happened to his 'room-mate' (*contubernalis*), Cuthbert Mayne, chaplain at St John's, who joined the seminary at Douai in 1573, a year after Campion had left Douai for Rome. Mayne was arrested in his native Cornwall, tortured and executed on four counts: carrying the bull of 10 May 1574 (which proclaimed the Jubilee), 'bringing in the Agnus Dei', 'saieng of the Masse', and 'extolling the Romane Aucthoritie': he was disembowelled at Launceston on 30 November 1577.[73]

---

[71]   The last four words of Thomas Hardy, *The Mayor of Casterbridge*, ed. Dale Kramer (Oxford: University Press, 2004), p. 310. The novel was first published in the *Graphic* and *Harper's Weekly* in 1886.

[72]   Kilroy, *Memory and Transcription*, p. 167 and translation on p. 187, lines 484–9.

[73]   *Cause of the Canonization of Blessed Martyrs John Houghton, Robert Lawrence, Augustine Webster, Richard Reynolds, John Stone, Cuthbert Mayne, John Paine, Edmund*

Campion's interview with Mercurian allowed him to voice his profound concerns about the effect of the papal bull, and on 14 April, Campion went with Persons and Oliver Mannaerts, the Assistant for France, Germany, Poland, Flanders and England, to an audience with Pope Gregory XIII.[74] Campion and Persons submitted in advance the text of 19 questions, 14 of which relate to the bull, *Regnans in Excelsis*, and the reply is contained in a document in the Secret Vatican Archives.[75] The central issue was whether Catholics were still bound by the bull, which absolved them from obedience to the Queen. Should Catholics continue to obey the Queen of England while she is in power, or are they obliged by the bull to take up arms against her? The answer given at the beginning of this secret document, which must represent what the Pope said at their audience on 14 April, is unequivocal:

> At the outset, it would seem expedient, in order to remove many difficulties which have arisen from the bull, to make clear that by the pope's authority the Catholics of England are not bound under pain of sin or of excommunication by virtue of the bull published by Pius V. In the meantime, however, we have come to believe (*Nos tamen interim credimus*), whatever may be argued concerning the sufficiency of the bull's promulgation, and concerning the bull's comments about the so-called queen, that Catholics are excused from the obligations laid down, and from excommunication, nor do they suffer any detriments by virtue of the bull.

> First since the bull was published in favour of Catholics and of religion, and since it is clear that great harm (*magnum damnum*) befalls Catholics and religion from observance of the bull – a result which was not intended by the legislator. This must always be considered because what was done out of charity ought not to militate against charity.[76]

Such a significant reply must have been approved by both Gregory XIII and the Cardinal of Como, his Secretary of State. The fourth answer hints at the northern rebellion of 1569 as the now vanished context:

> Fourth, because the precept and the obligation seem to have been laid down as time and place required – no more and no less – within which there was

---

Campion, Alexander Briant, Ralph Sherwin, and Luke Kirby (Rome: Vatican Polyglot Press, 1968), p. 122 and p. 146, which reprints in full the brief printed among *The MSS of his Grace the Duke of Rutland* (London: HMC, 1888), vol. 1, pp. 113–14.

[74]   McCoog, *Fashioning Jesuit Identity*, p. 68.

[75]   Vatican City, Archivio Segreto Vaticano, Armadio 64, vol. 28, fols 179r–v and 184r–187v. Printed in *Recusancy and Conformity in Early Modern England: Manuscript and Printed Sources in Translation*, ed. Ginevra Crosignani, Thomas M. McCoog and Michael Questier (Toronto: Pontifical Institute of Medieval Studies, 2010), pp. 90–100 (p. 97). I have translated *interim credimus* as 'we have come to believe', rather than 'we have believed meanwhile'.

[76]   Crosignani, *Recusancy and Conformity*, p. 97.

hope of recovery of that realm by that way and manner. Therefore, since such occasion has disappeared and the hope has been frustrated, and that avenue has been entirely blocked, it follows that the time of that precept has passed by and that obligation therefore ceases; it would seem to be contrary to reason to use a method and a most inconvenient way to something practically impossible.[77]

If these truths were in the minds of the Pope and his Secretary of State, why was the bull not rescinded, and why was that information not passed to the English Privy Council? The answer must be that while Sander was in Ireland, under a papal banner, the Pope could not rescind the bull, whose original purpose was to endorse the restoration of Catholicism in just such a way.[78] The news reaching Allen, the Cardinal of Como and the Pope in October still suggested that Sander's expedition would succeed. At the end of this audience, Campion must have been glad he had declined to be superior of the mission. One can only speculate what his response would have been, or whether Mercurian himself would have yielded to Allen's request for Jesuit involvement, if the Secretary of State had informed them that Sander's expedition had already landed in Ireland under a papal banner.

Instead of this forthright but secret answer, the public faculties that were granted to Campion and Persons contained a sentence that spins equivocally on a participle: *rebus sic stantibus*: Catholics were not obliged to obey the bull 'things being as they are', a 'mitigation' that was to be intercepted, and derided, by the Privy Council. It implied that Catholics could take their swords out in armed rebellion as soon as things stood differently. This led to the formulation of the so-called 'bloody question': what would you do if the pope and an army invaded? Sander's papal banners at Dingle in county Kerry gave immediacy to this question. The mission's instructions, lifting the obligation from Catholics to obey the bull as things stood, came as England prepared to meet an invasion launched from Ireland. How would things stand, if the King of Spain were to provide adequate naval support, and the Irish rebels were to reach the Dorset coast, three days' sailing from Smerwick? If Campion's doubts about the bull were adequately expressed in the 14 questions put to the Pope on 14 April, they were not adequately answered by a conditional mitigation, nor did the suspended present of the ablative absolute convince the Privy Council that Campion and Persons were in England only to save souls. The Privy Council soon obtained a copy of the faculties granted to Campion and Persons, which were published in Burghley's *Execution of Justice* (1584), and printed again in Holinshed's 'Continuation' of 1587 as damning evidence.[79]

---

[77]   Crosignani, *Recusancy and Conformity*, p. 98.

[78]   It is also true that no bull has ever been rescinded, as Thomas McCoog reminded me.

[79]   The (mutilated) document is calendared under its date of 14 April, along with two further copies, *CSP Domestic, 1547–1580*, 12/137/26–8, p. 651. These copies may have been made by agents abroad, but must have reached England before Campion landed; Holinshed, *Chronicles* (1587), III. 1362.b.35–73.

While Campion was riding post-haste from Padua to Rome, the Queen of England's ships were demolishing a fort in Ireland. The skirmishes of August 1579 had confirmed the difficulty of moving poorly motivated troops across inhospitable country, so the Privy Council turned to using their latest ships as artillery platforms. Throughout August 1579, they made arrangements for fitting out warships, requisitioning merchant ships for the transport of troops from Liverpool and Bristol, and for manning the castles and bulwarks in coastal towns.[80] By Good Friday, 1 April 1580, shortly before Campion arrived in Rome, Chief Justice Pelham was able to report that, on Maundy Thursday, he and Admiral Sir William Winter, with a fleet of four of the latest ships, *Revenge*, *Foresight*, *Swiftsure* and *Achates*, armed with over 100 cannon and culverins, had completed their two-day bombardment of the Desmond fort at Carrigafoyle, on the mouth of the Shannon.[81] Some 60 Irish, and 16 of Sander's Spanish soldiers under Captain Julian, a Spanish engineer, had little chance against this onslaught. The Earl of Ormond reported blood running down the castle walls and, within two days, they had all been put to the sword. The Irish women were hanged immediately, Captain Julian three days later.[82] This bloody end to Holy Week became a template for future action. The policy was supplemented by what Pelham calls 'waste and execution', which brought about the surrender of some 30 forts, including Askeaton, to Sir Humphrey Gilbert, the experienced head-hunter of the first Desmond rebellion.[83] From April to July, the Privy Council was raising musters in every county in England to meet the threat of invasion: in Dorset, 4,000 men to protect the coastline, 10,749 men in Suffolk, 9,260 in Norfolk, 4,000 men in Somerset and 2,120 men in Surrey.[84]

Campion exhibited 'so harty aversion from medling' that Persons was put in charge.[85] Campion was a natural leader, always chosen to speak first; his request not to be in charge of the mission is profoundly significant, and followed the interview with Mercurian. Bombino was clear that the instructions from the General for their conduct in the mission were that 'nothing was more precisely forbidden them then the intermeddling with state matters' (*Nihil vero sibi severius interdictum sciant, quam publicae rei administrationem*).[86] By the time Campion discussed his mission with Mercurian, between 10 and 14 April 1580, Admiral Winter had shown what his ships could do, and the musters in English counties were under way. On 13 May, the Pope granted a plenary indulgence to all those who assisted the Earl of Desmond: Spanish ships, men and, above all, cannon, would have been more useful, and less theologically offensive.[87]

---

80 *CSP Domestic, 1547–1580*, 12/131/65–83, pp. 630–31.
81 *CSP Ireland, 1574–1585*, 72/28, p. 214.
82 Lennon, *Incomplete Conquest*, p. 225.
83 *CSP Ireland, 1574–1585*, 72/28–33, pp. 214–15. For Gilbert, see Chapter 3.
84 *CSP Domestic, 1547–1580*, 12/137/3 to 12/140/13.1, pp. 649–65.
85 ABSI Collectanea P. I, fol. 105b.
86 Bombino, *Vita et Martyrium*, p. 61; Bodl. MS Tanner 329, fol. 27r.
87 CRS 26, p. 46.

Catholic historiography has largely ignored the first year of Sander's invasion. The result of reducing the invasion of Ireland to the reinforcements sent in 1580, is to disguise the criminal folly of sending the English Jesuit mission into a country that was already facing the two greatest horrors for the Elizabethan state: rebellion and invasion under a papal banner. Simpson is surely correct to say that, 'The policy of combining these two expeditions is hard either to be justified or to be understood', but he too writes as if Sander's fleet 'reached Ireland about the same time that Persons and Campion were entering England'.[88] In fact, by the time Campion landed at Dover on 25 June 1580, Sander had been in Ireland a whole year, the death toll from the rebellion was mounting, and English forces were 'wasting' everything in sight. The Spanish Ambassador, Bernadino de Mendoza, reported to his King on 18 June 1580, six days before Campion crossed the Channel, 'the calling out of the militia, which had been under orders to muster for the last four months, and the vigilant watching night and day from the beacon-towers'.[89] On 15 July 1580, Lord Burghley drafted a proclamation in his own hand 'against spreading seditious rumours of the approach of a Spanish fleet, and a projected invasion of England by the Pope, the King of Spain and other Princes'.[90] Burghley feared that a mere rumour of invasion would be enough to rouse Catholics in England, 50,000 of whom had been listed as 'recusant'.[91] On 19 July 1580, James Eustace, Viscount Baltinglass, who had been educated in London and spent time in Rome, raised the papal banner in Leinster.[92] The whole of southern Ireland, from Dingle to the outskirts of Dublin, was now under arms. When Campion landed in England, he might as well have walked onto a battlefield carrying an umbrella.

Campion sent this summary from Bologna to his beloved Rector:

> In this expedition are two fathers of the Society, Robert Persons and I, seven other priests and three laymen, one of whom is also of our Society. All I see are so prodigal of their life and blood, that I am ashamed of my own cowardice (*ignaviae*).[93]

With two such charismatic figures at the centre, it is not surprising that others were drawn to join the expedition, but Persons attributed the 'desire and appetite in divers others' to Campion's 'devout & christian preparation towards the same

---

[88]   Simpson, pp. 143–4.

[89]   *CSP Spanish, 1580–1586*, p. 35.

[90]   Paul L. Hughes and James F. Larkin, C.S.V., eds, *Tudor Royal Proclamations*, 3 vols (London and New Haven: Yale University Press, 1969), II. 469–71, no. 650; *CSP Domestic, 1547–1580*, 12/140/18, p. 665.

[91]   CRS 39, pp. 50 and 58: Persons, in letter of 17 November 1580; see John Lingard, *The History of England: From the First Invasion by the Romans to the Accession of William and Mary in 1688*, 10 vols (London: C. Dolman, 1855), VI. 166.

[92]   *CSP Ireland, 1574–1585*, 12/74/66, p. 237.

[93]   *Opuscula*, p. 404.

by visiting the holy places of Rome'.[94] When Campion and Persons came to leave Rome, there were, much to Campion's delight, three Jesuits, three priests from the English College, four chaplains and two laymen, so that Campion

> was wonderfully comforted with the number of twelve, desiring God that seeing it was an apostolical number and cause, that they might have alsoe apostolical grace to stand and persever in the same, and if any should fall or fainte by human frailty that it might be rather the fall of S. Peter to repentance then of the other to desperation.[95]

Ralph Emerson, the Jesuit 'co-adjutor' (lay brother) was to prove remarkably constant.[96] The mission 'putt a great desire in so many priests of the College as were any way ready in respect of their studies to goe'.[97] Those who joined 'alsoe of their own free choice and election' were four 'ancient and grave priests', who had been chaplains of the English Hospital 'before it was a seminary'.[98] These were Dr Edward Brombery, William Gilbert, Thomas Crane and William Kemp. These were much older than the young Oxford scholars that made up the Jesuit and English College contingent. Kemp was 'captured and held in York, Dr Brombery died in England 'having laboured very faithfully', while Fr Crane, 'being a very aged man', came back to Rouen and 'there died most godly'; Fr Gilbert was likewise 'captured, imprisoned, banished and died in Rome'.[99]

The three members of the Society had been 'appointed to go by their superiors', as were the three priests and two 'scholars' from the English College. The three seminary priests were Ralph Sherwin, born in Derbyshire, Fellow of Exeter College, Luke Kirby, a Yorkshireman who was a graduate of Louvain, and Edward Rishton, a Lancashire-born graduate of Brasenose College, who would later edit the works of Dr Sander. The two Oxford scholars were Thomas Briscow, from Yorkshire, and John Paschal, 'who had been a scholar to Mr Sherwin in Oxford', presumably in Exeter College.[100] Persons is full of admiration for Briscow, who 'was taken also about a year and a half after his entrance [to England] and kept six yeares prisoner in the Tower of London and sixteen weekes together in a dark dungeon under the ground'.[101] Paschal, however, after torture, 'yielded to goe

---

[94] ABSI Collectanea P. I, fol. 106b.

[95] ABSI Collectanea P. I, fol. 107a.

[96] ABSI Collectanea P. I, fol. 8r.

[97] ABSI Collectanea P. I, fol. 8r.

[98] ABSI Collectanea P. I, fol. 106b.

[99] ABSI Collectanea P. I, fol. 150a (my translation).

[100] The Oxford bias in the party was reinforced by the priests who had already been sent to England. Alexander Briant, who had arrived in 1579, and was active in Somerset, was M.A. of Hart Hall, John Colleton had been a member of Lincoln College, and was working in Oxfordshire; Laurence Johnson (*alias* Richardson) and John Short (Shert) were both Brasenose men.

[101] ABSI Collectanea P. I, fol. 107b, cross-referenced by Grene to fols 150b and 115b.

to church & to make a certain abjuration in the Guildhall of London'.[102] Allen's own preferences are present not just in the choice of Oxford men, but also in his selecting scholars already known for their skills at oratory and disputation.

Two other key figures earnestly requested the Pope to allow them to join the mission. Thomas Goldwell is portrayed by Persons and Bombino simply as 'an ancient Catholic Confessor & Bishop in Q. Mary's time of St Assaph', but he had been assistant to Cardinal Pole during the restoration of the hierarchy in England during Mary's reign, active at the Council of Trent, and instrumental in securing the excommunication of Elizabeth.[103] He was joined by Dr Nicholas Morton, Papal Penitentiary, 'a man of ample power in cases of conscience', who had helped 'trigger' the northern rising in 1569, telling the earls that the Queen was 'excommunicated already'.[104] Gregory XIII reluctantly gave Goldwell permission to travel as far as Rheims, but Morton clearly thought he was going to England, since he sold all his possessions before leaving Rome.[105] The Pope's reservation was not just the age of Bishop Goldwell, but also the fear that sending the bishop to England might seem a direct challenge to the established church. Goldwell and Morton, therefore, were told to 'goe very privately and before the rest and no farther than Rhemes', where they would discuss with Dr Allen whether it was wise to continue or return, so they travelled ahead of the party, on horseback.[106] Despite this precaution, the Privy Council intercepted a letter sent from Rome to Dr Ely which described the 'departure of my Lord of St. Asaph and Mr D. Morton', and noted, on 18 April, that 'this day many of his countrymen depart from Rome, and withal good Father Campion'.[107]

The large party left Rome by the Ponte Molle. The departure was an emotional event. Most of the priests had decided to abandon their 'long apparell for better travelling a foot': Campion insisted on wearing 'old buckram under an old cloke' throughout the whole journey, even though 'God Almighty sent continual rain for the first eight or ten daies', and 'F. Campian travelled in the wett with that evil apparell, and often times stuck so fast in the myre in those deep and fowl waies as he was scarce able to gett out againe'.[108] The coarse, heavy material became caked

---

[102]   ABSI Collectanea P. I, fol. 108a.

[103]   ABSI Collectanea P. I, fol. 106b; Bombino, *Vita et Martyrium*, p. 62; Bodl. MS Tanner 329, fol. 22v. Persons and Bombino emphasize the age and frailty of Goldwell, but he was bound to be seen as a serious threat by the Privy Council, *ODNB*, 'Thomas Goldwell' (d. 1585), by T.F. Mayer.

[104]   *ODNB*, 'Nicholas Morton' (1520/21–1587), by Peter Holmes.

[105]   Holmes, 'Nicholas Morton'.

[106]   ABSI Collectanea P. I, fol. 9a–b. Richard Challoner, *Memoirs of Missionary Priests*, ed. J.H. Pollen, S.J. (London: Burns Oates & Washbourne, 1924), p. 30, suggests that Sherwin was intended to be Goldwell's chaplain, but 'the Bishop falling sick at Rhemes', Sherwin 'went forward towards *England*'. This may have influenced Sherwin's view of the mission.

[107]   *CSP Domestic, 1547–1580*, 12/137/38, p. 651.

[108]   ABSI Collectanea P. I, fol. 106a.

with mud. When challenged, Campion defended his 'evil apparell' by saying that 'to him that went to be hanged in England any kinde of apparell was sufficient'.[109]

On '18th day of April of the year 1580', they took their leave 'att the church of S. Peter, went all twelve out together on foot' even though they took some horses for the older men, and in case anyone was ill.[110] Persons's leg had been 'greevously wrenched' by a fall in Rome, so he needed to use a horse, but Campion used a horse only for one day in the whole journey, when suffering from 'fever and bloody flux', which 'his much travaile had procured'.[111] 'They were led out beyond the City's walls in a kind of triumph by all the English who were in Rome', including Sir Richard Shelley, Grand Prior of the Knights of St John of Jerusalem: this was a dramatic farewell.[112] On the Ponte Molle, 'they were at length divorced unwillingly from their deare countrymen, who kissed their garments at parting' and wept.[113] The presence of the English Prior of the Knights of Jerusalem is significant, and suggests that the spiritual nature of the mission was accepted in Rome, since Shelley, a bitter opponent of Stuckley, was opposed to Dr Allen's 'militant Catholic strategy'.[114]

The journey was regulated by a routine cycle of daily prayers. Each day started with the *Itinerarium*, followed by meditations and mental prayer, then the office of the breviary.[115] When they found a church, one of them would say Mass; after dinner, they said Vespers, Compline and Matins for the next day; finally, they said 'their rosary, or their beades and divers sortes of Letanies'.[116] Each day, Campion would take 'himselfe to his journey on foote so swiftly, that within a short time he lost the very sight of them that followed him'.[117] This solitary walking gave him time for 'silent contemplation of divine matters', and then an hour to his 'vocall prayer', never omitting 'the solemn litanie of sayntes', so that 'betwixt some two or three howers he spent in prayer & meditation'.[118] He only rejoined the party when he 'had fully finished his devotions', about an hour before dinner, when he 'would stay to goe in company with the rest & would be so merry & talke of

---

[109] ABSI Collectanea P. I, fol. 109a.

[110] ABSI Collectanea P. I, fol. 109a: Persons twice mentions the date.

[111] ABSI Collectanea P. I, fol. 109a; Bombino, *Vita et Martyrium*, p. 74; Bodl. MS Tanner 328, fol. 27r.

[112] Bombino, *Vita et Martyrium*, p. 63. Bombino's 'Thoma Scellaeo' is obviously incorrect. Strangely, the Prior's presence is not mentioned by the translator of Bodl. MS Tanner 329, fol. 22v.

[113] Bombino, *Vita et Martyrium*, p. 63; Bodl. MS Tanner 329, 22v–23r.

[114] *ODNB*, 'Sir Richard Shelley' (1513–87), by Michael Mullett.

[115] ABSI Collectanea P. I, fol. 109b. The *Itinerarium* was a prayer for priests to say when travelling, which was contained in the breviary. I am grateful to Thomas McCoog, S.J., and Joseph Munitiz, S.J., for this information.

[116] ABSI Collectanea P. I, fol. 109b.

[117] Bombino, *Vita et Martyrium*, p. 75; Bodl. MS Tanner 329, fol. 23r.

[118] Bombino, *Vita et Martyrium*, p. 75; Bodl. MS Tanner 329, fol. 23r.

suffering for Christ with such comfort ... as a man might easily perceave, with whom he had had conversation in his praiers before'.[119] The same pattern was repeated in the evening, when he 'out-went his fellows agayne' and 'spent as long time in divine considerations' before rejoining his companions.[120] On this long 'travail', Campion united himself with Christ in the Eucharist, meditated on the suffering of Christ, and, perhaps dreading the ordeal ahead, invoked the help of all the saints.

Persons supplies enough details for us to know that their route from Rome was essentially the ancient pilgrimage route, the *Via Francigena*. Campion was retracing the route he had taken in 1573. The route was first described by Sigeric, Archbishop of Canterbury in the tenth century.[121] Campion and Persons travelled due north heading for Bologna, passing through Viterbo, Perugia, Arezzo and Florence, before reaching the home-town of Cardinal Gabriele Paleotti (1522–97), Bishop of Bologna.[122] Paleotti was a veteran of the Council of Trent, where he had mediated between reformers and conservatives. He must have nearly finished the first two volumes of his *Discorso intorno alle imagini sacre e profane* (1582), a work on the role of iconography in the church.[123] They stayed 'a whole weeke', partly because Persons's leg was 'much swolne'; after dinner each evening, Paleotti invited his chaplains, 'according to a laudable custom', to propose some spiritual theme, and then invited the guests to take part in impromptu debate in Latin.[124] Campion and Sherwin excelled at these after-dinner 'spiral conferences'; Campion took Cicero's *Tusculan Questions* as his text, arguing that Christians were confronted not just with the gap between nature and virtue, but that in the life of a Christian, 'the labours were greater, the helps more potent, the end more high and the reward more excellent'.[125]

In Bologna, Campion wrote a long letter to his rector, which gives us a clear idea of his state of mind 12 days into the journey.[126] He tells Campani he has taken the space of his long pilgrimage from Rome to meditate on his own 'cowardice' (*ignavia*), and pray for the strength to embrace the commands of his superiors as if they were 'divinely commanded' (*divinitus imperata*); he ends by saying, 'I beg you, as long as I live, to keep me in your thoughts and prayers' (*Obsecro vero te, ut dum vivo, tibi curae sim*).[127] This is joined to some reflections on how much he

---

[119]   ABSI Collectanea P. I, fols 109b–110a.

[120]   Bombino, *Vita et Martyrium*, p. 75; Bodl. MS Tanner MS 329, fol. 23r.

[121]   BL MS Cotton Tiberius B. V, fols 23v–24r.

[122]   Persons calls him Cardinal Archbishop, but the see was made an archdiocese only in 1582.

[123]   Gabriele Paleotti, *Discourse on Sacred and Profane Images*, intro. Paolo Prodi, trans. William McCuaig (Los Angeles: Getty, 2012).

[124]   ABSI Collectanea P. I, fol. 110a; 'Memoirs', CRS 2, p. 197.

[125]   ABSI Collectanea P. I, fol. 110b; 'Memoirs', CRS 2, p. 197.

[126]   *Opuscula*, pp. 400–407.

[127]   *Opuscula*, pp. 401–4.

values a mutual prayer pact with John Aquensis (who copied out all his sermons in the manuscript now at Cieszyn), Gabriel and 'Stephen, the Dalmatian', who was a fellow-novice at Brno: Campion says 'they will be able especially to help him now that he is surrounded with infinite dangers'.[128] This is about as vivid an indication we have of Campion's assessment of the mission, especially as Campion also uses the image he repeats again to Mercurian that, 'Even if we fall in the first rank, the army is full of recent recruits, whose victory our spirits will delight in'.[129] At the end of the letter, Campion tells his rector that he is sorry he has not been able to write individually to all his pupils, and to all those in his sodality because he was worn out when he arrived in the colleges, hardly had time to draw breath in the inns, and was worked off his feet in the eight days he had in Rome. Nevertheless he will be glad to get another letter from him before he crosses to England, and tells him to send it to Rheims, Paris or Douai. Apparently sceptical about his survival, he ends by writing a will, where the legacy is far from material:

> As I am not sure whether you will ever see me again, I am writing a will: I leave
> to you and to all the kiss of charity and the bond of peace. Farewell.[130]

They walked north from Bologna, through Modena and Piacenza, to Milan, where they spent 'divers days' with Cardinal Charles Borromeo.[131] Another veteran of Trent, Borromeo had organized many of the final sessions, and drafted the Tridentine Catechism. As a powerful reformer, 'whose rare sanctity', Persons writes, 'is known to the whole world', he was nothing 'but skinn and bone through continual paines fasting & pennance'.[132] 'Greatly edifyed and exceedingly animated' by the saintly cardinal, they turned west from Milan to travel the 100 miles to Turin, then part of the kingdom of Savoy.[133] Here they heard the disturbing news that the route through Savoy to Lyons, which crossed the Alps by Mont Cenis, was full of decommissioned Spanish soldiers on their way from the Netherlands, where Don John of Austria, governor-general, had made a truce. To avoid this danger, they decided to change their route, and travel by Geneva 'notwithstanding it was a place so different from us in religion'.[134]

What followed in Geneva was a pleasant interlude with moments of unplanned comic relief. Several in the party expressed the fear that they might be arrested by 'the magistrates of Geneva, being in confederation with the Queen of England',

---

[128]   *Opuscula*, p. 403.

[129]   *Opuscula*, p. 404.

[130]   *Opuscula*, p. 407.

[131]   ABSI Collectanea P. I, fol. 110b. Bombino, *Vita et Martyrium*, p. 76, followed by Simpson, p. 157, says 'eight days'; a week with each cardinal would leave only 26 days for walking 900 miles.

[132]   ABSI Collectanea P. I, fol. 110b.

[133]   ABSI Collectanea P. I, fol. 110b.

[134]   ABSI Collectanea P. I, fol. 110b–111a.

and sent as prisoners by the 'waters of the Rhine' to England.[135] Should they say who they were? Campion and Sherwin were for open declaration. When they came to the city, they were led immediately to the magistrates in the marketplace, since the inhabitants of the fortified hilltop city were also worried about hungry Spanish soldiers.[136] When they said they were Englishmen, the first question they were asked was 'of what religion'; when Thomas Briscow answered that they 'were Catholics', the magistrates replied 'So are we also', but Briscow insisted that they were 'Roman Catholics'.[137]

The magistrates expressed surprise that they were not of the same religion as the 'Queen and realm', who, they confidently affirmed, 'are of our religion'. Someone (apparently Campion) wittily replied that it was hard to say whether the Queen was 'of your religion or no considering the variety of opinions that this age has brought forth, but sure we are, she is not of ours'.[138] When they explained that they had come to Geneva for fear of the Spanish soldiers, the magistrates now asked them 'no more questions about religion, but rather about the Spaniards, wherein we could give them very small advises'.[139] Won over by their frankness, the magistrates sent them to a 'very fair Inne bearing the sign of the city', where they 'willed that we should be very wel used'.[140]

After dinner, Campion, Persons, Sherwin and Paschal decided to go to visit the famous Calvinist theologian, Theodore Beza, in his house.[141] They found that the house where he lived with Candida, the mistress he had made 'famous by his verses' (not 'his lawfull wife'), was 'poorely furnished, sordid alltogether, & nastie'.[142] This surprising observation on home furnishing seems to be using domestic arrangements as a moral emblem. Candida kept them standing, while Beza, alerted by the magistrates to their presence, reluctantly emerged from his study. Campion kept himself at the back, disguised in 'a servile habit', and one of 'our men' began a disputation by asking Beza to define the differences between Calvinists and Lutherans. Beza insisted they were all 'children of the same Gospell', and that any differences were small.[143] Campion asked if he thought that sacraments were 'but light and triviall', since Lutherans and Calvinists agreed 'neither about their number, origen, efficacie, manner of receiving or delivering'.[144]

---

[135]   ABSI Collectanea P. I, fol. 111a.

[136]   ABSI Collectanea P. I, fol. 111a.

[137]   ABSI Collectanea P. I, fol. 111b.

[138]   ABSI Collectanea P. I, fol. 111b.

[139]   ABSI Collectanea P. I, fol. 111b.

[140]   ABSI Collectanea P. I, fol. 111b.

[141]   ABSI Collectanea P. I, fol. 112a.

[142]   Bombino, *Vita et Martyrium*, p. 78; Bodl. MS Tanner 329, fol. 47r. Bombino appears to have an additional source for this episode, as his account contains many striking physical details not in Persons.

[143]   Bombino, *Vita et Martyrium*, p. 78; Bodl. MS Tanner 329, fol. 24r.

[144]   Bombino, *Vita et Martyrium*, p. 79; Bodl. MS Tanner 329, fol. 24v.

As Beza struggled to extricate himself from this trap, he gave a signal ('not so secret') to Candida, who came in with 'another packet of letters (a matter set between them we suspected)', which he pretended to read silently. As they made no move to depart, Beza dismissed them with an offer to send another minister to their inn.[145] This man was the tutor to the son of George Hastings, Earl of Huntingdon, who had been sent to Geneva for godly instruction.[146] He was accompanied by an Englishman, 'a very civil gentleman though a Protestant', named Pooley, who turned out to be an Oxford contemporary, known to both Campion and Persons.[147] They soon fell to disputing, and Persons:

> had them goe abroad, under pretence of walking and taking the benefit of the ayre. Now night began to come upon them disputing, the seazon was hotte, more like somer then spring (it being farre in May), the moone shone all night, the heat of the weather, the free concourse of the people, the silence of the night, all things made for the battell, in so much that they disputed at pleasure all over the citty, with such fervour of mind & alacrity that they filled all about them with noyse, all the streets with clamour.[148]

Pooley warned them of the danger of arousing the anger of the magistrates and damaging the chances of Catholics in the future, so Persons decided it was time to 'sound the retreat'. Realizing that they have passed a good part of the night, they retired to get what rest they can.[149] Their policy of cautious openness had upset Beza, but otherwise won them friends.[150]

As they left Geneva in the morning, Persons sent Campion ahead, lest he be detained by Pooley joyfully recognizing him. Campion, accompanied by Thomas Briscow, saw in the fields

> a man of a severe aspect, grave in habit, freely walking and expatiating the fieldes. His bigge lookes, often poynting with his finger, & clapping his handes, his gate now quick, now slow, often stopping and staying, shewd as if he were meditating a sermon.[151]

Their deduction (that he was a minister) turned out to be correct, and Campion could not resist the desire to 'buckle with him', and so started by asking him how

---

[145]   ABSI Collectanea P. I, fol. 112a.

[146]   Bombino, *Vita et Martyrium*, p. 80; Bodl. MS Tanner 329, fol. 25r.

[147]   ABSI Collectanea P. I, fol. 112b; Bombino, *Vita et Martyrium*, p. 80; Bodl. MS Tanner 329, fol. 25r.

[148]   Bombino, *Vita et Martyrium*, pp. 80–81; Bodl. MS Tanner 329, fol. 25r.

[149]   Bombino, *Vita et Martyrium*, p. 82; Bodl. MS Tanner 329, fol. 26r.

[150]   Peter Lake and Michael Questier, 'Puritans, Papists, and the "Public Sphere" in Early Modern England: The Edmund Campion Affair in Context in Context', *The Journal of Modern History* 72 (September, 2000), 587–627 (p. 613), read this visit as 'a dress rehearsal for the hoped-for confrontation in England'.

[151]   Bombino, *Vita et Martyrium*, p. 83; Bodl. MS Tanner 329, fol. 26r.

the church of Geneva was governed; when the minister asserted that no man can be in charge of a church, Campion told him that the Queen of England claimed sovereignty over the church.[152] The minister refused to believe this, when Persons arrived and confirmed that 'all first fruits of benefices were paid to her use'.[153] Driven into a corner, the minister exclaimed that Campion was 'no Englishman, but a Papist'.[154] Campion, 'mindfull of his superiours command', slipped away at the height of his 'rayling', leaving the minister 'his eyes glowing as yet in his head, a threatening countenance, the man muttering, rather then playnely uttering, certayne barbarous speeches', and swearing that the man who had just left him was 'starke madde. A man? nay rather a divell'.[155] The accidental encounter is proof that for Campion, disputation, nurtured ever since he was a schoolboy, had become as natural as walking. Campion's sense of the absurd was aroused by the comic incongruity of the situation.

The rest of the party took their leave of the courteous Pooley, and looking back on 'the miserable city of Geneva', sang a '*Te Deum laudamus*' for 'delivering us from them'.[156] Before the final leg of their journey, they decided to do penance 'of our curiosity that we had to passe that way', and made a difficult journey into the hills to the royal shrine of St Clovis which was only 8 or 9 miles away, across the border in France.[157] Campion may have been doing penance for unnecessarily enraging a Calvinist minister.[158] They travelled the remaining 300 miles through Dole, Dijon and Troyes, and reached Rheims on 27 May.[159] The journey had taken just 40 days in all, an astonishing feat for the 900 miles they had walked, which included crossing the Alps. If they spent a week in Bologna and Milan, they must have covered more than 25 miles a day.

Persons recounts the joy with which they were received, and how Campion 'was exceeding welcome both to Mr Dr Allen the President, and to all the rest for that he had been one of them before in Douay, and they had not seen him now for the full space of 8 years or more'.[160] After the ecstatic greeting – 'there was no end of their embracing' – the mood changed rapidly. There were two pieces of worrying news. The first was of a new proclamation by the Queen, against a conspiracy by the Pope, King of Spain, Duke of Florence and other princes to invade the country, which they

---

[152]   Bombino, *Vita et Martyrium*, p. 83; Bodl. MS Tanner 329, fol. 26v.

[153]   ABSI Collectanea P. I, fol. 113a–b.

[154]   ABSI Collectanea P. I, fol. 113b.

[155]   Bombino, *Vita et Martyrium*, p. 85; Bodl. MS Tanner 329, fol. 27r.

[156]   ABSI Collectanea P. I, fol. 113b.

[157]   ABSI Collectanea P. I, fol. 113b.

[158]   The largely amicable, and often comic, quality of this unplanned visit, does not support Lake and Questier, 'Edmund Campion Affair', p. 613, who argue from the 'polemical line they adopted when haranguing Genevan ministers' that they 'intended the regime in England to know they were coming'.

[159]   Knox, *Douai Diaries*, p. 166.

[160]   ABSI Collectanea P. I, fols 114a–115b.

took 'to be a plaine preface & introduction to the rigour of the persecution which they meant to use towards us'.[161] The second was even more disturbing.

> We were told also by Mr Dr Allen how he had understood by fresh letters from Spaine that Dr Sanders by order of his holinesses Nontio lying there was niewly gon into Ireland to comfort & assist certain Catholic Irish Lords as namely the Earl of Desmond the Vicont Baltinglas & others that were said to have taken armes a little before for defence of their religion & had asked help counsail & comfort of his Holiness therin for which journey of Doctor Sanders though being made by order of his superiors it belonged not to us to mislike, yet were we hartily sorry, partly for that we had just cause to suspect and feare that which came to passe, that so rare and worthy a man should be lost in that action; and secondly for that we did easily foresee that this would be layd against us and other priests that should be taken in England as though we had been privy or partakers therof, as in very truth we were not, nor ever heard or suspected the same until this day.[162]

Persons's memory (perhaps aided by Allen's narrative) has distorted the facts here: Sander had landed not 'niewly', but earlier; he had initiated, rather than supported, the rebellion; and Baltinglass did not enter the lists till 19 July 1580.[163]

Sander's expedition justified the Privy Council's fear that the papal bull of 1570, *Regnans in Excelsis*, was no dead letter. The 'clamour' that heralded the arrival of the Jesuit mission in 1580, was occasioned not just by the bull, but by its active manifestation in Sander's expedition[164] Campion was found guilty by association with Sander, and the views expressed in his book that the 'so-called queen' must be deposed and disobeyed. Allen's own aims were equally militant.[165] As early as 10 August 1572, Allen and several other Louvainists, including Thomas Harding and Thomas Stapleton addressed a letter to Giovanni Morone, the Cardinal Protector of England, which contained an appeal to the new pope, Gregory XIII, for his support in ousting the so-called queen (*praetensam reginam*).[166] Allen does not, in that letter, talk about the method (*de modo hic nihil dicemus*), but recommends further discussion with three men in Rome: Bishop Thomas Goldwell, Dr Nicholas Sander and Dr Nicholas Morton.[167] In 1576, he and Sir Francis Englefield, who were in Rome for an audience with the Pope, drafted a detailed plan for immediate invasion and replacement of the 'so-called

---

[161]   ABSI Collectanea P. I, fol. 114a.

[162]   ABSI Collectanea P. I, fol. 114b.

[163]   See Chapter 6 for full account.

[164]   Campion to Mercurian, 20 June 1580 (St Omers), in Henry More, *The Elizabethan Jesuits*, ed. and trans. Francis Edwards, S.J. (Phillimore: London, 1981), pp. 77–9.

[165]   *ODNB*, 'Willam Allen', by Eamon Duffy.

[166]   CRS 58, *Letters of William Allen and Richard Barret 1572–1598*, ed. P. Renold (London: Catholic Record Society, 1967), pp. 275–84.

[167]   CRS 58, p. 279. All three men had been involved in the excommunication, and in political action against Elizabeth.

queen' by Mary, Queen of Scots.[168] The 'pretext of the war' (*praetextus vivus belli*) was to be the bull of excommunication.[169] The preparation for the invasion was to be done by 'trustworthy and prudent men, chiefly priests' (*viri fidi et prudentes, praecipue sacerdotes*).[170] In 1576, Allen was involved in a plan for Don John of Austria to put Mary, Queen of Scots, on the throne and, in 1583, he was given a role in the projected invasion by the Duc de Guise; he was named as papal legate and appointed bishop of Durham if the invasion succeeded.[171] On 16 April 1584, after the discovery of the Throckmorton plot had thwarted this plan, Allen expressed to the Cardinal of Como his feeling that if an invasion of England were 'not carried out this year, I give up all earthly hope and the rest of my life will be bitter to me' (*Si hoc anno non geratur, omnem humanam spem abjicio, et reliqua vita mihi acerba erit*).[172] In 1585 he was in Rome to give the new Pope an elaborate memorandum on how easily an invasion of England might be accomplished, and in 1586, he told the Pope that the

> 'daily exhortations, teaching, writing and administration of the sacraments … of our priests' had made the Catholics in England 'much more ready' for an invasion, and that no good Catholic now 'thinks he ought to obey the queen as a matter of conscience, although he may do so through fear, which fear will be removed when they see the force from without'.[173]

After the death of Mary, Queen of Scots, on 8 February 1587, Allen became 'the only conceivable figurehead for a crusade'.[174] Allen's consistent refrain that none of the 471 seminary priests sent to England had any political involvement was true, but it was also an equivocation. The man who sent those priests to England on a spiritual mission was, at the same time, deeply involved with the House of Guise (who protected the seminary in Rheims), the Spanish King and the Pope, in attempts to depose a ruler whom he saw as illegitimate, and to restore a Catholic monarch to England. Significantly, it was in the run-up to the Spanish Armada, that Allen was created Cardinal on 7 August 1587. He argued in the very year of Campion's martyrdom that he had 'three or foure hundred ready to die for Gods cause'.[175] As Eamon Duffy pithily writes, 'Allen cannot entirely be absolved of responsibility for the disasters of Catholicism in the 1580s and 1590s'.[176]

---

[168]   CRS 58, pp. 284–94.

[169]   CRS 58, p. 284.

[170]   CRS 58, p. 286.

[171]   *ODNB*, 'William Allen', by Eamon Duffy.

[172]   Allen, *Letters and Memorials*, p. 233.

[173]   *ODNB*, 'William Allen', by Eamon Duffy.

[174]   *ODNB*, 'William Allen', by Eamon Duffy.

[175]   William Allen, *An Apologie and True Declaration of the Institution and endevours of the two English Colleges, the one in Rome, the other now resident in Rhemes: against certaine sinister informations given up against the same* (Rheims: n.p. 1581), STC 369, ARCR II. 6.

[176]   *ODNB*, 'William Allen', by Eamon Duffy.

Allen had known that Sander had landed for at least eight months, long before he received letters the following May from Spain.[177] Yet he did not tell Campion before he set out from Rome. Even Persons says that Sander's expedition 'made the whole cause of the priests that were sent on mission to England more odious'.[178] It would not have taken long for Campion to deduce that Allen must have known of Sander's expedition before his 'provost', Mercurian, agreed to their mission:

> This difficulty then being passed ouer F. Campian went to the President Mr Dr Allen and sayd Well Sir heer now I am: you have desired my going to England and I am come a long journy as you see from Praga to Rome and from Rome & do you think my labors in England may countervail all this travail as also my absence from Boemia, where though I did not much, yet I was not idle nor unemployed, and that also against hereticks.[179]

Campion's cold formality contrasts with the affectionate intimacy of Allen's letter begging Campion to come quickly to Rome. The fluid accumulation of clauses leads to one overwhelming question, whether his 'labors in England' will 'countervail all this travail'.[180] Allen, apparently ignoring the intensity of Campion's language, including the bleak 'absence from Boemia', blandly replied that Campion's talents would nowhere be better employed than in England. In his own account, Allen subtly softened Campion's language, as

> he demaunded of D. Allen whether he thought that any service he could do in England the time being as it is, were like to be worth al these long labours and hazardes past and to come: or might countervaile the lacke that those should seeme to have by his absence from whence he came.[181]

Schmidl makes no mention of Sander, but has Campion politely ask Allen whether it would be more useful for him to work in England 'where everything seemed desperate', or Bohemia, 'where there was such a fertile field to plough'.[182]

---

[177]   Michael E. Williams takes the same view in 'Campion and the English Continental Seminaries', *The Reckoned Expense*, p. 372 n. 2.

[178]   CRS 2, *Miscellanea II*, 'Father Persons' Memoirs' (London: Catholic Record Society, 1906), p. 199.

[179]   ABSI Collectanea P. I, fol. 114b.

[180]   The word 'travail' derived from the Latin *trepalium*: an instrument of torture.

[181]   [William Allen], *A Briefe Historie of the Glorious Martyrdom of Twelve Reverend Priests, executed within these twelve monethes for confession and defence of the Catholike Faith. But under the false pretence of Treason* ([Rheims: Foigny], 1582), STC 369.5 (formerly 13526), ARCR II. 7, sig. d3v.

[182]   Schmidl, *Historiae*, I. pp. 438–9. Bombino, *Vita et Martyrium*, 88, makes no mention of the interview.

Rheims is the moment when the spiritual intentions of Campion confronted the unwelcome 'political and polemical contexts', which were to shape its outcome.[183] Faced by a grotesque human muddle, diplomatic deception and the political 'meddling' he abhorred, Campion had little choice but to surrender himself in obedience to God's will:

> As for me, sayd father Campion, all is one and I hope I am & shal be ever indifferent for all nations & functions whereinsoever my superiors under God shal imploye me. I have made a free oblation of my self to his divine maiesty for life and death, and I trust that he wil give me grace and force to perform, and this is all I desire.[184]

Campion's tone suggests that he was far from the naïve and impetuous martyr his critics sometimes allege.[185] Persons says that they decided their only course was 'to goe forward with the spiritual action', aware that they would be charged 'under a wrong tytle', with political subversion.[186]

Campion was not going 'led by his own will' (*sua voluntate inductus*), as William Whitaker's hostile English edition of the *Rationes Decem* suggests.[187] Nor was he 'careless of his own life'.[188] Nor was the mission a series of 'rehearsed public performances', where the two men 'courted publicity' and 'had not employed the prudence demanded by their general'.[189] The mission was imperilled not by Campion's recklessness, but by Sander's invasion. Patrick McGrath is surely right to blame Dr Allen for the double message that destroyed any chance of the mission's success:

---

[183] Michael L. Carrafiello, 'English Catholicism and the Jesuit Mission of 1580–1581', *Historical Journal* 37.4 (1994), pp. 761–74 (pp. 764 and 774), argues retrospectively, from Persons's later political writings and activities, that Catholic historians have 'misunderstood' the mission, naively accepted its 'pastoral objectives', and ignored its political 'intent'. By contrast, Lake and Questier, 'Edmund Campion Affair', p. 603, argue ('*pace* Michael Carrafiello') that the mission itself was not political, but 'structured by certain political and polemical contexts'; I agree completely with this interpretation.

[184] ABSI Collectanea P. I, fol. 115a. Evelyn Waugh, *Edmund Campion* (London: Longman, 1935), p. 97, quotes only these last two sentences, turning Campion into a saint who *is* too good to be true.

[185] John Bossy, 'The Heart of Robert Persons', in *The Reckoned Expense*, 187–207, talks of Campion's 'angelism', p. 187. Lake and Questier, 'Edmund Campion Affair', p. 603, talk of 'a first flush of youthful charismatic enthusiasm'. Campion was 40 years old when he left Prague, more like Edward Thomas ('uncle'), than Wilfred Owen. See Chapter 12.

[186] ABSI Collectanea P. I, fol. 114b.

[187] William Whitaker, *Edmundi Campiani Jesuitae Rationes Decem* (Lichae: Wolfgang Kezel: 1604), ARCR I. 156, sig. A2r.

[188] Bossy, 'Heart of Robert Persons', p. 193.

[189] Lake and Questier, 'Edmund Campion Affair', p. 614; Jessie Childs, *God's Traitors: Terror and Faith in Elizabethan England* (London: Bodley Head, 2014), p. 57, explicitly follows this interpretation.

And yet Allen was himself deeply involved in plans for the overthrow of government by force, and there can be no doubt that if England had been invaded by a foreign army seeking to restore Catholicism, he would have called upon English Catholics to assist the invader ... The missionary priests, carefully avoiding politics and ministering to Catholics at the risk of their lives, were caught between a murderous crossfire from a papacy prepared to use temporal as well as spiritual means for religious ends, and a government determined to conceal its mixed political and religious aims by smearing its victims with what Campion called 'the odious name' of traitor.[190]

Allen diverted Campion by telling him 'the desire of the whole company of that house to heare some sermon of his in English before his departure', and Campion yielded to the request more readily because 'he was willing to take an occasion to exercise againe his English toung before he went into England whereof he had no publick use for many yeares before'.[191] It is significant that Campion's first sermon in English focused on the destruction of the monasteries and churches in England, and

the hurts that this fier had already donne in our country; how many goodly churches, monasteries & other monuments of piety it had devoured in an instant which our catholick ancestors had erected in so many hundred yeares before, how many holy orders of religion it had dissolved in both sexes.[192]

It is a reminder of how much of his life Campion has spent in restored monastic ruins. Persons said he could not remember the Gospel text, so Bombino mistakenly concluded that Campion was preaching on the text, 'I have come to bring fire to the earth' (*Ignem veni mittere in terram*), and even recounts the (obviously apocryphal) story that he repeated the word 'fire' so often that passers-by in the *Rue des Anglais* (completely destroyed in the First World War), started to rush in with buckets to put out the fire in the College.[193]

Important changes in the party occurred in Rheims: Bishop Goldwell became ill, and Allen detained him, while awaiting further instructions from Rome: 'he was a blessed man in all his life and actions', says Persons, 'and dyed some 3 or 4 years after in Rome'.[194] Dr Morton also decided to return to Rome so as not to 'infuriate the privy council'.[195] The damage, as we have seen, had already been done. As Goldwell and Morton dropped out, three men, who reinforced its Oxford weighting, took their place. The first was Dr Humphrey Ely, brother of William

---

[190]   McGrath, *Papists and Puritans*, pp. 185–6.

[191]   ABSI Collectanea P. I, fol. 115a.

[192]   ABSI Collectanea P. I, fol. 115a.

[193]   Bombino, *Vita et Martyrium*, p. 88; Bodl. MS Tanner 329, fol. 28v.

[194]   ABSI Collectanea P. I, fol. 116a. Mayer, 'Thomas Goldwell', argues Allen had a 'low opinion' of Goldwell; Waugh, *Edmund Campion*, p. 94, describes Goldwell as a man 'accustomed to soft living and deferential treatment'.

[195]   *ODNB*, 'Nicholas Morton', by Peter Holmes.

Ely, the President of St John's, and a former fellow of the college, who was not yet ordained but taught law at Douai and Rheims.[196] The second was Fr John Hart, brother of Fr William Hart who was later martyred at York.[197] The third was the newly ordained Thomas Cottam, S.J., who, like Rishton, was a Brasenose man with Lancashire roots, and had left Douai to join the Jesuits in Rome, on 8 April 1579. Unfortunately, his health began to deteriorate, and he was sent to Lyons to recover. He was unlucky enough to travel from Lyons to Rheims in the company of the spy, Charles Sledd, who left a description of him as 'lean and slender of body, his face full of freckles'.[198] He was ordained priest at Soissons on 28 May 1580, in time to join Campion's party. and he crossed from Dunkirk to Dover with John Hart and Edward Rishton.[199] His brother, John Cottam, taught at the grammar school in Stratford-on-Avon.[200]

The missionaries now had to decide how to cross the Channel safely. The original twelve, augmented by the three men from the English College in Rheims, decided to split into five groups to minimize the danger that Campion's notoriety brought to the rest. Dr Brombery and Briscow went via Dieppe; Sherwin and his pupil, Paschal, went to Rouen; the three other chaplains, Gilbert, Crane and Kemp, went to Boulogne; Dr Ely, Kirby, Hart and the two Brasenose men, Rishton and Cottam, went via Douai to Dunkirk.[201] The three Jesuits, Campion, Persons and Emerson, made up the fifth group, and went to the Jesuit college at St Omer, there to decide on the next step and which of three possible ports (Dunkirk, Gravelines or Calais) they were to use.

The journey to St Omer proved 'perilous', because 'all those countries were troublesome and full of soldiers at that time'.[202] They arrived, much to the amazement of the Flemish fathers at St Omer, 'in health & safety', but bad news awaited them.[203] They now heard that the 'loose lads' who had infiltrated the English College in Rome – Charles Sledd, Anthony Munday and Nowell – had given detailed descriptions to the Privy Council, which 'advised divers ways of our coming' and had passed to the searchers at the ports, 'our very pictures and retracts'.[204]

---

[196]   Hegarty, *Register*, pp. 50–51.

[197]   Godfrey Anstruther, O.P., *The Seminary Priests*, 2 vols (Ware: St Edmund's College, n.d.), I. 153–5.

[198]   Anstruther, *Seminary Priests*, I. 90.

[199]   See Chapter 6 for the fate of Cottam.

[200]   Stephen Greenblatt, *Will in the World: How Shakespeare became Shakespeare* (London: Jonathan Cape, 2004), pp. 97–104; René Weis, *Shakespeare Revealed: A Biography* (London: John Murray, 2007), pp. 34–5; Peter Milward, S.J., *Shakespeare in Lancashire* (Tokyo: Renaissance Pamphlets, 2000), p. 3.

[201]   ABSI Collectanea P. I, fols 115b–116a.

[202]   ABSI Collectanea P. I, fol. 116a.

[203]   ABSI Collectanea P. I, fol. 116b.

[204]   ABSI Collectanea P. I, fol. 116b.

The fathers of the college and George Chamberlayn, a member of the Oxfordshire family (linked to the Stonors, Dormers and Owens), who was now resident in St Omer, confirmed the rumours, and advised careful deliberation before proceeding. Persons and Campion replied that there could be deliberation only 'on the manner, way, place & time & other such like circumstances'.[205] After discussing with Chamberlayn the danger of the Privy Council knowing their names and 'apparel', they concluded that the spies would have had too little time to make pictures of them and have copies made.[206] Delay would only make the matter worse. Their conclusion was, 'that they would commend the matter to God', change their apparel and submit to 'the pleasure of almighty God & meaning of our superiors in Rome.[207] Persons offered to cross separately, and send word back to Campion if he 'found security'.[208] Persons went disguised as a captain returning from the wars in Flanders, while Campion was to go as a 'marchant of Jewels'.[209] Chamberlayn lent Persons his own captain's uniform of buff 'layd with lace' and a 'hatt with feather'.[210]

Campion waited anxiously for word from Persons, as he explained to Mercurian, his general, in a letter he began on 17 June and finished on 20 June, but kept open in case news arrived. The letter is a rare glimpse of Campion's feelings:

> Father Robert, accompanied by his brother George, left Calais with a very favourable wind after midnight the day before I started writing this. We hope, therefore, that he made Dover yesterday morning, June 16th. He went disguised as a soldier. He was so well made up and showed such a choleric disposition that he would have eyes, indeed, who could discern beneath that costume, face and gait the goodness and modesty that lay in hiding. We are worried all the same. I will not say by mere rumours but by something positively like a clamour that heralds our approach. Only divine Providence can counteract this kind of publicity, and we fully acquiesce in its dispositions. Following orders, I have stayed on for a while, so that, if possible, I can find out from the captains and certain merchants who are due here how Father Robert got on before I set sail myself. If I hear anything I may make fresh plans. I have decided to make the attempt whatever happens so that I can strike a blow for the cause even if it means death. It often happens that a conquering army's first troops in take a thrashing. Certainly, if our Society pushes on with this campaign, it will be necessary to overcome much ignorance and sheer wickedness. For which cause, in any case, the war was declared. I am thinking of 20th of the month for going to Calais.[211]

---

[205] ABSI Collectanea P. I, fol. 116b.

[206] ABSI Collectanea P. I, fol. 117a.

[207] ABSI Collectanea P. I, fol. 117a.

[208] ABSI Collectanea P. I, fol. 117a–b.

[209] ABSI Collectanea P. I, fol. 117b.

[210] ABSI Collectanea P. I, fol. 117b.

[211] Campion to Mercurian, 20 June 1580, in More, *Historia Missionis*, pp. 77–9. For George Persons, see CRS 39, pp. 257 and 259.

Campion apologizes for spending so much money on their disguises (as well as the four horses they will have to buy in England), but acknowledges that money is the least of their problems. The letter ends:

> Today the wind is dropping so I shall move off quickly for the sea. I have been most kindly entertained here at St Omer's College, and helped in all things needful. Indeed along the whole route we have received extraordinarily good treatment in all our houses. To this was added the hospitality of the illustrious Cardinals Paleotto and Borromeo, and of the Arch-priest Collensis. We deliberately avoided Paris and Douai. We seem safe enough, provided we are not betrayed in these coastal regions. I have waited a further day, but since there is still no news either way of Father Robert, I persuade myself he got through safely. I pray God to watch over your Reverence, your Assistants and the whole Society. Farewell, June 20th 1580.[212]

While Campion waited for a wind, he heard news that the presence of Bishop Goldwell, 'noised abroad in letters and conversation' had made the Privy Council think the mission was 'something big'.[213] Persons had arrived in Dover on the morning of 16 June, and luckily struck up a good relationship with the 'searcher' (Customer), asking him to treat his friend, 'Mr Edmonds', a merchant from St Omer who was following, with kindness.[214] The searcher even organized a horse and provisions for Persons's 60 miles journey overland, to Gravesend, and arranged for the delivery of a letter from Persons to 'Mr Edmonds', which told him 'to make hast for utterance of Jewels which he could help him to sell if he made hast after him'.[215] Campion, because 'of the new troubles raised in that country by Dr Sanders', had finally agreed to abandon 'the name of his old protector in Ireland', Saint Patrick, in case he might be taken for an 'Irish man'.[216] The letter was 'faythfully delivered to Campian at St Omers', and 'added, as it were, winges to him', as he hastened to Calais.[217]

Persons reached Gravesend late that evening and, in the dark, embarked on a tilt-boat, one of the Thames pleasure-boats that, under a canvas awning, plied back and forth from Tilbury. This one had been hired by a group of 'gentlemen of the Inns of Courts' and 'some of the Queens household', who had been down 'to make merry in Kent' with 'diverse musicians and a great variety of instruments'.[218] Persons, realizing the danger, was afraid that, when dawn came, one of his Oxford

---

[212]   More, *Historia Missionis*, p. 79.

[213]   Campion to Mercurian, 20 June 1580, in More, *Historia Missionis*, p. 78.

[214]   Persons mistakes the dates of his own journey; he says that he arrived at Calais 'on St Barnabas Day, as I remember, being 11 June', and 'next morning arrived at Dover', ABSI Collectanea P. I, fol. 117b.

[215]   ABSI Collectanea P. I, fol. 118a.

[216]   ABSI Collectanea P. I, fol. 109b.

[217]   Bombino, *Vita et Martyrium*, p. 94; Bodl. MS Tanner 329, fol. 61r.

[218]   ABSI Collectanea P. I, fol. 118a.

contemporaries might recognize him, but luckily, the musicians played for most of the night, and at 4 o'clock in the morning, with the revellers finally sleeping, he hailed a passing wherry, slipped off the tilt-boat unrecognized, and asked the boatman to take him to the Southwark side.[219] There he and his man could find nowhere to stay, partly because he had no horse, partly as a result of the 'new proclamations and rumours against suspicious people', and partly because he looked like a foreigner (the feathered hat may not have helped).[220] Persons abandoned the search for lodgings, and went to the Marshalsea prison to look for Thomas Pounde, the first cousin of the Earl of Southampton.

There was at last a favourable wind at Calais, and on the night of 24 June 1580, Campion embarked, glad that he was crossing on the feast of St John the Baptist, the patron of his old Oxford college.[221] The boat reached Dover in the early morning of 25 June 1580, and when it beached on the sand, Campion flung himself on his knees behind a rock, so that he could 'commend his cause & whole coming to Almighty God whether it were to life or death as He should think best'.[222]

---

[219] ABSI Collectanea P. I, fol. 118a–b.

[220] ABSI Collectanea P. I, fol. 118b.

[221] ABSI Collectanea P. I, fol. 119b.

[222] ABSI Collectanea P. I, fol. 119b; Bombino, *Vita et Martyrium*, p. 95, '*Humi stratus*'; Bodl. MS 329, fol. 31v ('casts himself on his knees'). Persons and the translator think Campion fell on his knees, Bombino that he prostrated himself.

Chapter 6
An Immense Harvest

Once ashore, Campion, accompanied by Ralph Emerson disguised as his servant, set off to find the friendly searcher, 'perswading himself that he should finde him in so good a mood as Fr Persons left him: but the time was changed', and the Privy Council had reprimanded both the Mayor of Dover and the Customer 'for that it had bin understood that certain priests had come that way into England of late daies'.[1] Between Persons's landing on 16 June 1580 and Campion's arrival on 25 June 1580, musters had been held in St Alban's, Chester, Wales, Lichfield, London, Buckingham, Hertfordshire, Worcester, Stamford, Oxfordshire and Nottingham; Oxfordshire submitted 5,000 horse and foot in late June, and Berkshire a number of demi-lances and light horse on 6 July.[2] In Kent itself, '12,131 men, consisting of pikemen, gunners, archers, billmen, pioneers, carpenters, smiths, masons and wheelwrights', had been mustered: a formidable force, designed to defend Dover and the other Cinque Ports against invasion from Ireland.[3]

Sledd had alerted the Council to the possibility that Gabriel Allen, Dr Allen's brother, might enter the country, and there was always a worry that an invasion might use Furness Fells as a port of entry, and be supported by Dr Allen's Lancashire network of relatives. Campion matched the description of Mr Allen, 'as indeed they were somewhat like', and he was arrested. Sledd's description of Gabriel Allen is:

> Gabriell Alline, brother to Doctor Alline. About 45 yeres of adge – of reasonable stature & well timbred. He is a very clowneshe man in his behaviour & speaketh northerly. His bearde of a flaxen collor – he hath a wife and children. Is dwellinge neare unto furnes feles in Lankasher.[4]

As Sledd describes Dr Allen as 'tall of stature and slender', we have to suppose that his brother is of medium height, solidly built and with a fair beard.[5]

---

[1]   ABSI Collectanea P. I, fol. 119b.

[2]   *CSP Domestic, 1547–1580*, 12/139/21–52, pp. 660–63.

[3]   *CSP Domestic, 1547–1580*, 12/139/43, p. 662.

[4]   BL Add. MS 48029, fol. 127v. Sledd left with the party that included Gabriel Allen, 'which departed from Rome the 25 of Febuary 1579 [1580] in which company I travelled all the waye'. Sledd (or, perhaps, Norton) added Campion's name (with no description) in a different ink, fol. 128r, since Campion arrived in Rome after he had left; printed in CRS 53, p. 207. See Chapter 5 n. 15, for more on this manuscript.

[5]   Neither 'flaxen' used here, nor 'auburn' used by Charles Weld of Campion's beard, is an exact word. 'Auburn' used to mean 'white' (from the Latin *albus*), but changed its meaning in the seventeenth century to 'reddish brown'.

The 'watch-men of the port' took Campion to the Mayor, who interrogated 'Mr Allen', accusing him of being a traitor, of having gone abroad for his religion and returning to spread it, and of having changed his name. The Mayor ordered him to be taken to the Privy Council; while two horses champed outside the door, Campion waited in his house and took to prayer, particularly calling upon John the Baptist. Suddenly, the Mayor, 'an old man', came out of his room, told Campion he could find no reason to detain him, and that he was free to go.[6] It was only nine years since Campion had been held and released at Dover, on his way from Ireland to Douai. Campion himself could not explain this release, except as an act of grace; it made him even more aware that he would 'be taken, but only when it pleases the greater glory of God, and not before'.[7]

Campion 'forthwith' hired the horses still standing at the Mayor's door, 'he & his man mounting them, posted in a few houres to Gravesend, where striking into the thickest of the Thames water-men, who were ignorant of him, with a payre of oares he arrived in London betime the next morning'.[8] Bombino says that he was 'carried in a wherry against the current' (*flumine adverso lintre subvectus*); rowing upstream a distance of about thirty miles must have taken them most of the night, since they arrived in London 'early in the morning' of 26 June.[9] By now Campion and Emerson had been travelling for two nights and, in the wherry, would have passed through one of the arches of London Bridge, and landed, probably on the steps of the Temple.

Persons, accompanied by Henry Orton, had already left London to start his mission in 'a shire nigh adjoyning', at the request of 'certain principal Catholick gentlemen', so had organized Thomas James, to keep a look-out for Campion.[10] James did this by passing 'up and down in a small boat on either side of Gravesend', and recognized the description of his 'apparel' and the appearance of his 'little man', Emerson.[11] As Campion was coming into land, James stepped to the side of the wherry, held out his hand, and said, 'Mr Edmonds (for so he was called), give me your hand. I stay here for you to lead you to your friends'.[12] On the landing steps, Campion, James and Emerson could have merged with the throng of lawyers and their clerks carrying bundles from Lincoln's Inn and the Temple, as they walked up the steep slope from the river to Chancery Lane.

James, whom Campion describes as his 'good angel', led him to the house where Persons had been lodged. Persons had not been idle since his arrival in

---

[6]   Bombino, *Vita et Martyrium*, pp. 95–7; Bodl. MS Tanner 329, fols 31v–32v.

[7]   *Opuscula*, 410. Campion's accent may have marked him out as from London.

[8]   Bombino, *Vita et Martyrium*, p. 97; Bodl. MS Tanner 329, fol. 32v.

[9]   Bombino, *Vita et Martyrium*, p. 97; Bodl. MS Tanner 329, fol. 32v. Henry More says that he was due to arrive 'on the second day after leaving Dover', More, *Historia Missionis*, p. 80.

[10]   ABSI Collectanea P. I, fol. 120b.

[11]   More, *Historia Missionis*, p. 80.

[12]   ABSI Collectanea P. I, fol. 120b.

London. Through Thomas Pounde, he had been introduced to Edward Brooksby, who had taken him 'to a Catholic house in the city, where he lodged and found other priests and other gentlemen'.[13] With amazing insouciance (and considerable irony), George Gilbert had rented a house in Chancery Lane from Mr Norris, the chief pursuivant, and secured, with bribes, the connivance of both Norris and Dr Adam Squire, former Master of Balliol, and son-in-law of John Aylmer, Bishop of London.[14] Here he was surrounded by 'many noble young gentlemen' who 'greeted me, clothed me, decorated me, armed me, and last of all, sent me out of the city on horseback'.[15]

Gilbert, at his own expense, first furnished each priest with two suits of clothing, two 'very good horses', and sixty pounds.[16] Before the mission arrived, he 'had organized a group of young Catholic laymen to receive arriving clergy' and to escort them round the country and provide for all their material needs.[17] This included Henry Vaux, son and heir of Lord Vaux, Charles Arundell, Charles Bassett (a grandson of Sir Thomas More) Gervase Pierrepoint, William Tresham, brother of Sir Thomas Tresham, Thomas Fitzherbert, John Stonor, James Hall, Anthony Babington, Chidiock Tichborne, Charles Tilney, Edward Abington, Thomas Salisbury, Francis Throckmorton, his two brothers, Thomas and Edward, Godfrey Foljambe, Nicholas Roscarrock, Stephen Brinkley, Richard Stanihurst, Edward Fitton, Jerome Bellamy, William Griffith and his brother Richard, who along with William Brooksby and Arthur (Joseph) Creswell, subsequently joined the Jesuits.[18] It is a formidable list of the Catholic nobility and gentry, which reveals the massive stretch and penetration of this network.

Campion was immediately asked to preach on the forthcoming feast of St Peter and Paul, 29 June. The difficulty was to find a private house large enough, but they settled on the great hall of Lord Paget's palace near Smithfield, outside the city walls near Ludgate. He took as his text Peter's confession of faith (*Tu est Christus filius Dei vivi*) and Christ's reply (*Tu es Petrus et super hanc petram*), and 'moved

---

[13]   McCoog, *Fashioning Jesuit Identity*, p. 202. More, *Historia Missionis*, pp. 53–62, recounts Pounde's long resistance and imprisonment. Foley, *Records*, III. 565–657, provides fascinating details of his membership of the Society of Jesus, and his extraordinary life. For Brooksby see below.

[14]   Thomas Norris was present when Topcliffe ransacked William Carter's house in July 1582, BL MS Harley 422, fol. 161r. McCoog, *Fashioning Jesuit Identity*, p. 202, notes that Squire had sided with Persons's opponent, Christopher Bagshaw, in the Balliol dispute, a further irony.

[15]   *Opuscula*, p. 411.

[16]   ABSI Collectanea, P. I, fol. 125b. For the remarkable Gilbert, see H. Foley, S.J., *Records of the English Province of the Society of Jesus*, vol. 3 (London: Burns and Oates, 1878), pp. 658–704, and *ODNB*, 'George Gilbert', by Thompson Cooper, rev. Thomas H. Clancy.

[17]   McCoog, *Fashioning Jesuit Identity*, pp. 201–2.

[18]   ABSI Collectanea P. I, fol. 126a.

many teares' as he 'animated them to the true confession of Christ'.[19] Many of the young men agreed to protect those coming to hear the sermon, but when news of the event spread, the 'search began to be very great for his apprehension'; the Council sent out spies who pretended to be devout Catholics, keen to hear the Jesuits; luckily, some 'principal persons of the courte' alerted Campion to the danger, and he 'retyred himself more carefully & took great heed with whome he conversed and imployed himself only in privat conference & exhortations in particular & secret friends houses until F. Persons returned to London'.[20] Danger was everywhere in London, with large numbers of spies looking for the priests from abroad. Whoever the 'principal persons of the courte' were, Campion took note of the spirit and letter of their advice, and never again preached 'so publickly'.[21] As false reports arrived of the King of Spain assembling 40,000 men in Portugal, and a fleet of '20 sail in Biscay', it became clear that Sander's invasion of Ireland had created conditions that rendered almost impossible the original plan of preaching and sacramental ministry. [22]

Persons recalls that ordinary people tried to reconcile the hostile propaganda of the government, that the priests were a danger 'to the realme', with their perception that they had 'come without weapons only to preach & teach the old ancient doctrine of their forefathers'.[23] The earthquake that had struck London the Kent coast, Antwerp, Bruges, Rouen and much of Normandy on 6 April 1580, caused further confusion, especially as it was followed by a series of disturbing *prodigia*.[24] Many interpreted black figures in the sky as representing the clash between 'these preests coming from forrain countries' and the 'ministers and clergy of England', Persons tells us, but 'the ignorant people stood astonished

---

[19]   ABSI Collectanea P. I, fol. 121a.

[20]   ABSI Collectanea P. I, fol. 121a; Richard Challoner, *Memoirs of Missionary Priests*, ed. John Hungerford Pollen, S.J. (London: Burns Oates and Washbourne, 1924), p. 21. Daniel Bartoli, S.J., *Europeae Historiae Societatis Iesu Pars Prior Anglia*, trans. Ludovicus Janinus (Lyons: A. Demen, 1671), p. 98, records everyone weeping as Campion talked of the long and glorious history of the Catholic church, and compared the 'lamentable appearance of the Anglican church (*Anglicanae Ecclesiae*) with that old, beautiful and universal church, rich in heavenly blessings'. Robert E. Scully, *Into the Lion's Den: The Jesuit Mission in Elizabethan England and Wales, 1580–1603* (St Louis: Institute of Jesuit Sources, 2011), p. 74, asserts that Campion was 'not particularly prudent', in using the sermon to 'laud papal supremacy'.

[21]   ABSI Collectanea P. I, fol. 121a.

[22]   *CSP Ireland*, 1574–1585, 73/45.1 and 60, pp. 226 and 228.

[23]   ABSI Collectanea P. I, fol. 122a.

[24]   John Stow, *The Chronicles of England, from Brute unto this present yeare of Christ, 1580* (London: Henry Bynneman, 1580), STC 23333, 1210. The earthquake in Rouen, where many were hurt by falling tiles and slates, is described by a friend of Sir Henry Cobham in a letter forwarded to London, *CSP Foreign 1579–1580*, pp. 227–9. ABSI Collectanea P. I, fol. 124b. Scully, *Lion's Den*, pp. 73–4, also links the interpretations to the arrival of the Jesuits.

& knew not what to believe nor say.[25] He concludes that 'the most part of them especially those that live in the country out of townes are generally wel affected to the Catholick religion' and disillusioned with 'their ministers' so 'were glad to here of the coming of these other preachers & desirous to hear them'; but 'the fury of the persecution making their cause to be treason & their ayders and receavers to be traytors did terrify the weaker sort'.[26]

As soon as Persons heard Campion had arrived, he returned from the country, and found 'Father Campion retyred for his more safety into a certain poor mans house in Southwark neer the Thames where men might repare without great shew or suspicion both by land & water'.[27] Although Campion now 'lived more warily & more retyredly', large numbers of young men 'of great zeale & forwardnesse in matters of religion', and of a certain 'estate and parentage', flocked to the house.[28] The Jesuits held a conference there with 'certaine of the gravest', and learned, Marian priests that were still in London (Edward Chambers and George Blackwell are named), 'others newly come from beyond the sea', and some leading Catholic laymen.[29] The 'synod of Southwark' (as it is often called) took place in a riverside house, near St Mary Overy, west of London Bridge.[30]

The central issue of the conference was the same as the 'difficulty' raised by the Jesuit superiors: how were they to deal with the rumour that 'this late coming in of Jesuits & priests' was 'for treason conspiracy & matter of state & not for religion', which would only bring 'all their spiritual and ecclesiastical functions' into disrepute, and increase the cruelty with which priests and Catholics in general were used.[31] The defence they proposed against the charge of 'meddling' was to reveal their instructions to deal only in spiritual matters, and to assert that, when it came to Sander's expedition, 'they knew no more hereof then the child niewborne, but only heard therof at their passage by Rhems'.[32] While they think this will satisfy Catholics, they recognize it is not likely to convince the Privy Council and bishops of the religion now professed. For them, their only answer is more protestation and a trust that if they are brought to trial, no jury of 'twelve English substantial men' would condemn them. When some argue that hatred against them is such that 'conjectures' will be enough to convict them, their answer is that

---

[25]   ABSI Collectanea P. I, fol. 124b.

[26]   ABSI Collectanea P. I, fol. 124b.

[27]   ABSI Collectanea P. I, fols 125a.

[28]   ABSI Collectanea P. I, fol. 125a.

[29]   ABSI Collectanea P. I, fol. 128a.

[30]   Michael Questier, *Catholicism and Community in Early Modern England: Politics, Aristocratic Patronage and Religion, c. 1550–1640* (Cambridge: University Press, 2006), pp. 161–3, suggests a possible link of the house to the Southwark estate of Viscount Montague; see McCoog, *Fashioning Jesuit Identity*, p. 203. The 'poor mans house' is confirmed by the later story of the seizure of the books (see end of this chapter).

[31]   ABSI Collectanea P. I, fol. 128b.

[32]   ABSI Collectanea P. I, fol. 128b.

'if forraine princes' had sent men on 'matters of state they would have chosen other manner of men, then we who all our lives have bin meer schollars'.[33] This belief that men with treasonous intent would not 'have come on foot and soe poorly appareled from Rome', passed over the fact that one 'meer' Oxford scholar was stirring up rebellion in Ireland.[34]

The synod dealt with two other issues. Should Catholics, under pressure from laws and fines, be granted a dispensation to attend Protestant churches? The answer to this, originally formulated at the Council of Trent, on the advice of Nicholas Sander and Bishop Goldwell, was a resounding negative.[35] But, as Persons says, 'now was the question much more revived upon the coming in of the foresaid Fathers', and was to surface again at Uxbridge in November.[36] As we have seen, 'the true opinion of not going to heretical services came not from the Jesuits', but from 'a secular priest's shop'.[37] On the second issue, whether English Catholics, who had more fast days than those on the Continent, should fall in line with the guidelines of Trent, they decided to continue to allow local variation in fasting.[38] Persons mentions that a 'grave and ancient priest', called Wilson, came with a petition 'to persuade the said Fathers out of England againe' till 'a more calmer time', but left 'well contented'.[39]

Events now overtook theory. The 'searchers of London' and 'the spyes' became so 'frequent' and 'diligent' that, 'every hower almost', they began to hear of people arrested upon suspicion, and they were advised by their friends to 'abreviate our stay in London'.[40] The danger was brought home to them when Charles Sledd, the 'Roman' spy, recognized Henry Orton in Holborne on his way to the meeting, and offered 'the Constable' 3 pounds if he would arrest Orton without giving him away while he hid in 'a pelting Inne'; the no-nonsense constable hauled Sledd into the

---

[33] ABSI Collectanea P. I, fol. 129a.

[34] ABSI Collectanea P. I, fol. 129a.

[35] Veech, *Sanders*, pp. 33–41, outlines the acute difficulties, as far back as 1561, of English Catholics on this painful issue, the long discussion at the Council of Trent, the subsequent promulgation in England through Laurence Vaux, and the argument made by Sander in *A Treatise of the Images of Christ* (Louvain: Fowler, 1567), STC 21696, ARCR II. 696, p. 39, that Catholics who attended schismatical services put in 'hasard their everlasting salvation'. See Chapter 3.

[36] CRS 2, pp. 178–81, and CRS 4, pp. 2–7, for Mr Edward Chambers's letter, dated 6 November 1580, which occasioned Persons's answer to Alban Langdale's 'manuscript book'.

[37] Wood, *Athenae Oxonienses*, I. 470, quoted by Veech, p. 41. Childs, *God's Traitors*, p. 57, repeats a commonly held belief that it was the Jesuits who first insisted upon 'absolute recusancy'.

[38] CRS 2, pp. 27, 176–7; Persons lists this issue second, but gives it enormous prominence.

[39] CRS 2, pp. 177–8; see Scully, *Lion's Den*, p. 75, for a version of this.

[40] ABSI Collectanea P. I, fols 127b–128a.

open, 'with straw about his eares'.[41] If Sledd had waited till Orton crossed the river, he would have found the entire group.[42] At about the same time, Sledd also spotted Fr Robert Johnson, a 'very grave and godly man', as he went through Smithfield with Mrs Talbot, wife of Mr John Talbot of Grafton and sister of Sir John Petre, and arrested him.[43] Sledd had travelled with Johnson and Thomas Cottam from Lyons to Rheims, heard Hart preach at Rheims, and sent descriptions of Cottam and Hart to the port of Dover. Sledd gave his 'A generall discorse of the Popes holynes devises' to Walsingham on 26 May 1580, one month before Campion landed.[44] Descriptions were circulated, and both Hart and Cottam were arrested as they arrived at Dover. Dr Humphrey Ely, under the alias of Howard, managed to stand surety for Cottam, and had him released. Cottam then had scruples about bringing trouble on others, and twice consulted Campion and Persons. They finally agreed with him that he might endanger the lives of others, and he joyfully gave himself up to Mr Andrews, a deputy of Lord Cobham 'at the sign of the Star in New Fish Street'.[45]

Persons and Campion agreed to have a final meeting in the house in Hoxton of a gentleman 'who was at that time no Catholick though his wife were'.[46] Many prominent Catholics had their houses in this area close to Spitalfields, and to the house of the Portuguese ambassador, where they could hear Mass, so the house could have been that of Sir William Catesby, Sir Thomas Tresham or Mr Gardiner, 'the well-known tenant of Hoxton', all recently reconciled by the missionaries.[47] The end of Trinity term marked a good point at which to leave London, since 'the most part of gentlemen were retyred home into their countries', and 'the searches & other dangers grew to be so many and manifest in London', and the 'two poore priestes' had been 'hemd-in so long, as it were, in the walls of London', that they now decided to 'divide themselves into sundry shires to preach and teach the Catholic religion', though even in the country, information provided by the spies Sledd and Munday, meant there was little respite.[48]

---

[41]   Allen, *A Briefe Historie*, sig. b.1v–b.2r.

[42]   ABSI Collectanea P. I, fol. 128a and fol. 151b. As Fr Grene notes in the margins, the first account suggests the incident happened before the conference; the second is ambiguous.

[43]   ABSI Collectanea P. I, fols 131b–132a.

[44]   BL Add. MS 48029, fols 121r–142v; CRS 53, pp. 193–245. Allen, *A Briefe Historie*, sig. b.2r–v, attacks Sledd's credibility, adding that Norton read 'this booke at the barre which was pretended to be *Sledds*'.

[45]   ABSI Collectanea P. I, fol. 133a.

[46]   ABSI Collectanea P. I, fol. 135b.

[47]   CRS 2, p. 27; Simpson, p. 224; More, *Historia Missionis*, p. 87; McCoog, *Fashioning Jesuit Identity*, p. 203.

[48]   ABSI Collectanea P. I, fol. 135a; Bombino, *Vita et Martyrium*, p. 121; Bodl. MS Tanner 329, fol. 40v. It seems strange that Persons should mistakenly call it 'Hilary' term, but the dominance of the culture of the Inns of Court is again apparent.

George Gilbert furnished the missionaries with horses men, money, clothes, books, vestments and 'all other furniture for the church' and, in the guise of a servant, acted as guide to Persons, while Gervase Pierrepoint escorted Campion.[49] After being trapped in a riverside tenement, Campion must have been glad at the idea of escaping to the country 'to preach and teach the Catholic religion according to their profession and cause of their coming'.[50] They had met at night 'so that they might depart more secretly', and were on the point of departure early the next morning, 19 July 1580, when Thomas Pounde, currently in the Marshalsea prison, arrived, accompanied by a group of unnamed Catholic friends, saying he had scarcely slept for anxiety about the priests.[51] They were concerned by the rumours put about by the Privy Council that the Jesuits had come into England 'for rebellion & matter of state': such rumours would only increase when they went into the country, as more Catholics were converted by their preaching and the administration of the sacraments, which 'would more & more exasperate the Queen and Councell'.[52] If either of the missionaries were caught, when 'it was very probable that he should be made away guilefully or openly be slaundered, and after his death books should come forth to deface him according to the fashion of our government in these daies'.[53] Their proposal, to counter what they called 'these inconveniences', was a declaration in writing, to be made by each missionary, signed, and left 'with some certain and sure friend, fast sealed until the day we might be taken or putt to death'.[54] In the face of the inevitable slander by the state, the friend would be able to publish a document that should have the 'sincerity and integrity of truth' of a 'last will and testament'.[55] Campion, 'a man of a singular good nature', quickly agreed:

> he arose from the company with whome he was & taking a penne in his hand wrote presently upon the end of a table that stood by in lesse I suppose then half an houre this declaration following.[56]

Campion kept the original and gave a copy to Pounde, imploring that it be kept secret until the necessity they had agreed (his arrest or death) should require it. This was a fond hope: 'wonderfull many copies were taken thereof in a small time'.[57] Within months the document had two books attacking it, and Campion's

---

49   ABSI Collectanea P. I, fol. 135a; McCoog, *Fashioning Jesuit Identity*, p. 203.
50   ABSI Collectanea P. I, fol. 135a.
51   ABSI Collectanea P. I, fol. 151b.
52   ABSI Collectanea P. I, fol. 135b.
53   ABSI Collectanea P. I, fol. 135b.
54   ABSI Collectanea P. I, fol. 135b.
55   ABSI Collectanea P. I, fol. 136a.
56   ABSI Collectanea P. I, fol. 136a.
57   ABSI Collectanea P. I, fol. 138a.

gift for rhetoric had made him the 'champion' the Privy Council wished to seize.[58] Although Persons wrote (in Latin) his own *Confessio fidei* ('Confession of faith for the London magistrates'), at the same time, it has never attracted as much notice.[59]

In 'The Letter to the Council', Campion assures the Queen and her Privy Council that his intentions are honourable and peaceful, but there is a very personal warmth, even in the last section where the dominant note is one of defiance in the face of death. This was not bravado, still less was Campion being careless about capture.[60] It is true that, as a result of the publication of the letter, 'the mission became a highly public challenge to the basic categories under which the Elizabethan regime organized its treatment of Catholicism'.[61] The defiance was the courage of a man who feels he had little to lose because the situation was already so desperate. Sledd's effective spying had already led to the arrest of Orton, Johnson, Hart and Cottam; Campion and Persons had narrowly escaped capture themselves. If they stayed in London, it was only a matter of time before they were arrested on a charge of treasonable practice against the state.

The 'Letter to the Council' was intended as a last testament, like the one Christian de Chergé wrote as he awaited the violent death, which came on 21 May 1996, at the hands of *mujahideen* in Tibhirine, Algeria.[62] In its very form, the letter was a tacit admission of how beleaguered and threatened they felt, but its epistolary genre is no literary trope, but central to Campion's characteristically personal form of address. Two copies of the 'Letter to the Council' (both with signs that they have been folded and carried like letters) are among the Foxe

---

[58]   Lake and Questier, 'Edmund Campion Affair', pp. 603–8, question the 'inadvertent manuscript publication', and argue that it was part of a pattern of 'seeking a disputatious showdown' that 'exceeded the remit given to the two Jesuits'. The attempts of the missionaries to preach in the country, and to keep a low profile in Southwark, suggest otherwise.

[59]   Leo Hicks, in CRS 39, pp. 28–41, prints and translates Persons' Latin document; Holmes, *Resistance & Compromise*, pp. 36–7, and discusses Persons' 'willingness to discuss political matters'. Carrafiello, 'Jesuit Mission', pp. 766–8, discusses *only* the letter of Persons, which he uses to argue that 'the toppling of Elizabeth's "tyrannical" regime' was the 'first priority' of the missionaries. A cornerstone of his 'careful reading' is the 'political' meeting in Rome in the Jubilee year, 1575, of English exiles (pp. 764–5). Yet Persons tells us that he wasted his time in Rome that year on 'trifles', visiting classical monuments; he only joined the Society on 25 June ['perhaps July', as Fr Grene says], CRS 2, pp. 24–5. He was not even a priest at the time of the meeting, nor was Sander present, being 'detained at Madrid', Veech, *Sanders*, p. 218.

[60]   As argued by Bossy, 'Heart of Robert Persons', pp. 193–4.

[61]   Lake and Questier, 'Edmund Campion Affair', p. 607.

[62]   Freddy Derwahl, *The Last Monk of Tibhirine: A True Story of Martyrdom, Faith and Survival* (Brewster, MA: Paraclete Press, 2013), prints the testament, finished in January 1994, in full, pp. 169–71.

papers, bound next to the papers seized by Richard Topcliffe and Thomas Norris, the chief pursuivant.[63] The tone of determined spiritual vulnerability with which Campion transformed the irenic purpose of the 'Letter to the Council' was in keeping with everything he had done since receiving the command of Mercurian to leave Prague. While seeing little chance of the overall success of the mission, Campion had submitted himself to his superiors, and agreed to do what he knew best: 'to preach the gospell, to minister the sacramentes, to instructe the symple, to reforme synners, to refute errors, and in briefe to crye all arme Spirituall, against fowle vyce, and proude ignorance wherewith my poore countrie men ar abused'.[64] In Hoxton, away from the damp slum next to the Thames where he had been holed up since his arrival at the end of June, Campion finished his letter 'To the Right Honourable Lords of Her Majesties Privy Council' with a defiant flourish:

> Many Innocent handes ar lyfted upp to heaven for yow dailye and howerlie by those English Studentes, whose posteritie shall not dye, which beyonde the Seas, gatheryng vertew and sufficyent knowledge for the purpose, are determyned never to give yow over, but either to wyn yow to heaven, or to dye uppon your pykes. And touchinge our Societye, be it knowen unto yow that we have made a league, all the Jesuites in the worlde, whose succession and multytude must over reach all the practises of England, cherefullie to carrye the crosse that yowe shall laye uppon us, and never to dispair your recoverie, while we have a man lefte to enjoy your Tybourn, or to be racked with your tormentes, or to be consumed with your prisons. The expence is reconed, the enterpryse is begunne; it is of god, it may not be withstode. So the faith was planted, so it must be restored.[65]

Campion here turns the political power of the Privy Council into a disadvantage, and transforms the exile of the priests into a potent image of their likeness to the cross-carrying Saviour, and their continuity with Saint Augustine's first mission to the Anglo-Saxons. Campion, in one short document, takes up the central issue of the controversy launched by Bishop Jewel, and asserts that, while the Catholics in exile are the true church, the members of the 'new religion' are in need of conversion as much as their Anglo-Saxon ancestors. It is not the Jesuit mission that is a practice against the state; here 'practises' (plots or conspiracies) are 'of England'.

The tone of the 'Letter to the Council' is remarkable. At its heart is the Ignatian language of *mission*: being 'sent' is central to Campion's Jesuit conception.[66] But some of the vocabulary is glitteringly chivalric, and echoes that of medieval

---

[63]   BL MS Harley 422, fols 132r–135r.

[64]   Harley MS 422, fol. 132r. See A.C. Southern, *Elizabethan Recusant Prose 1559–1582* (London; Sands & Co., [1968]), pp. 153–5, for a printed version.

[65]   Harley MS 422, fol. 132v–133r; Southern, *Elizabethan Recusant Prose*, p. 154.

[66]   O'Malley, 'Mission and the Early Jesuits', in *Saints or Devils Incarnate?*, p. 219, argues the Jesuits inaugurated the new sense of the word, derived from the Latin word *missus* (sent).

romances. Campion has 'adventured' himself like a knight on 'a special kynde of warfare, under the banner of obedience' into 'this noble Realm' ('my deare Countrie'), and he describes the Queen as 'my Sovereigne Ladye', offering to preach 'in her or your hearing'.[67] This knightly task is combined with a vivid sense of the tenderness of his own body, its fragility in the face of torture and death. So many times in the course of the piece Campion imagines what he is soon to suffer: God will 'deliver my body into durance', the missionaries will 'spend the best blood in their bodies', 'be racked with your tormentes' and 'be rewarded with rygor'. Just as Christian de Chergé prayed in his 'testament' that he and his assassin might meet, 'like happy thieves, in Paradise', Campion ends by praying that 'we maye be frendes in heaven where all injuryes shalbe forgotten'.[68] The effect of this is to cast the Council as lost in error, and in possession only of the weapons of tyrannical power, 'howsoever they face men down in *their* pulpettes'.[69] Campion's generosity, like that of a knight errant ('having runne thowsands of myles to do yow good'), acts as an indictment of churlish councillors. While he can 'cherefully carry the Crosse', the Privy Council is linked in apostrophe to 'your Tybourn', 'your tormentes' and 'your prisones': he predicts accurately that such cruel punishments will be administered by the people addressed in this letter.[70] Finally, in the midst of a national panic about armed invasion by a foreign power, Campion turns the debate back to theology. This was a daring challenge, but definitely not on the Privy Council's political terms. In the fifth point, Campion specifies the three audiences he seeks: the first before the Council itself, the second, of 'more account, before the doctors and Masters and chosen men of both Universities', and the third 'before the Lawyers, Spiritual and Temporal'.[71] This 'Letter to the Council', improvised in crisis, is a prologue to the *Rationes Decem*. What exasperated the authorities, as it moved audiences in his sermons, was that Campion chivalrously asked for 'safe conduct into the heart of the regime to debate the crucial doctrinal issues before the queen'.[72] If, by September, the Council felt compelled 'to concede' Campion 'at least the appearance' of a debate, they ruined the festivity of tournament by the brutality of 'resort to torture'.[73]

Campion wrote this letter fluently; he had enjoyed the patronage of the Queen, and knew personally several members of the Privy Council, including the Earl of Leicester and Sir Henry Sidney. One copy was found in the possession of Sr Elizabeth Sander, the sister of Dr Sander, who was examined on 18 November

---

[67]   BL MS Harley 422, fol. 132r; Southern, *Elizabethan Recusant Prose*, pp. 153.
[68]   BL MS Harley 422, fol. 133r; Derwhal, *Last Monk of Tibhirine*, p. 171.
[69]   BL MS Harley 422, fol. 134v (my emphasis for this significant variant in the second letter).
[70]   BL MS Harley 422, fol. 132v.
[71]   BL MS Harley 422, fol. 134v; Southern, *Elizabethan Recusant Prose*, p. 154.
[72]   Lake and Questier, 'Edmund Campion Affair', p. 606.
[73]   Lake and Questier, 'Edmund Campion Affair', pp. 620–21.

1580, at St Cross, by the Bishop of Winchester.[74] The 'Letter' was carried abroad, since the King of Poland, Stephen Báthory, on 21 April 1581, thanked the Apostolic Delegate, Cardinal Caligari, for sending him a copy, and saying that he would get it translated into Polish to encourage his own 'preachers' (*evangelicis*).[75]

Persons says that, 'presently after our departure' from London, the Privy Council published its proclamation of 15 July.[76] This edict, about 'Suppressing Invasion Rumours', written by Lord Burghley and corrected in his hand, indicates the level of fear in England; Campion wrote his 'Letter to the Council' four days later, just before Mendoza reported on 23 July 1580 that the fear that 'Catholics may rise' in England had inspired the proclamation, and further that all Catholics released on bail had been ordered to surrender themselves on pain of death within 20 days, and that very many had already done so.[77]

This phase of the mission lasted little longer than the summer vacation, since Persons and Campion met again in October in Uxbridge, after 'passing over many shires'.[78] Where Campion went during these three months has been much debated. It seems that in 'somer 1580', he visited the houses of Lord Vaux, Sir Thomas Tresham and Sir William Catesby.[79] He cannot have gone far north, since Persons explicitly says that Campion later considered visiting the Catholics of Lancashire, whom he 'had not had time or commodity to reach in his former circuit'.[80] He seems instead to have travelled through Berkshire, Oxfordshire, Northamptonshire and Warwickshire.[81] Campion was certainly in the Thames Valley in the summer of 1580.[82] He said Mass at the house of Francis and Anne Morris, 'the mansion house of Great Coxwell', Wiltshire, on 30 July 1580, and in Ashbury Manor, Oxfordshire, formerly a lodge of the Abbey of Glastonbury, and then the home of Alice Wicks, on 8 August 1580.[83] He also exploited both the Vaux family network

---

[74] *CSP Domestic, 1547–1580*, 12/144/31, 18 November 1580, p. 688.

[75] *Monumenta Poloniae Vaticana: Continet I.A. Caligari Nuntii Apost. in Polonia Epistolas et Acta* (Krakow: Academy of Letters, 1915), vol. 4 (1578–81), p. 619. The editorial footnote to this letter assumes that the King is referring to a copy of *Rationes Decem*, which had not been written at this date.

[76] ABSI Collectanea P. I, fols 138a and 139b; Hughes and Larkin, *Tudor Royal Proclamations*, no. 650, II. 469–71. See below for the way Persons confuses this with the proclamation of 24 January 1581.

[77] *CSP Spanish, 1580–1586*, p. 43.

[78] ABSI Collectanea P. I, fol. 141b.

[79] BL Lansdowne MS 30, no. 78, fol. 201r. Burghley has annotated and endorsed these notes. See Chapter 8 for details.

[80] ABSI Collectanea P. I, fol. 145a.

[81] McCoog, *Fashioning Jesuit Identity*, p. 334.

[82] Michael Hodgetts, 'Campion in the Thames Valley, 1580', *Recusant History* 30 (2010), 26–46.

[83] Godfrey Anstruther, O.P., *Vaux of Harrowden: A Recusant Family* (Newport: R.H. Johns, 1953), discusses this phase of the mission, p. 115, citing King's Bench 9/654/58 and 9/654/57.

(which included Edward and Eleanor Brooksby) and the St John's College properties, since he first stayed that summer at Lowches Farm, Long Wittenham, which Henry Russell leased to Justinian Stubbs.[84] William West's letters to Henry Russell, Campion's exact contemporary at St John's, who resigned as Principal of Gloucester Hall in the summer of 1580, accuse him of being 'Campion's companion both before and after the proclamation [of 24 January 1581] for the apprehension of the traitor Campion'.[85] Campion's choice of this area may owe something to George Chamberlayn, but probably more to Campion's own Oxford connections. Persons's account, vague about the locality, is clear about the rich harvest of souls the two missionaries reaped as 'they confirmed and gained to the Catholick religion very great numbers of all sorts of people', because those in the country, including 'the better of the English nobility and gentry', far from 'the infection of ministers', find it easier to remember 'the virtuous life'.[86] During the same period, Persons, accompanied by George Gilbert, visited Northampton, Derby, Worcester, Gloucester and Hereford.[87]

The Council, informed of the mission's rural rides by 'their spies and other persons whom they apprehended', quickly 'sent divers pursuivants after us into most shires of England'.[88] The Jesuits stayed in the houses of gentlemen and nobles, the only houses large enough to conceal them and to hold the considerable congregations that gathered, often in the upper rooms, for Mass. This was a policy which had practical advantages, not (as some scholars have suggested) 'a strategy for disaster' leading to the transformation of Catholicism into a 'seigneurially structured minority'.[89] The nobility and gentry provided the religious, economic and social structure for the surrounding population, and it is hard to see what else the disguised missionaries could have done. 'The network' established by the Jesuits was a tight one, 'based on personal relations and contacts'.[90]

---

[84]   For more detail on this first visit to Lowches Farm, see Hodgetts, 'Campion in the Thames Valley', pp. 30–31, and Kilroy, 'The Queen's Visit to Oxford in 1566: A Fresh Look at Manuscript Sources', in *Recusant History* 31.3 (2013), 331–73 (p. 369). For the second visit, see Chapter 7.

[85]   Michael Hodgetts kindly passed to me his transcript of the first letter, 25 April 1584; the second quotation comes from the letter, dated 23 August 1584, in *Little Malvern Letters: I, 1482–1737*, ed. Aileen M. Hodgson and Michael Hodgetts (Woodbridge: Boydell Press for Catholic Record Society, 2011), p. 53.

[86]   ABSI Collectanea P. I, fol. 141b.

[87]   ABSI, Collectanea P. I, '*Notae Quaedam Pro Scribenda Vita Sua*', fols 222b–233b (fol. 227b); CRS 2, Persons's 'Autobiography', p. 27.

[88]   ABSI Collectanea P. I, fol. 138b.

[89]   Christopher Haigh, 'From Monopoly to Minority: Catholicism in Early Modern England', *Transactions of the Royal Historical Society*, 5th Series, 31 [1981], 129–47 (p. 147); Carrafiello, 'Jesuit Mission', pp. 772, writes (anachronistically), 'Persons gloried in his association with the upper classes'.

[90]   McCoog, *Fashioning Jesuit Identity*, p. 223.

Persons's account focuses on the intimate and emotional nature of this mission as they 'entered' in the guise of friends or relatives of 'some person that lived within the house', changed into priest's 'apparel and furniture, which ever we carried with us', heard confessions usually that evening and sometimes 'a good part of the night', said Mass the 'next morning', sometimes before dawn if both 'heretikes & Catholikes lived together as many times they did', after which ('a comfort & solace was it to them all, to heare him preach') there was an 'exhortation', and they made themselves 'ready to depart again', or 'stole privately thence, before any heretike, fast asleepe … perceived what was done', and 'no one ever parted from him but unwillingly'.[91] This was the life of passionate pastoral ministration intended by Everard Mercurian, but the missionaries were risking their lives to reconcile individual Catholics: recusants and schismatics alike.[92] Campion's own letter to Mercurian in November reveals both how dangerous it was, and how desperate Catholics were for help.[93] Although the Latin text shows Campion at his most humorously self-deprecating, the final quotation from Psalm 118 succinctly specifies Campion's deepest feelings:

> I ride through some part of the country almost every day. The harvest is altogether immense. As I sit on my horse, I meditate my little sermon and, once I have entered the house, put the finishing touches to it. I speak with all those who come up to me, and hear those who wish to confess. In the morning I say Mass, and then preach. They listen intently, like men thirsty for the word; very many receive the sacraments. In ministering these we are everywhere helped by priests whom we find wherever we go, which means that the people are satisfied, and this region is won for us with much less effort. Our indigenous priests, themselves outstanding in doctrine and holiness, have aroused such a high opinion of our order that I hesitate to record it. So, even more can we see that the helpers we badly need should be of the same quality, so that they can maintain all these things worthily. Above all, let them be experienced in preaching. We cannot long escape the hands of the heretics, since all around us are so many spying eyes, so many wagging tongues and so many traps of our enemies.
>
> I wear a completely ridiculous outfit, which I change as frequently as I change my name. I myself read letters which announce on the first small page: *that Campion has been captured*. This chant has now become so familiar wherever I come, and so rings in my ears, that fear itself has taken away my fear. *Anima mea in manibus meis semper* (My life is every moment in danger).[94]

---

[91]   Bombino, *Vita et Martyrium*, pp. 123–4; Bodl. MS Tanner 329, fol. 42r.

[92]   Carrafiello, 'Jesuit Mission', p. 761, uses later 'correspondence and memoirs' of Persons to argue that, 'Pastoral contact with individual recusants was therefore a secondary and consequential concern'.

[93]   The letter was written before he left Uxbridge, on 16 November 1580.

[94]   *Opuscula*, pp. 411–13 (my translation). I have left the last phrase, a quotation from the Vulgate translation of Psalm 118, verse 109, in Latin, since the following verses make clear the meaning: his life is in immediate peril from the snares of surrounding enemies.

This letter was written as the Irish rebellion reached a shocking climax. In July 1580, Sander had been in Ireland a year, and the Spanish ambassador, Bernadino de Mendoza, reported to his King, on 18 June, 'the calling out of the militia which had been under orders to muster for the last four months, and the vigilant watching night and day from the beacon-towers'.[95] On 19 July 1580, James Eustace, Viscount Baltinglass, stirred Leinster into revolt, and on 26 July 1580, Captain John Zouche described the Baltinglass rebellion as 'the more dangerous because he coloureth it with religion'.[96] Mabel Browne, Countess of Kildare, provided a refuge for Fr Robert Rochford, S.J., Fr Nicholas Eustace (cousin of Baltinglass) and Fr Compton, all linked to the rebellion.[97] If Catholicism could unite Anglo-Irish Palesmen against the English crown, there were fears it could do the same in England.

On 27 July 1580, Sir Nicholas Malbie wrote despondently from Limerick to say that 'if foreign aid come, few will stick with her majesty'.[98] On 21 August 1580, Mendoza again reported that 'fear of a rising of Catholics here as well as in Ireland' had prompted the Queen to order 'a hundred Catholic gentlemen' to be imprisoned in various castles and strongholds.[99] In Ireland, the main problem was victualling the growing force, which by October, included 6,437 soldiers and 1,344 mariners.[100] On 25 August, in the muddy pass of Glenmalure in the Wicklow mountains, Baltinglass inflicted a humiliating defeat on Arthur Grey, newly appointed Lord Deputy, and on 31 August, Lord Grey himself wrote to Walsingham that 'the conspiracy through Ireland is so general, that without a main force it will not be appeased'.[101]

Of course, there were false rumours (a fleet and 15,000 Spanish troops assembling in Biscay).[102] But Munster and Leinster were in rebellion, the Pale was splintering and Dublin was under threat.[103] About 10 September, Admiral Winter, patrolling the south coast of Ireland, had to return to England to revictual

---

ARSI Fondo Gesuitico 651, no. 612, contains the copy Campion sent to the new general, Claudio Acquaviva, on 9 July 1581, of this letter to Mercurian (who had died), which had clearly gone astray. Allen, *A Briefe Historie*, sig. e2v–e6r, gives text, with the translation made canonical by Simpson, pp. 246–50. See Foley, *Records*, III. 671–3; compare Persons to Agazzari, in CRS 39, pp. 85–6.

[95]   *CSP Spanish, 1580–1586*, p. 35.

[96]   *CSP Ireland, 1574–1585*, 74/66, p. 237.

[97]   Vincent Carey, *Surviving the Tudors: The 'Wizard' Earl of Kildare and English Rule in Ireland, 1537–1586* (Dublin: Four Courts Press, 2002), p. 76 (with detailed sources). See Chapter 3.

[98]   *CSP Ireland, 1574–1585*, 74/75, p. 238.

[99]   *CSP Spanish, 1580–1586*, p. 50.

[100]   *CSP Ireland, 1574–1585*, 75/55, 56, 62, 77/25; Paul E.J. Hammer, *Elizabeth's Wars: War, Government and Society 1544–1604* (Basingstoke: Palgrave Macmillan, 2003), p. 109.

[101]   *CSP Ireland, 1574–1585,* 75/79–83, p. 247.

[102]   *CSP Ireland, 1574–1585*, 72/44, p. 217.

[103]   *CSP Spanish, 1580–1586*, 7 August 1580, p. 44.

his fleet (the armaments on the latest ships left little room for food and drink), and so missed the arrival of a flotilla of six ships that had sailed from Ferrol on 28 August.[104] Only the flagship under Colonel Sebastiano di San Giuseppi was of any size (400 tons). The other 4 ships ranged from 50 tons to 120 tons, and there was one small galley of 20 oars. On board the fleet were the Bishop of Killaloe, Fray Mateo de Oviedo and the Pope's commissary, Don Fernando de Ribadeneira.[105] The soldiers, all raw recruits, had been hired locally, and consisted of 200 men from Asturias, 200 Biscayans, some Italians and a further contingent of Irish swordsmen.[106] These variously commissioned and refitted ships proudly flew the Pope's arms from their main-tops, and King Philip's arms from their fore-tops. Two ships (one carrying Charles Browne, half-brother of Viscount Montague) became separated in a storm and returned to Spain.[107]

The scale of Lord Burghley's response indicates the danger perceived. Nine of the Queen's latest warships were fitted out. The flagship, *Revenge* (580 tons) had 42 guns.[108] The Vice-Admiral, Captain Bingham, was in *Swiftsure* (360 tons), supported by the *Aid* (300 tons), the *Achates* (100 tons) the *Bull* (200 tons), the *Lion* (200 tons), the *Foresight* (300 tons, commanded by Captain Frobisher), the *Tiger* (200 tons) and the *Merlin* (50 tons).[109] The admiral of this formidable fleet, which deployed 252 guns, had to shelter from a storm in Kinsale on 15 October, but Bingham in *Swiftsure*, separated from the main fleet by the storm, put his sails to the wind and, in 60 hours from Portland Race, reached Smerwick on 17 October.[110] After firing some of his guns, Bingham was forced to wait impatiently for Admiral Winter, and reported accurately to Walsingham that two of the enemy ships had returned to Spain with 200 sick soldiers.[111] Two days later, on 19 October 1580, Sander wrote to Sega to say that, when he saw that his reinforcements consisted of 400 raw recruits, no artillery and very little money, 'a greater despair than ever seized upon the minds of all'.[112] On the same day, Sander wrote a letter to Mendoza in London, signed by the Earl of Desmond and Viscount Baltinglass, asking for: '6 bronze cannons, 6 demi-cannons with all necessary apparatus, 2 culverins, a quantity of powder, some artificial fire, 25 bombadiers', 8,000 footmen, 2,000 harquebuses, 1,000 broad swords, and victuals'.[113]

---

[104]   *CSP Ireland, 1574–1585,* 76/55, p. 254, 23 September 1580.

[105]   CRS 26, pp. 46–7.

[106]   CRS 26, pp. 46–7.

[107]   CRS 26, pp. 46–7.

[108]   Hammer, *Elizabeth's Wars*, p. 94.

[109]   BL MS 6265, fol. 12r–v; collated with J.J. College and Ben Warlow, *Ships of the Royal Navy: The Complete Record of all Fighting Ships of the Royal Navy from the 15th Century to the Present* (London: Chatham House, 2006).

[110]   *CSP Ireland, 1574–1585,* 77/51, p. 262.

[111]   *CSP Ireland, 1574–1585,* 77/51, p. 262.

[112]   CRS, 26, pp. 48 and 52.

[113]   *CSP Spanish, 1580–1586,* pp. 57–9.

Sander was beginning to despair of Spanish help, and left the fort 'with 2,000 ducats' to try to raise an Irish army; he engineered a meeting in nearby Tralee between the Earl of Desmond, Viscount Baltinglass and Sir John of Desmond, but no coordinated action followed; Desmond was a largely fugitive leader.[114]

On 23 October 1580, Mendoza reported from London that the Queen and Council were 'much troubled about affairs in Ireland', and 'five hundred Catholic gentlemen have been imprisoned here on the charge of being Catholic, there being fears that they may rise in consequence of the news in Ireland'.[115] Although the uncoordinated Irish rebels lacked artillery, the Privy Council feared what would happen if they were properly led and decently armed, so they carefully controlled the news coming from Ireland. As the rebellion spread, anxiety grew about the loyalty of both the O'Neill in Ulster and the Earl of Kildare, and there was no certainty that the Spanish troops could be dislodged if Baltinglass and Desmond (who had 4,000 men) joined forces. Campion's November letter to his general (so often quoted without the context of the Irish invasion) describes the effect in England:

> While I am writing this, a truly monstrous persecution is raging (*immanissima saevit persecutio*). The house where I am staying is full of grief: they either forecast their own death, or capture, or imprisonment or seizure of all their property. Nevertheless, they press on bravely.[116]

Perhaps more bravely than the Asturians and Biscayans at Smerwick, who at this very time were shivering in the isolated iron-age fort, Dún an Óir, and waiting for the inevitable; a few fortunate men died first of the damp and cold. The Lord Deputy himself complained of the foul weather as he camped nearby. As soon as the Admiral and his artillery reached Smerwick on 7 November, he put his heavy guns ashore; Grey moved this ordinance into position overnight (Plate 2).[117] The bombardment, by land and sea, began on the morning of 8 November, and lasted till 4 p.m. on 9 November, when the Spanish colonel finally despaired of help from Desmond, and displayed a white flag. On 10 November 1580, he came to Lord Grey, with 12 of his officers trailing furled ensigns, to surrender.

Grey's secretary was Edmund Spenser, who describes him 'selfe being as neare them as any'.[118] In his elegant italic hand he transcribed Grey's report, dated 12 November, for the Queen.[119] Don Sebastiano, he records, requested that his

---

[114]   Colm Lennon, *Sixteenth-Century Ireland: The Incomplete Conquest* (Dublin: Four Courts, 1995), pp. 225–6.

[115]   *CSP Spanish, 1580–1586*, p. 62.

[116]   *Opuscula*, p. 418.

[117]   Holinshed, *Chronicles* (1587), II. 171.a.52–64.

[118]   Spenser, *A View of the State of Ireland*, p. 75.

[119]   Andrew Hadfield, *Edmund Spenser: A Life* (Oxford: University Press, 2012), figure 7 on p. 166, a photograph of the first page of Lord Grey's letter to the Queen, written in Spenser's hand.

men should be spared 'according to the custome of Warre, and the Law of Nations'; Grey rejected the appeal on the grounds that the Desmonds and their supporters 'were no lawfull Enemies, but Rebells and Traytours, and therefore they that came to succour them, no better than Rogues and Runagates, specially comming with no licence, nor commission from their owne King'.[120] The result, Spenser related, was that 'they craved onely mercy, which it being not thought good to shew them … there was no other way but to make that short end of them as was made'.[121] Mendoza reported that Lord Grey took 'possession of the fort, on 10th, and they slaughtered 507 men who were in it, and some pregnant women, besides which they hanged 17 Irish and Englishmen'.[122] Many of the Spaniards were beheaded, and their heads thrown into the sea. Friar Laurence Moore, Oliver Plunkett and Sander's English secretary, William Wollick, were taken to a forge for torture, their legs and arms broken, the priest's thumb and forefingers cut off. John Hooker described the role of Walter Raleigh in the revised 'Irish Historie' he dedicated to Raleigh:

> When the capteine had yeelded himselfe, and the fort appointed to be surrendered, capteine Raleigh together with capteine Macworth, who had the ward of that daie, entered into the castell, & made a great slaughter, manie or the most part of them being put to the sword.[123]

The massacre, completely contrary to the *ius gentium*, reflected 'Grey's hatred of Catholicism' and the 'fear of an international Catholic conspiracy', and caused shock and outrage across Europe.[124]

Sixteen years later, in *A View of the State of Ireland*, Spenser defended Lord Grey 'in that sharpe execution of the Spaniards'; Grey, far from deserving 'the name of a bloody man', was 'most gentle, affable, loving and temperate'.[125] This is not convincing. Grey had cudgelled his neighbour, John Fortescue, almost to death in Fleet Street, and was as committed to repression of Catholics as his father had been when, during the Oxfordshire rebellion in 1549, he hanged priests from Bloxham and Chipping Norton steeples.[126] Now the Lord Deputy and the Earl of

---

[120]   Spenser, *A View of the State of Ireland*, p. 75.

[121]   Spenser, *A View of the State of Ireland*, p. 75.

[122]   *CSP Spanish, 1580–1586*, p. 69.

[123]   Holinshed, *Chronicles* (1587), II. 171.b.67–73. *ODNB*, 'John Hooker [Vowell]', by S. Mendyk, Hooker (1527–1601) reveals that Hooker had witnessed the brutal suppression of the Western Rising in 1546.

[124]   Lennon, *Incomplete Conquest*, p. 226; Hammer, *Elizabeth's Wars*, p. 109; Carey, *Surviving the Tudors*, p. 180; *ODNB*, 'Arthur Grey', fourteenth baron Grey of Wilton (1536–1593), by Julian Lock.

[125]   Spenser, *A View of the State of Ireland*, p. 74.

[126]   Philip Caraman, *The Western Rising 1549: The Prayer Book Rebellion* (Tiverton: Westcountry Books, 1994), p. 81; Susan Brigden, *New Worlds, Lost Worlds: The Rule of the Tudors, 1485–1603* (London: Penguin, 2000), p. 191, confirms the practice; *ODNB*, 'Arthur Grey', by Julian Lock, confirms the order.

Ormond laid Munster waste. Spenser, recommending this as a way of quelling rebellion, describes how hunger so gripped the Irish that

> they would quickly consume themselves and devoure one another. The proofe whereof, I saw sufficiently exampled in these late warres of Mounster, for nothwithstanding that the same was a most rich and plentifull countrey, full of corn and cattle, that you would have thought they should have been able to stand long, yet ere one yeare and a halfe they were brought to such wretchedness as that any stony heart would have rued the same. Out of every corner of the woods and glynnes they came creeping forth upon their hands, for their legges could not bear them. They looked like anatomies of death, they spake like Ghosts crying out of their graves; they did eat the dead Carrions, happy were they could find them; yea, and one another soone after, insomuch as the very carcasses they spared not to scrape out of their graves. And if they found a plot of water-cresses or Shamrocks, there they flocked as to a feast for the time, yet not able long to continue therewithall; that in short space there were none almost left, and a most populous and plentifull country suddenly left void of man and beast, yet sure in all that warre, there perished not many by the Sword, but all by the extremitie of famine, which they themselves had wrought.[127]

John Hooker's 'Supplie of the Irish Chronicle' ends its catalogue of rebellions in Ireland with the just punishment of Sander's expedition: the famine in which more than 50,000 people died.[128] On the last page, he describes how one could travel across the waste land stretching from Waterford to Smerwick 'about six score miles' and not meet 'anie man, woman, or child … nor yet see anie beast, but the verie wolves, the foxes … a heavie, but a just judgement of God upon such a Pharoicall and stifnecked people'.[129] Hooker's peroration ends with that 'antichrist of Rome' who has 'suborned his unholie & traitorous Jesuits, under colour of holiness, to range from place to place through her majesties realmes'.[130] 'The Continuation of the chronicles of England' in Holinshed begins its 47-page account of Campion's trial with the papal bull and Dr Sander:

> The like was put in practise in Ireland through doctor Sanders and other traitors, who there joined themselves togither under the popes standard, to bring to passe their secret appointment in this realme. Through their persuasions and dealings, the people were mooved in the popes name to fight against their lawfull princesse under his banner; and to rebell against hir so notoriouslie as they might. The incouragement to this great disobedience they received through doctor Sanders a fugitive and ranke traitor to his prince and countrie as also through diverse Jesuits both English and Irish.[131]

---

[127]   Spenser, *A View of the State of Ireland*, p. 72.

[128]   The figure is the lowest estimate, *Incomplete Conquest*, p. 227.

[129]   Holinshed, *Chronicles* (1587), II. 183.a.24–5.

[130]   Holinshed, *Chronicles* (1587), II. 183.b.8–10.

[131]   Holinshed, *Chronicles* (1587), III. 1322.b.40–50.

Sander's expedition to Ireland, like a suffocating blanket, robbed the Jesuit mission of the air it required to live and breathe. By the time Campion landed at Dover, Sander's invasion had unleashed death and destruction across Munster, and raised the spectre of a Catholic rebellion and invasion in England. The proclamation against Jesuits of 24 January 1581 explicitly states this: 'Her highness therefore, foreseeing the great mischief that may ensue by such wicked instruments, whereof experience hath been overlately seen in the realm of Ireland …'[132]

Persons, in his 'Life and Martyrdom of Father Edmond Campian', makes only three passing references to Sander's expedition: his account of the news of it in Rheims does suggest that 'they were hartily sorry'.[133] Otherwise, Persons simply recounts that Campion finally agreed to give up his alias, Mr Patrick, because of it, and that they decided at the Hoxton conference to make it clear that they knew nothing of Sander's expedition before they heard of it in Rheims.[134] The increased level of spying and oppression of Catholics is made to seem like a response to the arrival of the Jesuits themselves. Most surprisingly of all, Persons replaces the proclamation of 15 July 1580 (about invasion rumours) with the proclamation of 24 January 1581 'Ordering Return of Seminarians, Arrest of Jesuits'.[135] Bombino follows him in this.[136] This suppression (even if unconscious) has effectively shaped all subsequent Catholic historiography of the first Jesuit mission, so that the damaging effect of the Irish expedition has been expunged from the Campion story.[137] It is not mentioned in the *Concertatio* of 1588, where Sander is listed simply as a major source and an *academicus*: neither his tragic death nor the colossal catastrophe occasioned by the invasion is mentioned.[138] Yet the Irish invasion was not merely a damaging backdrop to the first Jesuit mission: it was the stage on which it was unwillingly played, and the prism through which it was viewed. Campion wrote his 'Letter to the Council' and Persons his 'Confession of Faith' on the same day, 19 July 1580, as Viscount Baltinglass declared his rebellion, which drowned Campion's voice in a sea of violent political rhetoric, at the very moment when his intellectual challenge forced the state to respond with 'inherently contestable' debates.[139]

---

[132]   PRO SP 12/152/3: *Tudor Royal Proclamations*, no. 655, II. 481–4 (483).

[133]   ABSI Collectanea P. I, fol. 114b.

[134]   ABSI Collectanea P. I, fol. 109b.

[135]   ABSI Collectanea P. I, fol. 139b. The proclamation was dated 10 January, published on 24 January 1581.

[136]   Bombino, *Vita et Martyrium*, p. 121; Bodl. MS Tanner 329, fol. 40v.

[137]   Scully, *Lion's Den*, p. 73, links the proclamation of 15 July with fears of a 'Jesuit invasion'.

[138]   [John Gibbons and John Fenn], *Concertatio Ecclesiae Catholicae in Anglia* (Trier: Bock, 1588), ARCR I. 525, fol. [404]v.

[139]   Lake and Questier, 'Edmund Campion Affair', p. 623.

Irish historians give full weight to the terrible events of 1579 to 1583.[140] English historians, who tend to follow Lord Burghley in making Campion carry the blame for the fear of papal invasion, end up arguing that the mission itself was surreptitiously political. Some, while characterizing the mission as 'fundamentally political', completely omit the invasion of Ireland.[141] Others describe the mission itself as militant: 'when Robert Persons and Edmund Campion launched the mission to England in June 1580 ... the Jesuits sought to foment rebellion against Elizabeth and prepare the way for a foreign invasion to restore Catholicism by force'.[142] In the most original and influential account of the mission, Lake and Questier refer only once to 'the recent military adventurism of Sander in Ireland'.[143] Patrick McGrath's verdict, 40 years on, still seems a more accurate assessment:

> Allen, like the pope who relied so much on his advice in English affairs, failed to see that he could not have it both ways and that he was placing the missionary priests in an impossible situation when he sent them to work for the Catholic cause by spiritual means while at the same time he was supporting attempts to overthrow the Protestant regime by force.[144]

Edmund Campion had used his two visits as a pilgrim to Rome to voice his disagreement with the papal bull, as he asserted vehemently at his trial.[145] His conception of the church was a thousand miles apart from the visible monarchy of Dr Sander; he always 'acknowledged her Majestie (both *facto* & *Iure*), to be Queene', and his model was Aesculapius, the healer-god, not Aeneas, Virgil's mythical hero.[146] It is no wonder that he spent most of his long journey to England in solitary prayer.[147]

By the time Persons returned to London at the end of October, he found 'the persecution so hott, and especially against Fr Campian by name, by reason that his

---

[140]   Lennon, *Incomplete Conquest*; Carey, *Surviving the Tudors*; Cieran Brady, *The Chief Governors: The Rise and Fall of Reform Government in Tudor Ireland, 1536–1588* (Cambridge: University Press, 1994).

[141]   Carrafiello, 'Jesuit Mission', pp. 761–74; Scully, *Lion's Den*, p. 312, mentions an invasion of Ireland as a theoretical possibility only in a footnote on, p. 64 n. 64, and couples Sander with Campion.

[142]   Hammer, *Elizabeth's Wars*, p. 107.

[143]   Lake and Questier, 'Edmund Campion Affair', p. 623. McCoog, *Fashioning Jesuit Identity*, pp. 70–74, examines how much Persons knew, and couples it with fear of a 'papal league'. Highley, *Catholics Writing*, pp. 123–37, compares Sander's 'ethnically inclusive, British-Irish reconversion effort', with Campion, who 'exploited Ireland and its symbols in his acts of self-fashioning'.

[144]   Patrick McGrath, *Papists and Puritans under Elizabeth I* (London: Blandford, 1967), p. 271.

[145]   BL MS Harley 6265, fol. 17r.

[146]   BL MS Harley 6265, fol. 19r.

[147]   Bombino, *Vita et Martyrium*, p. 75; Bodl. MS Tanner 329, fol. 23r.

paper of challenge, as they called it, was come abroad and infinite copies taken thereof' that it was not thought safe for him to 'enter the citty'.[148] Persons wrote to Alfonso Agazzari, S.J., at this time:

> The causes of this persecution are not known with certainty, but not a few are suggested: as for instance the ill-success of the English in Ireland against the army of the Supreme Pontiff.[149]

Campion went to the comparatively safe house near Uxbridge (15 miles from London), which was rented by William Griffith from Sir George Peckham (who lived at Denham).[150] The meeting in Uxbridge was a large one, attended by several senior priests, many members of the Catholic nobility including two grandsons of Thomas More, George and Charles Bassett and the two equerries, Gilbert and Pierrepoint. There, they recounted what 'mercies God had shown unto them', and Campion wrote his letter to Mercurian. While they discussed what to do next, Captains Raleigh and Mackworth were following Grey's orders; the Jesuits may not have heard the cries of the dying Spaniards, but Campion would have to use all his logical and rhetorical skills to try to distinguish his mission from the reality Sander's expedition had given to the Privy Council's nightmare of a papal invasion.

The Uxbridge conference marks the end of the first phase of the mission: indeed the end of the mission as originally conceived and planned. Even in the country, the search, especially for Campion, had intensified to the point where such a ministry was almost impossible. Although 'light & spirit were brought back agayne to poore England', the priests and the whole Catholic community found 'that a rigid persecution was at their heeles'.[151] They decided that the only way they could reach a wider audience was by writing, which effectively opened a second front for the two hunted priests.[152]

Those at Uxbridge suggested that Campion 'besides his occupations of preaching & instructing to write something also in the Latin toung unto the universities'.[153] Campion thought about their request and asked them what they would suggest; there were as 'many matters' proposed as there were 'divers men'. Some proposed writing 'some consolation unto Catholics in this time of

---

[148]   ABSI Collectanea P. I, fol. 144b. Persons is referring to the title '*The great bragge and challenge*', which Meredith Hanmer gave to Campion's 'Letter to the Council': see below.

[149]   Letter of 17 November, CRS 39, p. 56.

[150]   ABSI Collectanea P. I, fol. 144b; CRS 2, p. 27; McCoog, *Fashioning Jesuit Identity*, p. 205. For more on William Griffith, see Anna Maria Orofino, '"*Coelum non animum mutant qui trans mare currunt*": David Stradling (1537–c. 1595) and his Circle of Welsh Catholic Exiles in Continental Europe', *Recusant History* 32.2 (2014), pp. 139–58 (p. 155).

[151]   Bombino, *Vita et Martyrium*, p. 126; Bodl. MS Tanner 329, fol. 43r.

[152]   Bombino, *Vita et Martyrium*, p. 129; Bodl. MS Tanner 329, fol. 45r.

[153]   ABSI Collectanea P. I, fol. 145a.

persecution'; others to encourage the weak to make a stand; others that he should 'write of some points of controversy'. When Campion had heard their views, 'he paused awhile', said they were all good ideas, but that if it were 'his own choice' he would write '*de haeresi desperata*, to show that heresy did now despaire in England'. When they laughed, given that it seemed 'most to flourish in England & to threaten persecution', Campion replied calmly that 'their cruel proceeding by terror is the greatest argument that may be of their desperation'.[154] This perception is central to Campion's view of the regime, and is visible in the *Praefatio* of *Rationes Decem*: '*tormenta non scholas parant antistites*' (the high priests are preparing instruments of torture not scholastic debates).[155] The word itself runs in anaphora diagonally (Figure 6.1) across the first leaf, sig. A1: *Desperatio … Desperatio … Desperatio … Desperatio*, as a repeated answer to a series of rhetorical questions about what has driven the heretics to reject books of the Bible that do not fit their ideas.[156]

It was decided that Campion should 'return again to the country until the present tempest of persecution' was 'blown over'.[157] Which part of the country resolved itself into a choice between two counties that he had not been able to visit before: Norfolk or Lancashire. They settled on Lancashire, first because 'it was more distant from London & more generally affected to the Catholic religion', and secondly because 'there was more hope for him to finde commodity of books for him to write or answer the heretics'. They assumed that, since his 'challenge' was now 'spread over England' and the main subject of conversation in inns, taverns and public meetings, it would soon be answered.[158]

In his later 'Notae breves', Persons mentions that 'as Campion was leaving (*discedens*), seeing that many books full of lies would be published against him, he strongly recommended that we should see about setting up a press'.[159] Campion's liminal afterthought transformed the mission and how it would be perceived. Almost immediately, Stephen Brinkley offered his help. Brinkley, pensioner of St John's College, Cambridge, had organized the secret printing in 1579, by William Carter, of his own translation of Gaspar Loarte's *Exercise of a Christian Life*, and several other books.[160]

---

154 ABSI Collectanea P. I, fol. 145b.

155 *Rationes Decem*, sig. 3r. For quotation, see Sir John Harington, York Minster Library MS XVI.L.6, p. 239. There is a deliberately pejorative tone to the word Campion chooses for bishops: *antistites*.

156 *Rationes Decem*, sig. A1v; see also, ABSI Collectanea P. I, fol. 146a.

157 ABSI Collectanea P. I, fol. 144b.

158 ABSI Collectanea P. I, fol. 145a.

159 ABSI Collectanea P. I, fol. 152b.

160 Brinkley's birth and background remain obscure, but after his release from the Tower on 24 June 1583, he went abroad and helped Persons on his secret press at Rouen. His translation of Loarte – revised for a second edition in 1584 – may have inspired Persons's *Christian Directory*. It seems likely that he was involved in the publication of *Leicester's*

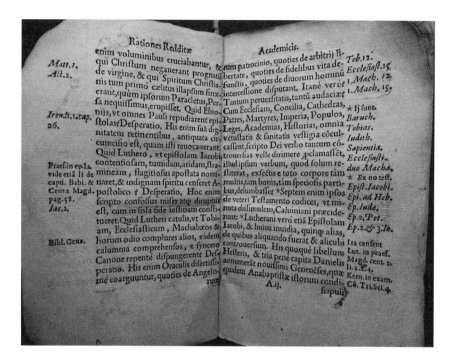

Figure 6.1　*Rationes Decem*, Stonor Park edn, ARCR I. 135.1, Winchester
copy (WN⁴), sig. A1v–A2r. With permission of the Bishop and
Trustees of the Catholic Diocese of Portsmouth and the Parish
Priest of Hampshire Downs Parish.

Although Campion suggested the printing press, Persons was the first to use
it. The decision of the Hoxton conference in July had been to maintain the stance
that Catholics should not attend Protestant services. Before they left Uxbridge in
November, Persons received a letter from Fr Edward Chambers telling him that an
anonymous manuscript was being circulated among leading Catholics arguing that
Catholics could attend Protestant services without sin. The book had apparently
already convinced several leading Catholics, including Lord Paget, Ralph
Sheldon, Lord Compton and Sir William Catesby.[161] Chambers asked to meet

---

Commonwealth, which was carried to England by Ralph Emerson, S.J., in September 1584.
See 'Stephen Brinkley', by D.M. Rogers in *The New Catholic Encycopaedia* (New York:
McGraw-Hill Book Company, 1967). William Carter was incarcerated between December
1579, when his press was raided and his house ransacked for books, and June 1581, which
explains why he was not involved at this stage. T.A. Birrell, 'William Carter (c. 1549–84):
Recusant Printer, Publisher, Binder, Stationer, Scribe – and Martyr', *Recusant History* 28.1
(2006), 22–42 gives a full account of Carter's life and printing; see also, *ODNB*, 'William
Carter', by Ian Gadd.

[161]　CRS 2, pp. 179–81.

Persons, 'at the first Inn upon the right hande when you are past Holborne Bridge going towards Newgate', where they would talk 'of all these matters and divers poynts I reserve to word of mouth', and suggested bringing along an unnamed person (Fr George Blackwell) to be 'there about sixe of the clocke when it shall be somewhat darke'.[162] After the meeting, Persons and Blackwell set out to answer the pamphlet and, like good scholars, started their research at the house of 'a certaine merchant' who had purchased Dr Young's library, 'but finding his books ould and of evill print and edition', they 'departed thence againe quickly, crossed the 'River to Southwarke and procured to have a sight of the library of Mr Doctor Langdale, who was absent in the country with the Lord Montague, and there they found not only sufficient bookes, but also the same places coated [glossed] and marked which were alleadged in the pamphlet newly sett forthe'.[163] They realized that Langdale, Viscount Montague's chaplain, was their opponent, and they were looking at the very books he had annotated as he 'had made that booke, or at least gathered the notes for it, for that they were wrytten with his owne hande'.[164]

Stephen Brinkley took charge of the whole printing process. He found a man willing to sell a press 'at a round rate' and 'all that belonged unto it' (types, formes, ink), and (given the need for absolute secrecy) put together a team of Marian (*antiquiores*) priests: Edward Chambers, Nicholas Blackwell, William Maurice, Nicholas Tyrwhitt, Nicholas Gwynn, Richard Norris and Nicholas Birkett.[165] To avoid suspicion, he dressed them all as footmen, and rode about the streets of London with them in this uniform, and then took them back to Greenstreet House, East Ham, seven miles out of London, where they climbed out of their costumes.[166] The house belonged to Edward and Eleanor Brooksby; Eleanor was the daughter of William, Lord Vaux and younger sister of Henry, whom Campion had tutored 'when he was eight years old' (presumably around 1567).[167] Within a month of Campion's suggestion, Brinkley and Persons had set up a printing press.

Here Fr Persons printed, within a month, his answer to Langdale, the first book off the new press: *A Brief Discours contayning certayne Reasons Why Catholiques refuse to goe to Church*.[168] He says that on his way to Greenstreet House, he was

---

162 CRS 2, p. 180.

163 CRS 2, p. 180.

164 CRS 2, p. 180.

165 ABSI Collectanea P. I, fol. 152b.

166 Bombino, *Vita et Martyrium*, pp. 137–8; Bodl. MS Tanner 329, fol. 49v.

167 The probable date of his birth, 1559, is taken from John J. LaRocca's *ODNB* article. The letter, dated from Oxford as 'v. Kalend. Sext. M.D. LXX' (June 1570) gives us an idea of how deep is Campion's admiration for the whole family and is printed in the *Opuscula*, pp. 341–7.

168 [Robert Persons], *A Brief Discours contayning certayne Reasons Why Catholiques refuse to goe to Church. Written by a learned and vertuous man, to a frend of his in England. Dedicated by J. H(owlet, pseud.) to the queenes majestie* (Doway, J. Lyon [East Ham: Greenstreet House], 1580), STC 19394, ARCR II. 613. The date of this has to be between 16 November when the Uxbridge conference finished and Christmas, since the press had

'once stayed by the watche'.[169] They were trying to keep the sounds and signs of the press from leaking out, which was difficult because Brooksby's tenant had no idea what was happening in his house. But paper, rather than noise, proved to be the weak link. As they were nearing the end of printing the first book, sometime in early December, Brinkley's servant gave something away in buying paper 'carelessly' (*incaute*), was arrested, 'sent to the Tower in London and racked', so, fearing a raid, they were 'constrayned to fly with print, presse, paper & all'.[170] Persons and Gilbert returned next day and sent Persons's servant, Robert Alfield, to 'scout around'; when Robert failed to return, they fled a second time. When Robert came back the next day, Persons was still worried, but he and Brinkley said to each other that 'if the work was of God etc.', so despite all these difficulties, Brinkley finished the printing, dismantled the press and came to Persons thinking he would spend the night in celebration, only to find him 'extremely gloomy' (*maestissimum*).[171]

The reason was that Campion's handwritten 'Letter to the Council', of which there had been 'an infinite number of copies', had received two printed replies.[172] The first by William Charke, *An answere to a seditious pamphlet lately cast abroade by a Iesuite, with a discoverie of that blasphemous sect*, was published by the royal printer on 17 December.[173] The second followed on 2 January 1581. Meredith Hanmer printed Campion's letter, chapter by chapter, with Campion's text in roman type and his reply in what was then called English (which we now call black letter), the font casting *M. Champion* (playing on the name) as foreign. Hanmer was the first to call it by the title that has (misleadingly) stuck: *The great bragge and challenge of M. Champion a Jesuite*.[174] From now on, Campion was treated as the 'Champion', the leading fighter on the gladiatorial campus. The sobriquet was conferred by his adversaries, not his supporters.

Brinkley offered to reassemble the press, and Francis Browne, brother of Viscount Montague, provided Henley Park, where they moved the dismantled

---

been dismantled by the time the Charke and Hanmer books were both out, 2 January 1581. In *Letters and Memorials of Father Persons, S.J.*, ed. Leo Hicks, S.J., CRS 39 (London: Catholic Record Society, 1942), p. xxxii n. 49, Hicks argues that December is the true date of this first book, and that Persons has muddled the dates.

[169]   CRS 2, p. 29.

[170]   ABSI Collectanea P. I, fol. 153a (*ex coempto incaute papyro*); CRS 2, p. 29.

[171]   ABSI Collectanea P. I, fol. 153a.

[172]   ABSI Collectanea P. I, fol. 153a.

[173]   William Charke, *An answere to a seditious pamphlet lately cast abroade by Iesuite, with a discoverie of that blasphemous sect* (London: Christopher Barker, 1580), STC 5005.

[174]   Meredith Hanmer, *The great bragge and challenge of M. Champion a Jesuite, commonlye called Edmunde Campion latelye arrived in Englande, contayninge nyne articles here severallye laide downe, directed by him to the Lordes of the Councell confuted and aunswered by Meredith Hanmer* (London: T. Marsh, 1581), STC 12745.2. Hanmer's pejorative title is now widely used; 'Letter to the Council' is more appropriate to the genre.

press.[175] Here Persons wrote, printed and published, within 10 days, in January 1581, under a false imprint, *A brief censure uppon two bookes written in answere to M. Edmonde Campions offer of disputation.*[176] After moving the press again in March, Persons followed this with a third book, *A discoverie of J. Nichols.*[177] In this, Persons exposed the renegade priest John Nichols, who had been trading on his time at the English College in Rome to become a celebrity spy and informer on all his former priest colleagues, before finally repenting and fleeing to Rouen.[178] So while Campion was travelling north to Yorkshire and Lancashire, Persons was transforming the public face of the mission in the south, using the press as an instrument of controversial literature.[179] As Victor Houliston shows, Persons 'set great store by written propaganda' and sought in all three books to brace the English Catholic community, to stiffen their faith and resolution.[180] The focus of the second phase of the mission was now divided. Still firmly at the centre of Campion's mission, as he made his way north, was preaching, hearing confession and saying Mass.[181] 'He preached once a day at least, often twice, and sometimes thrice', and even allowing for some days when 'he had to withdraw from the throng of besiegers to write', Campion may have preached to between 30,000 and 50,000 people during his missionary year.[182]

Campion left Uxbridge on 16 November 1580. The month is made clear both by his own letter to Mercurian, written after he had started on this phase (*quintum iam mensem in his locis dego*) and the date by Persons, who says in his letter to

---

[175]   See Questier, *Catholicism and Community*, p. 514, for the extent of properties owned by the Brownes. The house is just north of Henley.

[176]   McCoog, *Fashioning Jesuit Identity*, p. 206. See also D.M. Rogers, on 'Stephen Brinkley', in *Catholic Encyclopaedia*, p. 804.

[177]   [Robert Persons], *A discoverie of J. Nichols minister, misreported a Jesuite* ([Stonor Park: Greenstreet House press, 1581]), STC 19402, ARCR II. 625. This is the third book on the press, apparently moved in March to Stonor Park.

[178]   CRS 39, pp. xxxv–xxxvii, where Hicks gives a full account.

[179]   Dom Hilary Steuert, 'The Place of Allen, Campion and Parsons in the Development of English Prose', *Review of English Studies*', 20.80 (1944), 272–85 (p. 283), compares Persons with Hooker, and identifies 'the tradition of plain, direct, and yet dignified prose statement'; Southern, *Elizabethan Recusant Prose*, p. 157, praises his 'simplicity of utterance'.

[180]   Victor Houliston, *Catholic Resistance in Elizabethan England: Robert Persons's Jesuit Polemic, 1580–1610* (Rome; Aldershot, UK and Burlington, VT: Ashgate and IHSI, 2007), pp. 27–8 (p. 27) gives a superb account of the gradual evolution of Persons's writing.

[181]   Lake and Questier, 'Edmund Campion Affair', pp. 603–8, treat the missionaries' own account with a 'little healthy skepticism', and focus on the 'highly public challenge' to the regime.

[182]   Challoner, *Missionary Priests*, p. 21; More, *Historia Missionis*, p. 92. My estimate allows for a minimum of 300 days of preaching once a day to congregations with an average of 100 people.

Agazzari, written on 17 November, that Campion left 'yesterday'.[183] Campion was still travelling on horseback (*obequito quotidie*), as he tells Mercurian, staying in each house long enough to say Mass, preach and hear confessions. His route took him through Oxfordshire (a day's ride from Uxbridge), Warwickshire, Worcestershire and Northamptonshire, where he stayed again with his old friends. He seems to have gone through Warwickshire staying with Edward and Eleanor Brooksby at Baddesley Clinton, Lord Vaux at Harrowden, the home of Ralph Sheldon of Beoley, Worcestershire, Sir William Catesby at Lapworth (Campion is said to have assisted Richard Catesby, an uncle of Sir William, 'in dying a holy death'), Sir Thomas Tresham at Rushton Hall, Northamptonshire.[184] He seems then to have stayed with the Throckmortons at Coughton Court.[185] The visit to Northamptonshire would explain Tresham's lifelong devotion to Campion, which cost him some 15 years of imprisonment because he refused to swear that Campion had *not* been in his house.[186]

Campion's letter, and his later confessions, suggest it was his normal pattern to stay only one day in each house, and hope to elude capture by moving on before any spy could relay the information, although Bombino suggests that where the household was wholly Catholic, Campion would stay 'two, three or four dayes together'.[187] The three notable exceptions, which we know of, are the long Christmas visit to Holme Pierrepoint, a prolonged Easter visit at the Yorkshire home of William Harrington (where he wrote the *Rationes Decem*), and his final visit to Lyford Grange, when he returned to the same house with fateful consequences. All these houses were remote, and appeared to be protected by connections with the local justices of the peace.

By Christmas, Campion reached Holme Pierrepoint, Nottinghamshire, where he stayed with Gervase and Henry Pierrepoint, till after Twelfth Night. Although the proclamation of 24 January 1581, making it a capital offence to shelter Jesuits, made Persons instruct Campion to use inns rather than the houses of Catholics, it seems clear from his subsequent itinerary that Catholic families were still begging Campion to stay with them. Burghley's notes of the interrogations record that 'The Proclamacion made for theis Jesuites etc. was the 24 daie of January', and glosses that 'all following receaved Campyon after that proclamacyon'.[188]

---

[183]   *Opuscula*, p. 408; CRS 39, p. 52 (trans. p. 59).

[184]   McCoog, 'Edmund Campion and William Shakespeare', *Reckoned Expense*, p. 178; More, *Historia Missionis*, pp. 87–8.

[185]   *APC*, 13, 1581–82, pp. 155–6 (p. 477), p. 176 (p. 493).

[186]   BL Add. MS 39828, fols 42v–43r, printed in Kilroy, *Memory and Transcription*, pp. 130–31; see also Tresham's vigorous defence transcribed in Bodl. MS Eng. th. b. 1–2, II. 822.

[187]   Bombino, *Vita et Martyrium*, p. 124; Bodl. MS Tanner 329, fol. 42r.

[188]   BL MS Lansdowne 30, no. 78, fol. 201v. I have accepted Burghley's date for this.

Campion was still preaching every day.[189] As late as 1660, Henry More, S.J., found that 'Campion's memory has remained green in the North even down to our own day' and people remembered the topics of his sermons ('the Angelic salutation, on the ten lepers, on the king setting out for a far country, on the last judgment'), the crowds that 'flocked' to hear them 'with such enthusiasm' that 'men in numbers and of notable families would pass whole nights in neighbouring barns in order to be present' the next morning.[190]

> They were not merely captivated by his eloquence or elocution, although in both respects he was admirable. Rather was it the warmth with which he spoke, and some hidden force in his way of speaking which, as it was believed, proceeded from nothing less than the Holy Spirit. He preached every day, except when he had to withdraw from the throng of besiegers in order to write.[191]

When Campion wrote to Mercurian, as we have seen, he specifically asked that those coming should be trained in preaching.

So what was it in a Campion sermon that made people desire it so intensely as to risk all to hear it? We can get some idea from the rhetorical features he uses in the surviving prose, as A.C. Southern says:

> The force, and indeed the charm, of the writing lies in the extreme simplicity of the structure and vocabulary. Though the style is not epigrammatic, yet everything is brief and to the point. Its sureness is reflected in the words, which are those which men used in their daily talk, and where emphasis is sought it is by the position and weight of the word in the sentence only.[192]

Campion does use parallel clauses, apostrophe and anaphora, but the rhetorical tropes are very restrained. As Southern concludes, 'The writing is, indeed, aglow with the writer's own keen spirit, and from this springs its consistency and luminosity, and on this depends the vigorous march of the elocution'.[193] The real power was very personal and very *affective*. We know that Campion's first sermon at Lord Paget's had people weeping, and last sermon at Lyford Grange had everyone in tears, and even the Judas-figure, George Elyot, wondering whether he would repent or not.[194] Round the sick bed of Mrs Yate, the mistress of Lyford Grange, everyone was weeping, but filled with joy, during Campion's final

---

189   More, *Historia Missionis*, p. 92.

190   More, *Historia Missionis*, p. 91. The four topics remembered are the Annunciation, the ten lepers, the parable of the talents ('a man going into a far country' in the Douay-Rheims translation Matt. 25.14), the Last Judgement: all seem concerned with the generosity of the divine invitation and, with the exception of the first, the variable human response. Once again, the Marian theme takes precedence, see Chapter 4.

191   More, *Historia Missionis*, pp. 91–2.

192   Southern, *Elizabethan Recusant Prose*, pp. 155–6.

193   Southern, *Elizabethan Recusant Prose*, p. 156.

194   Bombino, *Vita et Martyrium*, p. 170; missing in Tanner translation.

exhortation.[195] All those in the audience thought that they were being addressed personally. Sometimes, this is explicit, as in the speech to the Queen and the Earl of Leicester, or in the funeral eulogy on Maria Cardona:

> For which one of you (I call to witness the most intimate conscience of each one of us) would not prefer to have the last day of this most illustrious and distinguished lady, than the pleasures of Sardanopolis, the victories of Alexander or the riches of Croesus or the power of Julius Caesar?[196]

From Christmas onwards, we have a better idea of some of Campion's journey, from his confessions under torture in the Tower, preserved among Lord Burghley's papers.[197] Campion left Holme Pierrepoint on the Tuesday after Twelfth Night (10 January), and headed north, through Derbyshire. He spent one night only at the house of Henry Sacheverell, another with the Langtons, and a third with Lady Fulton, a fourth with the Powtrells, and, finally, just before 24 January, a night with the Eyres of Dronfield, Derbyshire. 'A sennight after twelfth day' he met 'by former appointment' with a certain Tempest (no Christian name is supplied), who was probably related to Robert Tempest, Sheriff of Durham, one of the northern rebels.[198] He then travelled 'Northward' with Tempest for 'aboute six daies and will confesse no place of their being but at Innes'.[199] At 25 miles a day, Tempest could have covered about 150 miles, and taken Campion into Yorkshire.

The campaign to prosecute recusants in Yorkshire, begun when the Earl of Huntingdon became President of the North after the rising of the northern earls in 1569, had reached hysterical intensity. Thanks to an army of informers, 120 families in the West Riding were presented for recusancy in 1580–82.[200] The gentry became skilled at evading attempts to make them conform, including 'vagrancy' (moving from house to house across the county borders). Recusancy was so widespread among the gentry (and the 'lowest officials' were often their tenants) that men 'wold not troble their neighbors'.[201] Between 28 January and the middle of Lent (the beginning of March) Campion stayed with several Yorkshire recusants, most of whom had more than one house, in more than one county, making Campion's route hard to determine. The Privy Council accused him of staying with John

---

[195] Bombino, *Vita et Martyrium*, p. 178; Bodl. MS Tanner 329, fol. 68r.

[196] *Opuscula*, pp. 298–9.

[197] BL Lansdowne MS 30, no. 78, fol. 201r–202r. For the debate about the truth of these, see Chapter 8.

[198] Alan Davidson, 'Roman Catholicism in Oxfordshire from the Late Elizabethan Period to the Civil War (c. 1580–c. 1640)', Bristol Ph.D. thesis, 1970, p. 411.

[199] BL Lansdowne MS 30, no. 78, fol. 201r. Of course, Campion could be protecting his friends.

[200] Hugh Aveling, 'The Catholic Recusants of the West Riding of Yorkshire 1558–70', *Proceedings of the Leeds Philosophical and Literary Society*, vol. 10 (1963), 190–306 (p. 222).

[201] Aveling, 'Recusants of the West Riding', p. 214.

Rokeby at Yafforth in the North Riding, with Dr Thomas Vavasour of York, Mrs Bulmer ('either at Thirsdale in county Durham or Marrick in Richmondshire'), Sir William Babthorpe of Osgodby in the East Riding, but none of these four seems to have been prosecuted.[202] He does seem to have stayed with Thomas Grimston of Nidd, William Hawksworth and Askulph Cleasby, who were related to Dr Allen and had property both sides of the county border.[203] It seems likely that the bulk of Campion's stay in Yorkshire was passed discreetly in a few very remote houses in Allertonshire organized by two priests, William Wattes and Richard Holtby.[204] He may have chosen to pass by the Babthorpes of Osgodby to avoid going through York itself.

In the third week of Lent, Tempest handed over to another guide, Mr Smyth, who took Campion to Mount St John, an isolated house in the parish of Felixkirk, now in the North Riding, and the home of his brother-in-law, William Harrington. Ironically, the house (the ancient commandery of the Knights Hospitaller of St John) 'was leased by the Harringtons of the Archbishop of York, and Felixkirk in some way formed a member of the Archbishop's Liberty of Ripon'.[205] It was secluded, but not far from Thirsk, and must have seemed comparatively safe, since the Harringtons belonged to a family of sheriffs and lord mayors of York, with a strong foothold among the registrars and attorneys of York's ecclesiastical courts, that had not come under suspicion for religion since 1562. They were, incidentally, also related to William Fawkes, notary public of York, whose grandson was Guy Fawkes.[206] It was here that Campion began writing the *Rationes Decem*, as, under interrogation, William Harrington admitted:

> Campyon: That he was ther xiiii daiees aboute Easter last made ther parte of his latyn Booke, brought thither by Smyth Mrs Harringtons Brother, Mr Harrington confesseth he came to his house aboute the Tewssday the 3rd sweeke in lent last staied there aboute xii daies knew him not for Campyon untill he was uppon departure.[207]

The schedule on the verso confirms that 'At Eas[ter la]st he was at one Mr Haringtons house in Yorckshire. There he was busy at his study, and made a good pece of his Latin booke' and that 'He sent his Latin booke to Mr Parsons by one

---

[202]   Hugh Aveling, O.S.B., *Northern Catholics: The Catholic Recusants of the North Riding of Yorkshire 1558–1790* (London: Geoffrey Chapman, 1966), p. 60.

[203]   J.C.H. Aveling, *Catholic Recusancy in the City of York 1558–1791* (London: Catholic Record Society, 1970), p. 42, points to 'a very small but definite and well-instructed group of Catholic recusants', thanks to Dr Thomas Vavasour, who 'had been exercising an apostolate in York through his medical practice'.

[204]   Anstruther, *Seminary Priests*, I. 175, notes that Holtby entered the Society of Jesus in 1582/3.

[205]   Aveling, *Northern Catholics*, p. 58.

[206]   Aveling, *Northern Catholics*, p. 59.

[207]   BL MS Lansdowne 30, no. 78, fol. 201v.

Rychardson. He sent it to Rychardson by one Robinson, who delivered it at Mr Claisbyes house in Yorckshire'.[208] If he was there from the third week of Lent till Easter (26 March) his stay must have lasted nearly three weeks. The reason why Campion's stay in Yorkshire 'differed so markedly from his travels in Lancashire' is that he felt protected from pursuivants by a triple layer of seclusion, extensive links with the justice system and the appearance of conformity.[209]

Henry More's account of Campion's withdrawing only to write suggests that the writing of *Rationes Decem* was a pastoral adjunct of the preaching, which may account for the clarity and personal freshness of the style.[210] The original plan to write the book in a house with a large library in Lancashire obviously yielded to a work begun in Mount St John and completed in Lancashire. As the writing accompanied preaching to dawn congregations in halls and barns, it could have been spread over several weeks.

From Mount St John to Lancashire, he was guided by a former Oxford pupil, a 'Mr More living near Sheffield' (most probably, 'Edward More, another grandson of Sir Thomas More, of More Hall').[211] Persons singles out two large family networks in Lancashire: one of Mrs Allen of Rossall, the mother of Dr Allen, the other of the Worthingtons, where, on one occasion, the pursuivants so nearly caught him that a quick-thinking maid pushed Campion into a pond to maintain his disguise.[212] He also stayed with John Talbot of Salesbury, Sir John Southworth of Salmesbury, Bartholomew Hesketh of Maines, John Westby of Mowbreck Hall and John Rigmaiden of Wedacre.[213] The Privy Council asked for all these men to be interviewed in August 1581.[214] Since Campion later wished to retrieve his books from Lancashire, and since the Privy Council early gave orders to search 'especiallie the house of Richard Houghton, where it is said the said Campion left his bookes', he must have taken his notebooks (with quotations culled from Luther and Calvin in Munich) from Mount St John, and finished the *Rationes Decem* at Park Hall, the house of Richard Hoghton, on the banks of Yarrow Water.[215]

---

[208] BL MS Lansdowne 30, no. 78, fol. 202v. This Richardson was not Fr Laurence Johnson (who used the name as an alias), as Campion made clear on the scaffold, see Chapter 11.

[209] Aveling, *Northern Catholics*, 60.

[210] More, *Historia Missionis*, p. 92.

[211] Aveling, 'Recusants of the West Riding', p. 204.

[212] ABSI Collectanea P. I, fol. 154a; Foley, *Records*, III. 670.

[213] I thank Dr Wilfred Hammond for all his help with these families and houses.

[214] *APC, 1581–82*, pp. 257, 270, 335, 336. See CRS 60, *Recusant Documents from the Ellesmere Manuscripts*, ed. Anthony G. Petti (London: Catholic Record Society, 1968), pp. 37–41 for the search, in 1592, of Sir John Southworth's house and lodge: 37 dependent servants were interrogated.

[215] *APC, 1581–82*, pp. 148–9. The map of Lord Burghley (reproduced as a frontispiece to CRS 4, *Miscellanea IV* (London: Catholic Record Society, 1907), confirms the ownership of 'the Parke' at Charnock Richard, p. 192. See Chapter 8.

This Lancashire phase lasted from Easter (26 March) to Whitsun (14 May): about seven weeks.[216]

Then, after sending down the manuscript, presumably during Whitsuntide, he returned south, summoned by Persons who had 'procured another place for a print', Stonor Park, the house of Dame Cecily Stonor 'standing in a wood fast by Henley'; here Brinkley 'was prefect of the printers', while Fr William Maurice was 'procurator to buy the paper and other necessaries', in London.[217] When Persons received the manuscript, he was struck by the marginal glosses:

> Persons, at first sight, was much moved at the world of testimonies, which he saw (as the manner is) in the margent of the booke, fetchd from all antiquity and coated out of their severall places, where they were to be found in ancient writers; in so much that they all most filled the whole margent of the booke.[218]

Persons was conscious that the 'adversaries would search, canvas, & examin, till their very hearts ak'd' the references 'fetched from all antiquity', and so wrote to Campion to ask if he was sure that all his citations were correct.[219] Campion replied that he was, but he asked (as a further indication of his scholarly 'diligence') that they should 'try even to the quicke' all the references.[220] Persons engaged Thomas Fitzherbert to help check the citations. Fitzherbert, who 'by reason of his noble extraction and learning' had 'all the London libraries at his command', says that Persons gave the manuscript to him 'in written hand to be printed', and told him

> that it was Father Campion's, and therefore recommended yt to me not only to read but also to examine the places of the Fathers alleadged therein (because I might have more free recourse to publick libraryes in London than priests or religious could have) besides that after yt was printed Father Campion himself gave me one of the first printed coppyes as his owne worke.[221]

Fitzherbert was in Viscount Montague's household, so this must again have been his first place of research. Although Montague's brother, Francis Browne, had provided a second home to the printing press, Persons obviously decided that Henley Park was no longer safe, and they had dismantled and moved the press to its third base at Stonor Park, only three miles away (Figure 6.2).

---

[216]   Simpson, p. 284, must be correct in arguing that Campion 'could not have been with Persons till the middle of May'. E.E. Reynolds, *Campion and Parsons: The Jesuit Mission of 1580–1* (London: Sheed and Ward, 1980), p. 101, apparently influenced by Pollen, asserts that Campion sent the manuscript to Persons 'at the end of March, 1581', which would negate the Lancashire phase of the writing.

[217]   CRS 2, p. 29.

[218]   Bombino, *Vita et Martyrium*, p. 132; Bodl. MS Tanner 329, fol. 46v.

[219]   Bombino, *Vita et Martyrium*, p. 132; Bodl. MS Tanner 329, fol. 46v.

[220]   Bombino, *Vita et Martyrium*, p. 133; Bodl. MS Tanner 329, fol. 47r.

[221]   Pollen, *Acts of English Martyrs*, p. 37.

Figure 6.2   Stonor Park, near Henley. Photograph by the author.

Stonor Park nestles deep in a valley between high outcrops of the Chilterns, as John Leland described it: 'a fayre parke, and a waren of connes, and fayre woods. The mansion place standithe clyminge on an hille, and hathe 2. courtes buyldyd withe tymbar, brike and flynte'.[222] The woods in Campion's time came down almost to the house itself, *domus silvestris*, as Persons says.[223] The house, still standing today, and still in the Stonor family, is built into the side of the hill. The major appeal of the house was its closeness to the Thames at Henley, and 'by that meanes accommodated with navigation', so all 'necessaries' (especially paper), could be discreetly conveyed there (Plate 3).[224] It is significant that it was Fr William Maurice, 'a learned and experienced priest' who was in charge of procuring the paper, who found the house.[225]

---

[222]   John Leland, *The itinerary of John Leland in or about the years 1535–1543*, ed. Lucy Toulmin Smith, 5 vols (London: G. Bell, 1906–10), V.72. I thank James Carley for his help with the reference, which is cited in part by Robert Julian Stonor, O.S.B., *Stonor: A Catholic Sanctuary in the Chilterns from the Fifth Century till To-day* (Newport: Johns, 1951), p. 216.

[223]   ABSI Collectanea P. I. fol. 155a.

[224]   Bombino, *Vita et Martyrium*, pp. 138–9; Bodl. MS Tanner 329, fol. 50r.

[225]   CRS 4, p. 17.

The physical location of the house was only one factor in the choice. Generations of Stonors had been Sheriffs of Oxfordshire, as was Dame Cecily Stonor's son, Francis, at the time of Campion's capture in Berkshire. The Brownes and the Stonors were also connected by marriage. Cecily Stonor was the sister of George Chamberlayn, who had helped equip Persons and Campion in St Omer.[226]

> Having searched very diligently, he [Fr William Maurice] with great difficulty found the house of a widow named Stonor, which stood in the middle of a wood, twenty miles from London, and in which she was not then living. To which house he had everything necessary carried, viz. type, presses, paper etc., and this not without many dangers. Mr Stephen Brinkley before mentioned, a gentleman of excellent parts in letters and virtue, took charge of the printing. So Father Campion on coming to London with his book already revised, went at once to stay at the said house in the wood, where the book was printed and then published.[227]

Campion must have joined Persons at Stonor before the end of May, for they were together on 3 June when Persons received a letter from the new Jesuit General, Claudio Acquaviva:

> With what sentiments we read this letter, I can not tell you! (Providentially we were gathered together at that time. I had called my father [Campion] from distant parts. I had not seen him for eight whole months.) I will say only: we read it; reread it; a third and a fourth time we read it; we showed it to our friends; we were exultant, delighted. May God thank you for so great a consolation.[228]

The intensity of this response reveals the sense of danger the two men felt. While Campion and Persons were together again, Campion preached every day in London, where his 'ardent eloquence', both 'in the citty' and suburbs, 'upheld' men from 'tottering'; he would 'ever & anon interrupt his speech with teares of joy streaming down his cheekes'.[229]

The dangers involved, both in the preaching and in the printing, a task involving so many skills and so many materials, hardly need stating. A long tradition at Stonor locates the press in the roof. A room in the central gable over the front porch had secret doors into the roof. Persons tells us that there was a large team, and there was enough space here for several men to work, and they would probably have fixed the press by crossed beams to the roof (Figure 6.3).[230] The original team of 'older priests' had now given way to seven men, who are named in the *Concertatio* (1588): the printer Stephen Brinkley, Fr William Hartley who was in charge of the

[226]   Simpson, p. 171.

[227]   CRS 4, p. 17.

[228]   ARSI Fondo Gesuitico 651/640; quoted by McCoog, *Fashioning Jesuit Identity*, p. 207 n. 34. Everard Mercurian had died on 1 August 1580.

[229]   Bombino, *Vita et Martyrium*, p. 135; Bodl. MS Tanner 329, fol. 47v.

[230]   As can still be seen in the presses in the Plantin Moretus museum in Antwerp.

Figure 6.3   A hand-press, Plantin Moretus Museum, Antwerp. Photograph by
              the author.

distribution, John Stonor, Dame Cecily's other son, and four servants, all called John: John Harris, John Harvey, John Tucker and John Compton.[231]

Although the steep elevation of the attic roof makes it possible to stand in the centre of the roof-space, there cannot have been much room to move, and the place would have been full of half-sheets of printed paper drying. This must, nevertheless, have been one of the most rewarding periods in Campion's year in disguise, in which he was busy preaching and seeing his book through the press. The continuous camaraderie of fellow priests and laymen assistants, resembling the collegiate life in Oxford and Prague, combined with the sounds and smells of a printing-press, must have brought back many good memories from his youth and childhood.

The printing of *Rationes Decem* took the best part of a month, from late May till late June. This book, in all its aspects, bears Campion's stamp. The font of *Rationes Decem* can be distinguished from that of Persons's *A Brief Censure*, which came from the same press at Henley Park, where Persons had used 'English' type (or black letter).[232] Campion chose to use roman type throughout, 10 years before it became standard in England, although it was normal for Latin texts.[233] Persons's black letter text is only relieved by the quotations and marginal glosses in roman; Campion's roman type has the contrast of wide margins, and carefully differentiated glosses: italics for the citations from the scriptures and patristic sources, but only lower case roman for Luther, Calvin and Beza. For a secret press this is remarkable. The title page (Figure 6.4) has the same *impresa* as *A Brief Censure*, but with the IHS oval now enclosed by an irenic quotation from Luke in a rectangular border in italics: 'I will give you speech and wisdom that all your opponents will not be able to resist or contradict'. This suggests the triumph of rational argument. In addition to the decorated capital at the start of the text, the whole text is prefaced by an elaborate epistle (in italic) to the 'very learned Academics now flourishing at Oxford and Cambridge'. This is a book printed by a stationer's son with an eye for an aesthetically pleasing *mise-en-page*.

Dr Allen's letter of 23 June 1581 makes it clear that he has heard of, but not yet seen, Campion's book: 'He has seven men continually at work at a press outside of London (where the noise of the machine is less likely to betray it)'.[234] The printers were working round the clock at Stonor Park, to have Campion's intellectual challenge ready for the University Act, a three-day celebration of speeches and prizes, which began in St Mary's Church, Oxford on 27 June 1581. The church of St Mary the Virgin was arranged for the Commencement (as it was also sometimes called) with scaffolding 'in maner of a theater' (as for the Queen's visit in 1566)

---

[231] [John Gibbons and John Fen], *Concertatio ecclesiae Catholicae in Anglia Adversus Calvinopapistas et Puritanos* (Trier: Henry Bock, 1588), ARCR I. 525, fol. 408r.

[232] See above for details.

[233] See Steven K. Galbraith, '"English" Black-Letter Type and Spenser's *Shepheardes Calender*', in *Spenser Studies*, 23 (2008), 13–40; Kilroy, 'Advertising the Reader', p. 64.

[234] Allen, *Letters and Memorials*, p. 98.

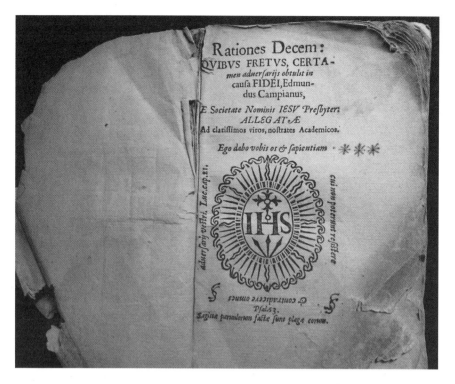

Figure 6.4   Title page of *Rationes Decem*, Stonor Park edn, ARCR I. 135.1,
              Winchester copy (WN⁴). With permission of the Bishop and
              Trustees of the Catholic Diocese of Portsmouth and the Parish
              Priest of Hampshire Downs Parish.

with an upper tier added to hold the crowd.[235] So popular was the event, Bombino
tells us, that the benches were filled several hours before the candidates presented
their dissertations and received their prizes.

Persons says that 'his book was printed and most parte of the copies sent to
Oxforde'.[236] Fr William Hartley (1557–88), a former chaplain of St John's, and
now a Catholic priest, took 400 copies to Oxford for binding by Rowland Jenkes,
who was nationally notorious as a Catholic binder, after the sensational events at
his trial (in July 1577), which afterwards became known as the Black Assizes.[237]

---

[235]   Bombino, *Vita et Martyrium*, p. 141; Bodl. MS Tanner 329, fol. 51r.

[236]   CRS 2, p. 29.

[237]   John Stow, *The Chronicles of England, from Brute unto this present yeare of
Christ, 1580* (London: Ralph Newberie, 1580) STC 23333, pp. 1164 [1190]–1191. [The
pagination has gone awry here.]

Stow begins the 'Continuation' of Holinshed's *Chronicles* by relating that Jenkes had been sentenced in Oxford to lose his ears for publishing recusant material; almost immediately, the entire court was struck with a deadly fever (whose medical causes Abraham Fleming discusses) and 'there died in Oxforde 300. persons', including Sir William Babington and Anthony Pollard.[238] Their widows, Lady Babington, who had one house at Twyford, close to the county boundary, and another in Whitefriars, and Mrs Pollard, another sister of Ralph Sheldon of Beoley, both sheltered Campion in their houses.[239] When these copies of *Rationes Decem* had been 'bound up with speed' in Jenkes's shop (probably close to St Mary's), Hartley began his mission:

> He cleverly attached himself to those he knew and those he did not, distributing more than four hundred books. Some realized what was happening, as he gave the book to them, so that little by little they were drawn by a desire to read what had been put in their hands. Other copies he left during the night in the theatre itself, as if they had been scattered there. The whole of the Oxford establishment was struck dumb. When it grew light, there was a wonderful spectacle, and very unusually, complete silence of the academics throughout the theatre: the eyes of all were intent on their furtive reading of the book they had found in their hands. I have heard some say that they have never experienced such a cold atmosphere in any assembly. The officials sitting on the dais, unaware of the reason, were amazed at what seemed like a shameful silence.[240]

The place, the timing, the language and even the font of this book were significant. This was a challenge in Latin from a leading Oxford scholar now famous in Prague and Rome, placed in St Mary's, the location for major academic disputations. Campion may have written the book secretly, but this was a chivalric challenge in print addressed especially to the Queen. Campion names a succession of emperors and kings in Europe. In a very personal apostrophe, Campion invites Elizabeth to join them:

> *Erunt Reges nutricii tui & Reginae nutrices tuae.* Hear, Elizabeth, most puissant Queen (*Audi, Elizabetha, Regina potentissima*), the great prophet is addressing you, and teaching you your role. One heaven cannot hold both Calvin and the princes I have named. Join those princes who are worthy of your ancestors, your intelligence, your learning, your honours and your good fortune.[241]

---

[238] Holinshed, *Chronicles* (1587), III. 1270.a.52–b.18. The first page of the 'Continuation' is marked in the margin by the initials of John Stow and the paraph of Abraham Fleming.

[239] Davidson, 'Catholicism in Oxfordshire', p. 604.

[240] Bombino, *Vita et Martyrium*, pp. 141–2 (my translation); Bodl. MS Tanner 329, fol. 51r.

[241] *Rationes Decem*, sig. I4v–K1r. The text is from Isaiah, 49.23, in the Latin Vulgate. Gregory Martin's Rheims translation (1582) is, 'And kings shall be thy nursing fathers, and queens thy nurses'.

On the last day (*Veniet, Elizabetha, dies, ille ille dies*), the Queen will discover whether it is 'the Society of Jesus, or Luther's brood, that has loved her the most'.[242] This is not 'a public challenge to the authority, and even the legitimacy, of the regime'.[243] Campion ignores the debate over the pope's right to depose monarchs that had filled more than 500 pages in Sander's book; instead, with knightly courtesy, he addresses the Queen as a prince among princes, an equal among European monarchs, just as Sidney in his *A Letter to Queen Elizabeth Touching her Marriage with Monsieur* of 1579, had addressed her as 'the excellentest prince in the world', and 'the ornament of this age'.[244] Campion, as if remembering her offer in Oxford 'to care & provide for' him, explicitly recognizes her right to rule, tacitly rejects Sander's attack, in the seventh book of *De Visibili Monarchia*, on the Queen's legitimacy, and courteously offers 'good counsel'.[245] There is no record of the Queen's anger with the manner of Campion's address.[246]

The book is unusually short for controversial literature.[247] There are just over 80 octavo pages of about 100 of text on each page; the conciseness and simplicity of the language, in short sentences, is balanced by the 250 detailed references in the margins to the scriptures, Fathers of the church, and reformers. The division into 10 chapters allows the book to build up a sense of the combined weight of 1,500 years of tradition, confronting the novel views expressed by the reformers. The first two chapters, on the Scriptures, show Campion undermining a central plank of the reformers' position: they may appeal to the Scriptures but they do so only by eliminating many texts (like the Epistle of St James) that resist their position. The next five chapters on the Church, the Councils and the Fathers, show what a long and learned tradition confronts reformers whom Campion places in succession to an uninspiring list of heretics from Arius to the Lollards, Wycliffe and Hus. Campion follows this with a collection of the most controversial *Paradoxa* and *Sophismata* of the reformers. He starts with Calvin's assertion that God is the 'author and cause of sin' (sig. F2v), and moves to another Calvinist statement that 'the image of God has been completely wiped out in man' (sig. F4v). The finale is a climactic tenth chapter on the formidable list of witnesses in heaven and on earth who make up the Catholic church, which even shows how the church has inspired the laws, the stained glass, the dress: 'settled in the very roots' of English culture (sig. K1v–K2r). The word 'witnesses' (*testes*) runs in an unusually extended anaphora, beginning

---

[242]   Edmund Campion, *Rationes Decem* ([Stonor Park: Brinkley, 1581]), STC 4536.5, ARCR I. 135.1, fols 36v–37r.

[243]   Lake and Questier, 'Edmund Campion Affair', p. 613.

[244]   Worden, *Sound of Virtue*, p. 128.

[245]   Sander, *De Visibili Monarchia*, pp. 730–32. See Chapter 2 for the offer of patronage in Oxford.

[246]   The situation is less clear with Sidney, see Chapter 12.

[247]   Edmund Campion, *Ten Reasons*, ed. John Hungerford Pollen, S.J., trans. Joseph Rickarby, S.J. (London: Manresa Press, 1914), prints both the Latin and a translation, and contains a long introduction.

seven long paragraphs, and culminating in a final flourish of 10 clauses, each beginning with *testes* from every aspect of life in Europe:

> Witness the Universities, witness the laws, witness the customs of ordinary people, witness the election and enthronement of emperors, witness the coronation rites and anointing of kings, witness the orders of knights and the very cloaks they wear, witness the stained glass windows, witness the coins, witness the gateways of cities and the public buildings, witness the fruits of our ancestors and their way of life, witness every trivial detail: there is no other religion but ours in the world, and it has become embedded in the very roots of our culture.[248]

It is not surprising that Campion signed off the *Rationes Decem* with the word *Cosmopoli* (city of all the world).[249] He succeeded in making the entire establishment feel that it had to enlist the most learned to answer his theological challenge. John Aylmer, Bishop of London, when asked by Lord Burghley to find theologians to respond to Campion, replied with a list of deans and learned churchmen, but adds (in a third letter on the topic) that he thinks 'none of our church mean to defend Luthers hyperbolas or all thinges that have passed the pennes of Calvin or Beza'.[250] To answer this Ignatian knight errant, therefore, Aylmer drafted in Laurence Humphrey and William Whitaker, the regius professors of divinity at Oxford and Cambridge, and several 'overtly Puritan, indeed Presbyterian, authors' like William Charke and Meredith Hanmer.[251] Campion had found the Achilles heel of the newly established church, since the Queen clearly loathed some of Calvin's doctrines and despised the Calvinists, and the Treasurer and the Bishop were having difficulty finding deans willing to answer Campion.

Others were excited and moved by the intellectual content of the argument:

> In a word, all the bookes, the prayses whereof were soone knowen & spread abroad, invited men to read them, in so much that scarcely was there any one, to whom this booke was either by chaunce, or purposely offered, but it went forthwith from hand to hand, amongst many. Neither can it be easily imagined, or readily sayd, what a name this one only booke procured Campian, what prayse it added to the society, or to the whole Catholike cause. Many men, having but once read it, layd aside their heresie, many were enflamed with a desire to see the writer, & looke what wholsome spirit they had conceived in reading, in *hearing* Campian.[252]

---

[248]   *Rationes Decem*, sig. K1v (my translation).

[249]   *Rationes Decem*, sig. K3r.

[250]   BL MS Lansdowne 33, fols 35r–38r. The third letter is endorsed, 'His opinion concerning Campions cavilles'.

[251]   Lake and Questier, 'Edmund Campion Affair', p. 624; see Thomas M. McCoog, S.J., 'The Role of Disputation', in *Reckoned Expense*, pp. 138–63 (p. 150–52) for the impact of the 'Letter to the Council'.

[252]   Bombino, *Vita et Martyrium*, pp. 141–2; Bodl. MS Tanner 329, fol. 52r–52v (my emphasis).

Prevented from preaching publicly, Campion, like Persons, had succeeded in preaching on paper and moving his readers; the writing was a continuation of the preaching, the central aim of the mission.[253] This is a book that invites response from its hearers in its wide margins, and blank pages.[254] It moved them in many different ways, but always as if they were part of a continuing debate in which they involved others:

> Others there were ambiguous and wavering in matter of Religion, whom you might observe, with a pensive silence hummingly to revolve the matter with them selves, & rather buzz & mutter amongst their friendes, then speake their mindes playnely.[255]

Campion's theological argument was suffused with his personal warmth, and written in a compellingly elegant style. Marc-Antoine Muret (1526–85), the highly respected authority on Ciceronian style, inscribed his copy 'on its first page, in capital letters: "LIBELLUS AUREUS VERE DIGITO DEI SCRIPTUS" (a golden book truly written by the finger of God), an inscription visible in the copy bequeathed to the English College in Rome'.[256]

For a brief moment the two Jesuits could feel that their mission, which had been forced into the inner secrecy of Catholic households, was at last able to take the debate to the hearts of the people and of the authorities. Hartley returned 'cherefully' (*laetus*) to Campion and Persons, but the elation was as transitory as the dawn light in St Mary's.[257] Bombino records that a few days later, Hartley casually mentioned that he had heard that Jenkes's journey-man, in 'brauling' (*iurgium*), had threatened to report his master for the 'Catholike bookes, & written by a Catholike', which he had helped Rowland bind in a 'certayne strangers chamber' in London, and had 'immediately' set off for London in a rage:

> As Hartley was thus discoursing, Persons, who all this while had heard him with change of countenance, his colour often coming and going, asked him how many dayes it was since he heard of this newes; & Hartley answering, it was some foure dayes since, & withall perceiving Persons so betroubled; demanded, whether the matter anything concerned either him, or Campion? Yea verily doth it, sayd Persons, in manner, wholy concerne me. For know you, the chamber you

---

[253]   More, *Historia Missionis*, p. 92.

[254]   Blank pages were not uncommon, but the extra gathering seems generous.

[255]   Bombino, *Vita et Martyrium*, p. 142; Bodl. MS Tanner 329, fol. 52r ('hummingly' is added by the translator).

[256]   Bombino, *Vita et Martyrium*, p. 132; Bodl. MS Tanner 329, fol. 46v. This was also noted by Johannes Lorinus, S.J., *In Actus Apostolorum Commentaria* (Cologne: A. Hieratus, 1609), p. 758: '*His dignus est quem adiungas, Edmundi Campiani Martyris nostri aureus libellus, decem rationes continens, ad Anglicos Academicos. Huic libello sua M. Antonius Muretus manu non dubitauit ascribere: Libellus diuino SPIRITV scriptus*'. I thank Arnold Hunt for this reference.

[257]   Bombino, *Vita et Martyrium*, p. 143; Bodl. MS Tanner 329, fol. 52v.

speake of into which Ginkx so unluckily brought that fellow, is mine; mine the bookes, which you say were there bound up; my selfe am the stranger who sette them a worke; & by and by, taking Campion to a side, told him: Assuredly, if Hartley say truth, your bookes are all lost, & both you and I in danger.[258]

The Tanner manuscript's translation, 'your bookes are all lost' (for *rerum suarum iacturam*: overthrow of his affairs), highlights a previously overlooked aspect of the reception of *Rationes Decem*, that in addition to the 400 copies (the 'most parte') taken to Oxford, a second batch was shipped down river to Southwark, for binding by Rowland Jenkes and his hired journey-man, who travelled there for the purpose. There are five extant copies: only one of these, the Winchester copy, which has recently reappeared, is still in its original binding, a parchment wrapper (Figure 6.5).[259] The parchment manuscript is a fragment of a lease of property belonging originally to 'Sir [Tho]mas Docwra, Prior of the late hosp[ital of St John]' of Clerkenwell, and dated to 1562.[260] Since the lease mentions 'Rycharde', 'William' and 'Dorethe' Bellamy, and the parish of 'Kyngsbury & hendon', there is a strong London provenance.[261] Campion and Persons regularly rested in Mrs Bellamy's 'well furnishd Librarie' in Harrow, which was the first port of call for Fr Weston three years later.[262]

---

[258]   Bombino, *Vita et Martyrium*, pp. 144–5; Bodl. MS Tanner 329, fol. 53r–v.

[259]   This copy, measuring 100 by 140 mm, was preserved by successive parish priests (at least as far back as Cannon Gunning, in 1909) of St Peter's Roman Catholic Church, Winchester, now part of the Parish of Hampshire Downs. It had been cut professionally, but untrimmed later. The other copies, now trimmed and re-bound, have shadows of the stitching holes, and are in the library of the Marquess of Bute, Stonyhurst College, Campion Hall, and Durham University Library (transferred from Bamburgh Castle). STC in 1986 listed them as follows: 'O37 [Campion Hall]. BUTE. DUR. (Bamb.) ST. W [St Edmund's Ware]'. ARCR, apparently misled by STC, lists the Winchester copy as 'W (formerly WN⁴)'. John Hungerford Pollen was aware of only two copies when he wrote, 'Blessed Edmund Campion's "Decem Rationes"', in *The Month* 105 (1905), 11–26. Four years later, he became aware of the 'new discovery', and wrote a short additional note, 'Campion's *Decem Rationes*', *The Month* 114 (1909), 80. Pollen discusses all three copies in his edition of the *Ten Reasons* (1914), p. 18. Evelyn Waugh apparently took his information from Pollen, see Donat Gallagher, 'Five Editions of Evelyn Waugh's *Edmund Campion*', in *The Book Collector* 61.4 (2012), 531–49 (p. 536), who quotes the American edition of Waugh's life to explain the origins of the Campion Hall copy, found in 1936 in 'the sixpenny-box of a second-hand bookseller'; Waugh remained unaware of the Bamburgh Castle copy, as David Rogers pointed out in a letter to *The Tablet*, 5 May 1962, p. 534. Reynolds, as late as 1980, *Campion and Parsons*, p. 106 n. 3, still thought there were only four.

[260]   *ODNB*, 'Sir Thomas Docwra' (d. 1527), by Andrew A. Chibi.

[261]   I thank Professor Henry Woudhuysen for all his help with interpreting this copy, and reading its manuscript wrapper.

[262]   Bombino, *Vita et Martyrium*, p. 135; Bodl. MS Tanner, fol. 48r; Pollen, *Ten Reasons* (1914), pp. 21–2; William Weston, *The Autobiography of an Elizabethan*, trans. Philip Caraman (London: Longmans, Green, 1955), p. 3.

Figure 6.5   *Rationes Decem*, Stonor
Park edn, ARCR I. 135.1, Winchester
copy (WN[4]): binding. With permission of
the Bishop and Trustees of the Catholic
Diocese of Portsmouth and the Parish
Priest of Hampshire Downs Parish.

Everything suggests this copy was one of the Southwark batch, and that some of the Bellamy family of Uxenden Hall, Harrow, helped with the sewing and binding.[263] Whatever is the case, this copy provides invaluable, and very rare, evidence of the binding of recusant books in England.[264] The method used was clearly chosen for speed: it was stab-stitched, a technique which involves the loss of the gutter. By looking along the outer surfaces of this copy, one can see that the head and tail of the book were cut professionally (with a plough) and burnished (by Jenkes), while the fore-edge has been left uncut, ensuring that the margins provide space for annotation. Did Alexander Nowell have his margins annotated for the first Tower disputation in St Peter ad Vincula? Bombino records that all the ministers were carrying a copy of *Rationes Decem*, the pale parchment bindings standing out against the black of their gowns.[265]

One would not know, to look at the book, with what difficulty it was produced; it is 'distinctly well got up', as Pollen argues.[266]

---

[263]   Pollen, 'Campion's *Decem Rationes* (1909)', p. 80, suggested the manuscript was 'a deed brought home [Stonor Park] from Harrow by one or other of the missionaries', and that 'Mrs Bellamy was ready to give away old deeds'. Both seem unlikely. Reynolds, *Campion and Parsons*, p. 106 n. 3, suggests that the book was 'surely imprudently' bound with this 'parchment deed'.

[264]   I thank Nicholas Pickwoad for his invaluable advice on all the aspects of binding discussed here.

[265]   Bombino, *Vita et Martyrium*, p. 217; Bodl. MS Tanner 329, fol. 89v; BL MS Add. 39828, fol. 38r. These copies of *Rationes Decem* may have come from the batch of books seized in Southwark.

[266]   Pollen, '*Decem Rationes*' (1905), p. 22.

Perhaps the most striking features of the book are the elegance of the Latin, the neatness of the print, the wide margins full of glosses, and the heavily thumbed corners: worn to a used roundness as it was passed greedily from 'hand to hand'.[267] The book is octavo in fours, in 11 gatherings, printed on half-sheets of 8 pages, because of the paucity of roman type and of Greek letters; some type ran short before the end of each gathering.[268] Each sheet had to be printed before the next forme could be set up. The paper appears to have come from Troyes.[269] The last leaf of signature K is blank, and has been supported by two sets of bearer type, one centimetre high, at the top and bottom of the page (Figure 6.6). This is followed by two blank endpapers of a new gathering, providing six blank pages (as well as wide margins), possibly for annotation and response, possibly to protect the text.[270]

Immediate danger now surrounded them: fearing that his chamber would be ransacked by the Privy Council, Persons asked Gilbert to saddle his horse and ride as fast as he could from Stonor to London, and 'covertly dissembling the matter', ride down the street past the rented lodging to try to find out what was happening.[271] It was two days' ride to Southwark (Figure 6.7). Gilbert came back to report that he had 'first passed through the street, & found it bristling with sorrowful silence, except for the sound, in some of the houses, of women weeping; the most notable for her grief being the landlady [of Persons's lodgings]'.[272] From her, Gilbert found out that 'the night before', Sir Thomas Wilkes, secretary to the Council, 'with an hundred armed men' had 'entred the lodging', which her

---

[267]   Bombino, *Vita et Martyrium*, p. 132; Bodl. MS Tanner 329, fol. 46v.

[268]   Pollen, *Ten Reasons*, p. 20. There is one signature for the *Praefatio*, followed by 10 from A1 to K4, with 2 blank flyleaves at the beginning and 2 at the end, making 48 leaves altogether. There is a curious *s semé* on the title page and at the end of the printed text (sig. K3r), as if it were some sign of approval.

[269]   The watermarks are mostly concealed by the binding, but they reveal a left-handed pot surmounted by a flowery crown, like Briquet 12801 with initials, 'P O', and with initial 'D', which may be part of 'P D' (12791) or 'P D B', Philippe de Bosy (Briquet 12794). See Nancy Pollard Brown, 'Paperchase: The Dissemination of Catholic Texts in Elizabethan England', in *English Manuscript Studies*, vol. 1 (Oxford: Blackwell, 1989), 120–43, for de Bosy's paper being used later. Pollen, *'Decem Rationes'* (1905), p. 22, and *Ten Reasons* (1914), describes the watermark as 'the ordinary English sign', and the book as '16mo', using half folio sheets.

[270]   Sig. L1–2. There were two flyleaves at the front of the book, but they are very damaged in the Winchester copy. They do not appear to have been wrapped around the spine under the parchment.

[271]   Bombino, *Vita et Martyrium*, p. 145 *'hominem Catholicum quem in famuli speciem trahebat secum'*; Bodl. MS Tanner, fol. 53v. This must refer to George Gilbert, whom Persons was already pressing to leave England for his own safety, but he may have decided to stay till the printing and distribution of *Rationes Decem* was completed, Foley, *Records*, III. 691.

[272]   Bombino, *Vita et Martyrium*, p. 145 (my translation); Bodl. MS Tanner 329, fol. 53v.

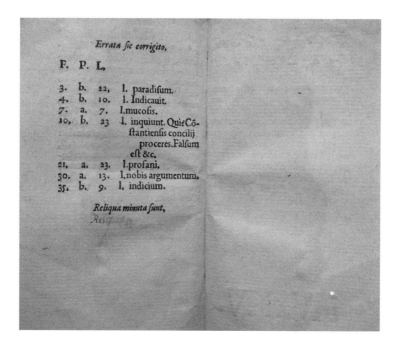

Figure 6.6   *Rationes Decem*, Stonor Park edn, ARCR I. 135.1, Winchester
copy (WN⁴): sig. K3v–K4r. With permission of the Bishop and
Trustees of the Catholic Diocese of Portsmouth and the Parish
Priest of Hampshire Downs Parish.

husband let to 'a certain strange gentleman' (Persons had not given his name),
where they had seized 'a world of pardons & indulgences from the pope, beades,
graynes, & Agnus Deies: & out of her bedde', dragged her husband, and in the
next house, 'apprehended a fine young man for a priest, as it is rumourd': Persons
knew this was Alexander Briant, his favourite pupil, who had come to England in
1579.[273] The news that Gilbert brought back to Stonor Park is a vivid reminder of
what Elizabethan England could be like for the ordinary Catholic.

---

[273]   Bombino, *Vita et Martyrium*, pp. 145–6; Bodl. MS Tanner 329, fol. 54r. Bombino
(and the Tanner translator) follow Persons in connecting Briant's capture with the distribution
of *Rationes Decem*. Simpson, pp. 284–5, concludes that Persons was mistaken, and takes
the dates *assumed* for Hart's 'Tower Diary', attached to Nicholas Sander, *De Origine ac
Progressu Schismatis Anglicani*, aucti per Edouardum Rishtonum (Romae: Bonfadini,
1586), ARCR I. 973, sig. 216v–7r, as correct: that he was brought to the Tower from another
prison on 27 [March/April], and thrown into the Pit on 6 [April/May]. Anstruther, *Seminary
Priests*, I. 50, follows this, and corroborates with letters of the Privy Council ordering the
arrest of Jenkes (28 April) and instructing the Lieutenant of the Tower about the torture
of Briant (3 May), *APC, 1581–82*, pp. 35–7. But the dates of these letters appear to have
been added later. Allen's letter describing the capture to Agazzari, *Letters and Memorials,*

Figure 6.7   Map of London, 1572, by Georg Braun and Frans Hogenberg, BL
Maps 215, f. 1, pl. 1. © The British Library Board.

In a contemporary motet, William Byrd set to music Jeremiah's lamentation
(Jer. 31:15–17) *Haec dicit Dominus*; it perfectly describes the silent street, women
weeping, midnight searches and men snatched from their beds:

> Thus says the Lord: the voice of lamentation, grief and wailing, has been heard
> in heaven, Rachel weeping for her children, and not wishing any consolation,
> because they are no more.[274]

---

p. 95, is dated 23 June, but Persons does not mention Briant's capture till his August letter,
CRS 39, pp. 72–90. He does not mention it in a letter dated 24 June (sometimes dated
14 June, as in CRS 4, p. 12), recommending George Gilbert to Pope Gregory XIII, Foley,
Records, III. 676–7. With so many conflicting dates, others left blank or added later, it
seems safer to follow Bombino's account, supported by Persons in his 'Notae breves',
ABSI Collectanea P. I, fol. 155a, which links the story of Briant's arrest with the printing
and distribution of *Rationes Decem*. The story depends on the combined presence of
Hartley, Campion, Persons and Gilbert, and the binding of printed copies of Campion's
book in Southwark, which makes late June or early July more likely. But, with Persons as
a key witness, certainty about the date of such an important event is likely to be elusive.

[274]   Joseph Kerman, *The Masses and Motets of William Byrd* (London: Faber and
Faber, 1981), p. 42. John Harley, *William Byrd: Gentleman of the Chapel Royal* (Aldershot,
UK and Burlington, VT: Ashgate Publishing, 1997), p. 223, dates *Haec dicit* to 1582–83.

Chapter 7
Captive Good

The news of Briant's capture and torture changed everything.[1] Persons was particularly attached to Alexander Briant, another Somerset man, born in Stogursey, two miles from Nether Stowey, where Persons used to walk to school. Briant had moved from Hart Hall to Balliol to be with Persons, whose 'Notae breves' slide in macaronic discord from Latin to Spanish, as he explains why he was so affected by the news of Briant:

> Como fue Brianto mi discipulo y pupillo en Oxonio y sempre inclinado a la virtud despues sacerdote en Rhemis de grandissimo zelo scrivio al P. Richardo Gibbonio cum esset ingressurus Angliam an posset matrem suam adire: reconciliavit patrem meum et a latere meo nunquam in Anglia discedere voluit.

> [As Briant was my disciple and pupil in Oxford and always inclined to virtue, and later a priest of the greatest zeal in Rheims, when he was about to come to England [on 3 August 1579], I wrote to Fr Richard Gibbons to ask whether he could visit his mother. He reconciled my father and wished never to leave my side in England.][2]

Persons's redoubtable mother, Christina Persons (who died 26 April 1600, aged 92), was a determined recusant, but the sacramental anointing of his dying father must have cemented the bond with Briant. The two days that followed news of his capture (as Bombino makes clear) filled Campion with foreboding, and were deeply engraved on Persons's mind:

> For two nights they spent without sleepe, & two most carefull dayes, while ever & anon they heare of Briant's wracking, & other torments, many things false, some true, by many men's speeches & letters. But Campian (as Parsons told me when I was writing this) continued those two dayes, for the most part in prayer, without taking any rest in the nights: & what little time he spard from prayer spent it in talke concerning this subject: how he shoulde carry himselfe at his arraignement, what he should say, what countenance, or mind he should put on, when he fell into his enemies handes.[3]

---

[1]   ABSI Collectanea P. I, fol. 155a, and CRS 2, p. 182.

[2]   ABSI Collectanea P. I, fol. 155a.

[3]   Bombino, *Vita et Martyrium*, p. 147; Bodl. MS Tanner 329, fol. 54v.

Stonor Park was now too dangerous. 'Since many were now looking for Campion, everyone agreed he should now go to Norfolk'.[4] Persons had letters from several counties inviting Campion to come to them, but Norfolk was chosen; it was remote from London, full of large estates belonging to Catholic families like the Kitsons, Bedingfelds, Cornwallises and Pastons. Campion agreed, as long as he could fetch his books first, 'for so much as his bookes were in Lancashire, without which Campian alleadged he could not well live'.[5] Persons gave permission for this detour (about three hundred miles) to collect them from Park Hall, the house of Richard Hoghton, but not to linger in Lancashire, to stay in 'publike Innes' and not 'Catholikes houses', and then to carry his books to Norfolk.[6]

Surrounded by danger, and anguished by daily news of Briant's torture, they at least had a plan, and Campion sat down on Sunday, 9 July 1581, to write to the new general, Claudio Acquaviva, conscious that his last letter in November to Mercurian (who had died on 1 August 1580) had not arrived.[7] Campion talks as if he is a soldier facing, with fear and defiance, the prospect of imminent death. Enclosing a second copy of the November letter, Campion first explains why he has not written more:

> I live in an armed camp, limited by many factors. My eyesight is weaker, and that which is worth your reading is not safe to commit to paper ... Although our enemies have never been more inhuman than they are now, Christ's cause has never been in a better or safer place. They have put forward no other arguments than those which are drawn from the rack, starvation or cursing; these very things have destroyed the dignity of our enemies, and made Catholics the focus of everyone's concern. The only thing our cause lacked was that to our books written in ink, others should succeed, as many do now daily, inscribed in blood.[8]

At first light on Monday 10 July, the two men mounted their horses and prepared to leave Stonor: Campion for Lancashire, Persons for Kent. Campion had as companion the faithful Emerson, Persons the indefatigable George Gilbert. Campion's route would have taken him up the long incline through the woods towards the high escarpment that marks the edge of the Chiltern hills.[9] It was an emotional farewell, as Persons describes:

---

[4]   ABSI Collectanea P. I, fol. 155b.

[5]   Bombino, *Vita et Martyrium*, p. 147; Bodl. MS Tanner 329, fol. 54v.

[6]   Bombino, *Vita et Martyrium*, p. 147; Bodl. MS Tanner 329, fol. 55r.

[7]   Claudio Aquaviva (1543–1615), was elected the fifth Superior General on 7 February 1581.

[8]   ARSI Fondo Gesuitico 651, no. 612 (my translation); see Daniel Bartoli, S.J., *Dell'Istoria Della Compagnia Di Giesu L'Inghilterra Parte Dell'Europa* (Rome: Varese, 1667), p. 145; (part) trans. Simpson, p. 306.

[9]   Bombino, *Vita et Martyrium*, p. 147; Bodl. MS Tanner 329, fol. 55r.

As if with some premonition that we would never see each other again, we renewed our vows, confessed and received communion. At length, on the tenth of July we embraced, exchanged hats as a sign of love, and departed from each other.[10]

The appearance of following an orderly plan was soon shattered. Bombino's account, built clearly on Persons's recollections, is vivid:

Having spurred their horses in different directions, neither man had proceeded very far, when suddenly Persons heard his name being called out from behind him with a very loud voice. It was Campion, who had followed to ask him if he could have permission to divert from the agreed route towards the house of a nobleman called Yates.[11]

Francis Yate was in prison for his beliefs, and had been writing to Campion, pressing him to visit his family, especially because 'noble virgins from the holy order of St Bridget' were living in his house.[12] It seems that it was only when Campion asked Emerson what route they were to take, that he realized they would pass by Lyford Grange. Persons knew that 'if but once they gotte Campian amongst them, how hard it would be to gette him away', and agreed only after Campion suggested that Emerson should be made his superior to ensure that Campion would not be constrained to stay longer.[13]

Campion and Persons parted a second time. The journey took Campion and Emerson through south Oxfordshire and into what contemporary maps describe as 'the Vale of Whythors' (White Horse). The vast plane that opened up before them, as they rode towards the Thames at Wallingford, was a patchwork quilt of lands belonging to Catholic families. They were travelling through one of the most Catholic areas of the country, and certainly one where there were many active priests, both Marian and seminary. A wide swathe of land that stretched from Berkshire to Oxfordshire belonged to a group of some 40 gentry families, interlinked by marriage. Even more significantly, one of the most powerful landowners, Sir Francis Englefield (who had two relatives among the Bridgettine nuns), remained in exile, while the leading lawyer in the the country, Edmund Plowden, managed his land and successfully protected it from sequestration by the crown.[14] Other large landowning families, the 'Fermors, Stonors, Chamberlaynes,

---

[10]   ABSI Collectanea P. I, 'Notae breves', fol. 155b. This hat has not survived, but the Archives in Farm Street have a fragment, taken from a hat in Prague, apparently given in an exchange between Campion and Fr Francis Borgia, Item 234. I thank Thomas McCoog and Jan Graffius for alerting me to this.

[11]   Bombino, *Vita et Martyrium*, pp. 148–9 (my translation).

[12]   Bombino, *Vita et Martyrium*, p. 149.

[13]   Bombino, *Vita et Martyrium*, pp. 151–2; Bodl. MS Tanner 329, fols 56v–57r.

[14]   Edmund Plowden (1519/20–1585) is still regarded as one of the greatest lawyers of the sixteenth century.

Fettiplaces of Swyncombe, Appletrees, Symeons, Belsons, Hildesleys, Nappers and Powells were Catholics throughout the period studied'.[15] The Sheriffs of both Oxfordshire and Berkshire, and many of the Justices, came from these families, and repeated attempts by the Privy Council to ensure their conformity reflect official frustration with a region whose 'spirit of inward resistance' had been if anything increased by Lord Grey's savage reprisals during the Prayer Book rebellion of 1549.[16]

The Yates of Berkshire, Buckinghamshire, Oxfordshire, Gloucestershire and Wiltshire were descended from the 20 children of John Yate of Charney Bassett and Lyford, a wealthy Merchant of the Staple who died in 1541. Edward Yate, another grandson, was master of nearby Buckland Manor (where some of the Fettiplaces were living), and a Master of Arts of Oxford University.[17]

The journey to Lyford Grange from Stonor Park is only 25 miles, but Campion and Ralph Emerson took 'two or three days journey' to get there, so they must have stopped on the way.[18] The route to Lyford took them past Swyncombe House, the ancient home of the Fettiplaces, with its eleventh-century chapel, St Botolph's, still virtually hidden in a wooded fold of the hills. Then they would have ridden through Long Wittenham, on the west bank of the Thames, opposite Dorchester. Sir Thomas White, Campion's patron, had bought land at Long Wittenham in July 1565, outlining his purpose in a letter to the President of St John's that names Campion and Gregory Martin.[19] It was here that Justinian Stubbs held a lease from Henry Russell on Lowches Farm.[20] Henry Russell, his brother Rowland, Justinian Stubbs and Francis Willis, President of St John's from 1577, were accused in three letters of William West that have recently come to light, of knowing 'where all the papists are that passeth or do come from Rome and where they live, and who were confederate with Campion's libells'.[21] It seems that the farm at Long Wittenham

---

[15]   Davidson, 'Catholicism in Oxfordshire', pp. 6–7.

[16]   Brigden, *New Worlds*, p. 191; Caraman, *Western Rising*, pp. 80–81; see Chapter 6.

[17]   CRS 22, *Miscellanea XII*, ed. Patrick Ryan, S.J., and J.H. Pollen, S.J. (London: Catholic Record Society, 1921), pp. 86, 108–12, where the 1577 recusant returns for the Salisbury and Oxford dioceses show the family spread across several villages: John Yate of Ganfielde, Francis Yate of Hormer and Ocke, Richard Yate of Lyford, Anthony Yate of Deddington, Francis Yate of Kencot and his wife and Mabyn, the wife of James Yate of Stanlake. The Yates were also intermarried with the Askehams. An 'Askeham of Lyforde, a thousande markes by the yeare' is included in the 1577 recusant returns, and John Ayshcombe is honoured by a tombstone in a nearby village that lists him as Justice of the Peace and High Sheriff.

[18]   CRS 4, p. 17.

[19]   Stevenson and Salter, *Early History of St John's*, pp. 417–18. White's intention from the start may have been a safe house.

[20]   Michael Questier, *Catholicism and Community in Early Modern England: Politics, Aristocratic Patronage and Religion, c. 1550–1640* (Cambridge: University Press, 2006), p. 154; Michael Hodgetts, *Secret Hiding Places* (Dublin: Veritas, 1989), pp. 54–5 and 79.

[21]   Hegarty, *Register*, 168, citing the Berington Collection, WRO 705:24/29 (1).

was a safe house for priests. West continues 'The President was your surety to have a faithful friend's house to keep [secret] such as [are] Campion's fellows'.[22] Francis Willis, Vicar of nearby Cumnor and Rector of Kingston Bagpuise during Campion's mission, a close friend of Henry Russell, and a contemporary fellow of St John's with Campion, is described as being 'always a privy succourer of seminary priests', and 'traitor Campion's companion'.[23] West, who was trying to recover the farm for an evicted widow, accused Willis of sheltering Campion at the time he 'threw his traitorous libel abroad'.[24]

Lyford Grange, about eight miles from Oxford, and 50 from London, was a substantial Catholic household. 'The house was very large, built in manner of a castle, with a wall & moat about it'.[25] Only three sides of the courtyard house, and three sides of the moat, survive. There appears to have been a gate-tower, as at Hoghton Tower, in the fourth side that could look out over the fields to the north. It is still a quiet part of the country, just over two miles from Kingston Bagpuize, and less than two miles from the small villages of West and East Hanney. Surrounded by open, flat countryside typical of the area, the house was as much protected by the marriage links that made the Yates part of the network of justices of the peace and sheriffs of Berkshire and Oxfordshire as by its moat.

Within the walls of Lyford Grange, originally a manor of Abingdon Abbey, Francis Yate 'maintayned many years' eight Bridgettine nuns, 'fitly accommodating a certayne part of his house for their use, where he ordained them a quire, an altar, and all furniture belonging thereunto'.[26] His widowed mother looked after the nuns, who wore their habits in the house, and came from Syon Abbey, originally one of the richest and most influential communities in England. They were re-founded under Mary, dissolved again under Elizabeth, exiled into Flanders, where they settled in Mechlin, under the protection of Sir Francis Englefield; during the siege, eight were sent back to England in 1578, to try to raise money for their survival, and more followed after the fall of Mechlin in 1580, when they threw themselves on the Queen's mercy.[27] The Queen first lodged these noble ladies

[22]   Berington Collection, 29/1; William West to Henry Russell, 25 April 1584 (transcript kindly supplied by Michael Hodgetts).

[23]   Aileen M. Hodgson and Michael Hodgetts, *Little Malvern Letters I: 1482–1737* (London: CRS 83, 2011); Berington Collection, 29/2, p. 52.

[24]   Berington Collection, 29/1.

[25]   Bombino, *Vita et Martyrium*, p. 149; Bodl. MS Tanner 329, fol. 55v.

[26]   Bombino, *Vita et Martyrium*, p. 150; Bodl. MS Tanner 329, fol. 56r; Daniel Bartoli, *Dell'Istoria Della Compagnia Di Giesu L'Inghilterra Parte Dell'Europa* (Rome: Varese, 1667), p. 149. Simpson, p. 310.

[27]   Ann M. Hutchison, 'Some Historians of Syon', in *Syon Abbey and Its Books: Reading, Writing and Religion, c. 1400–1700*, ed. E.A. Jones and Alexandra Walsham (Woodbridge: Boydell Press, 2010), pp. 228–51 (p. 236); John Rory Fletcher, *The Story of the English Bridgettines of Syon Abbey* (Bristol: Syon Abbey, 1933), pp. 49–54.

with Protestant theologians, but finally allowed them to stay in small groups with willing Catholic hosts.[28]

Among the nuns who came to Lyford Grange at the beginning of 1579 was Sister Elizabeth Sander, the younger sister of Nicholas Sander, 'and of Margaret, who had been Prioress of Syon', but who had died at Mechlin in 1576.[29] Sister Elizabeth's letters to Sir Francis Englefield, now in Valladolid, give us a vivid picture of her life, sufferings and daring escapes from Winchester castle.[30] Her letter describing 'her beying in England' to Sir Francis does not explain why she had left Lyford Grange in the summer of 1580, but it is likely that she wished to protect the community from the effect of her brother's rebellion in Ireland, as the fear of invasion grew.[31] She went to stay with another sister, Mrs Henry Pits of Alton, where she was arrested on 18 November 1580, shortly after her nephew, William Pits, was arrested in Bath for distributing Campion's 'Letter to the Council'.[32] The Pits of Alton, whose sons John and William were both priests, were another branch of the recusant family of Iffley, where both Mrs Arthur Pits and her priest son, Robert, figure in the 1577 recusant rolls.[33] John Pits became a celebrated Catholic bibliographer.[34] Neither Sister Elizabeth nor Mrs Pits could have heard of the horrific massacre at Smerwick a week earlier, but they would have feared for their brother. News of Sander's solitary death, 'probably from dysentery', in the hills of Limerick, which occurred sometime between March and June 1581, seems not to have reached the Queen in England before November 1581, but must have been presumed before then.[35]

The 'quire' provided for the nuns suggests that the liturgy was sung antiphonally.[36] There was certainly a musician in the house, John Jacob, who was

---

[28]   Bombino, *Vita et Martyrium*, p. 149; Bodl. MS Tanner 329, fol. 56r.

[29]   Hutchison, 'Historians of Syon', p. 234.

[30]   Royal English College, ACSA, Series II L.5, nos 12 and 13. See Betty S. Travitsky, 'The Puzzling Letters of Sister Elizabeth Sa[u]nder[s], in *Textual Conversations in the Renaissance: Ethics, Authors, Technologies*, ed. Zachary Lesser and Benedict S. Robinson (Aldershot, UK and Burlington, VT: Ashgate, 2006), 131–45; Fletcher, *The English Bridgettines*, 58–69. Sr Elizabeth Sander escaped to Rouen after six years in prison in Winchester.

[31]   ACSA Valladolid, Series II L.5, no. 12.

[32]   The arrest is recorded in *CSP Domestic, 1547–1580*, 12/144/31, 688, and by Ann Hutchison, p. 236. Foley, *Records*, III. 645–8, shows Pits offered copies to 'one Lichpoole'.

[33]   CRS 22, 'Recusant Returns, 1577', p. 113.

[34]   *ODNB*, 'John Pits' (1560–1616), by F. Blom and J. Blom. They defend the independence of *Relationum Historicarum de Rebus Anglicis Tomus Primus* (Paris: Thierry & Cramoisy, 1619), ARCR 1. 907, usually known by its running title, *De illustribus Angliae Scriptoribus*.

[35]   *ODNB*, 'Nicholas Sander' (c.1530–1581), by T.F. Mayer.

[36]   Emilie K. Murphy, '*Adoramus te Christe*: Music and Post-Reformation English Catholic Domestic Piety', in *Religion and the Household*, *Studies in Church History*, vol. 50 (Woodbridge: Boydell, 2014), pp. 240–53 (pp. 248–9), argues convincingly that

captured with Campion.[37] He was still in Bridewell in 1583, when John Gerard found him in fetters for praising Campion, beaten, 'wasted to a skeleton', and with lice swarming on him 'like ants on a mole-hill'.[38] Sister Elizabeth Sander's description of what followed her arrest, a life of humiliating interrogation – on one occasion her headgear was wrested from her head – and imprisonment, including '23 weeks' in Bridewell, 'a place indeed for rogues', is a moving and pitiful story.[39] She was questioned in a particularly aggressive way by John Watson, Bishop of Winchester, who implied 'that bothe I and others mo were sent by my brother Dr Saunders hyther into England, and put in hope, that our Relygion and order should come upp agayne'; accused of aiding him, she replied that she had not 'seene my brother in many years and scarsly heard from hym att any tyme'.[40] His name was enough to bring obloquy on her and, on at least one occasion in her letter, it is hard to tell whether she was being addressed rudely as 'Saunders', or her brother apostrophized. Since, it seems that Campion's primary purpose was to see the nuns, '*ut videret monachas*', it seems possible that Campion was concerned to console Sister Elizabeth for the catastrophe that had enveloped her brother's expedition, and did not know that she had already left Lyford.[41]

At Lyford also were two remarkable seminary priests. Fr John Colleton was a Lincoln College man.[42] He was ordained in Binche, Flanders, in June 1576, returned to England the following month, and spent two years at the Sutton Courtenay home of James Braybrooke, a barrister of the Inner Temple, 'notoriouslye suspected to be obstinately bent to papestrie', who heads the Berkshire recusant rolls as the earliest conviction for recusancy.[43] The second priest was Fr Thomas Ford, a contemporary of Campion's, and fellow of Trinity, who was at Douai with Cuthbert Mayne and Gregory Martin, ordained before he returned to England in 1576, and shares at least two torture warrants with Campion, on 14 August and 29 October 1581.[44]

---

antiphonal singing helped transform domestic into sacred space, and uses as evidence the mirror-image score of 'Adoramus te Christe' in Bodl. MS Eng. th. b. 1–2, II. 137.

[37] George Elyot, *A very true report of the apprehension and taking of that Arche Papist Edmond Campion* (London: T. Dawson, 1581), STC 7629, sig. C4v. John Jacob may have been the son of James Jacob, surmaster of Paul's School, and the grandson of Henry Jacob, stationer; see below.

[38] John Gerard, *The Autobiography of an Elizabethan*, trans. Philip Caraman (London: Longmans, Green, 1951), p. 5.

[39] ACSA Valladolid, Series II L.5, no. 12, fol. 1r.

[40] ACSA Valladolid, Series II L.5, no. 12, fol. 1r.

[41] ABSI Collectanea P. I, fol. 154v.

[42] Anstruther, *Seminary Priests*, I. 82–5. See Chapter 12 for more on Colleton.

[43] CRS 22, p. 104; 'Berkshire Recusants in Pipe Rolls & Recusant Rolls, 1581 to end of Elizabeth's Reign', Downside Library, acc. no. 85313, Deck B80G (Box).

[44] *APC, 1581–1582*, pp. 171, 249; implied perhaps on p. 145. Langbein, *Torture*, pp. 106–7; Anstruther, *Seminary Priests*, I. 121 (who discusses the problems with the exact date of his ordination).

Campion and Emerson arrived at Lyford on Wednesday, 12 July; it seems they had spent two nights at Long Wittenham. Campion was greeted enthusiastically when he arrived, the nuns going down on their knees and, 'withe teares streaming down their cheekes, begd to kisse his sacred hand, nor would any of them rise' (however much Campion begged them) 'before he had made the signe of the crosse on them'.[45] Campion told them he would have to leave soon, and heard their confessions that evening. The following morning, Thursday, 13 July, he said Mass and preached, 'stayd no longer then dinner', and 'according as he had been commanded, departed, amidst the teares & humble supplications of the sorrowfull house, whereat him selfe after was somewhat moved'.[46]

Colleton accompanied Campion and Emerson, as they set off for Lancashire, and took them to a 'publike Inne' (*publicum hospitium*) near Oxford.[47] The northward route would have taken them by the former Godstow Priory hostelry, which then formed part of the estate of Richard Owen, and is now a riverside inn, on the other side of the river from the ruins of the priory. By then another large group of Catholics (gentlemen, matrons and maidens, says Bombino) had gone to Lyford, heard that he had 'preached altogether divinely', but stayed only one night, and begged Fr Ford to help recall him so that they too could hear him.[48] Bombino implies their arrival is 'by chance', which seems unlikely, especially as he goes on to say how much they had all been seeking an occasion to hear Campion.[49] Ford, who was 'so extremely addicted to Campion' (*Campiano addictissimus*), was only too happy to ride after him and, apparently knowing where Colleton was taking Campion, caught up with him at the 'publike Inne' near Oxford, surrounded by 'a notable troope of principall Catholikes' and 'many university men', among whom a lively discussion was taking place.[50] It sounds as if the university men had been warned of the route of Campion, and this inn, like the Star and the Catherine Wheel, was a well-established recusant centre.[51] It was now the evening of Thursday, 13 July. Ford explained his errand to Colleton, who communicated it to the large gathering. Campion had resisted their requests for him to say Mass and hear confessions, arguing that both the time and the place were too dangerous, so they realized that if Campion could be persuaded to go back to Lyford, they could all come to enjoy his oratory in the more secluded setting of Lyford Grange.[52]

Campion now found himself under siege from a large, vocal and persuasive crowd, which may have included Richard Owen, and men from the Corpus contingent – Miles Windsor, Thomas Twyne, Jerome and Edmund Rainolds –

---

[45]   Bombino, *Vita et Martyrium*, pp. 152–3; Bodl. MS Tanner 329, fol. 57r–v.

[46]   Bombino, *Vita et Martyrium*, p. 153; Bodl. MS Tanner 329, fol. 57v.

[47]   Bombino, *Vita et Martyrium*, p. 154; Bodl. MS Tanner 329, fol. 58v.

[48]   Bombino, *Vita et Martyrium*, p. 153; Bodl. MS Tanner 329, fol. 58r.

[49]   Bombino, *Vita et Martyrium*, p. 153; Bodl. MS Tanner 329, fol. 58r.

[50]   Bombino, *Vita et Martyrium*, p. 154; Bodl. MS Tanner 329, fol. 58r–v.

[51]   Reynolds, *Campion and Persons*, p. 116, rightly questions chance as the explanation.

[52]   Bombino, *Vita et Martyrium*, p. 155; Bodl. MS Tanner 329, fol. 58v.

the displaced professors, Thomas Neale and George Etheridge, and the leading Aristotelian, John Case.[53] Campion invoked the command of Persons, but this large group of intelligent men, who 'unanimously conspire' to persuade him, pointed out the spirit of commands, not the letter, had to be obeyed, that Persons had never imagined such a large number begging for his help, that, having granted one day to 'a few nuns and matrons' (*pauculis virginibus, matronisque*) in going to Lyford, he could hardly turn down the prayers of so many 'distinguished men' and 'such a knott of speciall friendes' for two or three days.[54] They were asking him, they concluded, only to return to Lyford for two days: arrive by midday on the Friday, stay for the Saturday and for Mass on Sunday, '& after this goe freely whither soever he pleasd'.[55] Campion, 'of an exceeding sweet and facill disposition' (*ingenij facillimi*), almost in tears because he was so 'movd with the intreaties of so many of his friendes', fell back on his 'final defence' (*postremum effugium*): the arrangement agreed with Persons precisely to defend him from this sort of pressure.[56] When he pointed out that he was under obedience to Ralph Emerson, his auditors turned the full force of their intellect on Emerson. If the issue was collecting books from Lancashire, why not, they proposed, split the tasks? If Campion went, they argued, he would be forced to spend many days there since, 'when they had once heard the name of Campian, a world of old friendes would flocke unto him'.[57] Emerson could go by himself to fetch the books (about six days' ride, as Persons later says), and arrange to rejoin Campion in Huntingdonshire. That way they were still following the *spirit* of Persons's orders. It was a perfectly logical argument, and Emerson yielded to their pressure: he would fetch the books, and go to Norfolk.[58] Campion agreed to ride back to Lyford the next day, stay till Sunday, and then depart for Norfolk. On the morning of Friday, 14 July 1581, Emerson set out for Lancashire, and Campion, surrounded by a large party of distinguished academics and local gentry, all 'with joyfull heartes', and 'in a manner triumphant' (*in speciem triumphi*), returned to Lyford.[59]

A large number of Catholics was able to discourse with him.[60] Henry Russell and another St John's man, Justinian Stubbs, were certainly there, so it is likely

---

[53] Bombino, *Vita et Martyrium*, p. 155; Bodl. MS Tanner 329, fol. 59v.

[54] Bombino, *Vita et Martyrium*, pp. 155–6; Bodl. MS Tanner 329, fol. 59v. The phrase, 'knott of speciall friendes', is not in the Latin original. This was clearly a very masculine group.

[55] Bombino, *Vita et Martyrium*, p. 156; Bodl. MS Tanner 329, fol. 58v.

[56] Bombino, *Vita et Martyrium*, p. 156; Bodl. MS Tanner 329, fol. 59v.

[57] Bombino, *Vita et Martyrium*, pp. 156–7; Bodl. MS Tanner 329, fol. 60r.

[58] Bombino, *Vita et Martyrium*, p. 157; Bodl. MS Tanner 329, fol. 59v.

[59] Bombino, *Vita et Martyrium*, p. 157; Bodl. MS Tanner 329, fol. 60r.

[60] Waugh talks of the 'pious women' of Lyford Grange, repeats several variants on the phrase 'good women', and ends with the patronizing, 'Campion was lionised and cosseted by the good ladies', Waugh, *Edmund Campion*, pp. 152–4. See Bombino, *Vita et Martyrium*, p. 156; Bodl. MS Tanner 329, fol. 59v.

that Francis Willis was with them.[61] William Hildesley (Ilsley), who was the son of Margaret Hildesley (née Stonor), and came from the large family that had property in Crowmarsh Gifford, just next to Wallingford, was also there.[62] Hildesley would be arrested, in 1582, for carrying into England some controversial Catholic books from William Rainolds to his Calvinist brother, John, at Corpus.[63] Also in Lyford Grange were Humfrey and Edward Keynes, who appear to have been Catholic 'vagrants', exploiting the ownership of houses in different counties, since they came from the large Catholic family of Compton Pauncefoot, near Bruton, Somerset.[64] For two days, Lyford Grange must have been one of the most vibrant houses in Oxfordshire, echoing to the sound of lively intellectual debate and a sung liturgy. The Mass on Sunday morning was to be the climax of these two days, but the force of destiny, or as Bombino asserts, the wisdom of providence, was preparing a very different ending to Campion's triumphant arrival.[65]

George Elyot was the man appointed to betray Campion.[66] Elyot had been a steward in several Catholic households, and acquired the sobriquet 'Judas' because he came from the heart of the Catholic community. He was a kinsman of William Moore of Haddon, and had worked in three leading Catholic households. He had been causing trouble as far back as 1564, when he was dismissed by Viscount Montague after an angry exchange over shooting one of his deer. Montague related in a letter to William Moore how Elyot had woken him and his wife 'atte one of the clocke after mydneightt', had caused him to lose his temper, and 'in the mydell of my anger and displeasaunt speache, he moved to me a sute to recomende him for mariage'. Later, on the same day, 'he commeth to me smylinge', and told Montague that he had 'strykenid a bucke in my parke here with a gonne', which Montague took badly because he had recently given him 'a bucke'.[67]

Ejected from the Montague household, Elyot moved first to Thomas Roper, Thomas More's grandson, who was related to the Montagues through Roper's marriage to Lucy Browne, and then to the household of Lady Petre, the widow of Sir William Petre, at Ingatestone Hall.[68] Persons's account in the 'Notae breves' supplies the details of Elyot's time in the Roper household, giving as his source,

---

[61]   Elyot, *A very true report*, sig. C4v; Questier, *Catholicism and Community*, p. 154.

[62]   Elyot, *A very true report*, sig. C4v; Davidson, 'Catholicism in Oxfordshire', pp. 187 and 191.

[63]   Davidson, 'Catholicism in Oxfordshire', p. 191 citing PRO SP 12/157/68.

[64]   'Berkshire Recusants', Downside Library manuscript, acc. no. 85313.

[65]   Bombino, *Vita et Martyrium*, pp. 158–9; Bodl. MS Tanner 329, fol. 60v.

[66]   Elyot's name is spelt variously; I have chosen the spelling used for his own book.

[67]   Questier, *Catholicism and Community*, p. 196, citing Surrey History Centre, Loseley Manuscripts 6729/8/13.

[68]   *L'Histoire de la Mort que le R. P. Edmond Campion Prestre de la compagnie du nom de Iesus, & autres ont souffert en Angleterre pour la foy Catholique & Romaine le premier jour de Decembre, 1581*. Traduit d'Anglois en Francois (Paris: Chaudiere, 1582), ARCR I. 197, sig. A3r; Questier, *Catholicism and Community*, p. 196.

Roper's cousin, Charles Bassett, who knew Elyot as an 'always arrogant' (*semper superbus*) servant in the house; Bombino confirms that Elyot lived a comparatively blameless life in the Roper household 'for many years'.[69] After he was 'entised' by Fr John Paine 'to serve my Lady Peters, to whom the sayd Paine served craftily as Steward of her house', at Ingatestone Hall, he (in his own words) 'continued almost two yeares' during which time, 'being myself bent somewhat to that religion', he frequented 'the company of a number of Papists'. At Lady Petre's house he was charged with murder and embezzlement, and was saved from prison only by Thomas Roper, who stood bail for him, on condition of residence in the Roper house.[70] Elyot was ordered to appear at the next local assizes, where Sir John Petre would probably have been the Justice.[71] While on bail, Elyot seduced a girl living in the house, and even persuaded her that he had a priest waiting to marry them, and led her from the sleeping Roper household in the middle of the night.[72] So 'a girl of good family left terrified by the nocturnal horror, the present booty of a madman, the future spoil of an unholy rapist'.[73]

Elyot and his unfortunate prey made haste to London, where Elyot sought out Fr Paine, and asked him to marry them; Paine, shocked at what Elyot had done, refused, and told him to take the girl back home. Elyot was struck dumb, but astonishment 'gave way to fury' (*stupori furor*).[74] Munday confirms that Elyot had 'long since committed a murder', for which reason he went 'to one of the cheefe Lordes in the Court', and negotiated release from the murder charge if he delivered 'into his handes the Father Edmund Campion'.[75] Desperate because of his impending trial, he claimed he had, after years of living in the darkness of the Catholic faith, now seen the truth of Calvin by the light of the Gospel.[76] Elyot made clear his knowledge of the entire Catholic community in a list 'by me

---

[69]   Bombino, *Vita et Martyrium*, p. 160 (this section of the Tanner manuscript is wanting).

[70]   A[nthony]. M[unday]., *A breefe Aunswer made unto two seditious Pamphlets, the one printed in French, and the other in English. Contayning a defence of Edmund Campion and his complices, their most horrible and vnnatural Treasons, as gainst her Maiestie and the Realme* (London: E. White, 1582), STC 18262, sig. B3v.

[71]   Bombino, *Vita et Martyrium*, pp. 160–61.

[72]   Bombino, *Vita et Martyrium*, p. 161.

[73]   Bombino, *Vita et Martyrium*, pp. 161–2.

[74]   Bombino, *Vita et Martyrium*, p. 162.

[75]   Anthony Munday, *A breefe Aunswer made unto two seditious Pamphlets, the one printed in French, and the other in English* (London: John Charlewood, 1582), STC 18262a, sig. B2r, and sig. B4r, where Munday quotes Elyot naming the Earl of Leicester. Bombino, *Vita et Martyrium*, p. 165, specifies Walsingham; *L'Histoire de la Mort*, pp. 5–6, talks of a nameless '*Seigneur*' who was '*grandement Calviniste*'.

[76]   BL MS Lansdowne 33, fol. 145r. Simpson takes this as decisive evidence that it was Leicester, pp. 313–14. Walsingham seems more likely, but it is possible Leicester simply passed Elyot to Walsingham, as Reynolds, *Campion and Parsons*, p. 118, implies. With two practised deceivers as sources, it is hard to decide where truth lies.

exhibited to the right honorable, my good l. therle of Leycester', and added two long paragraphs outlining a fictitious plot by Fr Paine to assassinate the Queen, which Burghley, to whom the list was passed, has glossed in his own hand: 'payne to be examyned'.[77]

Walsingham gave Elyot royal authority to seek out all those plotting against the Queen, and for all magistrates to take instructions from him, by providing a messenger of the Queen's Privy Chamber, David Jenkins, 'one of those old catchpolls, a crafty undermining fellow, under the honourable show of assistant, but indeed as a perpetuall spie over that punie Ghospeller'.[78] Walsingham, rather than doubting his 'faith' as Bombino assumes, may have sensed that Elyot was an unbalanced individual, who required a 'minder'. Mrs Yate was also to allocate someone to keep watch over him. Elyot's own narrative begins when he and Jenkins leave London.[79] The 'smylinge' Elyot must have been sufficiently plausible to work his way through three major Catholic houses. The combination of impudence, social resentment and raw cunning, allowed him to denounce many Catholic families including that of Viscount Montague, his son-in-law, the Earl of Southampton, Lady Petre, and his former employer and protector, Sir Thomas Roper.[80] Elyot, accompanied by Jenkins who was 'very vilely slaundered with a Booke set out by one Anthony Munday', was employed to track Campion down.[81] Elyot went straight to William Moore's house at Little Haddon, where on Sunday, 2 July 1581, he saw Fr Paine saying Mass for the whole household, and on Tuesday, 4 July, Fr George Godsalf saying Mass.[82] He returned to London and

---

[77] BL MS Lansdowne 33, fol. 147r–v. David Mateer, 'William Byrd, John Petre and Oxford, Bodleian MS Mus. Sch. E 423: An Index and Commentary', *Research Chronicle* 29 (1996), 21–45 (p. 30), describes the close connection of Byrd with the old Lady Petre until her death on 10 March 1582, 21 days before the execution of her former chaplain, Fr John Paine.

[78] Bombino, *Vita et Martyrium*, p. 165; Bodl. MS Tanner 329, fol. 61r.

[79] Elyot, *A very true report*, sig. A2v.

[80] Elyot's list of Catholics he claims to have known (perhaps copied by Thomas Norton) is in BL MS Lansdowne 33, no. 60, fols 145r–149r. He starts with 'Mr Yates' of Berkshire and 'Mr Moore' of Oxfordshire, and includes 'The ould la. Peter' and 'Sir Thomas Rooper', fol. 146r.

[81] Elyot, *A very true report*, sig. A2v.

[82] BL Lansdowne MS 33, fol. 149r: Elyot's report of who was present at the Mass, which included 'Mistress Tempas', on 2 July 1581 'at Mr Wllm Moore his howse at haddon'. Robert Tempest was one of six gentlemen in charge of musters for the Chiltern Hundreds, Davidson, 'Catholicism in Oxfordshire', p. 174. I thank James E. Kelly, who alerted me to TNA, E351/142, mem.23d, which describes Paine's arrest, and shows the Moore household was part of the extended network of the Petre family; see his 'Conformity, Loyalty and the Jesuit Mission to England of 1580', in *Religious Tolerance in the Atlantic World: Early Modern and Contemporary Perspectives*, ed. Eliane Glaser (Palgrave Macmillan, 2013), pp. 149–70 (pp. 154 and 156). The Moores had links with the Nappers (Napiers) of Holywell Manor and the Waldegraves. Fr Godsalf was ordained at Cambrai on 20 December 1576,

reported to Walsingham; the two priests were arrested in Warwickshire, without breaking Elyot's cover. Having proved his worth, Elyot proposed:

> What do I get if I bring a Jesuit to you? You'll get everything (*Tu summa omnia*), replied Walsingham, and straightway, with witnesses suborned, they agreed the deal.[83]

All charges against him would be dropped, Walsingham replied, if he could find either Persons or Campion. Lady Petre had dismissed Elyot, and Fr Paine had refused to sanction his elopement: now he took his revenge on Paine and the entire Catholic community.[84]

'About eight of the clocke in the morning' of Sunday 16 July 1581, Elyot rode through the fields towards Lyford.[85] Elyot tells us that he had left London on 14 July, and arrived at Lyford Grange after seeing the house from a distance with his fellow 'messenger'.[86] His success at Little Haddon two weeks earlier, indicated what a good day Sunday was for catching priests saying Mass. Although Munday says that Elyot's commission was explicitly to find Campion, Elyot argues that the commission he and Jenkins received was for 'the apprehension of certaine lewde Priestes, and other seditious persons of like sort, wheresoever wee shoulde happen to finde them within Englande', and that, by chance, he thought to contact Thomas Cowper, an old 'acquaintance' of his, now working as a cook 'to one maister *Yates*' at Lyford Grange.[87] Bombino, following Persons, supports Elyot's (barely credible) assertion that he had no specific knowledge of any priest when he began his search.[88]

> When he saw the house from a distance, he exclaimed: 'If anyone could get access to that house he would surely find a priest'. Then he remembered that the cook was an old friend of his, so he was allowed into the Mass and Campion's sermon.[89]

Elyot's account of Campion's arrest at Lyford Grange gives us a vivid picture of life among the servants in a Catholic household, of kitchen dialogue and backstairs

---

but still in the Tower at Christmas 1583; he moved to the Marshalsea on 12 February 1584, and was banished in September 1585.

[83]   Bombino, *Vita et Martyrium*, p. 165 (most of ch. 34 is missing in MS Tanner 329).

[84]   BL MS Lansdowne 33, fols 145–9. Mateer, 'William Byrd', pp. 29–30, studies the links between Byrd, the Petre family, John Bolt, Jane Wiseman, Lady Penelope Rich, the Pagets and the Earl of Worcester.

[85]   Elyot, *A very true report*, sig. B1v.

[86]   Elyot, *A very true report*, sig. B2r.

[87]   Elyot, *A very true report*, sig. A4v.

[88]   Bombino, *Vita et Martyrium*, p. 166: '*incertum vagumque maleficium*'; ABSI Collectanea P. I, fol. 156a: '*non n. certo sciebat ubi aliquis esset*'.

[89]   ABSI Collectanea P. I, 'Notae breves', fol. 156a.

intrigue. He had worked alongside Thomas Cowper, who had had left the Roper household to be the cook at Lyford Grange. Bombino devotes 10 chapters (one sixth of his biography) to the capture at Lyford Grange and the procession to the Tower (chapters 33 to 42), and chooses to end this long sequence with a discussion of his sources:

> It is the most assured authority of Fr: Parsons that I insist upon, who him selfe receivd the whole relation, from that man that was present in the very heat of the businesse, that selfe same man that was willed (as before I shewd) to accompany Eliotte; which long since he faythfully, & carefully sette downe in writing, & gave me those notes as guides, whilst I was writing this at Rome.[90]

While Elyot supplies vivid physical detail, in the convoluted prose of a paid informer, Mrs Yate's servant has given us, via Bombino, a vivid eyewitness account, which conveys all the fearful emotions of the search.

Elyot arrived at Lyford Grange, shouted his arrival to his old friend Cowper, the cook, who had the bridge over the moat lowered, and ran to greet Elyot warmly.[91] Elyot, pleading his need as a Catholic to participate in 'the fruit of the salvific host' (*salutaris hostiae fructu*) – an echo of the language of St Thomas Aquinas's hymn – asked if he could be admitted to the Mass which he was sure was taking place there.[92] Cowper told him to wait at the kitchen door, and raced upstairs to ask permission of the mistress of the house. The kitchen chimney is still visible at Lyford (Figure 7.1), and that side of the house is less altered than the two remaining wings. Mrs Yate sensed danger: 'Honest cooke, wee must walke warily; thou knowst well what a treasure we have in our house'; but the cook, 'solemnely assuring her that the man was very well knowen to him, and that without any danger he might be admitted, and that he was so approved a good Catholic', Mistress Yate finally 'bids him, admitte him'.[93] The cook, 'leading him in by the hand, in a great jolity', now told Elyot how fortunate he was, since he would 'heare Campian both say Mass and preach', and Elyot 'shewd such signes of unusuall joy, both in voyce & countenance' which 'were currently taken for evident signes of piety and devotion'.[94] Elyot pretended that he had just remembered some important business, excused himself and returned to his companion to fetch the Queen's commission. His plan was, in the name of the Queen, to arrest Campion in the middle of Mass or preaching. After he had tucked the commission into his chest, he returned 'to the secret chapell of the house' (*arcana aedium*).[95] Elyot takes up the story:

---

[90] Bombino, *Vita et Martyrium*, pp. 182–3; Bodl. MS Tanner 329, fol. 70v.

[91] Bombino, *Vita et Martyrium*, p. 167; Bodl. MS Tanner 328, fol. 62r.

[92] Bombino, *Vita et Martyrium*, p. 167; Bodl. MS Tanner 328, fol. 62r.

[93] Bombino, *Vita et Martyrium*, p. 168; Bodl. MS Tanner 329, fol. 62v.

[94] Bombino, *Vita et Martyrium*, p. 169; Bodl. MS Tanner 329, fol. 62v.

[95] Bombino, *Vita et Martyrium*, p. 169; Bodl. MS Tanner 329, fol. 63r.

Figure 7.1   Lyford Grange, from the kitchen side, where George Elyot entered.
Photograph by the author.

And so perforce there was no remedie but stay wee must, and having lighted
from horsebacke, and being by him brought into the house, and so into the
buttery, and there caused to drink: presently after, the said Cooke came and
whispered with mee, and asked whether my friende (meaning the said Jenckins)
were within the Church or not, therein meaning whether he were a papist or no,
to which I answered, he was not, but yet (said I) hee is a verie honest man and
one that wisheth well that way. Then saide the Cooke to mee will you goe up, by
which speeche, I knewe hee woulde bring mee to a Masse, and I answered him,
and saide, yea for Gods sake, that let mee doe, for seeing I must needes tarry,
let mee take some thing with mee that is good. And so wee left Jenckins in the
Buttery, and I was brought by the Cooke through the hall, the dining Parlour, and
two or three other odde roomes, and then into a faire large chamber, where there
was at the same instant one Priest called *Satwell* [Thomas Ford] saying Masse,
two other Priestes kneeling by, whereof one was *Campion*, and the other called
Peters alias Collington, three Nunnes, and xxxvii [37] other people.[96]

---

[96]   Elyot, *A very true report*, sig. B2v–B3r.

Elyot's account gives us some idea of how Catholic households were organized. Bombino adds that Campion had just finished hearing confessions and had come in to vest for Mass.[97]

From the moment Elyot gained access to the room, Campion's fate was sealed. Persons adds some interesting details apparently supplied by the servant whom Mistress Yate had allocated as a guide to Elyot. His picture of Elyot as a highly erratic, disturbed individual, makes the drama of all that followed even more painful. His volatile personality is confirmed by Bombino, who heads his chapter, 'George Elyot sets out from London to the shires to track down martyrs, driven by the furies of his own crimes'.[98] Campion's sermon blended the text of that Sunday, the ninth after Pentecost, from 'Luc. 19':41–7, where Jesus, vividly aware that his own death is to come soon, laments the obduracy of Jerusalem (here identified with England), and weeps over it, with another passage where Jesus would 'have gathered' the mistaken children of Israel 'as the bird doth her brood under her wings', from Luke 13:34:

> *Jerusalem, Jerusalem, quae occidis prophetas*! Hierusalem, Hierusalem, which killeth the prophets! so movingly to all the audience, & expressing so great sense in him selfe, that afterward they that were present there affirmed they verily thought, no mortall man, to that day, ever heard the like. All the standers by shedde teares in abundance, especially when they saw, as it were, felte before their eyes, by the lively speeche of the preacher, the cruell image of their country, glutted, as a man may say, & yet not satiated, with holy mens blood.[99]

Campion clearly saw that he would soon be part of the catalogue of cruelty, but he also revealed his passionate desire for England to return to the old faith. The identification with Christ's entry into Jerusalem was now complete, the fruit of meditation of the last few months on the long road from Rome to Dover. Elyot's own account confirms this:

> When Satwell [Ford] had finished his Masse, then Campion hee inuested himselfe to say Masse, and so hee did, and at the ende thereof, made holy breade and deliuered it to the people there, to euery one some, togeather with holy water, whereof hee gaue to mee parte also. And then was there a chayre set in the chamber some thing beneath the Aulter, wherein the said Campion did sit downe, and there made a Sermon very nigh an houre long, the effect of his text being as I remember, *That Christe wept ouer Jerusualem, &c.* And so applied the same to this our Countrie of England, for that the Pope his authoritie and doctrine did not so floorishe heere as the saide *Campion* desired.[100]

---

[97]   Bombino, *Vita et Martyrium*, p. 169; Bodl. MS Tanner 329, fol. 63r.

[98]   Bombino, *Vita et Martyrium*, p. 166 (my translation).

[99]   ABSI Collectanea P. I, 156a; Bombino, *Vita et Martyrium*, p. 170; Bodl. MS Tanner 329, fol. 63r–v. The quotation is from an earlier passage, Luke 13:34.

[100]   Elyot, *A very true report*, sig. B2v–B3v.

Persons tells us that, as Campion feelingly described Christ's desire for Jerusalem's repentance, all wept, Elyot with the rest; Bombino presents this as an hypocritical contrast with his forthcoming dry-eyed contribution to that very wickedness, but adds that Elyot kept alternating between the desire to flee and, especially during the sermon, the impulse to arrest Campion on the spot.[101] He suggests he was restrained, perhaps by the size of the gathering, or by its solemnity or simply by consciousness of his own wickedness. Persons, in the 'Notae breves', says he was weeping because he was 'wondering whether he should convert, immediately arrest Campion or, like Judas, go out to fetch a magistrate. He chose the last of these options'.[102] Had Elyot tried to arrest Campion at Mass, there would have been a violent scene, Bombino asserts, because 'those Catholikes which were present, men & women of all degrees, whereof many of them were not alltogether of the discreetest in their zeale to Religion, & affection towards their Ghostly Father, would have torne him in pieces'.[103] Campion apparently preached for nearly an hour, the standard length for Catholic sermons, and Elyot stayed till the end.[104] When Mass was over, Elyot rushed off. The cook caught up with him and told him that 'it was not the use of the house to suffer any guestes, which came for the service of God, to depart away before dinner; goes about to detayne the man, but could not, hee seeming mightily distracted in mind, voyce & countenance, covering his desire of hasting away about his wicked project'.[105] Having caught sight of his intended victim at Mass, Elyot was keen to fetch the nearest Justice of the Peace.

Once everyone was seated for lunch, apparently in several rooms, Mistress Yate began to realize, as she looked into all the rooms, that Elyot was no longer there.[106] She asked the cook what had happened. Although Cowper reassured her, he himself was worried by Elyot's agitated departure. Bombino's account catches the full drama:

> Meanewhile Mrs Yates, with some of her kinswomen, [did] take an exact survey, of all the tables in severall roomes, where her guestes were at dinner. But her chiefest care was, over that stranger, which she suspected, & therefore sought to eye-out none more diligently, in all the company. But when shee saw he appeard not, and had notice by the cooke, that brought him in, of his suddayne departure, shee was greevously strooken in mind, mistrusting presently some false measure, yet, not to disturbe the company of her friendes, she kept the

---

[101] Bombino, *Vita et Martyrium*, p. 170; Bodl. MS Tanner 329, fol. 63v.

[102] ABSI Collectanea P. I, fol. 156a: '*Quomodo admissus est ad missam et concionem P. Campiani. qua aestuatione animi fluctuabat, si converteretur vel si statim caperet, vel si ut Iudas exiret ad magistratus et elegit posterius*'.

[103] Bombino, *Vita et Martyrium*, pp. 170–71; Bodl. MS Tanner 329, fol. 63v.

[104] The standard length for Protestant sermons seems to have been two hours; Catholic sermons had to allow one hour for the Mass itself.

[105] Bombino, *Vita et Martyrium*, p. 170; Bodl. MS Tanner 329, fol. 64r–v.

[106] ABSI Collectanea P. I, fol. 156a.

matter closely. Never the lesse, to prevent the worst, she sette one to watch upon the highest tower of her house, least peradventure that whirle-wind might chaunce to raise a storme.[107]

About one o'clock, the lookout in the tower saw 50 armed horsemen approaching with a justice of the peace, and ran down to tell the mistress of the house.[108] The cook now realized what Elyot had done, and came 'armed and garded with a band of armed men' to try to kill him.[109] He was restrained 'by some good and pious men', but then tried to turn the sword on himself, so his friends had to dissuade him from damning his own soul.[110]

The Justice of the Peace was '*Maister Fettiplace*', most probably Humfrey Fettiplace of Buckland who, 'within one quarter of an houre', had 'put himselfe in readinesse with fortie or fiftie men very well weaponed'.[111] Bombino makes it clear that these were light horsemen of the trained band of Berkshire.[112] That Fettiplace was able to muster 50 horsemen so quickly was due to the success of the 1580 musters, in which the justices were given wide powers to prepare 'large numbers of armed men, organising them into bands under officers'.[113] The trained band of Berkshire, in November 1580, numbered 10 demi-lances and 171 light horse.[114] By a terrible irony, the light cavalry mustered to meet Sander's invasion force, would now support the arrest of Campion. Since Elyot had first arrived about eight in the morning, and both Thomas Ford and Campion had said Mass, and Campion preached for an hour, the liturgy cannot have finished much before noon. The short distance (three miles) to Buckland enabled Elyot to return with Justice Fettiplace within an hour.

The Fettiplaces and the Yates were related by marriage several times over, and clearly lived in each other's households.[115] Sir Francis Englefield, sheriff for

---

[107]   Bombino, *Vita et Martyrium*, pp. 171–2; Bodl. MS Tanner 329, fol. 64r–v.

[108]   ABSI Collectanea P. I, fol. 156a.

[109]   Bombino, *Vita et Martyrium*, p. 171; Bodl. MS Tanner 329, fol. 64r.

[110]   Bombino, *Vita et Martyrium*, p. 171; Bodl. MS Tanner 329, fol. 64r.

[111]   Elyot, *A very true report*, sig. B3v. Reynolds, *Campion and Parsons*, p. 122, says it was Edward Fettiplace of Denchworth, but offers no source. One local tradition favours Denchworth, but another proposes Besselsleigh, 8 miles away.

[112]   Bombino, *Vita et Martyrium*, p. 174 ('*constituta Barchiensis provinciae militia*'); Bodl. MS Tanner 329, fol. 65v, translates as 'the trayne band of Barkeshire'. Simpson, p. 315, talks of a *posse comitatus*.

[113]   Roger Vella Bonavita, 'The English Militia, 1558–1580: A Study in Relations between the Crown and the Commissioners of Musters', M.A. thesis in the Victoria University of Manchester, April 1972, p. 233.

[114]   Bonavita, 'The English Militia', pp. 300–309, citing *CSP Domestic*, 12/111/5.1, p. 664. It is clear that there was widespread resentment of the 'rates' applied by the commissioners, which were difficult to enforce against Catholic 'vagrants' who crossed county borders to avoid recusancy charges.

[115]   Davidson, 'Catholicism in Oxfordshire', p. 137.

Oxfordshire and Berkshire till his exile in 1559, and protector of the Bridgettine community in Flanders, had been married to Katherine Fettiplace until her death, at Compton Beauchamp, eight miles away, in 1579.[116] In the recusant return for 1577, when John Yate was still alive, Buckland Manor housed not only the older Mrs Yate, and their daughters and son Thomas, but 'Peter and Humfrey Phetiplace', none of whom 'Come to the Churche nor receive the Communion'.[117] In the Pipe Rolls, 22–3 Eliz. (1582), Francis Yate and his wife Jane of Lyford were convicted as recusants alongside Edward Keynes and his wife Katherine, of Hampstead Norris, Berks and Compton Pauncefoot, Somerset; in 1588, the recusant returns record Humfrey Fettiplace of Buckland and Dorothy, wife of Robert Fettiplace of Buckland, alongside Jane, wife of Edward Yate of Buckland.[118] The tensions between Justice Fettiplace, who was clearly trying *not* to find anyone, and the pathologically disturbed pursuivant, Elyot, must have been severe, even before they erupted into the open at the end of the day. Elyot continues:

> Aboutes one of the clocke in the afternoone of the same day, before wee knocked at the gates (which was then as before continually accustomed to bee fast shut, the house being moted rounde about, within which Mote was great store of fruite trees and other trees, with thicke hedge rowes, so that the danger for feare of loosing of the saide *Campion* and his associates was the more doubted). Wee beset the house with our men rounde about without the Mote in the best sorte wee coulde devise, and then knocked at the gates, and were presently heard and espied, but kept out by the space of halfe an houre (In which time as it seemeth, they had hidden Campion, and the other two priests in a very secrete place within the saide house, and had made reasonable purveiance for him as heereafter is mentioned).[119]

Bombino tells us that, when the look-out in the tower brought news to the mistress in the hall, 'some were strooken with feare, some ran hither & thither distractedly, other some stood in a helplesse manner, pitifully weeping & wringing their handes'.[120] Campion immediately offered to free the house of further trouble by handing himself over to the magistrate, but they 'all drenchd in teares, lay hold of him; & cry out; Deare Father, it is not one mans perill alone but the spirit & life of us all dependes upon your safety'.[121] The priests and 'all the churche stuffe likewise' (including chalices, vestments and habits), were bundled into a hiding hole.[122] Mistress Yate finally opened the gate:

[116]   *ODNB*, 'Sir Francis Englefield' (1522–96), by A.J. Loomie.
[117]   CRS 22, p. 85.
[118]   'Berkshire Recusants', Downside Library ms., acc. no. 85313.
[119]   Elyot, *A very true report*, sig. B4r.
[120]   Bombino, *Vita et Martyrium*, p. 172; Bodl. MS Tanner 329, fol. 64v.
[121]   Bombino, *Vita et Martyrium*, p. 172; Bodl. MS Tanner 329, fols 64v–65r.
[122]   Bombino, *Vita et Martyrium*, p. 173; Bodl. MS Tanner 329, fol. 65r.

> and then they let us into the house, where came presently to our sightes mystrys *Yates*, the goodwife of the house, five Gentlemen, one Gentlewoman, & three Nunnes, (the Nunnes being then dignified in Gentlewomans apparell not like unto that they hearde Masse in).[123]

Mistress Yate emerges as the heroine of this story. She and the nuns, Elyot tells us, denied that they had been at Mass. Elyot saw three nuns in their habits at Mass, and two, Sister Juliana Harman and Sister Catherine Kingsmill, he was able to identify, so they were arrested, and thrown into Reading gaol, where they still were a year later; as for the third, Elyot's marginal gloss simply says: 'One Nunne got away in country maides apparell'.[124] The letter to 'the Sheriffe of the countie of Berkes' from the Privy Council on 26 July 'touching the women latelie apprehended in the house of Mistress Yate in that shire, and committed to his charge' requires him 'to geve order that Mrs Yate remaine in the common gaole untill the next Sessions', and 'to take bandes with good sureties in good summes to her Majesties use of Gillian Harman, Katherin Kingesmill, and the wiffe of Edward Keynes (if they can putt in anie) for their forth cominge appearaunce at the said next Sessions, and theruppon to sett them at libertie, or els detaine them in prison still'.[125]

Elyot and Jenkins, 'her Maiesties messenger', began searching the house, 'where' (he says) 'wee founde many secrete corners, continuing the search (although with no small toyle) in the Orchardes, hedges, and ditches, within the Mote and divers other places'.[126] Where Elyot before 'came creeping, like an humble suppliant unto the altar', he now 'peept into and ransackd every corner'.[127] Although they failed to find Campion and the other two priests, Ford and Colleton, they did find Edward Yate of Buckland, and two other 'countriemen', John Mansfield and William Weblyn, 'fast locked togeather in a pidgeon house'.[128]

The tension between the search party and the pursuivants, Elyot and Jenkins, was extreme. The young men of Berkshire's trained band were 'used to live peacefully at their owne homes', and 'nothing trayned in such wicked service'.[129] Weary with turning everything upside down, they gave up; even Elyot agreed it was fruitless.[130] Before they left, the 'captaynes & officers', presented themselves to Mrs Yate, and begged pardon for 'this their needlesse vexation'; 'an upstart captayne', they explained, 'this base conditioned fellow', had 'seduced them', and

---

[123]   Elyot, *A very true report*, sigs B4r–C1r.

[124]   Elyot, *A very true report*, sig. B4r–v.

[125]   *APC, 1581–1582*, p. 136.

[126]   Elyot, *A very true report*, sig. C1r.

[127]   Bombino, *Vita et Martyrium*, p. 173; Bodl. MS Tanner 329, fol. 65r.

[128]   Elyot, *A very true report*, sig. C1r. At the end, sig. C4r, Elyot lists 'Iohn Maunsfielde' and 'William Weblyn' as 'Husbandmen and neighbours'. Simpson, p. 320, describes Mansfield and Webley as 'yeomen'; Waugh, *Edmund Campion*, p. 157, calls them 'two yokels'.

[129]   Bombino, *Vita et Martyrium*, p. 174; Bodl. MS Tanner 329, fol. 65v.

[130]   ABSI Collectanea P. I, fol. 156a.

'it went much against their mindes to be any way assistant to such a perfideous rogue'.[131]

Mrs Yate, eager only to have them all out of the house, willingly granted them pardon in the most fulsome terms she could muster. 'Full of indignation' they led the humiliated and volatile Elyot outside. They had apparently crossed the bridge, when some of the young cavaliers, now free from the restraint of the house, began 'to deride and revile' Elyot for leading them on this wild goose chase.[132] The light horse came from the best families of Oxfordshire and Berkshire, which had close ties to the Yates and, unwisely, they now treated Elyot with the contempt they felt he deserved:

> When some of the officers had mounted their horses, and had began to mock and berate Elyot for this wasted work, he, like a demon, ran in fury against them and threatened that he would accuse them before the Queen for not searching diligently.[133]

As the officers continued to 'revile and deride' him, and challenged Elyot to say what more they could have done, the cornered Elyot replied, 'Come on, my doughty searchers (sayd hee) what wall did any one of you beat down?'[134] The captain retorted that he had no warrant for smashing walls. Elyot replied that *he* did, and pulled out the Queen's warrant from his chest, and began to read aloud; 'a young man', coming up behind him and looking over his shoulder, saw he was making up the text. It is not clear, Bombino says, whether the officers, suspecting fraud, sent the young man or whether he did this on his own account.[135] Elyot ordered this man to be arrested 'as a champion of the Jesuites'; the men were struck dumb, so Elyot 'puffed up with pride' ordered them back to conduct a more thorough search.[136] The wording of the royal warrant did in fact give the bearer authority over magistrates, but his immediate capitulation suggests that Fettiplace felt vulnerable to the charge that he had done too little. The Berkshire light horse now trooped back into the house, a disconsolate band.

Within the house, there had been 'marvellous rejoicing'.[137] The priests had come out of their hiding-hole, and the household was giving thanks to God for their unexpected escape, with mutual congratulations and much embracing. They had closed the doors, put up the small drawbridge and were returning to normal, when terrified messengers announced the soldiers were coming back again. Panic returned. While Campion showed composure in his face, words and demeanour,

---

[131]   Bombino, *Vita et Martyrium*, p. 174; Bodl. MS Tanner 329, fol. 65v.

[132]   Bombino, *Vita et Martyrium*, p. 174; Bodl. MS Tanner 329, fol. 65v.

[133]   ABSI Collectanea P. I, fol. 156b.

[134]   Bombino, *Vita et Martyrium*, p. 175 (*egregii quaesitores*); Bodl. MS Tanner 329, fols 65v–66r; see ABSI Collectanea P. I, fol. 156b.

[135]   Bombino, *Vita et Martyrium*, p. 176; Bodl. MS Tanner 329, fol. 66r.

[136]   Bombino, *Vita et Martyrium*, p. 176; Bodl. MS Tanner 329, fol. 66v.

[137]   ABSI Collectanea P. I, fol. 156b.

the rest 'fledde to their usuall refuges; the women to their teares, the priestes to their secret places', and the small household to 'their straggling up & downe'.[138] Mrs Yate now took charge, using her wits to do what she could to save Campion. More of an Esther than a Judith, she seems to have adopted a deliberate policy of theatrical distraction. She lay on her bed, sick, she claimed, in mind and body and summoned 'the captayne of the trayne band of Barkeshire', asking him why they should return to a house they had freed from suspicion if they were not intent on killing a woman already afflicted with sickness.[139] She acknowledged that God was punishing her sins, and, with studied irony, praised their 'goodly manhood' in gaining a cheap triumph by killing a woman; they would find that she would receive praise for enduring this 'scourge of almighty God'.[140] Bombino praises her as 'a woman of extraordinarie courage', who was able to act a part, 'shedding teares, & with her whole body turning discontentedly from the standers by'.[141] The embarrassed captain, moved by this superb performance, begged her not to blame the evil of this most wicked informer on him; he was obliged (he said) to obey the royal warrant, which had been handed to a complete madman (*hominem ultimae dementiae*), whose furies they could only avoid, not moderate.[142] He guaranteed, that if she chose any part of the house for her own peace and quiet, 'no souldier of his should come neare those roomes'.[143] It was now getting dark when, calmed with that announcement, Mrs Yate selected the part of the house where the priests were hiding. She was led with great 'reverence' to that part, and 'betooke her selfe to her bedde', while the rest of the house was being searched, and walls were prodded and broken down.[144] It was a bravura performance.

As the evening of Sunday drew in, Elyot sent for the High Sheriff of Berkshire, Humfrey Forster.[145] Elyot, having fallen out with Fettiplace, was apparently trying to find men to outrank him, but Forster, reputed to have strong Catholic sympathies, could not be found. Instead, Justice Edmund Wiseman, perhaps sent by Forster, arrived with a further 10 to 12 'very able men and well appointed'.[146]

Mistress Yate plied the militia, now completely exhausted by the search, with food and drink; after an hour or so, they 'layd them all soundly asleepe, here & there, wheresoever it chaunced to surprise them'.[147] The household servants pretended to be asleep so they could watch all the movements of the soldiers.[148]

---

[138] Bombino, *Vita et Martyrium*, p. 176; Bodl. MS Tanner 329, fols 66v–67r.

[139] Bombino, *Vita et Martyrium*, p. 176; Bodl. MS Tanner 329, fol. 67r.

[140] Bombino, *Vita et Martyrium*, p. 176; Bodl. MS Tanner 329, fol. 67r.

[141] Bombino, *Vita et Martyrium*, p. 177; Bodl. MS Tanner 329, fol. 67r.

[142] Bombino, *Vita et Martyrium*, p. 177 (my translation).

[143] Bombino, *Vita et Martyrium*, p. 177; Bodl. MS Tanner 329, fol. 67v.

[144] Bombino, *Vita et Martyrium*, p. 177; Bodl. MS Tanner 329, fol. 67v.

[145] *Vice-Comitis* is usually translated as High Sheriff, but Bodl. MS Tanner 329, fol. 71r calls Forster 'the Lieutenant of Barkeshire'.

[146] Elyot, *A very true report*, sig. C1r.

[147] Bombino, *Vita et Martyrium*, p. 178; Bodl. MS Tanner 329, fol. 67v.

[148] Bombino, *Vita et Martyrium*, p. 178; Bodl. MS Tanner 329, fol. 67v.

Plate 1   Panorama of London by William Smith, 1588, BL MS Sloane 2596, fol. 52. © The British Library Board.

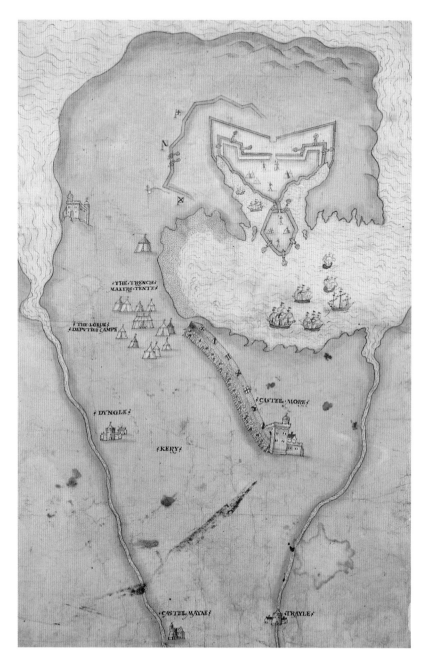

Plate 2   Smerwick Harbour, 1580: contemporary map, from collection of George Legge, Master General of the Ordnance, F2046. © The National Maritime Museum.

Plate 3   Henley-on-Thames (1698), by Ian Siberechts, b. Antwerp 1627, d. London 1703.
© The River and Rowing Museum, Henley.

Plate 4   Jesuits at the court of Akbar, the Mughal Emperor, in 1580, from *The Book of Akbar*. © The Trustees of the Chester Beatty Library, Dublin, In 03.263b.

Once it was established that the men were fast asleep, Mrs Yate asked Campion to come out of hiding, and speak words of comfort to them.[149] There were protests at this 'perillous piece of piety', but Mrs Yate won the day by saying it might be their last chance to 'speak together' and hear Campion.[150] 'So with this sweet kind of violence they were forced to obey her obstinate piety', the priests came out, and the household gathered round the bed, 'many being present & abundantly weeping'.[151] With mortal danger hanging over their heads, Campion gave them 'a short exhortation', and 'they tooke so deepley into their mindes joy & comfort, that forgetting allmost their dangers, they behavd them selves over freely for besieged persons'.[152] Indeed, one of the priests, on returning to the hiding place, 'stumbled grievously', as he had done on his way out; the soldiery were aroused and, forgetting their compact, began to search 'the secret corners' of Mrs Yate's room, but the priests had managed to hide themselves again.[153]

Early the next morning, Monday, 17 July, another local Justice of the Peace, Christopher Lydcote, arrived 'with a great sort of his owne men'.[154] There were now some 70 or more armed men in, or around, the house, but the soldiers were beginning to give up and leave, so Elyot's shame at treachery had now converted to manic behaviour. Filling the whole house with his 'roaring & clamour', he seemed 'rather a beast then a man'; not one part of his being was constant, even his eyes 'rowling, & glowing'.[155] The servant whom Mrs Yate had 'set over him, as as a spie' (and our source for this account) was now going down the stairs when Elyot pointed to a section that overhung the stairs (the very section where the priests were hiding), turned to him and asked, 'Nay, but for all this, yonder is a wall was never as yet stirred'; Elyot saw the servant 'confounded in countenance, & silent contrarie to his former custome'.[156] He repeated the very same words even more fiercely 'to see if he could gather out of his face, what was in his heart'.[157] The servant replied that there had surely been enough demolition and damage, and 'tooke him by the arme & gently sought to lead him away'. Elyot 'stood still', and replied that 'he would destroy the whole house if he list, & leave them nothing but ruines'.[158] There was complete silence. Those who knew the danger stood transfixed with silent dread; those unaware just stared at the fury of the man, as, with insane shouts, he asked for a crow-bar. The wall was only just held on by a plaster cornice: the informer, 'as if he had bene madde', drove the crow at this

---

[149]   ABSI Collectanea P. I, 'Notae breves', fol. 156b.

[150]   Bombino, *Vita et Martyrium*, p. 178; Bodl. MS Tanner 329, fol. 67v.

[151]   Bombino, *Vita et Martyrium*, p. 178; Bodl. MS Tanner 329, fol. 68r.

[152]   Bombino, *Vita et Martyrium*, pp. 178–9; Bodl. MS Tanner 329, fol. 68r.

[153]   Bombino, *Vita et Martyrium*, p. 179; Bodl. MS Tanner 329, fol. 68r–v.

[154]   Elyot, *A very true report*, sig. C1v.

[155]   Bombino, *Vita et Martyrium*, p. 180; Bodl. MS Tanner 329, fol. 68v.

[156]   Bombino, *Vita et Martyrium*, p. 180; Bodl. MS Tanner 329, fol. 69r.

[157]   Bombino, *Vita et Martyrium*, p. 180; Bodl. MS Tanner 329, fol. 69r.

[158]   Bombino, *Vita et Martyrium*, p. 180; Bodl. MS Tanner 329, fol. 69r.

with the maximum force.[159] Although Elyot omits any hint of his own irrational behaviour, his *rabies* (madness) is at the centre of Bombino's long account. Elyot could scarcely believe the miracle of his unexpected luck and stared, stupefied; the silence broken only by 'the servants of the house all groaning pittifully' and 'the confused murmuring' of the soldiers.[160] Revealed was the hiding place of the three priests lying on a narrow bed, their eyes, faces and hands, Bombino tells us, held in prayer.[161] One can only guess what had been the visceral fear of the three priests as they heard through the thin partition the demented cries of the pursuivant. In fact, they had each heard the others' confessions, and at that point, had imposed on each other the penance that for the stains of their sins they should, at this crisis, 'devoutly supplicate allmighty God in these words, *fiat voluntas tua*, thy will be done'.[162] The time was about 10 o'clock in the morning of Monday, 17 June 1581.[163]

Fettiplace and his men had done their best, but Elyot's manic cunning had won the day. Justice Fettiplace must have been trying hard not to catch the eye of Mrs Yate or the nuns (whom he probably knew) and not to notice anything suspicious. Elyot asked again for the High Sheriff to come, and this time Forster came quickly, and took the three priests into his custody.[164] Forster seems to have done all he could to mitigate the suffering of the priests: he had admired Campion since he was a child, and 'had bene eye-witnesse, how much hee swayed in the schooles at Oxford'.[165] Persons adds that 'this Forster came of very Catholic stock and acted more mildly'.[166] The Sheriff sent for instructions from the Privy Council, but treated his captives (whom Elyot lists) with great courtesy:

1 Edmond Campion Jesuite and Prieste
2 Thomas Satwell [Ford]
3 John Peters alias Collington }Priestes
4 William Fylbye
5 Edward Yates
6 Edward Keynes
                   } Gentlemen
7 Humfrey Keynes
8 John Cotton

---

[159]   Bombino, *Vita et Martyrium*, p. 181; Bodl. MS Tanner 329, fol. 69r.

[160]   Bombino, *Vita et Martyrium*, p. 181; Bodl. MS Tanner 329, fol. 69v.

[161]   Bombino, *Vita et Martyrium*, p. 181; Bodl. MS Tanner 329, fol. 69v. Elyot's account attributes the find to Jenkins, and omits the dramatic tell-tale signs on his minder's face, Elyot, *A very true report*, sig. C2r–v.

[162]   Bombino, *Vita et Martyrium*, p. 181; Bodl. MS Tanner 329, fol. 69v.

[163]   Elyot, *A very true report*, sig. C2r.

[164]   Elyot, *A very true report*, sig. C2v.

[165]   Bombino, *Vita et Martyrium*, p. 185; Bodl. MS Tanner 329, fol. 71v.

[166]   Bombino, *Vita et Martyrium*, p. 185 calls him 'Fredus Frosterus' (*sic*); Bodl. MS Tanner 329, fol. 71v, has been (mistakenly) revised to 'Fred^erike Foster'; in ABSI Collectanea P. I, fol. 156b, Persons calls him 'Humfredus Forster'. Humfrey Forster came from Aldermaston and Edmund Wiseman from Steventon.

9 William Ilsley
10 John Jacob
11 John Maunsfielde   } Husbandmen and neighbors therby
12 William Weblyn.[167]

The nuns, and Mrs Yate, were taken to Reading for trial. Six years later, on 12 February 1587, Edward Unton wrote to Walsingham that, searching for 'Arden and other prisoners, who had escaped, he found in the house of Francis Yeates of Lyfford, many popish relics and books, and arrested there two of his servants, John Doe and Richard Buckly'; both confessed to hearing mass and being reconciled to Rome when Campion was at Lyford.[168] Many, it seems, were at this mass, including all ranks in the household, and the repercussions lasted for several years.

On Thursday 20 June, the command came from the Council to escort the prisoners to London, so a huge party set out. The Sheriff and, it seems, the three Justices, were sympathetic to their charges, and treated their prisoners like princes in need of armed escort. With 60 armed men (horse and foot), 4 captive priests and 9 laymen, Forster led an extraordinary procession followed by Mrs Yate's servants 'weeping and wailing most pitifully'.[169] It is clear that Forster treated Campion with great respect and courtesy, and that Campion independently won the affection of his guard, so that 'they seemd to honour the prisonour, as if he had been their maister'.[170] Persons ascribes some of the qualities of a royal progress to the journey to London of the four arrested priests in the custody of a sympathetic Sheriff:

He [Forster] treated him kindly, and while they were passing such places and towns as Abingdon and Henley a great crowd of men came out to see him and some sought Campion's blessing while the guard was looking the other way. At Abingdon, the nearest town to Oxford, many scholars came out to see him as he passed, and he spoke to them with a cheerful countenance (*hilari vultu*) and said that he would preach to them if he were allowed to. There and at meals, Elyot complained that he was the only person that Campion did not look upon with cheerful countenance.[171]

Persons refers to the *Concertatio* for Campion's answer, but Dr Allen first related it:

God forgeve thee *Eliot* (said he) for so judging of me, and in token thereof I drinke to thee, yea and if thou wilt repent and come to confession I will absolve thee: but large penance thou must have.[172]

---

[167] Elyot, *A very true report*, sig. C4v.
[168] *CSP Domestic, 1581–1590*, 12/198/12 and 12.1, pp. 384–5.
[169] Bombino, *Vita et Martyrium*, p. 186; Bodl. MS Tanner 329, fol. 72r.
[170] Bombino, *Vita et Martyrium*, p. 186; Bodl. MS Tanner 329, fol. 72r.
[171] ABSI Collectanea P. I, fols 156b and 157a.
[172] Allen, *A Briefe Historie*, sig. d5v, 'Preface'; see [John Gibbons and John Fenn], *Concertatio ecclesiae Catholicae in Anglia Adversus Calvinopapistas et Puritanos* (Trier:

The first night of the journey from Lyford to the Tower was spent at Henley, a good day's ride. When they reached Henley, they were close both to Stonor Park, where Brinkley and the others were still manning the press, and to Henley Park, where Persons was sheltering: he risked only sending his unreliable servant, Robert Alfield, whom Campion recognized, and with 'a cheereful aspect of his eyes, & bowing of his head, saluted him, for unsafe it was to use any speech'.[173] Neither Hartley nor Brinkley could risk coming in disguise to Henley. Fr William Filby did, and, 'behaving himself somewhat unwarily', was arrested.[174] Elyot describes the night at the inn:

> Wee went that day to Henly upon Thames where wee lodged the night, & about midnight wee were put into great feare by reason of a very great crie and noyse that the saide *Fylbye* made in his sleepe, which wakened the moste that were that night in the house, and that in such sorte that every man almost, thought that some of the prisoners had beene broken from us and escaped, although there was in and aboute the same house a very strong watch appointed and charged for the same … it was founde no more, but that the saide *Fylbye* was in a dreame, and as he saide, he verily thought one to be ripping downe his bodie, and taking out his bowels.[175]

Filby was to suffer the gruesome fate he imagined in his proleptic dream, on 30 May 1582. The second night was spent at Colnbrook, then a major resting place, with 10 coaching inns.[176] This seems to have been the site of another large gathering of people of all classes, including sympathetic nobles, this time from London; the crowd was so great that there was scarce room for the large party of soldiers and prisoners; but even here, Campion managed to address his friends discreetly, by nods and signs, while apparently speaking to his keeper.[177] It was here that the Sheriff received instructions from the Privy Council for the last part of their journey through London. The prisoners were passing outside the jurisdiction

---

Henry Bock, 1588), ARCR I 525, sig. O3v (with minor differences). Bombino omits, as does Simpson. Reynolds, *Campion and Parsons*, pp. 125–6, paraphrases, but does not specify his source.

[173]   Bombino, *Vita et Martyrium*, p. 189; Bodl. MS Tanner 329, fol. 74r.

[174]   Bombino, *Vita et Martyrium*, p. 188; Bodl. MS Tanner 329, fol. 73v. Simpson, *Edmund Campion*, p. 321, follows Bombino, but adds, p. 539 n. 246, that there is a divergent tradition that Filby was 'taken at Lyford, and dreamed at Henley'.

[175]   Elyot, *A very true report*, sig. C3r.

[176]   Elyot, *A very true report*, sig. C3v. Allen, *A Briefe Historie*, sig. d5r, says that they were only two days in the custody of Mr Forster, and that an additional stop was made at Abingdon. Simpson, *Edmund Campion*, p. 322, follows Allen in asserting there were three stops, but Elyot in saying that Forster had to wait till the fourth day (Thursday the 20th) for instructions from the Council (p. 321). Elyot, the informant, is generally reliable on forensic detail. All agree that they entered London on Saturday, 22 July. For the 10 coaching inns recorded in Colnbrook in 1577, see National Archives, D–X 401–500.

[177]   Bombino, *Vita et Martyrium*, p. 190; Bodl. MS Tanner 329, fol. 74v.

of the Sheriff of Berkshire, and the escort was instructed to treat the prisoners differently. For the final stage in their journey, they were to have their elbows tied behind their back, their hands in front, and their legs tied under their horses' bellies. The clearest description of this last stage is to be found in Fr Persons's letter to Acquaviva, sent from London on 30 August 1581:

> By letters from the Council of State orders were given for him to be led through all the length of London, a matter of two to three miles, and to pass through the open squares, and finally to be put in the fortress which we here call the Tower. The order of the cavalcade was as follows: In front of everybody came the Sheriff of the County of Berkshire, for the reason that they were captured in that county, holding in his fist the white staff of Justice. Immediately after him came Fr. Campion, on a very tall horse, without cloak on his back, his arms tied behind his loins, and his feet confined by a rope beneath his horse's belly. On each side rode two lancers, close by his side guarding him lest he should speak to anyone or anyone to him. Around the hair of his head they encircled an inscription, written in great big capital letters: EDMUND CAMPION, THE SEDITIOUS JESUIT. The others followed after him, all likewise bound, but without the title: Fr. Campion was the only one to be honoured in that way. Behind them, in addition to a guard of 50 horsemen who accompanied him on the whole journey, came a large crowd of other people, some on horseback, some on foot, who had come out to witness the spectacle and did not desert the Father until his entrance into the fortress. A good many of these related to me with how fearless and glad a countenance Fr. Edmund and the others endured that ignominy. They wore at all times a look full of peace, and smiled also at times. It happened that they passed by the cross of Cheapside, that is to say the market place in the middle of which it was situated. It was the only one in all the kingdom which, on account of its great beauty, they had not knocked down; and as soon as Campion caught sight of it he made much account of it, inclining his head to it in sign of reverence, and as well as he could with his hands tied behind him, he made the sign of the cross. And in the same way as he did, so likewise did his companions who came after him. This being noticed by the populace, occasioned much wonder; nor were they on that account mocked at, except by a few.[178]

The image of the Virgin at the foot of this cross had just been defaced, on 21 June 1581, but the Cross, which Campion must have passed every day as a child, still retained its figure of Christ, and so 'in the best maner he could being pinyoned, he christianly made the signe of our Saviour upon his brest: and with like humilitie, deeply bent his bodie for reverence towardes Christs image there'.[179] Bombino tells us that the common people 'laught at this superstition, as they calld it, hissed, stampd and exclaymd against it, as the madde common people used to doe in

---

[178]   CRS 39, pp. 92–3. I have changed Fr Leo Hicks's translation of '*atterata*' from 'thrown down' to 'knocked down', and 'of the upper class' to 'noblemen'.

[179]   Allen, *A Briefe Historie*, sig. d6r. Stow, *Survay of London* (1603), p. 168, says that 40 crowns were offered as a reward for revealing the desecrator, but none was found.

shewing their dislike'.[180] Richard Stonley's diary confirms that 'this day report was made that one Campion was brought through Chepside & so to the Tower ... with a paper upon his hatte'.[181] Allen's account in *A Briefe Historie* is full of outrage that he was being treated, contrary to legal custom, as if he had been convicted.[182]

> And to take their further pleasure of him, order was geven, they should stay at Colbrucke a good peece of Friday and al night that thence they might bring him and his fellowes upon Saturday in triumph through the citie and the whole length thereof, specially through such places where by reason of the markets of that day, the greatest concourse of the common people was, whom in such matters they seeke of pollicie most to please, which was executed accordingly: all London almost beholding the spectacle, the simple gasing and with delite beholding the noveltie, the wise lamenting to see our country fallen to such barbarous iniquitie, as to abuse a sacred man so honorable in al nations for his lerning, and of so innocent a life.[183]

Allen is not slow to point out the parallel between this ritual humiliation by the 'Herodians' and that of Christ; Campion's journey is already being construed as a *via dolorosa*. Those with any sense of spiritual values, Bombino tells us, deplored 'their countries blindnesse' that it should humiliate men who were 'her chiefest lightes and ornaments' in this popular way.[184] Persons explains how an earlier version of this 'spectacle' was stage-managed by the authorities, when Cuthbert Mayne and several Catholic prisoners were moved from their prison in Launceston to London. With no saddle or bridle, their arms 'bounde fast behinde them' and the horses tied head to tail, they were led some 200 miles:

> When they came neare to anie citie or towne: one was appointed to ryde before, and to geve warning to the inhabitants, that there were cominge at hand, certein papists, foes to the Gospel, and enemies to the common weale. Uppon which notice, the people beinge sturred upp, dyd runne in flocks foorth of their houses in to the stretes, and welcome the commers with as spitefull contumelies as they could.[185]

The spectacle of public humiliation ordered for Campion's party was obviously modelled on this earlier crowd-pleaser. John Hart's 'Tower Diary', added to Rishton's edition of Sander's *De Origine Schismatis* in 1586, a report that Campion was brought to the Tower 'with great celebrity' (*magna celebritate*).[186]

---

[180]   Bombino, *Vita et Martyrium*, p. 193; Bodl. MS Tanner 329, fol. 76r.

[181]   Folger MS V.a.459, fol. 10v.

[182]   Allen, *A Briefe Historie*, sig. d5v.

[183]   Allen, *A Briefe Historie*, sig. d6r.

[184]   Bombino, *Vita et Martyrium*, p. 192; Bodl. MS Tanner 329, fol. 75v.

[185]   Persons, *An Epistle of the Persecution*, pp. 81–2.

[186]   Nicholas Sander, *De Origine ac Progressu Schismatis Anglicani, aucti per Edouardum Rishtonum* (Romae: Bonfadini, 1586), ARCR I. 973. [Additions by Persons, including John Hart's 'Diarium Rerum Gestarum in Turri Londinensi'], sig. I.i.7.

It is characteristic of Campion, that even as his mind must have been full of the horrors ahead, he chivalrously turned to the men who had escorted him from Berkshire, before being delivered into the charge of the Keeper, Sir Owen Hopton:

> At the gate of the fortress, or rather prison, Fr. Edmond turned round, and thanked those very kindly who had accompanied him, and prayed for their salvation with admirable courtesy. This action of such peaceful civility melted the hearts of a number of Catholics, mainly young noblemen, to such an extent that, being unable to keep back their tears at the spot, they returned to their homes, and preserving the memory of this outstanding man, then continued for many days afterwards to weep.[187]

Bombino says that Campion turned 'with a pleasing countenance' to the militia who had guarded him, forgiving those who had inflicted any 'contumely' on him, and asking God to 'enlighten your darknesse'; then he entered the Tower.[188]

There must have been a strange sense of release: the moment Campion had dreaded since he received the summons in Prague had at last arrived. All the accounts agree on this: that Campion constantly showed a grace of composure, a serenity of expression, throughout the journey, to the large crowds that turned out everywhere to see them, talk to him and hear him.[189] What he must have been most aware of, going into the Tower, was the horror that lay within. Persons and Campion (as we have seen) had talked for two days and nights of Briant's tortures. Bombino has a whole chapter contrasting two figures in the procession: the leading Oxford scholar 'with great grace of countenance' winning the affection of the crowds that everywhere followed them, being led to the Tower by George Elyot, whose 'shameful over-weening' drew universal opprobrium, and who was to boast of his exploit.[190] This really was 'captive-good attending Captaine ill'.[191]

The dramatic capture at Lyford Grange is one of the best-documented events in Campion's life. It is also a study in miniature of the complex relations between the Catholic community, the local judiciary and the Privy Council. It highlights the peculiar situation of the university of Oxford, where the attempt by the Privy Council to tighten its grip on Catholics had succeeded only in producing a diaspora of private halls and safe houses in the surrounding county. The strong Catholic character of Berkshire and south Oxfordshire blended into the underground world occupied by Catholic scholars. This system normally offered Catholics a measure of security, broken here only because Elyot was a *transfuga*: a traitor, who had very personal reasons for crossing the lines. The Privy Council, on 26 July 1581,

---

[187]   Bartoli, *Europeae Historiae Societatis Iesu*, p. 145 (my translation).

[188]   Bombino, *Vita et Martyrium*, p. 194; Bodl. MS Tanner 329, fol. 76v.

[189]   More, *Historia Missionis*, p. 108.

[190]   Bombino, *Vita et Martyrium*, pp. 186–7; Bodl. MS Tanner 329, fols 71r and 72v.

[191]   William Shakespeare, *Sonnets*, ed. Stephen Booth (New Haven: Yale University Press, 1977), Sonnet 66, p. [58]. This is the spelling and punctuation of the first edition, which was edited by Thomas Thorpe in 1609.

elected to pay the Sheriff of Berkshire the sum of £23 for 'bringinge upp of one Edmund Campion, a Jesuite, iij other Popishe priestes and viii other persones taken in that shire, and by their Lordships' order committed to the Tower'.[192] On 8 September 1581, on the Queen's authority, William Parker, the man who had supervised the state-sponsored kidnapping in Antwerp of Dr Story on 25 May 1571, signed a warrant to pay Elyot a reward of £100; the charges against him of murder, attempted rape and embezzlement were dropped.[193]

---

[192]   *APC, 1581–1582*, p. 136.

[193]   Sacred Congregation of Rites, *Cause of the Canonization of Blessed Martyrs John Houghton, Robert Lawrence, Augustine Webster, Richard Reynolds, John Stone, Cuthbert Mayne, John Paine, Edmund Campion, Alexander Briant, Ralph Sherwin, and Luke Kirby* (Rome: Vatican Polyglot Press, 1968), p. 195, citing TNA PRO, London: E. 404/124, Box 3. This colossal sum is not for the arrest of John Paine. For the kidnapping of Story, see Sander, *De Visibili Monarchia* (1571), p. 737. Sander was writing in June 1571 about an event that had happened at the end of the previous month.

Chapter 8
On the Rack

When Edmund Campion entered the Tower of London, he entered a realm where the 'sound of all speche, and mourning of the afflicted is shutt upp from the eares of them that are abroade'.[1] The paradoxes of this interior space are startling. Because torture was outside the common law, its practitioners required indemnity from the Privy Council. Campion has the distinction of having his name on four warrants for torture, more than any other person in English legal history.[2] The number of warrants indicates the level of anxiety about using, on such a renowned scholar, a procedure deplored by three of the great legal authorities of the period. In contrast to the horrors of modern torture, conducted by anonymous agents in extra-territorial space, the commissioners who presided over this aberrant procedure were senior figures in the established church and state.

Two contemporary pillars of English common law had condemned the practice: Sir John Fortescue, who wrote around 1460, was translated by Robert Mulcaster, and printed only in 1567, and Henry de Bracton, who wrote soon after Magna Carta, was printed in 1569; Tottell published both.[3] Campion knew the passage in Fortescue condemning the practice of torture, as we shall see. Although Sir Thomas Smith's condemnation of torture was not published till 1583, it circulated in manuscript from 1565.[4] Smith too asserted that torture was 'not used in England, it is taken for servile', and concluded that 'the people not accustomed to see such cruell torments, will pitie the person tormented, and abhorre the Prince and the Judges', since 'the nature of our nation is free, stout, haughty, prodigall of life and blood; but contumely, beating, servitude, and servile torment and punishment, it will not abide'.[5] There was a strong legal and cultural resistance to torture during the period when Campion was captive, which explains why he was able to win such immediate public sympathy when he exposed the government's use of it, and why the last warrant, on 29 October 1581, included the top law officers of the land

---

[1]   Persons, *An Epistle of the Persecution*, p. 87.

[2]   John H. Langbein, *Torture and the Law of Proof: Europe and England in the Ancien Regime* (Chicago and London: University of Chicago Press, 1977), p. 106.

[3]   Sir John Fortescue, *A Learned Commendation of the Politique Laws of Englande*, trans. Robert Mulcaster (London: Tottell, 1567), STC 11194 (Latin text in roman type, English text in black letter); Henry de Bracton, *De Legibus & Consuetudinibus Angliae* (London: Tottell, 1569), STC 3475.

[4]   Sir Thomas Smith, *De Republica Anglorum: A Discourse on the Commonwealth of England* (London: G. Seton, 1583), STC 22857.

[5]   Smith, *De Republica Anglorum*, pp. 85–6.

in an attempt to give legitimacy to this 'servile' practice, and to strengthen the immunity from prosecution.

While the Privy Council expected that his torture, which was repeated throughout August and at the end of October, would be 'kept from the knowleige of them that are withoute', Campion, both by his appearance and his words, ensured that it was disclosed at every public appearance: in his first disputation on 31 August, at his arraignment on 14 November and at his trial on 20 November 1581. The state itself, far from asserting its power over the subject's body and mind, ensured that what happened in that 'close and straite warde' became the most discussed, disputed and notorious part of Campion's life, even before the posthumous image of Campion on the rack, engraved by Verstegan and Cavallerii, accompanied the accounts, in poetry and prose, circulating in every court and capital of Europe throughout the 1580s.

After the Privy Council had tried to penetrate the interior space of Campion's heart, it sought to diminish his celebrity by questioning all who had sheltered him, and telling them he had confessed. This had the paradoxical effect of involving the Catholic nobility and gentry the length and breadth of the land, from London to York, from Oxfordshire to Lancashire, in Campion's long process leading to trial and execution. The Privy Council issued over fifty letters, instructing city and county officials to question those suspected of sheltering Campion and to restrict the movement of prominent papists.[6] On the last day of August, the Privy Council instructed the sheriffs of 14 counties and the cities of York and London to draw up lists of recusants.[7] 31 August was the day when they allowed Campion his first public disputation in the Tower: a *spectaculum* intended to humiliate him, at which he immediately raised the issue of his torture.[8] If the regime 'enabled Campion to play to the gallery', it also provided the theatre where he could win over a national audience.[9]

While the Council's commissioners tried to make Campion speak in the darkness of the torture chamber, the 'dolefull voice of the afflicted' (as Persons called it) evoked a stunned and sympathetic silence in the Tower chapel.[10] Nothing could better illustrate the incoherence of the Privy Council's policy than the fact that they chose to interrogate Campion secretly on the rack at least twice in August, then allowed him four public disputations from the end of August to the end of September, and finally tortured him even more severely at the end of October, before putting him on public trial in November.

Torture was officially used in England only during a brief period, from 1540 to 1640. Eighty-one warrants for torture issued by the Privy Council survive, of which 53 belong to the reign of Elizabeth, and most of those to the period after

---

[6]   See below.

[7]   *APC, 1581–1582*, 'Ultimo die Augusti', p. 189.

[8]   Bombino, *Vita et Martyrium*, pp. 225–7; Bodl. Tanner MS 329, fols 94r–95r.

[9]   Lake and Questier, 'Edmund Campion Affair', p. 621.

[10]   See Chapter 9.

1570, the year of the papal bull *Regnans in Excelsis*, and before 1610, when Sir Edward Coke declared torture 'directly against the common lawes of England'.[11] Most relate to what one might call state crime. We know (from diaries and other sources) that there were more cases of torture than the warrants.[12] The warrants are important because they reveal that the power to torture did not derive from the royal prerogative; instead, the warrants grant the commissioners a temporary share in the protection from prosecution enjoyed by the sovereign, because 'without immunity the use of torture would have exposed the torturer to liability for civil and criminal trespass'.[13]

The fact that most of those tortured were priests, many were Jesuits, and most cases occurred after the publication of *Regnans in excelsis* in 1570, suggests that insecurity over papal deposition, fear of invasion and fear of Catholic rebellion, lay behind the Privy Council's resort to a practice consistently described as having no place in the English judicial system by English jurists from Bracton in the thirteenth century to Lord Bingham in the twenty-first century.[14]

Under Roman law, the basis of law on the Continent, torture was a part of the legal process, because 'the most serious crimes carrying the death penalty could only be proved by the evidence of at least two eyewitnesses to the crime or by the accused's own confession', so there developed 'a jurisprudence of torture with its own rules, treatises, and learned doctors of law'.[15] The looser rules of evidence required for jury trials under common law in England meant that torture was a departure from normal practice, and 'English torture remained an exclusively executive function used only in cases where the Crown had a special interest'.[16] Torture was 'occasionally used as an engine of state, not of law'.[17] As Lord Bingham argued,

> Torture was not indeed practised so systematically in England as on the continent, but the fact that the most powerful court in the land sanctioned it, was bound sooner or later to have a demoralising effect upon all those who had prisoners in

---

[11]   Langbein, *Torture*, p. 81; Danny Friedman, 'Torture and the Common Law', *European Human Rights Law Review* 2 (2006), 180–99 (p. 187), gives the figure as 101, based on evidence, from other sources, of a further 20 cases; see Catherine Drinker Bowen, *The Lion and the Throne: The Life and Times of Sir Edward Coke* (Boston: Little Brown, 1956), pp. 91–2.

[12]   Elizabeth Hanson, *Discovering the Subject in Elizabethan England* (Cambridge: University Press, 1998), p. 156 n. 17.

[13]   Langbein, *Torture*, p. 130.

[14]   Langbein, *Torture*, pp. 81–121, lists the warrants.

[15]   Langbein, *Torture*, p. 1; Friedman, 'Torture and the Common Law', p. 182.

[16]   Hanson, *Discovering the Subject*, p. 27.

[17]   Sir William Blackstone, *Commentaries on the Laws of England*, 4 vols (Oxford: Clarendon Press, 1775), IV. 320–21.

their power. Once torture has become acclimatised in a legal system it spreads like an infectious disease.[18]

When Sir Edward Coke, who had participated in torture on a number of occasions, saw that the authority derived from the Crown, he changed his mind, and in his *Third Institute*, asserts that 'there is no law to warrant tortures in this land, nor can they be justified by any prescription lately brought in'.[19] If it was meant to boost the standing and security of the sovereign, it must be accounted a failure, since 'the use of torture in Elizabethan England was a brief departure from a legal tradition that abhorred and ridiculed the highly organized practice of judicial torture on the Continent'.[20] Jesuits and seminary priests constituted by far the largest group of victims, and Catholics were the most vocal critics of what they portrayed as a 'fraudulent method of discovery'.[21]

Elizabeth Hanson suggests that the Elizabethan government's recourse to the 'aberrant, quasi-juridical, quasi-political phenomenton' of torture in the case of Catholic priests suggests that the threat posed by Catholicism was relevant to the goals of torture as a means of investigation in a way that other threats to Elizabethan authority were not.[22] If the torture of Catholic priests was an aberration, the case of Edmund Campion was unique. He was the only victim to be granted four warrants, the only priest in the Elizabethan period to be granted public disputations and the only person whose torture the Privy Council felt obliged to justify in print, in three separate books, and in five different languages.

The darkened torture chamber, in which three Cambridge-educated lawyers confronted a leading Oxford scholar over a 'pain bank', is one of the most grotesque incongruities of this period (Figure 8.1). Spread over three months, the torture involved at least four, and probably five, separate sessions in which he was interrogated on the rack. In addition to the Lieutenant of the Tower, whom the warrants sometimes name, the warrants instruct three 'Commissioners'. Dr John Hammond (1542–90), civil lawyer, and brother-in-law of Alexander Nowell, Dean of St Paul's, is reputed to have drawn up the questions, and was later to censor Holinshed's *Chronicles*. Thomas Norton (1532–84), had translated Calvin and Peter Martyr (de Vermigli), tutored the children of Edward Seymour, Lord Protector, married Thomas Cranmer's daughter and after she died, her cousin, the daughter of Edmund Cranmer.[23] He also drafted some of the questions for the

---

[18]   Lord Bingham, in *A v Secretary of State for the Home Department*, [2005] UKHL 71; [2005] 3 W.L.R. 1249. He is relying on Sir William Holdsworth, *A History of English Law*, 17 vols (London: Methuen, 1922–72), V. 194, as Friedman, 'Torture and the Common Law', p. 191, points out.

[19]   Sir Edward Coke, *Third Institute*, pp. 34–5, cited by Hanson, *Discovering the Subject*, p. 28.

[20]   Hanson, *Discovering the Subject*, p. 24.

[21]   Hanson, *Discovering the Subject*, p. 26.

[22]   Hanson, *Discovering the Subject*, p. 30.

[23]   *ODNB*, 'Thomas Norton', by Marie Axton.

Figure 8.1 Campion on the rack. Giovanni Battista Cavallerii, *Ecclesiae Anglicanae Trophaea*, Rome, 1584, ARCR I. 944, plate 31. By permission of the Folger Shakespeare Library.

torture, and organized the disputations. He was singled out by Robert Persons as 'the Rackmaster', a charge that became so famous by 1582 that Norton felt he had to defend himself against it by claiming, disingenuously, that 'the doing was by the handes only of the quenes servauntes, and by Mr Lieutenant'.[24] Norton had obviously been too busy to read Fortescue, since Fortescue is adamant that a system where the judge presides over the torture of an innocent is 'the highe waye to the devill' since the wound in the mind of the judge 'wyll never be healed agayne specially while he remembreth the extremitie of the paines systeyned by the poore wretche in those miserable tourments'.[25] The third was Robert Beale (1541–1601), Clerk to the Privy Council and brother-in-law to Sir Francis Walsingham. He was named in the warrant of 30 July, 7 August and 14 August, but not 29 October 1581. Thanks to John Strype, we know that he later published 'seditious books' (now lost) which, according to Archbishop Whitgift 'condemneth without exception of any cause racking of grievous offenders as being cruel, barbarous, contrary to law and the liberty of English subjects'.[26]

The Privy Council gave specific instructions to the three named interrogators that Campion be asked (on an oath taken on a St Jerome translation of the Bible, 'for avoidinge of losse of time and also of further cavill') whether he accepts her Majesty as his lawful Queen, whether he has had any contact with Robert Rochford, S.J., a chaplain of Viscount Baltinglass (sheltered as we have seen by the Countess of Kildare), and then to put to him questions based on Dr Sander's *De Visibili Monarchia* and Richard Bristow's 'Motives'.[27] The common thread behind these questions is fear that Campion is executing the papal bull, is in touch with the rebels in Ireland, and is stirring rebellion among Catholic subjects here. The instructions on 7 August 1581 indicate that 'their Lordships' are not satisfied with his answers, and wish questions (which Robert Beale is 'to signifie unto them' verbally) to be put to him 'againe' that he might make 'a more plaine and direct answere'.[28] On 14 August 1581, the Council wrote again:

> to the Lieutenant of the Tower, Mr Doctor Hammond, Robert Beale or to anie 3 or 2 of them, thancking them for their paines taken in th'examinacions taken of Campion, and further requiring Mr Lieutenant to remove Filby and Jacob unto the prison of the Marshallsea; they are required to examine Campion, Peters [Colleton] and Forde, who refuse to confesse whether they have said anie Masses or no, whome they have confessed, and where Parsones and the other priestes be, touching those pointes, and to putt them in feare of the torture if they shall refuse to answer directly therto; and touching Keynes, Hildersey and Cotton, who have confessed the hearinge of a Masse at Mr Yate's & to understande from

24 *ODNB*, 'Thomas Norton', by Marie Axton, 27 March 1583, PRO, SP 12/152/72.

25 Fortescue, *A Learned Commendation*, fols 49r–50v.

26 John Strype, *Life and Acts of John Whitgift*, 3 vols (Oxford: University Press, 1822), I. 401–2, cited by Hanson, *Discovering the Subject*, p. 31.

27 *APC, 1581–1582*, pp. 144–5.

28 *APC, 1581–1582*, p. 165.

them what other persones were present then in their companie; touching Paine, seing there are vehement presumptions that he is guiltie of the fact wherewith he is charged &c, they are to proceade to the torture with him and to examine him theruppon; concerning the persones apprehended in the Ladie Stoner's house they are to examine them severallie upon the Interrogatories inclosed &c.[29]

On 29 October 1581, the warrant was addressed to a larger team, the Attorney General, Sir John Popham, and the Solicitor General, Sir Thomas Egerton, the Lieutenant of the Tower, Dr Hammond, Thomas Wilkes and Thomas Norton, and instructs them to examine Edmund Campion, Thomas Ford and others, to 'put them to the Rack &c., according to the minute remayning in the Councell Chest'.[30]

The warrants initially focused on political issues, but shifted quickly to interrogation on religious sacraments. While the power of the Council to reveal truth was limited, the power of the victims to proclaim their torture after the event was not. As Hanson argues, 'If the English authorities had the power to torture their victims to appropriate their speech, Catholics had the power to appropriate the scene of torture as a subject of representation in their pamphlets'.[31] As Persons says:

> Our adversaries bestowe no small diligence in this point, that the afflictions and torments which are there practiced within doores, be not brought to the knowledge of them that are withoute: but buried rather in darknesse, and cleane hyd in blynd and obscure dungeons … Yet at lengthe the truthe of the matter came to light when maister Campion himselfe did utter it in an open audience.[32]

During the first public disputation on 31 August 1581, in which Campion revealed that he had been tortured, Catholic sympathizers took advantage of their entrance into the Tower to smuggle out a letter by Alexander Briant with one of the most detailed accounts of torture by a victim to have emerged, which Persons published because he 'thought good to place yt woord by woord taken oute of the Authors owne handwriting'.[33] No such letter from Campion exists, so only his public comments provide evidence of what he felt on the rack.

The most notorious of the questions put to Campion was what he called the 'bloody question', devised by Burghley 'to try the truth or falsehood of any such seditious person'.[34] This was the question of which side, if a papal or Spanish force landed in England, the defendant would support? The bulk of the questions could fairly be said to relate to what Bacon called 'discovery', of where he had stayed.

---

[29]   *APC, 1581–1582*, p. 172.

[30]   *APC, 1581–1582*, p. 249.

[31]   Hanson, *Discovering the Subject*, p. 35.

[32]   Persons, *Epistle of the Persecution*, p. 87.

[33]   Persons, *An Epistle of the Persecution*, sig. L7v.

[34]   Hanson, *Discovering the Subject*, p. 39, citing Burghley, *Execution of Justice*, as mediated through Allen, *A Modest Defence*, p. 38,

This issue was brought into sharp focus by Campion's letter to Thomas Pounde, which was read at his trial:

> It greyveth me much to have offended the catholike cause so highlye as to confesse the names of those gentlemen and frends in whose houses I had beene entertayned, yet in this, I greatlye cheryshe & comforte my selfe that I never discovered anye secretes there declared, and that I will not come Racke come Rope.[35]

Here, Campion hints at the analogy between sacramental confession (which had been made a treasonable offence) and the confession being sought by the torturing interrogator. Campion admitted to the damage done by his confession of the names of his hosts, while defending his right never to disclose sacramental secrets. Campion's distinction was reinforced by Thomas Cottam's assertion that his rack masters were 'searchers of secrets', and had asked him 'what penance I was enjoined by my ghostly father' and further 'what my sins were for which that penance was enjoined me (a loathsome and unchristian question)'.[36] Cottam's confession completely refutes the alleged comment of Queen Elizabeth that she would not open windows into men's souls, the most probable source for which is a letter of Francis Bacon, who supervised at least five tortures.[37] Bacon goes to some length to justify torture on the grounds that it was not used to gather evidence or obtain confessions: 'By the laws of England no man is bound to accuse himself. In the highest cases of treason, torture is used for discovery and not for evidence'.[38] When Alexander Briant was tortured, the questions slide from the whereabouts of the press to sacramental confession: 'And because he would not confesse where he had seene F. Parsons, how he was mantained, where he had said Masse, and whose confessions he had hard: they caused needles to be thrust under his nailes'.[39]

The earliest account of Campion's tortures seems to be Allen's *A Briefe Historie*. Allen, relying on reports sent to him in Rheims, tells us what happened to Campion between 22 July, when he entered the Tower, and 12 November 1581, when he was arraigned. Allen accepts the Privy Council's view that the first racking, apparently on 31 July, contained 'no great rigor in the torment'.[40] It seems that, when they could not obtain what they wanted, they issued two warrants of 7 and 14 August 1581 for intense interrogation 'of relieving with money the Irish

---

[35]   BL MS Harley 6265, fol. 18r.

[36]   Hanson, *Discovering the Subject*, pp. 50–51, citing Allen's *A Modest Defence*, p. 72.

[37]   Langbein, *Torture*, pp. 117–25.

[38]   Hanson, *Discovering the Subject*, p. 37, quotes Bacon's defence from Spedding, *Letters and Life*, III. 114.

[39]   Allen, *A Briefe Historie*, sig. f5r.

[40]   See Philippa Berry, *Shakespeare's Feminine Endings: Disfiguring Death in the Tragedies* (Cambridge: University Press, 1999), p. 36, who argues that the precise dating in *Romeo and Juliet* relates to Campion's capture and torture.

rebells, of conspiring the Queenes death, invasion of the realme'[41] The repeat warrant of 7 August shows that the moment the torturer 'applied force to the victim's body (the point at which he broke with English legal traditions) marked the limit of his discursive hegemony'.[42] Allen describes how Campion then 'used to fal downe at the rackehowse dore upon both knees to commend him selfe to Gods mercie, and to crave his grace of patience in his paines', and 'when his body was so cruelly distent and streached upon the torment that he did hang by his armes and feete onely, he most charitably forgave his tormenters and the causers thereof, and thanked one of the rack men meekely for putting a stone under his backe bone'.[43] This cannot be dismissed simply as hagiography, especially as Allen adds, 'He said to the keeper after his last racking that it was a preface to death'.[44]

Most violent of all were the sessions on 31 October and 2 November 1581. For 'afterward upon his second or third racking he was so benommed, that he could neither take the cuppe and lifte it to his mouth, nor drawe of his cuffe at the barre'.[45] At his arraignment, on 14 November, Campion was unable to lift his hand.[46] If his appearance at the arraignment can be taken as evidence, the bandaged hands suggest that, as Bernadino de Mendoza, the Spanish Ambassador, concluded, nails were thrust between his nails and the quick.[47] The 'Tower Diary' for 31 October 1581 confirms that 'Edmund Campion was put to the rack for the third time after the disputations, and on this occasion the most seriously of all'.[48] A letter of Dr Allen of 14 December 1581 to Agazzari, confirms that 'There is talk of the torture of the rack given to Campion on the vigil of All Saints [31 October] and again on All Souls [2 November]'.[49] It seems that this last torture was precipitated by the letter Campion wrote to Thomas Pounde (quoted above), which was intercepted and read aloud at the trial. When the Queen's Counsel interpreted these 'secretes' to be treason, Campion made clear that he 'solemnlye tooke a vowe unto god never to disclose anie secretes confessed'.[50] The secular state's chamber of forced

---

[41]   Allen, *A Briefe Historie*, sig. d6v.

[42]   Hanson, *Discovering the Subject*, p. 34.

[43]   Allen, *A Briefe Historie*, sig. d6v.

[44]   Allen, *A Briefe Historie*, sig. d6v.

[45]   Allen, *A True, Sincere and modest Defence of English Catholiques that suffer for their Faith both at home and abrode: against a false, seditious and slaunderous Libel intituled THE EXECUTION OF JUSTICE IN ENGLAND* (Rouen: George Flinton, 1584), STC 373, ARCR II. 14, p. 15.

[46]   Allen, *A Briefe Historie*, sig. d8r.

[47]   *CSP Spanish, 1580–1586*, no. 119, 12 August 1581, p. 153.

[48]   The full title is: '*Rerum pro religione Catholica ac in Turri Londinensi gestarum, ab anno Domini 1580 ad annum usque 1585 Indiculus seu Diarum, ab eo observatum atque collectum qui toto illo tempore captivus interfuit*' [John Hart]: added to Nicholas Sander's *De Origine et Progressu Schismatis Anglicani* (Romae: Bonfadini, 1586), ARCR I. 973, 14 unnumbered pages, in double columns.

[49]   CRS 58, p. 36.

[50]   BL MS Harley 6265, fol. 18r.

confession under torture here met the limit of its power to penetrate the secrets of men's hearts as revealed in sacramental confession. Bombino describes the torture chamber as infernal, interior and secret:

> Far beneath the earth, a vast and wide cavern horrible to look at, foul in stench and squalid in its site, that is used for instruments of torture. It is so dark that the torturers need torches to operate their machines, and the interrogators need light to take down the words of the victims.[51]

Campion was in the Tower for four months from 22 July to 1 December. During this time, the policy of the Privy Council evolved, in part at least, as a result of political struggles within the Privy Council. The most important elements of the political context were the fear of the rebellion in Ireland spreading to England, and the complex marriage negotiations with the Duke of Anjou.[52] Neither Campion nor the authorities predicted how things would turn out. What has been read ever since the earliest accounts by Thomas Alfield and Cardinal Allen as a straightforward and unequal contest between a tyrannical Protestant state and victimized Catholic priests, leading to inevitable martyrdom, was actually a complex series of fits and starts. Only five days after Campion's execution, Norton, the Rackmaster, was arrested and thrown into the Tower, apparently for his opposition to the Anjou marriage.[53]

The affection that Campion had generated with his preaching ensured that the state's attempt to humiliate him merely enhanced his celebrity, and implicated Catholics the length of the country in harbouring him: it made him their champion in every possible sense. In what is more than an etymological accident, the manuscript account of the trial consistently writes his name as 'Champion'.[54] Only gradually did the state realize the scale of Campion's achievement, since his theological challenge also challenged the state's attempt to control popular opinion. Assuming that they had to win the argument only on the public stage in London, they underestimated the extent of Campion's fame across Europe. They paraded him through the streets with his hands tied behind his back: a clear breach of de Bracton's *De Legibus et Consuetudinibus Angliae* that a person who is 'to be produced before a justice, ought not to be produced with his hands tied', since 'it ought not to appear that he has been brought to undergo an expiation'.[55] By holding a show trial of seven priests and one layman on one day, they hoped to diminish

---

[51]   Bombino, *Vita et Martyrium*, p. 200.

[52]   McCoog, *Fashioning Jesuit Identity*, pp. 55–88; Worden, *Sound of Virtue*, pp. 41–3, 146–54, 88–114, 187, 285–6; *ODNB*, 'Sir Philip Sidney' (1554–1586), by Henry Woudhuysen. See Chapter 12, for the sustained ironic parallelism between executions and marriage negotiations in three contemporary chronicles.

[53]   Allen, *A Briefe Historie*, sig. c5v–6r.

[54]   It was an alternative spelling, and both are derived from *campianus*: the champion of the campus.

[55]   *De Legibus et Consuetudinibus Angliae*, II, fol. 385.

Campion by force of numbers, but found that Campion emerged as a superb defence counsel for them all. It became manifest that the crown's case rested on the evidence of paid spies and informers. The execution, planned as a Saturday spectacle of a representative Jesuit (Campion), a student of Dr Allen's college in Rheims (Alexander Briant) and a student of the English College in Rome (Ralph Sherwin), became the stage on which English injustice was presented to the world.

The most exciting recent contribution to Campion studies has encouraged us to see the state and Campion struggling for control of the narrative in the public sphere.[56] Campion's challenge to debate is part of a 'rehearsed' strategy, where the state eventually responds to Campion's 'effective propaganda war' in 'a disputatious game' devised by the Catholics, where 'the battle is continued 'through the medium of public performance' in the disputations, trial and execution.[57] Yet, Campion's determination to stay in the spiritual sphere of the sacraments of the mass and confession, accompanied by preaching addressed to the interior soul, aroused the intense fear of the state that its insistence on external conformity was being undermined from within. Sacramental confession, with its emphasis on reconciliation, became the focus for the fear that loyalty to the Queen could be eroded in secret whisperings. The struggle, therefore, was less for the public sphere than for the *private*. The state resorted to torture to try to penetrate the area that its public test of loyalty could not reveal.

The real battleground for control was not the theatre of the gallows, but the dark interior of the Tower, where the rack was used to gain access to the interior self, even to the interior knowledge gained in the sacrament of confession. At his trial, the prosecution could point only to external signs. So it was that Campion found himself bizarrely defending his disguises, and having to assert that he was 'not indicted upon the statute of Apparel'.[58] Campion, in his distinction between external reality and inner truth, sounds as if he is asserting that he has 'that within which passes show'.[59] It is not at all clear what knowledge the state gained by the torture, and Hanson talks of the 'epistemic instability of the investigation, the inconsistency between the kind of evidence it yielded and the truth it ultimately sought'.[60]

---

[56]   Peter Lake and Michael Questier, 'Puritans, Papists, and the "Public Sphere" in Early Modern England: The Edmund Campion Affair in Context', *The Journal of Modern History* 72 (September 2000), 587–627.

[57]   Peter Lake with Michael Questier, *The Antichrist's Lewd Hat: Protestants, Papists & Players in Post-Reformation England* (New Haven and London: Yale University Press, 2002), pp. 255–62 (p. 255).

[58]   BL Add. MS 6265, fol. 18r.

[59]   *Hamlet*, I.2.85–6.

[60]   Hanson, *Discovering the Subject*, p. 41.

'Treason, then, is a crime that occurs in the imagination', as Katharine Eisaman Maus has argued.[61] So, in his defence of the torture, *The Execution of Justice*, Lord Burghley argues that it does not matter that these men are not dressed like traitors and carry no weapons: 'neyther their tytles, nor their apparel doth make them traitours, but their traiterous secret motions & practices'.[62] For 'these disguised persons (called schollars or Priestes)', he argues, 'came hither by stealth in time of warre and rebellion' to be 'secret espialls & explorers in the Realme for the Pope'.[63] He ends his pamphlet by mocking the learning of 'these Seminaries, secret wanderers, and explorators in the darke'.[64]

This was not a debate stirred up by agitators in the public sphere, a 'dare' to which the government responded with violence, but an extra-juridical attempt to penetrate the mind of its subjects, to portray the external facts (like absence of weapons and apparel) as deceptive disguises of hidden treason. The torture in the cave so dark it requires torches for the torturers to operate the machine is not an incidental feature of the treatment of Campion and his fellow priests; it is not even a prelude to the theatre of the scaffold. Rather it is the space that dramatizes the limits of the state's power. Completely outside the tradition of English common law, only the answers on the papal power of deposition were used by the Crown in the courtroom. For the priests themselves, the space became the point at which their interior beliefs met the sharp needles of the state's power. Willing to yield names of his hosts, Campion held fast on the secrets of the confessional, and challenged the state's attempt to appropriate religious practice as a function of the state.

At the end of five months of torture, terror and arrests, nobles and gentry were brought before the Star Chamber, only to be released if they promised that 'they would hereafter duely and orderlie resorte unto the churche to heare Divine Service and sermons as shoulde become good and duetifull subjectes'.[65] After months in which the fundamental principles of the common law were flouted, the state reverted to accepting external conformity as an indication of loyalty. It was a high price to pay for a return to the *status quo ante*.

There is every indication that the practice of torture, so recently introduced into England, was as revolting to contemporaries as it is to us. Persons's *An Epistle of the Persecution* and Burghley's defence in *The Execution of Justice* indicated

---

[61]   Katharine Eisaman Maus, 'Proof and Consequences: Inwardness and Its Exposure in the English Renaissance', *Representations* 34 (Spring, 1991), 29–52 (p. 34).

[62]   *The Execution of Justice in England for maintenaunce of publique and Christian peace, against certeine stirrers of sedition, and adherents to the traytors and enemies of the Realme, without any persecution of them for questions of Religion, as is falsely reported and published by the fautors and fosterers of their treasons, xvii Decemb.* ([London:] 1583), STC 4902, sig. E2v.

[63]   *The Execution of Justice*, sigs E3v–E4r.

[64]   *The Execution of Justice*, sig. E4v (the last page).

[65]   *APC, 1581–1582*, pp. 261–2.

what a sensitive issue it was.[66] The irrefutable evidence is that the Privy Council tried to ensure that the torture practised in secret 'be not browght to the knowleige of them that are witheoute'.[67] The information about religious loyalties provided by the interrogations, far from producing a compliant conformity only produced a more determined recusancy and varying degrees of hypocrisy.

The racking of Campion and the violent torture of Alexander Briant remain disgraceful episodes in the history of English law and government.[68] The Queen's Counsel, Edmund Anderson, did not mention the torture at the trial, and recent studies have focused on the moments when Campion was allowed to speak in public: at the disputations, the trial and on the gallows. Yet the dark secrets of the torture chamber are at the heart of the issue; its horrors still haunt the corridors of the Campion narrative. For the Privy Council's resort to torture indicates not the extent of its power, but its limitation. In the end, it could not see into men's hearts, and its attempt to do so tarnished its reputation in Europe. While carrying out the torture in secret, it publicized it by interrogating perhaps as many as 500 Catholic gentry and nobility on whether they had 'entertained' Campion, as he had confessed, in their houses.

Under this repeated, excruciating pressure, an ordeal he had always dreaded, we know that Campion did reveal information, but not how much. Campion, in the letter to Pounde, and on the scaffold, confessed that he had given away the names of many of his hosts, 'desiring all them to forgeve him whome he had confessed upon the racke'.[69] When Allen reprints this with his *A Briefe Historie*, he adds a parenthetic explanation, '(for upon the commissioners othes, that no harme should come unto them, he uttered some persons with whom he had been)'.[70] Paolo Bombino also includes Campion's request for pardon, saying he desired forgiveness of 'all whom he had in any way injured'.[71] Persons, however, began a long tradition that treated the 'confessions' as part of the government's ministry of untruth:

> But they have yet an other stratageme or politike shyft, familiarlie acquainted in this tower: that is, to surmise and forge what they lust of the prisoner, & to publishe it to his shame, and for a trapp to beguile other Catholiques. The thing is evident, and hathe plenty of examples: but because I purpose to be breefe, I will touche but a few.

---

[66] See Chapter 12 for a full discussion of the controversy that followed Campion's death.

[67] Persons, *An Epistle of the Persecution*, p. 87.

[68] This is not to say that these were the only departures from humanity and justice in the sixteenth century. As Campion argued (see Chapter 9), his intention was not to 'compare' his treatment with any other.

[69] Alfield, *A true reporte*, sig. C1r–v; Allen, *A Briefe Historie*, sig. d1v, reprints this, with minor variations in spelling.

[70] Allen, *A Briefe Historie*, sig. d1v (Allen's emphasis).

[71] Bombino, *Vita et Martyrium*, pp. 290–91.

When maister Campian had bene afflicted with torments: it was reported that he had confessed what soever they had demaunded of him: specialie at whose howses, & in what places he had bene. And (to geve to the lie his right shape and perfection) it was further bruted abrode, that he had promised a recantation of I know not what. But that tale no man thowght to be probable: yet there were that doubted thereof, because the adversaries had so earnestlye affirmed it. For many gentlemen, and some of the nobilitie were called up to London, frome their owne howses, and charged with a supposed confession of maister Campian: And yet in verie truthe (as afterward it well appeared) he never yeelded one worde to his torments.[72]

Sir Thomas Tresham is, of course, one of the 'gentlemen' summoned to London, and his account of the examination ends with a characteristically forceful phrase:

and if Mr Campion or his like shoulde saye yt, as by reason of the untruth of the thinge I will never beleeve yt, yet am I to answere for the deedes of Sir Thomas Tresame and not for the wordes of Mr Campion: and therfore in his behalf I make no accounte what hee or any other shall saye of me, no not the least heare of my head: for he that pisseth cleare needeth not the phisicians helpe.[73]

In Tresham's account of the first disputation in the Tower, he records Campion as denying any confession:

Let any man (quoth Mr Campion) within this realme charge me with woorde or fact but concerninge conscience and religion, and I yelde toe determinacion/ wherunto was made no answere/ and then he shewed that his punishment was for that he would not bewraie the places and persons with whome he had conversed and dealt with and concerninge the Catholike cause alleaging an example of primitive Christians who choose rather to abide merterdome than that they wold yelde up the books which Catholike pastures [pastors] had given and distributed amonge them/ (much more said hee) I ought to suffer any thinge rather than to betraie the bodies of those that mynistered necessaries to supplie my lacke.[74]

Richard Simpson wisely said, 'There is no authentic account of what Campion said or did at this racking'.[75] Yet he follows Persons in trying to show that the government version is a forgery. At the centre of his argument is the fact that, during the first disputation, Campion said 'he might not betray his Catholic brethren, which were, as he said, the temples of the Holy Ghost'. The manuscript

---

[72]   *An Epistle of the Persecution*, pp. 88–9.

[73]   Bodl. MSS Eng. th. b. 1–2, II. 822. This page is facing an engraving of Tresham's coat of arms, tipped in (125 by 150 mms), and a space for another.

[74]   BL Add. MS 39828, fols 38r–41r (fol. 38v), printed in HMCR, 55, III. 8–16 (p. 9). The piece has recently been published by James V. Holleran, *A Jesuit Challenge: Edmund Campion's Debates in the Tower of London in 1581* (New York: Fordham University Press, 1999), pp. 82–93.

[75]   Simpson, p. 340.

version of this exchange I have put above. Simpson's argument is a strong one, that the rackmasters were all present at the disputation – Beale, Hammond, Hopton and Norton – and could easily have contradicted Campion.[76] While Evelyn Waugh follows Simpson in quoting this argument, and while he comes up with a formula that corresponds closely to Campion's own statements – 'Two things seem certain, that Campion told something and that he told very little' – he ignores the distinction that Campion made in what he revealed and concealed.[77] For he says later that 'Campion very rarely admitted to having performed any priestly office'.[78]

As Waugh argues, only now 'can we begin to pierce the subterranean gloom and guess at the atrocious secrets of the torture chamber'.[79] There is a clear account in a surviving manuscript of Lord Burghley, annotated in his own hand, of some of the interrogations.[80] While the state had many lists of Catholics, from which they could have concocted the searches that followed, the hunt for the books at Park Hall and the press at Stonor Park do suggest particular information.[81] It would have been hard to obtain this from any other source, as we see on 2 August, when the Privy Council instructs the Sheriff of the countie of Lancaster and others:

> requiringe them forthwithe, &c to repair unto the dwellinge houses of certaine persones in their Lordships letter mentioned, havinge ben harbourers of Edmonde Campion latelie sent from Rome contrarie to her Majesties Proclamacion, and to cause the said persones to be examined whether the said Campion hathe ben there or no, whether he said anie Masse there, together with such other particularities as they shall thincke meete to be enquired of; and further to cause the said houses to be searched for bookes and other supersitious stuffe, and especiallie the house of Richard Houghton, where it is said the said Campion left his bookes, and to enquire what is become of the said bookes, and also of Raffe Emerson, his man, and to understande from whence he cam thither, how he was accompanied, and whether he went, and what thinges the said Campion or Emerson caried thence.[82]

---

[76]   Simpson, p. 351.

[77]   Waugh, *Edmund Campion*, p. 174.

[78]   Waugh, *Edmund Campion*, p. 179.

[79]   Waugh, *Edmund Campion*, p. 166.

[80]   BL MS Lansdowne 30, fols 201r–202r.

[81]   See Kilroy, *Memory and Transcription*, pp. 126–32, and correspondence in the *TLS* (8 September and 1 December 2006), in response to John Bossy in the *TLS* (18 and 25 August, 2006), who argued that Campion had confessed the names of some hosts; I now think that he was right, and I was mistaken in following Tresham, Persons and Simpson on this matter.

[82]   *APC, 1581–1582*, pp. 148–9. The house of Richard Hoghton was Park Hall. See Chapter 12 for more on this.

More letters follow on 4 August 1581.[83] The first is to the Earl of Huntingdon to search 'such places in the countie of Ebor [Yorkshire] as are specified in their Lordships' letter unto him that 'Edmund Campion hath, upon his examination here taken, confessed that he hath bene at, and to apprehend the parties and to search their houses for bookes and other superstitious stuffe'. A second is to London Aldermen, 'Mr Alderman Martin, Mr Doctor Hammond and Mr Norton to enquire after one Nashe and one Eden, some times an attorney in Guild Hall, in whose houses Edmunde Campion hathe confessed that he was lodged at his being in London, and to examine them bothe touching the said Campion's beinge in their said houses, &c, what is become of Gilbert, which is said to have brought Campion unto them, and of Short, a priest, who resorted to the said Nashe's house, what other Jesuites or priests have ben harboured there, &c … '. A third is to Sir Walter Mildmay, Sir Henry Darcie and Sir Edmonde Montague, knightes, asking that:

> thei make their repaire uppon the sodaine unto the house of one Mr Price, in Huntingdonshire, whether Edmund Campion hath confessed that he appointed his man, Raffe Emersonn, which attended on him, to bring certaine bookes and papers which he left at the house of one Richard Houghton, in the countie of Lancaster, and that they cause the same house to be diligentlie and substantiallie searched for the said Emersonn, and such bookes and other supersititious stuffe as maie be founde there.[84]

More ominously, there is a fourth letter telling Sir Henrie Nevill and Raffe Warcoppe:

> to repaire unto the Ladie Stoner's house and to enter into the same, and there to make diligent searche and enquire for certain Latin bookes dispersed abroad in Oxford at the last commencement, which Edmund Campion uppon his examinacion hathe confessed to have ben there printed in a wood, and also for such other English bookes as of late have been published for the maintenance of Poperie, printed also there as it is thought by one Parsones, a Jesuite, and others; and further for the presse and other instrumentes of printinge, &c, thought also to be there remaininge, and to examine such persones as they shall finde in the house of their knowledge touchinge the said bookes and printinge, how many there were printed, and of what sortes, &c, what Masses to have ben there said, what reconciliations, &c., used, &c., and of their conformitie in Religion.[85]

That the information was coming out gradually suggests that Campion was being racked on successive days. On 6 August 1581, there is another letter instructing Sir Walter Mildmay:

---

[83]   *APC, 1581–1582*, pp. 150–54. Simpson, Downside MS 30 A, fols 60r–75r, copied out all the letters.

[84]   *APC, 1581–1582*, pp. 152–3.

[85]   *APC, 1581–1582*, p. 154.

to send for the Lord Vaux (at whose house Edmunde Campion hath uppon his examinacion confessed he hathe ben) and to examine him touchinge the said Campion's beinge there, or if one Parsones, or anie other Jesuite or priest ... he is to take the like course in takinge of th'examinacion of Sir Thomas Tresham and Mr [William] Griffith uppon the like pointes ... and to proceede in like sorte with Sir William Catesby'.[86]

On 7 August 1581, the Privy Council sent several letters to the Earl of Shrewsbury to search Mr Sachaverell's house in Derbyshire 'touching Campion the Jesuites beinge there', in Warwickshire, to Sir Fulke Greville, Sir Thomas Lucy and others to examine Sir William Catesby; in Buckinghamshire, to Sir Robert Drury, Lord Norris, Richard Fiennes and Anthony Cope, to examine Edward East of Bledlow, Mrs Penne of Penne, Lady Babington at Twyford, Mrs Pollard and Francis Morris: 'in whose houses the said Campion hathe also confessed that he hath ben'.[87] 'Mr. Griffin of South Mines in the countie of Middlesex' and 'Mrs Brideman (at whose house in Westminster Campion hathe confessed to have ben)' are also to be questioned.[88] This is the day when the commissioners are instructed to press Campion and 'his fellowes' to 'make a more plaine and directe answer'.[89]

A letter on 14 August 1581, 'to the Vicechancelour and Doctors of the Universitie of Oxford' highlights the special role of the the university:

three Masters of Artes, namelie one [Henry] Russell, [Justinian] Stubbes and [Edward] Yate, at the time of th'apprehending of Campion the Jesuite at the house of one Yate of Liforde in that shire, were then in the said house, forasmuch as their Lordships finde by experience that most of the Seminarie Priestes which at this present disturbe this Churche have ben heretofore schollers of that Universitie.[90]

Their lordships also complain that 'one Jacob, a musitian taken in Campion's companie', has been 'tolerated there manie yeres without goinge to churche and receavinge of the Sacramentes', and ask that 'diligent searche and enquirie to be made in all the Colledges and Houses of Learninge within that Universitie after such suspected persones in Religion'.[91] A further letter on that day instructs Thomas Pounde, formerly removed from the Marshalsea to 'some other place', to be brought to the charge of the Lieutenant of the Tower.[92] Equally, [William] Filby and John Jacob are to be taken from the Tower to the Marshalsea. Sir Jervis Clifton and Sir Thomas Stanhope are to go to the Pierrepoints' house, where Campion has confessed

---

[86]   *APC, 1581–1582*, pp. 155–6.
[87]   *APC, 1581–1582*, pp. 163–4.
[88]   *APC, 1581–1582*, p. 164.
[89]   *APC, 1581–1582*, p. 165.
[90]   *APC, 1581–1582*, p. 170.
[91]   *APC, 1581–1582*, p. 170.
[92]   *APC, 1581–1582*, p. 172.

to having spent 13 days last Christmast last, and search the house 'for bookes and other supersitious stuff and suspected persones', and to arrest the two Pierrepoint brothers and keep them from having any 'conference among them selves'.[93]

A further letter of 'xi' [probably xxi] August makes it clear Catesby has refused to swear that Campion has not been in his house, and another that Pounde is to be interrogated 'touching his acquaintance and dealinges with Jesuites, priestes and suspected persones &c', another to the Knight Marshal to receive (into the Marshalsea) the Stonor Park team: 'William Hartley, priest, John Harrys, John Harvey and John Tucker, printers, and to kepe them aparte close prisoners so they have no conference together or with anie others'.[94] All had been arrested when the press was seized, before 13 August, and brought to the Tower; only Compton yielded under the threat of torture.[95]

Robert Persons, who was lying low in Henley Park, the home of Francis Browne, avoided capture, and now escaped to Sussex, and 'almost by chance', to Michelgrove, the coastal house of William Shelley, and from there crossed to France before 21 August 1581, partly 'to printe some books which I had written in England or was in wryting, as the *Defence of the Censure*, the latin *Epistle of Persecution* and *The Book of Resolution* in the first edition all which were printed at Roan this winter'.[96] It is clear from his 'Autobiography' that Persons now saw publishing books as central to the mission, even if 'the capture and execution of Campion certainly shifted Persons's priorities from missionary to military strategy'.[97] One of the central figures of Catholic resistance, he founded seminaries at Valladolid (1589) and Seville (1592) in Spain, and made major contributions to political thought (including the debate over the succession) until his death in 1610.[98]

On 30 August 1581, the Privy Council wrote to the Earl of Derby and others involved in Lancashire, thanking them for information on Thomas Southworth, Richard Hoghton and Bartholomew Hesketh (all hosts of Campion), asking for them to try to arrest Haddocke of Lancaster and Randall his man, and

---

[93]   *APC, 1581–1582*, pp. 170–71.

[94]   *APC, 1581–1582*, p. 177. John Compton yielded as they entered the Tower, as the 'Tower Diary', added to *De Origine Schismatis* (1586), entry makes clear. Although the entry is recorded under the heading of 13 August, it is possible that they had been brought there earlier (*in turrim perducti fuerunt*).

[95]   *Concertatio* (1588), fol. 408v. See Chapter 8 for the letter of 4 August, ordering the search.

[96]   CRS 2, p. 30 (titles standardized): all were printed on 'Father Persons's press', by George L'Oyselet for George Flinton (see Bibliography); see CRS 4, pp. 26–7, for Persons's own accounts of his escape. For his letter of August 1581, see CRS 39, pp. 72–90, and pp. ix–lxxvi (p. xxxix), for the narrative of Leo Hicks, S.J.

[97]   Houliston, *Catholic Resistance*, p. 35, provides the best scholarly assessment of the way Persons's thought and action developed during this critical period.

[98]   [R. Doleman (pseud.)], *A Conference about the Next Succession to the Crowne of Ingland, divided into two partes. Where unto is added a genealogie* (Antwerp: Arnout Coniunx, 1594 [1595]), STC 19398, ARCR II. 167.

further, to re-examine Richard Houghton and his wiffe touching Campion's being there and Raffe Emerson, his man, and his bookes, and also touching the bookes sent downe by Rishton and dispersed in that shire; touching Mr Talbot and Mrs Allen, they shall perceave who they be by a parcell of Campion's examinacion taken sith the receipt of their letters and now sent unto them, wheruppon they are to proceade accordinge to the tenour of their Lordships' former letters.[99]

Another letter concerns Haddocke of Lancaster and his man Randall; a further letter is to Lord Norris and Anthony Cox,

adverstisinge them of the receipt of their letter of xixth of this present, together with th'examinacions of the Ladie Babington, Mrs Pollard and Mrs Morreys; touching the Ladie Babington, it is thought meete that she remaine in her house, according to the bande by them taken of her, untill her Majesties further pleasure shalbe knowen, since by Campion it has ben confessed sondrie times that he hath ben both in her house at Oxford and in the White Friers in London; the like order they are to take with Mrs Pollarde, save that they shall cause one Pollarde who (as it is said) shalbe her heire, and is servant unto th'Erle of Bedforde, to be sent unto their Lordships or bounde with good suerties, &c. for his appearance at a daie to be by them limited; concerning Francis Morrice, if he be retorned to his house, in case he shall not confesse the trothe of Campion's being there, they are required to sende him unto their Lordships under suer guarde of some trustie persones; the chest of Papisticall bookes nailed and sealed upp by them at the said Morreyces they are required to cause them to be viewed and an inventorie made of them all ...[100]

The same day there are letters to Mr Frauncis Hastinges and Mr Adrian Stokes about Mrs Beaumont who persists 'in her deniall of Campion's being with her' and 'the Massinge stuffe their Lordships thincke meete to be defaced'.[101] On the 31 August 1581, there are 16 letters directed to the Sheriffs, *Custos Rutulorum* or his deputy, and the Justices of the Peace of Somerset, Dorset, Devon, Oxfordshire, Wiltshire, Lincoln, Middlesex, Berkshire, Buckinghamshire, Southampton, Stafford, Sussex, Salop, Hereford, the Lord President of York and Lord Mayor of London, with a schedule of recusants, requiring the sheriffs to make sure the bonds are kept.[102]

On 5 September 1581, a letter to Sir Henrie Nevill is sent with instructions to allow Lady Stonor to return from the custody of her son, Francis, to her own house on certain bonds.[103] Another letter of the same date is addressed to Mr Alderman Martin, that Gervase Pierrepoint, shortly to become sheriff, hitherto confined to his house until he conforms, is now to be sent to the Marshalsea, and a letter is

---

[99]   *APC, 1581–1582*, pp. 184–5.
[100] *APC, 1581–1582*, pp. 186–7.
[101] *APC, 1581–1582*, p. 187.
[102] *APC, 1581–1582*, p. 189.
[103] *APC, 1581–1582*, pp. 189–90.

sent to the Knight Marshall for that purpose.[104] Thomas Roper of Orpington and Edward Griffin of Dingley are to be set at liberty, as they have entered into bonds of £500 to

> resort to the parish church, and not to admit unto his house or societie, or him self to haunte or resorte unto the house or societie of anie Massing Priest &c., or persones knowen to him to be Recusantes in not coming to the churche, and, further, not to kepe anie servauntes forbearing to resorte to the churche, &c.[105]

On 10 September 1581, John Pollard, in whose house Campion has confessed that he was present, gave a bond and agreed to appear before their Lordships.[106] A further letter of the same day thanks Lord Norris and others for seizing books at the house of William Moore of Haddon.[107] The allegiance of Justices of the Peace was not always certain: a letter of 12 September 1581 is sent to Mr Keynes, Justice of the Peace in Somerset, whose sons were in the 'Campion the Jesuites companie', and are now in the Tower; if he fails to send them money for their diet, they are to be thrown into the common gaol.[108] On 21 September, William Tresham, brother of Sir Thomas, swears that he never saw, or spake with Edmund Campion, prisoner in the Tower.[109] On 3 October, Edward Griffin of Dingley, Northamptonshire, is required to pay a bond of £500. On 9 October, the terms of bonds for Thomas Roper and Henry Pierrepoint are agreed.[110]

A revealing letter is sent on 15 October 1581 to the vice-chancellor and others on 'Popery in Oxfordshire':

> Whereas their Lordships are enformed that in divers howses and places within that countie of Oxon there are dailye sundrye meetinges and conventicles had of Papistes and Massing priestes to verie disordered purposes, in which houses and places are also to be found hidden vestementes and suche lyke tromperie for Massing in great quantities.[111]

The recipients of the letter are instructed to search all these houses, 'apprehend the persones and seas the tromperie'.[112] On 25 October 1581, a letter is sent to the Bishop of Hereford about 'sundrie persons ... excommunicated for not comyng to churche, who with many others notoriously addicted to Papistrie have their ordinary meetings and secret conventicles within that countie, where they are

---

[104]   *APC, 1581–1582*, p. 194.
[105]   *APC, 1581–1582*, p. 196.
[106]   *APC, 1581–1582*, p. 200.
[107]   *APC, 1581–1582*, p. 201.
[108]   *APC, 1581–1582*, pp. 205–6.
[109]   *APC, 1581–1582*, p. 216.
[110]   *APC, 1581–1582*, p. 225.
[111]   *APC, 1581–1582*, p. 234.
[112]   *APC, 1581–1582*, pp. 233–4.

resorted unto, as it is enformed, by certen Jesuites and Massing Priestes'.[113] On 28 October, Henry Pierrepoint and John Penne of Penne in the countie of Bucks, appeared before their Lordships as ordered by their bonds.[114] On 1 November, there are instructions for Henry Sachaverell and Walter Contrell, Derbyshire, to appear before the Star Chamber; on 5 November William Tyrrwhit, John Thimelby and Robert Tyrrwhit, who had appeared before their Lordships, were sent to the Fleet.[115] More sinister is the instruction for a number of named recipients to go to the Uxbridge house of William Griffith 'at Southland in the county of Bucks', to whose house 'one Morris has conducted Campion, Persons and others of that confederacie', and:

> with all diligence upon the receipt hereof to resorte unto his house and there to apprehend him, the said Gryffithe, his wyfe, and as many of his brethern as they shall fynde there, as also Morrys, and as many other as shalbe found within the howse as persones carying suspicion, and after their apprehensyon to search the howse for papers, bookes, letters and writinges concerning Campion and the rest, and forthwith to send the parties, &c.[116]

Further instructions follow on the same day to the Earl of Derby and others to take bonds from leading Lancashire recusants: Sir John Southworth, John Talbot, Bartholomew Hesketh, Richard Hoghton of Park Hall, John Rigmaiden, John Westby and Mrs Allen, mother unto Doctor Allen.[117] These are followed by instructions to Lord Norris to take bonds of Mr Morris and Mrs Pollard, and to the Earl of Shrewsbury to send up Langford and Ayre.[118] A letter is sent to Lord Norris to apprehend one Edmunds in Oxfordshire, 'which Edmundes is by Campion and others detected to have ben a receiver and harbourer of the said Campion and other of the Jesuites and Seminary Priestes'.[119]

Several members of the Privy Council were active on the Star Chamber, which began the long task of trying all those accused of harbouring Campion the day after his arraignment. On 15 November, as Stonley noted in his diary, they interviewed Lord Vaux, Sir Thomas Tresham and Sir William Catesby and nameless others; Stonley notes the following day that Vaux was fined the staggering sum of £1,000, the other two 1,000 marks each, while unnamed others were fined 500 marks each.[120]

---

[113]   *APC, 1581–1582*, p. 245.

[114]   *APC, 1581–1582*, pp. 247–8.

[115]   *APC, 1581–1582*, p. 252.

[116]   *APC, 1581–1582*, p. 253.

[117]   *APC, 1581–1582*, pp. 256–7. Richard Hoghton's house, Park Hall, is consistently mentioned as the place where Campion left his books. All those named were known recusants, listed in the 1577 recusancy return, CRS 22, pp. 69–73.

[118]   *APC, 1581–1582*, p. 257.

[119]   *APC, 1581–1582*, pp. 249–50.

[120]   Folger MS V.a.459, fols 30v–31r.

By 24 November, immediately after the trial of Campion, the Star Chamber started to arraign many of the rest of those arrested:

> Edward Griffyn of Dingley in the countie of Northampton, Henry Parpointe of Holbecke Woodhouse in the countye of Nottingham, and Henry Sachaverell of Hopwell in the countie of Darby, esquiers, and John Penne of Penne in the countie of Bucks, gentleman, detected by the confession of Edmund Campyon the Jesuite, lately convicted for Highe Treason, for receyving into their howses and harboring of the said Edmunde Campyon … confessed and acknowledged their offence … promising from this tyme forthe to be of good and duetifull behaviour towardes her Majestie and her estate, and that they would hereafter duely and orderlie resorte unto the churche to heare Divine Service and sermons as shoulde become good and duetifull subjectes.[121]

On 27 November, while Campion waited for his execution, the Privy Council was instructing Sir Henry Nevill and Radulphe Warcupp to allow Lady Stonor to move back to 'Stonar Howse', as long as she receives the parson of Henley, 'or some other learned man'; a process that seems risibly miscalculated to make any impact on the formidable Dame Cecily Stonor (née Chamberlayn).[122] Given her defence of recusancy a few years earlier, we might rather sympathize with the parson:

> I was born in such a time when Holy Mass was in great reverence, and was brought up in the same faith. In King Edward's time this reverence was neglected and reproved by such as governed. In Queen Mary's time it was restored with much applause, and now in this time it pleaseth the state to question them, as now they do with me, who continue in this Catholic profession. The State would have the several changes, which I have seen with mine eyes, good and laudable. Whether it can be so I refer to your Lordships' consideration. I hold me still to that wherein I was born and bred, and find nothing taught in it but great virtue and sanctity, and so by the grace of God, I will live and die in it.[123]

There are instructions that David Jenkins, the Queen's Messenger, is to receive 'the presse, letters and other implementes for printing' found in her house at the time of the arrest of Brinkley and the rest, as part of his reward.[124]

On 30 November and 6 December 1581, there are instructions for the examination and taking of bonds of three recusants from Yorkshire, John Rokeby, William Harrington and Thomas Grimston, and Mr Morris and Mrs Pollard from Oxfordshire. Mrs Pollard is to be 'conferred with by Dr James, Vicechauncelor of Oxon', while Morris, still refusing to aunswer is to be proceeded with.[125]

---

[121]   *APC, 1581–1582*, pp. 261–2.

[122]   *APC, 1581–1582*, p. 234.

[123]   Dom Julian Stonor, *Stonor*, p. 259.

[124]   *APC, 1581–1582*, pp. 264–5.

[125]   *APC, 1581–1582*, p. 267.

On 6 December, bonds are taken of Thomas Grimston of Grimston and William Harrington of Mount St John in the countie of Yorke, esquires,

> for their apparence before the Lord President and Justices of Assise at the next Assises at Yeorke, there in the open Courte to acknowledge and confesse their offence committted unto her Majestye in receaving into their howses and harboring of Edmunde Campion the Jesuite, latelie condemned and executed for Highe treason.[126]

It is reasonable to ask what these 50 letters from the Privy Council, from 2 August till the end of December to sheriffs and county officials instructing them to arrest nobility and gentry, have achieved. Many of the letters reveal how little control the Privy Council has. The letter to Lord Norris of 10 September makes clear that the Privy Council thinks that in Oxfordshire

> it is enformed that there are divers other Recusantes in coming to churche within that shire, in whose house it is vehementlie suspected there is much badde stuffe to be founde, they are required upon the sodaine at some convenient time to cause the houses of the persones whose names are noted on the backside of the said letter to be searched, and such priestes and others suspected persones there to be founde to commit to safe custodie as they shall see cause, and to take such supersitious stuffe as maie be there founde into their handes, and of their doinges to advertise their Lordships.[127]

Within days of Campion's execution, there are instructions to the city of Chester and the Gatehouse, which show the whole system is groaning under the numbers of recusants. The recusants in the Gatehouse on 4 December present a petition, saying that 'shutte from all charitie and relief in their wantes ... by their straight and close keeping, wanting open ayre, moste of them were fallen into sicknes, and thereby their lives endaungered'.[128] At Chester, the Privy Council suggests moving all the prisoners to Manchester, where there are fewer recusants, and they need only have one preacher, since the prison is 'more convenient for that purpose than the Castle of Chester'.[129]

For six months, the Privy Council has been implicating the entire Catholic population (not for political sedition, but for continuing to practise their proscribed religion) in the Campion interrogations. Judged on utilitarian grounds, the torture has been a massive waste of effort; as a propaganda exercise it has exposed England to contempt throughout the rest of Europe. By the end of the trial, not only Catholics, but the leading judges and lawyers in the land were appalled by the process.[130]

---

[126] *APC, 1581–1582*, p. 282.
[127] *APC, 1581–1582*, p. 201.
[128] *APC, 1581–1582*, p. 275.
[129] *APC, 1581–1582*, p. 279.
[130] See Chapter 10.

Michel Foucault has described public executions as 'the culmination of the ritual of investigation and the ceremony in which the sovereign triumphed'.[131] The torture revealed only the names of those with whom Campion had stayed, but failed to make him reveal the secrets of the confessional, clearly not matters of state. The round-up of Catholic gentry throughout the land, the rituals whereby they were induced to promise attendance at church, seems a pathetic end to such a violent assault by the state on its citizens. The promise of outward conformity did nothing to address the possibility that those promising to attend church might still harbour treasonable thoughts. While Campion, Sherwin, Briant, Ford, Johnson, Short, Filby, Kirby and Paine had, by the end of May 1582, all been publicly butchered, the Privy Council had handed to its opponents perfect propaganda material: the power to represent, in print and engraving, a chamber of state cruelty. There is absolutely no evidence that, as Stephen Alford argues, 'the instruments of the state' (the rack and propaganda), applied to a renowned European scholar, allowed 'Elizabeth to die in her bed'; far from being 'the politics of raw survival', the house searches and interrogation of Catholic gentry revealed no plots, but alienated many 'perfectly loyal English Catholics'.[132]

The reason why torture came to be practised so often in this period, and largely against Jesuit priests, stemmed from the insecurity of the monarch herself, prompted by the papal bull, which excommunicated her and exempted subjects from loyalty to her. The Jesuits and the seminary priests were seen as emissaries of a foreign deposing power, and torture was meant to wring out of them their secret desire to overthrow her. Dr Sander did pose a military threat, which the Crown was fully justified in meeting with force, but the use of torture merely confirmed what was already known: the existence of a vast network of residual loyalty to the Catholic sacraments. The disgraceful treatment of leading European scholars and Oxford fellows shows that the government felt it was losing the argument. Campion's premonitory preface to his *Rationes Decem* (and his original choice of title, *De haeresi desperata*) reflected his perception of how desperate the authorities were, and correctly predicted: 'the high priests prepare tortures not disputations' (*tormenta non scholas parant antistites*).[133]

It is not surprising that the story of Campion, from the time of his arrest to his death, contains credible anecdotes of the Queen trying to intervene, and of 'Monsieur', the Duc d'Alencon failing to intervene.[134] As Bernadino de Mendoza wrote to the King of Spain on 7 November:

---

[131]   Michel Foucault, *Discipline and Punish: The Birth of the Prison*, trans. Alan Sheridan (Harmondsworth, 1979), p. 48, cited by Anne Dillon, *The Construction of Martyrdom in the English Catholic Community 1535–1603* (Aldershot, UK and Burlington, VT: Ashgate, 2002), p. 73.

[132]   Alford, *The Watchers*, pp. 319–20.

[133]   Campion, *Rationes Decem*, STC 4536.5, sig. ¥2 (Praefatio).

[134]   For the context of the Anjou marriage negotiations, see Chapter 5.

It is a great consolation for the Catholics here, in their affliction, that your Majesty should favour them; as by your hand they hope that God will release them from this captivity. I tell them what your Majesty orders, and do my best to alleviate their sufferings. After having terribly tormented Campion of the Company of Jesus, they have 'indicted' him, as they call it here, as a traitor, with sixteen others, mostly clergymen. They are in prison, and it is to be feared they will be executed, Campion not yet having been brought to trial, as he is all dislocated and cannot move.[135]

The fear of invasion, the rebellion in Ireland, the presence of Anjou in London, and the fear of a return to 'popery' all conspired against the priests. Mendoza ends the same letter of 7 November with news that 'the Queen has again received confirmation from Ireland of the death of Dr Sander from illness.[136] Since Sander could not now be brought to London for exemplary punishment, someone had to pay the price for his rebellion.

In the end, this was a bitter personal struggle being fought by the Queen and her Councillors with the King of Spain, Pius V, Dr Allen, Dr Morton, Dr Sander and Sir Francis Englefield, who *were* harbouring plans for rebellion and invasion. The Privy Council was right to fear them; right to worry about the strength of catholicism in the university, city and county of Oxford, and to conclude 'that most of the Seminarie Priestes which at this present disturbe this Churche have ben heretofore schollers of that Universitie'.[137] They were wrong to attempt to solve it by the torture and execution of an Oxford scholar and many other priests against whom there was no evidence of treason. Campion's desire to debate the theological arguments in the two universities was far more rational than the *ad hoc* brutality authorized by the Privy Councillors of the Queen.

Persons summarizes the inconsistency of the Council's approach to Campion by indicating three distinct phases:

At first they began to tempt him with every kind of flattery, stated that he would soon be of their religion. Walsingham was publicly saying this in Paris to various Englishmen, and even swore solemnly that he knew it to be so. Then they stretched him with tortures, and then admitted him to disputations.[138]

We now know that the two main phases of torture ended in a final attempt at flattery.[139] During the first week in captivity, 22–29 July, Campion was offered

---

[135]   *CSP Spanish, 1580–1586*, no. 160, p. 210.

[136]   *CSP Spanish, 1580–1586*, no. 160, p. 211.

[137]   *APC, 1581–1582*, p. 170.

[138]   ABSI Collectanea P. I, fol. 157r ('Notae breves'): '*Principio omnibus blanditijs tentare eum coeperunt et affirmaverunt eum suae religionis fore: Walsinghamus publice dicebat Parisijs diversis Anglis, et iurabat solemniter se hoc scire. Deinde cruciatibus exercuerunt bis, deinde ad disputationes admiserunt*'.

[139]   Bombino, *Vita et Martyrium*, confirms this pattern with his heading for chapter 43, p. 194: 'Undaunted, he first endures their flatteries, and then their tortures' (*Blandientes primo, mox torquentes hostes invictus frangit*).

allurements to conform. Allen records in a letter that Campion was taken by boat, on the fourth day (26 July), 'from the Tower' to the house of the Earl of Leicester, and was interviewed in his presence by 'the Earl of Bedford and two Secretaries of State'.[140] The interview with Leicester is certainly confirmed by a letter that Lord Burghley wrote from Greenwich on 6 August 1581 to the Earl of Shrewsbury, but the location was not Leicester's house:

> I think your Lordship hath heard how Campion the Jesuit was taken in Berkshire at one Yate's house and 3 other massing priests with him. He is in the Tower and stiffly denieth to answer any question of moment, having been corrected before my Lord Chancellor [Sir Thomas Bromley], my Lord of Leicester and Mr Vice-Chamberlain [Sir Christopher Hatton] at my Lord Chancellor's house.[141]

This interview was, therefore, at York House, the Lord Chancellor's house, not Leicester House, and Allen mistook the persons present, since there were no Secretaries of State present.[142] Marion Colthorpe has successfully relocated this interview, and shown that the Queen was not present at this early attempt to win Campion by flattery.

The Queen herself *was* present, however, after the torture. Simpson (apparently influenced by Bartoli) was mistaken only in concluding that it was in July, and at Leicester's house.[143] Persons indicates that Cottam told Thomas Briscow that, on the night before the trial, Campion was led out under a blanket for a secret interview with the Queen herself.

> Cottam said that Campion said in public at the trial that he had spoken to the Queen, face to face, and said what he thought of the power of the Pope to excommunicate princes. This agrees with those authorities who say that on the same night that they led him out covered with a cloak of Hopton's servant he was led to the Queen and to Cecil (ask Orton) and that the Queen offered him a bishopric.[144]

Bombino has added autograph glosses to his own copy (deletions shown and additions in italics), now in the Jesuit archives in Rome, which refer to the night before the trial:

---

[140]   Allen, *Letters and Memorials*, p. 102.

[141]   Marion Colthorpe, 'Edmund Campion's Alleged Interview with Queen Elizabeth I in 1581', *Recusant History* 17 (1985), 197–200 (p. 198), citing G.D. Owen, ed., *Calendar of the Manuscripts ... at Longleat*, vol. V, *Talbot, Dudley and Devereux Papers (1980)*, p. 35.

[142]   Colthorpe, 'Campion's Alleged Interview', p. 198, shows that Thomas Wilson had died in June, and Walsingham had left for France.

[143]   Louise Imogen Guiney, *Blessed Edmund Campion* (London: Macdonald and Evans, 1908), includes a picture of the scene opposite page 144; Waugh, *Edmund Campion*, p. 171, perhaps inspired both by this and Simpson, imagined a scene in Leicester House, where that 'The vast red wig nodded acknowledgement'.

[144]   ABSI Collectanea P. I, fols 157v–58r (my translation).

Neque hoc subticuerim, inde famam increbuisse, nocte, quae priorem hanc praegressa est actionem deductum ad Reginam Campianum, ~~veste~~, *pallio famuli Odoni Hopton contectum*, ne quid turbaret inscios ~~famulitia~~, ea coram et Caecilio multa de religione disseruisse: iterumque ab ipsa Regina, *et Archiepiscopatus aliorum* praemiorum spe, frustra tentatum. ~~esse~~.

[Nor should I be silent about a story, whose strength has increased, that on the night before the trial Campion was led to the Queen, *covered with the cloak of a servant of Owen Hopton*, lest anything should disturb those who did not know what was going on, and that in her presence and that of Cecil, he talked much about religion, as did the Queen herself, and that he was tempted with the offer of *an archbishopric and the hope of other* prizes.][145]

Bombino received independent confirmation of Persons's note after the second edition was printed, perhaps from a prisoner released from the Tower where Briscow was kept for several years.[146] The Queen and Cecil made one final attempt, before the trial, and after her Council and its delegates had tortured him, to offer Campion an archbishopric. Nothing better illustrates the political instability of the monarchical republic and its established religion, than its inconsistent and illegal treatment of Campion. The state had stumbled erratically towards a conclusion that shamed the country's judicial system before its European neighbours.

Meanwhile, the rebellion in Ireland continued to spread, and pinned nearly 6,000 troops down till the end of 1582.[147] The English armies burnt all the crops and cattle, so that the garrison had to be victualled from Chester; the total costs for the war since August 1579 were estimated, on 30 September 1581, to be more than £200,000.[148] While Campion was being tortured again at the end of October, the Queen was complaining about the costs of the Irish rebellion being 'far greater than looked for'.[149] There was increasing disillusionment with that 'bloody man', Lord Grey, and 'great antipathy between Grey and the people of all sorts'.[150] Grey himself boasted that he had executed 1,500 'chief men and gentlemen … not accounting those of the meaner sort', between September 1580 and August 1582.[151]

Campion's torture was a legal anomaly which reflected a government terrified both of invasion and of rebellion by its Catholic nobility and gentry; Campion was used *in terrorem*, when the loyalties of English Catholics, *rebus sic stantibus*, remained uncertain.

---

[145] Bombino, *Vita et Martyrium* (1620, editio annotata), ARSI Vita I. 35, p. 266.

[146] Anstruther, *Seminary Priests*, I. 51.

[147] *CSP Ireland, 1574–1585*, 86/47, p. 327. On 1 November, the garrison was estimated as 5,644 men.

[148] *CSP Ireland, 1574–1585*, 85/45 and 68, pp. 319 and 321.

[149] *CSP Ireland, 1574–1585*, 85/43, p. 326.

[150] *CSP Ireland, 1574–1585*, 86/60, p. 328.

[151] Hammer, *Elizabeth's Wars*, p. 109.

Chapter 9
Upon the Publike Stage

After torturing him, the Privy Council brought Campion out of the dungeons, and began four public 'disputations' or 'conferences' in the Tower. The first, on 31 August 1581, was staged in the chapel of the Tower, appropriately named *St Peter ad Vincula* (St Peter in Chains), a room grand enough to accommodate Campion's fellow prisoners and a large audience. Ostensibly in answer to Campion's request for a disputation, this was more of a popular trial by academic ordeal. Campion's opponents were two prominent Protestant divines, Dr Alexander Nowell, Dean of St Paul's, and Dr William Day, Dean of Windsor. Campion and his fellow prisoners, who were summoned to dispute with no warning, no knowledge of the agenda and no books, sat on simple stools in the middle of the room, surrounded by armed soldiers. The effect of this 'unequal dealing' was to make Campion, clearly damaged by torture, the focus of the audience's sympathy. Campion turned what looked like a disadvantage into a triumph of the oppressed individual over the authority of the state. The iconography of the room, clearly intended to suggest a courtroom, reinforced the sense of injustice; a man whose body was physically broken, could hardly fail to remind onlookers of portraits of the crucifixion, with armed Roman soldiers surrounding the three crosses, as at Rushton Hall. The representatives of the newly established church, far from emerging as the superior intellects, appeared to need every prop they could get: both the books which loaded the tables in front of them, and the armed support of the civil power.

This is also one of the few events where we have first hand accounts of the impact of Campion's oratory on his hearers, and even his opponents provide evidence, unwittingly, of Campion's power to gain the affection of a hostile crowd. The reactions of the large audience (a crowd apparently of the kind that attended Paul's Cross sermons) were recorded by a witness, and included hissing, coarse ribaldry, clapping and, when won over, a 'soothing murmur'. When Alexander Nowell, who regularly answered the Louvain theologians from Paul's Cross during the 1560s, rose to start the disputation, he spoke in English (not in Latin, the language of academic discourse): this event was staged as a crowd-pleaser.

What seems to have taken everyone by surprise is that Campion's physical state, which the government calculated would weaken his wits, had the effect of exposing the Privy Council's policy of using extra-juridical torture. He was in a shocking condition in front of a large audience, and the authorities were forced to admit in public that he had been racked. The attempt to gain advantage by using extra-juridical methods had hoist the government with the petard of its own cruelty. This trial of Campion by popular audience, dressed up as a theatre of intellectual discussion, and staffed by men used to managing crowds at Paul's Cross, turned into an embarrassing revelation of the government's pre-trial procedures. Many people seem to have been converted into ardent Campionists by this encounter, including Philip Howard, Earl of Arundel.[1]

A smooth transition from torture to theological dispute was helped by continuity in the personnel. There were strong family links between Campion's opponents and the torturers. Alexander Nowell, Campion's first opponent, was John Hammond's uncle, while another nephew of Nowell's, William Whitaker, acted as notary for the first disputation. Thomas Norton, the 'Rackmaster', helped stage-manage the disputations, and acted as notary for the fourth conference. Within the first hour, the issue of Campion's torture had derailed the government's plan, and Campion had reduced the audience to stunned silence. Stephen Vallenger, a prebendary from Sussex, seems to have been one of the audience, although this is one of the two conferences for which we do not have an autograph account by him.[2]

The reaction of the authorities supports the Catholic claim that Campion, despite being deprived of books and despite his physically broken state, won over the hearts and minds of the audience, and shamed his opponents. For when three further disputations took place, the audience was reduced, the venue was no longer public and the opponents were changed. For the second and third conferences on 18 and 23 September, Dr William Fulke and Dr Roger Goade were Campion's opponents, in the private quarters of Sir Owen Hopton. The final debate on 27 September also took place here, but with another change of opponents. This time, two Calvinist reformers, Dr John Walker and Dr William Charke were selected. Charke, who had acted as a notary in the earlier conferences, may have been chosen because he was one of the first men to reply to Campion's 'Letter to the Council' with his *An answere to a seditious pamphlet*.[3] On 31 August 1581, six weeks after his capture, Campion emerged from the darkness of his imprisonment and the uncertainty created by the government rumour-mill, to be thrust into the public arena for the first time since his capture. Persons, in *An Epistle of the Persecution*, provides more details of the atmosphere surrounding the first disputation. The authorities, confident that the bookless and racked prisoner would be worsted by Nowell and Day, opened the doors of the Tower to an invited audience. All the Privy Council's attempts to stage-manage what Campion describes as a duel or fencing-match dissolved before the actual event.

There were at least five manuscript accounts of various portions of the four disputations written by Catholic observers, and many contemporary poems and

---

[1]   Bombino, *Vita et Martyrium*, p. 255. *The Life of St Philip Howard*, ed. Francis W. Steer (London: Phillimore, 1971), p. 8; a new edition is being prepared by Earle Havens and Elizabeth Patton.

[2]   Questier, *Catholicism and Community*, p. 160, n. 57.

[3]   William Charke, *An answere to a seditious pamphlet lately cast abroade by a Iesuite, with a discoverie of that blasphemous sect* (London: C. Barker, 17 December 1580), STC 5005. Persons seems to have seen this and Hanmer's book at the same time, in early January, so the December date may be notional.

ballads.[4] The only extant manuscript account of the first conference is among the Tresham papers.[5] Tresham's hospitality to Campion and his steadfast defence of his freedom of conscience transformed his life.[6] He showed his devotion to Campion by leaving behind an extraordinary monument of his learned piety in piles of manuscripts that, wrapped in white sheets and sealed, were buried on 28 November 1605.[7]

The official printed account by Alexander Nowell and William Day, *A true report of the Disputation or rather private Conference had in the Tower of London*, published on 1 January 1583, differs significantly in substance and tone from the manuscript accounts.[8] As their preface 'To the Reader' makes clear, they had originally thought that 'Master Campion being now dead' and his 'whole booke being confuted' (by William Whitaker and Laurence Humphrey) there was no reason to publish; with a sigh of satisfaction, they 'laid aside their notes'.[9] But the two Deans now see themselves as having to 'defende our selves against the backebitings of so many slaunderous reporters, who doe yet live and lirke in every corner' and who claim that '*The Catholikes ... did get the Goale*'.[10] The metaphor of backbiting leads effortlessly to a fear that, because there had been changes of opponents, they would be seen as biting curs who, one by one, were thrown off:

> This was foorthwith by reportes and pamphlets every where so framed and dispersed, as though Campion like some great beare, or Lyon rather (as they would have him seeme) had shaken us all off like cowardly curres one after another.[11]

The repetition of the Catholic criticism was something of an own goal. By the start of 1583 they argue, the situation had changed: these 'untruths and impudencie' have been in 'so many lyes so braggingly advouched, and in print in the Latin tongue

---

[4] Sir Thomas Tresham's account, not as good as Bombino's on crowd reaction, is in BL Add. MS 39828, fols 38r–41r. See below for the other three disputations, and the manuscript accounts, which have recently been published (posthumously) by James V. Holleran, *A Jesuit Challenge: Edmund Campion's Debates in the Tower of London in 1581* (New York: Fordham University Press, 1999). For the poems and ballads, see below and Chapter 12.

[5] BL MS Add. 39828, fols 38r–41r (with endorsement on fol. 41r).

[6] See Kilroy, *Memory and Transcription*, pp. 121–45, for a full account of Tresham's memorials in manuscript and stone to Edmund Campion.

[7] *Memory and Transcription*, p. 121.

[8] *A true report of the Disputation or rather private Conference had in the Tower of London with Ed. Campion Jesuite, the last of August, 1581. Set downe by the Reverend learned men themselves that dealt therein* (London: Christopher Barker, 1 January 1583 [1584]), STC 18744.

[9] Nowell and Day, *A true report*, sig. A2r.

[10] Nowell and Day, *A true report*, sig. A2r–v.

[11] Nowell and Day, *A true report*, sig. A2v.

published to the world'.[12] The book shows every sign of uncertain composition, since it passes straight from signature A2v to C1r, where the heading is made to seem as if it is the original heading for a previously unpublished version of the first conference. There is a grander title page for the last three conferences.[13] At the end of the first disputation is 'A brief recital of certain untruths scattered in the pamphlets, and libels of the papists, concerning the former conferences: with a short answer to the same'.[14] This 'brief' appendix contains nine pages, which print some of the manuscript accounts by the Catholics, and specify the charges made by Catholic pamphleteers:

> First, they leave no circumstances of Master Campions imprisonment, his racking, sicknes, lacke of his note bookes, of his librarie, our sodaine comming upon him &c untouched.[15]

To these charges, they answer, remarkably, that they gave him the books when he needed them, having found the places for him 'to ease his travell in seeking of them', and that he himself 'showed no token of any either sicknesse or weaknesse'.[16]

When it comes to 'uncourteous wordes', they counter that Campion 'did rise up from the forme whereon he sate, and fling with his handes and armes', that he affirmed 'that all our printed bookes were false' and 'that he would procure true copies to be sent from the Emperours Majestie, & from the Duke of Bavaria, and from an other prince (whom we remember not)', and that in response they switched to Latin so that the 'common auditorie' would not understand the insults.[17] Campion's tortured state makes the arm-flinging impossible, and they admit saying: '*Os impudens*' (Loud-mouth) but justify that because of Pounde's 'mockings, wordes and lookes', and admit that they said, '*Siccine tam multos oggannire & obstrepere?*' (Do you not see so many growl and screech?), but think that was mild, under the circumstances.[18] It is surprising that the two deans, who have the full backing of the state and are publishing their account with the Queen's printer, should sound so defensive.

Our best witness for the first disputation, on 31 August 1581, is Paolo Bombino, because, while he 'was writing these things at Rome', he had 'the good hap to light upon' a 'note-book' in the English College, written by 'a zealous Catholike, who underhand ventured amidst the thickest of them, to note downe whatsoever passed betwixt the disputants on both sides, as well the first day, as the other dayes

---

12 Nowell and Day, *A true report*, sig. A2r.
13 Nowell and Day, *A true report*, sig. C1r. The second title page is on sig. G4r.
14 Nowell and Day, *A true report*, sigs F3r to G3r.
15 Nowell and Day, *A true report*, sig. F3r.
16 Nowell and Day, *A true report*, sig. F3r.
17 Nowell and Day, *A true report*, sig. F3r–v.
18 Nowell and Day, *A true report*, sig. F3v.

following'.[19] Even the writing of this, presumably in a table book or on a wax tablet, was a brave deed. This manuscript (translated into Latin for him) enabled Bombino to provide details of how the audience 'turnd their eyes upon Campian', and a vivid impression of their 'murmour'.[20]

Bombino's eyewitness describes the staging. Seats were arranged in benches down both sides of the church; on the north side there were two grand thrones, occupied by the two deans, Nowell and Day, and in front of them, so that they had easy access to it, was a table laden with an immense pile of books; behind them was seating of a more modest kind (*levioris armaturae*) for the Protestant ministers who were all carrying a copy of *Rationes Decem*.[21] On another dais opposite, was even more prominent seating, reserved for the Privy Council and the nobility. Among these were seats for two divines appointed as notaries: William Charke who had written such a scornful answer to Campion's 'Letter to the Council', and Nowell's nephew, William Whitaker, regius professor of divinity at Cambridge, whose reply to the *Rationes Decem* had apparently been held back by the Privy Council. In front of them was another table, covered with all the paraphernalia of copying (pens, ink, paper, sand, knives for scraping and cutting paper). In the minimal space left between these rows of seats and tables in 'the theatre' were several stools for Campion, Ralph Sherwin and James Bosgrave and several other unnamed Catholic prisoners. The arrangement already suggested that this was a *spectacle*, a trial by wit, rather than an evenly matched debate. When the prisoners (Campion, Sherwin and Bosgrave), entered, they had difficulty reaching their stools, even though they were guarded by armed men, since there was a multitude as many as the space would permit; the authorities were hoping for maximum publicity for what they foresaw would be an easy victory. Bombino says that

> News that the disputation would take place very soon had spread far beyond those who were immediately involved. Excitement at the forthcoming spectacle had filled not just London, but nearly the whole of the kingdom.[22]

As Campion, stooped from his racking, with his hands bandaged, came into the Tower Chapel of St Peter ad Vincula, the impact, according to Bombino, was dramatic:

> It is scarcely possible to describe how quickly Campion drew all eyes to himself. The rumour of the tortures he had suffered, stories about him, so many and so various, spread abroad, the longstanding veneration of the man, his immense

---

[19] Bombino, *Vita et Martyrium*, pp. 217–18; Bodl. MS Tanner 329, fol. 90r.

[20] Bombino, *Vita et Martyrium*, p. 218; Bodl. MS Tanner 329, fol. 90r–v. This is no longer extant.

[21] Bombino, *Vita et Martyrium*, p. 217; Bodl. MS Tanner 329, fol. 89v; BL MS Add. 39828, fol. 38r. These copies of *Rationes Decem* may have come from the stack of books seized in Southwark.

[22] Bombino, *Vita et Martyrium*, p. 215 (my translation).

reputation among his adversaries: all drew a crowd eager to look on him. Most powerful was the desire to see how strong his spirit was, what state of mind, what colour and movement of the body, so affected by that torture, he would bring to this almost theatrical arena. The alertness of the martyr exceeded everyone's expectation, to such an extent did the flower of his vigorous mind seemed to have green shoots in a body almost dead before its time.[23]

While the audience tried to deduce his state of mind from his body, we can only guess at Campion's appearance from Persons' description of how he looked at his trial in November, when his hands were 'folden in lynnen clothe, and with that feblenesse, as he was neyther able to pluck of his owne mytton of freese nor lyft a cupp of drink to his mouthe withoute helpe'.[24]

When the prisoners sat down, and 'the murmoure of the multitude allayed', Nowell began his 'long preamble', to his 'quaint oration, much before premeditated & artificially trimmed', in English.[25] Campion is a 'Golias' who, in the 'impunity' of his 'lurking-places' has dared to 'chalenge all the English Divines, to publike combat', and now is finally brought 'at last into the light, & upon the publike stage'. Campion's indignant reply accepts the metaphor of combat, but argues that, while they have accepted 'the place', they have withdrawn his 'weapons': the place consists of 'the poynts of Religion', but the weapons are 'bookes and study'.[26]

> Whereas therefore you vauntingly challenge mee, naked and unarmed as I am, to dispute of these poynts, you accept in deed of the place I have appoynted for the combat, but withdraw my weapons. For otherwise, why should not I have the use of bookes as well as you, either before this time appoynted, or at leastwise even now, when I see those that are brought hither, not so much as to be touchd or looked upon by any of us, without your leave? And in very deed I (spent though I am, and allmost exhausted with payne and miseries) could hardly forbeare laughter, to heare you go about to perswade how equall my conditions were with yours, unlesse you thinke I might as well be prepard for a learned disputation by being three times racked, as you by turning bookes.[27]

Campion says he never imagined he would have to dispute

> with my body torne with torments, all disjoynted & destitute of bookes? I have muchc adoe (Nowell) to keepe life, to retayne any spirit; my very soule, through torments, is even allmost on my lippes, is it so easy a matter, amidst all this, to have my wittes about me?[28]

---

[23]   Bombino, *Vita et Martyrium*, pp. 218–19 (my translation).

[24]   Persons, *An Epistle of the Persecution*, sig. M3r.

[25]   Bombino, *Vita et Martyrium*, p. 219; Bodl. MS Tanner 329, fol. 90v.

[26]   Bombino, *Vita et Martyrium*, p. 220; Bodl. MS Tanner 329, fol. 91r.

[27]   Bombino, *Vita et Martyrium*, p. 224; Bodl. MS Tanner 329, fol. 93v.

[28]   Bombino, *Vita et Martyrium*, p. 224; Bodl. MS Tanner 329, fol. 94r.

When Nowell asserts that for every 'one Catholike, which perhaps was hardly handled' there were 'whole hundreds of protestants, burnt by Catholikes', Campion replies that, when he complained of their cruelty, he never 'went about to compare it with any other'; since some of those who 'kindled the fires' under Queen Mary are still alive, Nowell should 'treat this business with them':

> If you will have mee (who have so lately felt your torments) speake my opinion,
> I verily thinke your hellish torment of the racke, was never wont to be exercisd
> agaynst any of yours, with such violence, with such cruelty, as it is now by your
> men agaynst us; which torment I esteeme more cruell than any one single death.[29]

Campion seems to be remembering a quotation from Sir John Fortescue, whose *De Legibus Angliae*, in the recent Mulcaster translation, argues:

> But whoe is so harde harted, whiche beynge once released out of so cruell
> a Racke, though he bee innocent, and faultles, woulde not yet rather accuse
> himselfe of all kindes of offences, then agayne to commyt himselfe to the
> intollerable crueltie of the tourment once proved: and hadde not rather dye at
> ones (seeinge deathe ys the ende of all miseries) then so often to be kylled, and
> to sustaine so manye hellyshe furies, paynfuller then death it selfe?[30]

Campion's passionate assertion elicits a response from the Lieutenant of the Tower, Sir Owen Hopton, that leads to the most dramatic moment in the disputation:

> Hopton, looking upon him, counterfeiting laughter in his countenance and voyce,
> sayd; verily, Campian, you are one of these nice, these delicate Jesuites, who
> being but favourably stretched; call this gentle strayning, this small extention
> wherewith you were examined, a formidable torment: thus unseasonably did
> this spouting companion, seeke to stir up laughter upon so dolefull a subject. But
> merry only as he was in cruelty and mischiefe, his mirth, at the time, succeeded
> accordingly and Campians insuing speech, moved all there present to pity him.
> Very well, Sir, sayd he; yet when the question is of the extremity of the racke;
> much better may his testimonie be taken, who hung upon it, then his, that looked
> on. And I would have you know, I complayne not so much of my owne particular
> torments, in declaring the torment of the racke to be more terrible than death, as
> of the common miserie of Catholikes, which I deplore, seeing them dayly racked
> and torne, examined like thieves and murtherers. Upon which wordes, one of the
> Noble men, seeing the whole assembly much moved, asked; And Campian shall
> we suffer thee to delude so great a multitude as this, as if forsooth, thou seemdst,
> to suffer all these punishments for thy religion, whereas, indeed thou didst it
> for thy most greevous offences? dost thinke, that though thou obstinately didst
> suppresse them, when thou was examined, they are not manifest enough to the
> whole state, and those that were thy judges? be thy religion Campian whatsoever
> it will be it was thy wicked conspiracies agaynst thy country, that haled thee to

---

[29] Bombino, *Vita et Martyrium*, p. 225; Bodl. MS Tanner 329, fol. 94r.

[30] Fortescue, *De Legibus Angliae*, fol. 47r–v.

these torments. This mans loud and desperate lye, provd profitable to the cause of Campian, and his companions. Forthwith, for the love he bare to truth, he summond all the forces he had remayning to his poore and afflicted body, and with a mighty fervour of his invincible mind, which sparkeled even through his eyes, rose up, and sayd, If any one, setting my Religion aside, dare charge me with any crime whatsoever: I aske no favour, make me an example to the whole Kingdome, discharge on me all the cruelties you can. This when he had sayd, with a countenance all enflamed, the deep silence which insued, even amongs the Lords themselves, and the whole assembly, gave a most evident testimonie to the truth whefore after this no one ever contradicted him.[31]

Far from treason, Campion declared that he was tortured to find out: 'to whom according to the rites of the Catholike churche he had communicated the Sacraments, and with whom he had commerce in matter of Religion'.[32] The script of this event, so carefully prepared by the state, has gone badly awry even before it has begun.[33]

Nowell opened the disputation itself by doubting Campion's assertion in the *Rationes Decem* that Luther had attacked the Epistle of St James as 'contentious, swelling, dry, strawie, and to esteeme it unworthy an Apostolicall spirit?'[34] Bombino and Tresham agree that Nowell slipped into Latin for the insult, and 'with many bigge words he had ambitiously exaggerated, with a loud voyce' he concluded thus, in Latin, '*Ergo impudentissime mentiris Campiane*' (therefore Campian, thou lyest most shamefully): a breach of academic decorum that 'moved all the audience', especially as 'what he had written, he had read in Latin in Luthers owne booke'.[35] Nowell argues that Luther never said any such thing:

> and Nowell ended this debate, by beginning his former complaynt, how fouly Luther had bene defamed, prosecuting it so vehemently, and with such shameful rayling, that he snatched up the booke of Luthers, which was suspected, opend it, and with a solemne oath affirmed, that there was no such reproach agaynst the sacred Epistle of St James, in that whole booke, and that Campian falsely belyd him, nor was able to shew any coppy of the worke, now extant in London, that did not witnesse agaynst him, to be a most impudent lyer.[36]

This was true of the revised London editions, but Campion replies that 'ere long' he can send for copies from the Emperor and the Duke of Bavaria, of the original edition that does contain the phrase.[37] Although the official version

---

[31]   Bombino, *Vita et Martyrium*, pp. 225–7; Bodl. MS Tanner 329, fols 94r–95r. See also, BL Add. MS 39828, fols 38r–41r (fol. 38v), printed in *HMCR*, 55, III. 8–16 (p. 9).

[32]   Bombino, *Vita et Martyrium*, p. 227; Bodl. MS Tanner 329, fol. 95r–v.

[33]   Bombino, *Vita et Martyrium*, p. 227; Bodl. MS Tanner 329, fol. 95v.

[34]   Bombino, *Vita et Martyrium*, p. 221; Bodl. MS Tanner 329, fol. 92r.

[35]   Bombino, *Vita et Martyrium*, pp. 227–8; Bodl. MS Tanner 329, fols 95v–96r.

[36]   Bombino, *Vita et Martyrium*, p. 227; Bodl. MS Tanner 329 fol. 95v.

[37]   Bombino, *Vita et Martyrium*, p. 228; Bodl. MS Tanner 329 fol. 96r.

of this debate concealed the narrow chauvinism of the Dean by omitting all references to London editions, the ribald reaction to Campion's offer to obtain copies of the first edition from the Emperor, Rudolf II, and the Duke of Bavaria (who had inherited the Fugger library's collection), shows that England's borders have become closed to more than Jesuits and seminary priests. Campion had recently (as we have seen) been in the Duke's library, and had 'copied those words very faithfully', citing Luther's text 'in the margin of his little book'.[38] This exchange confirms how many scholarly hours Campion had spent in two of the best libraries in Europe.

Nowell, thinking that the debate was going their way, and that Campion's desperation was shown by needing to go as far as Germany, brought out the two books in question. The first was the preface to the Epistle of St James; the second was Luther's *De captivitate Babylonica*: on the Babylonian captivity. Campion found the place from which the sentence had been erased and, close by, the verdict that supported it: '*Affirmant nonnulli epistolam Iacobi Apostolico spiritu indignam*' (some argue that the Epistle of St James is unworthy of the apostolic spirit).[39]

'Foure whole howres were spent in this first disputation'.[40] It is easy to see why Catholics felt their champion had won this first bout. Campion had gained the sympathies of the audience with his irrefutable argument that, without books either before or during the debate, it was not 'equal dealing'. Secondly, Campion had succeeded in bringing onto 'the publike stage', not his treason, but his torture for religion. Finally, when it came to editions of Luther or Fathers of the Church, Campion had shown himself to have a more international textual knowledge.

One detail preserved in Nowell and Day is that Campion 'answered, that he wrote his booke as he traveiled, and that he coulde not, we knewe, cary a librarie about with him, and therefore he was forced to give credite to his notes'.[41] The effect was to emphasize the manifest disadvantage the authorities had tried to put Campion under. Bookless as he was, he emerged as a better scholar than men who seemed unaware of the changes Luther's text had undergone since his first challenge to the church. The argument reveals the textual nature of scholarship at this period. Years later, William Whitaker admitted that the offending sentence was

---

[38] *Rationes Decem* ([Stonor Park: Brinkley, 1581]), STC 4536.5, ARCR I 135.1, sig. A1v; Daniel Bartoli, S.J., *Dell'Istoria Della Compagnia Di Giesu L'Inghilterra Parte Dell'Europa* (Rome: Varese, 1667), identifies the edition: 'Father Campion had copied those words very faithfully from the works of Luther, from the old edition of Jena in Thuringen of Saxony, a city quite devoted to that heretic, as having been among the first to receive the evil seed of his errors', quoted in Holleran, pp. 203–4. Nowell and Day, *A true report*, sig. C2r–C4v.

[39] Bombino, *Vita et Martyrium*, p. 229; Bodl. MS Tanner 329, fol. 97r.

[40] Bombino, *Vita et Martyrium*, p. 230; Bodl. MS Tanner 329, fol. 97r.

[41] Nowell and Day, *A true report*, sig. C4v.

in the 1529 Jena edition; as Bombino puts it, 'the very hereticall ministers them selves, amongst which Whitaker was one, openly confessed, that those madde speeches of Luther were found in his old originall coppies'.[42]

The afternoon session introduced the issue that was to dominate: *sola fides* (faith alone); the Epistle of St James is again central. Whereas the morning session slipped between two languages, Latin and English, the afternoon discussion moved between three: Greek, Latin and English. Bombino chooses this point to detail his source originally in English, and turned into Latin for him. He says he intends eventually to publish an account of all four dispuations separately; he specifies his interest in the reactions of the audience:

> The place of the disputation, the authours and mayntayners I will declare, what also was acted even in the meeting, of what thing disputed, with what effect of the audience, with what judgment of the wiser sort transacted.[43]

A true report of the conference merely indicates a difference in Campion's demeanour. Nowell and Day note 'his gentle and milde behaviour, and speach' in the afternoon conference, in comparison with 'his bragging and lewde wordes used in the forenoone'.[44] *A true report* suggests that the session passed quickly to the central issue of *sola fides*, 'the justifying by faith only', with a brief diversion to a sentence in Gratian that the church's doctors and councils are to be trusted as much as the scriptures.[45] Bombino, by contrast, shows the afternoon began with another attempt to humiliate Campion that spectacularly failed. William Day had taken over from Nowell, and to press home his opening attack on Campion's refutation of Luther, offered Campion a Greek edition of the New Testament. Campion, who 'knew the Greek text to be wickedly corrupted by heretikes, answered (I thank you sir) and without opening the booke, layed it aside'.[46] If this was Beza's translation, complete with his annotations, Campion's refusal would have had added piquancy.[47] Someone in the audience derisively shouted, '*Graecum est non legitur*' (he can't read Greek), and the chant was rapidly taken up:

---

[42]   Bombino, *Vita et Martyrium*, p. 231; Bodl. MS Tanner 329, fols 97v–98r. William Whitaker, *An answere to the ten reasons of E. Campian. Whereunto is added the summe of the defence of those reasons by John Duraeus the Scot, a jesuit, with a reply unto it*, trans. Richard Stocke (London: Kyngston, 1606), STC 25360; Holleran, pp. 46–7.

[43]   Bombino, *Vita et Martyrium*, p. 232; Bodl. MS Tanner 329, fol. 98r–98v.

[44]   Nowell and Day, *A true report*, sig. D4r.

[45]   Bombino, *Vita et Martyrium*, p. 232; Bodl. MS Tanner 329, fol. 98v.

[46]   Bombino, *Vita et Martyrium*, p. 233; Bodl. MS Tanner 329, fol. 99r.

[47]   Beza had produced many editions with extensive annotations, but one Greek text had just been published in Geneva, *Iesu Christi Domini Nostri Novum Testamentum, Graecum et Latinum* (Geneva: H. Stephanus, 1580).

a wonder it is with what laughter, with what base jestes, what hissing, they both often inculcated the old saying, and heaped upon it many quippes and byting tauntes. Meanwhile Campian tolerated this frequent disgrace with marvelous patience.[48]

Bombino explains this as part of the Protestant contempt for what they see as Catholic ignorance of Greek and Hebrew, indicating that the taunt was a generic insult frequently used against Catholics. Campion was just biding his time. After the discussion has turned to the heart of the debate, the use of the word *sola* by doctors of the church, Campion's adversaries were keen to present him with another Greek text. Two fathers of the church were cited: Hilary in Latin, and Basil in Greek. Bombino's account captures the theatricality of the moment, more like a tense moment in a duel than a theological discussion:

> and to the end they might fall agayne to make themselves mery with jesting and hissing at Campian, they pitchd more willingly upon the Greeke. Wherfore with their eyes and whole aspectes, swimming as a man may say, and sauced with saucie laughter, they ran many of them by heapes, to thrust Basill upon Campian. Now began the whole multitude of people, that were present, to murmur, and rayse upon themselves, as it were, upon tiptoes, ready to clappe their handes, by way of derision. When Campian, without any trouble, or shew of distemper at all, takes up the booke, and with a serene and setled countenance (as if he had minded nothing lesse, then them that watchd to disgrace him) began to read the place designed; whereby he first repressed those eyes of theirs, that were so boldly cast upon him, then restrayned their laughter wherewith they were brimfull, and even ready to have burst forth. But when after they saw him (with the selfe same confidence and constancie) read the whole place in Greeke, and render it word for word in English, so, not only properly, but even elegantly, that he seemed, as well to all his enemies, as friendes, equally maister of both languages; his enemies began to wax pale, to hang their heads, and never afterward would so much as well endure to behold him, or the multitude about him. Meanewhile, Campian with a resolute countenance closed the booke, and redeliverd it, with these wordes: you henceforth I suppose, will beare me witnesse, I somewhat understand Greeke. At which speech the whole audience were even ready to have given their applause, but suddaynely turnd it into a kind of festivall and soothing murmur, admiring no lesse his modesty, then learning; and as the common sort, are for the most part, on either side, immoderately changeable, they exceeded no lesse in too much favouring and applauding him then they did before in disgracing and hissing at him.[49]

Campion had outpaced his opponents both in learning and in coolness under fire.

The discussion now turned to the proposed topic: justification by faith alone (*sola fides*). After the issue had been explored and fathers cited, Campion

---

[48]   Bombino, *Vita et Martyrium*, p. 234; Bodl. MS Tanner 329, fol. 99v.

[49]   Bombino, *Vita et Martyrium*, p. 235; Bodl. MS Tanner 329, fol. 100r–v. The 'festivall and soothing murmur' is not in the Latin original.

after the manner of Logitians, briefely darted agaynst them this argument. If fayth only justify, it justifies without charity, but without charity, if wee beleeve St Paul, it justifies not: therefored Fayth only justifies not.[50]

Campion's adversaries were, not unnaturally, keen to close the discussion, but first had to silence Ralph Sherwin who had wanted to intervene. Perhaps to prevent further interference from Sherwin, Campion was asked his opinion, and expounded the theology of the church:

> with so great approbation of all the audience, that Nowell, seeing men's mindes inclined so much to favour our cause, and fearing the overthrow of theirs, interrupted him craftily in his speech.[51]

The session was dissolved. The only victory of Campion's opponents in the morning, that they could not find an edition with the phrase he had attributed to Luther, was to be short-lived.[52] The dominant events for the audience must have been the two big dramas of Campion's assertion of his torture in the morning and his reading of Greek in the afternoon. If this was, as Campion imagined, a fencing match, he had won both bouts, revealing his ability to win round a large public crowd deliberately incited against him. The hardest thing to recapture, four centuries on, is the sound of Campion's voice, the spell he seemed to cast over an audience, whether the congregation at Lyford, the royal court in Prague, or this diverse crowd of nobles, protestant ministers and many of the 'vulgar sort'.

What is remarkable is that Campion, powerless and tortured, has succeeded in having a disputation, not on the authority of the Queen or the power of the Pope, but on the topics he had chosen for his printed challenge – *sola fides*, transubstantiation, the authority of the scriptures – and on Luther, Calvin and Beza. The Privy Council had agreed to a disputation on truly theological issues, and not the 'blouddye questions and verye Pharesaicall' ones of allegiance, the right of the sovereign over the spiritual realm or the pope over the secular power.[53] The *Rationes Decem* had shown no interest in these questions, which dominate Book VII of Sander's *De Visibili Monarchia*. Instead, Campion has managed to have a debate on the central issues of European reformation theology. Campion 'shows himself consistently uninterested in the theoretical question' of the Pope's power to excommunicate the Queen.[54] Campion defined all the issues surrounding this question at his trial as 'merelye spirituall poyntes of doctrine and disputable in schooles'.[55]

---

[50]   Bombino, *Vita et Martyrium*, p. 236–7; Bodl. MS Tanner 329, fol. 101r.

[51]   Bombino, *Vita et Martyrium*, p. 238; Bodl. MS Tanner 329, fol. 102r.

[52]   Bombino, *Vita et Martyrium*, p. 231; Bodl. MS Tanner 329, fol. 98r.

[53]   BL MS Harley 6265, fol. 19r.

[54]   Stefania Tutino, *Law and Conscience: Catholicism in Early Modern England, 1570–1625* (Aldershot, UK and Burlington, VT: Ashgate, 2007), 46.

[55]   BL MS Harley 6265, fol. 19r.

Remarkable too is the skill with which Campion conducted the disputations without a copy of his own book. If it is unclear whether anyone 'had the goal', it is certain that Campion, even after torture and without books, has not been discredited. There is some evidence that many, including the Earl of Arundel and Stephen Vallenger, 'prebendary of Selsey', were won over during Campion's first disputation in the Tower.[56] Vallenger, at any rate, became the major source of our knowledge of the disputations, and went on to transcribe Thomas Alfield's life for the printer, and to write at least one of the four poems printed in that book.[57]

There are several indications, as Bombino argues, that the Privy Council was pleased neither with the conduct of the first disputation nor with its advocates. First, they published false accounts; secondly, they changed the location from the chapel to the private quarters of Owen Hopton, so it was easier to keep a large crowd away than from the public chapel of the Tower; thirdly, they changed the two protagonists, Nowell and Day, substituting William Fulke and Roger Goade.[58] Finally, 17 days elapsed, 'a surprisingly lengthy interval'.[59] When Campion was brought into the hall of Owen Hopton, he immediately noticed 'the whole face of the theater changed, for the auditours were but few at most not above thirty persons'.[60]

Campion began the second disputation on 18 September with a complaint and an appeal:

> Campian took occasion briefely to complayne, that heere he was brought altogether unprovided to encounter with them that were armed and prepared, moreover he expostulated more and saw himselfe much aggrieved, that he understoode they had caused many thinges to be falsely printed, and promulgated concerning their former disputation; for that he heard his adversaries published those things to be sayd by him in disputation, which he never so much as dreamt of. Beside, they should call to mind, what his request was, and what they ought to aford him in common duty, to wit, not any private or chamber disputations, but publike, and Academicke.[61]

The key word here is the last one. These debates are not being conducted like 'academic' debates in the University of Oxford.

For the second, third and fourth disputations we have the manuscripts, mostly written by Stephen Vallenger, who as a prebendary, may have been one of the

---

[56] Questier, *Catholicism and Community*, p. 160. Anthony Petti, 'Stephen Vallenger (1541–1591)', *Recusant History* 6 (1962), 248–64, discusses the authorship of the four poems.

[57] See Chapter 12 for more details.

[58] Bombino, *Vita et Martyrium*, p. 239; Bodl. MS Tanner 329, fol. 102r–v.

[59] These are the conclusions of Holleran, pp. 57–8.

[60] Bombino, *Vita et Martyrium*, p. 240; Bodl. MS Tanner 329, fol. 103r.

[61] Bombino, *Vita et Martyrium*, pp. 241–2; Bodl. MS Tanner 329, fol. 103v.

ministers at the table, and able legitimately to take notes for a more detailed commentary.[62] It certainly seems that Vallenger had decided to record the disputations, and prepare them for the Catholic printer, William Carter. Vallenger was sentenced to lose his ears by the Star Chamber, presided over by Sir Walter Mildmay, on 16 May 1582.[63] The manuscripts were seized by the pursuivant, Richard Topcliffe, in July 1582, in Carter's house.[64] From Topcliffe, the manuscripts passed to John Foxe, and were then lent by William Willys, an executor of one of Foxe's descendants, to John Strype, who, in 1709, sold them to Humfrey Wanley, Robert Harley's librarian, whence they passed (as part of the Harley collection) to the British Library in 1753.[65] A second manuscript of these three disputations has survived, (with 'one Mr Nortone barrester Notarie'), so similar that it appears to have been copied from the same source.[66] Thomas Norton copied out a detailed account of the books seized at William Carter's house.[67]

There was clearly a radical shift of tone between the first disputation and the last three conferences, although this may be because Vallenger took more seriously the theological discussion. For the second conference, Dr Fulke and Dr Goade were 'syttinge at a table havinge ther certayne Bookes aboute them' (accompanied by Mr Charke and Mr Field as notaries), while Campion was opposite them 'uppon a stoole'.[68] Fulke certainly provided Campion with his most able adversary. Vallenger confirms what Bombino relates, that Campion began by complaining of the inaccurate reporting:

---

[62]   See above for Vallenger.

[63]   Folger MS. X.d.338, an account endorsed by Mildmay. See Chapter 12 for Carter's fate.

[64]   Harley MS 422 (vol. 7 of the Foxe papers). There is a fair copy, fols 148r–60r, in Vallenger's hand of the second conference, with numbered arguments, revisions and speakers' names in the margin, followed by a rough draft, fols 161r–67r. The third conference, 'Confessed by Carter to be Vallengers hande', fols 168r–172v, has a gloss in Richard Topcliffe's hand, indicating the manuscript was 'Taken in Carter's house, a printer, in the presence of Mr Payne, Mr Norris, the persevant, etc.'. The fourth conference, in another hand, now comes first (with a similar gloss by Topcliffe), fols 136r–147r.

[65]   T.A. Birrell, 'William Carter (c. 1549–84): Recusant Printer, Publisher, Binder, Stationer, Scribe – and Martyr', *Recusant History* 28 (2006), 22–42 (p. 39), Holleran, p. 225; and *ODNB*, 'William Carter' (c. 1549–1584), by Ian Gadd. This is a remarkably complete, and surprising, provenance.

[66]   Bodl. MS Rawl. D. 353, fols 1r–35r. The manuscript is badly damaged, but in a large and legible secretary hand, and the disputations are in the same eccentric order as in BL MS Harley 422: fourth, fols 1r–13r; second, fols 14r–25v; third, fols 25v–35r. I have used Harley MS 422 as my principal text, see Holleran, pp. 227–8.

[67]   BL Add. MS 48029, fols 58r–59v. I am grateful to Dr Mark Rankin for his analysis and transcription of this section (in Norton's own hand) of his 'Chayne of Treasons' in the same manuscript that contains the reports of Charles Sledd.

[68]   Bodl. MS Rawl. D. 353, fol. 14r.

> There were at that time [the first conference] such as did note and afterwards reported our conference: but I understand, there be many thinges published thereof more than truth is, and that I am belyed in print, so that I thinke it scarce good and just dealing, wishing I had at this time a notarye on my part.[69]

Fulke defended the published reports: 'There is nothing published in print, but that which is indifferent' (impartial), and claims that Campion was informed on Saturday that there would be a debate, and had been given the opportunity to choose which part of his book he would defend.[70] Campion retorted that, if they had really been looking for the truth, they would have made sure that both sides were equally prepared (he complains that before Fulke is 'a table full of bookes readie before you prepared for the same') to search the scriptures and antiquity; he nevertheless proposed that they proceed.[71] Bombino reports that both parties fell sharply to it, and that Goade was soon in trouble, faltering 'both in tongue and argument', so that he had to be rescued by Fulke.[72]

The topic chosen for the morning debate was that of Campion's third *Ratio*: the nature of the church. In this sense alone, the disputations followed some kind of order, having dealt with '*Sacrae Literae*' (scripture), Campion's *Prima Ratio*, in the first conference. Calvin had argued that the church was invisible, and made up of the elect, and Campion had no difficulty deflecting Fulke from discussing the church in heaven. While the exchanges between Fulke and Campion are sharp and fast, those between Campion and Goade are good-humoured and compassionate. On one occasion Goade could not

> readily turne to the places, it was appointed it should be prepared against after diner. Campion: I would, Mr Goade, that you and I might shake hands together of St Jeromes religion, that we might meet together with him in heaven.[73]

On another, Goade could not remember which Council of Nicaea, the first or the second, had approved of images, or whether it was the first council of Constantinople or the second that had condemned them, and so 'that day they proceeded no further'.[74]

Two wider cultural points are interesting. One is that Campion twice refers to the 'persecution' in Queen Mary's time, without in any way diminishing the suffering of Protestants. In the first they are included in an historical survey of persecutions.

---

[69]   BL MS Harley 422, fol. 148r–v; Holleran, p. 95.

[70]   BL MS Harley 422, fol. 148v; Holleran, p. 95.

[71]   BL MS Harley 422, fol. 148v; Holleran, p. 96.

[72]   Bombino, *Vita et Martyrium*, p. 242; Bodl. MS Tanner 329, fol. 104r.

[73]   BL MS Harley 422, fol. 152r; Holleran, p. 103.

[74]   BL MS Harley 422, fol. 156r; Holleran, p. 112.

Campion: For in the time of persecution under Diocletian certaine escaped from prison, as Silvester and others, as in time of Queene Mary many did, and in this Queenes time doo.

Goade: You meddle too much with the state of this time.
Campion: I meane as well Queen Maries time, as this time.[75]

Again Campion refers to the practice recommended in Matthew of attempting to reprove a brother and if he does not listen, taking it to the church (*dic ecclesiae*), and Goade attempts to argue that this remedy is not available during persecution:

Campion: For although persecution be in one place, yet this complaint may be done in divers other places: as for example: The protestantes in Queene Maryes time being persecuted in Inglande, yet they might have this remedie in Germanie, where their relligion was used.[76]

On another occasion, Campion argues that there are different opinions on whether one should converse with Protestants:

Campion: I knowe not: It might be that Peter was of opinion that it was lawfull for him to kepe company with the Jewes onely so yeelding something more thereby to their weaknes: which St Paule, being more strict, did not allowe of: as if one Catholike should holde, that it were lawfull to be conversant with Protestantes, and another doth holde the contrary. Which opinions, being but onely touching conversation, is no matter of fayth. St Jerome also doth thinke that Peter was not reprehensible in that acte, although St Augustine should seeme to be of the contrary opinion.

Goade: Take heede of dissuading men from companying together, least you incurre the daunger of some Statutes.

Campion. I hope, Mr Goade, you came not to threatten me: I say nothing but that some men are of opinion that Catholikes ought not to be conversant with Protestantes. What then of this?[77]

Goade's intervention makes it clear that he understands Campion to refer to the advice to Catholics not to attend the Protestant church. Campion's reply means that he does not see this as a matter of faith, but only an accident of the current situation. One might even interpret his 'some men are of opinion' to mean that it is not his view.

In the afternoon, the central issue of whether the church of Christ may err in matters of faith was disputed before 'a companye to the number of sixtie'.[78]

---

[75]   BL MS Harley 422, fol. 150v; Holleran, p. 101.
[76]   BL MS Harley 422, fol. 152v; Holleran, p. 104.
[77]   BL MS Harley 422, fol. 157r; Holleran, p. 115.
[78]   Bodl. MS Rawl. D. 353, fol. 18v.

At only one absurd point is there the kind of audience reaction common in the first debate: hissing.

> Fulke: Mans justification groweth by performance of the lawe, which is it not possible for any man to performe. ergo.

> Campion: The lawe may be fulfilled by this meanes, in loving God above all things, and thy neighbour as thy selfe, which a man may well doo by the grace of God.

> Goade: Note this absurditie, for no man can keep his commaundementes, and therewith some in affirming the same did hisse.

> Campion: Because there was a hisse geven, in that I saide, the commaundementes might be performed, I beseeche you geve me leave to explane my minde howe they may be performed: and that is, to love God with all the heart, so farre forth as it is required at his handes; that is, to love him above all thinges, to preferre him before all riches, to forsake all thinges for his sake, so that he would renounce the worlde, and also his life, to cleave and sticke to God, and the other to love his neighbour, that is to be understanded, to preferre him before any riches, and withall to be readie to pleasure him in that that lyeth in him; and in vaine was it commaunded to be performed, if it were impossible to be performed. And all this may be performed by the assistance of almightie God.[79]

Campion's reaction shows him perfectly able to handle a crowd, meet their objections, and explain the issue in simple terms. It seems as if the audience is less rowdy, more combative and more academic than those at the first disputation; it is certainly smaller. While the discussion is more academic, there are still some attempts to show that Campion is not really learned. Campion himself refers again to the attempt to assert that he cannot read Greek, a charge that he describes as 'very childishe'.[80] On another occasion, at the end of the debate, Fulke charges Campion with ignorance of St Augustine; Campion's reply is appropriately robust, offering to meet Fulke on his own territory:

> Fulke: You seem not to have read St Augustine.

> Campion: Seeing you charge me with ignorance in St Augustine, I challenge you before this company to dispute with you in St Augustine in the universitie of Cambridge.[81]

---

[79] BL MS Harley 422, fol. 155r–v; Bodl. MS Rawl. D. 353, fol. 21r; Holleran, p. 110.

[80] BL MS Harley 422, fol. 159v; Holleran, p. 120.

[81] BL MS Harley 422, fol. 160; Holleran, p. 121.

Campion tries to change the order of proceedings and challenges Fulke to justify what he has written in his 'booke against Mr Doctor Bristowe'.[82] Campion challenges Fulke to send him the book he has written via the Lieutenant of the Tower, and 'I will the next day shewe the thinges that I have saide; or I would you would maintayne it against me in Cambridge'.[83] Bizarrely, when Fulke gives him a book it turns out to be another book against Heskins and Saunders, and Campion says 'I demanded your booke expressely against Bristow'.[84] These seem petty attempts to deprive Campion of the chance of proving his intellectual prowess.

Later, when Fulke criticizes Campion's confidence in challenging the whole kingdom, Campion sounds weary with always having to answer arguments that seemed designed to trap him, rather than reveal the truth:

> To prove that the Sunne is Sunne, and the daye is day, I dare challenge all the whole world: and I praye you, seing I have beene pressed to answere all this day, that eyther nowe or the next time I may be admitted to appose also.[85]

Clearly Campion is never going to be allowed to 'appose', or set the topics for discussion.

The next conference occurred comparatively soon, on 23 September, and Campion confronted the same opponents. This suggests that the Privy Council was happier with the outcome of the second disputation than of the first. This time, it is Fulke who begins by complaining of false reports (presumably circulating in manuscript) of the second debate:

> Fulke: At our last conference Mr Campion, you answered our argumentes with multitude of wordes, similitudes, comparisons, and distinctions. Whereupon it was reported, that we could say nothing. But this day, Campion, we mean to cutt you shorter.[86]

Yet the day began by Fulke and Goade going back to issues in the previous debate. To Goade, who could not remember again which Council of Nicaea had allowed images, and when Campion asked him to show which council it was, he fumbled

---

[82]   BL MS Harley 422, fol. 158; Holleran, pp. 116–17. In response to Richard Bristow's *Motives to the Catholike Faith* (STC 3799, ARCR II. 67), first published in 1574, and revised for a second edition in 1576, called *Demaundes to bee proponed of Catholickes to the Heretickes* (STC 3800.5. ARCR II. 69), Fulke had written *Two Treatises written against the Papistes* (STC 11458), published in 1577. Bristow's answer to this was printed secretly: *A reply to Fulke, in defense of M.D. Allens scroll of articles, and book of purgatorie* (Louvain: John Lion [East Ham: Greenstreet House], 1580), STC 3802, ARCR II. 72. Fulke's reply to this, *A Rejoynder to Bristows Replie* (STC 11448), was registered only on 14 February 1581, so it was very recent.

[83]   BL MS Harley 422, fol. 158; Holleran, p. 117.

[84]   BL MS Harley 422, fol. 158v; Holleran, p. 117.

[85]   BL MS Harley 422, fol. 160r; Bodl. MS Rawl. D. 353, fol. 25v; Holleran, p. 121.

[86]   BL MS Harley 422, fol. 168r; Holleran, p. 122.

for his notes; Campion patiently explained the difference between a general Council and 'an assemblye or conventicle':

Campion: What Councell of Nicea?

Goade: What Councell, said Goade? I had it in my paper, but I cannot finde it. I will remember the Councell, and bring the booke against the next conference; and hereupon he brought the booke, and showed that the Council of Constance disallowed of Images, which the seconde Councell of Nicea did allow.[87]

But there are no lapses in memory when Fulke and Campion clash over the issue decreed for the day: the Real Presence, where the discussion focuses on the substance and accidents of the Eucharist. The discussion is fast, and fiercely conducted according to the rules of logic, especially the syllogism. Campion frequently replies, 'I denye your minor', or 'I denye the antecedent', while Fulke aggressively moves from 'Is this your answer?' to 'Your answer is absurd' and 'Your answer is no answer'.[88] Campion, understandably says that there is no reason why he should 'forbeare' Fulke's rudeness: he is 'the Queenes prisoner and not yours. And if you use such wordes, I will returne them'.[89] Nowell and Day confirm Campion's claim to be 'the Queenes prisoner', but have him complaining that Fulke is coming 'to appose me as if I were a scholer in the Grammar schoole'.[90] An even more choleric exchange occurs when Fulke challenges Campion to put his case in writing, and Campion asks Fulke to 'procure me that I may have libertie to write', and to 'appose once' (propose the topics).[91] For someone as experienced a disputant as Campion, this one-sided debate must have been very frustrating.

Neither the content (philosophical arguments over substance and accidents and theological niceties over whether Christ's physical body be present or not) nor the style (a very scholastic argument that proceeds by major, minor and antecedents in syllogisms) is easily accessible to the modern reader. Yet what is clear, in both Vallenger's account and that of Nowell and Day, is that between the two former scholars of St Paul's there is real hostility. For the debate 'After dynner', which is meant to continue on the topic of transubstantiation, begins with another sharp exchange, because Campion has asked for Fulke's book on Dr Allen, and been given another of his books; a cheap, obstructive tactic. The issue is whether Fulke has said the church may err in matters of salvation:

Fulke. Would you have us knowe what book you meant. I hold not that the true church may erre in matters of salvation.

---

[87]   BL MS Harley 422, fol. 168r; Holleran, p. 124.
[88]   BL MS Harley 422, fols 168v–169r; Holleran, pp. 126–7.
[89]   BL MS Harley 422, fol. 169r; Holleran, p. 127.
[90]   Nowell and Day, *A true report*, sig. O2r.
[91]   Nowell and Day, *A true report*, sig. R4r.

> Campion. It is no great matter for the booke, for everyone that hath read it, doth know that you holde that the Church erred in teaching prayer for the deade, and invocation of Saintes, which you crye out on in the pulpet, saying that it is Idolatrye. And do you make it no matter of salvation, to teache, or not to teache Idolatrie?[92]

This debate shows the close interaction of print and pulpit in controversies.

The style of argument was an elaborate form of intellectual fencing, as Campion's metaphors constantly suggest. Campion was given the field, but denied the weapons. This was a horrible parody of disputation, where the form of the debate – scholastic exchange in the manner of logicians – has been harnessed to a base purpose. Campion was never allowed to appose (to put forward the topics) but always cast in the role of defender. He was never allowed free access to books, and the only occasions when he was given books, he was either given the wrong book, or given a book in Greek designed to show his ignorance of the language. Only in the first debate do we have a witness who is interested in the reactions of the audience; Vallenger does mention hissing once, but neither he nor Fulke and Goade give us any consistent sense of the reactions of the audience. The third day's conference, according to Fulke and Goade, ended in a prayer, not for truth, but for the preservation of truth from the ignorance of heretics. The prayer seems less about asking for God's help than about the side in power (Fulke and Goade) proclaiming that they are of God's party.

The fourth and final debate took place in Sir Owen Hopton's hall on 27 September.[93] The Privy Council replaced the aggressive Fulke and forgetful Goade with John Walker and William Charke, two godly preachers, both notable for their extreme views. Charke's answer to Campion's 'Letter to the Council' had won him notoriety, and perhaps some favour.[94] Although Persons had answered Charke's book with his *A Brief Censure*, printed at Francis Browne's house at Henley Park in early January, Campion must have been glad to confront such ignorant preachers. Charke had been expelled from St Mary's, Cambridge, for preaching that Satan had introduced bishops, while Walker had protested against ornaments in the cathedral.[95] Holleran even suggests that the Queen may have 'secretly hoped that the debates would bring discredit to both the Catholics and the Puritans alike and thus demonstrate the wisdom of her earlier decision to found the national church on religious compromise'.[96] The Privy Council seemed more desperate to find men willing to oppose Campion than to represent the religion

---

[92]   BL MS Harley 422, fol. 170v; Bodl. MS Rawl. D. 353, fol. 30v; Holleran, p. 133.

[93]   BL MS Harley 422, fols 136r–147v. This scribe's spelling is eccentric and his punctuation minimal.

[94]   William Charke, *An Answere to a seditious pamphlet lately cast abroade by a jesuite with a discoverie of that blasphemous sect* (London: Christopher Barker, 1580), STC 5005.

[95]   Holleran pp. 72–3.

[96]   Holleran, p. 73.

now established. 'It was to such men that they naturally turned … when the chips were down'.[97]

The quality of this debate is inferior to the Fulke debates, and reverts randomly to the topics of the first debate: which scriptures are canonical, and *sola fides*. Walker opens the proceedings with a prayer and a threat:

> And nowe it hath pleased the Queenes majestie to send us to see whether yower doctrine be sound and trewe, or corrupted, accordinge as your wrytinges are. The clemencie of the prince and great mercifullnesse dothe herein appear, and howe lothe she would be to deale with rigore against yowe, as she might justly doe. She had rather torne you by fayre meanes then to showe justice agaynst yowe, but take hede lest her mercie be torned into rigor, throwghe your own dealinge, for *quamdiu abutere nostra patientia Catalina*. (then holdinge Mr Campiones booke in his hand) he said so little as this pamphlet is, yet it hathe bredd great troble.[98]

Campion ignores the risible allusion to the most famous Roman traitor, Catiline, and merely picks out the way they are not distinguishing different questions:

> Upon Sunday last I received a letter from yowe bothe, wherby I did understand that yowe were in mynd to dispute with me touchinge the orthoritie of holly scriptures, for even so were the wordes of your letter which I intended to be touchinge the authoritie of the authenticall scriptures, and not to call in question and to dispute which be authenticall nether whether all thinges necessarie to salvacon be conteyned in scripture, for that were to dispute of the sufficiency of scriptures and not of the authoritie, which questiones yowe nowe seme to bringe in.[99]

The account of the fourth disputation shows Campion able to run rings round his opponents, and quietly to deride their arguments. The tone is very different from the tense and bitter exchanges with Fulke, and, if the account is to be believed, the audience shared Campion's disdain for his opponent. Charke's methods are those of the popular preacher at Paul's Cross, and he suffers the fate sometimes accorded to those who play the crowd. Before preaching at Paul's Cross, John Foxe wrote to Bishop Grindal of his fears that in that 'renowned theatre (*tam celebre theatrum*) he would "either draw upon myself the mockery of the crowd or be driven off the stage by their hisses"'.[100]

---

[97] Lake and Questier, 'Edmund Campion Affair', pp. 624–5.

[98] BL MS Harley 422, fol. 136r–v; Holleran, p. 145.

[99] BL MS Harley 422, fol. 136v; Holleran, p. 146.

[100] BL MS Harley 417, fol. 131r, cited by Arnold Hunt, 'Preaching the Elizabethan Settlement', in *Handbook of the Early Modern Sermon*, ed. Peter McCullough, Hugh Adlington and Emma Rhatigan (Oxford: University Press, 2011), pp. 366–86 (p. 383).

The people treated Charke's arrogance – and his ignorance – with contempt. At one point he proudly asserted, again and again, that he had an argument Campion would not be able to answer. At first, Campion responds with gentle mockery:

> Campion: Smylinge at this argument said, is this your doughty argument that cannot be answered? take this answer: I deny your argument, prove it.
>
> Charke: What do yowe scoff? Yowe knowe not where you are nor into what place yowe are brought? I doubt not but you shall be broght to a place where you shall learne better to behave your selfe.
>
> Campion: I have a terrible adversarie of yowe, Mr Charke, but what dothe this prove your argument?[101]

Undeterred, Charke continues to assert that his argument cannot be answered:

> Then lookinge a side upon the people, he said, this is an argument which all the world can not answer ... and therewithall there was a great murmuringe amongest the people and some of them did hisse before the argument was either repeated or answered.[102]

The crowd grew impatient, and Mr Norton, the notary, interrupted and had to be told to 'hold his peace' by Owen Hopton, Lieutenant of the Tower.[103] 'These are the comedies that you exercise to get the applause of the people', as Persons argues in a vivid apostrophe to Charke in his *A Defence of the Censure*, where he ridicules his habit, 'most ridiculous, and fytt for a stage', of 'often turning to the people & requesting them to reioyce, & thank the Lord, that he had gyven you suche an argument agaynst the papistes as now you had to propose'.[104] When the argument 'came forth it proved not woorth three egges in Maye: for that M. Campian dispatched it oftentymes in less than halfe three woordes'; it was 'a pitie' that they did not make 'these fewe disputations publik so more men might have laughed'.[105] When Campion asks for a copy of the books he 'noted in the margent of his booke' (his sources), Walker simply says, 'I can not let yowe have those bookes you speake of'.[106] This is an apparently pointless deprivation.

In the afteroon, the *sola fides* debate was resurrected by Dr Walker, and then taken up by Charke. Campion admits that 'some of these fatheres, havinge to

---

[101]   BL MS Harley 422, fol. 146v; Holleran, p. 166; Persons, *A Defence of the Censure*, p. 8.

[102]   BL MS Harley 422, fol. 146v; Holleran, p. 167.

[103]   BL MS Harley 422, fol. 146v; Holleran, p. 167.

[104]   [Robert Persons], *A Defence of the Censure, Gyven Upon Two Bookes of William Charke and Meredith Hanmer mynysters* ([Douai: Georges Flinton], 1582), STC 19401, ARCR II. 624, p. 8.

[105]   *A Defence of the Censure*, p. 8.

[106]   BL MS Harley 422, fol. 137r; Holleran, p. 146.

deale with pagans and Jewes, as St Paule had, for abbolishing of their Jewesse ceremonies and the Gentiles moralites' used the phrase, but by 'faith' they meant 'religion'.[107] In the course of this, Charke says, 'Campion, I do yeld to yowe on one thinge, that yowe have one of the stingingeste styles that ever I redd, which is the only thinge yowe broght to England with yowe'.[108] It is clear that Charke is outclassed by the clarity of Campion's logic, The debate ended on an inconclusive, but bizarre note, as the audience started to leave:

> Charke. All your answeres are sett downe and I hope the audience do nowe see howe foolishe they are therefore let us thanke God, and some being ready to depart, Mr Charke commanded the doors to be shut till after prayer, which was to this effect: to thank God that he hath at this time brought this solemn action to such success, to the confirmation of the faithful and confusion of the enemy, etc., which being ended all departed.[109]

Persons remembers that Charke asked the audience to pray, 'to thanke the lorde for your victorie that daye gotten uppon M. Campian'.[110] It is not surprising that 'many smylde in their sleeves to beholde this hypocrisie'.[111] The fourth disputation was an intellectual muddle, and it may be significant that Vallenger did not bother to record it. Campion was confronted by opponents who were flat-footed, outclassed both in theology and in the skill of disputation.

The official account of the fourth disputation in Nowell and Day is unconvincing. The muddle and chaotic repartee is replaced by laboured politeness. So when Campion asks if, for once, he can 'appose', a request immediately refused in the manuscript, the official version makes Charke concede and Campion pause a long time, before he can construct a syllogism. The manuscript says that Charke 'interrupted him sayinge yowe must not be apponent'.[112]

A fifth conference was scheduled for 13 October, but cancelled, because the Bishop of London, John Aylmer, another radical reformer and Marian exile, perceived that things were neither going well nor serving the government's purpose. On 29 September, Aylmer wrote to Burghley:

> Touching the conference with Campion in the Tower, I wrote unto Mr Lieutenant of my misliking that so many were admitted to it, whose authoritie is not to be directed there by me, but by hir Majestie and your Lordship. And for the ill opinion I have of it, I sent to staie it.[113]

---

[107]   BL MS Harley 422, fol. 145v; Holleran, p. 165.

[108]   BL MS Harley 422, fol. 145v; Holleran, p. 165.

[109]   BL MS Harley 422, fol. 147r; Holleran, p. 168.

[110]   *A Defence of the Censure*, p. 8.

[111]   *A Defence of the Censure*, p. 8.

[112]   BL MS Harley 422, fol. 145v; Holleran, p. 164.

[113]   BL Lansdowne MS 33, no. 24, fol. 48v.

The following day, the 30 September, in a message that reflects the real sense of urgency attached to the Campion affair by Lord Burghley, Thomas Norton, Campion's 'Rackmaster', who had acted as notary at the fourth conference, wrote:

> My dutie most humbly done to your Lordship. Immediately upon my comyng to London about iiii this afternoone I received your Lordships letter to have my notes of the last conference with Campion sent unto you. Whereupon I did forthwith goe to your Lordships house to present it unto you. Bicause you were gone to the courte, I have according to my dutie sent it you with as good spede as I can, and the rather this mornyng that it may seme time enough if your Lordship do thereupon gather any cause with the rest of the most honourable to think of any amendment of the order in that course or treatie that hath ben [taken] with that Jesuite.
>
> I pray your Lordship to pardon me to say that I think the course hitherto taken, either by lack of order or moderation or convenient respect of admitting men to be hearers, hath been both fruitless and hurtful, and subject to great harm by reportes.[114]

Laurence Humphrey, Regius Professor of Divinity at Oxford, was preparing to travel to London for the event. When he was told to stand down, he concluded correctly that intellectual dispute was to be abandoned for a blunter instrument:

> It was then, perhaps, smelt out that a different course was to be taken with the Jesuits, and that they would have to plead not for religion, but for life, and be accused not of heresy, but of treason.[115]

What was intended to demonstrate the weakness of Campion, and to enhance the authority employed by the state, became a powerful piece of theatre, in which Campion emerged as the tragic champion. He was given a public platform, even before his trial and execution, on which his oratory, his silent resistance and his relentless emphasis on real theological issues, won him adherents on every occasion.

Campion had seen off six leading opponents. With every resource the Queen's advisers could muster, they had failed to silence an opponent whose intellect, memory and patience had kept them all at bay. The Privy Council now turned back to torture, and a trial for treason against the state. Unable to ridicule him, it would take him apart at Tyburn. Order had been given 'to put them to the rack &c', again on 29 October, and there followed a whole series of searches and Star Chamber trials of those involved in guiding him or 'entertaining' him in their houses.[116]

State papers from the period after the disputations reveal that among Catholics there was triumphant response to Campion's performance. The regime had clearly underestimated the strength of Campion's inner resources, and really thought

---

114   BL Lansdowne MS 33, no. 61, fol. 150r.
115   Simpson, p. 360.
116   *APC, 1581–1590*, pp. 249–50.

they could win 'at the odds'. There were several unintended consequences. The disputations made public Campion's torture, and brought discredit on the state, particularly among lawyers. More importantly, they showed the state's attempt to manipulate 'reportes': public opinion. Campion, for all his powerlessness as a prisoner and victim of torture, had succeeded in moving the debate away from the issues that dominated Elizabethan monarchical republic's relations with Rome and onto the genuinely theological issues of the reformation.

Ballads appeared that reflect the period between September and the trial on 20 November. One, written in a fluent secretary hand, is endorsed as 'A libell touching Campion'. Too sophisticated in its etymology, plural voices and use of irony to be called popular, it combines admiration for Campion's intellectual superiority with scorn for the theatricality of the disputations and a sense of outrage at the racking:

Campion is a Champion
him once to overcome
the rest be well drest
the sooner to mumme

he lokes for his liffe
they saye to dispute
and doubts not our doctrine
he bragges to confute

yf in steede of good argument,
we deale by the racke,
the papistes maye thinke
that learninge we lacke

come forthe, my fine darlinge
and make him a dolt
you have him full fast
& that in strong holte

A Jesuite, a Jebusite wherefore I you praye
because he dothe teache you the onely right waye
he professeth the same by learninge to prove
and shall we from learninge to racke him remove

his reasones were redie, his groundes were most sure
the enemie cannot his force long endure
Campyon in camping in spirituall feild
in godes cause his liffe is reddy to yeld

our preacheres have preached in pastime & pleasure
and nowe they be hated farre passinge all measure
there wives and their wealthe have made them so mute
they can not nor dare not with Campyon dispute

let reason rule & rackinge sease
orels for ever hold your peace
you cannot withstand godes powre and his grace,
no not with the tower nor the rackinge place

A golden verse which truly saithe
let reason goe hold fast thy faithe
A mayde to be a mother & god a man
let reason go mum & beleve thowe the mother
set faithe above & lett reason goe under[117]

Voices proclaiming Campion the victor continued to circulate long after the event. After Campion's trial, a letter, dated 26 november 1581, and endorsed as 'A Letter from a Jesuit upon Campions Condemnation', was intercepted that interprets the trial as revenge for Campion's victory. It appears to be from a learned priest who has travelled with Campion whom he calls 'my deare brother Mr C'. He writes to those he calls 'my dearly beloved' fellow Catholics:

There is nothinge happened to him which he loked not for before, and whereof he made not oblacon to god before he ever sett foote to goe towardes England / I looked for this ende of his disputacones also, and suerelie when I heard howe prosperouslye god turned them to the glorye of his cause I suspected that he would have his lief also, for that yt was like the adversaries would never putt upp so great a blowe without revengement upon his bloude /... The pretended duste of fayned treason wherewith they go about to cover his bloud is blowen away with eny litle ayre of consideracon that commeth nere yt ...

The crosse appeares, Christ doth approve
    a comfort for us all
for whom to suffer or to dye
    is grace celestiall
be therefore of good corage nowe
    in your sharpe probacon
which shall you bring to glory greate
    and myghty consolacon
yf you persever to the ende
    of this sharpe storme in deede
you shall confounde both foe and frend
    and heaven have for meede[118]

---

[117] PRO SP 12/150, no. 72, fol. 137r–v: a single sheet folded in four, and clearly confiscated. Simpson, pp. 378–9, prints in three parts; cf. *CSP Domestic 1581–1590*, p. 31 (one verse only). See Alison Shell, *Oral Culture and Catholicism in Early Modern England* (Cambridge: University Press, 2007), p. 132. Simpson, in Downside MSS, notebook 30 A, fol. 75r, copied the entire poem from the State Papers without adding the divisions he put in the printed text.

[118] PRO SP 12/150, no. 67, fols 122r–123v; *CSP Domestic, 1581–1590*, p. 31; Simpson, Downside MS 30 A, fols 66r–68r. I have checked my reading against that of Simpson who (as was his practice) modernized the text as he transcribed.

After Campion's death, it is not only about his trial and execution that there is dispute, but also about the disputations. In the parish of St Andrew in Holborne, a certain Oliver Plunkett was hauled before 'a wardmott inquest' on 28 December 1581:

> as touchinge certayne speache, which the said Plunkett had used, to one Thomas Pirene, in holborne concerninge certayne Dysputations held in the Tower, betwene certayne Doctors of Devenities and one Campion the prysoner there, who as we doe understand, is executed for treason, which Disputation was had before dyvers persons of worshipp, as we doe juderstand by credable reportt, in which speech the said Plunkytt did affirme that the said Campyon was both dyscrett, and learned, and dyd saye verie well, and the he thought in his consciens that he was an honest man, and that the said Campyon would have convinced them, yf that he might have bene hard with indifferencye. All which speache the said Plunkytt beinge then demaunded by the forman, whether he had used any such, he answered the he had heard disputation and he thought in his consciens that Campyon was discret and learned, and said verie well, and he thought hym to be an honest man, whereunto the fforman answered, said, Neighbor Olyver yf yow thinke soe well of hym that is judged for treason, we doe not think well of you.[119]

Fifteen days later, William Fleetwood, Recorder, put his signature to this exchange and committed Plunkett 'to ward'. Since speech was so dangerous, it is no wonder that silence became a mode of protest. Oliver Plunkett was right: Campion had been both discreet and learned, and would have convinced men, if he had been given an impartial hearing.

As Lake and Questier argue, 'What is really remarkable is the fact that this extraordinary event should have been allowed to take place at all', showing 'how effective Campion's campaign for a fair hearing had been'.[120] The Privy Council had certainly failed to humiliate Campion, and he had succeeded in wresting the argument – if only for a brief moment – from the political into the theological sphere, where, as the leading Catholic disputant of his day, he was perfectly placed to challenge the doctrines of the still new and uncertain Elizabethan settlement.

---

[119]   BL MS Lansdowne 33, no. 63, fol. 153v. He is not to be confused with the seventeenth-century saint.

[120]   Lake and Questier, 'Edmund Campion Affair', pp. 621–2, a more optimistic assessment of the impact of the disputations than Thomas M. McCoog, S.J., '"Playing the Champion": The Role of Disputation in the Jesuit Mission', in *The Reckoned Expense*, pp. 139–63 (pp. 162–3), who thinks that 'Charke and Hanmer were right: the time for discussion had passed'.

Chapter 10
The Lawes of England

After Norton had advised Burghley, on 30 September 1581, to abandon the theatre of disputation, the Privy Council spent a month uncertain what to do next. Occupied with Ireland, the Anjou match and ordering searches in Oxfordshire and Hereford for 'hidden vestementes and suche lhyke tromperie for Massing', they decided to revert to the rack only at the end of October.[1] It is not clear exactly when the decision was taken to put Campion on trial, but it may not have been till after the final racking on 2 November.[2] The fourth warrant for torture was issued on 29 October 1581, and apparently implemented on the 31 October and 2 November, All Souls Day.[3] By now the Campion pageant was firmly hitched to the struggle in the Privy Council over the Anjou marriage.[4] William Camden, who had access to Burghley's papers, says that it was only when the Queen 'yielded to insistent entreaties' (*importunis precibus evicta*) that she finally agreed to put Campion on trial.[5]

But under what statute was he to be tried? Campion, and many of the priests, had entered the country several months before the proclamation of January 1581 against Jesuits and seminarists.[6] The Crown settled on treason under a statute of Edward III, of 1352, but two draft indictments preserved in Burghley's papers make clear that the initial indictment was for Campion alone, while the second was for Campion and 19 others.[7] In the second draft, which is headed 'Inditement of Campion and others', five overseas (and therefore absentee) defendants head the list; the Crown intended to damn Campion by association: with William Allen, Nicholas Morton, Humphrey Ely, Robert Persons and George Osliffe, linked by a chain of treasons stretching back to the northern rebellion of 1569.[8] If Sander had been alive, he would certainly have joined Allen, whose name runs like a refrain through the whole draft.[9] In addition to Campion, there are 14 others who will be present in court, in two separate batches. The second draft, which seems to

---

[1]   *APC, 1581–1582*, 15 October 1581, p. 234; 29 October 1581, p. 249.

[2]   Simpson, p. 390, takes this view.

[3]   CRS 58, Allen to Agazzari, 14 December 1581, p. 36 (see Chapter 8).

[4]   See Chapters 5, 8 and 12 for more detail on this long saga.

[5]   William Camden, *Annales Rerum Anglicarum et Hibernicarum* (London: Stansby, 1615) STC 4496, p. 326.

[6]   Hughes and Larkin, *Tudor Royal Proclamations*, II. 481–4, no. 655.

[7]   BL MS Lansdowne 33, nos 64 and 65, fols 154v–64v.

[8]   BL MS Lansdowne 33, no. 65. fol. 157r.

[9]   BL MS Lansdowne 33, no. 65 fols 157v–64v.

have been accepted, shows that the division of the 15 defendants into two groups occurred at an early stage, although John Hart was added later.[10]

The Coram Rege rolls are the official record of the trial and sentences.[11] They show that the arraignment, before the King's Bench at Westminster, was also spread over two days. The first seven priests and one layman – Edmund Campion, Ralph Sherwin, Thomas Cottam, Robert Johnson, Luke Kirby, James Bosgrave, Edward Rishton (all priests) and Henry Orton, a layman – were arraigned on Tuesday 14 November.[12] The diary entry of Richard Stonley (a teller of the Exchequer) for that day confirms this:

> This day one Campion & Sherwyn with others were brought to the Kinges Benche to have byn arrayned of Treyson, but the Quens Maiestie of hir gracious goodnes and marcye gaue them further respite to consider ther estate & to take good delyberacion before they shuld Answer for them selves.[13]

When Campion was asked to take the oath, 'being pitifully by his often cruel racking benummed before of bothe his armes, and having them wrapped in a furred cuffe, he was not able to lift his hand so high' so one of 'his fellowes humbly kissing his sacred handes, so wrounged for the confession of Christ, took of his cuffe, and so he lifted up his arme as highe as he coulde pleading not guiltie'.[14] They were

> Indicted of hyghe treason, namelye that they in the dayes of the last March and Aprill, Anno 22 Eliz: [1580] at Champaine Rhemes Rome and other places beyonde the Seas, had conspired the death of the Queenes Majestie, the overthrowe of the Religion nowe professed in England, the subvertion of the state, and that for the attempt therof, they had stirred up straungers to invade this Realme: moreover that the viiith daye of Maye nexte followinge, they tooke there Jorneye from Rhemes towardes England, to perswade and seduce the Queenes subjectes to the Romyshe Religion, obedience to the Pope, from there duetyes and allegiaunce to her Highnesse, and that the ffyrst of June, they arrived in this countrye for the selfe same purpose.[15]

Campion's reply to these charges was simple:

---

[10]   BL MS Lansdowne 33, no. 65, fol. 157v.

[11]   PRO, Coram Rege rolls, K.B. 27/1279, Crown side, rot. 2 and 3, are printed in full in *Cause of the Canonization of Blessed Martyrs John Houghton, Robert Lawrence, Augustine Webster, Richard Reynolds, John Stone, Cuthbert Mayne, John Paine, Edmund Campion, Alexander Briant, Ralph Sherwin and Luke Kirby* (Rome: Vatican Polyglot Press, 1968), 293–300.

[12]   Allen, *A Briefe Historie*, sig. d8r, confirms the date.

[13]   Folger MS V.a.459, fol. 30v (with abbreviations silently expanded). I thank Alan H. Nelson for his transcription.

[14]   Allen, *A Briefe Historie*, sig. d8r–v.

[15]   BL MS Harley 6265, fol. 14r.

I proteste before the livinge Lord, and the tribunall seate of God (which heare before my eyes I see represented), that it was unpossible for me to be guyltye of the leaste of theis accusations.[16]

They were brought before the court again on 16 November, and remanded. On the same day, a second group of seven more priests was indicted: Alexander Briant, Thomas Ford, John Short (or Shert), William Filby, Laurence Richardson, John Colleton and John Hart.[17] They too were brought before the court on the following day, 17 November. The Coram Rege rolls, rot. 2 'cites the indictment of the twenty and then records the proceedings and sentence of the first group; rot. 3 repeats the indictment of the twenty and then records the trial proceedings and sentence of the second group'.[18] Arraigned 'severally', every one pleaded not guilty in the same way.

The first group (Campion and seven others) was tried on Monday 20 November; all were sentenced to death. The second group (Briant and six others) was tried on the following day, 21 November, and all but Colleton sentenced to death: The Coram Rege rolls record the punishments in an abbreviated marginal gloss repeated 14 times: '*T[ractus] et S[uspensus]*' and one final '*Quiet[us]*'.[19] John Colleton affirmed that, when he was alleged to be in Rheims, he was in London 'à l'hostel que l'on dit Graiesynne, avec un gentil-homme appellé Lankaster'.[20] Fortunately, '*Maister Lankaster* of *Grayes Inne*' was in court to confirm this, and Colleton alone was acquitted.[21]

The indictment focuses on the fact that this is a plot from across the seas, *in partibus transmarinis*; specifically that they conspired in Rome and Rheims, both laden with hostile significance, to come to England to detach Her Majesty's subjects from their lawful allegiance.[22] While it is hard now to see how the jury reached, after one hour, their guilty verdict on seven priests and one layman, a careful reading of the indictment reveals the fear of foreign invasion led by priests.

---

[16]   BL MS Harley 6265, fol. 14r.

[17]   Richardson was the *alias* for Laurence Johnson who, like Cottam and Rishton, was a Lancashire man, educated at Brasenose, where he became a fellow in 1569. Like so many others, he left Oxford and arrived at Douai in 1573, and was ordained in 1577. He conducted his ministry in his native Lancashire, so the accusations of the 'pretended plot of Rhemes and Rome' were particularly inapposite in his case since, 'he was in England at the time that he was asserted to have been plotting at Rhemes', Challoner, *Missionary Priests*, pp. 59–60; Anstruther, *Seminary Priests*, I. 190.

[18]   *Cause of Canonization*, pp. 293–300. The Latin word for roll is *rotula*.

[19]   *Cause of Canonization*, pp. 298 and 300.

[20]   *L'Histoire de la Mort que le R. P. EDMOND CAMPION Pretre de la compagnie du nom de Jesus, et autres ont souffert en Angleterre pour la foy Catholique & Romaine le premier jour de Deccembre, 1581. Traduit d'Anglois en Francois* (Paris: Chaudiere, 1582), ARCR I. 197, p. 22.

[21]   Munday, *A breefe Aunswer*, sig. C2v (paraphrasing *L'Histoire de la Mort*).

[22]   *Cause of Canonization*, p. 295. Rheims was where Clovis was baptized and French kings were crowned.

The effects of Sander's invasion (frequently invoked in the trial) were still being felt. On 23 November 1581, reports were sent from Dublin of the escape of 'James Eustace, late Viscount Baltinglass', and his chaplain, to Spain, and the execution of his 'confederates' within the Pale.[23] Campion's life and death were, right up to the end, determined by Sander's writings and actions.

The first printed account of the trial was published in the *Complete Collection of State Trials and Proceedings for High Treason* by T.B. Howell in 1816.[24] There appears to be no official record of the trial before this date, since the Coram Rege rolls give no details of the trial itself.[25] Howell's source survives in three different manuscripts, all of which appear to derive from a missing original.[26] Since his printed version contains many substantial errors, the most flagrant of which repeats the scribal misreading of 'Riston' as 'Bristow', the two best manuscripts will be the principal source for all that follows. Several other documents give details of the torture, but say nothing of the trial.[27] Additional information is supplied by William Allen, Thomas Fitzherbert and Henry Walpole.[28] Walpole tells us: 'I was present during his arraignment in Court and indictment, and stood near him when sentence was passed'.[29] Walpole specifically mentions that Chief Justice Wray treated Campion with great courtesy, that the trial was sometimes so noisy that he could not hear everything, and that Campion and his seven companions 'stood at the bar from eight in the morning till seven in the evening'.[30] Fitzherbert was present neither at the trial nor the execution, but he was in London, and heard valuable testimonies, especially from other lawyers.[31] Bombino seems again to

---

[23]   *CSP Ireland, 1574–1585*, 86/79, p. 330.

[24]   *Complete Collection of State Trials and Proceedings for High Treason and other Misdemeanours from the earliest period to the year 1783, with notes and other illustrations*, compiled by T.B. Howell (*Cobbett's State Trials*), 33 vols (London: R. Bagshaw, 1809–28), I. 1049–67.

[25]   PRO K.B. 27/1279, Crown side, rots 2 and 3, Coram Rege indictments, pp. 292–300, printed in *Cause of Canonization*, pp. 292–300.

[26]   BL MS Harley 6265, fols 14r–22v, my copy-text, being the best complete manuscript, is clearly copied from the same source as BL MS Sloane 1132, fols 2r–13v, but it contains several errors; Bodl. Add. MS C. 303, fols 67r–73v, in a beautifully neat hand that is very similar to Vallenger's, is impeccable, but incomplete, lacking the first half of the trial. I have specified the point at which I have been able to use this. In BL MS Harley 6265, Campion's name is always written as 'Champion', and the arraignment is given as '15 November 1582', where both the day and the year are erroneous.

[27]   Simpson gives a vivid account of the trial, pp. 393–442, but does not specify his source or sources.

[28]   Printed in Pollen, *Acts of English Martyrs*, pp. 35–48.

[29]   Pollen, *Acts of English Martyrs*, p. 41.

[30]   Pollen, *Acts of English Martyrs*, pp. 41, 42 and 45.

[31]   Pollen, *Acts of English Martyrs*, pp. 41–2.

have had an eyewitness source (perhaps Colleton), and it is clear that the celebrity of the event had drawn an exceptional crowd.[32]

The Privy Council arrayed against Campion the principal law officers of the realm: Edmund Anderson, the Queen's Serjeant; the Chief Justice, Sir Christopher Wray; the Attorney General, John Popham; and the Solicitor General, Thomas Egerton. As Henry Hallam writes 'If we may confide in the published trial, the prosecution was as unfairly conducted, and supported by as slender evidence, as any perhaps which can be found in our books'.[33]

Westminster Hall (Figure 10.1) was then filled by raised wooden tiers, like those of a choir or parliament, where the audience was facing each other, and looking down on the defendants, and perhaps on the Queen's Counsel. The judges were on a raised wooden platform towards the far end; the King's Bench normally sat 'in the Southest corner' (at the far end).[34] This ancient building would have intimidated anyone not used to large public occasions. While most of the prisoners were brought on foot from the Marshalsea and Gatehouse, Campion was brought by boat from the Tower, so he and his escort had to make their way through the crowd. As he reached the Hall, Campion's arrival at the west door produced a moment of rapt attention:

> Campion, held up by the huge crush of people pressing to hear him, arrived later than the others at the doorway of the hall. You would have thought a new planet had appeared, the eyes of all turned towards him as if he were the only person on trial. Surrounded by his guards and executioners, he had a countenance very different from the style of his clothing; they say he seemed to have an even more composed expression (*constantiore vultu*). He was dressed in a long, heavy, coarse garment made from rags that reached to his ankles, which they call Irish. He kept his arms and hands, now utterly without feeling, and completely dislocated by the long and brutal tortures, within the sleeves of that tunic. He was unable to respond to those surreptitiously greeting him, except to show them the characteristic serenity of his face (*frontis, orisque serenitate*): calming the hostile, reassuring the friendly. When he finally reached the Bar, he provided a new and extraordinary spectacle: how great a light of the Catholic faith Edmund would be, as he was applauded by many, approved by all. As he arrived at the Bar, the rest of the martyrs who had preceded him and were already standing there, bowed deeply, as if to a prince at the head of their column.[35]

---

[32] Bombino, *Vita et Martyrium*, p. 267.

[33] *Cause of Canonization*, p. 339, citing Hallam, *The Constitutional History of England from the Accession of Henry VII to the Death of George II* (London: 1827), I. 156–7.

[34] Stow, *Survay of London* (1603), p. 472.

[35] Bombino, *Vita et Martyrium*, pp. 267–8 (my translation).

Figure 10.1   Trial in Westminster Hall of Henry Dundas, 1st Viscount Melville, 1806, aquatint by John Hill, from drawing by Augustus Charles Pugin (1762–1832) and Jean Claude Nattes (1765–1839). © The British Library, BL Maps K. Top. 24.24.l.

The Chief Justice, Sir Christopher Wray, presided, 'assisted by two of his puisnes (juniors), William Ayloff and Thomas Gawdy'.[36] The jury entered, and the Crown Clerk read the indictment. The jury was instructed that if any of those absent were found guilty of treason, they 'should then Inquire what Lands, Tenementes, Goods or Chatells, they had at the tyme of the Tresone committed, or at anie tyme sithens'.[37]

When each of the accused responded to the reading of his name, Sherwin extracted Campion's hand from its protective covering, kissed it and then raised it for him. Even more important were the names of those who were not present. The reading of the indictment, starting with William Allen, Nicholas Morton, Humphrey Ely and Robert Persons, made clear that this was essentially a trial of the Pope, Dr Allen's seminary and Dr Sander. Campion first responded to the nature of the indictment, making the reasonable point that the jury would be confused by the fact that they were all on the same charge sheet:

> My Lord forasmuche as our surmised offences are severall, for that the one is not to be taynted with the cryme of thother, the offence of one not beinge the offence of all, I could have wyshed lykewise, that for the avoydance of confusione we myght alsoe have been severallye indicted, and that our accusacions carryinge soe great importance and soe neerlye unto us as our lives, eche one might have had one daye for his triall, for albeit I acknowledge the Jurye to be wyse men, and much experienced in suche cases, yet all evidence beinge given, or rather handled at once, must needs breed a confusion in the Jurye, and perhapps suche a mispritione of matters as they may take the evidence agaynst one to be agaynst all, and consequently the cryme of the one for the cryme of the other, and finally the guyltye to be saved and the guiltlesse to be condemned, wherfore I would it had pleased your Lordshippe that the indictment had been severall, and we myght have severall dayes of tryall.[38]

When the Queen's Counsel, Mr Anderson, sardonically commented that Campion seemed to have had his 'counsell', Campion replied that he has had 'Noe counsell but a pure conscience'.[39] The Chief Justice, however, acknowledged the force of the argument, admitting that he would have preferred each of the defendants to have had a 'severall day assigned him had the tyme soe permitted'.[40] The judge gave no explanation as to why time was so short that justice had to be flouted, and the Crown opened its case. Campion, as well as making use of his logical and rhetorical skills, seems uncommonly aware of the basic principles of English

---

[36] Geoffrey de C. Parmiter, *Edmund Plowden: An Elizabethan Recusant Lawyer* (Southampton: Catholic Record Society, 1987), p. 141.

[37] BL MS Harley 6265, fol. 14r. These speeches provide a rare opportunity to hear Campion speaking in English.

[38] BL MS Harley 6265, fol. 14r. I have expanded 'thone' and 'thother', this scribe's elision.

[39] BL MS Harley 6265, fol. 14r.

[40] BL MS Harley 6265, fol. 14v.

common law. After pointing out that they should have had 'one learned in your law to answer for us', Campion, aged 41, found himself conducting not only his own defence, but that of the other young and inexperienced men who were included in the indictment.[41] Despite the fact that he was mocked for using the terminology of scholastic logic, he conducted the defence in a way that impressed several lawyers who were friends of Thomas Fitzherbert and Henry Walpole, himself a Gray's Inn lawyer.[42]

Edmund Anderson, for the Crown, opened with a carefully prepared speech that started by praising the Queen, listed a chain of rebellions which sprang from the 'well it selfe the pope', and finally swung into a rhetorical series of parallel clauses:

> What then? Are we to thinke these latest and present conspiracies to have been done, eyther unwittinge or unwilling the pope? shall we denye eyther champion or his companione, without the Popes assent or consent, to have conspired these matters beyond the Seas themselves, whye, had they not entertainment at his handes? did he bestowe nothinge upone them for ther maytenaunce? Was ther noe cause why he should eyther doe for them or they for him? They Papistes, he Pope; they flyinge ther countrey, he receavinge them; they Jesuites, he their founder; he supreme head, they sworne members; he ther cheyfe provoste, they his dearest subjectes.[43]

Twenty-three years of peace under Queen Elizabeth have been broken only by 'secret and pryvye practising of sinister devises', which Anderson proceeds to list, from the 'Rebellion in the north', through the 'bill of pius Quintus' to Dr Sander:

> yea, which is more, and yet sticketh in our stomackes, they efforded soe large commendacions to Saunders, lykinge and extollinge his late proceedinges in Ireland, that it cannot be otherwyse entended, but that thereof, they also have been partakers?[44]

This emotive rhetoric must have aroused the audience to increasingly voluble agreement that they were traitors; the defendants were 'troblesomlye affected' and, in a noisy scene, they cried out that they were true and faithful subjects. Campion 'bare it out best', and having 'heard the exaggerations of the Attorney and lawyers attempting to please the Government … seemed wonder-stricken; then, lifting up his eyes to heaven, and recollecting himself, he began his answer'.[45] Campion 'demanded of Mr Anderson', whether he came 'as an orator to accuse them or as a pleader to give in Evidence'.[46] It was a well-deserved, but polite,

---

[41]   Pollen, *Acts of English Martyrs*, p. 43.
[42]   Pollen, *Acts of English Martyrs*, pp. 38 and 43: see below for details.
[43]   BL MS Harley 6265, fol. 14v.
[44]   BL MS Harley 6265, fol. 15r.
[45]   Pollen, *Acts of English Martyrs*, p. 44.
[46]   BL MS Harley 6265, fol. 15r.

rebuke to the Crown's representative, and it provoked Justice Wray into defending the Queen's Serjeant: these 'be but inducements to the poynte it selfe, and thereto every one shall have his severall Aunswere'.[47]

Campion's reply started with a statement of the basis of English law that could have come straight from Sir John Fortescue; continued with a parody of the swinging rhythm of Anderson's rhetorical questions and, by linguistic analysis of the word 'reconcile', highlighted the injustice of making sacramental confession a treasonable crime; and concluded by contrasting 'proof' with 'conjectures' (the very last word):

> The wysdome and providence of the Lawes of England (as I take it) is such as proceedeth not to the tryall of man, for lyfe and death, by shiftes of probabilities, and conjecturall surmises, without profe of the cryme, by sufficient Evidence and substantiall witnesse. For otherwyse it had beene verye unequally provided, that upone the descante and florishes of affected speeches a mans lyfe should be brought into daunger and extremitye, or that upon the perswatione of anie orator or vehement pleader without wytnes (*viva voce*) testifying the same, a mans offence should be Judged or Reputed mortall. Yf soe I see not to what end Mr Serjeants oration tendes, or if I see an end, I see it but frustrate, for be the cryme but in tryfles, the lawe hath his passage; be the thefe but of an halfpennye, witnesses are produced, soe that probabilities, agravations are not the Ballance wherin Justice must be weyghed, but witnesses oathes, and apparent guyltines. Wherto then apperteyneth these objections of treasone? he barelye affirmeth; we flatly denieth them. But let us examyne them, how will they urge us? we fledde our countrye: what of that? The pope gave us interteynment, how then? We are catholykes, what is that to the purpose? We perswaded the people, what followeth? We are therfore traytors: wee denye the sequell, this noe more necessarye, then if a sheep had been stolne, and to accuse one you should frame this reason: my parents are theeves, my companions suspected persones, and my selfe an evill liver, and one that loveth mutton: therfore I stole the sheepe. Who seeth not but that these be odious cyrcumstances to bringe a man in hatred with the Jurye, and necessarye matter to conclude him guyltye? Is that to the purpose? We perswaded the people: what followeth? we are therfore traytors. Yea, but wee seduced the Queenes subjectes from ther alleigiance to her Majestie, what can be more unliklye? We are dead men to the world, soe onelye traveled for soules, we touched neyther state nor pollicye, we had noe such commission. Wher was then our seducing? Nay, but we reconciled them to the Pope: nay then what reconciliation can ther be to him, sithen reconciliation is onely due to god? This word soundeth not to a lawyeres usage, and therfore it is wrested agaynst us unaptlye; the reconciliation that we endevored was onelye to god, and as Peter sayeth, *reconciliamini Domino*. What resteth then agaynst us? that we were pryvye to the rebellion in the north, instruments to Storye, ministers to ffeltone, partakers with Saunders? How soe? forsouth it must be presumed. Why? because we commended some, some we rejoyced at, concerning some we gave counsell and conference. How appeareth that bye our own speeches? nothing lesse. God is our witnesse, we never ment

---

[47]   BL MS Harley 6265, fol. 15r.

it, we dreamed it not. These matters ought to be proved and not urged, declared by evidence and not surmysed by anye. Notwithstanding it ought to be soe, yet muste all circumstances note us for trators, indeed all yet that is layed agaynst us be but bare cyrcumstances and noe sufficient argumentes to prove us traytors: in soe much that we thinke our selves somwhat hardlye delte with, that for wante of proofe must aunswer to cyrcumstances. Well, circumstaunces or other, as I remember this was all, and if this were all, all this were nothing, wherfore in gods behalf we praye that better proofe may be used, and that our lyves be not brought in prejudice bye conjectures.[48]

It was a magisterial opening to the defence, confirmed by Walpole's account:

Reason, moreover, requires that we should have one learned in your law to answer for us, and time to meet such long accusations, especially seeing that it is not only we here present, who are accused at this bar, but also the greatest princes in the world – the Pope, the King of Spain and all the Catholics in the world. For what you say against myself and these others, about the Northern Rising, the book of Doctor Bristow, and the coming of Doctor Sander to Ireland, does not affect us more than all the rest of our religion. Again, where you call us traitors, you ought to prove, first, that those acts were traitorous, and then that we were their authors. This you have not done, and have therefore arrived at a conclusion without establishing your premisses. When one of the Court took him up: 'If you want to dispute as though you were in the schools, you are only proving yourself a fool'. 'I pray God make us both wise', was Campion's polite reply.[49]

Despite Campion's defence that the prosecution's argument was based on *circumstances* and *conjectures*, his demolition of the prosecution's attempt to tar him with a general brush may not have been enough to prevent the audience thinking that Campion and his fellow prisoners were part of a long line of papal conspirators that stretched back to Felton, Story and the northern earls. Sander's expedition was particularly damaging, as Campion was charged with having brought £3,000 to support his expedition.[50] In his version of the trial, Anthony Munday, another Roman spy and one of the Crown's witnesses, preserves a strikingly idiomatic phrase that may be Campion's:

For us that be heere at his instant, you must eyther saye: thou Campion dyddest this thing, or thou (naming some of the other) committedst this offence, and thereupon bring your proofes and witnesses, otherwise you shall never be able to touch us. As for these assertions, for the strength they have against us, I wyll not esteeme it woorthy a penyworth of Pippins.[51]

---

[48]   BL MS Harley 6265, fol. 15r–v.

[49]   Pollen, *Acts of English Martyrs*, pp. 44–5.

[50]   *L'Histoire de la Mort*, p. 17.

[51]   Anthony Munday, *A Discoverie of Edmund Campion and his Confederates ... Whereunto is added, the Execution of Edmund Campion, Ralphe Sherwin, and Alexander*

The Queen's Counsel now passed to a more detailed attempt to link Campion and his fellow defendants with the most destructive elements of papal policy. Campion's replies to each of the charges offer fascinating insights into life and practice among English exiles abroad. His defence is spirited and precise, patiently exposing the logical flaws in an argument that insisted on linking all plots to them.

Anderson's first general charge is that it is the custom of 'all *Seminarye* men' to take two oaths to the text of 'Brystoes Motives'. An attempt to summarize Dr Allen's articles, Richard Bristow's *Motives unto the Catholike faith* was first published in 1574, and it was on items from this book (alongside Sander's *De Visibili Monarchia*) that Campion and the other defendants had been interrogated.[52] Campion first pointed out that only 'yonge striplinges that be under tuition' take the oath of allegiance to the pope in the book, and that the 'men of ryper yeares' have plenty of other books to study, and are 'farr better imployed then they otherwyse could bee, in Readinge English Pamphlettes'.[53] Campion was not being pejorative to Bristow, who had debated with Campion before the Queen in Oxford, and arrived in Douai just before him. Rather, it distinguished between lightweight religious pamphlets intended for wide consumption, and serious theological debate in Latin. The very fact that these 'pamphlets' were in English indicated that they were not intended for an academic audience. The English colleges in Rheims and Rome aimed to turn out respectable students of theology. Campion's fellow defendant, Luke Kirby, declared that there were no more than 'fowre Bookes of those Brystoes motives in all the Seminaryes', and 'Thereupone they all cryed that wheras they were indicted of treasone, they feared least under vizarde of that, they should be condemned of religione'.[54]

Campion immediately set out logical support for their plea by showing that they had all been offered liberty if they went to church, that Paschal and John Nicholls had accepted the offer and been set free and that since they could acquire liberty by conforming, religion must be the issue. The Attorney General intervened to argue that other matters have come to light since Nicholls was set free, and that their religion 'myght be anie cloake or colour of suche treasons'.[55]

Anderson now asserted that there was a material link with the Pope. Each of them had received money from this enemy of the Queen, some '200 crownes some more, some less'; and that the only purpose of such a gift, must be 'the pryvye inveygling and persuations to sette on foote his devises and treacheryes'.[56]

Briant, executed at Tiborne the 1 of December (London: Edward White, 29 January 1582) STC 18270, sig. B5r.

[52] Richard Bristow, *A Brief Treatise of diverse plaine and sure wayes to finde out the truthe in this doubtful and dangerous time of Heresie: conteyning sundry worthy Motives unto the Catholike faith* (Antwerp: J. Fowler, 1574), STC 3799, ARCR II. 67.

[53] BL MS Harley 6265, fol. 16r.

[54] BL MS Harley 6265, fol. 16r.

[55] BL MS Harley 6265, fol. 16r.

[56] BL MS Harley 6265, fol. 16r.

Campion's reply was simple: 'what end should that bee? marye to preach the Gospell, noe devises noe treacherye, noe suche end was intended'.[57]

The first witness was produced, a spy called 'Caddye or Caddocke', who claimed he has heard 'beyond the seas' of a plan to send 200 priests who have all taken a vow 'for the restoring and establishing of Religione in England', and that Sir Richard Shelley, Grand Prior of the English Knights of St John, had been approached to see if he would lead an army into England. Sir Richard had answered, 'that he would rather drinke poyson with Demostenes then see the overthrow of his countrye, and added further that he thought the catholikes in England would fyrst stand in Armes agaynst the Pope, before they would joyne such an enterpryse'.[58] Campion pointed out that 'this deposition is more for us than agaynste us': there was no evidence they were part of the 'two hundred', and if Sir Richard did not consent, how much less would they be willing, who are 'dead men to the world'?[59] Sir Richard Shelley was renowned for his fierce loyalty to the Queen, and for his opposition to militant Catholics.[60]

Anderson now directed at Campion a particular charge that some years ago, he talked with Cardinal Gesualdi about the Papal bull of excommunication, and that this 'doth flatte prove yow A Traytor'.[61] Campion's answer began with a characteristically personal appeal to the jury – 'Yow men of the Jurye I praye yow listen' – and an admission that the Cardinal had offered him preferment, which (as we have seen) he politely declined.[62] When the Cardinal asked his opinion of the papal bull, and Campion replied that 'it procured much severytye in England', the cardinal agreed that it should be 'mitigated' so that Catholics could obey 'their Queene without daunger of excommunication'.[63] Campion's opinion of the bull could hardly be clearer: it had been an unmitigated disaster for Catholics in England. If his view was justified in 1573, it was even more so when he saw the Pope, on 14 April 1580, to plead for changes to the bull.[64] When Anderson still says that a 'mitigation' is not outright opposition, and that it shows Campion's complicity in the bull, Campion asserted forcefully that 'My pryvitye enforceth not my consenting, nay rather it proved my disagreement in that I sayd it procured much severytye'.[65]

---

[57]   BL MS Harley 6265, fol. 16r.

[58]   BL MS Harley 6265, fol. 16r–v. The scribe has given his name as 'Ralph', presumably a mistaken expansion of an initial; see *ODNB*, 'Sir Richard Shelley' (c. 1513–1587), by Michael Mullett.

[59]   BL MS Harley 6265, fol. 16v.

[60]   *ODNB*, 'Sir Richard Shelley', by Michael Mullett.

[61]   BL MS Harley 6265, fol. 16v.

[62]   BL MS Harley 6265, fol. 16v. See Chapter 3.

[63]   BL MS Harley 6265, fol. 16v.

[64]   See Chapter 5.

[65]   BL MS Harley 6265, fol. 17r.

Anderson moved to a second charge, that Campion had conferred with the Bishop of Ross, 'a professed Papist, and a mortall enymye to the state and queene of England'.[66] We know that the bishop, the Queen of Scots' agent, had dined in the Clementinum in October 1578, but Campion utterly denied any 'conference past between him and me'.[67] Campion's reply is completely credible, since it is hard to imagine much common ground between these two men.

Anderson now moved to corrupted material evidence, a letter he claims is 'from Dr Allen unto Dr Sander in Ireland'. The Queen's Counsel here uses an encrypted letter from Sander to Allen, dated 6 November, 1577, which had been in the government's hands for some time, to allege that Campion must have known of 'an army and hoste of men the Pope by the aid of the King of Spain and the Duke of Florence had levied for the overthrow of this Realme, the destruction of her majestie, and the placing of the Scotishe Queen as governesse in England'.[68] Anderson accuses Allen of having written that '[the *king of Spaine*] feared the warres as a chyld doth the rodde', and that '[the *pope*] at all tymes will be readye with two thousand to ayde him'.[69] This distorted letter certainly incriminates the man who sent it, Sander, but the Crown has reversed the authorship to make Allen appear to be conspiring with the pope and Sander, two of the leading enemies of the Queen.[70] Anderson alleges that, because Campion came from Rome and visited Dr Allen in Rheims, Campion must have been 'pryvye' to such schemes, and indeed came as 'procurator from the Pope and Dr Allen'.[71] Campion, apparently unaware that the Crown has tampered with the evidence to make Allen the author, rejects the charge, saying that he came 'but as a priest to minister the sacraments and to heare confessions', and that nothing indicates *his* involvement with this plan.[72] Campion's defence is prefaced by a rehearsal of his three vows to the Society of Jesus, and a solemn declaration that it was on the third 'vowe injoyning obeydiance I came (being sent for) from Prage to Rome, having not soe much as the smallest inkling of those supposed armyes nor the least inclinacion, to put anie such thinge in practise'; that the Pope had 'with charge and commandment' expressly 'excused me from matters of state', that while he dined with Allen in Rheims, and 'after dinner' he had 'walked in his garden', he talked 'not one jot' of 'the crowne or state

---

[66]   BL MS Harley 6265, fol. 17r.

[67]   BL MS Harley 6265, fol. 17r; Clementinum Diaries, Strahov MS DC.III.16, fol. 99r; see, D. McN. Lockie, 'The Political Career of the Bishop of Ross, 1568–80', *Historical Journal of the University of Birmingham* 4–5 (1953–6), 98–145 (109–11). There is a need for a detailed study of John Leslie's visits to, and reception at, the court of Rudolf II in Prague.

[68]   BL MS Harley 6265, fol. 17r. See BL Add. MS 48029, fol. 50r; printed in CRS 26, pp. 13–14.

[69]   BL MS Harley 6265, fol. 17r.

[70]   See Chapter 4 for full quotation from the letter of Sander to Allen on 6 November 1577.

[71]   BL MS Harley 6265, fol. 17r.

[72]   BL MS Harley 6265, fol. 17r–v.

of England' and, most tellingly of all, that Dr Allen was not his superior.[73] If (and Campion insists this is not the case),

> Dr Allen had communicated such affayres unto me, yet for that he was not my superior it had been full apostacye in me to obeye him. Dr Allen for his learninge and good religione I reverence, but neyther was I his subject or inferior, nor he the man at whose commaundment I rested.[74]

It was in obedience to his 'provost' that Campion has made the voyage to England 'as a Preyst to minister the sacraments, to heare confessions', as he would have, had he 'been sent to the Indians or uttermost regions of the world'.[75] Francis Xavier had landed in India in 1542, and Akbar, the Mughal emperor, invited the Jesuits in Goa to send three learned fathers to him in September 1579.[76] Thomas Cottam later discloses that he was originally among those destined for the Indians, and that he had come back to England only for health reasons. Three Jesuits (Fr Rudolfo Acquaviva, Fr Antonio Monserrate and Fr Francis Henriquez, a Persian-speaking interpreter) were sent, and arrived at the Mughal court on 27 February 1580, a week after Campion left Prague for Rome (Plate 4).[77] Mercurian had agreed to send Campion to England, only on condition that his priests did not meddle in affairs of state. Campion sounds as if he had imagined going to India. He had refused to take any overall responsibility for the English mission, which he knew (at least after Rheims) was to be only the spiritual wing of Allen's 'stowte assallynge of England'.[78] Anderson was definitely going beyond any evidence, but he was also probing Campion's most sensitive area as a Jesuit under vow of obedience to his 'provost', but seconded to Dr Allen's mission.

Anderson now employed the populist language of anti-Jesuit discourse. The Jesuits have been 'lurking and lying hid in secret places', wearing disguises, changing their names. Are clothes such as 'a buff leather jerkin and velvet Venetians' appropriate for men 'dead to the world' (as Campion had earlier claimed)? No, if their intentions had been good, they would never have 'wrought a hugger mugger' and 'hated the lyghte'; their 'budging decyphers their treason': this is no spiritual mission.[79] The demotic register, and the fashion flourish of the 'buff leather jerkin' made its impact, since the authorities later wanted Campion

---

73 BL MS Harley 6265, fol. 17r.

74 BL MS Harley 6265, fol. 17v.

75 BL MS Harley 6265, fol. 17r–v.

76 Daniel Bartoli, S.J., *Missione Al Gran Mogor Del P. Ridolfo Aquaviva Della Compagnia Di Gesu Sua Vita e Morte E D'Altri Quattro Compagni Uccisi in Odio Della Fede In Salsete Di Goa* (Rome: Salvione, 1714), pp. 37–56; Sir Edward Maclagan, *The Jesuits and the Great Mogul* (London: Burns Oates and Washbourne Ltd, 1932), pp. 24 and 26.

77 Bartoli, *Missione al Gran Mogor*, p. 38; depicted in the Chester Beatty Library, Dublin. In 03.263.

78 Sander, in letter of 6 November 1577, *Letters and Memorial of Cardinal Allen*, p. 38.

79 BL MS Harley 6265, fol. 17v.

to be humiliated by wearing it on his way to the scaffold.[80] This shorthand for disguise and deception was a convenient metaphor for the 'lurking and lying' of the Jesuit missionaries. To Anderson's populist rhetoric, which must have roused the crowd in Westminster Hall, Campion replied with scriptural understatement. Yes, they have changed their names and worn disguises, as did the Apostle Paul, because he feared that, if he were known, he would be arrested:

> I chaunged my name, I kept secretlye, I imytated Paule, was I thenne a Traytor? but the wearing of a Buffe Jerkine, a velvet hatt, and suche like, is much forced agaynste me, as though the wearing of anie apparell were Treasone, or that I in soe doing were ere the more a Traytor. I am not indicted upone the statute for apparell, nether is it anye parte of this present arraignment in deed. I acknowledge an offence to godwards for soe doinge, & therof it did earnestly repent me, and therfore doe now pennance as yow see me.[81]

Campion was dressed very differently now, the manuscript tells us: 'He was newlye shaven in a rugge gowne and a great black nyghte cappe coveringe halfe his face'.[82]

Anderson next produced a piece of evidence that was to form an important part of all subsequent discussions: Campion's letter to Thomas Pounde, first cousin to the Earl of Southampton. No transcript of this oft-quoted letter has survived:

> The Clerk of the Crown read a letter sent from Champione unto one Pounde, a Catholike, part of the contentes whereof was this. It greyveth me muche to have offended the Catholike cause so highly as to confesse the names of those gentlemen and friends in whose houses I had been entertayned. Yet in this, I greatly cheryshe and comforte my selfe that I never discovered anye secretes there declared, and that I will not, come Racke, come Rope.[83]

Campion's promise that he would not give away any secrets was read by the prosecution as evidence that Campion was concealing 'some heinous matter and very pernicious', whereas he was referring to the vow he took as a priest 'never to disclose anie secrets confessed'.[84] Campion's admission that he had disclosed the names of his hosts, and that he derived comfort from the fact that he has withheld the secrets of the confessional and his priestly ministry, cost him two final bouts of racking.

Campion clearly did yield the names of those he had stayed with, but equally he drew the line at revealing the names of those who had been present at Mass or

---

[80]   Bombino, *Vita et Martyrium*, pp, 287–8. See Chapter 11 for the full story.

[81]   BL MS Harley 6265, fols 17v–18r.

[82]   BL MS Harley 6265, fol. 18r. Howell printed this as 'a great blacking strap covering half his face': eccentric apparel, even for Campion.

[83]   BL MS Harley 6265, fol. 18r.

[84]   BL MS Harley 6265, fol. 18r.

whose confessions he had heard.[85] It was a distinction that might have been hard for the 12 members of the jury to understand. Anderson passed to another piece of material evidence: written copies of oaths to be administered to people to 'alien the hartes of her subjectes from her Majestie, renouncinge there obeydience to her' and 'swearing subjection to the Pope'.[86] These documents, Anderson argues, had been found in the houses Campion has visited; therefore, he must be the person who put them there. This is almost a textbook example of false logic, and Campion quickly dismissed this 'naked presumption', pointing out that Anderson's 'reason is imperfecte'.[87] Anderson responded by pouring scorn on Campion's scholastic language ('minor and conclusion') as inappropriate to a courtroom.[88]

The prosecution ended by asserting that Campion had refused 'to sweare to the supremacie, a notorious token to an evillwiller to the crowne' and to answer the commissioners on whether the Pope's excommunication was valid or not.[89] Campion had replied that these were 'blouddye questions' such as the Pharisees put to Jesus to trap him, and Hammond and Norton confirmed Campion's answer. Campion was perfectly correct: under English common law, a defendant had a right not to incriminate himself, a right defended by all the great jurists of the period, including Francis Bacon, who wrote to King James that 'By the laws of England no man is bound to accuse himself'.[90]

Campion now launched a devastating counter-attack. He contrasted his private conversation with the Queen to the artificial 'interrogatories' put to him on the rack. It was a masterly performance, a finely discriminating study of papal powers and one of the clearest answers ever given on this 'blouddye' question:

> Not longe sithens it pleased her Majestie to demaund of me whether I did acknowledge her to bee my Queene or noe. I answered, that I did acknowledge her highnes: not onelye as my Queene but alsoe, as my most lawfull governesse, and beinge further required of her Majestie whether I thought the Pope might lawfully excommunicate her / Or noe, I aunswered I confesse my selfe an insufficient umpire betweene her Majestie and the Pope, for soe highe a controversie, wherof nether the certentye is as yet known, nor the best divines in christendome stand fullye resolved. Albeit I thought that if the Pope should doe it, yet it might bee insufficiente, for it is agreed *Clavis errare potest*: but the divines of the catholyke churche doe distinguishe of the Popes authoritye attributinge unto him *ordinatam et inordinatam potestatem. Ordinatam*, wherbye he procedeth in matters merely spirituall and pertinent to the churche, and bye that he cannot excommunicate anie Prince or potentate, *inordinatam*, where he passeth by order of lawe, as bye appeales and such like, and soe as some thinke, he maye excommunicate &

[85]   See Chapter 8 for discussion of this complex issue.
[86]   BL MS Harley 6265, fol. 18v.
[87]   BL MS Harley 6265, fol. 18v.
[88]   BL MS Harley 6265, fol. 18v.
[89]   BL MS Harley 6265, fol. 18v.
[90]   Hanson, *Discovering the Subject*, p. 37, quoting Spedding, *Letters and Life*, III. 114.

depose Princes. The selfsame Articles were required of me, bye the commisioners but muche more urged to the poynte of supremycye, and to further supposalls then I could thinke of. I sayd in deede they were blouddye questions and verye Pharesaicall undermininge of my lyfe, wherunto I answered as Chryst did to the Delemma: give to *Cesar* that which is due to *Cesar* and to God that to god belongeth. I acknowledged her Highness as my governes & Soverayne, I acknowledged her Majestie (both *facto & Iure*), to be Queene.[91]

Campion, in distinguishing between the Pope's power in spiritual matters where his authority is naturally exercised, and his power in political matters where he must pass by due process of law, draws on language formulated to discuss God's power (best known through William of Ockham, but made current by Luther and Calvin) to create an analogy with papal power.[92] Henry More's paraphrase confirms this, perhaps making the distinction between the Pope's powers clearer, by saying that 'In matters purely spiritual, as the theologians admit, the Pope cannot err when he is publicly teaching the Church in matters pertaining to faith, but he can err in judging practical situations'.[93]

The sceptical tone on the power of excommunication ('as some thinke') makes it clear that scholarly opinion was divided; that if the Pope acted in the temporal sphere, he had to proceed according to the rule of law, with time allowed for appeal (which was certainly ignored in the bull of 1570), and that lay members of a jury were 'temporall and unfitte Judges' to decide such theological questions, since 'theis matters be merelye spirituall poyntes of doctrine and disputable in schooles.[94] Campion ended by asserting that he has given an unequivocal acceptance of the Queen's sovereignty 'both *facto & Iure*'.[95]

Canon law required that the Pope issue a warning before any excommunication, and that a sentence of deposition be separated by a year's delay from the sentence of excommunication.[96] In 1570, both sentences were pronounced together; and

---

[91]   BL MS Harley 6265, fol. 18v–19r.

[92]   Donna B, Hamilton, *Anthony Munday and the Catholics, 1560–1633* (Aldershot, UK and Burlington, VT: Ashgate, 2005), pp. 40–46, presents Munday's account in *A discoverie of Edmund Campion* (STC 18270) as a skilful piece of 'Catholic sophistry' using 'typographical' consistency to hide his own 'equivocation': we must all become 'different, if not better, readers than Alfield was'. We are asked to believe Munday's unique report, that on the critical issue of 'loyalty to the pope', Campion, a celebrated orator, resorted to mumbling: 'somewhat drew in his woords to himselfe' (*A discoverie*, sig. F8v). Hamilton offers insufficient evidence to reverse Allen's verdict, which she quotes of 'that damned traitor, Munday' (p. 52), as 'the offal of the world' (*A brief historie*, sig. A7r), or Campion's that he was not a credible witness (see below).

[93]   More, *Historia Missionis*, p. 118.

[94]   BL MS Harley 6265, fol. 19r.

[95]   BL MS Harley 6265, fol. 19r. This contradicts the account in *A Particular Declaration*, sig. B4v.

[96]   Arnold Oskar Meyer, *England and the Catholic Church under Queen Elizabeth*, 2nd ed. (London: Routledge & Kegan Paul, 1967), pp. 77–90 (p. 79).

the bull circumvented the requirement for the warning period by referring, in the first part of the bull, to the *praetensa Angliae regina* (the pretended or so-called Queen of England). Although Pope Pius V 'showed a careful observance of form', beginning the process in the Apostolic Chamber on 5 February 1570, concluding the evidence on 12 February, and pronouncing judgement on 25 February, he did not inform the King of Spain.[97] Philip II expressed his astonishment at 'this sudden and unexpected step', and wrote to Elizabeth to tell her of his displeasure at the declaration.[98] It was 'at the last the work of a moment, called forth by the necessity for prompt action'.[99] To suggest that Elizabeth had no right to the throne because of her illegitimacy, might have seemed a casuistical way round the requirements of canon law but, as Arnold Oskar Meyer argues, it was 'indefensible from a strictly legal point of view'.[100] It was also a serious diplomatic failure, uniting Elizabeth's subjects in 'a blaze of loyalty', as the church's medieval manipulation of 'spiritual and temporal weapons' to restore unity 'recoiled on its authors with a force which no aggressive action against the church on England's part could have equalled'.[101]

The Holy Roman Emperor, Maximilian II, also wrote to Elizabeth to express his strong disapproval, and (at Elizabeth's request) asked the Pope either to withdraw the bull or to prevent its diffusion. Both requests were refused.[102] Campion's replies on the bull, *Regnans in excelsis*, suggest he also thought that it was unwise and, quite possibly, illegitimate. Many contemporaries, it seems, shared Campion's reservations, as a manuscript copied out 25 years later reveals:

> Notwithstanding, this we know that many Catholiques did thincke hardly of that deede (meaning the bull of pius 5. against Q. Eliz.) & did wishe that so great a matter & subject to dyvers suspitions had never bene commytted to writing, but reserved to higher powers & most cheifly to the judgment of god.[103]

Anderson now called two 'suborned' witnesses, George Elyot and Anthony Munday.[104] Elyot deposed that he had heard Campion preach in Berkshire on the text of Christ weeping over Jerusalem, and that he had heard him lament the many 'enormities here abounding in England, and namely heresies' and that he looked forward to 'a day of change, comfortable to the catholiques now shaken and

---

[97] Meyer, *England and the Catholic Church*, p. 78.

[98] Meyer, *England and the Catholic Church*, p. 78.

[99] Meyer, *England and the Catholic Church*, p. 78.

[100] Meyer, *England and the Catholic Church*, p. 82.

[101] Meyer, *England and the Catholic Church*, p. 86.

[102] Meyer, *England and the Catholic Church*, p. 78.

[103] Bodl. MSS Eng. th. b. 1-2, II. 477. The manuscript was transcribed shortly after 1605, and reflects an earlier opinion. See also Francis Harington's extremely harsh verdict in an epigram (in Latin and English), condemning the bull, *The Epigrams of Sir John Harington*, ed. Gerard Kilroy (Farnham, UK and Burlington, VT: Ashgate, 2009), p. 296.

[104] Pollen, *Acts of the English Martyrs*, p. 38. Fitzherbert's charge that they were 'suborned' is supported by the fact that Elyot had already been paid £100; see Chapter 7.

distressed and terrible to the heretickes here florishinge in the lande'.[105] Campion's sermon, as we have seen, blended the compassionate moment when Christ wept over Jerusalem (here understood as England) with sadness at the state's violence towards the priests: 'Jerusalem, Jerusalem, thou that killeth the prophets'.[106] Anderson asks what the 'day of change' could refer to, except the day when the Pope, the King of Spain and the Duke of Florence all invade 'this realm'.[107] Campion's emotional reply takes in the treachery of Elyot and the absurdity of converting religious change into violent political and military invasion:

> O Judas, Judas, noe other day was in my mynd, I protest, then that wherin it should please God to make a restitution of ffayth and religione.[108]

This slender piece of evidence is followed by Anthony Munday, the itinerant player who spent enough time in the English College in Rome to make money out of the experience with a scandalous book that came out the following year.[109] He 'deposed that he hard the Englishe men as the Doctors and others conspire of these treasons against England', and that 'Campion and others afterwards had conference with Dr Allen'.[110] Campion makes short work of the logical error by this 'stage player', pointing out, 'Here is nothing deposed agaynst me directlye'.[111]

The third phase of the prosecution's case was over. Anderson had used his opening speech to portray a chain of treasons, passed to general charges against all the accused, and finally to particular charges against Campion himself, based on two unreliable witnesses. Not one of these charges has passed Campion's scholastic analysis of the central logical flaw in the Crown's case: that no one has yet been able to charge him with a single crime. Anderson has simply painted him as guilty by association with the Pope, the king of Spain, Dr Allen and Dr Sander. Campion's clear disavowal of Allen as his superior provides the only hint of his frustration at being charged with the very policies he had done all he could to avoid.

---

[105] BL MS Harley 6265, fol. 19r.

[106] Luke 19:41–2 was blended with Luke 13:34 (cf. Matthew 23:37): see Chapter 7.

[107] BL MS Harley 6265, fol. 19r.

[108] BL MS Harley 6265, fol. 19r.

[109] Anthony Munday, *The English Romayne lyfe* (London: J. Charlewood for N. Ling, 21 jn.1582), STC 18272. The book, full of lurid details and sensationalist readings of Catholic practices, is more a precursor of the Gothic novel than reportage.

[110] BL MS Harley 6265, fol. 19v. Hamilton, *Munday and the Catholics*, p. 39, implies that Munday's testimony against Campion, 'Bristow' (*vere* 'Riston') and Henry Orton is not utterly untrustworthy, but produces no evidence that any of it is true. The charge against Rishton that he was an explosives expert is perhaps the least credible evidence in the trial. As Alford, *The Watchers*, pp. 62 and 87, admits, he had a 'nose for scandal' and 'a gift for telling exciting tales'.

[111] Alfield, *A true reporte*, sig. D4v–E1r; BL MS Harley 6265, fol. 19v.

As Anderson passed to the other defendants, Campion intervened to defend each of the young and vulnerable priests who have been retrospectively grouped in a conspiracy. Anderson first turned his fire on Ralph Sherwin, a former fellow of Exeter College, 'an excellent Grecian and Hebrician', according to Anthony Wood, who went on to Douai, and then to the English College in Rome.[112] 'Tall of stature and slender', he came with Campion's party from Rome, but arrived ahead of Campion, and was arrested in London on 9 November 1580 (the same day as the siege of Smerwick), in the house of Nicholas Roscarrock.[113] After a month in the Marshalsea, he was moved to the Tower on 4 December, offered a bishopric, racked severely on 15 and 19 December 1580, and kept in close confinement for almost a year.[114] He was now aged 32.

Anderson's charge against Sherwin is that, before the commissioners, he has refused to swear to the supremacy, did not give a plain answer on the papal bull, but admitted that he came to 'perswade the people to the catholique religion'.[115] *A Particular Declaration* dates the interrogation as 12 November 1580, one year earlier.[116] Sherwin defends his actions by appealing for the same 'tolleration' as the Apostles, who preached in 'Empires of Eathnick and heathen rulers' and were not sentenced to death, so he 'well hoped' for the same treatment 'in such a comon wealth, as wheare open christianitie and godlines was pretended'.[117] When the Clerk to the Crown read out a letter showing that 'by the fierside' in Rheims, he has talked of the best place for a foreign army to land, and mentioned Sir John Arundell in Cornwall, Sherwin replies that he 'never spake any suche matter (god is my recorde) neither was it ever the least part of my meaninge'.[118]

Anderson turned next to James Bosgrave, a Jesuit who had returned from Poland, aged 32. Bosgrave's position was unique. Upon arrival from Poland on 4 October 1580, he had been arrested by the mayor, as he landed at Orford in Suffolk, probably on information supplied by John Rogers (son of the Protestant martyr) who, on a diplomatic mission for the Queen to the King of Denmark, had met Bosgrave by chance at Elsinore.[119] The mayor paid £5 14s 4d to have Bosgrave

---

[112]   Wood, *Athenae Oxonienses*, I. 478; Folger MS V.a.459, fol. 30v, where Stonley, a clerk of the Exchequer, calls him a 'Knight'.

[113]   *Cause of Canonization*, p. 234.

[114]   'Tower Diary', sig. 214v; Anstruther, *Seminary Priests*, I. 312; *Cause of Canonisation*, 235.

[115]   BL MS Harley 6265, fol. 19v.

[116]   *A Particular Declaration*, sig. C1v.

[117]   BL MS Harley 6265, fol. 19v; Bodl. MS Add. C 303, fol. 67r. From this point, I have collated the Harley manuscript with the Bodleian manuscript, giving preference to the latter.

[118]   BL MS Harley 6265, fol. 19v; Bodl. MS Add. C 303, fol. 67r.

[119]   Paul Skwarczynski, 'Elsinore 1580: John Rogers and James Bosgrave', *Recusant History* 16.1 (1982), 1–16 (pp. 3–4); Thomas M. McCoog, S.J., 'The Mystery of James Bosgrave', in *Fashioning Jesuit Identity*, pp. 123–41 (pp. 128–9). For John Rogers, the martyr, see Chapter 1.

taken to London, where the Bishop of London questioned him.[120] Asked what he thought about going to the official church, Bosgrave had innocently replied that he thought it was sometimes permitted. Bishop Aylmer was delighted with this reply, and published all over London that one of the most learned Jesuits had given this very reasonable opinion. The news was broadcast while Campion and Persons were still in the country before they met at Uxbridge at the end of October 1580. Bosgrave who was used to the situation in Poland and Lithuania, where nobility and gentry could attend Protestant services without causing scandal, found himself shunned by his fellow Catholics, and could not understand why.

When his brother explained the situation to him, he instantly set about correcting the impression given by his original opinion.[121] He wrote an open letter to all English Catholics retracting his opinion, entitled 'The satisfaction of M. James Bosgrave', and another letter to the Bishop of London, 'to retract his promise of going to church, and deliver himself up to their hands'.[122] Bosgrave was immediately rearrested, and put in the Marshalsea. Anderson's charge now was similar to the one he had used with Sherwin, that he had denied the supremacy, 'staggered without anie perfect aunsweare unto the Bull', and admitted that he came 'to perswade and teache, acknowledginge hir majestie his Queen and temporall heade'.[123] His main charge is that Bosgrave has admitted that he 'hearde it reported how the Pope, the King of Spaine, and the Duke of fflorence would sende a great armie of men into Englande, to deprive the Queenes majestie bothe of lyfe & dignitye for the restitution of the catholicke religion'.[124] Because he heard of treasonable plans and did not disclose them, he has become party to treason. Bosgrave, completely nonplussed, replies: 'What? am I a traitoure, because I hearde it spoken of?'[125]

Campion 'perceaving Bosgrave merelie daunted with the matter', speaks up on his behalf, pointing out 'how brittle & slipperye a grownde, fame & reportes are wonte to be built on', because of the nature of 'fame' (closer to the Latin *fama*, or rumour):

> the cause is the nature and propertie of fame, which is never but uncertaine and sometimes but forged. For whoe findes it not by dailye experience how that in everye cittie, everie village, yea and in most barbours shoppes, in all England, manie speaches, both of states and commonwealthes, bee tossed, which wear never meant nor dreampt of in the court? yf it be soe in England shall we not alsoe looke for the like in Italie and Spaine? yes trulye. For though the countries doe differ, yet the nature of the men remainethe the same, namelie, allwaies desirouse & greadie of newes.[126]

[120] Skwarczynski, 'Elsinore', p. 7.

[121] Skwarczynski, 'Elsinore', p. 8.

[122] Skwarczynski, 'Elsinore', p. 8.

[123] BL MS Harley 6265, fol. 19v; Bodl. MS Add. C 303, fol. 67r–v.

[124] BL MS Harley 6265, fol. 19v; Bodl. MS Add. C 303, fol. 67v.

[125] BL MS Harley 6265, fol. 20r; Bodl. MS Add. C 303, fol. 67v.

[126] BL MS Harley 6265, fol. 20r; Bodl. MS Add. C 303, fols 67v–68r.

This superb analysis of the instability of rumour in social discourse must have struck a chord, not just with the jury, but also with the whole crowded hall (although one wonders when Campion last went to a barber's shop). Popham's response suggests that there has been prolonged applause, as he acknowledges that Campion has won this point, when he stands up to say that 'there is no cloathe so course, but Campione can cast a colour upon it', and he attempts to retrieve the situation by arguing that Bosgrave has admitted that he 'arrived into England to teache and perswade the people: And what perswasion should that be, but to prepare a readines for these warres?'[127] Campion makes short work of Popham's logical leaps:

> These be but faynt and bare implications, which move but urge not: affirme but prove not. Whereas yow ought not to amplifie and gather upon wordes, when the matter concernethe and touchethe a mans lyfe.[128]

Anderson now turned to the man who had given himself up. Thomas Cottam's childlike honesty seems strangely at odds with the ferocious powers the Elizabethan state turned on him. Anderson, after noting that Cottam had, in his examination, neither agreed to the supremacy nor answered directly on the Pope's authority, drove directly at Cottam by asserting that his coming to England at the same time as the others, means that he must be involved in 'the furtheraunce of these affaires'.[129] Cottam's reply is engagingly simple:

> Yt was neither my purpose, nor my message to come into Englande, neither would I have come, had not god otherwise driven me. ffor my journaye was appointed to the Indians, and thither I had gone, had my healthe bene therto answerable. But the meane whiles, it pleased God to visitt me with sickenesse, and being cownselled by the phisitions for my healthe sake, to come into Englande (for otherwise as they sayde, eyther remayninge theare or going els wheare, I shoulde not recover it).[130]

Poor Cottam came to England to restore his health, only to be racked, and later hanged. Campion immediately intervened to say that among Roman physicians it was a common opinion that, if an Englishman falls sick, there is no better way for him to recover than to 'take his naturall aier, which best agreethe with his complexion'.[131] Cottam, aged 32, asserts again that he has come to England only because of his health, and with no intention either to 'perswade or disswade: beinge otherwise by my provost charged to the Indians', and that all the time in

---

[127]   BL MS Harley 6265, fol. 20r; Bodl. MS Add. C 303, fol. 68r.
[128]   BL MS Harley 6265, fol. 20r; Bodl. MS Add. C 303, fol. 68r.
[129]   BL MS Harley 6265, fol. 20r; Bodl. MS Add. C 303, fol. 68r.
[130]   BL MS Harley 6265, fol. 20r; Bodl. MS Add. C 303, fol. 68v.
[131]   BL MS Harley 6265, fol. 20v; Bodl. MS Add. C 303, fol. 68v.

England he lived openly in Southwark and 'walked daylie in Paules': behaviour that 'betokened my innocencie'.[132]

Anderson had a further card up his sleeve. A book has been found in Cottam's 'budget' (bag): Dr Aspingueta's *Tractatus Conscientiae*, which deals with issues surrounding the supremacy, and offers model ways of answering questions or debating religious issues. Surely, Anderson argues, the only purpose of such a book is to persuade and dissuade? Presumably, the spy Sledd rummaged through his belongings when they were travelling together. Cottam was, understandably, thrown, and, presumably in blind panic, said that he 'knew nothing of that book, neither when nor how it came unto me'.[133]

Campion, 'seeing him driven to so narrow an exigent, as to denie that which was manifeste', again answered on his behalf, arguing first that things can get into a man's luggage either through the 'malice of others' or 'his owne negligence or oversyghte', but if that is not the case

> yet is it a custome, with all studentes beyounde the seas, when as anie man learned and well thought of draweth any treatise, touchinge either conscience or good behavioure, to coppye it owt, and carrie it abowt them, not therbye ayminge at anie faction or conspiracie, but for their owne instruction, and private direction.[134]

The Queen's Counsel then turned to Robert Johnson. Anderson began his case against Johnson with the same preamble as against Cottam, that he had not yielded on the issue of the supremacy, and had given no 'resolute' answers on the papal bull of excommunication. Elyot was immediately called as witness. Elyot's story is that during the Christmas festivities at Lady Petre's house, Ingatestone Hall, Fr Paine, who had been acting as steward and, appointed to be Elyot's bedfellow, became friendly with Elyot. Elyot harboured a pathological resentment towards Paine for refusing to marry him to the girl of Lady Petre's household with whom he had eloped.[135] Elyot now alleged that Paine had tried to persuade him to join a plot involving 50 armed men 'furnished with privy coates, pocket daggers, & two hande swords', who would attack the Queen and her ministers when they 'shuld take the ayre', and that Paine had thought killing the Queen as lawful as 'to kill a brute beaste'.[136] Fr Paine had been singularly unlucky in his bedfellow, since he was convicted and hanged at Chelmsford on 2 April 1582, on the evidence of this

---

[132] BL MS Harley 6265, fol. 20v; Bodl. MS Add. C 303, fol. 68v.

[133] BL MS Harley 6265, fol. 20v; Bodl. MS Add. C 303, fol. 69r.

[134] BL MS Harley 6265, fol. 20v; Bodl. MS Add. C 303, fol. 69r–v.

[135] The word 'pathological' is appropriate to Elyot's behaviour throughout the search, the trial and the two approaches to Campion, at Henley and in the Tower: see Chapters 7, 10 and 11.

[136] BL MS Harley 6265, fol. 20v–21r; Bodl. MS Add. C 303, fol. 69v.

sole witness, who was paid £4 on the day of his execution.[137] Elyot now alleged that Johnson arrived after Paine had left, told him that Paine had fled because he was worried that Elyot 'would discover his secretes', and warned him, upon pain of damnation, to reveal nothing.[138] Johnson can only say, in answer to this colourful fabrication, 'I never in my life had anie such talk with him, nor uttered any speache tendinge to such matter'.[139]

Anderson passed to an examination of Edward Rishton, like Cottam a Brasenose man, who 'acknowledged her Majestie his lawfull Queen & governesse', as Campion had done.[140] Anderson tried to imply that his mere arrival at the same time as the rest proves he was 'also a partie and a furtherer of their purpose'.[141] Rishton's defence is disarming:

> I have to my mother a poore wydowe, whoe besydes me had one other sonne with the companie of whom (during his life) she was well appaide & contented. But it pleased god afterwardes to dispose him, at his mercie, and to deprive my mother of hir further succoure. She takinge the matter verye heavelye, used what meanes she possiblie could for my returne, sent letters after letters, and those soe importunate that, will I, or nill I, I must needes come home. The which was the onelye cawse of myne arrivall and not anye other, god is my witnesse.[142]

This account, in its very particularity and emotion, is in keeping with the fact that Rishton had joined the party only in Rheims.[143] In addition, he is not charged with any priestly activity, but

---

[137] TNA E. 351/542, mem. 33, cited as Doc. XVII, in *Cause of the Canonization*, p. 301.

[138] BL MS Harley 6265, fol. 21r; Bodl. MS Add. C 303, fol. 70r; see Harley, *William Byrd*, p. 69.

[139] BL MS Harley 6265, fol. 21r; Bodl. MS Add. C 303, fol. 69r.

[140] This is the name in Bodl. MS. Add. C. 303, fol. 70r–v. Both BL MS Harley 6265, fol. 21r and BL MS Sloane 1132, misread the name of the next defendant as 'Bristowe', and this was followed by the printed account in Howell's *State Trials*, I. 1067, Simpson, 427–8, and most subsequent accounts. The name cannot be correct. Richard Bristow, the author of the famous 'Motives' (on which the other defendants had been questioned on the rack), had entered England because of his health only in 23 September of 1581, and died on 14 October 1581. He is said to have been sheltered by the Bellamy family in Harrow, and buried by them. Richard Bristow is not named in the indictment in the Coram Rege rolls, while 'Riston' is. Bodl. Add. MS C. 303 here has the correct 'Riston', and his *R* could easily have been mistaken for a *B*. Anstruther, *Seminary Priests*, I. 53, tries to solve the problem by suggesting that Bristow may have died a month later. *ODNB*, 'Richard Bristow' (1538–81), by Peter E.B. Harris, wrestles with the problem, and inclines towards the view that he was at the trial. But Campion lists Bristow among the many *absent* people unjustly tried (see below), and if Bristow had been in the dock, Anderson would certainly have pressed him hard on his politically subversive 'Motives'.

[141] BL MS Harley 6265, fol. 21r; Bodl. MS Add. C 303, fol. 70r.

[142] BL MS Harley 6265, fol. 21r; Bodl. MS Add. C 303, fol. 70r.

[143] See Chapter 5.

> Anthonye Mundaye deposed against Riston that he shoulde saye, that he was
> conninge in fireworkes, and that shortlye he would make a confection of wilde
> fire, wherewith he would burne her Majestie when she were upone the Thames
> in hir bardge. And the deponent swore further that he hearde it spoken beyond
> the seas, that who soever had not the watche worde (which was *Jesu Maria*)
> shoulde be slaine.[144]

Rishton's reply to this lurid pyrotechnical fantasy is that he calls 'god to witnesse
I never fostred suche thoughtes nor never had such conninge in fireworkes, &
therfore he swearethe the greatest untruthe that may be'.[145] Munday's charge that
a Brasenose scholar who has spent 10 of his 31 years studying in Oxford, Douai
and Rome, is an explosives expert, is even more risible than Elyot's tale, but it may
have been earned him some money.

The Queen's Counsel now turned to Luke Kirby, a Yorkshireman who had
studied in Louvain, and was now aged 33.[146] He is listed first in *A Particular
Declaration* among those to whom the 'Articles are put'.[147] Kirby is reported as
saying that he 'he cannot answer' whether the Pope had the power to authorize
the northern earls. He thinks that 'Doctour Saunders and Doctour Bristowe, in his
booke of Motives' might both 'be deceived in these points of their books' but that
matter 'he referreth to God'.[148] The main evidence against Kirby was provided
by the spy, Charles Sledd, who deposed that when he was on his sick-bed in the
English College in Rome, Kirby had come to his bedside and talked about 'a
greate day' when the Pope, the King of Spain and the Duke of Florence would
bring about 'a great alteration'. To cap this, Sledd says that 'one Tuder a familiar
freinde of Kirbies', had called the Queen 'that whore of Babilon, that Jesabell of
Englande', whom he wished to kill.[149] To this kind of evidence, where the most
incriminating accusation is what Sledd alleges that Kirby said, Kirby can only
swear that, as he hopes 'to be saved at the last doome, there is not one word of
this deposition (that concerneth me) either true, or credible'.[150] Poor Kirby, who
has had to endure the ministrations of 'Maister *Reignoldes* of Oxford' in prison,
was asked all these questions again on the scaffold, where 'many did speake unto
him', and his answers were very 'intricat', so the people cried, 'away with him'.[151]

---

[144]   BL MS Harley 6265, fol. 21r; Bodl. MS Add. C 303, fol. 70v.

[145]   BL MS Harley 6265, fol. 21r; Bodl. MS Add. C 303, fol. 70v.

[146]   Allen, *A Briefe Historie*, sig. a1v; Anstruther, *Seminary Priests*, I. 197–8.

[147]   *A particular declaration*, sig. C2v.

[148]   Allen, *A Briefe Historie*, sig. A2r; copied from *A particular declaration*, sig. C3r.

[149]   BL MS Harley 6265, fol. 21v; Bodl. MS Add. C 303, fol. 70v.

[150]   BL MS Harley 6265, fol. 21v; Bodl. MS Add. C 303, fol. 71r.

[151]   Allen, *A Briefe Historie*, sig. B4r–v. John Rainolds, theologian and President of
Corpus Christi College, was the only Calvinist among the five brothers who included Jerome
(expelled from Corpus), James of Exeter, Edmund (of Cassington) and William Rainolds
of New College. For details on the other brothers, see Kilroy, 'Queen's Visit to Oxford',
pp. 336–7; *ODNB*, 'John Rainolds' (1549–1607) by Mordechai Feingold; and Chapter 2.

For the last defendant to be named in this trial, the layman Henry Orton, Munday deposed that

> that he being in Lions in ffraunce sayed unto this deponent, that her majestie was noe lawfull Queen of England, and that he ought her noe kinde of obeydiaunce, the deponent sayd further that this Orton made suite unto Dr Allen, that he might be one of the Popes pensioners, wherunto Dr Allen would not agree unlesse Orton would become a preist or seminarye man, which Orton refused.[152]

Orton utterly denies that 'ever I had anie speech with the witnesse eyther at Lyons or els where' and goes on to say that Munday 'manifestlye forswearthethe himselfe as one that having neither honestie nor religion, careth for neither'.[153] The other defendants joined in the criticism of Munday as a turncoat and hypocrite, who had pretended to be a Catholic in Rome, even going to Communion:

> The same all the partyes indicted did afferme, and that he was an Atheist for that, beyonde the Seas, he gooth on Pilgrimage, and receaveth the Sacrament, makinge himelfe a catholicke, and here he taketh a newe face and playethe the protestant, and therefore is an unfit and unworthye wytnesse, to give Evidence, or depose agaynst lyfe.[154]

The defendants linked this attack on Munday's hypocrisy with a scathing attack on Elyot, who, because he was 'a murtherer, and had slayne two men alreadye' was 'noe sufficiente nor allowable witnesse'.[155] It was disgraceful that the state was relying on such men to convict priests, two of whom were good enough to be offered bishoprics.

This was the end of the formal evidence. The judge advised the jury that they have to choose to believe 'prisoners that speake for there lives' or 'the witnesses that come freelye to depose'.[156] Since Elyot had been paid £100 on 8 September 1581, 'freely' is perhaps the wrong word.[157] Such a payment, made before a trial, would now render the verdict unsafe, and certainly be grounds for appeal. The Lord Chief Justice, trying to be fair, it seems, offered the defendants the chance to speak.

---

[152]   BL MS Harley 6265, fol. 21v; Bodl. MS Add. C 303, fol. 71r.

[153]   BL MS Harley 6265, fol. 21v; Bodl. MS Add. C 303, fol. 71v.

[154]   BL MS Harley 6265, fol. 21v; Bodl. MS Add. C 303, fol. 71v.

[155]   BL MS Harley 6265, fols 21v–22r; Bodl. MS Add. C 303, fol. 71v.

[156]   BL MS Harley 6265, fol. 22r; Bodl. MS Add. C 303, fol. 71v.

[157]   *Cause of the Canonization*, p. 195 citing PRO E. 404/124, box 3, lists this under payments received for the betrayal of Fr John Paine. But Elyot was paid £4 for going as a witness to Paine's trial in Chelmsford on 2 April 1582 (*Cause of Canonization*, p. 202, citing PRO E. 351/542, no. 33). £100 is surely payment for capturing Campion, and down-payment for giving witness against him.

Yow that be here indicted, yow see what is alledged, agaynst yow, in discharge wherof, if yow have anie more to saye, speake on, and we will heare yow untill the morrowe morninge, we would be lothe that yow should have anie occasion to complaine of the courte. And therfore, if ought rest behinde untowlde that is availeable for yow, speake, and yow shall be heard with indifferencie.[158]

Campion, savagely racked three weeks before, had been standing at the bar for over nine hours on full alert in order to defend each of his companions. Yet he now delivered his most critical speech.[159] Mixing legal analysis with common idiom, he must have held the huge audience in Westminster Hall spellbound with a speech that, in its logical, legal and moral assessment of the evidence, neither Popham nor Anderson had at any point matched:

What charge this daie yow sustaine, and what accompt yow are to render at the dreadfull judgement (whereof I could wishe this also were a mirror), I trust there is not one of yow but knoweth: I doubt not but in like manner, yow forecaste howe deare the innocent is unto god, and at what price he howldethe mannes bloode. Here we are accused and impleaded to the deathe, here yow doe receave owr lives into yowr custodie, here must be yowr choice, eyther to restore them or condempne them. We have noe whither to appeale, but unto your consciences: wee have noe frends to make there but yowr heede and discretion. Take heede, I beseeche yow, let no colour or inducementes deceyve yow, lett your grownde be substantiall, for your buildinge is waightie. All this maye yow doe sufficientlye (we doubt not) if you will but marke intentivelye, what thinges have been treated. In three distinct and severall pointes, the speache and discourse of this whole daye consistethe. ffirst in presumpcions and probabilities: secondlye in matters of doctrine and religion: lastlye in oathes and testimonie of witnesses. The weake and forcelesse proofe that proceedeth from conjectures, ar neither worthye to carrie the verdict of soe manye, nor sufficient evidence for triall of mans life. The constitutions of the realme exacte a necessitie, / and will that noe man showld totter in the hazarde of likelihoodes. And albeit the strongest reasons of owr accusers, have been put in bare and naked probabilities, yet are they not matters for yow to relye on, whoe ought to regard what onelye is apparaunt. Sett circumstaunces asyde, set presumptions apart, set that reason for your rule, which is warraunted by certayntye. But probabilities were not the onelye matters, which impertinentlye have heere been discussed. Ther were alsoe poyntes of doctrine and religione, (as excommunicatione, bookes and pamphlettes) wherin a great part of the daye hath been as unfitlye consumed. In soe much that in this same verye daye yow have heard not onelye us, but also the pope, the kinge of Spaine, the Duke of fflorence, Allen, Sawnders, Aspingueta, Bristowe, and manie more arraigned. What force excommunications be of, what authoritye is due to the Bishoppe of Rome, how mennes consciences muste be

---

158   BL MS Harley 6265, fol. 22r; Bodl. MS Add. C 303, fols 71v–72r.

159   Since it is a rare chance to hear Campion speaking at length, I have printed this in full, taking Bodl. MS Add. C. 303 as my copy text, and marking the page breaks in that manuscript.

instructed, be no matters of facte, nor triable bye Jurors: but pointes yet disputed, and not resolved in Schooles. How then can they be determined by yow, though wise, yet laye, though otherwyse experienced, yet herein ignoraunt? But were it soe, that for your knowledge, and skill in dyvinitye, yow might seeme approved censors of soe highe a controversye, yet are they noe parte of our indictment, and therfore not to be respected by the Jurye. Yow perchaunce would aske (if these prove nought agaynst us) what then yow should enquire of, for these sett asidede, the rest is allmost nothinge. Pardon me, I praye yow, owr innocence is such that if all were cut off that have been objected, either weaklye or untruelye agaynst us, ther would indeede rest nothinge that might proove us guiltye. But I aunswear unto yow, that what remayneth be oathes: And those, not to rest / As prooffes unto yow, but to be duely examined and fully considered whether they be true, and their deposers of creditt. In common matters, we see witnesses oft times repelled, and if at anie tyme the creditt be little, it ought then to be least, when they sweare against life. Call, I pray yow, to remembraunce how faintlye some have deposed, how cowldlye others, how untrulye the rest, especiallye two (which have testified most). What truthe may yow expect from their mowthes? the one hath confessed himselfe a murtherer, the other well knowne a detestable atheiste. A prophane heathen, a destroyer of two men alreadye, on your consciences would you beleeve them? theye that had betrayed both God and man, they that have lefte nothing to swear by, nether religion nor honestye, though yow would beleeve them, could yow? I knowe your wisdom is greater, your consciences uprighter. Esteeme of them as they bee, examyne the other two, yow shall fynd neither of them to have proved directlye, that ever we conspired or practised ought accomptable as treason in the face of a commonwealthe. Hereof yow ought to be throughlye advised, and that not so much for us as your selves: yowr sentence for us is present and finall, for your selves it is to come, and everlastinge. God give yow the spiritt to discerne aright, have respecte to yowr selves, I will hould yow noe longer, I committe the rest unto goddes providence and your good discretions.[160]

As remarkable as the understated rhetoric is the clarity with which Campion directs the jury; with the authority of a judge, he divides the evidence and even the witnesses, into separate categories; he also treats the jury as if they were in need of his guidance, not the men who were to determine his life. Campion argues with devastating precision that the only relevant evidence is that of two witnesses – one a murderer, the other an atheist – whose credibility is seriously in doubt. Campion raises the stakes by making each of the jury feel responsible for the lives of the defendants, and for the eternal judgement they will face if they deliberately distort justice. It is a remarkable reversal of power.

Throughout the trial, Campion showed a greater grasp of the principles of justice than either the judge, who was clearly uncomfortable in his role, or the prosecuting counsel, whose case was so weak that he had to wrap it in well-worn rhetorical tropes. Campion's perception that the Pope was being arraigned is central to the injustice of this trial. While Dr Allen heads the list of those indicted,

---

[160]   BL MS Harley 6265, fol. 22r–v; Bodl. Add. MS C 303, fols 72r–73r.

it is significant that his name hardly ever occurs in the trial, whereas the Pope's name occurs 43 times.

Persons's 'Notae breves' make it clear that the general view of lawyers present was that Campion would be acquitted, so 'very clearly' (*liquidissime*) had he defended them against the charges.[161] Allen repeats the legal judgement that 'whilst the Jeurie were gone furth, divers wise and well learned lawiers and others, conjecturing and conferring one with anvother what should be the verdict, they all agreed that it was impossible to condemn *Father Campion*'.[162] Thomas Fitzherbert says that 'a lawyer, and an earnest Protestant, yet a friend of mine, who was present at the trial, told me the day after, that in truth the evidences that were given against Father Campion were so weak, and his answers so sufficient and clear, that he could not persuade himself that he should be condemned, until he heard the Chief Justice give the sentence of death'.[163] Walpole, who was present as a member of Gray's Inn, wrote:

> Thus the whole day passed, and the jury retired to consider whether they should find a verdict of guilty or of not guilty. I asked a lawyer called Strickland, a friend of mine, who stood near me, if he thought they would be condemned, and what he thought of Campion. 'As far as he is concerned', was the answer, 'he surely cannot be touched, his answers to all that has been laid to his charge have been so excellent. I should say the same of all the rest, except of one or two, who may be found guilty on the insinuations against them'. As this man is known to he a heretic, he cannot be suspected of partiality.[164]

The trial account simply says that 'The Jurye departed under ther warden, staied an hower in conference, and then returned, pronowncinge all guiltie'.[165] As Persons notes, 'It seemed that it had been decided beforehand that all should be condemned, and therefore no defence was effective'.[166] Westminster Hall must have been a noisy place while the jury and judges withdrew, leaving the lawyers and defendants in the middle to discuss the likely outcome. Someone offered Campion a drink, and because he could not lift the cup, held it for him.[167] No pause in a play could have been as dramatic as this. When the verdict was given, defendant by defendant, there must have been gasps of surprise. Bombino says that many wagers on Campion being acquitted had been taken.[168]

---

[161] ABSI Collectanea P. I, fol. 158a.

[162] Allen, *A Briefe Historie*, sig. e1r–v.

[163] Pollen, *Acts of English Martyrs*, pp. 38–9. See also Archives of Westminster Cathedral, Series A. II. 39, where it is quoted in *Cause of the Canonization*, p. 334.

[164] Pollen, *Acts of English Martyrs*, p. 43.

[165] BL MS Harley 6265, fol. 22v; Bodl. MS Add. C 303, fol. 73r.

[166] Letter to Agazzari, 23 December 1581, *Cause of the Canonization*, p. 302.

[167] ABSI Collectanea P. I, fol. 158a.

[168] Bodl. MS Tanner 329, fol. 105v.

Before passing sentence, the Chief Justice asked Campion and the rest what they can say as a reason why they should not die, Campion replied:

> Yt was not our deathe we ever feared: but we knew we were not lordes of our owne lives, and therfore for want of aunswere, would not be guilty of our owne deathes. The onelye thing that we have now to saye, is that if our religion doe make us traitours, we are worthye to be condemned, but otherwise, are & have been, and shall be as true subjectes as ever the Queen had anie.[169]

The judge then passed sentence, and all the prisoners 'stormed in countenance, crying they were as true and faithful subjects as ever the Queen had', but 'only Campion suppressed his affections'.[170] *L'Histoire de la Mort*, in 'a detail' that reached Paris during the printing, adds that Campion first replied to the judge that he 'hoped that God would be kinder to him in the last judgement than he had been', and ended, *Te Deum laudamus, te Dominum confitemur*, and then turned to the whole audience, and said:

> You see, my dearest brethren in Jesus Christ, how unjustly we are condemned to death, and this for religion alone. For even if I had been capable of as many crimes as I have been charged with, they would never have promised me from the day I became a prisoner, life and liberty with many other large promises on the sole condition that I found myself going once to their meetings in church or that I did something similar. I call as my witness the Lieutenant of the Tower of London, who is here present, and who cannot deny it.[171]

Campion's speech supports the evidence that, in addition to the offers made by Leicester in late July, the Queen herself had very recently made an offer, which was witnessed by Hopton.[172] If the Queen herself were ready not only to release Campion but to make him an archbishop (a 'large promise' indeed) if he conformed, the trial for treason was a charade.

Persons, in his letter to Agazzari, adds that as 'in a loud voice Fr Campion began to recite "*Te Deum laudamus*", Fr Sherwin began to say the Easter antiphon, "*Haec est dies quam fecit Dominus, exultemus et laetemur in illa*"' (This is the day which the Lord has made: let us be glad and rejoice therein).[173] One of the 12 jurors admitted to Fitzherbert that Campion had been unjustly condemned, but said he had felt impelled to give the guilty verdict 'for otherwise

---

[169]   BL MS Harley 6265, fol. 22v; Bodl. MS Add. C 303, fol. 73v.

[170]   BL MS Harley 6265, fol. 22v; Bodl. MS Add. C 303, fol. 73v.

[171]   *L'Histoire de la Mort*, p. 28; also in Bombino, *Vita et Martyrium*, p. 275.

[172]   ARSI Vita I. 35, p. 266. See Chapter 8 for more details.

[173]   Letter to Agazzari, *Cause of the Canonization*, p. 302. The text is Psalm 117:24 (Vulgate); trans. Douai-Rheims. See Chapter 12 for the tradition Sherwin seems to have established.

he should not have bin accounted the Queen's friend'.[174] As Chief Justice Wray was walking the next day, 21 November 1581, to pass judgement on the rest of the defendants, he turned 'with a sorrowful countenance' to 'the Queen's advocates', and said, 'If things goe on this day as they did yesterday, we shal all be discredited'.[175] Two of the jurors chosen to serve on the jury the next day, 'otherwise heretikes', refused to serve, saying they 'utterly abhorred this so great crime of betraying justice'.[176] Sir John Roper, who was sitting below Judge Ayloff, later told the Jesuit missionary, John Gerard, that Ayloff leant down to him and asked him if he had any blood on him; when Roper said that he did not, the Judge replied: 'Behold my hand and signet ring: they are full of blood' (*Ecce manus mea et sigillum plena sunt sanguinis*). John Gerard deposed this, on 25 January 1628, in the English College in Rome.[177]

Two days after Campion's trial, during the Accession Day celebrations, 22 November 1581, it is said that the Queen 'declared in public she would marry Anjou, kissed him on the mouth and gave him her ring'.[178] Ever since the proclamation of 24 January 1581, Burghley and other proponents of the marriage had been giving 'clear signals that there should be no tolerance for Catholics'.[179] The trial of Campion was not a mere footnote in the political saga of the Anjou negotiations, but a final, futile attempt to win over a hostile population to an unpopular marriage.[180] To Susan Doran's conclusion that 'royal policy' was 'ill-conceived and ill-executed', and brought conflict with Spain closer, has to be added the damaging way the marriage negotiations subordinated English justice to the crown's political interests.[181] If 'Elizabeth gravely underestimated the domestic opposition to the match', the Privy Council failed to predict the storm of protest Campion's treatment would cause in the courts of Europe.[182]

There is no doubt that Elizabethan justice itself was on trial. Edmund Plowden, the greatest Elizabethan lawyer, and 'commonly called the Father of the Lawe', having heard what had passed the previous day, entered the Hall at the start of the second day, and 'presented himselfe as a spectatour', but the Chief Justice caused him to be called aside and asked to leave the room, since the judges were ashamed

---

[174] Pollen, *Acts of English Martyrs*, p. 39; Bombino, *Vita et Martyrium*, p. 301; Bodl. MS Tanner 329, fol. 105r. Fitzherbert is the source of this story, but Pollen translated *juror* as *judge*.

[175] Bombino, *Vita et Martyrium*, p. 301; Bodl. MS Tanner 329, fol. 105r.

[176] Bombino, *Vita et Martyrium*, p. 301; Bodl. MS Tanner 329, fol. 105r–v.

[177] ABSI 46/2/9/4, 'Fr Gerard on Fr. Campion'.

[178] Doran, *Monarchy and Matrimony*, p. 187, citing 'several different accounts'.

[179] Doran, *Monarchy and Matrimony*, p. 180.

[180] See Chapter 12, where this is William Camden's verdict.

[181] Doran, *Monarchy and Matrimony*, pp. 190–94 (p. 192).

[182] Doran, *Monarchy and Matrimony*, p. 193.

of 'their so wicked proceeding'.[183] Persons gives, as his authority for this, one of the things Cottam told Thomas Briscow in the Tower.[184]

The 'iniquitie' of the trial was criticized first in 'private whisperings', then in 'public speeches', so that by the following spring, the Queen herself was defending its justice in a proclamation, dated 1 April 1582, against those who 'traitorously affected have of late by letters, libels, pamphlets, and books both written and printed falsely, seditiously, and traitorously given out that the said most horrible traitors were without just cause condemned and executed'.[185] Far from suppressing criticism, the edict 'enflamed' it, and people took 'this fond diligence of excusing, for an open confession of the crime'.[186]

The trial had lasted from eight in the morning till six in the evening.[187] If it was a sad day for English justice, it was a devastating blow for the whole Catholic community. As Lake and Questier argue:

> What was at stake in the 'Campion affair' was nothing short of the legitimacy of the Elizabethan state in its dealing with its Catholic subjects and, beyond that, the whole structure of the English monarchy as the English reformation had re-created it.[188]

As the defendants were led out of the hall, 'an incredible crowd of men' gathered round; all those who could were trying to kiss the hands or the clothes of Campion and his companions; as they were 'convayed from thence with Boates' to the Tower, those on the bank 'followed them with tears in their eyes, and with devoted prayers'.[189]

---

[183]   Bombino, *Vita et Martyrium*, pp. 301–2; Bodl. MS Tanner 329, fol. 105v. BL MS Harley 6265 and Bodl. MS Add. C. 303. Geoffrey de C. Parmiter, *Edmund Plowden: An Elizabethan Recusant Lawyer* (London: Catholic Record Society, 1987), p. 141, describes this incident, but his source is Simpson.

[184]   ABSI Collectanea P. I, fol. 158a. Fr Grene records this as an autograph marginal note of Persons. The only discrepancy is that Persons says this was '*primo die*' (on the first day), but Persons is not reliable on dates.

[185]   *Tudor Royal Proclamations*, II. 490.

[186]   Bombino, *Vita et Martyrium*, p. 302; Bodl. MS Tanner 329, fol. 106r.

[187]   Bodl. MS Add. C 303, fol. 73v. This account of the trial does not mention the second day.

[188]   Lake and Questier, *Anti-Christ's Lewd Hat*, p. 262.

[189]   Bombino, *Vita et Martyrium*, pp. 275–6; Munday, *A Discoverie*, sig. F5r.

Chapter 11
We are Made a Spectacle

The trial was followed by further indecision and disagreement.[1] The interim, between the end of the trial and the execution on 1 December, belonged to the Privy Council, which was bitterly divided about what to do and besieged by attempts at intercession, some from surprising quarters.

John Foxe, the leading Protestant martyrologist, 'interceded for Edmund Campion'.[2] Samuel Foxe confirmed that his father wrote several letters to the Privy Council on his behalf.

> I will speak a word or two of his moderation towards them [the papists]. I could produce letters of his wherein he persuadeth the lords and others who then held the places of chiefest authority, not to suffer Edmund Campion and his fellow-conspirators to be put to death, nor to let that custom continue longer in the kingdom that death rather than some other punishment should be inflicted on the papist offenders. And lest he might seem only out of the goodness of his nature, and not out of the judgment of his mind to have so spoken, he there endeavoureth to prove by many reasons how much it was to the weakening of the cause rather to follow the example of their adversaries in appointing punishments than their own mildness; and that they much rather ought to strive as well in mercy and clemency to overcome them, as they had already in the justice of their cause got the upper hand. This he repeated (*inculcabat*) often, adventuring, even till he was in danger of giving offence by his importunity, to entreat for them.[3]

Sadly, none of these letters has survived, but his appeal for clemency on behalf of five Anabaptists in 1575 starts from basic humanity ('since I myself am a man'), and proceeds to appeal, 'for Christ's sake', to the Queen to 'spare the lives of the wretched men at least so far that this horror may be stopped'. In one of the three drafts of this letter, Foxe uses the argument most suitable to Campion, that 'When men of false doctrine are killed, their error is not killed; nay it is all the more strengthened, the more constantly they die'.[4] Foxe cannot have been the only one to write to the Council or to urge moderation on the Queen. Shock at the

---

[1] Bombino, *Vita et Martyrium*, pp. 276–82.

[2] G.R. Elton, 'Persecution and Toleration in the English Reformation', *Persecution and Toleration*, vol. 21, *Studies in Church History* (Oxford: Blackwell, 1984), pp. 163–87 (p. 174); noted by Scully, *Lion's Den*, p. 96.

[3] J.F. Mozley, *John Foxe and His Book* (London: SPCK, 1940), p. 90. See also V. Norskov Olsen, *John Foxe and the Elizabethan Church* (Berkeley: University of California Press, 1973), p. 212.

[4] Mozley, *Foxe and His Book*, p. 87; Simpson, p. 444.

trial's verdict, and revulsion at the idea of an international scholar being butchered in this way appears to have affected many beyond the blurred boundaries of the recusant community: John Stow, Abraham Fleming, William Camden and Sir John Harington, all register disquiet.[5]

George Elyot used this time to visit Campion in the Tower and to ask his pardon, saying that he 'did never thinke' that the charge would be treason, or that 'they would picke matter of death' for Campion, and that he would not 'for any good have done so much', if he had thought 'any further harme or trouble then imprisonment'. The reply was as vigorous as it was priestly: 'Then repent thee Eliot for Gods sake said F. Campion, and al wil be to his glorie'. When Elyot revealed that he was worried about 'being killed of the Catholikes', Campion assured him he had nothing to fear, but that 'for your more securitie', he could provide letters of introduction to the Duke of Bavaria: 'I will send you to a Duke in Germany where you shalbe safe'.[6]

On the Privy Council, some put forward very strongly the opprobrium that the death sentence on a renowned scholar would bring them among other nations, especially when he had so clearly rebutted the charge of treason.[7] Apparently, 'they debated the day and the number, and, indeed, whether any of them, should be killed at all'.[8] Some on the Council thought the evidence had been 'based on mere interpretations', that the witnesses were unreliable, and that the prosecution had depended on the 'meretricious persuasiveness of corrupted eloquence'; others merely wished to 'concoct something for the ignorant mutltitude', thinking that a bad reputation gained by an unjust verdict 'could be reversed by the execution of an equally unjust sentence'.[9]

Delays also arose from the return of the Duke of Anjou to London, on 1 November 1581, for a final round of marriage negotiations.[10] Persons attributes the change in the treatment of the imprisoned priests, including the removal of many from the mild regime of the Marshalsea to the much harsher Tower, to the arrival of 'Monsieur'; the aim of a more severe policy was to 'destroy the hopes they had entertained that his coming might bring some alleviation'.[11] Anjou certainly dominates Lord Burghley's papers for this period: from 22 November

---

[5]   See Chapter 12.

[6]   Allen, *A briefe historie*, sig. b5v; paraphrased in More, *Historia Missionis*, p. 127.

[7]   Bombino, *Vita et Martyrium*, pp. 276–7.

[8]   More, *Historia Missionis*, p. 122.

[9]   Bombino, *Vita et Martyrium*, pp. 277–8; More, *Historia Missionis*, p. 123.

[10]   Bombino, *Vita et Martyrium*, pp. 282–7.

[11]   Persons, 'Punti Per La Missione d'Inghilterra', ed. J.H. Pollen, in *Miscellanea IV*, CRS 4 (London: Catholic Record Society, 1907), p. 33; supported by Scully, *Lion's Den*, pp. 97 and 308–9. McCoog, 'The English Jesuit Mission and the French Match', in *Fashioning Jesuit Identity*, pp. 55–88 (pp. 80–81) is particularly helpful in identifying subtle changes in November 1581. See Chapter 12, for support from the contemporary histories of Stow, Holinshed and Camden.

to 3 December, Cecil's papers deal with only three topics: the Duke of Anjou, the Scottish Queen and the situation in Ireland.[12] Proponents of the marriage argued that carrying out the execution while the marriage negotiations were still going on, would be seen as a grave offence to the Duke of Anjou and his brother, the French king.[13] Many Catholics tried to intercede with the French ambassador, Michel de Castelnau, but to no avail.[14] They turned to Mendoza, now Spanish ambassador in Paris, hoping he could persuade the Queen Mother to write to Anjou, her son.[15] Persons sent Fr Edward Gratley to Anjou's ambassador, Jean Bodin, who brushed aside their request: religion was not his concern.[16] In response, the Privy Council 'began to sharpen the persecution', while 'banquets, balls and masquerades' continued to promote the marriage.[17] Persons remembers an attempt to plead with Sir Philip Sidney.[18] Finally, on the morning of the execution, some Catholics called on the Duke of Anjou himself to plead with him. His chaplain went to pass on the message, found him on the tennis court, and put the request to him. He paused for a moment, then said, '*Jouez*'.[19] The 'authority of William Cecil', according to Bombino, 'was decisive' (*vicit tandem Gulielmi Caecili auctoritas*): Cecil regarded the 'case' of Sander and Campion as identical (*eandem Sanderi & Campiani causam*); what ought to have been decreed against that 'leader of sedition' (now dead), must be 'declared by the punishment of this man' (*huius supplicio declarandum*).[20] Campion had to pay the cost of Sander's crimes.

Although 14 of the 15 accused were sentenced to death, only three, Edmund Campion, Ralph Sherwin and Alexander Briant, were chosen to die before Christmas, but there was indecision about which day would have most impact. The Council first chose a market day, Saturday, 25 November, as suitable for the populist spectacle of the execution of three priests; then (perhaps fearing the crowds would be too big to control) delayed until 29th, only to realize that was the vigil of the martyrdom of St Andrew, and postponed till Friday, 1 December.[21] As the proclamation of 1 April 1582 says, these three were intended to be an exemplary

---

[12]   Hatfield House MSS, 149/195; 12/16; 162/93–5.

[13]   Bombino, *Vita et Martyrium*, p. 278.

[14]   McCoog, *Fashioning Jesuit Identity*, p. 80.

[15]   McCoog, *Fashioning Jesuit Identity*, p. 80, citing letter to the King of Spain, 7 November 1581, *CSP Spanish, 1580–1586*, p. 211.

[16]   Persons, 'Punti', CRS 4, p. 25.

[17]   Persons, 'Punti', CRS 4, p. 25; see Chapter 12, for the contrast in three contemporary chronicles.

[18]   ABSI Collectanea P. I, fol. 158r.

[19]   Paolo Bombino, *Vita et Martyrium Edmundi Campiani* (Mantua: Osanna, 1620), p. 311 (autograph addition in Bombino's own copy, ARSI Vita 1.35). See Persons, 'Punti', CRS 4, p. 35, and McCoog, *Fashioning Jesuit Identity*, p. 80.

[20]   Bombino, *Vita et Martyrium*, p. 279 (my translation).

[21]   Bombino, *Vita et Martyrium*, p. 281 (my translation); Simpson, p. 446, follows.

punishment; most of the rest were to die in batches in April and May 1582.[22] The choice of these three representatives of the Society of Jesus, the English College and the college in Rheims was, as Allen argued, deliberate; they were also the three most scholarly of a group of priests dominated by Oxford men. It looks as if Leicester and Knollys were sending a clear message to the old university, 'forasmuch as their Lordships finde by experience that most of the Seminarie Priestes which at this present disturbe this Churche have been heretofore schollers of that Universitie'.[23]

It seems as if James Bosgrave should have been on the hurdle with Campion but, on the morning of 1 December 1581, he was reprieved. The Polish King, Stephen Báthory had earlier intervened on his behalf. In a letter from Warsaw of 27 April 1581, the nuncio to Poland, Bishop Giovanni Caligari, tells the Cardinal of Como that the King 'has been so kind as to intercede with the Queen on behalf of the captured Jesuits' (*li Gesuiti captivi*), in England, in return for which kindness, Caligari tells Como that he has sent him a copy of Campion's 'Letter to the Council', which the King liked so much that he immediately gave it to the Chancellor of Lithuania, Prince Mikołaj Radziwiłł, to translate into Polish.[24] The King knew, and liked, Bosgrave, and intervened a second time on his behalf on 29 January 1583, pointing to the freedom enjoyed by English merchants in Poland, a freedom that could easily be rescinded.[25] The official account of the interrogations, *A Particular Declaration*, tried to explain Bosgrave's reprieve (and that of Henry Orton) as capitulation, so he is reported as saying that the bull 'was at no time lawfull', that the Queen was 'lawfull', that he condemned Sander's invasion and his 'bookes', denied the pope's deposing power, and that he would fight on the Queen's side in the event of any invasion.[26] Soon after this account was published, an anonymous manuscript was found, on the morning of 6 July 1582, in a church porch, which argued that the government was lying about

---

[22]   *Tudor Royal Proclamations*, II. 490.

[23]   *APC, 1581–1590*, 14 August 1581, p. 170.

[24]   *Monumenta Poloniae Vaticana: Continet I.A. Caligari Nuntii Apost. in Polonia Epistolas et Acta Tomus IV, 1578–1581* (Cracoviae: Academy of Letters, 1915), p. 626. Como thanks Caligari in an earlier letter for getting the King involved, p. 621. Thomas M. McCoog, S.J., 'The Mystery of James Bosgrave', in *Fashioning Jesuit Identity*, pp. 123–41, is the most recent account of Bosgrave. McCoog is sceptical about the role of the Polish king, Stephen Báthory, whose letter of 29 January 1583 is recorded, even though he admits that Báthory knew and liked Bosgrave.

[25]   More, *Elizabethan Jesuits*, p. 175, suggests that the charge of betrayal is untrustworthy, and that Báthory's intervention is critical, but McCoog, 'Mystery of James Bosgrave', pp. 138 and 141, argues that Bosgrave's reprieve owes nothing to the Polish king's intervention, and that he later did penance for his 'one mistake in England'. But his 'one mistake' could be his early blunder on church attendance. Bosgrave and the Polish background are fascinating areas deserving more research.

[26]   *A particular declaration*, sig. D2r–v.

both Bosgrave and Henry Orton.[27] The reprieved Orton remained devoted to Campion's memory.[28]

One final attempt was made to win Campion over. Three days before his death, his sister came to visit him, presumably encouraged to try to persuade him to yield.[29] The Lieutenant of the Tower added his own offer of 100 pounds a year if he conformed. The condemned priests, now in irons, waited in different cells in the Tower. The final decision to execute Campion, Sherwin and Briant on 1 December seems to have been taken at the last minute, since the Lieutenant of the Tower was looking for Campion's buff leather jerkin on the morning of the execution, but this attempt to humiliate Campion 'for the more disgrace of the man of God', failed because Hopton could not find the garment.[30] As Hopton was engaged in this 'despiteful' task, Campion met with his fellow prisoners in the Coleharbour Tower, and 'there passed much sweete speach and embrasing one another'.[31]

The Privy Council intended the execution of Campion to be exemplary, so an immense guard was provided. Munday says that

> Edmund Campion Jesuit, and Raphe Sherwin and Alexander Brian, Seminarie Preestes … were drawne from the Towre of London on hurdles, to the place of execution appointed, being garded with such a sufficient company, as might expresse the honour of Justice the larger in that behalfe.[32]

Campion was put 'alone on one herdle', Sherwin and Briant 'together on an other'.[33]

> Campion was tied full length on a hurdle of osiers, Sherwin and Bryant had another like it. All three were dragged along with their feet towards the horse's hooves. As they bumped along the cobble-paved streets, they were splashed with filth from the puddles, assailed by the shouts of an abusive mob, harassed further by the importunity of Protestant ministers who tried to make them change their minds.[34]

Persons names William Charke as the minister who 'followed him in person to the place of his Martyrdome with bygge lookes, sterne countenance, prowde

---

[27]   The full text of the pamphlet, copied by Dr John Hammond, is printed by Foley, *Records*, III. 292–4; McCoog, *Fashioning Jesuit Identity*, p. 137, quotes from it.

[28]   See Chapter 12.

[29]   Allen, *A Brief Historie*, sig. e2r. This may be the only recorded encounter with a member of his family.

[30]   Allen, *A Briefe Historie*, sig. e2r.

[31]   Allen, *A Brief Historie*, sig. e2r; Simpson, p. 447.

[32]   Munday, *A Discoverie*, sig. F7v.

[33]   Allen, *A briefe Historie*, sig. c8v.

[34]   More, *Historia Missionis*, p. 123.

wordes, and merciles behavyour'.[35] The three scholars were dragged along Tower Street and up Cheapside to Tyburn, a distance of nearly four miles, with their feet raised behind the horses, which must have been excruciating for their spines. The puddles were enough to splash their faces, which were nearest the ground. Alfield makes clear that while some bystanders shouted abuse, others 'called and cried unto him', and one man 'eyther for pity or affection wiped his face defiled with durt, as he was drawen most miserably through thick and thin, as the saying is, to the place of execution'.[36] 'Alfield drew the parallel between Campion's *via crucis* and that of Christ, recalling the established legend of Veronica wiping the face of Jesus'.[37]

All accounts agree that the crowd was unprecedented in its number. Among the crowd were the many 'most addicted' (*addictissimi*) admirers that Campion had acquired in a year's preaching up and down the country, who tried to help the wretched priests as they lay on the hurdles, and were not afraid to

> make their devotion plain ... They ran to them. They spoke to them. They begged their help and advice, and took turns to help them as far as they could in their extreme necessity.[38]

There were people lining the street all the way from the Tower, and at Tyburn a crowd that stretched further than the eye could see; Munday says there was a 'multitude of people, not heer to be numbered'.[39] Richard Stonley, one of the four Tellers of the Exchequer, and a close friend of Lady Petre, records encountering the procession in Cheapside, as if by chance:

> This day After morning preyer cuminge thorough Chepside ther came one Edmond Campyon Ralph Sherwyn & Briant drawen vpon hurdles to Tyborne & ther suffred execucion at which tyme a pamphlet boke was redd by wey of Aduertisment agenst all thos that were sausye flaterers favorers or whisperers in his cause After dyner I kept home with thankes to god at night.[40]

Stonley's four entries for the arraignment, trial and execution of Campion, together with his double entry for the Star Chamber trial of Lord Vaux, Sir Thomas Tresham and Sir William Catesby, make chance the least likely explanation. The Privy Council's delay, while they decided how the executions were to be carried out, had only enhanced the importance of the event. The Spanish ambassador put the guard at 3,000 horsemen and innumerable footmen; the militia from outside

---

[35]   Persons, *A Defence of the Censure*, p. 4.

[36]   Alfield, *A true reporte*, sig. B4r.

[37]   Dillon, *Construction of Martyrdom*, p. 96.

[38]   More, *Historia Missionis*, p. 124. Simpson, p. 448.

[39]   Munday, *A Discoverie*, sig. F7v.

[40]   Folger MS V.a.459, fol. 33v. I thank Alan H. Nelson for this reference and his transcription of Stonley; I have silently expanded abbreviations.

London must have been drafted in, if they were to control the crowds.[41] But even these numbers proved inadequate to keep the situation under control. The guards, unable to control 'the applause' with 'angry looks' or 'threats', ended up, as tacit 'witnesses' of the crowd's enthusiasm, acknowledging the fact that these 'victims' drawing such sympathy, 'had not in fact been traitors'.[42] Public execution was, as Michel Foucault argued, intended to be a 'ceremony in which the sovereign triumphed' but, as in the disputations and his trial, Campion showed his ability to disrupt the script of the state's theatre of cruelty.[43] What had been intended to strike terror into all Catholics (and especially into papists at the university of Oxford) was going badly wrong.

The route lay from one side of the walled city to the other, past the cross at Cheapside, where Campion had stopped on the way to the Tower to bow his head; the cross stood just outside Paul's Churchyard and his home. The route was almost a synecdoche of Campion's life in England: it passed close to his home, between his two schools, and finally along the Oxford road (now Oxford Street), then outside the city walls. Tyburn, now at Marble Arch, was in open fields, and the 'crowd stretched away on every side', and 'such a great number that no one had ever seen the like'.[44] Campion was the first to mount the cart beneath the 'triangular scaffold'. At first, everything went according to plan, as the hangman placed the noose round his neck. Then Campion turned to the immense crowd and began to preach, addressing the people as if he were in an open-air pulpit. Alfield, our witness, says that he was near the members of the Privy Council, Sir Francis Knollys, Lord Charles Howard and Sir Henry Lee.[45] Campion chose as a text, the words of St Paul and, 'with grave countenance and sweet voyce' said:

> *Spectaculum facti sumus Deo, Angeli[s], & hominibus* saying, These are the wordes of S. Paule, Englished thus: We are made a spectacle, or a sight unto God, unto his Angels, and unto men: verified this day in me who am here a spectacle unto my lorde god, a spectacle unto his angels and unto you men.[46]

No text could have more effectively risen above what Campion called his 'agony'. Associated with 'martyrological discourse' since the early church, St Paul's words placed everyone involved in this grotesque spectacle – guards, hangman, Privy

---

[41]   *CSP Spanish, 1580–1586*, p. 231.

[42]   More, *Historia Missionis*, p. 124.

[43]   Michel Foucault, *Discipline and Punish: The Birth of the Prison*, trans. Alan Sheridan (London: Harmondsworth, 1979), p. 48, cited by Dillon, *Construction of Martyrdom*, p. 73; see J.A. Sharpe, '"Last Dying Speeches": Religion, Ideology and Public Execution in Seventeenth-Century England', *Past and Present* 107 (May, 1985), 144–67 (p. 161).

[44]   *L'Histoire de la Mort*, p. 27 (my translation).

[45]   Alfield, *A true reporte*, sig. B4v.

[46]   Alfield, *A true reporte*, sigs B4v–C1r; *L'Histoire de la Mort*, p. 24. The Pauline text is from 1. Cor. 4.9 (Vulgate).

Councillors, noblemen and the vast crowd – within the sight of God.[47] The Latin
allows the word *spectaculum* to come first, his repetition in English highlighting
the way the state is choosing to *stage* its theatre of punishment, a modern circus
as old as the Roman *spectaculum* (show). Campion shows that he is aware that he
is being used to reassure Londoners fearful of a repeat of the Spanish marriage
of Queen Mary, that the Queen's projected marriage to the Duke of Anjou would
not mean toleration for Catholics. The English translation he immediately offers
starts in the passive voice: 'We are made': these men are not active 'traitors', but
passive 'victims' of the state's game. The choice of a Pauline text places Campion
within the apostolic tradition where the martyr 'followed scriptural injunctions
and promises'.[48] Sir Francis Knollys, Treasurer of the Household, 'and the sheryfs'
interrupted him 'some way into his sermon', and told him to confine himself to
acknowledging his treason and begging the Queen's forgiveness.[49] Campion
replied:

> I am guilty of no crime against the Queen unless the religion I profess be a crime.
> As a priest I undertook to spread this faith. For this cause I came to England. To
> it I have given myself wholly. Seeing that I must die for it, I do it willingly. I beg
> you to believe me in this last hour of my life; before the God who sees me and to
> whom I must render an account of my most inward thoughts.[50]

The Privy Councillors present needed a reason to make it appear that he was
worthy to die, since the state's script required repentance and conformity. So they
put questions to him about the papal bull, published by Pius V, but renewed by
Gregory XIII: were Catholics now still bound to obey this? Campion replied that
this was hardly the place to discuss such a question.[51] He had several times made
clear his opposition to the bull (on one occasion, as we have seen, to the Queen
herself), so it was quite unnecessary to ask this question again. 'But Being asked
whether he renounced the Pope, said he was a Catholike; whereupon one inferred,
saying: In your Catholisisme (I noted the worde) al treason is conteined'.[52]

Campion, instead, remembered some 'gentlemen' who felt damaged by the
false rumour that he had revealed in whose houses he had said mass or whose
confession he had heard, so he took this opportunity to dispel that belief. By no
trickery or torture, he explained, had he revealed the names of anyone whom he

---

[47]   Susannah Brietz Monta, *Martyrdom and Literature in Early Modern England*
(Cambridge: University Press, 2005), p. 25, traces it back to Origen's *Exhortation to
Martyrdom*.

[48]   Brad Gregory, *Salvation at Stake: Christian Martyrdom in Early Modern Europe*
(Cambridge, MA and London: Harvard University Press, 1999), 110.

[49]   Alfield, *A true reporte*, sig. B4v.

[50]   More, *Historia Missionis*, 124. I have removed an exclamation mark from the
translation.

[51]   *L'Histoire de la Mort*, 25.

[52]   Alfield, *A true reporte*, sig. C2r.

had absolved in confession or reconciled to the church, and this is what he had meant in his letter to Pounde, that he would never reveal such sacred knowledge, 'come rack, come rope'.[53] He then asked Sir Francis Knollys and the other nobility present to accept that the Richardson (the alias of Laurence Johnson) who was under arrest was not the person to whom he had entrusted the manuscript of his book. Campion's focus was on the welfare of those he had encountered on the mission.

At this point, Thomas Hearne, a schoolmaster, proclaimed 'openly with lowde voyce unto the people' the pamphlet the Privy Council had printed for the occasion: *An Advertisement*.[54] The decision to print a pamphlet to be read at the gallows followed the practice begun earlier in the year with Everard Haunse, which 'gave just feare of the like practice' to Thomas Alfield.[55] Alfield is outraged that this 'notable and most infamous libel' was 'published there, and openly read, printed abrode without authoritie of seen and alowed, a pamphlet, false, impudent, and farssed with lyes and untruthes, only to colour and shadowe with some face of equitie those strange proceedings'.[56] As Persons records, 'The crowd, however, seemed little impressed by this, and rather suspected a trick in this new and unusual artifice'.[57] This innovation shows the state trying to impose its own meaning, like a mask, on the event:

> M. Campion al the time of his reading devoutlye praying notwithstanding which advertisement or defence of theirs, aswel because they distrusted their own policie in publication therof, as that they did also disyre some better colour or faster vizard for their proceedings.[58]

As Campion prayed the *Pater Noster* in Latin, resigning himself to God's will, '*fiat voluntas tua*', one of the ministers willed him to pray with him in English:

---

[53]   *L'Histoire de la Mort*, p. 26: '*soit que la corde, soit que la torture marche*'.

[54]   *An Advertisement and defence for Trueth against her Backbiters, and specially against the whispring Favourers, and Colourers of Campions, and the rest of his confederats treasons* (London: C. Barker, 1581), STC 153.7. (This slight book, of one quarto in fours, was formerly attributed to Anthony Munday, and so listed as STC18259.) The Folger copy is annotated by John Wylkinson, who paid 'ixd (9d)' for it, and underlined much of it, apparently in agreement.

[55]   For the pamphlets published by Robert Crowley for Fr Haunse's execution, Munday's attempt to make money by rushing off his flawed account, *The araignement and execution of a wilfull and obstinate traitour, named E. Ducket, alias Hauns*, STC 18259.3, and Crowley's revised pamphlet, *A true report*, STC 12934, written to correct Munday's errors, see Dillon, *Construction of Martyrdom*, pp. 76–7, citing Alfield, *A true reporte*, sig. A4r. Alfield skilfully demolishes the credibility of Munday in a final 'Caveat to the reader touching A.M. his discovery', *A true reporte*, sigs D4v–E1v.

[56]   Alfield, *A true reporte*, sig. A4v.

[57]   More, *Historia Missionis*, p. 135.

[58]   Alfield, *A true reporte*, sig. C2r.

Willing him to saye, Christ have mercy upon me or such like prayer, so Campion, looking backe with milde countenance, humbly saide: You and I are not one in religion, wherefore I pray you content your selfe, I barre none of prayer, only I desire them of the houshold of faith to pray with me, & in mine agony to say one Crede.[59]

He was pressed further 'to praye in English, to whom he answered that he would pray in a language he wel understood'.[60]

At the upshot of this conflict he was willed to aske the queene forgiveness, and to praye for her. He meekely answered: wherein have I offended her? In this I am innocent, this is my last speache, in this geve me credite, I have and do pray for her. Then did the Lorde Charles Howard aske of him: For which queene he prayed, whether for *Elizabeth* queen. To whom he answered, Yea for *Elizabeth* your queene and my queene, unto whom I wish a long quiet raigne, with all prosperity.[61]

This chivalrous reply was 'extemely pleasing to several councillors present'.[62] *L'Histoire de la Mort* gives us his last words:

Mais bien supplia tres instamment tous les Catholiques presens que cependant qu'il seroit en l'agonie de la mort, ils voulussent pour luy dire de la meilleure affection qu'ils pourroient le symbole des Apostres, pour montrer qu'il ne mourroit pour autre chose que la foy Catholique & Apostolique, laquelle se retrouve seulement en l'Eglise Romaine.

[Then he earnestly begged the Catholics present that, although he was in the agony of his death, they would recite with as much fervour as they could the *Symbolum Apostolorum*, to show that he was dying for nothing other than the Catholic and Apostolic faith, which is to be found only in the Roman church.][63]

Even Munday agrees that he 'said his *Pater noster* in Latin, & desired all those of the householde of faith, to saye one *Credo* for him'.[64]

The choice of the *Symbolum Apostolorum* (the earliest *Credo*) could not be more appropriate, and is an indication of how quickly Campion's mind worked. In the middle of this makeshift stage constructed for the punishment of 'treason', the crowd became a congregation fervently reciting together one of the earliest known prayers of the church (originally used in baptism), a prayer that united Campion and his improvised *ecclesia* with the earliest 'Catholic and Apostolic church'.

---

[59]	Alfield, *A true reporte*, sig. C2r–v.

[60]	Alfield, *A true reporte*, sig. C2v.

[61]	Alfield, *A true reporte*, sig. C2v.

[62]	*L'Histoire de la Mort*, p. 27.

[63]	*L'Histoire de la Mort*, p. 26.

[64]	Munday, *A breefe Aunswer made unto two seditious Pamphlets*, sig. O3r. More, *Historia Missionis*, 124, paraphrases *L'Histoire de la Mort*.

For a moment Campion transformed the state's secular theatre into a moment of intense religious communion with the early church of the martyrs. The choice of prayer allowed the congregation to end with four soothing proclamations of faith, their murmuring Latin labials eliding into the thin December air: '*sanctorum communionem, remissionem peccatorum, resurrectionem carnis, vitam aeternam*' (the communion of saints, the forgiveness of sins, the resurrection of the body, life everlasting). Holinshed reveals that the communal prayer ended in a moment of religious silence: 'After a few silent praiers to himself, the cart was drawen awaie, and he committed to the mercie of God'.[65] As in St Mary's, Oxford, the Tower and in Westminster Hall, Campion had the ability to make an Elizabethan audience do what it very rarely did: stand silent.

The moment of silent prayer turned to 'unbelievable wailing and groaning' (*une plaincte et gemissement incroyable*) as Campion's body dropped into the empty air.[66] The drama was not over. As the executioner went to cut the rope, so he could 'perform the butchery on Fr. Campion while alive', Lord Charles Howard, with drawn sword, stepped forward and 'drove him away in great wrath, threatening him with death if he dared to touch him before he had drawn his last breath'.[67] Howard had been completely won over by Campion's loyalty. Munday confirms that he 'hanged till he was dead, when being cut downe, he was bowelled and quartered'.[68]

When Howard returned to the Court, the Queen asked him where he had been. Howard replied that he had 'come from the execution of the three Papists', so she asked him how that seemed to him:

> They seem to me to be very learned men and steadfast, and to have been put to death for no fault; for they kept praying to God for your majesty, they pardoned everyone, and they protested under pain of their souls in eternity that they had never even thought of doing any evil act against the state or against your Majesty.[69]

There must have been an awkward pause, until the Queen said, 'Is that so? Very well, that has nothing to do with us; let the men who condemned them see to it'.[70] The carefully drafted script of this state theatre of cruelty has failed so badly that the crowd was not convinced, courtiers were disenchanted and the Queen herself disowned it.

In the silence after Campion's death, broken only by the sound of weeping and groaning, Sherwin came up onto the cart. Sherwin's actions on the scaffold help

---

[65] Holinshed, *Chronicles* (1587), III. 1329.a.5–7.

[66] *L'Histoire de la Mort*, p. 27.

[67] Persons, *Letters and Memorials*, CRS 39, p. 134.

[68] Munday, *A Discoverie*, sig. G3v.

[69] CRS 39, p. 134. This is from a long letter, dated 1 March 1582, of Persons to the Rector of the English College.

[70] CRS 39, p. 134.

highlight by contrast how little theatre, and how much ritual, there had been in Campion's behaviour. Sherwin

> embraced the executioner, and kissed the gore on his hands. The crowd was very much moved by this, and there was a general murmur which dragged from the official in charge permission for this next victim to say what he wanted.[71]

In fact, Sherwin, like Campion, was interrupted repeatedly by Sir Francis Knollys with the request that he 'come to the poynt, and confess your treason'; Sherwin finally expressed impatience with Knollys, and said, 'Tush, tush, you and I shall answere this before an other Judge', and even Knollys was prompted to admit that he was 'no contriver or doer of this treason, for you are no man of armes, but you are a traytor by consequence'.[72] The state's attempt to persuade the public that these Oxford scholars were traitors has descended to the point where Knollys, the Treasurer of the Royal Household, has to admit that the second scholar is only a 'traytor by consequence'. This new legal category did not convince the crowd, who cheered him, saying 'Well done, Sherwin! God receive your soul!' as the noose was put on this neck, and 'the noise lasted quite some time' and did not 'die down even when he was dead'.[73]

Alexander Briant's execution, like his prolonged and degrading torture, was an affront to English common law and all civilized values. Briant was, apparently, 'exceptionally handsome', and it is hard to avoid the impression that there was sadistic pleasure, both in his torture and the execution.[74] Since he had arrived in England in 1579, the charges against him of conspiracy in Rome and Rheims in 1580 were manifestly false:

> Being in the cart prepared to death, began first to declare his bringing up in the Catholike faith & religion, his being in *Oxford*, upon which worde he was stayed by one, saieng: What have we to do with *Oxford*? come to the purpose, and confesse thy treason. Whereupon he answered, I am not guyltye of any suche death, I was never at Rome, nor then at Rhemes, when D. Sanders came into Ireland ... and thereupon protesting him selfe to dye a true catholike, saying *Miserere mei Deus*, was delivered of the carte with more payn by negligence of the hangman then either of the other, who, after his beheading, himself dismembred, his hart bowels and intrels burned, to the gret admiration of some, being layd upon the blocke his bellye downward, lifted up his whole body then remayning from the ground: and this I adde upon report of others, not mine owne sight.[75]

---

[71]   More, *Historia Missionis*, p. 134.
[72]   Alfield, *A true reporte*, sig. C3v.
[73]   More, *Historia Missionis*, p. 136.
[74]   More, *Historia Missionis*, p. 130.
[75]   Alfield, *A true reporte*, sig. D3r.

The style of the question suggests that Knollys again was the malevolent person to interrupt Briant's account of Oxford, and ask him to confess his treason.

An early eyewitness account of the executions comes from a letter of the Spanish Ambassador on 4 December 1581, who noted that, despite the 'printed statement' that 'they are not condemned for their religion, but for having plotted with the Pope to kill the Queen', and the fact that, at the execution 'Knollys, the treasurer of the household, and a Councillor' had 'cried out that this was not a case of religion but of treason', the people were not convinced by this and 'other like fictions', and that, 'both at the trial and before their death, all the men said some holy words, asserting their innocence and pardoning their persecutors'.[76] Lord Charles Howard, it seems, was not alone in being impressed: Mendoza also noted that

> When Campion was executed, it was noticed that all his nails had been dragged out in the torture. The behaviour of these priests has been so exemplary, and their firmness in suffering such fearful deaths has been so conspicuous, that they may be counted amongst the great martyrs of the Church of God.[77]

The Ambassador's servant, Pedro Serrano, told Donna Anna de Mendoza that Mendoza disguised himself in order to see the martyrs pass.[78]

Only one fact made the *Advertisement* plausible, and convinced 'John Wylkinson' (who 'payd nyne pence' for the quarto pamphlet) that these men were executed for 'Hygh treasons against her Majesties person not doctrine & religion': it was that '*D. Sanders* an errant and detestable Traitour' had 'notoriously attempted' to 'deprive her Majestie of her life, crowne and dignitie'.[79]

The orders that had gone out from the Privy Council to search homes in every county visited by Campion meant that, from the beginning of August onwards, almost every Catholic household in the country was personally implicated in the drama that was being played out on the public stage. By November, the Privy Council was using several lists of Catholics – Elyot's, Sledd's, Burghley's – and these included most of the major Catholic families in England.[80] It was supplemented by lists compiled from the 1577 recusancy returns, some confirmed by Campion under torture. The turning or defection of Elyot was the kind of event the Catholic community most feared, since his inside knowledge of priests, houses where Mass had been said, and even those with 'papist' sympathies, made him a deeply threatening mole. The dinner that Richard Stonley had with his neighbour and close friend, Lady Petre, on Monday 24 July could stand for the many anxious

---

[76] *CSP Spanish, 1580–1586*, p. 231.

[77] *CSP Spanish, 1580–1586*, p. 231.

[78] BL MS Egerton 2679, fol. 9r–v; translated in John Morris, S.J., 'A New Witness about B. Edmund Campion', in *The Month* 78 (1893), 3–11.

[79] *An Advertisement*, sigs A2v–A3r.

[80] BL Lansdowne MS 33, no. 60, fols 145r–9r, Elyot's list of papists throughout the country.

conversations between Catholics from 22 July (when Elyot brought Campion to London) to the end of August.[81] Elyot himself acknowledged this:

> There hath beene great murmuring and grudging against mee, about the committing of the foresaid maister Thomas Roper, and many faults have been found for the same … But whatsoever I did against him I would have doone against mine owne Father.[82]

Elyot's extraordinary defence fits the pattern pursued by paranoid exhibitionists when dealing with a crisis of their own making. The last two acts of Campion's drama were played out in the full glare of the streets of London, the end of a process by which the government groped uncertainly towards a policy. The battle for public opinion was fought on every level. Since Campion and Persons had been 'preaching almost every day' to large congregations for nearly a year when he was captured, many thousands were personally affected by his death.[83] In this public theatre of Tyburn, the spectators were also participants.

Henry Walpole, a sceptical young barrister at Grey's Inn, was standing near the cart; as Campion's quarters and head were thrown into the cauldron of boiling water, they splashed him. The drop of blood on Walpole's coat was a turning point in Walpole's own life, but it also reminds us of the reality that exists beneath the whirlpool of conflicting narratives.[84] He told Father Ignatius Basselier

> that when the body of the Rev. Father Edmund Campion was quartered at the place of execution, he, Father Walpole, then a heretic, stood looking on amongst the rest. As the executioner threw the quarters of the Martyr into a cauldron full of water, a drop of it, mixed with the blood of the Martyr, was splashed out, and fell on Walpole's coat. From a heretic he became a Catholic without delay, from a layman a religious of the Society of Jesus, from a spectator of martyrdoms a most admirable Martyr, the most distinguished among the ten thousand converts said to have been made by Campion's death.[85]

It seems necessary to emphasize this, because the latest post-modern view of martyrdom argues that 'the martyr is a retrospectively constructed figure created in and through literature'.[86] In an age sceptical about faith, it may be hard to perceive the reality, but at Tyburn on 1 December 1581, Edmund Campion, S.J., who had refused to bow to pressure from the state, was hanged till he was dead, cut down,

---

[81]   Folger MS V.a.459, fol. 10v.

[82]   Elyot, *A very true report*, sig. D2.

[83]   Persons, *Letters and Memorials*, CRS 39, pp. 74 and 83.

[84]   Pollen, *Acts of English Martyrs*, p. 40 (quoted in full in Chapter 12).

[85]   Pollen, *Acts of English Martyrs*, p. 40.

[86]   Alice Dailey, *The English Martyr: From Reformation to Revolution* (Notre Dame: University of Notre Dame Press, 2012), p. 3.

beheaded, disembowelled and quartered. While his body was being quartered, his blood splashed onto the coat of a young lawyer, Henry Walpole.[87]

The physical and metaphysical reality of martyrdom is easier to grasp in more recent examples. Evelyn Waugh and Graham Greene were both struck by the comparison of Campion's death with that of Fr Miguel Pro, S.J., who returned to Communist Mexico in disguise, and died with his arms outstretched, at the hands of a firing squad on 23 November 1927.[88] Examination of the vestments which Archbishop Oscar Romero was wearing at the altar when, on 24 March 1980, he was shot by a professional gunman, revealed not only bloodstains, but also the particles of sweat that must have come as Romero saw his assassin at the back of the church, and realized what he was about to do.[89] He did not leave the altar. In Communist Warsaw, Fr Jerzy Popiełuszko carried on preaching to immense crowds, even though he was put under intense pressure by the government, which interrogated him, staged a false accident intended to kill him, and finally bludgeoned him to death on 19 October 1984.[90] Fr Christian de Chergé and his fellow monks stayed at their monastery in Tibhirine, Algeria, even though they knew the dangers for at least two years. Seven of them were seized on the night of 26 March 1996, and beheaded on 21 May 1996, 16 months after de Chergé left a testament that ends with forgiveness of the man who might murder him and the hope that, God willing, they would meet 'like happy thieves in paradise' (*larrons heureux en paradis*).[91] None of these men chose to die, but all – Campion, Pro, Romero, Popiełuszko and de Chergé – understood the muddled political context, felt intense fear and stayed the course; all suffered shocking interruptions of a life of preaching and sacramental ministry; all bore witness to their faith *before* anyone told their story.

When Sir Francis Knollys interrupted Campion's sermon with the request that he acknowledge his treason, Campion asked him to 'suffer me to speake a woorde or too for discharge of my conscience'.[92] The request was not granted because Campion would not act his part in the state's drama. Nothing could pinpoint more

---

[87]   See Chapter 12 for Walpole's poetic response.

[88]   Michael G. Brennan, 'Graham Greene, Evelyn Waugh and Mexico', *Renascence*, 55.1 (2002), 7–23, offers a magisterial analysis of the impact of Pro and Campion on both writers.

[89]   Jan Graffius, 'Telling Romero's Story', http://www.thinkingfaith.org/articles, 22 March 2013. I am grateful to Jan Graffius for sending me this link.

[90]   'Fr Jerzy Popiełuszko', http://news.bbc.co.uk/onthisday/hi/dates/stories/october/30/newsid_4111000/4111722.stm.

[91]   Freddy Derwahl, *The Last Monk of Tibhirine: A True Story of Martyrdom, Faith and Survival* (Brewster: Paraclete Press, 2013), prints the 'testament', pp. 169–71; the sympathetic study of the monks in the film of Xavier Beauvois, *Of Gods and Men*, won the Prix de Cannes in 2011.

[92]   Alfield, *A true reporte*, sig. C1r.

sharply the moment where Campion's 'sweet voyce' was silenced.[93] As Susannah Monta argues:

> Attempts to silence martyrs fail spectacularly as the truth is everywhere proclaimed; the martyrs' triumph has already been inscripted in spaces and texts outside government control.[94]

Prevented from preaching, Campion chose Latin prayers that effectively united him with the early church of the Apostles and martyrs, when it gloried in its powerlessness. The next verse in the Latin text of the First Epistle of St Paul to the Corinthians, chapter 4, from which Campion is quoting is: 'We are fools for Christ's sake' (*nos stulti propter Christum*), while the preceding verse is one Campion must have meditated on frequently on his long travail to England: 'God has set forth us apostles, the last, as it were men appointed to death' (*Deus nos apostolos novissimos ostendit tamquam morti destinatos*).[95] It is not a text that offers immediate comfort, because it accepts the inevitability of a struggle with earthly power, a struggle that wins an immortal crown only at the cost of a mortal life.

On the night of Campion's execution, there must have been many streets in London (and across the country) where weeping was the only sound. Byrd's motet, *Deus venerunt gentes*, with its emphasis on butchered and unburied bodies, is certainly contemporary, and has been seen by many as a response to the deaths of these three Oxford scholars. The harsh disharmonies of the uninterrupted 'cry of alarm', carried through 266 breves, express unalloyed grief:

> Deus venerunt gentes in hereditatem tuam, polluerunt templum tuum, posuerunt Hierusalem in pomorum custodiam. 2a pars Posuerunt morticina servorum tuorum escas volatilibus coeli, carnes sanctorum bestiis terrae. 3a pars Effuderunt sanguinem ipsorum tanquam aquam in circuitu Hierusalem, et non erat qui sepeliret 4a pars Facti sumus opprobrium vicinis nostris, subsannatio et illusio his qui in circuitu nostro sunt.

> [O God, other nations have invaded your inheritance, polluted your holy temple, turned Jerusalem into an orchard of rotting apples. They have laid out the dead bodies of thy servants as food for the birds of the air, the flesh of thy saints for the beasts of the earth. They have poured out their blood like water around Jerusalem: and there was no one to bury them. We have been made a mockery to our neighbours, an absurd laughing-stock for those in our area.][96]

---

[93]   Alfield, *A true reporte*, sig. B4v.

[94]   Monta, *Martyrdom and Literature*, p. 27.

[95]   *The New Testament of Jesus Christ*, trans. Gregory Martin (Rheims: Jean Foigny, 1582), ARCR II. 173, I Corinthians, 4. 9–10.

[96]   Joseph Kerman, *The Masses and Motets of William Byrd* (London: Faber and Faber, 1981), pp. 42, 142–4; John Harley, *William Byrd: Gentleman of the Chapel Royal* (Aldershot, UK and Burlington, VT: Ashgate Publishing, 1997), pp. 228–9. Alison Shell,

Jerusalem has been dishonoured: the desecration of the unburied bodies of these young priests and scholars was as barbaric as the dumping of the battered body of Fr Popiełuszko in the river Vistula, or the beheading of the monks of Tibhirine.

In fact, 'our neighbours', in courts and cities across Europe responded compassionately. In Prague, which Campion had left less than two years earlier, the memory of Campion was still vivid. Philippe de Monte, now Kapellmeister of Rudolf II, sent music to William Byrd on the first four verses of Psalm 136 (Vulgate), 'By the waters of Babylon, there we sat and wept' (*Super flumina Babylonis, illic sedimus et flevimus*), but with the verses 'pointedly rearranged' (1, 3, 4 and 2) so that the second verse, comes last: 'On the willows in the midst thereof we hung up our harps'.[97] De Monte evoked a deep despair, so Byrd responded to his sympathetic gesture by starting with the fourth verse, *Quomodo cantabimus*, and ending with the next two verses, which become a defiant statement of loyalty, and a prayer:

> Quomodo cantabimus canticum Domini in terra aliena? Si oblitus fuero tui, Hierusalem, oblivioni detur dextra mea; adhaeret lingua faucibus meis, si non meminero tui. 2a pars Si non proposuero Hierusalem in principio laetitiae meae. Memor esto, Domine, filorum Edom in die Hierusalem.

> [How shall we sing the song of the Lord in a strange land? If I forget thee, O Jerusalem, let my right hand be forgotten. Let my tongue cleave to my jaws, if I do not remember thee: If I make not Jerusalem the beginning of my joy. Remember, O Lord, the children of Edom, in the day of Jerusalem.][98]

De Monte's motet, and Byrd's answer, were soon circulating together, 'lyrical expressions of sectarian defiance'.[99] Byrd and his family were frequently named for recusancy in the King's Bench records from 1581 to 1590.[100] The execution of Campion made the sound of grief stretch from London to Prague: the attempt to manipulate the people of London with a public execution of three scholarly priests from Oxford succeeded only in evoking weeping in England, and horror across Europe.

The story of Campion's martyrdom, in text and image, was quick to grow. The eyewitness accounts became mature martyr narratives in the expert hands of

---

Oral Culture and Catholicism in Early Modern England (Cambridge: University Press, 2007), pp. 118–19, locates the musical setting of texts within a larger context of ballads, anecdotes and 'oral commonality'.

[97] Kerman, *Masses and Motets*, p. 44.

[98] Kerman, *Masses and Motets*, p. 44. The Latin is the Vulgate of St Jerome, the English from the Douay translation of 1609; the quotation is from Shell, *Oral Culture*, p. 117.

[99] Harley, *William Byrd*, p. 225. The dating of this exchange is normally put as 1583 and 1584, but this is based on an annotation in an eighteenth-century manuscript. Both motets, in eight parts, on a three-part canon, were recorded together by the Cardinall's Musick, *The Byrd Edition* 3, in 1999.

[100] Harley, *William Byrd*, p. 69; Mateer, 'William Byrd', p. 37.

.

Robert Persons and Dr Allen. Galleries of images engraved by Richard Verstegan, Niccolò Circignani and Giovanni Battista de Cavallerii, came eventually to define the entire recusant Catholic community, and how it 'perceived itself'.[101] That posthumous construction is the subject of the last chapter. This one ends with the immediate impact of Campion's death:

> As the cart slipped away beneath Edmund and he fell, such a groan and sound of weeping from the whole crowd of spectators was heard immediately that you would have thought the whole of England had come, not to the death of a common traitor, but to the funeral of a shared parent.[102]

---

[101]   Dillon, *Construction of Martyrdom*, pp. 72–169 (p. 102), for an authoritative discussion of this.

[102]   Bombino, *Vita et Martyrium*, p. 295 (my translation).

Chapter 12
The Legacy

Campion's body hung till he was dead (Charles Howard's intervention secured that small mercy), but it was butchered while Sherwin and Bryant were being executed:

> While these martyrs were being torn asunder, the Catholics did their best to retrieve at least a few of their remains. But their enemies exercised great care to prevent this. One young gentleman, however, pushing through the people round him, let his handkerchief fall in order to get it soaked in Campion's blood, or at least that it might collect a few drops. But his attempt was instantly noticed, and he was seized and put in gaol. All the same, while he was being arrested, another took the opportunity in the general confusion to cut off Campion's finger and make off with it. That, too, was observed, but although a rigorous enquiry was set on foot, it proved impossible to find the man who did it. Another young man, when he saw that nothing could be taken surreptitiously, offered £20 of our money to the executioner for a single joint of Father Campion's finger, but he did not dare to give it. Their clothes were much sought after by Catholics, who tried to buy them, but so far they have not been able to get anything.[1]

The struggle that developed over the body and reputation of Campion was as fierce as that over Patroclus in the *Iliad*; the intensity of the desire of Catholics for relics was matched by the determination of the authorities to prevent them. The establishment's response indicates a regime that felt itself under siege from 'reportes and pamphlets every where so framed and dispersed'.[2] Broadsheets, ballads and poems challenged the official story:

> Countless is the number of books, dialogues, treatises, poems, satires, which have been composed and published, some in print, some in manuscript, in praise of these martyrs and in blame of their adversaries.[3]

Persons was not exaggerating. By April 1582, just four months after his death, there were at least four books in print, a broadsheet of engravings on Campion's execution, and many poems circulating in manuscript. The 'whisperings' that the trial was unjust developed into public discontent. The diary for early 1582 of Richard Madox, Warden of All Souls' College, Oxford, records twice being summoned to Lambeth, because two members of his college had 'libels about

---

[1] More, *Historia Missionis*, p. 137.
[2] Nowell and Day, *A true report*, sig. A2v.
[3] Persons, *Letters and Memorials*, CRS 39, p. 133.

Campion', and another was 'used' for saying that 'Campion was hardly delt withal'.[4] It remained dangerous to praise him. At the sign of the Bell in Henley, on 7 June 1585, Gregory Gunnes, a former chaplain of Magdalen College, Oxford, was arrested for saying, that Campion was 'the only man in all England'; he was unlucky to be talking to a servant of Sir Francis Knollys, who had presided at the execution.[5]

In the febrile period following Campion's execution, eight other priests were executed. John Paine was tried separately, and executed at Chelmsford on 2 April 1582, solely on the evidence of George Elyot.[6] Robert Johnson, Thomas Ford and John Short (or Shert), were executed at Tyburn on 28 May, Thomas Cottam, William Filby, Luke Kirby and Laurence Johnson (*alias* Richardson), two days later, also at Tyburn.[7] Eleven priests, nine with an Oxford background, had been executed by the end of May 1582. Six of the defendants were kept in prison and later banished, some under suspicion of collusion or capitulation. John Paschal had defected on 15 January 1581, attracting scorn and pity from the rest of his companions.[8] John Hart, whose father was well known to Sir Francis Walsingham, was taken off the hurdle on the way to execution, sentenced to spend three months with Dr John Rainolds, of Corpus Christi College, Oxford, and though resolute at the end of this time, finally banished in 1585: by then he had entered the Society of Jesus, and died peacefully at Jarislau, Poland.[9] James Bosgrave, for whom (as we have seen) the King of Poland had interceded, also died peacefully in Poland, at the Jesuit college in Kalisz, on 27 October 1623, aged 75.[10] Edward Rishton was banished on 21 January 1585, along with a large group of priests and the reprieved layman, Henry Orton; he arrived in Rheims on 3 March 1585, where he edited Sander's most famous work for Jean Foigny, *De Origine ac Progressu Schismatis Anglicani* (1585), but died soon afterwards.[11] Thomas Briscow appears to have

---

[4]   Folger MS M.a.244, fols 5r and 9r.

[5]   Davidson, 'Catholics in Oxfordshire', p. 377, citing *CSPD 1581–90*, p. 244, TNA PRO 12/179, no. 7.

[6]   *Cause of Canonization*, pp. 177–217.

[7]   Challoner, *Missionary Priests*, pp. 39–66; Anstruther, *Seminary Priests*, I, 82–5, 90–91, 116, 121, 190–91, 197–8, 310–11. For Thomas Cottam, S.J., see Foley, *Records*, II. 145–59 (p. 149).

[8]   Simpson, pp. 259–60.

[9]   ABSI Collectanea, P. I, fol. 132a–b. McCoog, *Fashioning Jesuit Identity*, p. 134, notes the attribution to Hart of the Tower Diary. Anstruther, *Seminary Priests*, I. 153–4 summarizes the evidence.

[10]   McCoog, 'Mystery of James Bosgrave', p. 140. See Chapter 11 for more on Bosgrave's reprieve.

[11]   Nicholas Sander, *De Origine ac Progressu Schismatis Anglicani, Editus & auctus per Edouardum Rishtonum* (Cologne [Rheims: John Foigny], 1585), ARCR I. 972. Rishton himself gives a moving account of the banishment of 20 priests and one layman (Henry Orton) in Nicholas Sander, *Rise and Growth of the Anglican Schism*, trans. David Lewis (London: Burns and Oates, p. 1877), pp. 326–30.

been held for longer before being exiled, but returned twice more to England, was sentenced to death again and again reprieved.[12] John Colleton, the only one acquitted at the trial, was kept in prison till 1585, when he was exiled with the rest, but returned to England. On 17 November 1600, he 'signed the appeal at Wisbech' and wrote a learned defence of the appellants.[13] In 1618, he wrote a treatise on behalf of the Archpriest William Harrison, which supported his argument against priests attending the theatre, but proposed lifting the ban in order to avoid division.[14] He is the most likely translator of Bombino's *Vita et Martyrium*.[15] He became chaplain of Sir William Roper, and died, at the age of 87, on 19 October 1635.[16]

The first book on Campion's martyrdom appeared within a month in France. 'Le Privilege du Roy' (printed as a colophon to this book) was granted on 30 December 1581. As it had been 'Traduit d'Anglois en François', one can assume that it had been written in English at least two weeks before this, and smuggled across the Channel. *L'Histoire de la Mort* was on the streets of Paris by 4 January 1582.[17] The English ambassador, Sir Henry Cobham, told Walsingham that the Bishop of Ross has 'caused the book of Campion, which I send you, to be printed'.[18] This octavo book has only 16 leaves, but promises the publication of '*un beau, riche & ample volume, qui sortira bien tost en compaigne contenant, & les cruautez que l'heresie la plus cruelle qui fut a exerce depuis dix & huict ans*'.[19] On the following day Cobham reported that the Bishop of Ross has presented 'a little book' to the King, Henri III, and enclosed 'herewith the book in French of Campion's and the other Jesuits' death, which is publicly sold in this town'.[20] As the presence of these four men indicates, the history of Campion's death was instantly swept into the swirling political currents of English exiles, the Guise

---

[12]   Anstruther, *Seminary Priests*, I. 51–2, gives the best account (although he confuses Briscow with Rishton at the trial). Briscow appears to have been sentenced to death in Lancaster in April 1605, and then banished again on 26 November 1605. He returned again to England and was still alive in 1620.

[13]   *A Just Defence of the Slandered Priests* ([London: Richard Field], 1602), STC 5557, ARCR II. 147. See *ODNB*, 'John Colleton' (1548–1635), by Theodor Hamsen.

[14]   This document is available only in manuscript, Folger MS V.a.244, fols 1–89. I am grateful to Dr Clothilde Thouret, of the Sorbonne, for showing me this, and a draft of her forthcoming chapter.

[15]   Bodl. MS Tanner 329, see Preface.

[16]   *ODNB*, 'John Colleton', by Theodor Harmsen.

[17]   *L'Histoire de la Mort que le R.P. Edmond Campion Prestre de la compagnie du nom de Iesus, & autres ont souffert en Angleterre pour la foy Catholique & Romaine le premier jour de Decembre, 1581*. Traduit d'Anglois en Francois (Paris: Chaudiere, 1582), ARCR I. 197 (8o, fols 16). Only one copy of an earlier edition, published in Lyons, survives at Chantilly, ARCR I. 196.

[18]   *CSP Foreign, 1581–1582*, no. 489, p. 440.

[19]   *L'Histoire de la Mort*, sig. A2v.

[20]   *CSP Foreign, 1581–1582*, no. 493, pp. 443–4.

family, Mary, Queen of Scots, and the French monarchy. On 14 January, Cobham reported to Walsingham that the book had caused a stir in France's capital:

> I sent you a small book of the death of Campion. They have been crying these books in the streets with outcries naming them to be cruelties used by the Queen of England ... The king has now given order to the Procurator-fiscal that there shall be a prohibition of the further sale of such books, and those punished who have used such unworthy outcries.[21]

L'Histoire de la Mort was translated into Italian (with editions in Turin, Milan, Bologna), into several different Latin versions, and then adapted to accompany the *Rationes Decem* in the ever-expanding *Concertatio*.[22] This 'little book' helped spread the details of Campion's death across Europe.

Walpole must have started writing the 30 stanzas of 'Why doe I use my paper, ynke and pen' soon after Campion's death. Manuscript copies of this and of another poem, 'And is he dead yn dead; ys vertew so forsett?', were circulating before they were printed alongside an English prose account.[23] The two poems have been copied in a beautiful italic hand on a roll that is itself an emblem of the recusant situation: six pieces of paper, each about a foot long and six inches wide, glued together and concealed within a parchment fragment of a medieval manuscript.[24] A large section of this second poem is occupied with Campion's Oxford learning:

> Saynt Marie churche can tell, and all the scholes do know,
> the walles may yet resound his praise, where he excelled soo
> how scharpe yn science sound, how rype yn skyll was he?
> how sweate for toung, how grave for trowthe, how deape for memoree?
> how skyll yn antique wryters, how rare yn everie arte. *excelled.*
> and how the bible yn eche poynte he coulde repeate by harte.
> And that wich most appearde, yet rarest for to fynde,
> the more of learnyng he possest, more humble was hys mynde.[25]

Musical settings for 'Why do I use my paper, ynke and pen' are extant (one in five parts, and another for lute belonging to Edward Paston), and it is clear that

---

[21] *CSP Foreign, 1581–1582*, no. 508, p. 454.

[22] See ARCR I. 196–203; for the *Concertatio*, see below and ARCR I. 524–7.

[23] Kilroy, *Memory and Transcription*, describes the manuscripts, pp. 59–88, and provides a collated text, pp. 195–207.

[24] Bodl. MS Laud 755 is 145 mm by 2070 mm; each piece is about 330 mm long. This version was printed, with introductory material on Walpole, by Augustus Jessopp, *One Generation of a Norfolk House: A Contribution to Elizabethan History* (Norwich: Miller and Leavins, 1878), pp. 96–103. Dr Augustus Jessopp, an Anglican clergyman, (1823–1914) wrote a handwritten index on fine paper to the first edition of Simpson's *Edmund Campion* (London: Williams and Norgate, 1867), had the composite volume beautifully bound in red boards, and had the paper edged in gold.

[25] Bodl. MS Laud 755, lines 59–66.

Byrd's composition had been played (and memorized) long before it was printed in *Psalmes, Sonets, & Songs of sadnes, and pietie, made unto Musicke of five parts, 1588.*[26]

Walpole's poem circulated outside the boundaries (however loosely defined) of the recusant community, for the remarkable period of 75 years. Sir John Harington quoted two stanzas from it 20 years later in the irenic manuscript (now known as *A Tract on the Succession to the Crown*), which he presented to Bishop Tobie Matthew in 1602:

> Relligion thear was treason to the Queene,
> Preaching of peanaunce, war agaynst the lande,
> preestes weare suche dawngerous men as had not beene,
> Prayeres and beads weare fyghte and force of hand,
> Cases of conscience bane unto the state,
> Soe blynde ys error, so false a witnes hate.[27]

Harington insisted that his father considered it the 'best Englishe verse', and that it was the 'last Englishe verse that ever he redd', praise not diminished by the disclaimer that 'he misliked both the man and the matter'.[28] Harington was not as detached as he pretended: he himself copied all 30 stanzas into what we now know as the Arundel Harington Manuscript, one of the three miscellanies started by his father, while three other manuscripts of his contain the only surviving copies of Campion's poem on the early church, the earliest from about 1568, the latest copied around (or after) 1605.[29] A spy called Guilpine reported to Sir Francis Walsingham from Bath, that 'yong harrington', in late 1583, the peak of

---

[26]   *Psalmes, Sonets, & Songs of sadnes, and pietie, made unto Musicke of five parts* (London: T. East, 1588), STC 4253, sig. F4v. Gurney, *Recusant Poets*, pp. 176–7, prints Byrd's version. For Paston's setting, see BL Add. MS 31992, fol. 19v, and for the four extant parts, BL Egerton MSS 2009–2012.

[27]   The poem is in Arundel Harington MS, fols 32r–34r. This was edited by Ruth Hughey, *The Arundel Harington Manuscript of Tudor Poetry*, 2 vols (Columbus: Ohio State University Press, 1960), I.179–82, II.193–9. Hughey's scribal attribution now needs revising, since this poem is definitely autograph Haringon. This 'plea for peaceble parley' is in York Minster Library MS XVI.L.6, pp. 237–8; Sir John Harington, *A Tract on the Succession to the Crown (A.D. 1602)*, ed. Clements R. Markham (London: Roxburghe Club, 1880), p. 105. For full discussion of both, see Kilroy, *Memory and Transcription*, pp. 67–71 and pp. 108–20.

[28]   York ML MS XVI.L.6, p. 237 (the manuscript has been badly paginated, missing the second hundred).

[29]   BL Add. MS 36529, Bodl. MS Rawl. 289, Holkham MS 437; for details, see Kilroy, 'Advertising the Reader: Sir John Harington's "Directions in the Margent"', *English Literary Renaissance* 41.1 (2011), 64–110 (list of manuscripts and scribes, p. 110), for a full account of Harington's devotion to Campion, and his close knowledge of Persons. His brother, Francis, who was at Corpus Christi College in 1581, and therefore in Oxford when Campion returned, helped copy Exeter College MS 166, and may have provided the link.

the controversy over Campion's disputations, torture and trial, was distributing smuggled copies of 'Edmund Campions bookes' through his one-eyed servant, James Baker, who had been in Rheims, and thought these copies of the *Rationes Decem* (which may have been one of the two Ingolstadt editions of that year) had come through Sir Matthew Arundell, at Wardour.[30] Harington quotes from the *Rationes Decem* as if by heart, and plays alliteratively on the title, arguing that men are 'lesse satisfied of the uprightness of the cause, where rackes serve for reasons and *Tormenta non Scholas parant Antistites*'.[31] Harington is a reminder that, as even Munday acknowledges, 'the learned looved the man' and Campion 'subdued many to affecte him verie much'.[32]

No one has yet suggested that Harington met Campion (although his brother, Francis, who helped transcribe many of the manuscripts and was at Corpus till 1581, could have done so), but Sir Philip Sidney certainly did in Prague, and may have been among those who modelled their speech on his style of eloquence when he went up to Christ Church in 1568.[33] Bombino, obviously following Persons, devotes much of his penultimate chapter to Sidney's guilt in not helping him in his 'agony', and says that 'digracefully, he broke his promise' (*fidem turpiter fefellit*).[34] This seems unjust; the winter of 1581 was a bad time for the Dudley circle. The world of his uncle, Leicester, was in tatters after his opposition to the Anjou match, and his secret marriage left him isolated and 'humiliated' by a queen who 'governed by tantrum', while Sidney himself drew the queen's 'dislike and aversion' after the circulation in manuscript of his *A Letter to Queen Elizabeth Touching her Marriage with Monsieur*, in late 1579.[35] There is no evidence that Leicester ever tried to help

---

[30]   *CSPD, 1581–90*, p. 142, PRO SP 12/164, no. 83; *CSPD, 1581–90*, p. 150, PRO SP 12/167, no. 8. Sir Matthew's brother was Charles Arundell, almost certainly the author of 'The Addycion' (to *Leicester's Commonwealth*), which Harington translated and transcribed in Exeter College MS 166, about two years later; see below. Wardour Castle was the place where *The Metamorphosis of Ajax* was 'first thought of', in 1594, as Harington's marginal gloss, in the copy he gave to Lord Lumley, makes clear: Folger STC 12779, p. 112. For Ingolstadt editions of *Rationes Decem*, see ARCR I. 140, 141.

[31]   York Minster MS XVI.L.6, p. 239; *A Tract on the Succession*, p. 106.

[32]   A[nthony]. M[unday]., *A Discoverie of Edmund Campion, and his Confederates ... Whereunto is added, the Execution of Edmund Campion, Ralphe Sherwin, and Alexander Briant, executed at Tiborne the I of December* (London: J. Charlewood for E. White, 29 January 1582), STC 18270, sig. G2r.

[33]   Katherine Duncan-Jones, 'Sir Philip Sidney's Debt to Edmund Campion', in *The Reckoned Expense*, pp. 97–117 (p. 100), suggests that Sidney may have been among the '"Campionists" who imitated the speech, gait and diet of the charismatic fellow of St John's'. Bartoli, Simpson's source for this information, limits the imitation to speech, see Chapter 2.

[34]   Bombino, *Vita et Martyrium*, c. 59, pp. 304–11 (p. 309); Bodl. MS Tanner 329, fols 106v–111r (fol. 109v), 'shamefully violating with him his fayth'.

[35]   Worden, *Sound of Virtue*, pp. 41–3, 112–14, 149, 187 (Languet's advice), 285–6, assesses Sidney's strategy, and its consequences; see *ODNB*, 'Sir Philip Sidney', by Henry Woudhuysen.

his former protégé, and he signed all four torture warrants.[36] Katherine Duncan-Jones suggests that 'Sidney knew that he could not save Campion', that the conduct of the trial at the end of the 'Old' *Arcadia* probably reflects the 'monstrously unjust trial of Campion', and that the dark tone at the end of the fifth book, which may have been written over Christmas 1581–82, reflects Sidney's 'secret misery at the execution of his friend Edmund Campion'.[37] Certainly, Sidney's Catholic friends seem to have absolved him of responsibility for Campion's death: many of those involved in transcribing Sidney's works – William Byrd, Edward Paston, Sir John Harington, the Huddlestons and Tollemaches – had 'a shared faith or at least a degree of sympathy towards Roman Catholicism'.[38] When Byrd's setting of 'Why doe I use my paper, ynke and pen' was printed, it was on the page facing a 'funeral song' for Sidney.[39]

Several eminent scholars have suggested that the young William Shakespeare met Campion on his mission through Warwickshire to Lancashire, and the possibility has enriched many recent Shakespeare biographies, produced detailed study of Shakespeare's Catholic schoolmasters, his neighbours in Henley Street, the Hathaway and Debdale families of Shottery, and led to fruitful exploration both of the influence of Jesuit drama and of the wider context of religious oppression.[40] In this highly contested area, there are few certainties. Thomas Cottam was carrying a letter for Robert Debdale; his brother, John Cottam, was the schoolmaster in Stratford grammar school; and William Greenway, a carrier from Middle Row, Stratford, did take two cheeses and 5s to the young Debdale

---

[36] See Chapter 8.

[37] Duncan-Jones, 'Sidney's Debt to Edmund Campion', pp. 112 and 114.

[38] H.R. Woudhuysen, *Sir Philip Sidney and the Circulation of Manuscripts 1558–1640* (Oxford: Clarendon Press, 1996), pp. 251–7 (p. 257), and 'A New Manuscript Fragment of Sidney's *Old Arcadia*: The Huddleston Manuscript', in *English Manuscript Studies*, vol. 11 (London: British Library, 2002), pp. 52–69, and Gerard Kilroy, 'Scribal Coincidences: Campion, Byrd, Harington, and the Sidney Circle', *Sidney Journal* 22.1–2 (2004), 73–88.

[39] *Psalmes, Sonets, & Songs of sadnes, and pietie* (1588), sig. F4v and 5r. See Kilroy, 'Scribal Coincidences', p. 85.

[40] Stephen Greenblatt, *Will in the World: How Shakespeare Became Shakespeare* (London: Jonathan Cape, 2004), explores the issue imaginatively, pp. 92–117, and provides an excellent bibliography, pp. 396–8; René Weis, *Shakespeare Revealed: A Biography* (London: John Murray, 2007), sympathetically explores the Stratford and Shottery connections, as well as the dramatic life of John Gerard, S.J., and the wider background of Catholic schoolmasters. Alison Shell, *Shakespeare and Religion* (London: Arden Shakespeare, 2010), offers many fascinating insights into contemporary criticism of Shakespeare. Peter Milward, S.J., *The Catholicism of Shakespeare's Plays* (Southampton: St Austin Press 1997), a passionate pioneer, lists earlier advocates. Clare Asquith, *Shadowplay: The Hidden Beliefs and Coded Politics of William Shakespeare* (New York: Public Affairs, 2005), explores many important allusions to Catholic belief and ritual in the plays and poems; Michael Wood, *In Search of Shakespeare* (London: BBC, 2003), gave visual form to Campion's missionary journeys.

(not yet a priest) in the Gatehouse, on 3 November 1581, the day after Campion was tortured in the Tower.[41] While there is now less enthusiasm for the theory that William Shakespeare was Alexander Hoghton's servant, William Shakeshafte, than when Ernst Honigmann first explored the idea, debate has increased over the authenticity of the Catholic 'testament' (left by his father, but now lost) in the roof in Henley Street.[42] That Campion was carrying such a document has been hotly disputed.[43] Allen reported on 23 June 1581 that Persons had requested 'three or four thousand English Testaments' (*tria vel quatuor millia ex Testamentis Anglicis*), because so many were asking for them.[44] Yet Campion, in his trial, made short work of Edmund Anderson's attempt to link him to 'certeyne papers conteyninge in them Oathes' found in Catholic houses.[45]

While the hypothesis has had many beneficial effects, it has also led to distortions, some minor, others serious. Campion left his books at Richard Hoghton's house, Park Hall (now sadly vanished), and although he certainly stayed at Salmesbury Hall, there is no evidence that he stayed at nearby Hoghton Tower (isolated in majesty above Preston), still less that he made it the 'headquarters of the English Counter-Reformation'.[46] The exploration has helped us understand the complexity of religious allegiance and practice among close networks of friends

---

[41] Greenblatt, *Will in the World*, pp. 97–8; Weis, *Shakespeare Revealed*, pp. 35, 47–9. Debdale was ordained at Rheims on 31 March 1584, and executed on 8 October 1586, Anstruther, *Seminary Priests*, I. 101; for his later exorcisms, see Kilroy, *Memory and Transcription*, pp. 25–37.

[42] E.A.J. Honigmann, *Shakespeare: The 'Lost Years'* (Manchester: University Press, 1985), presents the evidence for Shakeshafte in a careful and scholarly way. Robert Bearman, '"Was William Shakespeare William Shakeshafte?" Revisited', in *Shakespeare Quarterly* 53 (2002), 83–94, attempted to lay the question to rest; Honigmann replied, 'The Shakespeare/Shakeshafte Question, Continued', *Shakespeare Quarterly*, 54 (2003), 83–6. The strongest arguments for the testament are in Weis, *Shakespeare Revealed*, pp. 269–72, and Greenblatt, *Will in the World*, pp. 315–21.

[43] Thomas M. McCoog, S.J., and Peter Davidson, 'Edmund Campion and William Shakespeare: *Much Ado about Nothing*?' in *The Reckoned Expense*, 165–85, completely reject the arguments. For reserved judgements, see Shell, *Shakespeare and Religion*, pp. 86–7, and David Scott Kastan, *A Will to Believe* (Oxford: University Press, 2014), pp. 15–48.

[44] Allen, *Letters and Memorials*, p. 96, and p. 95 n. 1: '*Anglicis*' is missing from the two copies in PRO 12/149, nos 51 and 52; McCoog and Davidson, 'Edmund Campion and William Shakespeare', discuss this problem, p. 175, n. 38.

[45] BL MS Harley 6265, fol. 18r–v. See Chapter 10.

[46] Richard Wilson, *Secret Shakespeare: Studies in Theatre, Religion and Resistance* (Manchester: University Press, 2004), p. 56. While his 'Shakespeare and the Jesuits', *TLS*, 19 December 1997, 11–13, inspired many, McCoog and Davidson, 'Campion and Shakespeare', p. 174, argue that *Secret Shakespeare* revives the Elizabethan government's view of Jesuits as conspirators. There is no evidence I can find, apart from oral tradition, that Campion was at Hoghton Tower, or at Lea Hall, which were the residences of Alexander Hoghton, as Lord Burghley's map confirms, see CRS 4, pp. 175, 192–3, with folding map.

and relatives in early modern England, and revealed the continuing resonance of Catholic rituals (and suffering) in the poems and plays. The impulse to put the iconic Catholic martyr under the same roof as the nation's bard may express the desire, on all sides, to heal, four centuries later, a profound cultural dislocation; some decisive document may yet be found.

Anne Dillon portrays Tyburn as the location for a contest between the Elizabethan state and supporters of the victim hung above the cart; executions were 'vast propaganda exercises' by the state, intended to display the sovereign's power, with men placed among the crowd to lead the cries of 'away with them, away with them'.[47] 'The narratives associated with Campion's confrontation with the state became central,' Lake and Questier argue, in the 'evolution' of the war of ideas.[48] Because Campion's challenge was genuinely theological, the state was forced to wrench the argument back to the bloody (and confused) arena of papal sovereignty and royal supremacy.

While the state was focused on dispelling opposition to Anjou in a stubborn people at home, Campion's apologists, forced to flee over the Channel, found a wider audience. In woodcut, print and engraving, the exiles extended the battle for the public sphere from the audience at Tyburn to every capital in Europe. The new exiles, Robert Persons, Stephen Brinkley, Thomas Fitzherbert, Ralph Emerson and Richard Verstegan, were also driven by a personal sense of loss, and real indignation at Campion's treatment. Persons, as we have seen, portrays William Charke as a petty man gloating over his broken victim on the hurdle, and shows this has driven him, 'the Author of the Censure', to take up his pen 'for the honour of Christ hys martyre now in rest', even if the main impulse was a very academic desire to show Charke 'of what value you are in reason, learninge, and weight of argument by writing'.[49] Charke is pictured preaching from a book to Campion while he is on the hurdle in all three of Verstegan's engravings of the *via dolorosa* of the three martyrs.[50] But in joining Dr Allen, who had already taken part in detailed discussions in Rome for an invasion of England, and John Leslie, the Bishop of Ross, who was still campaigning for the restoration of Mary, Queen of Scots, the Campionists grafted their passionate personal remembrance

---

[47] Dillon, *Construction of Martyrdom*, pp. 72–113; Allen, *A briefe historie*, sig. c2r.

[48] Lake with Questier, *The Antichrist's Lewd Hat*, p. 255.

[49] *A Defence of the Censure*, p. 4; for engraving, see Robert Persons, *De Persecutione Anglicana Epistola. Qua explicantur afflictiones, aerumna, & calamitates gravissimae, cruciatus etiam & tormenta, & acerbissima martyria, quae Catholici nunc Angli, ob fidem patiuntur. Quae omnia in hac postrema editione aeneis typis ad vivum expressa sunt. 8o.* (Romae: Ferrarius [Venerabile], 1582), ARCR I. 876, plate 5.

[50] Dillon, *Construction of Martyrdom*, pp. 114–276, shows in detail the development of the images in Verstegan, and how he 'constructs his priest martyrs in the imitation of Christ' (p. 138).

onto a concerted political campaign intended to shame the English government and persuade its European neighbours of the need to intervene.[51]

According to Persons, there was such dissatisfaction with the trial that even 'Walsingham declared that it would have been better for the Queen to have spent forty thousand gold pieces than to put those priests to death', and 'both our adversaries and our own people cry aloud with one voice' that the three priests have done more by their deaths than they could have done had they lived to be a hundred.[52] A letter of 6 February 1582 was seized, which complained that 'Mr Campion & other holy martyrs might have been released' if they had 'yielded to go to church'.[53] For one of the charges against Vallenger was 'hyering of ffellowes to wright copies'.[54] In an unprecedented step, the Queen felt impelled to issue a proclamation on 1 April 1582, defending the justice of the trial on the basis of the edict published on 24 January 1581: the very justification avoided on the original indictment.[55] As Allen argues, such a 'strange course caused men to suspect far more'.[56] On 16 May 1582, Stephen Vallenger, whose house had been raided, was tried in the Star Chamber, for threatening the authority of the state with 'the kinde of libelling' that:

> reacheth to the hole state of the Realme sounding out most maliciously to the hole world, that this noble kingdome, so much reputed heretofore emongest all Nations for just and upright government, is no more worthie the name of a Monarchie, ruled by lawe, and ordre, but is become a mere Anarchie, without lawe, without Justice, without equitie, without regarde of conscience towardes god or honest fame towarde men.[57]

The judgement confirms that within a month of Campion's death, manuscript pamphlets, in prose and verse, asserting his innocence and the corrupt manner of his trial, were circulating. The trial shows that scribal copying worked alongside

---

[51]   *ODNB*, 'William Allen' (1532–94), by Eamon Duffy. Allen 'actively sought the armed implementation of the bull and the deposition of Elizabeth in 1572, 1576, 1583, 1586 and 1588'; see also *ODNB*, 'John Lesley [Leslie]' (1527–96), by Rosalind K. Marshall.

[52]   Persons, 'Punti', CRS 4, pp. 43–5.

[53]   Simpson, Downside MS 30 A, fol. 32r, copy of *CSP Domestic 1581–90*, p. 45, 12/152/39. The letter was seized and acknowledged before John Popham by Francis Egerman (Eyerman) on 12 February 1582.

[54]   Folger MS X.d.338, fol. 7r.

[55]   *Tudor Royal Proclamations*, II. 490; Leo F. Solt, *Church and State in Early Modern England, 1509–1640* (Oxford: University Press, 1990), p. 105; [John Gibbons and John Fenn], *Concertatio Ecclesiae Catholicae in Anglia, adversus Calvinopapistas & Puritanos* (Trier: Hatotus, 1583), ARCR I. 524, prints this as one of two edicts against priests before Allen's *Apologia* under a separate title page, *Duo Edicta Elizabethae Reginae* (Trier: Hatotus, 1583), pp. 10–15.

[56]   Allen, *A Briefe Historie*, sig. b7v.

[57]   Folger MS X.d.338, fols 2v–3r.

secret presses.[58] Because Vallenger would not disclose the source of the 'booke written in his owne hande', and because it contained the 'printed Libell before spoken of worde for worde without varienge in any thinge', Mildmay chose to assume he was the 'verie principall devisor of theis infamous libelles' and 'Autor and spreader of theis Libelles'.[59]

> first a booke, written with his owne hande, founde in his lodginge, shewed in this courte, and confessed by him, wherin emongest other thinges, is conteined all the printed Libell before spoken of worde for worde without varienge in any thinge, which by his owne confession was written in Januarye last, wheras by good triall yt is founde that the same was not printed till ffebruarye than next.[60]

This Star Chamber trial reveals the level of anxiety in the Privy Council about the damage to its public reputation. Vallenger was sentenced to stand 'upon the pillorye' one day in Westminster, and one day in Cheapside, 'to leese in eche place one of his eares'.[61] It is no wonder that scenes in which the ears of priests and other Catholics are perforated with burning hot pokers figure in every set of Verstegan's engravings.[62] Vallenger was also sentenced to 'Imprisonment during the Quenes pleasure' and a fine to the Queen of £100.[63] He lingered, mutilated, a crown debtor, in the Fleet prison for a further 10 years until he died in 1592, neither the first nor the last person whose life was irrevocably altered by Campion's mission.[64] The account of Vallenger's trial, a repetition of the government's view of what happened to Campion, is further evidence of the intensity of the struggle for control of the public sphere.

In early 1582, Richard Verstegan printed secretly in Smithfield the first English prose report of Campion's death, Thomas Alfield's *A true reporte of the deathe and martyrdome of M. Campion.*[65] Alfield, a priest who operated in the Inns

---

[58]   Folger MS X.d.338. This manuscript has Sir Walter Mildmay's endorsement, and so was presumably an official account of the trial. Another copy of this account is to be found in BL MS Harley 6265, fols 87v–89r, the manuscript that côntains a complete account of Campion's trial.

[59]   Folger MS X.d.338, fol. 6r.

[60]   Folger MS X.d.338, fol. 5v.

[61]   Folger MS X.d.338, fol. 6v; CRS 4, p. 39.

[62]   *Praesentis Ecclesiae Anglicanae typus* (n.p. [Rheims], 1582), plate 3; *Descriptiones Quaedam Illius Inhumanae et Multiplicis Persecutionis* (1584), plate 4. Both are copied in Dillon, *Construction of Martyrdom*, p. 129 and 156.

[63]   Folger MS X.d.338, fol. 6v.

[64]   Anthony Petti, 'Stephen Vallenger (1541–1591)', *Recusant History* 6 (1962), 248–64 (p. 256).

[65]   [Thomas Alfield], *A true reporte of the deathe and martyrdome of M. Campion Jesuite and preiste, & M. Sherwin, & M. Bryan preistes, at Tiborne the first of December 1581 Observid and written by a Catholike preist, which was present therat Wherunto is annexid certayne verses made by sundrie persons* ([London: Verstegan, 1582]), STC 4537, ARCR II. 4.

of Court, composed the book from the eyewitness accounts of two Gray's Inn lawyers, the brothers, Robert and John Dolman, edited by Stephen Vallenger and printed by Richard Verstegan.[66] If the regime exploited its dominance of the public sphere, the suppressed voice of the 'whispring Favourers' specified in the title of *An Advertisement*, was channelled into poetry circulating in manuscript or coming from a secret press. *A true reporte* concludes with four long elegiac poems on Campion; the first two are almost certainly by Henry Walpole, the third appears to be by Stephen Vallenger and the fourth by Richard Verstegan.[67]

The press was seized at the end of February 1582, as the Recorder, William Fleetwood, told Burghley:

> It fell owt that in the first wike of Lent [28 February] there was a booke cast a brood in commending of Campion and of his fellowes, and of theire deathe. I pursued the matter so nere that I found the press, the letters, the figures and a number of the bookes … I have sent unto Your Honor a box of such stuffe as these libelers use for thire printe.[68]

After the seizure of his press, Verstegan fled abroad, and by April 1582, had printed, in Rheims, a broadsheet of six woodcuts called *Praesentis Ecclesiae Anglicanae Typus*, describing the capture, torture and execution of Campion, Haunse and other priests.[69] Evidence suggests this came from the press of Jean Foigny at Rheims, which was being used by Dr Allen and John Leslie, Bishop of Ross.[70] In July 1582, the notorious priest-hunter, Richard Topcliffe, raided the Tower Hill house of the 'innocent artisan', William Carter, and seized manuscript

---

[66]   The book is octavo, and has 26 leaves of 125 by 80 mm, in fours, signatures A to F, and G$_2$. For composition, see A.C. Southern, *Elizabethan Recusant Prose, 1559–82* (London, 1950), pp. 377–9; for the press, its capture and Verstegan's subsequent career, see A.G. Petti, 'Richard Verstegan and Catholic Martyrologies of the Later Elizabethan Period', *Recusant History* 5 (1959), 64–90 (p. 67).

[67]   *A true reporte*, sigs E2r–G2r; see Southern, *Elizabethan Recusant Prose*, p. 376; Guiney, *Recusant Poets*, pp. 176–81 (extracts from all four poems); Pollen, *Acts of English Martyrs*, pp. 22–34 (fourth poem in modernized spelling); Anthony Petti, 'Richard Verstegan', pp. 66–8, and 'Stephen Vallenger (1541–1591)', *Recusant History* 6 (1962), 248–64 (p. 255), for authorship.

[68]   BL MS Lansdowne 35, no. 26, fol. 87; printed in full in CRS 5, *Unpublished Documents Relating to the English Martyrs*, ed. J.H. Pollen (London: Catholic Record Society, 1908) pp. 27–30; in part by A.G. Petti, 'Richard Verstegan and Catholic Martyrologies of the Later Elizabethan Period', *Recusant History* 5 (1959), 64–90 (p. 69), who suggests Verstegan may have 'assisted William Carter with his secret press', p. 66.

[69]   A.G. Petti, 'Additions to the Richard Verstegan Canon', *Recusant History* 8 (1966), 288–93, describes finding a copy of the broadsheet, *Praesentis Ecclesiae Anglicanae typus* (Rheims: Foigny, 1582), ARCR I. 1293, at St Edmund's College, Ware. Dillon, *Construction of Martyrdom*, p. 123 n. 1, records this as having now disappeared.

[70]   Petti, 'Additions', p. 288. The Bishop of Ross had published STC 15505, in 1569, on this press.

accounts of Campion's disputations, which Carter admitted were in Vallenger's hand.[71] Carter's signed admissions are still on the manuscripts, witnessed in Topcliffe's calligraphic hand.[72] A spy called P.H.W. claimed that 'there is ne[i]ther Jesuete, prieste, nor papyste of anye acompte in england but he [Carter] knowthe them', suggesting that Carter's knowledge might prove very helpful 'if this be Rypte to the bottom'.[73] On 15 November 1582, Persons reported that Carter had been 'stretched on the rack almost to death, but those most cruel torturers could extract nothing from [him] but repetition of the name of Jesus'.[74] Carter endured 18 months of interrogation under torture by John Hammond, Robert Beale and Thomas Norton, the same team that had interrogated Campion, before he was put on trial on 10 January 1584. Carter, who was paid £20 per annum by Nicholas Harpsfield, 'to write such thinges as Harpsfeild did dictate or deliver him copie', and worked for Lord Lumley, and as a printer for George Gilbert and Stephen Brinkley, was a nodal figure in Catholic scribal and print publication.[75] He is evidence of the intellectual threat these men posed to the Elizabethan state, and of the continuity with Harpsfield, a man 'at the heart of the Marian project', the author of the first life of Thomas More in 1557, who 'would play a seminal role in the formation of Elizabethan Catholic polemic'.[76]

Topcliffe's menacing manicules fill the margins in a printed book he seized in Carter's house, a copy of *A Treatise of Schisme*, written by Campion's closest friend at St John's, Gregory Martin, and printed in 1578 (under the false imprint of John Fowler in Douai) by Carter in London.[77] Six years later, it was used to convict not its 'auctor' (who was dead), but its 'prynter'; Carter was being used *in terrorem*, just as Burghley published *The Execution of Justice* and after Nowell and Day had published their account of the disputations, in response to criticism of Campion's trial. Topcliffe's marginal gloss (here in italics) overshadows a passage on Judith that he has underlined:

---

[71] See Chapter 9.

[72] BL MS Harley 422, 8 (not Vallenger), fols 136r–147r, nos 7 and 31 (Vallenger), fols 148r–172v.

[73] *ODNB*, 'William Carter', by Ian Gadd, quoting PRO, SP 12/154/62, fol. 107r.

[74] CRS 4, p. 74 (my translation), cited by *ODNB*, 'William Carter', Gadd; Birrell, 'William Carter', p. 26. There is no official record of the interrogation extant. Carter had printed the Jesus Psalter c. 1579, Birrell, 'William Carter', p. 34.

[75] Birrell, 'William Carter', pp. 35–8. 'Thomas Nortons Chayne of Treasons' begins with a fascinating record of the books and Harpesfield material found in Carter's house in BL Add. MS 48029, fols 58r–59v (title as endorsement on fol. 72v). I thank Mark Rankin for sharing his transcription and analysis of this.

[76] Eamon Duffy, *Saints, Sacrilege and Sedition: Religion and Conflict in the Tudor Reformations* (London: Bloomsbury, 2012), p. 209; *ODNB*, 'Nicholas Harpsfield' (1519–75), by Thomas S. Freeman.

[77] Gregory Martin, *A Treatise of Schism* (Douai: John Fowler [*vere* London: William Carter], 1578), STC 17508, ARCR II. 524.

<u>Judith foloweth, whose godlye and constant wisedome if our Catholic gentlewomen woulde folowe, they might destroye Holofernes, the master heretike, and amaze all his retinew and never defile their religion by communicating with them in anye smal poynt.</u>

A Tratorous meaning of the auctor & prynter to our
gentlewomen catholickes to becum
like Judith to destroy hol: to amayse etc.[78]

This was 'most unjustlie' the principal evidence of treason, for which Carter was sentenced to death.[79] Holinshed's 'Continuation of the Chronicles of England' includes an account of the trial and execution of William Carter, placed with precise irony (perhaps by John Stow), just before *A Declaration of the favorable dealing*:

> On the tenth of Januarie in the yeare 1584 at a sessions holden in the justice hall in the old bailie of London for goale deliverie of Newgate, William Cartar of the citie of London was there indicted, arreigned, and condemned of high treason, for printing a seditious and traitorous booke in English, intituled A treatise of schisme: and was for the same (according to sentence pronounced against him) on the next morrow, which was the eleventh of Januarie, drawne from Newgate to Tiborne, and there hanged, bowelled, and quartered. And forthwith against slanderous reports, spread abroad in seditious books, letters and libels, thereby to inflame the hearts of our countriemen, and hir majesties subjects, a booke was published, intituled, A declaration of the favorable dealing of hir majesties commissioners, &c.[80]

In early 1582, Robert Persons first published, in Rouen, his *De Persecutione Anglicana Epistola* (under the false imprint of Bologna), followed by an English translation (from a French edition), *An Epistle of the Persecution of Catholickes in Englande* (under the false imprint of Douai), both with the aid of George Flinton, and on the press of George L'Oyselet.[81] On 28 March 1582, Sir Henry Cobham reported the publication, with royal privilege, to Walsingham.[82] Even the title of this powerful rhetorical piece by Persons was polemical: an assertion that the brutality in England was a religious persecution and not the prosecution of traitors, as the government argued. Persons begins by listing the many 'penal laws' that

---

[78]   Martin, *Treatise of Schism*, in Topcliffe's annotated copy, Bodley 8 C. 95(3) Th, sig. D2r.

[79]   Allen, *A True, Sincere, and Modest Defence*, p. 10.

[80]   Holinshed, *Chronicles* (1587), III. 1357.a.57–1368.b.63.

[81]   *An Epistle of the Persecution of Catholickes in Englande. Translated out of frenche into Englishe, and conferred with the Latyne copie. by G.T.* (Douai [Rouen: L'Oyselet for Flinton, 1582]), STC 19406, ARCR II. 627, transl. of a French version, printed in Paris, ARCR I. 879, by 'G.T'., who may be Gabriel Thimbleby.

[82]   *CSP Foreign, 1581–1582*, no. 634, pp. 584–5, and no. 668, p. 622. Cobham mistakenly thought Allen was the author, and that Persons was still in London.

rob Catholics of land, liberty and money, but reaches a climax with the argument that 'all these lawes, doe concern religion onlye'.[83] Then follows a list of all the offences now classified as treason, together with graphic detail of the horrible punishments given to 'traitors'.[84] The fate of 'maister Edmund Campian of the Societie of Jesus, a great learned clerk, a harmelesse and verie Innocent man' is inserted into this list of outrages.[85] Persons argues that Campion was tortured and that the authorities tried to deny it:

> For twyse nowe of late Maister Campian hath bene pulled on the rack. And what adversarie dyd not utterlie denye yt? Yet at lengthe the truthe of the matter came to light, when maister Campian him selfe dyd utter it in an *open* audience, & in the hearinge of oure adversaries ...[86]

Persons recounts the attempt to seize imported books, and the way the authorities granted disputations to Campion only when he had been 'twise before that tyme racked, destitute of bookes, and unprovided of all things, saving onlie of a good cause, & of a well willing mynde'.[87]

In *An Epistle of the Persecution*, Persons places the trial, torture and execution of Campion in the wider context of the oppression of Catholics in England, and conveys the intrusively banal quality of the persecution. The horrors are so ordinary that any reader in Europe can imagine them, so tactile that all can feel them. 'These texts told Europe what was happening to the Catholic community in England'.[88] *An Epistle of the Persecution* shows the oppression of ordinary Catholics in their homes when 'at midnight oure adversaries oftentimes rushe in forcibly upon them' and 'goe throwgh all the house from place to place, veweing, tossing, & rifeling in every corner, chests, coffers, boxes, caskets and closetts', taking what they call 'churche stuffe' which 'they snatche away, by a priviledge of robberie'.[89] It was surely this passage which Verstegan chose to make the subject of the second of the five engravings that make up the *Descriptiones Quaedam Illius Inhumanae et Multiplicis Persecutionis: Nocturnae per domos inquisitiones*' (Figure 12.1). In this sombre engraving, annotated in an alphabetical table, officials, lit only by torches, are shown battering down doors and rifling trunks for treasure, invading the privacy of gentlewomen's chambers.[90]

---

[83] *An Epistle of the Persecution*, p. 62.

[84] *An Epistle of the Persecution*, p. 68.

[85] *An Epistle of the Persecution*, p. 82.

[86] *An Epistle of the Persecution*, pp. 87–8.

[87] *An Epistle of the Persecution*, p. 125.

[88] Dillon, *Construction of Martyrdom*, p. 82.

[89] *An Epistle of the Persecution*, pp. 127–8.

[90] *Descriptiones quaedam illius inhumanae et multiplicis persecutionis quam in Anglia propter fidem sustinent Catholici Christiani, engraved by de Cavallerii* (Romae: Francisco Zanetti, 1584), ARCR I. 1284, plate 2.

Figure 12.1   *Nocturnae per domos inquisitiones*: Night house searches,
engraved by Giovanni Battista Cavallerii for Richard Verstegan,
in *Descriptiones quaedam illius inhumanae et multiplicis
persecutionis*, 1584, ARCR I. 1284, plate 2, bound with ARCR I.
944. With permission of the Folger Shakespeare Library.

By the end of 1582, Verstegan was in Rome cutting six copperplate engravings
for a new, illustrated, edition of Persons's *De Persecutione Anglicana* produced
by the English College in Rome.[91] By 1583, the plates, which tell the story of
Campion's capture, journey to the Tower, torture, being drawn on the hurdle
and execution, had also been added to Martellini's edition of Allen's expanded

---

[91]   Robert Persons, *De Persecutione Anglicana* (Rome: English College, 1582).

Historia del glorioso martirio di sedici sacerdoti.[92] Verstegan's prints were now attached to prose works by two of the most powerful controversial writers of the period.

Verstegan was back in Paris by autumn 1583, and produced a further set of six engravings accompanied by a printed text in French, *Briefve description des diverses cruautez*, or Latin, *Descriptiones quaedam.*[93] These aim 'to solicit help' from continental Catholics, 'so that you … may sympathize with us, your afflicted brethren, and may join your prayers with us'.[94] Sir Edward Stafford, who replaced Cobham as English ambassador in September 1583, had an informer in the press, and heard of this work as it was being set up.[95] He reported to Walsingham on 23 November 1583, sending him 'the coppie of a leafe of a booke that is nowe in presse': the only leaf engraved so far.[96] On 8 January 1584, Stafford wrote that he had confiscated the plates and arrested both the printer and Verstegan, the 'Englishman that was the bringer of them to print'.[97] Stafford, who hoped to get 'both the printed pieces and the moulds', added that he would like to have had Verstegan hanged.[98] The papal nuncio, Mgr Girolamo Ragazzoni, persuaded Henri III to release Verstegan after only two weeks in prison, so Stafford pressed for his rearrest.[99] By 17 March 1584, all Stafford could do was remonstrate that Verstegan had been allowed to escape, and to offer to present to the French king a copy of Burghley's *Execution of Justice.*[100]

Verstegan reached Rome on 28 April 1584, and found just completed a series of murals of martyrs in the English college, from earliest times to Campion and his companions; this was apparently the idea of Fr William Good, S.J., supervised by the rector, Alfonso Agazzari, S.J., paid for by George Gilbert and painted by

---

[92]   William Allen, *Historia del glorioso martirio di sedici sacerdoti martirizati in Inghilterra* (Macerata: Martellini, 1583), ARCR I. 8.

[93]   Richard Verstegan, *Briefve description des diverses cruautez que les Catholique endurent en Angleterre pour la foy* ([Paris: n.p.d., 1583]), ARCR I. 1280; *Descriptiones quaedam illius inhumanae et multiplicis persecutionis quam in Anglia propter fidem sustinent Catholici Christiani* ([Paris: n.p.d., 1583]), ARCR I. 1283; See Petti, 'Additions', p. 290.

[94]   Dillon, *Construction of Martyrdom*, p. 150; Petti, 'Richard Verstegan', pp. 72–3.

[95]   Petti, 'Additions', p. 290.

[96]   *CSP Foreign, 1583–1584*, p. 231. The letter is printed in full in Petti, 'Richard Verstegan', p. 70.

[97]   Petti, 'Richard Verstegan', p. 71.

[98]   *CSP Foreign, 1583–1584*, pp. 299–300, 8 January 1584; Petti, 'Richard Verstegan', pp. 71–2.

[99]   *CSP Foreign, 1583–1584*, pp. 316–17, 18 January 1584; Stafford complains to Walsingham that 'it is generally put into men's heads that they are only executed in England for conscience and not for treason'.

[100]   *CSP Foreign, 1583–1584*, pp. 416–18, 18 March 1584; Paul Arblaster, *Antwerp and the World: Richard Verstegan and the International Culture of Catholic Reformation* (Leuven: University Press, 2004), pp. 34–5.

Niccolò Circignani.[101] These murals, designed to reclaim the Catholic history of the conversion of England from John Bale and John Foxe, were copied by Giovanni Battista Cavallerii, as 36 engraved plates in his *Ecclesiae Anglicanae Trophaea*. Ten of Cavallerii's plates portray the martyrs created since Henry VIII's break with Rome down to the most recent in March 1583.[102] Three of these portray Campion's *via crucis*: the first shows two young priests forced to observe Campion's racking (Figure 8.1), the second shows him being drawn on a hurdle to Tyburn (with Charke preaching to him from a book), and the third shows the martyrdom of Campion, Sherwin and Briant.[103] These engravings mark the moment when Campion joined his fellow Londoners, Thomas à Becket and Thomas More, as an icon of English Catholic martyrs. The collection was bound together with a new edition by Cavallerii of Verstegan's *Descriptiones quaedam*.[104] Cavallerii's clean, engraved lettering now contrasts with the darkness of the heavily inked scenes of the persecution, which show England living through one long tempest, where women and priests are dragged from their houses by night, their houses are ransacked and justice is linked to mutilation of the ears.[105] The fifth plate is a climax of cruelty in which priests are dragged on hurdles, hanged, disembowelled and quartered; halberds and a burning fire by the cauldron allow smoke to rise and hang over a benighted country. Verstegan and Cavallerii disseminated the image of a country 'without lawe, without Justice, without equitie'.[106]

Persons was waging a parallel campaign stemming from Campion's 'Letter to the Council'. While *A Brief Censure*, refuting the two books produced by Meredith Hanmer and William Charke, had been written, printed and published in 10 days at the beginning of 1581, on a press that had to be re-assembled in a new house, Persons's *A Defence of the Censure*, which was being prepared in August

---

[101]	More, *Historia Missionis*, p. 16 (Good); p. 100 (Gilbert); Dillon, *Construction of Martyrdom*, pp. 171–229, reconstructs the murals and their missionary purpose. The murals formed an important part of the evidence of 'public cult' in the canonization process, Sacred Congregation of Rites, *Cause of the Canonization of Blessed Martyrs* (Rome: Vatican Polyglot Press, 1968), p. xiii. Simpson, Downside MS, 30A, fols 37r–38r, recounts Gilbert's generosity, and his death in 1583; see Foley, *Records*, III. 658–704 for full account.

[102]	Dillon, *Construction of Martyrdom*, pp. 211–23, outlines their wide-reaching significance.

[103]	Giovanni Battista Cavallerii, *Ecclesiae Anglicanae Trophaea sive Sanctorum Martyrum, qui pro Christo Catholicaeque fidei Veritate asserenda, antiquo recentiorique Persecutionum tempore, mortem in Anglia sibierunt, Passiones Romae in Collegio Anglico per Nicolaum Circinianum depictae* (Romae: Bartholomei Grassi, [1584]), ARCR I. 944, bound with ARCR I. 1284, fols 31–3, described and illustrated in Dillon, *Construction of Martyrdom*, pp. 226–32.

[104]	*Descriptiones quaedam illius inhumanae et multiplicis persecutionis*, ARCR I. 1284, bound with ARCR I. 944.

[105]	Dillon, *Construction of Martyrdom*, pp. 182–242, reproduces most of these engravings.

[106]	Folger MS X.d.338, fol. 3r.

1581, had to wait several months before it could be printed in Rouen.[107] For the book was 'in greate parte dispatched ... redie for the printe' when the press was seized, in early August 1581, at Stonor Park, 'withall, not onelie all furniture there redy for the booke; but also for sundry other thinges, partlie printed and partlie in printing'.[108] The valuable press was given (as we have seen) to David Jenkins, the Queen's Messenger, on 27 November 1581, one week after the trial.[109]

A Defence of the Censure was a fractured production; as Persons says: 'Thus brokenlie we are enforced to deale'.[110] It gains its strength from the cry of the oppressed that it represents, turning the weakness of Catholics into a critique of the powerful, who 'putt in prison, rent on racke, put to death those whiche speake, or wryte, or stand in defence of trueth against you'.[111] Persons had acquired additional animus against Charke for the way he treated Campion 'in the Tower of London', with 'M. Norton the Rackmaister at your elbowe'.[112] Persons highlights the inequality of the debates, where Campion had to answer 'unbookt, unprovided, wearyed with imprisonment, and almost dismembred with the rack, threatned and terrified with deathe to come: appointed onely to answer, and never to oppose'.[113] *A Defence* is designed to make the reader feel indignation at this unequal dealing.

John Gibbons's work under the title, *Concertatio Ecclesiae Catholicae in Anglia Adversus Calvinopapistas et Puritanos*, first appeared in 1583.[114] A collated *Vita et Martyrium Edmundi Campiani* was now joined to accounts of the martyrdom of ten other priests drawn from various sources, and combined with the *Rationes Decem, the De Persecutione Anglicana*, and a Latin version of Allen's *Apologie* to fill more than 500 pages. Gibbons excused himself from the English mission on the grounds that he lacked the spiritual strength, as Persons recounts in his *Punti per la missione d'Inghilterra*, and instead put together this compendium.[115] Campion's 'Letter to the Council', the *Rationes Decem* and an expanded life, fill the first half of the book, so Gibbons's work had the effect of confirming Campion as the jewel in the crown of English Catholic martyrs. The second, much expanded, edition of the *Concertatio* appeared at Trier in 1588, with a full account of 'a hundred or more Catholic martyrs', and was clearly intended

---

[107]   *A Defence of the Censure given upon two bookes of William Charke and Meredith Hanmer mynysters, which they wrote against M. Edmond Campion* ([Rouen: L'Oyselet for Flinton], 1582), STC 19401, ARCR II. 624, p. 1.

[108]   *A Defence of the Censure*, p. 1.

[109]   *APC, 1581–1582*, pp. 264–5. See Chapter 8 for the full text.

[110]   *A Defence of the Censure*, p. 3.

[111]   *A Defence of the Censure*, p. 3.

[112]   *A Defence of the Censure*, pp. 7–8.

[113]   *A Defence of the Censure*, p. 9.

[114]   [John Gibbons and John Fenn], *Concertatio Ecclesiae Catholicae in Anglia, adversus Calvinopapistas & Puritanos* (Trier: Hatotus, 1583), ARCR I. 524; Simpson, Downside MS 30 A, fol. 18, analyses the Campion material contained.

[115]   CRS 4, pp. 109–11.

to reach English exiles and other European readers.[116]. All subsequent martyr accounts were sent to Gibbons, so the *Concertatio* became 'the fullest Catholic response to Foxe'.[117] At least 30 copies of the 2 editions survive. The primacy of Campion material indicates that Campion's trial and martyrdom had already achieved iconic status. Because Campion so perfectly fulfilled the conditions of martyrdom, the polemical strand in the descriptions (the assertion that he was a martyr not a traitor) came to be a kind of synecdoche for the whole Catholic community. It was soon complemented, in 1585, by Edward Rishton's edition of Sander's *De Origine ac progressu Schismatis Anglicani*, later expanded by Allen and Persons in 1586, to include the anonymous 'Tower Diary', added by John Hart.[118] When Catholics gathered secretly to sing Byrd's setting of 'Why doe I use my paper, ynke and pen', or members of the English college gathered in front of the murals of Campion's execution, they were celebrating the moment when the English Catholic community was redefined.[119]

The Privy Council, confronted by the literary skill of Allen and Persons, and the pictorial power of the engravings of Verstegan and Cavallerii, felt impelled to defend itself. The first attempt to justify the torture of Campion was the publication, in 1582, of the anonymous *A particular declaration*, which took seven extracts from Sander and Bristow, and reported the responses given by Campion and his fellow prisoners to interrogatories as to whether they agree with them.[120] If the state could not silence supporters of those it had hoped to 'eliminate', it could reconstruct what they said in the torture chamber, and align them with that 'ranke traitor', Sander. A year later, there was a more explicit defence of the torture in *A Declaration of the favourable dealing*.[121] This brief quarto, a single gathering of four leaves, seems to be the work of Thomas Norton who had, as we have seen, been called the 'Rackmaster' by Robert Persons in *A Defence of the Censure*, in 1582. Norton's justification of the torture, on 27 March 1583 suggests that Persons's book was already having its effect.[122] For the preface states:

---

[116] *Concertatio Ecclesiae Catholicae in Anglia, adversus Calvinopapistas & Puritanos* (Trier: H. Bock, 1588), ARCR I. 525; D.M. Rogers, in his introduction to the facsimile (Farnborough: Gregg, 1970), describes the much expanded contents, p. iii.

[117] Monta, *Martyrdom and Literature*, 24; Dillon, *Construction of Martyrdom*, pp. 81–2.

[118] Nicholas Sander, *De origine ac progressu schismatis Anglicani, liber ... Editus & auctus per Edoardum Risthonum* ([Rheims: Jean Foigny], 1585), ARCR I. 972. For second and third editions, ARCR I. 973 and 974, see Bibliography. Mark Rankin has found 318 copies of the first three editions, spread all over the world (private communication).

[119] Dillon, *Construction of Martyrdom*, pp. 225–9.

[120] [Anon.], *A particular declaration or testimony, of the undutifull and traiterous affection borne against her Majestie by Edmond Campion Jesuite* (London: C. Barker, 1582), STC 4536.

[121] [Thomas Norton], *A Declaration of the favourable dealing of her Maiesties Commissioners appointed for the Examination of certaine Traitours, and of tortures unjustly reported to be done upon them for matters of religion* ([London: C. Barker], 1583), STC 4901.

[122] See Chapter 8 for a full discussion of this issue.

Good Reader, although her Majesties most milde and gracious governement bee
sufficient to defende it selfe against those most slaunderous reportes of heathenish
& unnatural tyrannie and cruell tortures pretended to have bene executed upon
certaine traitors, who lately suffred for their treason, & others, as well spread
abroad by Runnagate Jesuites and Seminary men in their seditous bookes,
letters, & libels in forreine countries and Princes Courtes, as also insinuated into
the hearts of some of our owne countrie men her Majesties Subjectes.[123]

The opening, 'Touching the racke and torments', passes swiftly to 'the principall
offender, Campion himselfe, who was sent and came from Rome and continued
here in sundrie corners of the Realme', and argues that Campion was 'charitably
used, was never so racked, but that he was presently able to walke, & to write'.[124]
Particularly specious was the appeal to 'the generall lawes of nations', since
everyone was very clear about the differences between English common law
which did not permit the use of confession gained under torture, and Roman law,
which required either a confession or two witnesses.

After defending the cruelty to Alexander Briant by saying that he brought it
on himself by his 'impudent obstinacie', Norton uses six lines of argument. The
first is that those 'whose office and act it is to handle the rack' were 'specially
charged to use it in as charitable maner as such a thing might be'.[125] Secondly,
the defendants were never asked any point of doctrine or faith, 'as the Masse,
Transubstantiation'.[126] Thirdly, only those thought guilty, and fourthly, only those
who refused to talk, were racked and fifthly, 'the proceeding to torture was always
so slowly and unwillingly'. Finally, while 'by the more generall lawes of nations,
torture hath bene and is lawfully judged to be used in lesser cases', so it was very
reasonable to use it in a case of such danger to the state. In all this was to be seen
(and here the leaflet closes) 'the sweete temperature of her Majesties milde and
gracious clemencie', by whom 'nothing hath bene done, but gentle and mercifull'.[127]
The last three words are clearly intended to ring in the ears of readers.

Norton thought this a reasonable defence, able to quell the growing
condemnation in Europe. Sir John Harington, writing in the middle of the next
decade, lists Norton among those who blackened the name of Sir Henry Goodyeare
at the time of the Ridolfi plot by writing a caveat, '*Hic niger est, hunc tu Regina
caveto*' (this man is dangerous, watch out, Queen, for him), beneath his name,
and argues that Norton had had many 'young scholers' (glossed by Harington
in Lord Lumley's copy as '*Justice Young a promooter*').[128] Richard Young was
another notorious rackmaster, whom the urbane John Gerard describes as 'the

---

[123]   *A Declaration of the favourable dealing*, sig. Aa2r.

[124]   *A Declaration of the favourable dealing*, sig. A2v.

[125]   *A Declaration of the favourable dealing*, sig. Aa3r.

[126]   *A Declaration of the favourable dealing*, sig. Aa3r.

[127]   *A Declaration of the favourable dealing*, sig. Aa4–4v.

[128]   *A New Discourse of a Stale Subject, Called the Metamorphosis of Ajax* (London:
Field, 1596), STC 12779. Harington's autograph glosses in this copy (now in the Folger

devil's confessor'.[129] He tortured Henry Donne (younger brother of the poet, John Donne), and interrogated William Harrington, the son of Campion's Yorkshire host, on 21 May 1593.[130] 'Campion I desired to imitate, whome onely love to his countrey and zeale of the house of god consumed before his time', young Harrington declared in a moving letter to the Lord Keeper, John Puckering.[131] He was executed with spectacular brutality on 18 February 1594.

Norton's risible defence obviously failed to silence the critics, since, as the year 1583 closed, Lord Burghley himself published *The Execution of Justice*. Criticism of the trial and the torture was growing, and December 1583 seems to have been the turning point. To ensure that *The Execution of Justice* was read in the 'other princes courts', Burghley also published it in Latin, French, Flemish and Italian (mostly under false imprints).[132] The book asserts defensively that:

> all the infamous libels latelie published abroad in sundrie languages, and the slanderous reports made in other princes courts of a multitude of persons, to have beene of late put to torments and death onelie for profession of the catholike religion, and not for matters of state against the queenes majestie, are false and shamelesse, and published to the maintenance of traitors and rebels.[133]

The running titles of the English version focus on the key issue: '*Execution for Treason* (verso) / *and not for Religion* (recto)'. This iteration over 17 openings aptly culminates in the verso heading on the last quarto. Barker's black letter font has bled through several sheets, and yields appropriately to roman only for the 'Pope' or 'Rome'; Campion and Persons are mentioned by name only seven times, and most of those occur in the direct quotation from the faculties granted them

---

Shakespeare Library), sig. O6v, reveal that 'Justice young' is the '*stercus*' (excrement) in this allegorical piece.

[129]   Gerard, *Autobiography*, p. 92.

[130]   Anstruther, *Seminary Priests*, I. 149–50; Richard Simpson, *The Rambler*, 10 (1858), p. 399. A close connection with Ralph Emerson is confirmed by renewed interrogation of Emerson in 1593.

[131]   TNA PRO SP 12/245, no. 66, fol. 99r–v, Harrington's calligraphic letter to John Puckering, Lord Keeper.

[132]   [William Cecil, Lord Burghley], *The Execution of Justice for maintenance of publique and Christian peace, against certeine stirrers of sedition, and adherents to the traytors and enemies of the Realme, without any persecution of them for questions of Religion, as is falsely reported and published by the fautors and fosterers of their treasons xvii. Decemb. 1583* (London: [Barker], 1583), STC 4902. T. Vautrollier printed the Latin, *Justitia Britannica* (STC 4904), and French versions (STC 4906) in roman type, while 'G. Wolfio' [John Wolfe] printed the Italian version (STC 4907) in italic, C. Barker published the Flemish version (with the false imprint of 'R. Schilders in Middleburgh', STC 4905), all in London. The English edition, dated 'xvii. Decemb. 1583', is in black letter. The book was entered in the Stationers' Register on 2 January 1584. The title page of the French version gives its date as 'Le 30. de Janvier 1584'.

[133]   *Execution of Justice*, sig. C2r; Holinshed, *Chronicles*, III. 1363.a.40–48.

by the Pope, a word that drums its way through the text 55 times. Italics are used to highlight the Latin of the papal bull and the faculties granted to Persons and Campion by *Pius Quintus*, the only particular evidence that can link them to the Pope, and there is no attempt to repeat the charges of the trial, which Campion had called 'shifts of probabilities, and conjecturall surmises'.[134] The prose pummels the reader with a succession of parallel clauses. Thirty-seven pages rant against the Pope and repeat the catalogue of rebels – Dr Sander and the northern earls – barely touching on Persons and Campion. Even the summary of charges at the end refers to: 'These disguised persons (called schollars or Priestes)'.[135]

A pamphlet of this length that attempts to confirm the guilt of the executed in the face of outcries on the streets of Paris and Rome, and simmering resentment in the courts of Prague and Madrid, with nothing more than guilt by association, was no more likely to persuade critics than had Norton's *A Declaration of Favourable Dealing*, with which it was now bound. That Burghley thought he was going to win friends abroad, and silence the opposition at home, only revealed how far he had failed to grasp the intellectual ability of the men leading the campaign in print. Vautrollier's printing of the French version, *L'Execution de Justice*, is at least a more elegant work on better paper, using italics for names, marginal glosses and quotations. It prints Norton's *Declaration du Traictement Favorable* at the end; but the French translation, '*le comportement charitabl*e', can have convinced few in Paris.[136] Evidence of the international outcry comes from a long Spanish poem composed at this time by Fr Franciso de Herrera, a German Jesuit, on the deaths of Campion, Thomas Cottam, S.J., and 16 other priests; the dedication to Philip II of Spain makes clear its intention.[137]

The Earl of Leicester blamed Lord Burghley and *The Execution of Justice* for provoking the three responses that followed, all printed in Rouen by George L'Oyselet for George Flinton, the press sometimes called 'Fr Persons's press'.[138] Ralph Emerson, S.J., Campion's 'little man', had escaped to France, and (Persons tells us) 'introduced 4 priests and 810 books' across the Channel.[139] He was now involved in a major publishing campaign, along with Thomas Alfield, the author of *A true reporte*. Dr Allen's answer to Burghley, *A True Sincere and Modest*

---

[134] BL Harley MS 6265, fol. 15r.

[135] *Execution of Justice*, sig. E4r.

[136] *Declaration du Traictement Favorable*, sig. E4v.

[137] Bodl. MS 513, fols 5r to 132v. The poem is in seven-line stanzas, and beautifully transcribed. I thank Dr Clarinda Calma for alerting me to this.

[138] See ARCR II. 14, for example.

[139] D.C. Peck, ed., *Leicester's Commonwealth: The Copy of a Letter Written by a Master of Art of Cambridge (1584) and Related Documents* (Ohio: University Press, 1985), p. 6, misreads Persons's letter to Agazzari, 20 August 1584, CRS 39, p. 227. Emerson has not 'just' smuggled in 'four priests and 810 books', but over the last few years. See my 'Advertising the Reader', pp. 94–5.

Defence of English Catholiques,[140] and Persons's *The copie of a Leter* (later called *Leicester's Commonwealth*), still full of bitterness that Leicester's opposition to the Anjou marriage had 'bereaved the realm' of 'tolleration in religion', were printed and ready by the summer of 1584.[141] L'Oyselet also printed the third edition of John Leslie's *A Treatise Towching the Right Title of Marie, Queene of Scotland*.[142] Books, printed and engraved, now formed part of a concerted campaign to shake the beard of the Privy Council. Alfield, who had presumably come through Dover, distributed 'ffyve or six hundreth' copies of Allen's book in All Saints parish, Bread Street, between 10 to 20 September; he was arrested and indicted on 26 September 1584.[143] Emerson landed in Norfolk with 'no small number' of copies of *Leicester's Commonwealth*, but was arrested and his load impounded, when he arrived at Bishopsgate on the same day as Alfield was indicted.[144] He was to spend the next 19 years in prison, and was paralysed when he was released, in 1604.[145]

---

[140]　　William Allen, *A true Sincere and modest Defence of English Catholiques that suffer for their Faith both at home and abrode: against a false, seditious and slaunderous Libel intituled THE EXECUTION OF JUSTICE IN ENGLAND* ([Rouen: L'Oyselet for Flinton, 1584]), STC 373, ARCR II. 14. A Bodleian copy, 80 K. 12(3) Th., has Topcliffe's annotation, 'A false sedicious & immodest offence set out by of *A True, Sincere and Modest Defence* ... To be redd & used for Q. Elizabethes service & not Otherwise'.

[141]　　[Persons], *The copie of a Leter, wryten by a Master of Arte of Cambridge to his friend in London, conccerning some talke about some procedinges of the erle of Leycester and his friendes* ([Rouen: L'Oyselet for Flinton], 1584), STC 5742.9; ARCR II. 31. Leo Hicks, S.J., 'The Growth of a Myth: Father Robert Persons, S.J. and Leicester's Commonwealth', *Studies: An Irish Quarterly* 46 (1957), 91–105 (pp. 98–9), cites Persons to Alfonso Agazzari, 13 December 1584, CRS 39, pp. 266–8. Hicks's argument against Persons as author held sway for 25 years. Peter Holmes, 'The Authorship of "Leicester's Commonwealth"', *Journal of Ecclesiastical History* 33 (1982), 424–30, renewed the case for Persons. Alan H. Nelson, 'Who Didn't Write *Leicester's Commonwealth*? (Who Did?)', *English Manuscript Studies 1100–1700*, vol. 18 (London: The British Library, 2013), pp. 11–18, uses detailed stylistic evidence to show Charles Arundel is the author of the French 'Addition', and therefore cannot be the author of the main text. Kilroy, 'Advertising the Reader: Sir John Haringtons "Directions in the Margent"', *English Literary Renaissance* 41.1 (2011), 64–110 (p. 95 n. 113), argues from Exeter College, Oxford, MS 166, that 'everything in the style, content, motivation, context, printing and distribution points to Persons' as the author of *Leicester's Commonwealth*.

[142]　　John Leslie, Bishop of Ross, *A Treatise Towching the Right Title and Interest of the Most excellent Princesse, Marie, Queene of Scotland. And of the most noble king James, her Graces sonne, to the succession of the Croune of England Wherein is contened aswell a Genealogie of the Competitors pretending title to the same Croune: as a resolution of their objections* ([Rouen: L'Oyselet for Flinton], 1584), STC 15507, ARCR II. 503.

[143]　　CRS 5, pp. 112–20.

[144]　　William Weston, *The Autobiography of an Elizabethan*, trans. Philip Caraman (London: Longmans, Green, 1955), pp. 1–3, tells the story in graphic detail.

[145]　　CRS, 39, p. 256 n. 3. He died shortly after his release.

The affection Campion inspired in his life ensured that, after his death, close friends and admirers lovingly preserved his memory, even if some did so through the prism of a complex web of political interests. In 1581, the Privy Council may have seen itself as engaged in a propaganda contest it could win with sermons at Paul's Cross, and proclamations at Tyburn. By the time *A Declaration of the favourable dealing* and *The Execution of Justice* were reprinted in Holinshed's 'Continuation of the Chronicles of England' in 1587, Campion's execution was familiar across Europe, and the Privy Council was facing skilled continental printers and engravers.[146]

Three contemporary chronicles portray Campion's execution as inextricably bound together with the marriage negotiations of the Duke of Anjou. The most succinct account of Campion's trial is printed on a single opening in John Stow's *The Annales of England* (1605), which purport simply to record events annually.[147] Stow, whose 'memoranda are openly sympathetic to the Catholic clergy', here manipulates the chronological sequence.[148] The 'execution' (mutilation) of John Stubbe, whose *Discoverie of a Gaping Gulf* had condemned the proposed marriage of the Queen with the Duke of Anjou, actually took place on 3 November 1579. Yet Stow moves it forward in time so that it *appears* to take place two years later, immediately before Campion's execution on 1 December 1581, in the middle of a sequence that begins with the execution of 'Everard Haunce a seminarie priest' on 'the last of July' 1581, sentenced 'to be drawne, hanged, bowelled and quartered'. This is followed by fines of 'twentie pounds' imposed on 'sundrie' recusants, and a paragraph on the arraignment 'for writing, printing and dispersing a libell' of John Stubbe, and William Page who 'lost their hands by chopping off' on 'the third day of November' (Stow studiously omits the year), although the aged printer, Hugh Singleton, 'had his pardon'. This state savagery is followed by a short paragraph outlining the reception given in November 1581 to 'monsieur Francis Duke of Anjou, the French kings brother' – the subject of the libell – 'with banquetting and diverse pleasant shewes and pastimes, &c'.[149]

Each of the next two paragraphs reaches a climax with the words 'hanged, bowelled and quartered', as they chronicle the arraignment on 'the 20. of November' 1581 of Edmund Campion and his companions, and their executions on 1 December. There follows the elaborate pageant with which, on 'The first of

---

[146] Holinshed, *Chronicles* (1587), III. 1328–68.

[147] John Stow, *The Annales of England* (London: Bishop, 1605), STC 23337, pp. 1168–9. This patterning is completely lost in the two later editions continued by Edmond Howes, first until 1614 (London: Widow Bishop, 1615), STC 23338, then until 1631 (London: R. Meighen, 1631), STC 23340, where both Stubbe and Campion have been cut out of the narrative.

[148] Eamon Duffy, *Saints, Sacrilege and Sedition: Religion and Conflict in the Tudor Reformations* (London: Bloomsbury, 2012), 237; see also Peter Marshall, in 'Religious Ideology', in *Oxford Handbook of Holinshed's Chronicles*, pp. 411–26 (p. 414).

[149] Stow, *Annales* (1605), p. 1167, gives the cost of the banquet as £1744, 19s, 1d.

Februarie the Queenes majestie with her whole court, accompanied the monsieur Francis Duke of Anjou, from Westminster to Canterburie'. Monsieur is conducted to the coast, and given elaborate honours. Stow's marginal gloss is '*1582. Monsieur returneth to the sea*'. This long paragraph of empty ceremonies is followed by three lines detailing the execution in Chelmsford of 'John Paine, priest', being indicted of high treason for 'words by him spoken to one Eliot'.

The non-chronological sequence, printed on a single opening, alternates execution and pageantry. Six paragraphs of executions of priests and libellers against the marriage enclose two of empty Anjou pageantry. At the end of Anjou's long and ineffectual wooing of the Queen, Stubbe and Page have lost their hands, 12 priests have been 'drawne, hanged, bowelled and quartered' (Stow's formula) and Anjou has returned to the sea (where he belongs, Stow seems to imply). The ironic juxtaposition would not have been lost on contemporary readers: the godly Stubbe and the Jesuit Campion suffer because of the same marriage pageant. When Stow later decides 'to returne to Monsieur his successe after the great dignities, authorities and titles bestowed on him', we find that Anjou is driven out of Bruges by the citizens, loses Dunkirk and dies of 'sicknesse on 10. July 1583'.[150]

For more information on Campion's execution, Stow directs the reader to 'My continuation of Reine Woolfe's chronicle' (Holinshed's *Chronicles*, 1587). 'The Continuation of the chronicles of England, from the yeare of our Lord 1576, to this present yeare 1586' begins with Abraham Fleming's preface describing these 'observations of time' as 'meerelie & simplie Chronicles'.[151] Stubbe's mutilation is tactfully omitted, but the sequence is manipulated in the same way as in the *Annales*; now the grim fate of Campion and his fellow priests is interlaced with the pageantry and lavish entertainment of Monsieur across the length of 94 folio columns.[152] Holinshed's *Chronicles* compensate for their silence on Stubbe by alternating empty pageantry (staged allegories of mercy and pardon on 'artificially' erected scaffolds) with an unrelenting saga of state violence as it hangs, disembowels and quarters priests. 'Any thoughtful reader must have been able to perceive the ironic contrast between festive material and brutal punishments'.[153] Persons himself noted that the 'banquets, balls, masquerades and other amusements with the French' produced no respite in the 'cruelty against Catholics'.[154] Stubbe and Campion came from opposite ends of the religious

---

[150]   Stow, *Annales* (1605), p. 1173.

[151]   Raphael Holinshed, *The Third volume of Chronicles ... Now newlie recognized, augmented, and continued (with occurrences and accidents of fresh memorie) to the yeare 1586* (London: Harrison, Bishop, Newberry, Denham and Woodcocke, 1587), STC 13569, III. 1268.

[152]   Holinshed, *Chronicles* (1587), III. 1322.a.51–1368.b.63.

[153]   Annabel Patterson, *Reading Holinshed's Chronicles* (Chicago: University Press, 1994), 70.

[154]   CRS 4, p. 25.

spectrum, but they were both crushed, according to Stow and Holinshed, because of the Anjou marriage.[155]

When Holinshed's *Chronicles* were finished by the end of January 1587, as the colophon tells us, the Privy Council stayed publication and insisted on 'reformacyon' of the book.[156] On 1 February 1587, it appointed Dr John Hammond (one of the three interrogators of both Campion and Carter) and two others, to carry out the 'reformacyon'. One of Hammond's first actions (taken in the first week of February) was to eliminate Fleming's record of Catholic 'libels' about Campion's death.[157] Their original inclusion indicates that Fleming, an ardent Protestant, like Foxe, may have been shocked by the treatment of Campion.[158] Whereas the long account of Campion's execution (1322–68) had ended with the statement that his death was for religion not for treason, this whole sheet, (sig. 6M3 and 6M4, 1328/1329, 1330/1331) was removed and replaced by a single leaf (sig. 6M3) that retains *An Advertisement* on the recto (1328), but has a new verso (1330), which passes abruptly from 'this tragedie now at the last act', the quartering of Briant, Sherwin and Campion, to the departure of the Duke of Anjou. Pages 1329 and 1331 disappear, and with them 47 lines that, while condemning the 'libels' of these 'enimies to the state politike', actually give a just account of the Catholic position, and end: 'and yet this man forsooth (albeit notorious) died not for treason but for religion, as with fowle mouths they are not ashamed to saie: *Relligio crimen non mala vita fuit*'.[159] It is ironic that one of Campion's 'rackmasters' should be doing such violence (Fleming described it as a 'castration') to the Protestant editor's text in the week before the execution of Mary, Queen of Scots.[160] It is significant that several copies have retained this cancelland.[161] In the Trinity College Dublin copy, bound in two volumes, only the second has been attacked by worms, and their progress through the gatherings confirms that the sheets had already been folded when the publication was stayed, and shows that, while Fleming made

---

[155] McCoog, *Fashioning Jesuit Identity*, pp. 55–88 (p. 67), argues the projected marriage raised hopes at Rome at the end of 1579; J.A. Bossy, 'English Catholics and the French Marriage, 1577–81', *Recusant History* 5 (1959), 2–16, examines the different Court factions and the lasting bitterness.

[156] Clegg provides a clear and detailed account of the three stages of the censorship in 'The Peaceable and Prosperous Regiment', pp. 5–12.

[157] Fleming has marked the passage with his distinctive paraph (‡).

[158] Clegg, ed., 'The Peaceable and Prosperous Regiment', p. 4.

[159] Clegg, ed., 'The Peaceable and Prosperous Regiment', p. 10 and p. 17 n. 46. McLeod, p. 64, has a diagram of cancellation; Clegg, 'Censorship', in *Oxford Handbook of Holinshed's Chronicles*, p. 56, has a helpful table.

[160] *The Castrations of the Last Edition of Holinshed's Chronicle, Both in the Scotch and English Parts, Containing Forty Four Sheets; Printed with the Old TYPES and LIGATURES, And Compared Literatim by the Original* (London: William Mears, 1723).

[161] One copy is in the Huntington, two in the Bodleian (F.1.17 and Σ.10.44) and three are in Dublin: in Trinity College (D), Marsh's Library (D2) and the National Library of Ireland (D6).

arrangements to follow the other instructions, he made no provision to take out this sheet, marked with his distinctive paraph, whether through haste or, more likely, defiance.[162]

'The queen and her Privy Council', especially after the publicity disaster of the Campion execution, were determined to present 'a desirable image of Elizabethan power and rule, an image that still influences twentieth-century historians' understanding and misunderstanding of Elizabethan events'.[163] The censors of these texts were so concerned about public reaction to the execution of Mary, Queen of Scots that, in the week before her death, they 'reconstructed accounts of justice'.[164]

Holinshed's *Chronicles* stubbornly resisted the state's message. The 'Continuation' opens with the Oxford assizes of 1577, when Rowland Jenkes was sentenced to lose his ears, and a plague broke out that killed 'three hundred persons'.[165] Stow talks of 'My continuation', and the first column is marked with his initials, but Fleming has made additions, marked with his paraph.[166] One hundred pages later, the execution of Carter (as we have seen) immediately precedes – and subverts – a reprinting of two of the official defences of the torture of Campion, *A Declaration of the favourable dealing* and Lord Burghley's *The Execution of Justice*, which close the 94 columns dominated by Campion.[167] The sympathies of the prominent stationers who published the 1587 edition were, apparently, with binders, printers and sons of stationers: Jenkes, Carter and Campion.

On Monday 28 September 1579, the day after the royal proclamation banning Stubbe's *Discoverie of a Gaping Gulf,* John Aylmer, the Bishop of London, wrote to Sir Christopher Hatton to tell him that the Sunday preacher had praised the Queen:

> Whereat the people seemed even as yt were with a shoute, to geve God thankes, & as farr as I could perceave, tooke yt very well, that she was comended, for her zeale, and constancie. I have understoode synce the sermonde, that as the people well lyked of the commendation attributed to her majestie, with the greate hope of her continuance so to saye playnlye, they utterlye bente theire browes at the sharpe and bitter speeches, which he gave against the author of the booke, of whome they conceave, & reporte, that he is one, that fearethe God deereleye,

---

[162]   Holinshed, *Chronicles* (1587), STC 13659, TCD shelf-mark, Ng.b.12. Where changes were made, the adjacent gatherings were clearly left exposed, and the worms have had a field day. Cyndia Clegg, in personal communication, argues that haste was the most probable explanation for the omission.

[163]   Cyndia Susan Clegg, 'Which Holinshed? Holinshed's *Chronicles* at the Huntington Library', *Huntington Library Quarterly* 55 (1992), 559–77 (p. 567).

[164]   Clegg, ed., 'The Peaceable and Prosperous Regiment', p. 15 and p. 10.

[165]   Holinshed, *Chronicles* (1587), III. 1270.a.52–b.37.

[166]   Holinshed, *Chronicles* (1587), III. 1270.a.1 (I.S.) and 1270.b.19 (ǂ): the 'Black Assizes' of 1577.

[167]   Holinshed, *Chronicles* (1587), III. 1357.a.57–1368.b.63.

lovethe her majestie, intred into this course, beinge caryed with suspicion & jealousye of her persone, & safetye.[168]

Aylmer expressed anxiety about ministers in the country ('the further off the worse') preaching sermons against the Anjou marriage, and the effect on Londoners if they knew of the 'grudging and groaning abroad'.[169] The reaction of the Paul's Cross audience accords with William Camden's account, in his *Annales*, of Stubbe's mutilation on 3 November, which not only captures the silent resentment of an audience at this grotesque piece of state theatre but links it to Campion's trial:

> From there they proceeded to a scaffold set up in the market place at Westminster, where Stubbe and Page had their hands cut off by a butcher's knife being struck by a mallet on a chopping-block. The printer was spared. When Stubbe's right hand had been cut off (I remember because I was present), he took off his hat with his left hand, and in a clear voice said, Long live the Queen! The crowd that was round the scaffold was completely silent, whether in horror at this new and unusual punishment, or in pity for a man of unspotted life, or from hatred of a marriage which most men sensed would be destructive for religion.

> These events occurred after the arrival of Anjou in England, and while he was lingering here, the Queen, in order to take away the fear that had seized hold of the popular imagination that the religion was about to be changed, and Papists tolerated, gave in to insistent entreaties and allowed Edmund Campion, the Jesuit, as I have said, Luke Kirby and Alexander Briant, seminary priests, to be put on trial, and prosecuted, under the Treason Act of the 25th year of Edward III, for planning an attack on the Queen and the Realm.[170]

Camden here follows Stow in manipulating the chronological sequence, by placing Stubbe's execution under the marginal heading of 'M. D. LXXXI' [1581], on the same page as the execution of Edmund Campion.[171] The effect is to make the silent protest of the crowd embrace both the mutilation of a godly lawyer and the butchering of a Jesuit scholar. Camden, in the safety of 1615, makes explicit what is implicit in Stow and Holinshed.

Campion's execution inspired a propaganda campaign across Europe that had clearly taken the Queen and her ministers by surprise. It was not until the trial of Mary, Queen of Scots, that the Privy Council regained the initiative. Holinshed's 'Continuation' ends before the execution, with Elizabeth proclaiming

---

[168] BL Add. MS 15891, fol. 8v.

[169] BL Add. MS 15891, fols 8v–9r; printed in Sir Harris Nicolas, ed., *Memoirs of the Life and Times of Sir Christopher Hatton* (London: Bentley, 1847), pp. 132–4; cited by Arnold Hunt, *The Art of Hearing* (Cambridge: University Press, 2010), p. 7.

[170] William Camden, *Annales Rerum Anglicarum et Hibernicarum* (London: Stansby, 1615), STC 4496, p. 326.

[171] See F.J. Levy, *Tudor Historical Thought* (San Marino: Huntington Library, 1967), pp. 190–91, for the close relationship of Stow and Camden.

that, after 'manie advises' (expressed in multiple concessive clauses) she 'did yeeld' reluctantly to the sentence as the will of the people.[172] News of the secluded execution on 8 February 1587 was only gradually released in London (perhaps after 18 to 20 days), so the public heard of an executed Scottish Queen only when it could read of a merciful English Queen.[173] The 'reformacyon' of Holinshed's *Chronicles* in February 1587 indicates that the bruising experience of Campion's execution had made the Privy Council more aware of its continental audience, and of the power of print 'to make and break both international alliances and personal reputations'.[174]

In Antwerp, Verstegan was not so restrained. His *Theatrum Crudelitatum Haereticorum*, a pictorial survey of all the cruelties in England and elsewhere, begins with iconoclasm under Henry VIII, and ends (Figure 12.2) by showing the executioner, in an interior chamber lit by torches, with his axe raised over Mary, Queen of Scots: this was a deed of darkness.[175] In *Theatrum Crudelitatum Haereticorum*, published in 1587, the state's theatre of cruelty starts with pulling down crucifixes, burning books, statues and churches, and ends by killing queens.

The Elizabethan theatre of punishment may have been aimed at terrifying its Catholic opponents, but it played to a much wider and more discriminating audience whose views and sympathies were anything but simple. Fleming, Stow and Camden, far from endorsing the state's line that Campion was a traitor, suggest that the monarchical republic spilt the blood of both Stubbe and Campion on the altar of an unpopular marriage that, ultimately, never happened. The public was convinced neither by the state's rhetoric nor by its elaborately staged performances. Abraham Fleming, John Foxe, Sir John Harington and John Stow are among those outside the recusant community who helped preserve Campion's memory. John Foxe, who had pleaded with members of the Privy Council for Campion to be spared, somehow obtained from Topcliffe the manuscripts of three of the disputations in the Tower, and two different copies of Campion's 'Letter to the Council'; the greatest Protestant martyrologist helped to preserve the memory of a Jesuit martyr.[176]

While this very public battle over Campion's memory was being fought in London, Paris and Rome, Campion's grieving students and colleagues in Prague were constructing their own memorials. Two manuscripts now in the Prague Castle Archive of the Metropolitan Chapter, contain his dictated lecture notes, lovingly preserved and decorated after his death, on Aristotle's *Logic* and his *Physics*.[177]

---

[172]   Holinshed, *Chronicles* (1587), III. 1587.b.49.

[173]   Clegg, 'The Peaceable and Prosperous Regiment', p. 23, estimates it took 18 to 20 days for the news to 'become common knowledge in London'.

[174]   Clegg, 'The Peaceable and Prosperous Regiment', p. 15.

[175]   Richard Verstegan, *Theatrum Crudelitatum Haereticorum* (Antwerp: Hubert, 1587), ARCR I. 1297. This went through numerous editions in Latin and French, ARCR I. 1298–1304.

[176]   BL MS Harley 422, fols 132r–172v.

[177]   APMC M42 (*Logic*) and M65 (*Physics*), fol. 260v. See Chapter 4 for details.

85

Perfecutiones aduerfus Catholicos à Proteftanti-
bus Caluiniftis excitæ in Anglia.

Poft varias clades miferorum, & cadis aceruos
Infontum, comes exornat fpectacula mater
Supplicio, & regum foror & fidißima coniunx.
Illa Caledonÿs diademate claruit oris,
Sed micat in cœlo fulgentior, inde corona
Sanguinis, infandaq̦ manet vindicta fecuris.

L 3   NOMI-

Figure 12.2   Execution of Mary, Queen of Scots, 8 February 1587, at
Fotheringhay Castle. Richard Verstegan, *Theatrum Crudelitatum
Haereticorum*, 1587, ARCR I. 1297, p. 85. By permission of
Folger Shakespeare Library.

A third collection, now in Cieszyn, started life as a *Concionale*, and developed, as we have seen, into a unique manuscript record of his funeral elegy for Maria Cardona, and perhaps the first collection of other orations.[178] These three documents record Campion's words, whether in theology, philosophy or poetry, and reveal in material form the immense affection and admiration he evoked, which was further intensified by his martyrdom. Just as the students adorned their academic notes on Aristotle's *Logic* and *Physics* with Latin verses, quadrifolia, picturesque tables and figurative trees of knowledge, so the *Concionale* was enhanced with more of Campion's own words. These three manuscript collections began as working records by colleagues, friends and disciples, but became, after his death, personal memorials in paper, ink and pen.[179]

In the Strahov Monastery Library are preserved three copies of a printed *Elogium Historicum*, composed by 21 of his former (mostly noble) pupils, who list themselves as *Rhetores Academici Pragenses*, and who praise Campion, in five sections, as:

> Ardent In His Love Of Literature And Virtue / An Outstanding Poet And Orator / A Brilliant Theologian / An Excellent Philosopher / As Famous For His Martyrdom As For His Scholarship.[180]

A section of the praise is devoted to each branch of Campion's excellence, but his 'modesty and the cheerfulness of his expression' are singled out as inspiring others.[181] The praise for his poetic skills says that 'rather than composing, he seemed to pour forth' poems, and singles out his *Ambrosiana Tragoedia* for matching the style to the seriousness of the subject.[182] The book is a reminder how much Campion's virtues were valued in Prague. A portrait of him in the form of a plaster medallion on the ceiling of the Clementinum must have been placed there quite early, though it has been restored more recently.

The elegantly printed catalogue of Jesuit writers by Pedro de Ribadeneira, S.J., published in Lyons in 1609, was later updated by Philip Alegambe, S.J., as the *Bibliotheca Scriptorum Societatis Iesu* in 1643, and contains a long account of Campion, which describes him as 'a glorious martyr of Christ and the most famous of our age'.[183] His account of the martyrdom is not wholly accurate, since

---

[178] See Chapter 4 for full account of this manuscript, SZ MS DD.V.8.

[179] Fr John Aquensis, S.J., was one of those in a prayer pact with Campion: see Chapter 5.

[180] *Elogium Historicum*, Bibliotheca Regiae Canoniae Strahov: Variorii Panegyrici, Pragae, A.B.VIII.35/5; A.J. VIII. 80; E.Z. II.47, sig. B3.

[181] *Elogium Historicum*, sig. B2r (*Modestia, & vultus hilaritas in ore*).

[182] *Elogium Historicum*, sig. B3r.

[183] Pedro de Ribadeneira, S.J., *Illustrium Scriptorum Religionis Societatis Iesu Catalogus* (Lyons: Pillelotte, 1609), pp. 47–9; Philippe Alegambe, S.J., *Bibliotheca Scriptorum Societatis Iesu Post Excusum Anno M.DC.VIII. Catalogum R.P. Petri Ribadaneirae S.J.* (Antwerp: J. Meursius, 1643), pp. 97–8.

it says that he was 'cut down half-alive', but mentions that the French account of his martyrdom was translated into Latin by a Dutchman, called William East. He particularly praises conciseness as the stylistic feature of the *Rationes Decem*: in this 'very little book one can hardly believe how many doctrines of the faith he is able to compress in so few words'.[184]

It was in 1608 that Henry Orton (the only layman to be tried with Campion) visited Prague, and on being shown 'the room of Blessed Father Edmund Campion', fell on his knees and kissed the floor.[185] He was not alone. The historian of the Bohemian province, Boluslav Balbin, writes:

> As long as the old College in Prague was standing, in the room which Campion had occupied for some years there was an altar with a portrait placed on it, which I myself remember, and whenever they visited our college, Archdukes of Austria, royal and imperial ambassadors, would go there on bended knee, venerating Campion in heaven.[186]

In the same year, 1608, Thomas Coryate, whose father had been at Oxford with Campion, visited 'a Colledge of the Jesuites' in Lyons and found 'the picture of Edmund Campian, with an *Elogium* subscribed in golden letters, signifying why, how, and where he dyed' and a temporary shrine in the church, 'a very faire Altar beautified with most glorious pillers that were richly gilt'.[187] In 1608, Campion features in a book of engravings of Jesuit martyrs from 1549 to 1607 and one copy, owned by the Jesuit college in Lyons, has survived.[188] It seems clear that by 1608 the cult of Campion as a martyr was firmly established across Europe.

Sir Thomas Tresham put up more substantial stone monuments in England. After suffering nearly 15 years of imprisonment for refusing to swear that Campion had not been in his house, Tresham erected both the Triangular Lodge (1593–95), and Lyveden New Bield (unfinished in 1605).[189] The date, 1580, when Campion

---

[184] Alegambe, *Bibliotheca Scriptorum*, p. 98.

[185] Clementinum Diaries, Strahov Monastery Library, MS DC.III.16, fol. 1v.

[186] Boluslav Balbin, S.J., *Miscellanea Historica Regni Bohemiae Decadisi Liber IV Hagiographicus* (Prague: G. Czernoch, 1682), pp. 189–90 and 195.

[187] Thomas Coryate, *Coryats Crudities* (London: W. S[tansby], 1611), STC 5808, 62–3.

[188] *EFFIGIES ET NOMINA QVORVNDAM e Societate IESV QVI PRO FIDE vel Pietate sunt interfecti Ab anno 1549.ad annum 1607* (Rome: Greuter & Maopinus, 1608). The book belonged to the Lyons College, '*Colleg. Lugdunensis Ssae. Trinitatis Sciet. Iesu*', and no. 77 is of Campion. It is now in Georgetown University Library, Washington, DC.

[189] Both fully illustrated and discussed in Mark Girouard, *Elizabethan Architecture: Its Rise and Fall, 1540–1640* (New Haven: Yale University Press, 2009), pp. 218–39. See also Mark Bradshaw, *Lyveden New Bield* (London: National Trust, 2004), who has been recreating Tresham's theological garden design with the help of Tresham's previously immured manuscripts BL Add. MSS 39828–38, and Luftwaffe photographs from 1943.

changed Tresham's life, figures prominently on the Lodge.[190] In Rushton Hall, Tresham immured his papers, wrapped in a sheet and sealed; they are full of the codes he had devised, and fill 11 volumes in the British Library.[191] A tunnel, one mile long, from Rushton Hall to the Lodge, has recently been found, suggesting that the Lodge could have been used for Mass. The plaster relief of the Crucifixion in the interior chapel at Rushton Hall may portray the Elizabethan state, while the date, 1577, could refer to the martyrdom of Cuthbert Mayne, Campion's *contubernalis* (room mate). The first line on the relief, *Ecce salutiferum signum thau nobile lignum*, echoes Campion's poem on the church, links the cross with Aesculapius and salvation by the *corpus Christi*, while the lances of the Roman soldiers stand as a metaphor for the power of the state.[192]

At the centre of the Triangular Lodge is the upturned *tau* (the beam or *trestrum* supporting the three-sided chimney): Tresham uniting himself with the sacrifice of the Mass and the last letter of the Hebrew alphabet. Lyveden New Bield is almost a completion in stone of Campion's recital of the *Symbolum Apostolorum* on the scaffold: the seven instruments of the passion are transformed into the resurrection by the number eight, so that inscription, carvings and the very shape of the building work together to form 'an impresa'.[193] Both symbolic constructions in stone reflect Campion's effect on Tresham.[194] But while Sir John Harington was secretly transcribing his poems, and Sir Thomas Tresham constructing his memorials and immuring his manuscripts, Campion was fiercely denounced as a traitor. 'A simple glance at the entries in the State Papers Domestic from 1580 until the end of Elizabeth's reign indicates how obsessed the Council was both with Campion's name and those associated with him'.[195]

---

[190]   Mark Girouard, *Rushton Triangular Lodge* (London: English Heritage, 2004), p. 13.

[191]   A full discussion of the codes and buildings can be found in my *Memory and Transcription*, pp. 121–45 (plates 10 and 11), and my 'Sir Thomas Tresham: His Emblem', *Emblematica* 17 (2009), 149–79. The beautiful Brudenell manuscript, Bodl. MSS Eng. th. b. 1–2, I. 3, describes the intention 'to burye and intombe in their sepulchre' all the patristic material contained therein, which suggests the manuscript originated with Tresham, as I argued in *Memory and Transcription*, pp. 13–38, even though, of course, most (or all) of it was copied after he died; Emilie Murphy, '*Adoramus te Christe*', pp. 243–6, raises doubts.

[192]   This epigraph has been restored, and at least four of the words [printed in brackets] are mistaken, but the poem could be by Campion. See Chapter 4 for more on Campion's use of Ovid.

[193]   Mark Girouard, *Elizabethan Architecture: Its Rise and Fall, 1540–1640* (New Haven & London: Yale University Press, 2009), pp. 232–9 (p. 239), analyzes and illustrates the two buildings and their coded meanings.

[194]   For detailed analysis of the symbolism, see Kilroy, 'Tresham: His Emblem', pp. 149–79.

[195]   John L. Larocca, S.J., 'Popery and Pounds: The Effect of the Jesuit Mission on Penal Legislation', in *The Reckoned Expense* (2007), pp. 327–45 (p. 344). The *OED* attributes the first use of popery to Tyndale about 1534.

Among English Jesuits, Campion established a pattern, as John Gerard's account of his torture in the Tower reveals; when he says, 'I fell on my knees for a moment's prayer', he echoes Allen's account of Campion.[196] Gerard was particularly glad to find that his cell in the Clink was next to Ralph Emerson, who had been Campion's 'little man'.[197] When Fr Roger Nayler, S.J., and Fr Mark Barkworth were on their way to Tyburn, and again on the scaffold, they sang the Resurrection antiphon, sung by Sherwin at Campion's trial, which seems to have become, within 20 years, a liturgical text for martyrs:

> Father Barcoth sang this Antheme: *Haec est dies, haec est dies, haec est dies domini, gaudiamus et laetemur in ea*, always Father Fieldcock answered. *Et laetemur in ea.*[198]

The impulse to collect Campion's *opera*, scattered across Europe, grew gradually. By 1591, Robert Turner, S.J., a self-styled 'disciple', was already collecting his writings, but they were not published till 1602, after Turner's death, at Ingolstadt, with later editions at Cologne in 1615 and 1625 that included a *Narratio de Morte*.[199] The 1602 preface, 'Ad Lectorem', records Turner passionately collecting Campion's writings, and he implores Walter Gwinn that, just as Richard Stanihurst had generously passed to him some of Campion's letters, so he should 'beg, borrow or steal (*expilare*)' any of Campion's 'Speeches, Dialogues or Poems', whether autograph or in the hands of others.[200] Sylvester de

---

[196]   John Gerard, *The Autobiography of an Elizabethan*, trans. and ed. Philip Caraman (London: Longmans, Green, 1951), p. 108 n. 2.

[197]   Gerard, *Autobiography*, p. 78.

[198]   Bodl. MS Eng. th. b. 2, pp. 114–16, which includes the music for all four parts; see Kilroy, *Memory and Transcription* (pp. 13–38 (p. 21), which also discusses the musical setting of this antiphon attributed to William Byrd, first analyzed by John Morehen in 'Is "Byrd's" *Haec* a Faec?', *Early Music Review*, 24 (October 1996), 8–9. Shell, *Oral Culture*, p. 221 n. 29, points out that an earlier setting by Byrd was printed in *Cantiones Sacrae* (1591). Barkworth may be alluding both to Byrd and to Sherwin's use of this Easter antiphon at the trial of Campion (see Chapter 10).

[199]   Edmundi Campiani Societatis Iesu Martyris in Anglia [added to Robert Turner, *Posthuma*, under separate title page], *Orationes, Epistolae Tractatus de imitatione Rhetorica, a Roberto Turnero Campiani discipulo collecta* (Ingolstadt: A. Angermarius, 1602), ARCR I. 1263, 'Ad Lectorem', sig. [a]1v; *Orationes, Epistolae, Tractatus de imitatione Rhetorica, a Roberto Turnero discipulo collecta, et nunc primum e M. S. edita. Praemissa est narratio de vita & morte, quam in Anglia pro fide Romana Catholica Edmundus Campianus Soc. Iesu Pater, aliique duo constanter appetierunt, ex Italico sermone latine facta* (Cologne: J. Kinck, 1615), ARCR I. 1265–69. The *Narratio de Morte* is a Latin version of the Italian translation of the anonymous *L'Histoire de la Mort*, ARCR I. 197.

[200]   Turner, *Posthuma* (1602), Letter 150 to Dr Walter Gwinn, 18 May 1591, pp. 651–52: '*si quid Campiani scriptum possis emere, expilare, dono accipere, Orationes, Dialogos, Poemata ... sive scripta illius, sive laborem scribentium illa tibi representabitur a me bona fide.*'

Petra Sancta, S.J., edited the elegant 1631 edition of the *Opuscula* for Balthasar Moretus on the Plantin press, which printed several more pieces for the first time, combined the *Orationes* and *Epistolae* with the *Rationes Decem*, and remains unrivalled, if incomplete.[201]

In 1615, Campion was still being listed by opponents as the 'chiefe champion'.[202] In 1622, Richard Gibbons, S.J., edited Nicholas Harpsfield's *Historia Anglicana Ecclesiastica*, and included, for the first time in print, a fragment of Campion's *Narratio de divortio Henrici VIII. Regis ab Uxore Catherina & ab Ecclesia Catholica Romana discessione* (The story of the divorce of King Henry VIII from his wife, Catherine, and the secession from the Roman Catholic church), which he received from the 'very learned old man, Henry Holland'.[203] In the same year, a special edition of the *Vita beati patris Ignatii Loiolae* of Pedro de Ribadeneira, S.J., was published in Rome, and the engraved title page 'presents Ignatius as founder, as a holy father of holy sons'.[204] Campion appears at the top of the column, on the same level as the three Jesuit martyrs in India, 'Blessed Rodolfo Acquaviva and companions', who had been attacked on the way back from three years at Akbar's court by a 'Portuguese-hating (and therefore Christian-hating) mob and killed'.[205] Campion would have enjoyed the many months of theological discussions in Akbar's court (Plate 4), but their equally barbaric deaths place all these 'sons of Ignatius' on the same plane as missionary martyrs.

The *Rationes Decem*, unusual in controversial literature for its conciseness and theological clarity, attracted lengthy responses for many years. William Whitaker, Regius Professor at Cambridge, was the first to reply, in 1582, with *Edmundi Campiani Iesuitae Rationes Decem ... et ad eas Guilelmi Whitakeri ... Responsio*.[206] Over 300 pages respond in detail to Campion, even though Campion is described as 'not especially learned'.[207] Nearly 500 pages of the Jesuit John Durie's *Confutatio Responsionis Guilelmi Whitakeri* were printed in Paris, in the same year.[208]

---

[201]   Alegambe, *Bibliotheca Scriptorum*, p. 98.

[202]   Thomas Mason, *Christs Victorie over Sathans Tyrannie* (London: G. Eld and R. Blower, 1615), STC 17622, p. 395. I am grateful to Carole Levin for pointing this out to me.

[203]   Nicholas Harpsfield, *Historia Anglicana Ecclesiastica* (Douai: M. Wyon, 1622), ARCR I. 639. Holland had earlier entrusted Campion's books to a married sister at Cleeve, in Gloucestershire, Hegarty, *Register*, p. 73.

[204]   John W. O'Malley, *Saints or Devils Incarnate? Studies in Jesuit History* (Leiden: Brill, 2013), p. 293, prints the title page, which is a facsimile of a 1609 edition, now adorned with these medallions of martyrs, as figure 15.7.

[205]   O'Malley, *Saints or Devils*, p. 295. 'Rodolphus Aquavivus' is listed (alongside English Jesuit martyrs, Campion, Southwell, Walpole, Fieldcock, and Garnet) as 'killed by the Mahometans', in the Bodl. MSS Eng. th. b. 1–2, II. 254.

[206]   *Ad rationes decem Edmundi Campiani Iesuitae responsio* (London: T. Vautrollier, imp. T. Chard, 1581), STC 25358.

[207]   Dedication to Lord Burghley, dated 31 August 1581, sig. A2v.

[208]   John Durie, *Confutatio Responsionis Guilelmi Whitakeri ... ad Rationes Decem* (Paris: T. Brumenn, 1582), ARCR I. 334.

The response of Laurence Humphrey, Regius Professor at Oxford, came in two separate works, *Pars Prima Iesuitismi* in 1582 and *Iesuitismi Pars Secunda Puritanopapismi* in 1584: a total of nearly 900 pages.[209] Twenty-five years after Campion died, Whitaker was still publishing against Campion's book in English in 1606, with *An Answere to the Ten Reasons of Edmund Campian the Jesuit.*[210]

Within a short time of the Stonor Park edition of *Rationes Decem*, others followed: in Rome, Milan, Ingolstadt, Pont-a-Mousson, Cologne, Trier, Paris and many cities across Europe. In Vilnius in 1584, Prince Mikhołaj Radziwiłł published two Polish translations, one by Gaspar Wilkowski (Figure 12.3), another by Fr Piotr Skarga, S.J. (Figure 12.4), and a Latin edition that imitated the title page and binding of the Stonor Park edition (Figure 12.5), although there was a misprint in the title: *Raitones.*[211] By 1632, the *Rationes Decem* had been published in more than 70 different editions in almost every country in Europe, and translated into 8 modern languages.[212] A Cologne edition of 1600, preserved in the Dominican library in Krakow, was printed together with the *Adversus Prophanas Haereseon Novationes* of Saint Vincent Lerins, and acquired by a Dominican provincial, Fr Jan Damascene Lubieniecki, O.P. (1651–1714), while he was in Rome in 1703.[213] Fr Mathaeus Kozlowski, O.P. (1759–1839), Dominican Provincial Prior, and a professor at the Jagiellonian University, Krakow, was 'using' another edition, published in Vienna in 1676; he has annotated the text, and copied out by hand a page that had been lost from the apologetic text with which the book was bound.[214] More than two centuries after the book was printed on a secret press, it was being used by Polish Dominican professors. By this time, there had been some

---

[209]   *Iesuitismi Pars Prima sive de Praxi Romanae Curiae* (London: H. Middleton, 1582), STC13961; *Iesuitismi Pars Secunda Puritanopapismi seu doctrinae Iesuiticae Rationibus ab Ed. Campiano comprehensae & a Ioann. Duraeo defensae Confutatio* (London: H. Middleton, 1584), STC 13962.

[210]   William Whitaker, *An Answere to the Ten Reasons of Edmund Campian the Jesuit ... Whereunto is Added in Briefe Marginall Notes the summe of the defence of those reasons by John Duraeus, the Scot, being a Priest and a Jesuit ... and now faithfully Translated ...* by Richard Stocke (London: F. Kingston, 1606), STC 25360.

[211]   For the Latin edition, see Biblioteka Jagiellońska, Cim. 1155, ARCR I. 144. The Wilkowski and the Skarga translations, Cim. 920.11 and Cim. 1174 (ARCR I. 193 and 192), are in the Princes Czartoryski Library; Warsaw University Library also has a copy of Wilkowski, Sol. 614.329.

[212]   ARCR I. 135.1–193. Dr Clarinda Calma has been finding many editions published later, and I have been honoured to see these in libraries in Krakow, Warsaw, Munich and Dillingen.

[213]   *Rationes Decem* with Saint Vincent Lerins, *Adversus Prophanas Haereseon Novationes* (Cologne: Birckmann, 1600), ARCR I. 151.

[214]   *Rationes Decem R.P. Edmundi Campiani* (Vienna: Cosmerovius, 1676). This fine edition includes *Epistolae, Orationes* and a *Vita et Mors Edmundi Campiani*, and is clearly being used for apologetic purposes.

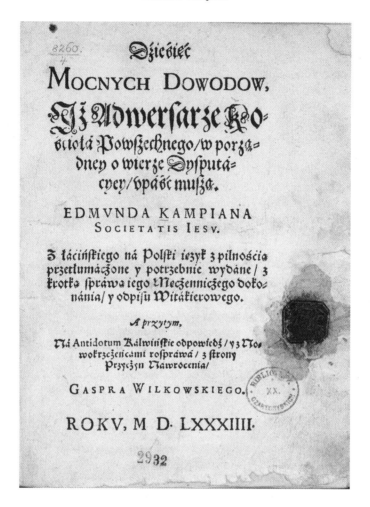

Figure 12.3   *Dziesięć Mocnych Dowodow*, trans. Gaspar Wilkowski ([Vilnius: M.K. Radziwiłł, 1584]), ARCR I. 193, title page. The item belongs to the collections of the Princes Czartoryski Foundation, Cim. 920 11.

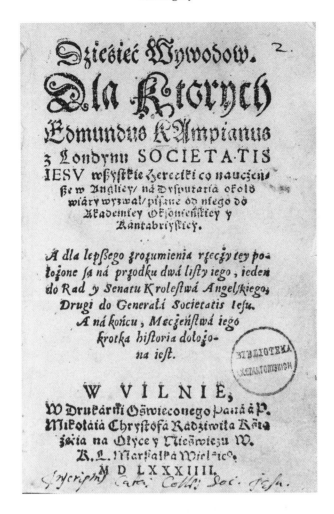

Figure 12.4   *Dziesięć Wywodów*, trans. Piotr Skarga, S.J. (Vilnius: M.K. Radziwiłł, 1584), ARCR I. 192, title page. The item belongs to the collections of the Princes Czartoryski Foundation, Cim. 1174.

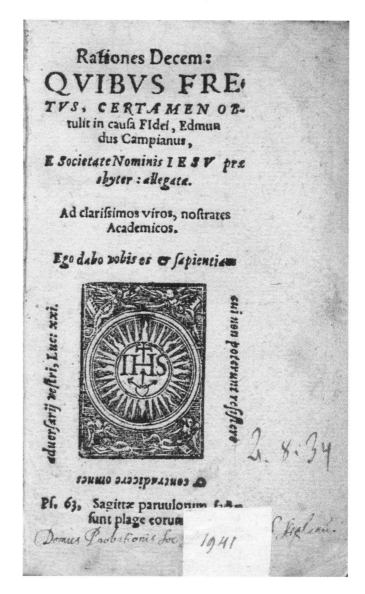

Figure 12.5   *Raitones* [*sic*] *Decem*, ([Vilnius: M.K. Radziwiłł, 1584]), ARCR I. 144, title page. By courtesy of Biblioteka Jagiellońska, Cim. 1155.

90 editions.[215] Campion's purpose was to defend the Catholic and Apostolic church, but the wide margins and generous blank end papers of the first edition show he was also inviting a real academic response. Campion's argument is based on scriptures, the doctors and councils of the church, and is not concerned with the intense political and parochial debate which was tearing England apart: whether the pope or the Queen had sovereignty, an issue central to the *De Visibili Monarchia* of Dr Nicholas Sander on which Campion was interrogated several times on the rack, but is instead pastorally focused on winning the hearts and minds of its readers.

Few other books have had such a long and geographically diverse publishing history. As suggested in 'The complaynt of a Catholike for the death of M. Edmund Campion', Campion was honoured abroad more than in England. The rhetorical simplicity, the pastoral concern, the lack of vitriol, and the scholarly focus on theological issues, made *Rationes Decem* survive long afterwards as a classic.

> Thy dolefull death O Campion is
> bewayld in every coste,
> But we live here & little knowe
> what creatures we have loste.
> Bohemia land laments the same,
> Rodolphus court is sad,
> With deepe regarde they now recorde
> what vertues Campion had
> Germania mourns, al Spayne doth muse,
> and so doth Italy,
> And Fraunce our friend hath put in print
> his passing tragedie.[216]

In 1660, the *Historia Missionis Anglicanae Societatis Iesu*, was published by Henry More, S.J., the great-grandson of Sir Thomas More. This account of the mission of Campion and Persons, gives us the most vivid picture of Campion's preaching, and the enduring popular memory it inspired.[217] In 1682, Boluslav Balbin, S.J., published his *Miscellanea Historica Regni Bohemiae Decadisi Liber IV. Hagiographicus*, which contains a succinct account of Campion's life and copies of both letters to the novices at Brno, and reveals the ardent affection in which *B.M.P. Edmundus Campianus* (the Blessed Martyr Father Edmund Campion) was held in Bohemia: despite being born and executed in England, Balbin asserts that he is *noster* (ours). Campion's admirers included the Emperor, Rudolf II, who often heard him preach, the Court and the Archbishop, Anthony Brus, who was a close friend and used to joke that, just as Wycliffe had brought all manner of evil to Bohemia, so God had sent another Englishman, Campion, to

---

[215] I thank Dr Clarinda Calma for this information.

[216] Alfield, *A true reporte*, lines 9–24, sig. F4v.

[217] *Historia Missionis*, p. 91. See Chapter 6.

clean it up.[218] Balbin claims to be one of the fifth generation of *discipuli* proud to trace their educational 'genealogy' back to Campion, and to count themselves as his metaphorical 'sons'.[219] Within the Bohemian province, it seems, there were no bounds to the way Campion was venerated and loved.

In 1689, Fr Christopher Grene, S.J., transcribed many of the papers of Persons, including his life of Campion.[220] In 1747, Joannes Schmidl, S.J., published his *Historiae Societatis Jesu Provinciae Bohemiae*.[221] Schmidl gives a vivid sense of the way the Clementinum was closely tied to the life of the court in Prague, and of the veneration in which Campion was held. Schmidl provides vital information on what Campion texts were still available in Prague before the suppression of the Jesuits in 1773, when the library of the Clementinum was scattered: some to the Strahov Monastery, some to the Prague Castle Archive, and others taken by Fr Szersznik to Cieszyn. While the texts of Robert Persons have been collected and edited, Campion's *oeuvre* has remained as dispersed, uncertain and elusive as it was in 1602.[222]

The first tentative steps towards collecting material for beatifying Campion as a martyr were taken as early as 1628 by Dr Richard Smith, chaplain to the second Viscount Montague and Bishop of Chalcedon, for a *Catalogue or Register of Martyrs*. Bishop Richard Challoner used this when he published the two volumes of his *Memoirs of Missionary Priests* in 1741 and 1742, in which Campion occupies 11 pages.[223] Urban VIII had in 1643 (the height of the Civil War) granted authority for beatification proceedings to begin, but when the papal brief to collect papers was seized by the English authorities and presented to Parliament, proceedings were suspended.[224] Two centuries later, in 1873, Cardinal Manning pressed for the case to be reopened, and proceedings began again slowly. Finally, after including the pictures of Circignani in the English College as evidence of the public cult of 54 martyrs, on 29 December 1886, Pope Leo XIII, in the decree, *Anglia Sanctorum Insula* (England, Island of Saints), confirmed the cult of Edmund Campion as one of the original list of five Henrician and six Elizabethan martyrs.[225] While Thomas

---

[218]   Boluslav Balbin, S.J., *Miscellanea Historica Regni Bohemiae Decadisi Liber IV Hagiographicus* (Prague: G. Czernoch, 1682), pp. 190–94.

[219]   Balbin, *Miscellanea*, pp. 195–6.

[220]   ABSI Collectanea P. I, fols 76b–160a ('Of the life and martirdom', with additional notes).

[221]   Joannes Schmidl, S.J., *Historiae Societatis Jesu Provinciae Bohemiae Pars Prima Ab Anno Christi MDLV Ad Annum MDXCII*, 2 vols (Prague: Charles University Press, 1747).

[222]   Turner, *Posthuma* (1602), sig. A2r, the editor describes Campion's writings as scattered (*scripta eiusdem sparsa*).

[223]   Richard Challoner, *Memoirs of Missionary Priests*, ed. J.H. Pollen, S.J. (London: Burns Oates and Washbourne, 1924), pp. 19–30.

[224]   Sacred Congregation of Rites, *Cause of the Canonization of Blessed Martyrs John Houghton, Robert Lawrence, Augustine Webster, Richard Reynolds, John Stone, Cuthbert Mayne, John Paine, Edmund Campion, Alexander Briant, Ralph Sherwin and Luke Kirby* (Rome: Vatican Polyglot Press, 1968), p. vii.

[225]   *Cause of Canonization*, p. vi.

More and John Fisher were canonized in 1935, it was not until 25 October 1970 that Campion and the rest of the 40 martyrs were canonized. The date is a further irony: four centuries and eight months after Pius V issued *Regnans in Excelsis*, the papal bull that led to the deaths of so many priests, Paul VI canonized a man who made public his disapproval of this use of the *potestas inordinata* of the pope, and who disapproved of 'meddling' in politics. Even the papacy, it seems, came to regret its policy. Towards the end of the reign of Louis XIII (1643), Cardinal Borgia solicited Urban VIII (1623–44) to excommunicate the King of France; the Pope replied that excommunication had been tried only twice, both in England, both politically inspired, once with Queen Elizabeth, and earlier with Henry VIII:

> But what was the result? The entire world can say: we are still weeping for it with tears of blood.
>
> [*Mais avec quel succès? Le monde entier peut le dire. Nous le déplorons encore avec les larmes de sang.*][226]

At the end of his biography, Richard Simpson concluded that 'the mission of 1580 into England was ultimately a spiritual failure' because 'the intention of its chiefs was not single', that 'the position of the Papacy towards England, as represented by Allen and Persons, was simply untenable', and that Campion and many of his fellow missionaries 'refused their deepest assent to the medieval views of the temporal prerogatives of the Holy See'.[227] Simpson published the first edition of his biography in 1867, after he had been forced by Cardinal Wiseman and Bishop Ullathorne to abandon the journal that he founded, *The Rambler*, for its opposition to precisely those Ultramontane tendencies in the church, and while troops of Pius IX were defending 'the temporal power of the Pope over the Papal States'.[228] He carefully distinguished Campion's spiritual aims from the political aims of Allen, Persons, and the papacy itself.

In our own time, several distinguished scholars have portrayed Campion as a political romantic who was careless of his own life, and accused him of 'turning a mission into a melodrama', seeking to 'play to the gallery', 'courting publicity' and 'actively seeking a disputatious showdown', and worst of all, of advocating 'a line on recusancy considerably stricter than anything advocated or acceded to by Rome'.[229] This has almost settled into a new orthodoxy, influencing popular studies, where Campion has been criticized for going 'further than

---

[226] Joseph Lecler, *Histoire de la tolerance au siècle de la Réforme* (Paris: Albin Michel, 1994), p. 719.

[227] Simpson, pp. 484 and 489.

[228] *ODNB*, 'Richard Simpson' (1820–76), by Josef L. Atholz; Eamon Duffy, *Saints & Sinners: A History of the Popes* (New Haven: Yale University Press, 1997), p. 224.

[229] Bossy, 'Heart of Robert Persons', pp. 187–94; Lake and Questier, 'Puritans, Papists and the "Public Sphere"', pp. 607–21. The writings of these scholars remain some of the most exciting and vital explorations of the mission.

Pope Gregory XIII', for not employing the prudence demanded by his General, and for wreaking havoc in the lives of ordinary Catholics by insisting on 'absolute recusancy'.[230] The evidence presented here suggests that Campion was reluctant to leave Prague and come to England, that he took every precaution to avoid capture (which he did for a whole year before Lyford Grange), that his ministry was charismatic but compassionate, and that he was intensely concerned for the welfare of his hosts, as his letter to Thomas Pounde and his request for forgiveness on the scaffold indicate.[231] The decision to maintain the recusant policy was taken by a representative body of English Catholics (including laymen and Marian priests) at the 'Synod of Southwark', even if there were dissenting voices, which Persons attempted to answer in the first book off the press.[232]

Campion's concern for others, even when he had 'most obediently' put the rope around his neck, came from a man who was 'now completely freed from all anxiety' (*omni solutus cura*), and possessed of 'an inner calm' (*aequitate animi*).[233] If Campion had first been reluctant to leave Prague, he had obviously achieved complete freedom (the liberation sometimes described by condemned men) on his long 'travail' to and from Rome. Despite 'his hands being so broken to pieces in the course of his tortures that he was unable to move them', he did not complain, but 'spoke very sweetly and lovingly and, with a joyful countenance, died smiling' (*vultu hilari subridens moriebatur*).[234]

Campion became the iconic martyr of the persecution in England because he was intent on saving souls, and clearly sent (*missus*) by the will of his superiors. Untainted as he was by 'meddling' in politics, he was fully aware (certainly by the time he reached Dover) of the political muddle into which he had been summoned. He undertook his missionary task with enthusiasm, perhaps even panache: to preach, minister the sacraments, dispute and write. His challenge was not to the secular state over the royal supremacy, but to the newly established church over its theological foundations in Luther, Calvin and Beza. Yet Campion's concise identification of the intellectual weaknesses in the 'religion now established', made him a serious challenge to the Protestant state. For the threat of popery 'was never purely political', as Lake and Questier argue, but 'ideological', and so 'popery in its foreignness and otherness threatened and hence, of course, helped to constitute the autonomy of a protestant England'.[235]

---

[230]   Jessie Childs, *God's Traitors: Terror & Faith in Elizabethan England* (London: Bodley Head, 2014), pp. 57–61.

[231]   See Chapters 10 and 11.

[232]   See Chapter 6 for the 'Synod of Southwark', for Dr Alban Langdale, and Persons's *Why Catholiques refuse to goe to Church* (1580).

[233]   Bombino, *Vita et Martyrium*, p. 290.

[234]   Persons, *Letters and Memorials*, CRS 39, pp. 129 (my translation). A monk in La Pierre-qui-Vire, Burgundy, who had been sentenced to death at the end of the war by the Russians, told me he experienced an intense feeling of liberation while he waited for death; he was later reprieved.

[235]   Lake with Questier, *Antichrist's Lewd Hat*, pp. 261–2.

The mission launched by Dr Allen may have strengthened Protestant identity, but the cost for the English Catholic community was high.[236] There is no question that the mission of 1580 'marked a turning-point', and that thereafter imprisonment, torture and executions became part of the fabric of the life of Catholics.[237] Eamon Duffy calculates that 'of the 471 seminary priests active in England in Elizabeth's reign, at least 294, 62 per cent, were imprisoned at some time or other; 116 were executed, 17 died in gaol, and 91 were banished'.[238] Many hundreds of Catholic laymen and some women were imprisoned, and more than 50 executed, three of whom were women.[239] Many suffered crippling financial fines: Tresham was not only imprisoned because of his connection with Campion, but also 'paid for his Recusancy (as it is said) 9000[li]'.[240]

The blame for this cannot be laid at Campion's door, nor even at the door of the Jesuits: Allen was the real architect of what is often called 'the Jesuit mission'. Attitudes of Catholics between 1580 and 1605, as Michael Questier has shown, were diverse and hidden, and only known with certainty among those who had chosen exile, but 'almost from its inception, the Catholic mission created controversies even within the community'.[241] This division later hardened into the bitter antagonism that we now call the Archpriest controversy, in which the 'Appellants reinterpreted the history of the English mission to highlight the disastrous influence of the Jesuits'.[242] It is significant that John Colleton, who was captured with Campion, signed the appeal on 17 November 1600 against Jesuit control.[243] Yet, if Campion was an unwilling participant in the mission, and unsympathetic to the political aims of Dr Allen, his spiritual enthusiasm, rhetorical brilliance and inspiring heroism ensured that the mission became the most serious Catholic challenge to the Crown since the papal bull of 1570. His magnetic charm turned a slow revival of the old faith into a blazing fervour that made recusancy the ideal, if not the norm, for English Catholics, and inevitably stiffened the

---

[236]   John Bossy, *The English Catholic Community 1570–1580* (London: Darton, Longman & Todd, 1975), pp. 15–19. This important and seminal study raises fascinating and provocative questions about Allen, the missionaries, and their effect.

[237]   Philip Hughes, *The Reformation*, 3 vols (London: Hollis and Carter, 1954), III. 353.

[238]   ODNB, 'William Allen' (1532–94), by Eamon Duffy.

[239]   Hughes, *Reformation*, III. 338 and 366.

[240]   Bodl. MS. Eng. th. b.1. p. 572. Recusancy fines of £9,000 help explain why his debts at the time of his death, came to £11, 495, see Mary Finch, *The Wealth of Five Northamptonshire Families* (Oxford: University Press for the Northamptonshire Record Society, 1956), p. 91. These are very large sums of money.

[241]   Questier, *Catholicism and Community*, pp. 178–80, 293–308, provides a masterly survey of the complexity, and of the growth, of the so-called 'appellant' controversy.

[242]   Thomas M. McCoog, S.J., 'Construing Martyrdom in the English Catholic Community, 1582–1602', in *Fashioning Jesuit Identity* (2013), pp. 371–406. See also Bossy, *English Catholic Community*, pp. 35–48; Questier, *Catholicism and Community*, pp. 250–65;

[243]   ODNB, 'John Colleton' (1548–1635), by Theodor Harmsen, Questier, *Catholicism and Copmmunity*, pp. 258–9; See Chapter 10 for more on Colleton.

persecution. It is hard to escape the impression that Allen exploited Campion's vow of obedience, as the Queen herself (according to Camden) appears to have believed:

> Certainly these times were such that the Queen, who never wanted force to be applied to men's consciences, thereby complained that she would have been forced to this by necessity if she had not preferred to show that destruction would be brought to herself and her subjects under the pretext of conscience and the Catholic religion. She did not, however, believe that most of these wretched little priests had been party to plotting destruction to their country. She did, on the other hand, believe that their *Superiors* used them as instruments of their wickedness since those who were being sent on a mission surrendered to their *Superiors* the complete and free disposition of their lives.

> [Ejusmodi certe haec tempora fuerunt, ut Regina, quae vim conscientiis afferendam nunquam censuit, subinde quereretur se ad haec necessario adactam fuisse, nisi sub quaesito conscientiae & Catholicae religionis praetextu sibi & subditis perniciem inferri maluisset. Plerosque tamen ex misellis his sacerdotibus exitii in patriam constandi conscios fuisse non credidit. *Superiore*s autem hos ut sceleris instrumenta habuisse, quandoquidem, qui mittebantur, plenam ac liberam sui dispositionem *Superioribus* relinquerent.][244]

There is little reason to doubt Camden, who portrays the Queen as having a remarkably informed and sympathetic understanding of religious obedience.

Campion was a scholar and a priest, and the most fruitful period of his life was after his ordination when he was able to combine these two aspects. He was clearly at full stretch in Prague; yet in England, his preaching moved tens of thousands as he journeyed from London to Lancashire. He returned to the university of Oxford, the Catholic part of which was scattered, for his last Mass, his last sermon and his last day of freedom. Even in captivity, he still touched the hearts of those who saw or heard him in the Tower, in Westminster Hall and on the scaffold at Tyburn. The final picture is conveyed by the surviving record of his words and their effect on audiences. Although Bombino ends his *Vita et Martyrium* with 'The prodigies wherewith Almightie God illustrated Fr Campian, as well in his life, as at his death', we do not need any miracles to appreciate Campion's remarkable courage in carrying out a mission whose wider political aims he did not share.[245]

Only a few secondary relics of Campion survive: the hat in Prague, the rope used for the hurdle, preserved at Stonyhurst, and two books that he owned and inscribed. One is a book presented to Campion Hall by Merton College in 1936, which contains two commentaries on Aristotle's *Physics*, both published in the 1480s, and has Campion's name inscribed three times, but also the name of

---

[244]   Camden, *Annales*, p. 327 (the italics are Camden's).

[245]   Bombino, *Vita et Martyrium*, p. 312; Bodl. MS Tanner 329, fol. 111v.

Dr Robert Barnes (1514–1604), a fellow of Merton.[246] The other is the three-volume *Summa* of Thomas Aquinas, which Campion inscribed in August 1571, when he arrived at Douai, and extensively annotated.[247] It is entirely appropriate that our best relics of Campion should be these Aristotelian and Thomistic books printed in Venice and Antwerp. In 1959, a very large *Agnus Dei* was found in the roof at Lyford Grange, wrapped in bombast, and originally carried in a leather pouch (now lost), with an image of the Transfiguration and the papal arms on the reverse; it is now lovingly preserved in Campion Hall, and the penitential weight makes it likely (though it cannot be proved) that it was Campion's.[248]

We may have no contemporary description or portrait of Campion, but one feature recurs in all the accounts: his composure. He is described as rising to address the Queen in Oxford, 'with a remarkably serene expression and composed demeanour' (*vultu gestuque adornatus composito*).[249] When he was being taken as a captive to London, all were struck by 'the modesty of his countenance, an aspect framed & composed according to the perfect image of all chastity, all

---

[246] Johannes de Janduno, *Quaestiones in libros Physicorum Aristotelis* (Venice, Santritter and de Sanctis, 1488), and Frater Gratia Dei Esculanus, O.P., *Questiones in libros Physicorum Aristotelis* (Venice: [H. Liechtenstein?], 1484), two commentaries on Aristotle in a composite book that has 'a sixteenth century blind-tooled Oxford binding', Dennis E. Rhodes, *Catalogue of Incunabula in All the Libraries of Oxford University Outside the Bodleian* (Oxford: Clarendon Press, 1982), no. 1030, p. 197, and no. 852, p. 163. Neither volume has a title page (though the first has a second cover with a table of contents) nor a formal colophon; instead the title is printed at the end of the text on the last leaf of each, fol. 185v in the case of Janduno, which ends with a section on the *Physics* by Elias of Crete with special reference to Averroes. The second volume is unpaginated. The marginalia do not appear to be by Campion, and only two of the three inscriptions of Campion's name appear to be autograph. The most convincing signature is at the top of the vellum pastedown of the lower board, *Edmundus Campyon*, indicating that the volume was already bound when Campion acquired it. Dr Robert Barnes (1514–1604) who was selected to speak in the disputation on medicine on Thursday 5 September 1566 before the Queen, but stood down for lack of time, gave the book to Merton College, along with 57 other books, on 29 November 1594, G.C. Brodrick, *Memorials of Merton College* (Oxford: University Press, 1885), p. 258. This suggests a possible link with Campion. The editors of the Nichols' project may to be mistaken in thinking that the 'Dr Barnes', who was ready to speak on medicine, was Richard Barnes (1532?–1587) of Brasenose College, who was in divinity, Nichols, *Early Modern Sources*, pp. 483, 530, 539. I thank Fr Joseph Munitiz, S.J., for passing to me his article, 'Three treasures of Campion Hall', *Letters and Notices* 100. 440 (2011), 321–8 (pp. 322–4), and Professor Henry Woudhuysen for his extensive help and advice on these incunabula.

[247] Thomas Aquinas, *Summa Totius Theologiae*, 3 vols (Antwerp: Christopher Plantin, 1569), see Chapter 3 for more details on the purchase and annotations.

[248] An oval of 17 cms by 13.7 cms, it weighs 236 grams. I thank Fr Jospeh Munitiz, S.J., for all his help with this. Charles Dingwall, the present owner of Lyford Grange, told me about the leather pouch, now lost.

[249] Bodl. Add. MS A. 63, fol. 9r.

cheerfullnesse' (*vultus ad omnem castae hilaritatis imaginem conformati*); he entered the Tower with 'singular, not only constancie, but even allacrity of mind & countenance' (*vultusque non modo constantia, sed etiam hilaritate*); when the crowd was jeering and hissing during the first disputation, he spoke with 'a serene & setled countenance' (*vultus summa serenitate*); when, bent with the effects of torture, he entered Westminster Hall, 'he calmed his friends with the serenity of his expression' (*orisque serenitate*); on the scaffold 'the beauty of his eyes and the cheerfulness of his face moved all who saw him' (*amoenitas oculorum orisque hilaritas omnium animos commovit*), and he spoke with 'constancy in his expression and speech' (*vultus, orationisque constantia*).[250]

Many colleges, provinces and societies across Europe still claim him as 'our own' (*noster*). It is not surprising that 'our Campion' should inspire such a distinctive term of endearment, or that a scholar who was the son of a Protestant publisher, who styled himself variously as *Anglus Londinensis* and *Oxoniensis,* who wrote sympathetically about Ireland, adopted St Patrick as his patron, studied in Flanders, walked as a pilgrim to Rome, who preached in the courts of Munich and Prague, the barns of Yorkshire and the halls of Lancashire, and finally on the scaffold at Tyburn, and who dreamt of being 'sent to the Indians', should put his faith in the 'witnesses' of a universal Christendom, and sign off his most famous work, the *Rationes Decem*, from the 'City of all the world': *Cosmopoli*.[251]

---

[250] *Elogium Historicum*, sig. B2r; Bombino, *Vita et Martyrium*, pp. 189, 194, 235, 268 and 290; Bodl. MS Tanner 329, fols 72v, 76v and 100r; the last two are my translation.

[251] *Rationes Decem*, sig. K3r; the translation is by John Hungerford Pollen, *Campion's Ten Reasons*, p. 145. In *De juvene academico*, SZ MS DD.V.8, fol. 400v, Campion, *Orationes* (1602), p. 31, Campion argues that the ideal scholar should be a citizen of the world' (*Patria quidem Cosmopolites*).

Bibliography

Manuscripts

London

Archivum Britannicum Societatis Iesu
Farm Street
ABSI Anglia A. I. fols 18r–27r: Autograph draft letters of Edmund Campion.
ABSI Anglia A. I. fols 28r–29v: Copy of Dr Allen's letter to Campion.
ABSI Collectanea P. I: Persons's 'Life and Martyrdom', 'Notae breves', 'Punti' (Fr Grene's copy).
ABSI Collectanea P. II: *Doctor Ironicus* & *Dialogus Mutus* (Campion); *Stratocles* (Jacob Pontanus).
ABSI MS A.V.1: Copy of faculties granted to Edmund Campion and Robert Persons.

Stonyhurst College, Lancashire
ABSI MS A.V.3: Campion's autograph *Anima*, and drafts of Corpus Christi dramas from Prague.
ABSI MS A.V.16: Campion's *Oratio pro festo Corporis Christi*, provenance, S. de Petra Sancta, S.J.
ABSI MS 46/2/9/4: John Gerard's deposition in Rome, 25 January 1628, on trial of Fr. Campion.

British Library
Add. MS 12049: Sir John Harington's *Epigrams*, with epigram by Francis Harington on papal bull.
Add. MS 15891: Letters to Sir Christopher Hatton, including Bishop of London's letter on Stubbe.
Add. MS 31992: Byrd lute setting of 'Why doe I used my paper, ynke and pen', Paston family.
Add. MS 36529: Harington MS, including Campion's poem, *Sancta salutiferi nascentia semina verbi*.
Add. MS 39828, fols 38r–41r: Tresham's account of first disputation in the Tower.
Add. MS 39831: Tresham papers translating theological ideas into mathematical codes for buildings.
Add. MSS 39828–39838: Tresham papers buried 28 November 1605, found in 1828 in Rushton Hall.
Add MS 48023 (Yelverton MS 26): Sledd's Roman diary (second book only).

Add MS 48029 (Yelverton MS 33): Sledd, 'Popes Holynes devices'; Norton, 'Chayne of Treasons'.

Add. MS 6995: Letter of Dr John Case to Robert Cotton, dated 28 December 1592.

MS Cotton Tiberius B. V, fols 23v–24r: *Via Francigena*, the itinerary of Archbishop Sigeric.

MSS Egerton 2009–2012: four parts of Byrd's setting of 'Why doe I use my paper, ynke and pen'.

MS Egerton 2711: Harington unique collection of autograph Wyatt poems.

MS Egerton 2679: Letter of Spanish ambassador describing Campion's execution, 4 December 1581.

MS Harley 417: John Foxe's letter to Bishop Grindal about Paul's Cross.

MS Harley 422: Second, third and fourth disputations; two copies of Campion's 'Letter to Council'.

MS Harley 859: Evidence from confession of Campion and letter to Pound.

MS Harley 3258: Collection of poems by Henry Holland, *In Chronologiam Edmundi Campiani*.

MS Harley 6265: Complete manuscript record of trial of 'Champion' and others in 1581.

MS Harley 6998: Examination of Ralph Emerson, S.J., Campion's helper, in 1593.

MS Harley 7033: Eighteenth-century copy of Robinson's Queen's visit in Folger MS V.a.176.

MS Lansdowne 28: Burghley papers: Aylmer's letter on book seized in William Carter's house on title of Queen of Scots.

MS Lansdowne 30: Burghley papers: Campion's confessions on the rack, endorsed by Burghley.

MS Lansdowne 33: Burghley papers: Aylmer's letters, Norton's notes, draft indictments, Elyot's lists.

Royal MS 2.D.XXI: *Rabbi Davidis Kimhi commentarii Latine redditi per Thomas Nelum*.

Royal MS 17.B.XXII: Sir John Harington's *A Supplie or Addicion* to Godwin's *Catalogue*.

MS Sloane 1132: Untidy and imperfect copy of trial of Campion.

Guildhall Library
MS 11.588: Grocers' Company Records.

Heythrop College Library
Aquinas, Thomas, *Summa Totius Theologiae*, 3 vols (Antwerp: Christopher Plantin, 1569): Campion's annotated copy.

London Metropolitan Archives
CLC/210/A/005: Indenture, covenant to the City of London for the relief of the poor in Christ's Hospital, Bridewell and St Thomas's Hospital, 12 June 1553.

CLC/210/A/006: Grant to the Corporation of London of the Manor of Bridewell and some Savoy lands for the maintenance of Christ's Hospital, Bridewell and St Thomas's Hospital, 26 June 1553.

COL/CA/01/1/11: Record of Court of Aldermen: hearing of 'Edmundus Campyon Stacyoner'.

The National Archives, Kew (TNA)

PRO SP 12/150, no. 72, 'Campion is a champion', ballad (October? 1581).

PRO SP 12/150, no. 67, 'Letter from a Jesuit upon Campions Condemnation', 26 Nov. 1581.

PRO SP 12/164, no. 83, Report on Harington and 'bookes from beyond the seas', 1 Dec. 1583.

PRO SP 12/167, no. 8, James Baker, John Harington and 'Edmund Campions bookes', 7 Jan. 1584.

PRO SP 12/179, no. 7, Interrogation of Gregory Gunnes in 1585, 8 June 1585.

PRO SP 12/245, no. 66, William Harrington's letter to the Lord Keeper, 28 May 1593.

Oxford

Bodleian Library

MS 13: Unique copy, with engravings, of Neale and Bereblock's 'Dialogus in Adventum Reginae'.

MS 513: Spanish elegy on '*Glorioso Martirio de Edmundo Campiano*', by Francis de Herrero, S.J.

MS Add. A. 63: Autograph narrative by John Bereblock of Queen's visit to Oxford.

MS Add. C. 303, fols 67r–73v: Incomplete, but impeccable, manuscript of Campion's trial.

MS Ashmole 1537: Latin and English anonymous complaint against Catholics at Oxford.

MS Eng. poet. b. 5: Poems and songs, including, 'Why doe I use my paper, ynke and pen'.

MSS Eng. th. b. 1–2: Two-volume Tresham alphabetical digest of theology, 'Brudenell manuscript'.

MS Jones 6: *Two Bokes of the Histories of Ireland*; bound with Thomas Otterbourne.

MS Laud 755 (roll): 'Why doe y use my papire, ynke and penne' and 'And ys he dead yn dead'.

MS Rawl. poet. 148: Thomas Watson, 'Why do I use my paper, inck and pen'.

MS Rawl. poet. 212: St John's College miscellany with poem excised.

MS Rawl. D. 111: 'Why do I take my paper, inke and penn' and 'What iron heart'.

MS Rawl. D. 272: Campion's orations for Thomas White, as Proctor and *coram Regina*.

MS Rawl. D. 289: Harington presentation copy of *Sancta salutiferi nascentia semina verbi*, c. 1605.

MS Rawl. D. 353: Another record of the second, third and fourth disputations; cf. BL MS Harley 422.

MS Rawl. D. 1071: John Bereblock's narrative of the Queen's visit to Oxford; annot. Hearne.

MS Rawl. Misc. 655: Garnet's 'Treatise of Equivocation', seized by Sir Edward Coke.

MS Tanner 329: Translation of Bombino by participant, but many chapters missing.

MS Top. Oxon. c. 73: Peter Whalley's notes to *Athen. Oxon.*, Bishop Matthew's apology.

MS Twyne 17: Brian Twyne's copy of Miles Windsor's 'Qu. Eizab: first Entertaynement'.

MS Twyne 21: Copy of Miles Windsor's 'A brief rehearsall' and Thomas Neale's 'Dialogue'.

MS Wood E.1: Wood's topographical notes on Oxford villages, including Cassington, and priories.

MS Wood D.10: Henry Jackson's list of Dr John Rainolds's books given to sundry persons.

MS Wood F 28: Wood's extensive collection and notes on Oxford colleges.

MS Wood F 29a: Wood's notes on the religious houses of Oxford and their suppression.

Oxford University Archives: Calendar and Register of Congregation and Convocation 1564–82.

Campion Hall

Johannes de Janduno, *Quaestiones in libros Physicorum Aristotelis* (Venice, Santritter and de Sanctis, 1488), and Frater Gratia Dei Esculanus, O.P., *Questiones in libros Physicorum Aristotelis* (Venice: [H. Liechtenstein?], 1484), Rhodes, nos 1030 and 852, composite book with 'Edmund Campyon' signatures.

Corpus Christi College

MS 257: Miles Windsor autograph draft and fair copy of Queen's visit.

MS 266: Miles Windsor's notes on Queen's visit, including speeches.

MS 280, 3 vols: collection of over 50 poems for Queen's visit, 1566, and copy of list of John Rous.

Exeter College

MS 166: Harington autograph, with Thomas Combe and Francis Harington, copy of *Leicester's Commonwealth*, with holograph translation of 'An addycion'.

Magdalen College

Jewel, John, *A Defence of the Apologie of the Churche of Englande, Conteininge an Answeare to a certaine Booke lately set foorthe by M. Hardinge, and*

Entituled, A Confutation of &c (London: Wykes, 1567), STC 14600: annotated copy, Magdalen College Library, 0.17.8.

St Peter's Church, Cassington, Oxfordshire
Shroud brass, 1590, of Thomas Neale, Regius Professor of Hebrew.

Downside Abbey Library, near Bath
MS 30 A: Richard Simpson, 'Collections for Life of Campion' (copies of original documents).
MS 30 D (25): Richard Simpson, 'Collections For the Life of Campion: Notes from Bombino'.
MS 30 D (26): Richard Simpson, 'Campion's Disputations in the Tower.
MS 30 D (27): Richard Simpson, 'Disputation between Campion &c'.
Berkshire Recusants in 'Pipe Rolls & Recusant Rolls, 1581 to end of Elizabeth's Reign', acc. no. 85313, Deck B80G: Box.

St Peter's Catholic Church, Winchester (WN[4])
Edmund Campion, *Rationes Decem: quibus fretus, certamen adversarijs obtulit in causa fidei, Edmundus Campianus* ([Stonor Park: S. Brinkley et al., 1581]), STC 4536.5, ARCR I. 135.1, bound in parchment wrapper of lease to Bellamy family of 1562. [This is now on loan to Stonor Park.]

York Minster Library
MS XVI.L.6: Unique manuscript of Sir John Harington's *A Tract on the Succession to the Crown*.

Arundel Castle, Sussex
Arundel Harington MS: 'Why doe I use my paper, ynke and pen', and 'fflower of Roses, Angells joy'.

Holkham Hall, Norfolk
MS 437: Harington presentation copy of *Sancta salutiferi nascentia semina verbi*.

Rushton Hall, Northamptonshire
Epigraph poem on altar relief: '*Ecce salutiferum signum thau nobile lignum*', 16-line elegy.

Hatfield House
MSS 149/195; 12/16; 162/93–5: Lord Burghley's papers for end of 1581.

Dublin, Ireland

Marsh's Library (incorporating Benjamin Iveagh Library in Farmleigh House)
Farmleigh MS IV.E.6: Campion's *Two Bokes of the Histories of Ireland*, and Giraldus Cambrensis, *Topographia*.

Chester Beatty Library
In 03.263: painting of Jesuits at the court of the Mughal Emperor Akbar, 1580–83, in *Book of Akba*.

National Library of Ireland
MSS D 2329, 2568, 2569, 2612: Ormond Papers (Deeds IV and V, and Indentures relating to property at Turvey, of Earl of Ormond and Sir Christopher Barnewall, 1540–56).

Washington, DC

Folger Shakespeare Library
Folger MS J.a.1: Copy of Campion's *Oratio Funebris* of Sir Thomas White.
Folger MS K.b.2: Alphabetical Commonplace book from about 1680, ref. to Campion, fol. 116v.
Folger MS M.a.244: Copy of BL MS Sloane 5008, diary of Richard Madox of All Souls.
Folger MS V.a.109: John Bereblock's narrative of the Queen's visit to Oxford: autograph.
Folger MS V.a.173: Campion's *Oratio Coram Regina* and *Oratio Funebris* for Sir Thomas White.
Folger MS V.a.176: Robinson's 'Of the Actes Done at Oxford' and Windsor's 'A Brief Rehearsall'.
Folger MS V.a.399: Commonplace book of verse and prose.
Folger MS V.a.459: Diary of Richard Stonley for June 1581 to December 1582.
Folger MS V.b.142: John Stubbe, his supplication, his words on scaffold, and letter to Lord Treasurer.
Folger MS V.b.214: Edmund Spenser's autograph copy of 'A View of the present estate of Ireland'.
Folger MS X.d.138 (7): Letter of Elizabeth to Rudolf II, 20 December 1597.
Folger MS X.d.338: Star Chamber trial of Stephen Vallenger, endorsed by Sir Walter Mildmay.
Harington, John, *A New Discourse of a Stale Subject, Called The Metamorphosis of Ajax* (London: Richard Field, 1596), STC 12779, Lord Lumley's copy with Harington's annotations.

Georgetown University Library
Georgetown Spec. Coll. GTC K 188: Lyons, S.J., *Collegium, Effigies Et Nomina Ssae. Trinitatis Sciet. Iesu Qvorvndam E Societate Iesv Qvi Pro Fide Vel Pietate Sunt Interfecti Ab Anno 1549. Ad Annum 1607* (Romae: Greuter & Maopinus, 1608): 102 engravings hand-tipped and annotated.

Dillingen, Bavaria

Studienbibliothek Dillingen
MS 219: Collection of 16 plays (including *Tragoedia cui nomen inditum Saul Galboaeus*), and two dialogues.
MS 221: Collection of 11 Jesuit plays including Campion's 'Ambrosia' (fols 135r–169v), and 'Isaac Immolatus', by Jacob Pontanus (fols 209r–231r).
MS 223: Collection of plays, poetry and dialogues made by Jacob Gretscher, S.J., including 'Stratocles' of Jacob Pontanus (fols 164v–174v).

Cologne

Historisches Archiv der Stadt Köln
MS Best. 150 (Universität), A 981, 'Liber Conseutudinum Scholae Coloniensis soc. Iesu', 1611–37, p. 71. Entry for 3 November 1621, records a performance of *Ambrosiana*.

Munich

Bavarian Staatsbibliothek
MS Cod. Lat. 308a: *Catalogus Librorum*.
MS Cod. Lat. 308b: *Catalogus Haereticorum* (including a 1564 Jena edition of Luther's works).
MS Cod. Lat. 1554: *Declamationes in Ducali Gymnasio Societatis Iesu Habitae, Monachii*, 1582.
MS Cod. Lat. 1606: Letters of Peter Canisius (some autograph) from 1556 to 1597, plus chart of life.
MS Cod. Lat. 2202: *Varia dramata* (1587–1690).

Krakow

Czartoryski Library
MS 2921.4: Manuscript of *Theatrum Virtutum* by Thomas Treter, dedicated to Cardinal Hosius.

Ignatianum Library
MS Jan Poplatek, S.J, 'Encyklopedia Jesuitow w XVI wieku, Pisane w latach 1946–1955' (compiled).

Cieszyn, Poland

Książnica Cieszyńska, Biblioteka Leopolda Jana Szersznika (Szersznik Library)
SZ MS DD.V.8: *Concionale* (notes of John Aquensis, S.J. on some 80 sermons by Campion), *Partitiones M.T. Ciceronis, Dialogus Mutus, Litaniae B.V. Mariae, Orationes: De tutela B.V. Mariae, De Iuvene Academico, In funere Mariae Cardonae, De S. Wenceslao, De foedere virtutis et scientiae* (untitled) *de sacramento Eucharistiae* (2 Orationes Joannis Aquensis).

Prague

Clementinum
UK MS I A I: 'Historia Collegii S.J., Pragensis ad S. Clementinum ann. 1555–1610'.

Castle Archive of Prague Metropolitan Chapter
M42: Notes on Campion's lectures on Aristotle's *Logic*, 2 November 1578 to 14 July 1579.
M65: Notes on Campion's lectures on Aristotle's *Physics*, 11 August 1579 to 9 February 1580.

Strahov Monastery Library
Elogium Historicum of Edmund Campion (3 printed copies): A.J. VIII. 80, E.Z. II.47, A.B.VIII.35/5.
MS DC. III. 16: Clementinum diaries, noting performances of *Ambrosiana*, visit of Henry Orton etc.
MS DC. III. 20: Clementinum diaries, from 1560 onwards.

Rome

Archivum Romanum Societatis Iesu
ARSI Anglia 38/1, fol. 31r–v: Copy of Campion's 'Examen', 26 August 1573, on entering Soc. Iesu.
ARSI Austr. 1/1a, pp. 240–41, 244, 255–6: Letters of Mercurian summoning Campion to Rome.
ARSI Austr. 1a, pp. 257–8: Letter of Everard Mercurian to Henry Blyssem.
ARSI Fondo Gesuitico 651/594: Letters of William Allen, 1575–86.
ARSI Fondo Gesuitico 651/612: Letters of Edmund Campion, 1580–81.
ARSI Fondo Gesuitico 651/628: Letter from Henry Holland to Campion, 14 February [1579?].
ARSI Fondo Gesuitico 651/636: Letters from Gregory Martin to Campion, 1575–79.
ARSI Germ. 158, fols 31v–32r, 47v: Letters from Henry Blyssem to Mercurian about Campion.

ARSI Germ. 158, fol. 84v: Letter of Giovanni Campani, Rector in Prague, on Campion's departure.

ARSI Vita 1.35: Autograph annotations in Bombino, *Vita et Martyrium* (1620).

Venerable English College
MS C-17-v: Copy of *Ambrosiana* (lacking beginning and end).

Uppsala

Universitets Bibliotek
MS R 380: *Collegii Posnaniensis Societatis Iesu* (collection of plays by Grzegorz Cnapius, S.J., et al.).

Valladolid, Spain

Royal English College
ACSA Series II L5, No. 12: Letter of Sr Elizabeth Sander to Sir Francis Englefield.

Early Modern and Primary Printed Sources

Alegambe, Philippe, S.J., *Bibliotheca Scriptorum Societatis Iesu, Post excusum Anno M.DC.VIII. Catalogum R.P. Petri Ribadaneira, S.J.* (Antwerp: Meursius, 1643).

[Alfield, Thomas], *A true reporte of the death and martyrdome of M. Campion Jesuite and preiste, & M. Sherwin, & M. Bryan preistes, at Tiborne the first of December 1581 Observid and written by a Catholike preist, which was present therat Whereunto is annexid certayne verses made by sundry persons* ([London: Verstegan, 1582]), STC 4537, ARCR II. 4.

Allen, William, *An Apologie and True Declaration of the Institution and endevours of the two English Colleges, the one in Rome, the other now resident in Rhemes: against certaine sinister informations given up against the same* ([Rheims: n.p.], 1581), STC 369, ARCR II. 6.

———, *A Briefe Historie of the Glorious Martyrdom of Twelve Reverend Priests, Father Edmund Campion and His Companions*, ed. J.H. Pollen, S.J. (London: Burns and Oates, 1908).

———, *A briefe historie of the glorious martyrdom of xij reverend piests, executed within these twelve monethes for confession and defence of the catholike faith* ([Rheims: Jean Foigny], 1582), STC 369.5 (formerly 13526), ARCR II. 7.

———, *Historia del Glorioso Martirio di Diciotto Sacerdoti Et Un Secolare, Fatti Morire in Inghilterra per la confessione, & difesa della fede Catolica, l'anno 1577, 1578, 1581, 1582. & 1583. S'e aggiunto al presente il martirio di cinque altri Sacerdoti Inglesi, martirizati quest'anno 1584* (Macerata: S. Martellini, 1585), ARCR I. 11.

————, *Historia del glorioso martirio di sedici sacerdoti martirizati in Inghilterra per la confessione, & difesa della fede Catolica, l'anno 1581, 1582 & 1583* (Macerata: S. Martellini, 1583), [with plates by Verstegan] ARCR I. 8.

————, *Letters and Memorials of William Cardinal Allen: 1532–1594*, ed. Fathers of the Congregation of the London Oratory with an historical introduction by Thomas Francis Knox (London: D. Nutt, 1882).

————, *A True Sincere and Modest Defence of English Catholiques that suffer for their Faith both at home and abrode: against a false, seditious and slaunderous Libel intituled THE EXECUTION OF JUSTICE IN ENGLAND* (Rouen: George L'Oyselet for George Flinton, 1584), STC 373, ARCR II. 14.

[Anon.], *An Advertisement and defence for Trueth against her Backbiters, and specially against the whispring Favourers, and Colourers of Campions, and the rest of his confederats treasons* (London: C. Barker, 1581), STC 153.7 (formerly STC18259).

[Anon.], *Canones, et Decreta Sacrosancti Oecumenici, et Generalis Concilii Tridentini Sub Paulo III, Iulio III, Pio IIII, Pontificibus Max.* (Romae: Paulus Manutius, Aldi F., 1564).

[Anon.], *Effigies Et Nomina Qvorvndam E Societate Iesv Qvi Pro Fide Vel Pietate Sunt Interfecti Ab Anno 1549. Ad Annum 1607* (Rome: Greuter & Maopinus, 1608). [No. 77 is of Campion.]

[Anon.], *L'Histoire de la Mort que le R. P. EDMOND CAMPION Pretre de la compagnie du nom de Jesus, et autres ont souffert en Angleterre pour la foy Catholique & Romaine le premier jour de Deccembre, 1581. Traduit d'Anglois en Francois* (Paris: Chaudiere, 1582), ARCR I. 197.

[Anon.], *Martyrium R.P. EDMUNDI CAMPIANI ... Per G. Estium e Gallico Latine redditum (Louvain: John Masius, 1582)* [translation by W. Est of *L'Histoire*], ARCR I. 203.

[Anon.], *A particular declaration or testimony, of the undutifull and traiterous affection borne against her Majestie by Edmond Campion Jesuite, and other condemned Priestes, witnessed by their own confessions: in reproof of those slanderous bookes & libels delivered out to the contrary by such as are malitiously affected towards her Majestie and the state* (London: C. Barker, 1582), STC 4536.

[Anon.], *A true report, of the Araignement and execution of the late Popish Traitour, Everard Haunse, executed at Tyborne, with reformation of the errors of a former untrue booke published concerning the same* (London: Henry Bynneman, 1581), STC 12934.

Balbin, Boluslav, S.J., *Miscellanea Historica Regni Bohemiae Decadisi Liber IV Hagiographicus* (Prague: G. Czernoch, 1682).

————, *Verisimilia humaniorum disciplinarum*, ed. Olga Spevak (Prague, 2006).

Bartoli, Daniel, S.J., *Dell'Istoria Della Compagnia Di Giesu L'Inghilterra Parte Dell'Europa* (Rome: Varese, 1667).

————, *Europeae Historiae Societatis Iesu Pars Prior Anglia*, trans. Ludovicus Janinus, S.J. (Lyons: Adam Demen, 1671).

———, *Missione Al Gran Mogor Del P. Ridolfo Aquaviva Della Compagnia Di Gesu Sua Vita e Morte E D'Altri Quattro Compagni Uccisi in Odio Della Fede In Salsete Di Goa* (Rome: Salvione, 1714).

Beza, Theodore, *Iesu Christi Domini Nostri Novum Testamentum, Graecum et Latinum* (Geneva: H. Stephanus, 1580).

Bombino, Paolo, S.J., *Vita et Martyrium Edmundi Campiani Martyris Angli* (Antwerp: Apud Heredes Martini Nutii et Joannem Meursium, 1618), ARCR I. 194.

———, *Vita et Martyrium Edmundi Campiani Martyris Angli, Editio Posterior ab Auctore multis aucta partibus, & emendata* (Mantuae: Fratres Osannas, 1620), ARCR I. 195.

Bracton, Henri de, *De Legibus & Consuetudinibus Angliae* (London: Richard Tottell, 1569), STC 3475.

Bristow, Richard, *A Briefe Treatise of Diverse plaine and sure wayes to finde out the truthe in this time of Heresie: conteyning sundry worthty Motives unto the Catholike faith* (Antwerp: J. Fowler, 1574), STC 3799, ARCR II. 67.

Byrd, William, *A gratification unto master John Case, for his learned booke, lately made in the praise of musicke* (London: T. East, 1589), STC 4246.

———, *Psalmes, sonets & songs of sadnes and pietie, made into musicke of five parts* (London: T. East, 1588), STC 4253.

Camden, William, *Annales Rerum Anglicarum et Hibernicarum, Regnante Elizabetha ad Annum Salutis M.D. LXXXIX* (London: William Stansby, 1615), STC 4496.

Campion, Edmund, S.J., *Campian Englished or A Translation of the* Ten Reasons, *in which Edmund Campian (of the Society of Jesus) Priest insisted in his Challenge to the Universities of Oxford and Cambridge, 16°* ([n.p. Rouen: Jean Cousturier], 1632), STC 4535, ARCR II. 116.

———, *Decem Rationes Propositae in Causa Fidei et Opuscula Eius Selecta*, ed. Sylvester de Petra Sancta, S.J. (Antwerp: Plantin Moretus Press, 1631), ARCR I. 170.

———, *Dziesięć Mocnych Dowodow*, trans. Gaspar Wilkowski (Vilnius: M.K. Radziwiłł, 1584), ARCR I. 193.

———, *Dziesięć Wywodów*, trans. Piotr Skarga, S.J. (Vilnius: M.K. Radziwiłł, 1584), ARCR I. 192.

———, *Edmundi Campiani ... Rationes decem redditae Academicis Angliae* (Ingolstadt: David Sartorius, 1583), ARCR I. 140.

———, *The Historie of Ireland, Collected by Three Learned Authors Viz. Meredith Hanmer, Edmund Campion and Edmund Spenser*, ed. Sir James Ware (Dublin: Societie of Stationers, 1633) STC 25067a.

———, *Two Histories of Ireland. The one written by E. Campion, the other by M. Hanmer. (A View of the State of Ireland. By E. Spenser)*, ed. Sir James Ware (Dublin: Societie of Stationers, 1633), STC 25067.

———, *Rationes Decem* (Romae: F. Zanettus, 1582), ARCR I. 136.

————, *Raitones* [sic] *Decem* (n.p.d. [Vilnius: M.K. Radziwiłł, 1584]), ARCR I. 144.

————, *Rationes Decem* (Cologne: Arnold Mylius, 1594), ARCR I. 151.

————, *Rationes Decem: quibus fretus, certamen adversarijs obtulit in causa fidei, Edmundus Campianus* ([Stonor Park: S. Brinkley et al., 1581]), STC 4536.5, ARCR I. 135.1.

————, *Rationes Decem with Adversus Prophanas Haereseon Novationes, by Saint Vincent Lerins* (Cologne: Birckmann, 1600), ARCR I. 150.

————, *Rationes Decem R.P. Edmundi Campiani, Orationes, Epistolae, Vita et Mors Edmundi Campiani* (Vienna: Cosmerovius, 1676).

————, *Ten Reasons*, ed. John Hungerford Pollen, S.J., trans. Joseph Rickarby, S.J. (London: Manresa Press, 1914).

————, *Two Bokes of the Histories of Ireland*, ed. A.F. Vossen (Assen: Van Gorcum, 1963).

————, [bd. w. Robert Turner, *Posthuma*] *Orationes, Epistolae, Tractatus de imitatione Rhetorica a Roberto Turnero Campiani discipulo collecta* (Ingolstadt: A. Angermarius, 1602), ARCR I. 1263.

————, [part of Robert Turner, *Orationum volumen primum*] *Orationes, epistolae et tractatus De imitatione Rhetorica* (Cologne: J. Kinckhes, 1615), ARCR I. 1265.

————, *Opuscula* (Barcelona: F. Rosalius, 1888).

Canisius, Peter, S.J., *Summa doctrinæ Christianæ. Per Quæstiones tradita, & in vsum Christianæ pueritiæ nunc primum edita* (Vienna: M. Zimmerman, 1554 [*vere* 1555]).

Cavallerii, Giovanni Battista, *Ecclesiae Anglicanae Trophaea sive Sanctorum Martyrum, qui pro Christo Catholicaeque fidei Veritate asserenda, antiquo recentiorique Persecutionum tempore, mortem in Anglia sibierunt, Passiones Romae in Collegio Anglico per Nicolaum Circinianum depictae* (Romae: Bartholomei Grassi, [1584]), ARCR I. 944, bd. w. ARCR I. 1284.

[Cecil, Lord Burghley William], *Atto dell giustitia d'Inghilterra. Translato d'Inglese in vulgare. Il 25 di Maggio 1584* (London: G. Wolfio, 1584), STC 4907.

————, *D'Executie van justitie* (Middleburgh [London]: R. Schilders [C. Barker], 1584), STC 4905.

————, *L'execution de justice faicte en Angleterre. Traduite en langue Francoise. Le 30. de Janvier 1584, & Declaration du traictement favorable* ([London: T. Vautrollier], 1584), STC 4906.

————, *The Execution of Justice for maintenaunce of publique and Christian peace, against certeine stirrers of sedition, and adherents to the traytors and enemies of the Realme, without any persecution of them for questions of Religion, as is falsely reported and published by the fautors and fosterers of their treasons. xvii. Decemb. 1583* (London: [C. Barker], 1583), ent. 2 Jan. 1584, STC 4902.

————, *The Execution of Justice*, 2nd ed., with small alterations (London: [C. Barker], January 1583[4]), STC 4903.

————, *Justitia Britannica. Per quam licet perspicue [etc.]* (London: T. Vautrollier, [March] 1584), STC 4904 (trans. of 4901 added).

Charke, William, *An answere to a seditious pamphlet lately cast abroade by a Jesuite, with a discoverie of that blasphemous sect* (London: C. Barker, 17 December 1580), STC 5005.

————, *A Replie to a Censure written against the two answers to a Jesuites seditious Pamphlet* (London: C. Barker, 1581), STC 5007.

Chronicle of the Grey Friars of London, ed. John Gough Nichols (London: Camden Society, 1852).

Churchyard, Thomas, *A generall rehearshall of warres, wherein is five hundred severall services of land* (London: Edward White, October 1579), STC 5235.

Cicero, M. Tullius, *Insignium Sententiarum elegans et perutile Compendium, post alias editiones plurimis locis auctum, brevibus scholiis illustratum* (Cologne: Soteres, 1552).

Clark, Samuel, *The History of the Glorious Life, Reign and Death of the Illustrious Queen Elizabeth* (London: H. Rhodes, 1683), Wing C4524.

Coryate, Thomas, *Coryats Crudities. Hastily gobled up in five moneths travells in France* (London: W. S[tansby], 1611), STC 5808.

Crato, Johannes, *Oratio Funebris de Divo Maximiliano Imperatore Caesare Augusto II* (Frankfurt: A. Wechel, 1577).

Dante, Alighieri, *Tutte le opere* (Rome: Newton Compton, 1997).

Dorman, Thomas, *A Proufe of Certyne Articles in Religion, Denied by M. Juell, Sett furth in Defence of the Catholyke Beleef therein* (Antwerp: J. Latius, 1564), STC 7062, ARCR II. 169.

Douay College: The First and Second Diaries of the English College, Douay, and an Appendix of Unpublished Documents, ed. Fathers of the Congregation of the London Oratory, intro. by T.F. Knox (London: D. Nutt, 1878).

Durie, John, S.J., *Confutatio Responsionis Gulielmi Whitakeri in Academia Cantabrigiensi Professoris Regii, ad Rationes decem, quibus fretus EDMUNDUS CAMPIANUS Anglus, Societatis Jesu Theologus certamen Anglicanae Ecclesiae Ministris obtulit in causa fidei* (Paris: Thomas Brummen, 1582), ARCR I. 334.

Elyot, George, *A very true report of the apprehension and taking of that Arche Papist Edmond Campion ... Conteining also a controulment of a most untrue former booke set out by one A.M. alias Anthonie Munday* (London: T. Dawson, 1581), STC 7629.

Erasmus, *Collected Works of Erasmus*, 24, *De Copia*, trans. Betty I. Knott; De Ratione Studii, trans. and annot. Brian McGregor (Toronto: University of Toronto Press, 1978).

————, *Collected Works of Erasmus*, 26, *De pueris Statim ac liberaliter instituendis declamatio, trans. and annot. Beert C. Verstraete* (Toronto: University of Toronto Press, 1985).

————, *Collected Works of Erasmus*, 39–40, *Colloquies*, trans. and annot. Craig R. Thompson (Toronto: University of Toronto Press, 1997).

————, *Familiarium Colloquiorum Formulae et Alia Quaedam* (Basel: Froben, 1518).

————, *De Ratione Studii, ac legendi, interpretandique auctores libellus aureus, Officium discipulorum ex Quintiliano. Qui primo legendi, ex eodem*, 2nd ed. (Strasbourg: Schurer, 1513).

Edrichus [Etheridge], George, *In libros aliquot pauli Aeginetae, hypomnemata quaedam, seu observationes medicamentorum* (London: T. East, 1588), STC 7498.

[Fleming, Abraham], *The Castrations of the Last Edition of Holinshed's Chronicle, Both in the Scotch and English Parts, Containing Forty Four Sheets; Printed with the Old TYPES and LIGATURES, And Compared Literatim by the Original* (London: William Mears, 1723).

Fortescue, John, *A learned commendation of the politique lawes of Englande, written in latine above an hundred yeares past*, trans. Richard Mulcaster (London: Richard Tottell, 1567), STC 11194.

Foxe, John, *The first (second) volume of ecclesiasticall history contaynyng the Actes and monuments*, 2 vols (London: J. Daye, 1570), STC 11223.

Fulke, William, *A Retentive to Stay good Christians, Against the Motives of R. Bristow* (London: T. Vautrollier for G. Bishop, 1580), STC 11449.

Gerard, John, S.J., *John Gerard: The Autobiography of an Elizabethan*, trans. Philip Caraman (London: Longmans, Green, 1951).

[Gibbons, John, S.J., and John Fen], *Concertatio Ecclesiae Catholicae in Anglia Adversus Calvinopapistas et Puritanos* (Trier, Edmund Hatotus, 1583), ARCR I. 524.

————, *Concertatio ecclesiae Catholicae in Anglia Adversus Calvinopapistas et Puritanos [anr. ed. enlarged]* (Trier: Henry Bock, 1588), ARCR I. 525.

————, *Concertatio Ecclesiae Catholicae in Anglia Adversus Calvinopapistas et Puritanos* (Trier: Henry Bock, 1588), ARCR I. 525 (facsimile), ed. D.M. Rogers (Farnborough: Gregg International Publishers, 1970).

Hanmer, Meredith, *The great bragge and challenge of M. Campion a Jesuite, commonlye called Edmunde Campion* (London: T. Marsh, 2 Jan.1581), STC 12745.

Harington, Sir John, *The Epigrams of Sir John Harington*, ed. Gerard Kilroy (Farnham, UK and Burlington, VT: Ashgate, 2009).

————, *A New Discourse of a Stale Subject, Called The Metamorphosis of Ajax* (London: Richard Field, 1596), STC 12779.

————, *A New Discourse of a Stale Subject, Called the Metamorphosis of Ajax*, ed. Elizabeth Story Donno (London: Routledge & Kegan Paul, 1962).

————, *Nugae Antiquae*, 2 vols, ed. Henry Harington and T. Park (London: Vernor and Hood, 1804).

————, *A Supplie or Addicion to the Catalogue of Bishops to the Yeare 1608*, ed. R.H. Miller (Potomac: Turanzas, 1979).

————, *A Tract on the Succesion to the Crown (A.D. 1602)*, ed. Clements R. Markham (London: Roxburgh Club, 1880).

Harpsfield, Nicholas [as Alan Cope], *Dialogi Sex Contra Summi Pontificatus, Monasticae Vitae, Sanctorum, Sacrarum Imaginum Oppugnatores, et Pseudo Martyres* (Antwerp: Plantin, 1566), ARCR I. 636.

————, *Historia Anglicana Ecclesiastica ... Adjecta brevi narratione de divortio Henrici VIII regis ab uxore CATHERINA, & ab Ecclesia Catholica Romana discessione ab Edmundo Campiano*, ed. Richard Gibbons, S.J. (Douai: Marcus Wyon, 1622), ARCR I. 639.

Hatton, Sir Christopher, *Memoirs of the Life and Times of Sir Christopher Hatton*, ed. Sir Harris Nicolas (London: Bentley, 1847).

Holinshed, Raphael, *The First and second volumes of Chronicles comprising The description and historie of England, The description and historie of Ireland, The description and historie of Scotland* (London: John Harrison et al., 1586), STC 13569.

————, *The First and second volumes of the Chronicles of England, Scotlande, and Irelande* (London: Henry Bynneman, 1577), STC 13568.

————, *The First volume of the Chronicles of England, Scotlande, and Irelande* (London: George Bishop, 1577), STC 13568a.

————, *The Historie of Irelande from the first inhabitation thereof, unto the yeare 1509, Collected by Raphael Holinshed, and continued till the yeare 1547 by Richard Stanyhurst* (London: John Hunne, 1577), STC 13568b.

————, *The Laste volume of the Chronicles of England, Scotlande, and Irelande, with their descriptions* (London: Lucas Harrison, [1577]), STC 13568.

————, *The Peaceable and Prosperous Regiment of Blessed Queene Elisabeth: A Facsimile from Holinshed's Chronicles (1587)*, ed. Cyndia Susan Clegg and Randall McLeod (San Marino: Huntington Library, 2005).

————, *The Second Volume of Chronicles: Conteining the description, conquest, inhabitation, and troublesome estate of Ireland ... augmented ... by John Hooker Whereunto is annexed the ... historie of Scotland* (London: John Harrison et al., 1586), STC 13569.

————, *The Third volume of Chronicles ... Now newlie recognized, augmented, and continued (with occurrences and accidents of fresh memorie) to the yeare 1586* (London: Harrison, Bishop, Newberry, Denham and Woodcocke, 1587), STC 13569.

Humphrey, Laurence, *Jesuitismi Pars Secunda: Puritanopapismi, seu doctrinae Jesuiticae aliquot Rationibus ab Ed. Campiano comprehensae & a Joanne Duraeo defensae Confutatio* (London: H. Middleton, 1584), STC 13962.

————, *Jesuitismi Pars Prima: Sive De Praxi Romanae Curiae contra Respublicam & Principes: Et De nova legatione Jesuitarum* (London: H. Middleton, 1582), STC 13961.

Hurlestone, Randall, *Newes from Rome concerning the blasphemous sacrifice of the papisticall Masse with dyvers other treatises very Godlye & profitable* (Canterbury: J. Mychell for E. Campion, [1548?]), STC 14006.

Leslie, John, Bishop of Rosse, *A defence of the honor of the right high, right mighty and noble princesse, Marie, queene of Scotland* (London [Rheims, J. Foigny], 1569), STC 15504, ARCR II. 500.

———, [as Morgan Philippes], *Ad nobilitatem, populumque Scoticum ... Ioannis Leslaei ... paraenesis;Scotorum historiae nuper ab eodem auctore editae, praefixa* (Romae: in aedibus populi Romani, 1578), ARCR I. 719.

———, *A Treatise Concerning the Defence of the Honour of the Right High, Mightie and Noble Princesse, Marie Queene of Scotland, and Douager of France, with a Declaration, as wel of her Right, Title and Interest to the Succession of the Croune of England: as that the regiment of Women is conformable to the lawe of God and Nature* (Liege [Louvain: J. Fowler]: Morberius, 1571), STC 15506, ARCR II. 501.

———, *A Treatise Towching the Right, Title, and Interest of the Most Excellent Princesse Marie, Queene of Scotland, And of the most noble king James, her Graces sonne, to the succession of the Croune of England Wherein is contained aswell a Genealogie of the Competitors pretending title to the same Croune: as a resolution of their objections* ([Rouen: George L'Oyselet], 1584), STC 15507, ARCR II. 503.

Lorinus, Johannes, S.J., *In Actus Apostolorum Commentaria* (Cologne: A. Hieratus, 1609).

Machyn, Henry, *The Diary*, ed. John Gough Nichols (London: Camden Society, 1848).

———, *A London Provisioner's Chronicle, 1550–1563*, ed. Richard W. Bailey, Marilyn Miller and Colette Moore (Michigan: University of Michigan, electronic version).

Martial, John, *A Replie to M. Calfhills Blasphemous Answer Made Against the Treatise of the Crosse* (Louvain: Fowler, 1566), STC 17497, ARCR II. 512.

Martin, Gregory, *A Treatise of Christian Peregrination. Wherunto is adjoined certen epistles* (Paris: R. Verstegan, 1583), STC 17507, ARCR II. 523.

———, *A Treatise of Schisme* (Duaci: Apud Johannem Foulerum [London: W. Carter], 1578), STC 17508, ARCR II. 524.

———, trans. (chiefly), *The New Testament of Jesus Christ* (Rheims: Jean Foigny, 1582), ARCR II. 173.

Mason, Thomas, *Christs Victorie over Sathans Tyrannie* (London: G. Eld and R. Blower, 1615), STC 17622.

Matthew, Tobie, *Concio apologetica adversus Campianum* (Oxford: Lichfield, 1638), STC 17657.

More, Henry, S.J., *The Elizabethan Jesuits: Historia Missionis Anglicanae Societatis Jesu (1660) of Henry More*, ed. and trans. Francis Edwards (London: Phillimore, 1981).

Munday, Anthony, *A breefe and true reporte, of the Execution of certaine Traytours at Tiborne, the xxviij and xxx dayes of Maye. 1582* (London: W. Wright, 1582), STC18261.

————, *A breefe Aunswer made unto two seditious Pamphlets, the one printed in French, and the other in English. Contayning a defence of Edmund Campion and his complices, their most horrible and vnnatural Treasons, as gainst her Maiestie and the Realme* (London: John Charlewood, 1582), STC 18262.

————, [anr. ed.] *A breefe Aunswer made unto two seditious Pamphlets* (London: E. White, 1582), STC 18262a.

————, *A breefe discourse of the taking of Edmund Campion, and his confederates* (London: [J. Charlewood] for W. Wright, 24 July 1581), STC 18264 [one extant copy originally owned by Bishop Bancroft, L²].

————, *A Discoverie of Edmund Campion, and his Confederates ... Whereunto is added, the Execution of Edmund Campion, Ralphe Sherwin, and Alexander Briant, executed at Tiborne the I of December* (London: [J. Charlewood] for E. White, 29 January 1582), STC 18270.

————, *The English Romayne lyfe* (London: J. Charlewood for N. Ling, 21 jn. 1582), STC 18272.

————, *A Watch-woord to Englande To beware of traytours and trecherous practises* (London: Thomas Hacket, 1584), STC 18282a.

Nichols, John, *A declaration of the recantation of John Nichols (for the space almost of two yeares the Popes scholer in the English Seminarie Colledge at Rome) which desireth to be reconciled and received as a member into the true Church of Christ in England* (London: Christopher Barker, 14 February 1581), STC 18533.

[Norton, Thomas], *A Declaration of the favourable dealing of her Majesties Commissioners appointed for the Examination of certaine Traitours, and of tortures unjustly reported to be done upon them for matters of religion* ([London, Christopher Barker], 1583), STC 4901.

Nowell, Alexander, *A Confutation, as wel of M. Dormans last Boke entituled A Disproufe. &c as also of D. Sander his causes of Transubstantiation* (London: Henrie Bynneman, 1567), STC 18739.

Nowell, Alexander and William Day, *A true report of the Disputation or rather private Conference had in the Tower of London, with Ed. Campion Iesuite, the last of August. 1581. Set downe by the Reverend learned men themselves that dealt therein* (London: C. Barker, 1 January 1583), Ent. 27 Dec. 1582, STC 18744.

————, *A true report of the Disputation* [anr. ed. with verso of tp. blank], 18744.5.

Ovidius Naso, Publius, *P. Ovidi Nasonis Metamorphoses*, ed. R.J. Tarrant (Oxford: Clarendon Press, 2004).

[Persons, Robert], S.J., *A brief censure upon two bookes written in answer to M. Edmonde Campions offer of disputation* (Doway: John Lyon [secretly at Francis Browne's house on Greenstreet House Press, 12 January] 1581), STC 19393, ARCR II. 612 (answers STC 5005 and 12745).

————, *A Brief Discours contayning certayne Reasons Why Catholiques refuse to goe to Church. Written by a learned and vertuous man, to a frend of his in England. And Dedicated by I. H[owlet, pseud.] to the Queenes most excellent*

Maiestie (Doway: John Lyon [secretly at East Ham: Greenstreet House Press], 1580), STC 19394, ARCR II. 613.

————, *A conference about the next succession to the crowne of Ingland. Where unto is added a genealogie.* Published by R. Doleman, *pseud.* (Imprinted at N. [Antwerp: A. Conincx], 1594 [1595]), STC 19398, ARCR II. 167.

————, *The copie of a Leter, Wryten by a Master of Arte of Cambridge, to his friend in London, concerning some talke ... about the present state, and some proceedings of the Erle of Leycester* ([Rouen: George L'Oyselet], 1584), STC 5742.9 (formerly 19399), ARCR II. 31.

————, *A Defence of the Censure Gyven upon Two Bookes of William Charke and Meredith Hanmer mynysters* ([Rouen: L'Oyselet for Flinton], 1582), STC 19401, ARCR II. 624.

————, *Discours de La Vie Abominable, Ruses, Trahisons, Meurtres, Impostures, empoisonnements, paillardises, Atheismes, et autres tres iniques conversations, desquelles a usé & use iournellement le my Lorde de LECESTRE Machiaveliste, contre l'honneur de Dieu, la Maiesté de la Royne d'Angleterre sa Princesse, & toute la Republique Chrestienne* ([n.p.d.] 1585).

————, *A discoverie of J. Nichols minister, misreported a jesuite. Wherin is contayned a ful answere to his recantation. There is added a reproof of an oration* ([Stonor Park: Greenstreet House Press, 1581]), STC 19402, ARCR II. 625.

————, *An Epistle of the Persecution of Catholickes in Englande. Translated out of frenche into Englishe, and conferred with the Latyne copie. by G.T.* (Douay [Rouen: G. L'Oyselet, 1582]), STC 19406, ARCR II. 627, trans. of ARCR I. 879.

————, *Epistre de La Persecution Meue en Angleterre Contre L'Eglise Chrestienne Catholique et Apostolique, et fideles membres d'icelle* (Paris: T. Brumen, 1582), ARCR I. 879.

————, *The First Booke Of The Christian Exercise, appertayning to Resolution* ([Rouen: L'Oyselet for Flinton], 1582), STC 19353, ARCR II. 616.

————, 'Of the Life and Martyrdom of Father Edmond Campian', trans. and ed. J.H. Pollen, S.J., 3 pts, *Letters and Notices* 11 (1877): 219–42, 308–39; 12 (1878): 1–68.

————, *De Persecutione Anglicana Epistola. Qua explicantur afflictiones, aerumna, & calamitates gravissimae, cruciatus etiam & tormenta, & acerbissima martyria, quae Catholici nunc Angli, ob fidem patiuntur* ([Rouen: L'Oyselet for Flinton, 1582]), ARCR I. 874.

————, *De Persecutione Anglicana Libellus. Quo explicantur Afflictiones, calamitates, cruciatus, & acerbissima martyria, quae Angli Catholici nunc ob fidem patiuntur. Quae omnia in hac postrema editione aeneis typis ad vivum expressa sunt* (Rome: G. Ferrarii, 1582), ARCR I. 876.

————, *De Persecutione Anglicana Libellus. Quo explicantur Afflictiones, calamitates gravissimae, cruciatus, & acerbissima martyria, quae Angli Catholici nunc ob fidem patiuntur. Quae omnia in hac postrema editione aeneis typis ad vivum expressa sunt. 8o* (Romae: George Ferrarius [English College], 1582), ARCR I. 876.

Pits, John, *Relationum Historicarum de Rebus Anglicis Tomus Primus* (Paris: Thierry & Cramoisy, 1619), ARCR I. 907.

Ribadeneira, Pedro de, S.J., *Bibliotheca Scriptorum Societatis Iesu post excusum Anno M. DC.VIII Catalogum R.P. Petri Ribadaneira, S.J.*, ed. Philippe Alegambe, S.J. (Antwerp: Meursius, 1643).

———, *Hystoria Ecclesiastica Del Scisma del Reino de Inglaterra En la qual se tratan las cosas que han sucedido en aquel Reyno tocantes a nuestra santa Religion, desde que comenco, hasta la muerte de la Reyna de Escocia* (Madrid: M. de Lyra, 1588).

———, *Illustrium Scriptorum Religionis Societatis Iesu Catalogus* (Lyons: J. Pillehotte, 1609).

———, *Vita beati patris Ignatii Loiolae Societatis Iesu Fundatoris* (Rome: [n.p.], 1622).

Sander, Nicholas, *A Briefe Treatise of Usurie, Made by Nicholas Sander D. of Divinitie* (Louvain: John Fowler, 1568), STC 21691, ARCR II. 691.

———, *De Origine ac Progressu Schismatis Anglicani, Editus & auctus per Edouardum Rishtonum* (Cologne [Rheims: John Foigny], 1585), ARCR I. 972.

———, *De Origine ac Progressu Schismatis Anglicani, aucti per Edouardum Rishtonum* (Romae: Bonfadini, 1586), ARCR I. 973. [Addns by Persons, incl. John Hart's 'Diarium Rerum Gestarum in Turri Londinensi', 'Tower Diary'].

———, *De Origine ac Progressu Schismatis Anglicani, aucti per Edouardum Rishtonum* (Ingolstadt: Ederus, 1587), ARCR I. 974.

———, *The Rise and Progress of The English Reformation* (Dublin: J. Christie, 1827).

———, *Rise and Growth of the Anglican Schism*, ed. and trans. David Lewis (London: Burns and Oates, 1877).

———, *The Rise and Growth of the Anglican Schism*, ed. and trans. David Lewis (Rockford: Tan Books, 1988).

———, *De Visibili Monarchia Ecclesiae, Libri Octo* (Louvain: John Fowler, 1571), ARCR I. 1013.

———, *De Visibili Monarchia Ecclesiae* (Antwerp: John Fowler, 1578), ARCR I. 1014.

Schelhornius, John George, *Amoenitates Historiae Ecclesiasticae et Literariae* (Frankfurt and Lipsiae: Daniel Bartholomaeus, 1737).

Schmidl, Joannes, S.J., *Historiae Societatis Jesu Provinciae Bohemiae Pars Prima Ab Anno Christi MDLV Ad Annum MDXCII*, 2 vols (Prague: Charles University Press, 1747).

Smith, Sir Thomas, *De Republica Anglorum: The maner of Governement or policie of the Realme of England* (London: G. Seton, 1583), STC 22857.

Spenser, Edmund, *A View of the State of Ireland* [ed. Sir James Ware] (Dublin: Soc. Stationers, 1633), STC 25067.

———, *A View of the State of Ireland, From the First Printed Edition (1633)*, ed. Andrew Hadfield and Willy Maly (Oxford: Blackwell, 1997).

Stanihurst, Richard, *Harmonia seu Catena Dialectica, in Porphyrianas Institutiones* (London: Reginald Wolfe, 1570), STC 23229.

Stow, John, *The Annales of England* (London: George Bishop, 1605), STC 23337.

———, *The Chronicles of England, from Brute unto this present yeare of Christ, 1580* (London: Ralphe Newberie for Henry Bynneman, 1580), STC 23333.

———, 'Historical Memoranda', in *Three Fifteenth-Century Chronicles*, ed. James Gairdner (London: Camden Society, 1880).

———, *A Survay of London* (London: John Wolfe, 1598), STC 23341.

———, *A Survay of London* (London: John Windet, 1603), STC 23343.

Strype, John, *The Life and Acts of John Whitgift*, 3 vols (Oxford: University Press, 1822).

[Stubbe, John], *The Discoverie of a Gaping Gulf Whereinto England is Like to be Swallowed by an other French mariage, if the Lord forbid not the banes, by letting her Majestie see the sin and punishment thereof* ([London: H. Singleton], 1579), STC 23400.

Tacitus, Publius Cornelius, *Tacitus in Five Volumes*, trans. M. Hutton et al. (London: Heinemann, 1970), Loeb classical series.

Thucydides, *History of the Peloponnesian War*, trans. C.F. Smith, 4 vols (London: Heinemann, 1919), Loeb classical series.

Turner, Robert, S.J., *Orationum Volumen Primum ... Accesserunt P. Edm. Campiani Orationes, Epistolae, & Tract. De Imitatione Rhetorica* (Cologne: John Kinckhes, 1615), ARCR I. 1265.

———, *Oratoris et Philosophi Ingolstadiensis Orationes XIV* (Ingolstadt: Sartoris, 1584), ARCR I. 1260.

———, *Posthuma. Orationes septemdecim ... Accesserunt Edmundi Campiani ... orationes, epistolae, tractatus de imitatione rhetorica a Roberto Turnero Campiani discipulo collecta* (Ingolstadt: Angermarius, 1602), ARCR I. 1263.

Verstegan, Richard, *Briefve description des diverses cruautez que les Catholiques endurent en Angleterre pour la foy* (n.p.d. [Paris: 1583]), ARCR I. 1285.

———, *Descriptiones quaedam illius inhumanae et multiplicis persecutionis quam in Anglia propter fidem sustinent Catholici Christiani* ([Paris: n.p.d, 1583]), ARCR I. 1283.

———, *Descriptiones quaedam illius inhumanae et multiplicis persecutionis quam in Anglia propter fidem sustinent Catholici Christiani, engraved by de Cavallerii* (Romae: Francisco Zanetti, 1584), ARCR I. 1284, bound with ARCR I. 944.

———, *Praesentis Ecclesiae Anglicanae Typus* ([Rheims: Jean Foigny, 1582]), ARCR I. 1293.

———, *Theatre des cruautes des hereticques de nostre temps* (Antwerp: Adrian Hubert, 1588), ARCR I. 1302.

———, *Theatrum Crudelitatum Haereticorum* (Antwerp: Adrian Hubert, 1587), ARCR I. 1297.

Weston, William, S.J., *The Autobiography of an Elizabethan*, trans. Philip Caraman (London: Longmans, Green, 1955).

Whitaker, William, *Ad rationes decem Edmundi Campiani iesuitae, quibus fretus certamen Anglicanae ecclesiae ministris obtulit in causa fidei, responsio Guilielmi Whitakeri, Theologiae in Academia Cantabrigensi professoris Regij* (London: Vautrollier, 1581), STC 25358.

————, *An answere to the ten reasons of E. Campian. Whereunto is added the summe of the defence of those reasons by John Duraeus the Scot, a jesuit, with a reply unto it*, trans. Richard Stocke (London: Kyngston, 1606), STC 25360.

————, *Edmundi Campiani Jesuitae Rationes Decem ... et ad eas Guilelmi Whitakeri Theologiae in Academia Cantabrigiensi professoris Regij Responsio* (Antwerp: Aegidius Radaeus, 1582), ARCR I. 139.

————, *Edmundi Campiani Iesuitae Rationes Decem ... et ad eas Guil. Whitakeri ... Responsio* (Lichae: Guolgang Kezelius, 1604), ARCR I. 156.

————, *Responsionis ad Decem illas Rationes, quibus fretus Edmundus Campianus certamen Ecclesiae Anglicanae ministris obtulit in causa fidei, Defensio contra Confutationem Joannis Duraei Scoti, Presbyteri, Iesuitae* (London: H. Middleton, 1583), STC 25362.

Wood, Anthony, *Anthony Wood's Survey of the Antiquities of the City of Oxford*, 3 vols (Oxford: Clarendon Press, 1890), Oxford Historical Society, 17.

————, *Athenae Oxonienses*, 2 vols, ed. P. Bliss (London: Rivington, 1813).

————, *Fasti Oxonienses*, 2 vols, ed. P. Bliss (London: Rivington, 1815).

Wriothesley, Charles, *A Chronicle of England*, ed. W.D. Hamilton, 2 vols (London: Camden Society, 1875).

Yepes, Diego de, *Historia Particular de la Persecution de Inglaterra* (Madrid: Louis Sanches, 1599).

Secondary and Modern Sources

Alford, Stephen, *Burghley: William Cecil at the Court of Elizabeth I* (New Haven and London: Yale University Press, 2008).

————, *The Watchers: A Secret History of the Reign of Elizabeth I* (London: Allen Lane, 2012).

Allison, A.F. and D.M. Rogers, *The Contemporary Printed Literature of the English Counter-Reformation between 1558 and 1640*, vol. 1: *Works in Languages Other than English*; vol. 2: *Works in English* (Aldershot, UK and Burlington, VT, 1989–1994).

Andersson, Daniel, 'How to Teach Philosophy', *TLS* (8 March 2013), 14–15.

Anstruther, Godfrey, O.P., *The Seminary Priests: A Dictionary of the Secular Clergy of England and Wales 1558–1850*, 2 vols (Durham: Ushaw College, [n.d.]), vol. 1, *Elizabethan 1558–1603*.

————, *Vaux of Harrowden: A Recusant Family* (Newport: R.H. Johns, 1953).

Arblaster, Paul, *Antwerp and the World: Richard Verstegan and the International Culture of Catholic Reformation* (Leuven: University Press, 2004).

Archer, Ian. W., *The Pursuit of Stability: Social Relations in Elizabethan London* (Cambridge: University Press, 1991).

Asquith, Clare, *Shadowplay: The Hidden Beliefs and Coded Politics of William Shakespeare* (New York: Public Affairs, 2005).

Aveling, Hugh [J.C.H., John], *Catholic Recusancy in the City of York 1558–1791* (London: Catholic Record Society, 1970).

———, 'The Catholic Recusants of the West Riding of Yorkshire 1558–70', *Proceedings of the Leeds Philosophical and Literary Society*, vol. 10 (1963), 190–306.

———, *Northern Catholics: The Catholic Recusants of the North Riding of Yorkshire 1558–1790* (London: Geoffrey Chapman, 1966).

Baker, David J. and Willy Maley, eds, *British Identities and English Renaissance Literature* (Cambridge: University Press, 2002).

Baldwin, T.W., *William Shakspere's Small Latine and Less Greeke*, 2 vols (Urbana: University of Illinois Press, 1944).

Basset, Bernard, S.J., *The English Jesuits: From Campion to Martindale* (London: Burns and Oates, 1967).

Bates, Peadar, *Donabate and Portrane: A History* (Dublin: Bates, 2001).

Beal, Peter, *Catalogue of English Literary Manuscripts 1450–1700* (CELM): digital online catalogue.

———, *A Dictionary of English Manuscript Terminology, 1450–2000* (Oxford: University Press, 2008).

———, *In Praise of Scribes: Manuscripts and Their Makers in Seventeenth-Century England* (Oxford: Clarendon Press, 1998).

———, *Index of English Literary Manuscripts*, vol. 1, *1450–1625* (London: Mansell, 1980).

Bennett, H.S., *English Books and Readers, 1558–1603: Being a Study in the History of the Book Trade in the Reign of Elizabeth I* (Cambridge: University Press, 1965).

Berry, Philippa, *Shakespeare's Feminine Endings: Disfiguring Death in the Tragedies* (Cambridge: University Press, 1999).

Bingham, Tom, *The Rule of Law* (London: Allen Lane, 2010).

Birrell, T.A., 'William Carter (c. 1549–84): Recusant Printer, Publisher, Binder, Stationer, Scribe – and Martyr', *Recusant History* 28.1 (May 2006), 22–42.

Blackstone, Sir William, *Commentaries on the Laws of England*, 4 vols (Oxford: Clarendon Press, 1775).

Blayney, Peter W.M., *The Bookshops in Paul's Cross Churchyard* (London: Bibliographical Society, 1990).

———, *The Stationers' Company and the Printers of London, 1501–1557*, 2 vols (Cambridge: Cambridge University Press, 2013).

———, *The Stationers' Company before the Charter, 1403–1557* (London: Worshipful Company of Stationers, 2003).

Blunden, Edmund et al., *The Christ's Hospital Book* (London: Hamish Hamilton, 1953).

Bohatcova, Mirjam, 'Book-Printing and Other Forms of Publishing in Prague', in *Rudolf II and Prague*, ed. Eliška Fučikova et al. (Prague, London, Milan: Thames and Hudson, 1997), pp. 332–9.

Bonavita, Roger Vella, 'The English Militia, 1558–1580: A Study in the Relations between the Crown and the Commissioners of Musters', History M.A. thesis, Victoria University of Manchester, 1972.

Bossy, John, *The English Catholic Community, 1570–1850* (London: Darton, Longman & Todd, 1975).

———, 'English Catholics and the French Marriage, 1577–81', *Recusant History* 5 (1959), 2–16.

———, 'The Heart of Robert Persons', in *The Reckoned Expense: Edmund Campion and the Early Jesuits*, ed. Thomas M. McCoog, S.J., 2nd ed. (Rome: IHSI, 2007), pp. 187–207.

Brady, Cieran, *The Chief Governors: The Rise and Fall of Reform Government in Tudor Ireland, 1536–1588* (Cambridge: University Press, 1994).

Brady, Cieran and Raymond Gillespie, eds, *Natives and Newcomers: Essays on the Making of Irish Colonial Society 1534–1641* (Dublin: Irish Academic Press, 1986).

Brennan, Michael G., 'Graham Greene, Evelyn Waugh and Mexico', *Renascence* 55.1 (2002), 7–23.

———, 'The Sidneys of Penshurst, the Earldom of Leicester, and the Monarchies of England, Spain and France', *Sidney Journal* 22.1–2 (2004), 25–45.

Brigden, Susan, *London and the Reformation* (Oxford: Clarendon Press, 1989).

———, *New Worlds, Lost Worlds: The Rule of the Tudors, 1485–1603* (London: Penguin, 2000).

———, 'Youth and the Reformation', in *The Impact of the English Reformation 1500–1640*, ed. Peter Marshall (London: Arnold, 1997), pp. 55–85.

Brodrick, J., S.J., *Saint Peter Canisius, S.J., 1521–1597* (Baltimore: Carroll, 1950).

Butterworth, Charles C., *The English Primers (1529–1545): Their Publication and Connection with the English Bible and the Reformation in England* (Philadelphia: University of Pennsylvania Press, 1953).

Buxton, John and Penry Williams, eds, *New College Oxford 1379–1979* (Oxford: New College, 1979).

Camm, Dom Bede, *Forgotten Shrines* (London: Macdonald & Evans, 1910).

Campion, Leslie, *The Family of Edmund Campion* (London: The Research Publishing Co., 1975).

Canny, Nicholas, *The Elizabethan Conquest of Ireland: A Pattern Established 1565–1576* (London: Harvester, 1976).

———, *Making Ireland British 1580–1650* (Oxford: University Press, 2001).

Caraman, Philip, *The Western Rising 1549: The Prayer Book Rebellion* (Tiverton: Westcountry Books, 1994).

Carey, Vincent P. and Ute Lotz-Heumann, *Surviving the Tudors: The 'Wizard' Earl of Kildare and English Rule in Ireland, 1537–1586* (Dublin: Four Courts Press, 2002).

————, *Taking Sides? Colonial and Confessional* Mentalités *in Early Modern Ireland* (Dublin: Four Courts Press, 2003).

Carrafiello, Michael L., 'English Catholicism and the Jesuit Mission of 1580–1581', *The Historical Journal* 37. 4 (1994) 761–74.

Catto, J.I. and Ralph Evans, *Late Medieval Oxford*, vol. 2 of *The History of the University of Oxford* (Oxford: Clarendon Press, 1992).

Challoner, Richard, *Memoirs of Missionary Priests*, ed. J.H. Pollen, S.J. (London: Burns Oates & Washbourne, 1924).

Clegg, Cyndia Susan, 'Censorship', in *The Oxford Handbook of Holinshed's Chronicles*, ed. Paulina Kewes, Ian W. Archer and Felicity Heal (Oxford: University Press, 2013), pp. 43–59.

————, 'Which Holinshed? Holinshed's *Chronicles* at the Huntington Library', *Huntington Library Quarterly* 55 (1992), 559–77.

Clegg, Cyndia Susan and Randall McLeod, eds, *The Peaceable and Prosperous Regiment of Blessed Queene Elizabeth: A Facsimile from Holinshed's Chronicles* (San Marino: Huntington Library, 2005).

College, J.J. and Ben Warlow, *Ships of the Royal Navy: The Complete Record of all Fighting Ships of the Royal Navy from the 15th Century to the Present* (London: Chatham House, 2006).

Coppens, Christian, *Reading in Exile: The Libraries of John Ramridge (d. 1568), Thomas Harding (d. 1572) & Henry Joliffe (d. 1573), Recusants in Louvain* (Cambridge: LP Publications, 1993).

Čornejova, Ivana, 'The Religious Situation in Rudolfine Prague', in *Rudolf II and Prague*, ed. Eliška Fučikova et al. (Prague, London, Milan: Thames and Hudson, 1997), 310–22.

Cressy, David, *Dangerous Talk: Scandalous, Seditious and Treasonable Speech in Pre-Modern England* (Oxford: University Press, 2010).

Crosignani, Ginevra, Thomas M. McCoog, S.J., and Michael Questier, *Recusancy and Conformity in Early Modern England: Manuscript and Printed Sources in Translation* (Toronto: Pontifical Institute of Medieval Studies, 2010).

Cross, Claire, 'Oxford and the Tudor State 1509–1558', in *History of the University of Oxford*, vol. 2, *Late Medieval Oxford*, ed. J.I. Catto and Ralph Evans (Oxford: Clarendon Press, 1992).

Crossley, Alan, ed., *Victoria County History, Oxford*, vol. 12, *Wootton Hundred (South) including Woodstock* (Oxford: University Press, 1990).

Cruickshank, C.G., *Elizabeth's Army* (Oxford: University Press, 1946).

Dailey, Alice, *The English Martyr: From Reformation to Revolution* (Notre Dame: University of Notre Dame Press, 2012).

Daly, Peter M. and G. Richard Dimler, *Corpus Librorum Emblematum: The Jesuit Series Part One* (Quebec: McGill-Queen's University Press, 1997).

Davidson, Alan, 'Roman Catholicism in Oxfordshire from the Late Elizabethan Period to the Civil War (c. 1580–c. 1640)', University of Bristol: Ph.D. dissertation, 1970.

Dent, C.M., *Protestant Reformers in Elizabethan Oxford* (Oxford: University Press, 1983).

Didiot, Canon, 'La "Somme" d'un Martyr', in *Revue des Sciences Ecclesiastiques* (1887), 193–212 and 289–304.

Dillon, Anne, *The Construction of Martyrdom in the English Catholic Community, 1535–1603* (Aldershot, UK and Burlington, VT: Ashgate, 2002).

———, *Michelangelo and the English Martyrs* (Farnham, UK and Burlington, VT: Ashgate, 2012).

Dobson, R.H., 'The Religious Orders 1370–1540', in *The History of the University of Oxford, 1555–1660*, vol. 2, ed. J.I. Catto and Ralph Evans (Oxford: Clarendon Press, 1992), pp. 539–79.

Dominguez, Freddy, '"We must fight with paper and pens": Spanish Elizabethan Polemics, 1558–1598', Princeton: Ph.D. dissertation, 2011.

Doran, Susan, *Elizabeth and Religion 1558–1603* (London: Routledge, 1994).

———, *Monarchy and Matrimony: the Courtships of Elizabeth I* (London: Routledge, 1996).

Drinker Bowen, Catherine, *The Lion and the Throne: The Life and Times of Sir Edward Coke* (Boston: Little Brown, 1956).

Duffy, Eamon, *Fires of Faith: Catholic England under Mary Tudor* (New Haven and London: Yale University Press, 2009).

———, *Saints, Sacrilege and Sedition: Religion and Conflict in the Tudor Reformations* (London: Bloomsbury, 2012).

———, *Saints & Sinners: A History of the Popes* (Italy: Yale University Press and S4C, 1997).

———, *The Stripping of the Altars: Traditional Religion in England, c. 1440–c. 1580* (New Haven and London: Yale University Press, 1992).

Duncan-Jones, Katherine, 'Sir Philip Sidney's Debt to Edmund Campion', in *The Reckoned Expense: Edmund Campion and the Early English Jesuits*, 2nd ed., ed. Thomas M. McCoog, S.J. (Rome: IHSI, 2007), pp. 97–117.

Durning, Louise, *Queen Elizabeth's Book of Oxford* (Oxford: Bodleian Library, 2006).

Dürrwaechter, A., 'Aus der Fruhzeit des Jesuitendrama. Nach Dillingen Manuskripten', in *Jahrbkuch des Historischen Vereins Dillingen, IX Jahrgang* (Dillingen: J. Keller, 1897), pp. 1–54.

Edwards, Francis, S.J., trans., *The Elizabethan Jesuits: Historia Missionis Anglicanae Societatis Jesu (1660) of Henry More* (London: Phillimore, 1981).

———, *The Jesuits in England from 1580 to the Present Day* (London: Burns and Oates, 1985).

Elliott, John R., 'Queen Elizabeth at Oxford: New Light on the Royal Plays of 1566', *English Literary Renaissance* 18.5 (1988), 218–29.

Elliott, John R. and Alan H. Nelson, *Records of Early English Drama: Oxford*, 2 vols (London: British Library, 2004).

Elton, G.R., 'Persecution and Toleration in the English Reformation', in *Persecution and Toleration*, vol. 21, *Studies in Church History*, ed. W.J. Sheils (Oxford: Blackwell, 1984) pp. 163–87.

Evans, R.J.W., *Rudolf II and His World: A Study in Intellectual History 1576–1612* (Oxford: Clarendon Press, 1973).

Fernandez-Armento, Felipe, *The Spanish Armada: The Experience of War in 1588* (Oxford: University Press, 1988).

Fielitz, Sonja, '*Timon* Revisited', in *Shakespeare. Satire. Academia. Essays in Honour of Wolfgang Weiss*, ed. Sonja Fielitz and Uwe Meyer (Heidelberg: Winter, 2012), pp. 29–46.

Fletcher, John Rory, *The Story of the English Bridgettines of Syon Abbey* (Bristol: Syon Abbey, 1933).

Friedman, Danny, 'Torture and the Common Law', *European Human Rights: Law Review* 2 (2006), 180–99.

Fučikova, Eliška, *Rudolf II and Prague: The Imperial Court and Residential City as the Cultural and Spiritual Heart of Central Europe* (Prague, London, Milan: Thames and Hudson, 1997).

Fučikova, Eliška, et al., eds, 'Prague Castle under Rudolf II, His Predecessors and Successors, 1530–1648', in *Rudolf II and Prague*, ed. Eliška Fučikova et al. (Prague, London, Milan: Thames and Hudson, 1997), pp. 2–71.

Galbraith, Steven K., '"English" Black-Letter Type and Spenser's *Shepheardes Calender*', *Spenser Studies* 23 (2008), 13–40.

Gallagher, Donat, 'Five Editions of Evelyn Waugh's *Edmund Campion*', *The Book Collector* 61.4 (2012), 531–49.

Gallard, Babette, *Via Francigena: Canterbury to Rome* (France: EURL, Pilgrimage Productions, 2013).

Gibbons, Katy, *English Catholic Exiles in Late Sixteenth Century Paris* (Woodbridge: Boydell Press for Royal Historical Society, 2011).

Girouard, Mark, *Elizabethan Architecture: Its Rise and Fall, 1540–1640* (New Haven and London: Yale University Press, 2009).

———, *Rushton Triangular Lodge* (London: English Heritage, 2004).

Graffius, Jan, 'Telling Romero's Story', http://www.thinkingfaith.org/articles, 22 March 2013.

Green, V.H.H., *Religion at Oxford and Cambridge* (London: SCM Press, 1964).

Greenblatt, Stephen, *Hamlet in Purgatory* (Princeton: University Press, 2001).

———, *Will in the World: How Shakespeare Became Shakespeare* (London: Jonathan Cape, 2004).

Gregory, Brad, *Salvation at Stake: Christian Martyrdom in Early Modern Europe* (Cambridge, MA and London: Harvard University Press, 1999).

Guiney, Louise Imogen, *Blessed Edmund Campion* (London: Macdonald and Evans, 1908).

———, *Recusant Poets: Saint Thomas More to Ben Jonson* (New York: Sheed & Ward, 1939).

Hadfield, Andrew, *Edmund Spenser: A Life* (Oxford: University Press 2012).

———, 'From Monopoly to Minority: Catholicism in Early Modern England', *Transactions of the Royal Historical Society* 5.31 (1981), 129–47.

———, *The Plain Man's Pathways to Heaven* (Oxford: University Press, 2007).

Haigh, Christopher, 'The Continuity of Catholicism in the English Reformation', *Past and Present* 93 (1981), 37–69.

———, *Elizabeth I* (London: Longman, 1988).

Hamilton, Donna B., *Anthony Munday and the Catholics, 1560–1633* (Aldershot, UK and Burlington, VT: Ashgate, 2005).

Hamilton, Donna B. and Richard Strier, *Religion, Literature and Politics in Post-Reformation England, 1540–1688* (Cambridge: University Press, 1996).

Hamilton, William Douglas, ed., *A Chronicle of England During the Reign of the Tudors From A.D. 1485 to 1559 by Charles Wriothesley, Windsor Herald*, vol. 2 (London: Camden Society, 1877).

Hammer, Paul E.J., *Elizabeth's Wars: War, Government and Society in Tudor England, 1544–1604* (Basingstoke: Palgrave Macmillan, 2003).

Hanson, Elizabeth, *Discovering the Subject in Elizabethan England* (Cambridge: University Press, 1998).

Hardy, Thomas, *The Collected Poems*, ed. James Gibson (London: Macmillan, 1976).

Harley, John, *William Byrd: Gentleman of the Chapel Royal* (Aldershot, UK: Scolar Press, 1997).

Heal, Felicity, *Of Prelates and Princes: A Study of the Economic and Social Position of the Tudor Episcopate* (Cambridge: University Press, 1980).

Heal, Felicity and Rosemary O'Day, *Church and Society in England: Henry VIII to James I* (London: Macmillan, 1977).

Heaney, Seamus, *New Selected Poems 1966–1987* (London: Faber and Faber, 1990).

Hegarty, Andrew, *A Biographical Register of St John's College, Oxford, 1555–1660* (Woodbridge: Boydell Press for Oxford Historical Society, 2011).

Highley, Christopher, *Catholics Writing the Nation in Early Modern Britain and Ireland* (Oxford: University Press, 2008).

Hodgetts, Michael, 'Campion in the Thames Valley, 1580', *Recusant History* 30 (2010), 26–46.

———, *Secret Hiding Places* (Dublin: Veritas, 1989).

Hodgetts, Michael and Aileen M. Hodgson, eds, *Little Malvern Letters: I, 1482–1737* (Woodbridge: Boydell Press for Catholic Record Society, 2011).

Holdsworth, Sir William, *A History of English Law*, 17 vols (London: Methuen, 1922–72).

Holleran, James V., *A Jesuit Challenge: Edmund Campion's Debates at the Tower of London in 1581* (New York: Fordham University Press).

Holmes, Peter, 'The Authorship of "Leicester's Commonwealth"', *Journal of Ecclesiastical History* 33 (1982), 424–30.

———, *Resistance and Compromise: The Political Thought of the Elizabethan Catholics* (Cambridge: University Press, 1982).

Honigmann, E.A.J., *Shakespeare: 'The Lost Years'* (Manchester: University Press, 1985).

———, 'The Shakespeare/Shakeshafte Question, Continued', *Shakespeare Quarterly*, 54 (2003), 83–6.

Houliston, Victor, *Catholic Resistance in Elizabethan England: Robert Persons's Jesuit Polemic, 1580–1610* (Rome; Aldershot, UK and Burlington, VT: Ashgate and IHSI, 2007).

Howell, T.R., ed., *A Complete Collection of State Trials and Proceedings for High Treason and other Crimes and Misdemeanours from the earliest period to the year 1783, with notes and other illustrations*, 33 vols (London: Hansard, 1816), I. 1049–67.

Hughes, Paul L. and James F. Larkin, C.S.V., eds, *Tudor Royal Proclamations*, 3 vols (London and New Haven: Yale University Press, 1969).

Hunt, Arnold, *The Art of Hearing: English Preachers and their Audiences, 1590–1640* (Cambridge: University Press, 2010).

———, 'Preaching the Elizabethan Settlement', in Peter McCullough, Hugh Adlington and Emma Rhatigan, eds, *The Oxford Handbook of the Early Modern Sermon* (Oxford: University Press, 2011), pp. 366–86.

Hutchison, Ann M., 'Some Historians of Syon', in *Syon Abbey and Its Books: Reading, Writing and Religion, c. 1400–1700*, ed. E.A. Jones and Alexandra Walsham (Woodbridge: Boydell Press, 2010), pp. 228–51.

Imhof, Dirk, *A Never Realized Edition: Balthasar Moretus's Project of a Polyglot Bible*, trans. Paul Arblaster and Levi Ruffle (Antwerp: Kockelbergh, 2014).

Jenkinson, Wilberforce, *London Churches before the Great Fire* (London: SPCK, 1917).

Jessopp, Augustus, *One Generation of a Norfolk House: A Contribution to Elizabethan History* (Norwich: Miller and Leavins, 1878).

Johnson, A.H., *The History of the Worshipful Company of Drapers of London*, 2 vols (Oxford: Clarendon Press, 1915).

Jones, E.A. and Alexandra Walsham, *Syon Abbey and its Books: Reading, Writing and Religion, c.1400–1700* (Woodbridge: Boydell, 2010).

Keith, A.M., *Play of Fictions: Studies in Ovid's Metamorphoses, Book 2* (Ann Arbor: University of Michigan Press, 1992).

Kelly, James E., 'Conformity, Loyalty and the Jesuit Mission to England of 1580', in *Religious Tolerance in the Atlantic World: Early Modern and Contemporary Perspectives*, ed. Eliane Glaser (Palgrave Macmillan, 2013), pp. 149–70.

Ker, N.R., 'Oxford College Libraries in the Sixteenth Century', *Bodleian Library Record* 6 (January 1959), 459–515.

Kerman, Joseph, *The Masses and Motets of William Byrd* (London: Faber and Faber, 1981).

Kilroy, Gerard, 'Advertising the Reader: Sir John Harington's "Directions in the Margent"', *English Literary Renaissance* 41.1 (Winter 2011), 64–110.

———, 'Edmund Campion in the Shadow of Paul's Cross: The Culture of Disputation' in *Paul's Cross and the Culture of Persuasion in England, 1520–1640*, ed. Torrance Kirby and P.G. Stanwood (Leiden-Boston: Brill, 2014), pp. 263–87.

———, *Edmund Campion: Memory and Transcription* (Aldershot, UK and Burlington, VT: Ashgate, 2005).

————, '"Paths Coincident": The Parallel Lives of Dr Nicholas Sander and Edmund Campion, S.J.', *Journal of Jesuit Studies* 1 (2014), 520–41.

————, 'The Queen's Visit to Oxford in 1566: A Fresh Look at Neglected Manuscript Sources', *Recusant History* 31.1 (2013), 331–73.

————, 'Scribal Coincidences: Campion, Byrd, Harington and the Sidney Circle', *Sidney Journal* 22 (2004), 73–88.

————, 'Sir Thomas Tresham: His Emblem', *Emblematica* 17 (2009), 149–79.

————, 'A Tangled Chronicle: The Struggle over the Memory of Edmund Campion', in *The Arts of Remembrance in Early Modern England*, ed. Andrew Gordon and Thomas Rist (Farnham, UK and Burlington, VT: Ashgate, 2013), pp. 141–59.

Kingdon, J.A., *Richard Grafton: Citizen and Grocer of London* (London: Rixon and Arnold, 1901).

Knowles, David, *The Religious Orders*, 3 vols (Cambridge: University Press, 1948–61).

Knox, T.F., ed., *The First and Second Diaries of the English College, Douay* (London: Nutt, 1878).

Lake, Peter with Michael Questier, *The Antichrist's Lewd Hat: Protestants, Papists and Players in Post-Reformation England* (London and New Haven: Yale University Press, 2002).

————, 'Puritans, Papists, and the "Public Sphere" in Early Modern England: The Edmund Campion Affair in Context', in *The Journal of Modern History* 72 (September 2000), 587–627.

Lang, R.G., *Two Tudor Subsidy Assessment Rolls for the City of London: 1541 and 1582* (London: London Record Society, 1993).

Langbein, John H., *Torture and the Law of Proof* (Chicago: University of Chicago Press, 1977).

Lecler, Joseph, *Histoire de la tolérance au siècle de la Réforme* (Paris: Albin Michel, 1994).

Ledvinka, Vaclav and Jiri Pešek, 'The Public and Private Lives of Prague's Burghers', in *Rudolf II and Prague*, ed. Eliška Fučikova et al. (Prague, London, Milan, Thames and Hudson, 1997), pp. 287–301.

Leland, John, *The itinerary of John Leland in or about the years 1535–1543*, ed. Lucy Toulmin Smith, 5 vols (London: G. Bell, 1906–10).

Lemprière, William, ed., *John Howes' MS.*, *"A brief note of the order and manner of the proceedings in the first erection of" The Three Royal Hospitals of Christ, Bridewell and St. Thomas the Apostle* (London: Christ's Hospital, 1904).

Lennon, Colm, 'Campion and Reform in Tudor Ireland', in *The Reckoned Expense: Edmund Campion and the Early English Jesuits*, ed. Thomas McCoog, S.J., 2nd ed. (Rome: Institutum Historicum, 2007), pp. 75–95.

————, 'Ireland', in *The Oxford Handbook of Holinshed's Chronicles*, ed. Paulina Kewes, Ian W. Archer and Felicity Heal (Oxford: University Press, 2013), pp. 663–78.

————, *Richard Stanihurst The Dubliner 1547–1618* (Blackrock: Irish Academic Press, 1981).

————, *Sixteenth-Century Ireland: The Incomplete Conquest* (New York: St Martin's Press, 1995).

Levy, F.J., *Tudor Historical Thought* (San Marino: Huntington Library, 1967).

Lingard, John, *The History of England: From the First Invasion by the Romans to the Accession of William and Mary in 1688*, 10 vols (London: C. Dolman, 1855).

Loach, Jennifer, 'Reformation Controversies', in *The History of the University of Oxford*, vol. 3 (Oxford: Clarendon Press, 1986), pp. 363–96.

Lockie, D. McN., 'The Political Career of the Bishop of Ross, 1568–80', *Historical Journal of the University of Birmingham* 4–5 (1953–56), 98–145.

Longhaye, G., *Campian: Tragédie en Quatre Actes* (Tours: Mame et fils, 1883).

Louthan, Howard, *The Quest for Compromise: Peacemakers in Counter-Reformation Vienna* (Cambridge: University Press, 1997).

MacCaffrey, Wallace, *Elizabeth I* (London: Arnold, 1993).

Maclagan, Sir Edward, *The Jesuits and the Great Mogul* (London: Burns Oates and Washbourne, 1932).

Mallett, Charles Edward, *A History of the University of Oxford*, vol. 2, *The Sixteenth and Seventeenth Centuries* (London: Methuen, 1924).

Marks, P.J.M., *The British Library Guide to Bookbinding: History and Techniques* (London: British Library, 1998).

Marshall, Peter, 'Religious Ideology', in *The Oxford Handbook of Holinshed's Chronicles*, ed. Paulina Kewes, Ian W. Archer and Felicity Heal (Oxford: Oxford University Press, 2013), pp. 411–26.

Mateer, David, 'William Byrd, John Petre and Oxford, Bodleian MS Mus. Sch. E 423: An Index and Commentary', *Research Chronicle* 29 (1996), 21–45.

Maus, Katharine Eisaman, 'Proof and Consequences: Inwardness and Its Exposure in the English Renaissance', *Representations* 34 (1991), 29–52.

McCabe, Richard A., 'Making History: Holinshed's Irish Chronicles, 1577 and 1587', *British Identities and English Renaissance Literature*, ed. David J. Baker and Willy Maley (Cambridge: University Press, 2002), pp. 51–67.

McConica, James Kelsey, *The Collegiate University*, vol. 3 of *The History of the University of Oxford* (Oxford: Clarendon Press, 1986).

————, 'The Catholic Experience in Tudor Oxford', in *The Reckoned Expense: Edmund Campion and the Early English Jesuits*, ed. Thomas McCoog, S.J., 2nd ed. (Rome: Institutum Historicum, 2007), pp. 43–73.

————, ed., *English Humanists and Reformation Politics Under Henry VIII and Edward VI* (Oxford: Clarendon Press, 1965).

McCoog, Thomas M., S.J., *English and Welsh Jesuits, 1555–1650*, 2 vols (London: Catholic Record Society, 1995 and 1995), CRS 74 and 75.

————, ed., *The Reckoned Expense: Edmund Campion and the Early English Jesuits*, 2nd ed. (Rome: IHSI, 2007).

————, *The Society of Jesus in Ireland, Scotland, and England 1541–1588; 'Our Way of Proceeding'* (Leiden, New York, Köln: Brill, 1996).

———, *"And touching our society": Fashioning Jesuit Identity in Elizabethan England* (Toronto: Pontifical Institute of Medieval Studies, 2013).

McDonnell, Sir Michael, 'Edmund Campion, S.J. and St Paul's School', *Notes and Queries* 194 (1949), 46–9, 67–70, 90–92.

———, *The Registers of St Paul's School 1509–1748* (London: privately printed, 1977).

McGrath, Patrick, *Papists and Puritans under Elizabeth I* (London: Blandford Press, 1967).

McKenzie, D.F., *Making Meaning: "Printers of the Mind" and Other Essays*, ed. Peter D. McDonald and Michael F. Suarez, S.J. (Amherst: University of Massachusetts Press, 2002).

McKerrow, Ronald B., *An Introduction to Bibliography for Literary Students* (Oxford: Clarendon Press, 1927).

Mears, Natalie, *Queenship and Political Discourse in The Elizabethan Realms* (Cambridge: University Press, 2005).

Meyer, Arnold Oskar, *England and the Catholic Church Under Queen Elizabeth*, 2nd ed., intro. John Bossy (London: Routledge & Kegan Paul, 1967).

Miller, John F., *Apollo, Augustus and the Poets* (Cambridge: University Press, 2009).

Milne, J.G., *The Early History of Corpus Christi College* (Oxford: Basil Blackwell, 1946).

Milward, Peter, S.J., *Shakespeare in Lancashire* (Tokyo: Renaissance Pamphlets, 2000).

Mitchell, David, *The Jesuits: A History* (London: Macdonald, 1980).

Monta, Susannah Brietz, *Martyrdom and Literature in Early Modern England* (Cambridge: University Press, 2005).

Morris, John, S.J., 'Blessed Edmund Campion at Douay', in *The Month*, 61 (1887), 30–46.

———, 'A New Witness about B. Edmund Campion', in *The Month*, 78 (1893), 3–11.

Morrissey, Mary, *Politics and the Paul's Cross Sermons, 1558–1642* (Oxford: University Press, 2011).

Mozley, J.F., *John Foxe and His Book* (London: SPCK, 1940).

Müller, Johannes, S.J., *Das Jesuitendrama in den Landern Deutscher Zunger vom Anfang (1555) bis Zum Hochbarock (1665)* (Augsburge: Benno Filser Verlag, 1930).

Murphy, Emilie K., '*Adoramus te Christe*: Music and Post-Reformation English Catholic Domestic Piety', in *Religion and the Household, Studies in Church History*, ed. John Doran, Charlotte Methuen and Alexandra Walsham, vol. 50 (Woodbridge: Boydell, 2014), pp. 240–53.

Nelson, Alan H., 'Who Didn't Write *Leicester's Commonwealth*? (Who Did?)', *English Manuscript Studies 1100–1700*, vol. 18 (London: The British Library, 2013), pp. 11–18.

Nelson, Alan H. and John R. Elliott, *Records of Early English Drama: Oxford*, 2 vols (London: British Library, 2004).

Nicholas, Sir Harris, *Memoirs of the Life and Times of Sir Christopher Hatton* (London: Bentley, 1847).

Nichols, John, *The Progresses and Public Processions of Queen Elizabeth*, 2 vols (London: Nichols, 1788); 3 vols (London: Nichols, 1823).

———, *The Progresses and Public Processions of Queen Elizabeth I: A New Edition of the Early Modern Sources*, 3 vols, ed. Elizabeth Goldring et al. (Oxford: University Press, 2014).

O'Malley, John W., *The First Jesuits* (Cambridge, MA: Harvard University Press, 1993).

———, *Saints or Devils Incarnate? Studies in Jesuit History* (Leiden: Brill, 2013).

O'Rahilly, Alfred, *The Massacre at Smerwick, 1580* (London: Longmans Green, 1938).

Pantin, W.A., *Oxford Life in Oxford Archives* (Oxford: Clarendon Press, 1972).

Parmiter, Geoffrey de C., *Edmund Plowden: An Elizabethan Recusant Lawyer* (London: Catholic Record Society, 1987).

———, *Elizabethan Popish Recusancy in the Inns of Court* (University of London: IHR, 1976).

Patterson, Annabel, *Censorship and Interpretation: The Conditions of Writing and Reading in Early Modern England* (Madison: University of Wisconsin Press, 1984).

———, *Reading Holinshed's Chronicles* (Chicago: University of Chicago Press, 1994).

Pearson, David, *Oxford Bookbinding 1500–1640: Including a Supplement to Neil Ker's Fragments of Medieval Manuscripts Used as Pastedowns in Oxford Bindings* (Oxford: Oxford Bibliographical Society, 2000).

Peck, D.C., ed., *Leicester's Commonwealth: The Copy of a Letter Written by a Master of Art of Cambridge (1584) and Related Documents* (Ohio: University Press, 1985).

Pešek, Jiri, 'Prague between 1550 and 1650', in *Rudolf II and Prague*, ed. Eliška Fučikova et al. (Prague, London, Milan: Thames and Hudson, 1997), pp. 287–301.

Pettegree, Andrew, 'Printing and the Reformation: The English Exception', in *The Beginnings of English Protestantism*, ed. Peter Marshall and Alec Ryrie (Cambridge: University Press, 2002), pp. 157–79.

Petti, A.G., 'Additions to the Richard Verstegan Canon', *Recusant History* 8 (1966), 288–93.

———, 'Richard Verstegan and Catholic Martyrologies of the Later Elizabethan Period', *Recusant History* 5 (1959), 64–90.

———, 'Stephen Vallenger (1541–1591)', *Recusant History* 6 (1961–62), 248–64.

Plomer, Henry R., *Abstracts from the Wills of English Printers and Stationers from 1492 to 1630* (London: Bibliographic Society, 1903).

Plummer, Charles, *Elizabethan Oxford* (Oxford: Clarendon Press, 1887).

Pollard Brown, Nancy, 'Paperchase: The Dissemination of Catholic Texts in Elizabethan England', in *English Manuscript Studies*, vol. 1 (Oxford: Blackwell, 1989), pp. 120–43.

Pollen, John Hungerford, S.J., *Acts of the English Martyrs Hitherto Unpublished* (London: Burns and Oates, 1891).

———, 'Blessed Edmund Campion's "Decem Rationes"', *The Month* 105 (1905), 11–26.

———, 'Campion's *Decem Rationes*', *The Month* 114 (1909), 80.

Potterton, Michael and Thomas Herron, eds, *Dublin and the Pale in the Renaissance c. 1540–1660* (Dublin: Four Courts Press, 2011).

Prest, W.R., *The Inns of Court under Elizabeth I and the Early Stuarts: 1590–1640* (London: Longman, 1972).

Questier, Michael, *Catholicism and Community in Early Modern England: Politics, Aristocratic Patronage and Religion, c. 1550–1640* (Cambridge: University Press, 2006).

Radle, Fidel, *Lateinische Ordensdramen des XVI Jahrhundert* (Berlin und New York, 1979).

Read, Conyers, *Lord Burghley and Queen Elizabeth* (London: Jonathan Cape, 1960).

Reynolds, E.E., *Campion and Parsons: The Jesuit Mission of 1580–1* (London: Sheed and Ward, 1980).

Ryrie, Alec, 'Counting Sheep, Counting Shepherds: The Problem of Allegiance in the English Reformation', in *The Beginnings of English Protestantism*, ed. Peter Marshall and Alec Ryrie (Cambridge: University Press, 2002), pp. 84–110.

Sacred Congregation of Rites, *Cause of the Canonization of Blessed Martyrs John Houghton, Robert Lawrence, Augustine Webster, Richard Reynolds, John Stone, Cuthbert Mayne, John Paine, Edmund Campion, Alexander Briant, Ralph Sherwin, and Luke Kirby* (Rome: Vatican Polyglot Press, 1968).

Scully, Robert E., *Into the Lion's Den: The Jesuit Mission in Elizabethan England and Wales, 1580–1603* (St Louis: Institute of Jesuit Sources, 2011).

Sharpe, J.A., '"Last Dying Speeches": Religion, Ideology and Public Execution in Seventeenth-Century England', *Past and Present* 107 (May 1985), 144–67.

Shell, Alison, *Catholicism, Controversy and the Literary Imagination, 1558–1660* (Cambridge: University Press, 1999).

———, *Oral Culture and Catholicism in Early Modern England* (Cambridge: University Press, 2007).

———, *Shakespeare and Religion* (London: Arden, 2010).

———, '"We are made a Spectacle": Campion's Dramas', in *The Reckoned Expense: Edmund Campion and the Early English Jesuits*, ed. Thomas McCoog, S.J., 2nd ed. (Rome: Institutum Historicum, 2007).

Simons, Madeline, 'Archduke Ferdinand II of Austria, Governor in Bohemia, and the Theatre of Representation', in *Rudolf II, Prague and the World: Papers from the International Conference, Prague, 1997*, ed. Lubomir Konečny (Prague: Artefactum, 1998), pp. 270–77.

————, 'King Ferdinand I of Bohemia, Archduke Ferdinand II and the Prague Court, 1527–1567', in *Rudolf II and Prague*, ed. Eliška Fučikova et al. (Prague, London, Milan: Thames and Hudson, 1997), 80–89.

Simpson, Richard, *Edmund Campion: A Biography* (London: Williams and Norgate, 1867).

————, *Edmund Campion: A Biography*, 2nd ed. (London: John Hodges, 1896).

Skwarczynski, Paul, 'Elsinore 1580: John Rogers and James Bosgrave', *Recusant History* 16.1 (1982), 1–16.

Solt, Leo F., *Church and State in Early Modern England, 1509–1640* (Oxford: University Press, 1990).

Sommervogel, Carlos, *Bibliothèque de la Compagnie de Jésus* (Paris: Picard, 1891).

Southern, A.C., *Elizabethan Recusant Prose 1559–1582* (London: Sands, [1950]).

Šroněk, Michal, 'Sculpture and Painting in Prague, 1550–1650', in *Rudolf II and Prague*, ed. Eliška Fučikova et al. (Prague, London, Milan: Thames and Hudson, 1997), pp. 353–75.

Steuert, Dom Hilary, 'The Place of Allen, Campion and Parsons in the Development of English Prose', *Review of English Studies* 20.80 (1944), 272–85.

Stevenson, W.H. and H.E. Salter, *The Early History of St John's College, Oxford* (Oxford: Clarendon Press, 1939), Oxford Historical Society (New Series) vol. 1.

Stonor, Robert Julian, O.S.B., *Stonor: A Catholic Sanctuary in the Chilterns from the Fifth Century till To-day* (Newport: R.H. Johns, 1951).

Travitsky, Betty S., 'The Puzzling Letters of Sister Elizabeth Saunders', in *Textual Conversations in the Renaissance: Ethics, Authors, Technologies* (Aldershot, UK and Burlington, VT: Ashgate, 2006), pp. 131–45.

Trollope, William, *A History of the Royal Foundation of Christ's Hospital* (London: William Pickering, 1834).

Tutino, Stefania, *Law and Conscience: Catholicism in Early Modern England, 1570–1625* (Aldershot, UK and Burlington, VT: Ashgate, 2007).

Valentin, Jean-Marie, *Le théâtre des Jésuites dans le pays de langue allemande, répertoire chronologique des pièces représentées et des documents conservés (1555–1773)*, 2 vols (Stuttgart: Hiersemann, 1983–84).

Veech, Thomas McNevin, *Dr Nicholas Sanders and the English Reformation* (Louvain: Bibliotheque de l'Université, 1935).

Vondraček, Radim, 'Bookbinding: Style and Ornament', in *Rudolf II and Prague*, ed. Eliška Fučikova et al. (Prague, London, Milan: Thames and Hudson, 1997), pp. 340–44.

Wabuda, Susan, *Preaching During the English Reformation* (Cambridge: University Press, 2002).

Walsham, Alexandra, *Church Papists: Catholicism, Conformity and Confessional Polemic in Early Modern England* (Woodbridge, Suffolk: Boydell, 1993).

————, *The Reformation of the Landscape: Religion, Identity and Memory in Early Modern Britain and Ireland* (Oxford: University Press, 2011).

Waugh, Evelyn, *Edmund Campion* (London: Longmans, Green & Co., 1935).

————, *Edmund Campion*, 2nd American ed. (Boston: Little, Brown, 1946).

————, *Edmund Campion*, 2nd ed. (London: Hollis and Carter, 1947).

_____, *Edmund Campion*, Penguin ed. (London: Harmondsworth, 1953).

————, *Edmund Campion*, 3rd ed. (London: Longmans, Green & Co., 1961).

Weis, René, *Shakespeare Revealed: A Biography* (London: John Murray, 2007).

Wells, Stanley, *Shakespeare: For All Time* (London: Macmillan, 2002).

Wiggins, Martin and Catherine Richardson, *British Drama, 1533–1642: A Catalogue*, 3 vols (Oxford: University Press, 2011–13).

Williams, Michael E., 'Campion and the English Continental Seminaries', in *The Reckoned Expense: Edmund Campion and the Early Jesuits*, ed. Thomas M. McCoog, S.J., 2nd ed. (Rome: IHSI, 2007), pp. 371–87.

Worden, Blair, *The Sound of Virtue: Philip Sidney's* Arcadia *and Elizabethan Politics* (New Haven and London: Yale University Press, 1996).

Woudhuysen, H.R., 'A New Manuscript Fragment of Sidney's *Old Arcadia*: The Huddleston Manuscript', in *English Manuscript Studies*, vol. 11 (London: British Library, 2002), pp. 52–69.

————, *Sir Philip Sidney and the Circulation of Manuscripts 1558–1640* (Oxford: Clarendon Press, 1996).

Younger, Neil, *War and Politics in the Elizabethan Counties* (Manchester: University Press, 1985).

Ziegler, Georgianna, ed., *Elizabeth I: Then and Now* (Washington, DC: Folger Shakespeare Library, 2003).

Catholic Record Society

CRS 2, *Miscellanea II*, 'The Memoirs of Father Robert Persons', ed. J.H. Pollen, S.J. (London: Catholic Record Society, 1906), pp. 12–218.

CRS 4, *Miscellanea IV*, 'The Memoirs of Father Robert Persons (concluded)', ed. J.H. Pollen, S.J. (London: Catholic Record Society, 1907), pp. 1–161.

CRS 5, *Unpublished Documents Relating to the English Martyrs, 1584–1603*, ed. J.H. Pollen, S.J. (London: Catholic Record Society, 1908).

CRS 9, *Miscellanea VII*, 'Some Correspondence of Cardinal Allen, 1579–83', ed. Patrick Ryan, S.J. (London: Catholic Record Society, 1911), pp. 12–105.

CRS 21, *Ven. Philip Howard, Earl of Arundel, English Martyrs*, vol. 2, ed. John Hungerford Pollen, S.J., and William MacMahon, S.J. (London: Catholic Record Society, 1919).

CRS 22, *Miscellanea XII*, 'Diocesan Returns of Recusants for England and Wales, 1577', ed. Patrick Ryan, S.J. (London: Catholic Record Society, 1921), pp. 1–114.

CRS 26, *Miscellanea XIII*, 'Some Letters and Papers of Nicholas Sander, 1560–1580', ed. John B. Wainwright (London: Catholic Record Society, 1926).

CRS 39, '*Letters and Memorials of Fr. Robert Persons, S.J.*, vol. 1 (to 1588)', ed. L. Hicks, S.J. (London: Catholic Record Society, 1942).

CRS 53, *Miscellanea: Recusant Records*, ed. Clare Talbot (London: Catholic Record Society, 1961). [Edited versions of Charles Sledd's reports, pp. 186–245.]

CRS 58, *Letters of William Allen and Richard Barret, 1572–1598*, ed. P. Renold (London: Catholic Record Society, 1967).

CRS 60, *Recusant Documents from the Ellesmere Manuscripts*, ed. Anthony G. Petti (London: Catholic Record Society, 1968).

Calendars of State Papers

Acts of the Privy Council, 1581–1582, ed. John Roche Dasent (London: HMSO, 1896), NS, vol. 13.

Calendar of the Patent and Close Rolls of Chancery in Ireland of the Reigns of Henry VIII, Edward VI, Mary and Elizabeth, ed. James Morrin (Dublin: Alex Thom, 1861).

Calendar of State Papers Domestic, Edward VI, Mary, Elizabeth I and James I, ed. R. Lemon and M.A.E. Green, 12 vols (London: HMSO, 1856–72).

Calendar of State Papers Foreign, 1579–1580, ed. Arthur John Butler (London: HMSO, 1904).

Calendar of State Papers Foreign, 1581–1582, ed. Arthur John Butler (London: HMSO, 1907).

Calendar of State Papers Irish of the Reign of Elizabeth, 1574–1585, ed. Hans Claude Hamilton (London: HMSO, 1867).

Calendar of State Papers Spanish, 1553, Edward VI and Mary, vol. 11 (Vienna, Simancas, Besancon and Brussels), ed. Royall Tyler (London: HMSO, 1916).

Calendar of State Papers Spanish, 1558–1567 (Simancas), ed. Martin A.S. Hume (London: HMSO, 1892), vol. 1 Elizabeth.

Calendar of State Papers Spanish, 1568–1579 (Simancas), ed. Martin A.S. Hume (London: HMSO, 1892), vol. 2 Elizabeth.

Calendar of State Papers Spanish, 1580–1586 (Simancas), ed. Martin A.S. Hume (London: HMSO, 1896), vol. 3 Elizabeth.

Calendar of State Papers Venetian, 1556–1557 (Venice), ed. Rawdon Brown (London: HMSO, 1881), vol. 6, part 2.

Monumenta Poloniae Vaticana: Continet I.A. Caligari Nuntii Apost. in Polonia Epistolas et Acta, ed. Ludovicus Boratynski (Krakow: Academy of Letters, 1915), vol. 4 (1578–81).

Index